FINANCIAL
ACCOUNTING
FOR DECISION MAKERS

Pearson

At Pearson, we have a simple mission: to help people make more of their lives through learning.

We combine innovative learning technology with trusted content and educational expertise to provide engaging and effective learning experiences that serve people wherever and whenever they are learning.

From classroom to boardroom, our curriculum materials, digital learning tools and testing programmes help to educate millions of people worldwide – more than any other private enterprise.

Every day our work helps learning flourish, and wherever learning flourishes, so do people.

To learn more, please visit us at **www.pearson.com/uk**

NINTH EDITION

FINANCIAL ACCOUNTING
FOR DECISION MAKERS

Peter Atrill
Eddie McLaney

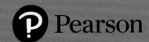

Harlow, England • London • New York • Boston • San Francisco • Toronto • Sydney
Dubai • Singapore • Hong Kong • Tokyo • Seoul • Taipei • New Delhi
Cape Town • São Paulo • Mexico City • Madrid • Amsterdam • Munich • Paris • Milan

PEARSON EDUCATION LIMITED
KAO Two
KAO Park
Harlow
CM17 9SR
United Kingdom
Tel: +44 (0)1279 623623
Web: www.pearson.com/uk

Second edition published 1999 by Prentice Hall Europe (print)
Third edition published 2002 by Pearson Education Limited (print)
Fourth edition published 2005 (print)
Fifth edition published 2008 (print)
Sixth edition published 2011 (print)
Seventh edition published 2013 (print and electronic)
Eighth edition published 2016 (print and electronic)
Ninth edition published 2019 (print and electronic)

© Prentice Hall Europe 1996, 1999 (print)
© Pearson Education Limited 2002, 2005, 2008, 2011 (print)
© Pearson Education Limited 2013, 2016, 2019 (print and electronic)

The Financial Times. With a worldwide network of highly respected journalists, *The Financial Times* provides global business news, insightful opinion and expert analysis of business, finance and politics. With over 500 journalists reporting from 50 countries worldwide, our in-depth coverage of international news is objectively reported and analysed from an independent, global perspective. To find out more, visit **www.ft.com/pearsonoffer**.

ISBN: 978-1-292-25125-7 (print)
        978-1-292-25131-8 (PDF)
        978-1-292-25130-1 (ePub)

British Library Cataloguing-in-Publication Data
A catalogue record for the print edition is available from the British Library

Library of Congress Cataloging-in-Publication Data
A catalog record for the print edition is available from the Library of Congress

10 9 8 7 6 5 4 3 2 1
23 22 21 20 19

Print edition typeset in 9.25/13 pt and Helvetica Neue LT W1G by Pearson CSC
Print edition printed and bound in Slovakia by Neografia
Cover image: © Shutterstock Premier/Allies Interactive

NOTE THAT ANY PAGE CROSS REFERENCES REFER TO THE PRINT EDITION

Brief contents

Contents

Lecturer Resources

For password-protected online resources tailored to
support the use of this textbook in teaching, please visit
www.pearsoned.co.uk/atrillmclaney

ON THE
WEBSITE

Preface

This text provides a comprehensive introduction to financial accounting. It is aimed at students who are not majoring in accounting as well as those who are. Those studying introductory-level financial accounting as part of their course in business, economics, hospitality management, tourism, engineering, or some other area, should find that the text provides complete coverage of the material at the level required. Students who are majoring in accounting should find the text a useful introduction to the main principles, which can serve as a foundation for further study.

The main focus of the text is on the ways in which financial statements and financial information can improve the quality of decision making. To ensure that readers understand the practical implications of the subject, there are, throughout the text, numerous illustrative extracts using commentary from company reports, survey data and other sources. Although some technical issues are dealt with in the text, the main emphasis throughout is on basic principles and underlying concepts.

In this ninth edition, we have taken the opportunity to make improvements, including those suggested by students and lecturers who used the previous edition. We have rewritten some material to make it more understandable to readers. We have updated and expanded the number of examples from real life. We have also incorporated developments to International Financial Reporting Standards, including the recently-published version of the Conceptual Framework for Financial Reporting. Recent developments in the area of corporate governance are discussed and explained. Finally, the discussion of the role of the auditor has been expanded.

The text is written in an 'open-learning' style. This means that there are numerous integrated activities, worked examples and questions throughout the text to help you to understand the subject fully. In framing these questions and tasks, we have tried to encourage critical thinking by requiring analysis and evaluation of various concepts and techniques. You are encouraged to interact with the material and to check your progress continually. Irrespective of whether you are using the text as part of a taught course or for personal study, we have found that this approach is more 'user-friendly' and makes it easier for you to learn.

We recognise that most of you will not have studied financial accounting before and, therefore, we have tried to write in a concise and accessible style, minimising the use of technical jargon. We have also tried to introduce topics gradually, explaining everything as we go. Where technical terminology is unavoidable we try to provide clear explanations. You will find all of the key terms highlighted in the text, and then listed at the end of each chapter with a page reference. All of these key terms are also listed alphabetically, with a concise definition, in the glossary given in Appendix B. This should provide a convenient point of reference from which to revise.

A further important consideration in helping you to understand and absorb the topics covered is the design of the text itself. The page layout and colour scheme have been carefully considered to allow for the easy navigation and digestion of material. The layout features a large page format, an open design, and clear signposting of the various features and assessment material.

We hope that you will find the text both readable and helpful.

Peter Atrill
Eddie McLaney

How to use this book

We have organised the chapters to reflect what we consider to be a logical sequence and, for this reason, we suggest that you work through the text in the order in which it is presented. We have tried to ensure that earlier chapters do not refer to concepts or terms that are not explained until a later chapter. If you work through the chapters in the 'wrong' order, you will probably encounter concepts and terms that were explained previously.

Irrespective of whether you are using the book as part of a lecture/tutorial-based course or as the basis for a more independent mode of study, we advocate following broadly the same approach.

Integrated assessment material

Interspersed throughout each chapter are numerous **activities.** You are strongly advised to attempt all of these questions. They are designed to simulate the sort of quick-fire questions that your lecturer might throw at you during a lecture or tutorial. Activities serve two purposes:

- to give you the opportunity to check that you understand what has been covered so far;
- to encourage you to think about the topic just covered, either to see a link between that topic and others with which you are already familiar, or to link the topic just covered to the next.

The answer to each activity is provided immediately after the question. This answer should be covered up until you have deduced your solution, which can then be compared with the one given.

Towards the end of Chapters 2–12 there is a **self-assessment question.** This is more comprehensive and demanding than most of the activities, and is designed to give you an opportunity to check and apply your understanding of the core coverage of the chapter. The solution to each of these questions is provided in Appendix C. As with the activities, it is important that you attempt each question thoroughly before referring to the solution. If you have difficulty with a self-assessment question, you should go over the relevant chapter again.

End-of-chapter assessment material

At the end of each chapter there are four **critical review questions.** These are short questions requiring a narrative answer or discussion within a tutorial group. They are intended to help you assess how well you can recall and critically evaluate the core terms and concepts covered in each chapter. Answers to these questions are provided in Appendix D at the end of the book.

At the end of each chapter, except for Chapter 1, there is a set of **exercises.** These are mostly computational and are designed to reinforce your knowledge and understanding. Exercises are graded as 'basic', 'intermediate' or 'advanced' according to their level of difficulty.

The basic-level questions are fairly straightforward; the more advanced ones can be quite demanding but can be successfully completed if you have worked conscientiously through the chapter and have attempted the basic exercises. Solutions to some of the exercises in each chapter are provided in Appendix E. A coloured exercise number identifies these questions. Here, too, a thorough attempt should be made to answer each exercise before referring to the solution.

Solutions to the other exercises are provided in a separate Instructors' Manual.

Content and structure

The text comprises twelve main chapters. The market research for this text revealed a divergence of opinions, given the target market, on whether or not to include material on double-entry bookkeeping techniques. So as to not interrupt the flow and approach of the main chapters, Appendix A on recording financial transactions (including activities and three exercise questions) has been placed after Chapter 12.

Lecturer Resources

For password-protected online resources tailored to support the use of this textbook in teaching, please visit **www.pearsoned.co.uk/atrillmclaney**

Acknowledgements

12–13 Telegraph Media Group Limited: Adapted extract from: Burn-Callander, R. (2015) Stupid errors in spreadsheets could lead to Britain's next corporate disaster, *Daily Telegraph*, 7 April, www.telegraph.co.uk. **18 Houghton Mifflin Harcourt:** Drucker, P. (1967) *The Effective Executive*, Heinemann. **23 National Express plc:** www.nationalexpress.com [accessed 2 January 2019]. **24 John Menzies plc:** www.johnmenziesplc.com [accessed 2 January 2019] **25 The Financial Times Limited:** Goyder, M. (2009) How we've poisoned the well of wealth, *Financial Times*, ft.com, 15 February. © The Financial Times Limited 2017. All rights reserved. **28 Vodafone plc:** Code of Ethics Vodafone plc Accessed 13 February 2019 www.vodafone.com **29 Guardian News and Media Limited:** Laville S., Barr C. and Slawson, N. (2015) Kids Company trustees accused of ignoring finance warnings, www.theguardian.com, 6 August. **59 Manchester United Plc:** Manchester United Plc, Annual Report 2017 **63 The Financial Times Limited:** Kay, J. (2015) Playing dice with your money, ft. com, 4 September. © The Financial Times Limited 2015. All rights reserved. **64 The Financial Times Limited:** Extracts from Garrahan, M. (2017) Daily Mail and General Trust shares drop 24%, ft.com, 30 November. © The Financial Times Limited 2017. All rights reserved. **65 Ted Baker plc:** Ted Baker plc, Annual Report and Accounts 2016/17, p. 90. **66 Crown Copyright:** Adapted from Balance sheets: the basics, www.businesslink. gov.uk [accessed 14 April 2010]. Available under the Open Government Licence v3.0, www.nationalarchives. gov.uk/doc/open-government-licence/version/3/. **95 Mothercare plc:** Extracts from Mothercare plc, Annual Report and Accounts 2017, p. 114, www.mothercare.com. **97 British Airways:** British Airways Annual Report and Accounts 2008/09, Note 15, www.britishairways.com. **105 The Association of Corporate Treasurers:** Extracts from The Treasurer (2016) UK SMEs write off £5.8bn of bad debt: Poll shows small firms are walking away from bad debt in droves, with almost one in 10 scrapping bills worth more than £100,000, Association of Corporate Treasurers, 15 September. www.treasurers.org/node/327677. **118 The Financial Times Limited:** Urquhart L. (2003) Monotub Industries in a spin as founder gets Titan for £1, *Financial Times*, 23 January. © The Financial Times Limited 2012. All Rights Reserved. **121 Crown Copyright:** Based on information in Companies Registration Activities 2012/13 to 2016/17, Table 1, www.companieshouse.gov.uk **122 Kantarworldpanel:** www.kantarworldpanel.com **130 Air Partner PLC:** Air Partner plc (2017), Statement from the business, 6 January. **134 Proactive Investors:** Adapted from 'Medusa Mining', www.proactiveinvestors. co.uk, 8 March 2010. **136 Rolls-Royce Holdings plc:** Rolls-Royce Holdings plc Annual Report and Accounts 2017 p. 148, note 15. **140 The Financial Times Limited:** Extracts from Hollinger, P. (2017) Cobham offers investors steep discount on rights issue, ft.com, 28 March. © The Financial Times Limited 2017. All rights reserved. **141 boohoo.com plc:** Boohoo.com plc (2017), Interim results for the six months ended 31 August 2017, 27 September **143 The Financial Times Limited:** Mance, H. (2014) Betfair admits to £80m payouts mistake, ft.com, 3 August. © The Financial Times Limited 2014. All rights reserved. **149 Telegraph Media Group Limited:** Extract from Armstrong, A. (2017) "Tesco to signal comeback with return to dividend", *Daily Telegraph*, 30 September. **150 Asos plc:** Asos plc, 2017 Annual report, p. 19. **169 The Financial Times Limited:** Extracts from Fleming, H. and Agnew, H. (2014) 'Bank annual reports too long or complex', ft.com, 8 June. © The Financial Times Limited 2014. All rights reserved. **171 IFRS Foundation:** Conceptual Framework for Financial Reporting, IASB **183 The Financial Reporting Council Limited:** Guidance on the Strategic Report, Financial Reporting Council, July 2018, p. 40 **184 VP plc:** Business Model and Strategy © Vp plc 2018 www.vpplc.com/investors/business-model-and-strategy [accessed 2 January 2019]. **188 A G Barr plc:** A G Barr plc Annual Report and Accounts 2017 p.128 **190 Times Newspapers Limited:** Based on information in 'Dirty laundry: how companies fudge the numbers', *The Times*, Business Section, 22 September 2002, News Syndication. **190–191 The Financial Times Limited:** Waters, R. (2014) Autonomy beset by revenues allegation, ft.com, 5 January. © The Financial Times Limited 2014. All rights reserved **193 Guardian News and Media Limited:** Extract from: Rio Tinto charged with fraud in US and fined £27.4m in UK, www.theguardian.com, 18 October 2017. **194 The Financial Times Limited:** Braithewaite, T. and Goff, S. (2012) StanChart accused of hiding Iran dealings, ft.com, 7 August. © The Financial Times Limited 2012. All rights reserved. **195 The Financial Times Limited:** Smith, S. (2005) It pays to read between the lines, *Financial Times*,

Bond, D. and Khan, M. (2017) BT appoints KPMG as auditor after Italian scandal, ft.com, 8 June. © The Financial Times Limited 2017. All rights reserved. **460 Ocado Group:** Independent Auditors Report, Annual report and Accounts 53 weeks ended 3 December 2017, Ocado plc **462 The Financial Times Limited:** Extracts from Cornish, C. (2017) Auditor merry-go-round fails to shake-up cosy market, ft.com, 29 May. © The Financial Times Limited 2017. All rights reserved. **463 The Financial Times Limited:** Mooney, A. (2018) SIG shareholders reject reappointment of Deloitte as auditors, ft.com 10 May. © The Financial Times Limited 2018. All rights reserved. **465 The Financial Times Limited:** Extracts from Crooks, E. (2014) Icahn signals a move on Hertz, ft.com, 20 August. © The Financial Times Limited 2014. All Rights Reserved **471 KPMG Channel Islands Limited:** Guide to Directors' Remuneration 2017, KPMG, Extracts from Summary, p. 2. **472 Guardian News and Media Limited:** Extracts from Goodley, S. (2018) Carillion's 'highly inappropriate' pay packets criticised, *Guardian*, 15 January. **479 KPMG Channel Islands Limited:** Guide to Directors' Remuneration 2017, KPMG, p. 59 **481–482 Crown copyright:** Ownership of UK Quoted Shares 2016, Table 4, Office for National Statistics, 29 November 2017. Office for National Statistics licensed under the Open Government Licence v.3.0. **484 The Financial Times Limited:** Extracts from Mooney, D. (2017) Ryanair faces fresh shareholder rebellion over executive pay ft. com, 7 September. © The Financial Times Limited 2017. All rights reserved. **487 Fidelity International:** Responsible Investment Policy Fidelity International, February, 2018 P.4 **488 The Financial Times Limited:** Smith, T (2015) Shareholder value is an outcome not an objective, ft.com 6 February. © The Financial Times Limited 2015. All rights reserved. **488 McKinsey & Company:** Preparing for bigger, bolder shareholder activists By Joseph Cyriac, Ruth De Backer, and Justin Sanders March 2014.

Chapter 1

INTRODUCTION TO ACCOUNTING

INTRODUCTION

We begin this opening chapter of the book by considering the role of accounting. We shall see how accounting can be a valuable tool for decision making. We shall also identify the main users of accounting information and the qualities, or characteristics, needed for accounting information to be useful for decision-making purposes. We shall then go on to consider the two main strands of accounting: financial accounting and management accounting. We shall discuss the differences between them and why these differences arise.

Since this book is mainly concerned with accounting and financial decision making for private-sector businesses, we shall devote some time to examining the business environment. We shall consider the purpose of a private-sector business, the main forms of business enterprise that exist and the ways in which businesses may be structured. We also consider what the key financial objective of a business is likely to be. These are all important factors that help to shape the accounting and financial information produced.

Learning outcomes

When you have completed this chapter, you should be able to:

- explain the nature and role of accounting;
- identify the main users of financial information and discuss their needs;
- identify and discuss the qualities that make accounting information useful; and
- explain the purpose of a business and describe how businesses are organised and structured.

WHAT IS ACCOUNTING?

Accounting is concerned with *collecting*, *analysing* and *communicating* financial information. The ultimate aim is to help those using this information to make more informed decisions. Unless the financial information being communicated can improve the quality of decisions that users make, there is really no point in producing it.

Sometimes the impression is given that the purpose of accounting is simply to prepare financial (accounting) reports on a regular basis. While it is true that accountants undertake this kind of work, it does not represent an end in itself. As already mentioned, the ultimate aim of the accountant's work is to give users better financial information on which to base their decisions. This decision-making perspective of accounting fits in with the theme of the book and shapes the way in which we deal with each topic.

A useful starting point in exploring the subject is to ask who uses financial information and for what kind of decisions it is useful. It is to these issues that we now turn.

WHO ARE THE USERS OF ACCOUNTING INFORMATION?

For accounting information to be useful, the accountant must be clear *for whom* the information is being prepared and *for what purpose* the information will be used. There are likely to be various groups of people (known as 'user groups') with an interest in a particular organisation, in the sense of needing to make decisions about it. For a typical private-sector business, the more important of these groups are shown in Figure 1.1. Take a look at this figure and then try Activity 1.1.

Several user groups have an interest in accounting information relating to a business. The majority of these are outside the business but, nevertheless, have a stake in it. This is not meant to be an exhaustive list of potential users; however, the groups identified are normally the most important.

Figure 1.1 Main users of financial information relating to a business

Ptarmigan Insurance plc (PI) is a large motor insurance business. Taking the user groups identified in Figure 1.1, suggest, for each group, the sorts of decisions likely to be made about PI and the factors to be taken into account when making these decisions.

Your answer may be along the following lines:

User group	*Decisions likely to be made*
Customers	Whether to take further motor policies with PI. This might involve an assessment of PI's ability to continue in business and to meet customers' needs, particularly concerning any insurance claims made.
Competitors	How best to compete against PI or, perhaps, whether to leave the market on the grounds that it is not possible to compete profitably with PI. This might involve competitors using PI's performance in various respects as a 'benchmark' when evaluating their own performance. They might also try to assess PI's financial strength and to identify significant changes that may signal PI's future intentions (for example, raising funds as a prelude to market expansion).
Employees	Whether to continue working for PI and, if so, whether to demand higher rewards for doing so. The future plans, profits and financial strength of the business are likely to be of particular interest when making these decisions.
Government	Whether PI should pay tax and, if so, how much, whether it complies with agreed pricing policies, whether financial support is needed and so on. In making these decisions, an assessment of PI's profits, sales revenues and financial strength would be made.
Community representatives	Whether to allow PI to expand its premises and/or whether to provide economic support for the business. When making such decisions, PI's ability to continue to provide employment for the community, its use of community resources and its willingness to fund environmental improvements are likely to be important considerations.
Investment analysts	Whether to advise clients to invest in PI. This would involve an assessment of the likely risks and future returns associated with PI.
Suppliers	Whether to continue to supply PI with goods or services and, if so, whether to supply these on credit. This would require an assessment of PI's ability to pay for any goods or services supplied at the due dates.
Lenders	Whether to lend money to PI and/or whether to require repayment of any existing loans. PI's ability to pay the interest and to repay the principal sum on time would be important factors in such decisions.
Managers	Whether the performance of the business needs to be improved. Performance to date may be compared with earlier plans or some other 'benchmark' to decide whether action needs to be taken. Managers may also wish to consider a change in PI's future direction. This may involve determining whether the business has the financial flexibility and resources to take on new challenges
Owners	Whether to invest more in PI or to sell all, or part, of the investment currently held. This would involve an assessment of the likely risks and returns associated with PI. Owners may also be involved with decisions on the rewards offered to senior managers. When doing so, the financial performance and position of the business would normally be taken into account.

Although this answer covers many of the key points, you may have identified other decisions and/or other factors to be taken into account by each group.

THE CONFLICTING INTERESTS OF USERS

We have just seen that each user group will have its own particular interests. There is always a risk, however, that the interests of the various user groups will collide. The distribution of business wealth provides the most likely area for collisions to take place. Take, for example, the position of owners and managers. Although managers are appointed to act in the best interests of the owners, they may not always do so. Instead, they may use the wealth of the business to award themselves large pay rises, to furnish large offices or to buy expensive cars for their own use. Accounting can play an important role in monitoring and reporting how various groups benefit from the business. Owners may, therefore, rely on accounting information to see whether pay and benefits received by managers are appropriate and are in line with agreed policies.

There is also a potential collision of interest between lenders and owners. Funds loaned to a business, for example, may not be used for their intended purpose. They may be withdrawn by the owners for their own use rather than used to expand the business as agreed. Thus, lenders may rely on accounting information to see whether the owners have kept to the terms of the loan agreement.

Activity 1.2

Can you think of *two* other examples where accounting information may be relied upon by a user group to check whether the distribution of business wealth is appropriate and/or in accordance with particular agreements?

Two possible examples that spring to mind are:

- employees wishing to check that they are receiving a 'fair share' of the wealth created by the business and that managers are complying with agreed profit-sharing schemes;
- governments wishing to check that the owners of a monopoly do not benefit from excessive profits and that any pricing rules relating to the monopoly's goods or services have not been broken.

You may have thought of other examples.

HOW USEFUL IS ACCOUNTING INFORMATION?

No one would seriously claim that accounting information fully meets all of the needs of each of the various user groups. Accounting is a developing subject and we still have much to learn about user needs and the ways in which these needs should be met. Nevertheless, the information contained in accounting reports should help users make decisions relating to the business. The information should reduce uncertainty about the financial position and performance of the business. It should help to answer questions concerning the availability of funds to pay owners a return, to repay loans, to reward employees and so on.

Typically, there is no close substitute for the information provided by the financial statements. Thus, if users cannot glean the required information from the financial statements, it is often unavailable to them. Other sources of information concerning the financial health of a business are normally much less useful.

What other sources of information might, say, an investment analyst use in an attempt to gain an impression of the financial position and performance of a business? (Try to think of at least four.) What kind of information might be gleaned from these sources?

Other sources of information available include:

- meetings with managers of the business;
- public announcements made by the business;
- newspaper and magazine articles;
- websites, including the website of the business;
- radio and TV reports;
- information-gathering agencies (for example, agencies that assess the creditworthiness or credit ratings of the business);
- industry reports; and
- economy-wide reports.

These sources can provide information on various aspects of the business, such as new products or services being offered, management changes, new contracts offered or awarded, the competitive environment within which the business operates, the impact of new technology, changes in legislation, changes in interest rates and future levels of inflation.

The kind of information identified above is not really a substitute for accounting information. Rather, it is best used in conjunction with accounting information to provide a clearer picture of the financial health of a business.

Evidence on the usefulness of accounting

There are arguments, and convincing evidence, that accounting information is at least *perceived* as being useful to users. Numerous research surveys have asked users to rank the importance of accounting information, in relation to other sources of information, for decision-making purposes. Generally, these studies have found that users rank accounting information very highly. There is also considerable evidence that businesses choose to produce accounting information that exceeds the minimum requirements imposed by accounting regulations. For example, businesses often produce a considerable amount of accounting information for managers that is not required by any regulations. Presumably, the cost of producing this additional accounting information is justified on the grounds that users find it useful. Such arguments and evidence, however, leave unanswered the question of whether the information produced is actually used for decision-making purposes, that is: does it affect behaviour?

It is normally very difficult to assess the impact of accounting on decision-making behaviour. One situation arises, however, where the impact of accounting information can be observed and measured. This is where the shares (portions of ownership of a business) are traded on a stock exchange. The evidence shows that, when a business makes an announcement concerning its accounting profits, the prices at which shares are traded and the volume of shares traded often change significantly. This suggests that investors are changing their views about the future prospects of the business as a result of this new information becoming available to them. This, in turn, leads them to make a decision either to buy or to sell shares in the business.

While there is evidence that accounting reports are seen as useful and are used for decision-making purposes, it is impossible to measure just how useful they really are to users.

We cannot say with certainty, therefore, whether the cost of producing these reports represents value for money.

It is possible, however, to identify the kinds of qualities which accounting information must possess in order to be useful. Where these qualities are lacking, the usefulness of the information will be diminished. This point is now considered in some detail.

PROVIDING A SERVICE

One way of viewing accounting is as a form of service. The user groups identified in Figure 1.1 can be seen as the 'clients' and the accounting (financial) information produced can be seen as the service provided. The value of this service to the various 'clients' can be judged according to whether the accounting information meets their needs.

To be useful to users, particularly investors and lenders, the information provided should possess certain qualities, or characteristics. In particular, it must be relevant and it must faithfully represent what it is meant to represent. These two qualities, relevance and faithful representation, are regarded as fundamental qualities and require further explanation.

■ *Relevance.* Accounting information should make a difference. That is, it should be capable of influencing user decisions. To do this, it should help to *predict future events* (such as predicting next year's profit), or help to *confirm past events* (such as establishing last year's profit), or do both. By confirming past events, users can check on the accuracy of their earlier predictions. This can, in turn, help them to improve the ways in which they make predictions in the future.

To be relevant, accounting information must cross a threshold of materiality. An item of information is considered material, or significant, only if its omission or misstatement would change the decisions that users make.

Ultimately, what is considered material is a matter of judgement. When making this kind of judgement, managers should consider how this information is likely to be used by users. If a piece of information is not considered material, it should not be included within the accounting reports. It will merely clutter them up and, perhaps, interfere with the users' ability to interpret them.

■ *Faithful representation.* Accounting information should represent what it is meant to represent. To do so, the information provided must reflect the *substance* of what has occurred rather than simply its *legal form*. Take for example a manufacturer that provides goods to a retailer on a sale-or-return basis. The manufacturer may wish to treat this arrangement as two separate transactions. Thus, a contract may be agreed for the sale of the goods and a separate contract agreed for the return of the goods if unsold by the retailer. This may result in a sale being reported when the goods are delivered to the retailer even though they are returned at a later date. The economic substance, however, is that the manufacturer made no sale as the goods were subsequently returned. They were simply moved from the manufacturer's business to the retailer's business and then back again. Accounting reports should reflect this economic substance. To do otherwise would be misleading.

To provide a perfectly faithful representation, the information should be *complete.* In other words, it should incorporate everything needed to understand what is being portrayed. Thus, information relating to a particular item would normally contain a description of its nature, some suitable numerical measurement and, where necessary, explanations of important facts. Information should also be *neutral,* which means that it should be presented and selected without bias. No attempt should be made to manipulate the information in such a way as to influence user attitudes and behaviour. Finally, it should be *free from error.* This is not the same as saying that it must be perfectly accurate. Accounting information often contains estimates, such as future sales or costs, which may turn out to be inaccurate. Nevertheless, estimates may still be faithfully represented providing they are accurately described and properly prepared.

Accounting information should contain *both* of these fundamental qualities - relevance and faithful representation – if it is to be useful. There is usually little point in producing information that is relevant, but which lacks faithful representation, or producing information that is irrelevant, even if it is faithfully represented. Nevertheless, a trade-off between relevance and faithful representation may sometimes have to be made. Where, for example, an estimate of some future financial commitment is highly uncertain, it may not reflect a totally faithful portrayal of the item. This estimate may, however, be the most relevant information available. In such a situation, it may be better for users to receive the estimate, along with a description of the uncertainties that surround it, rather than receive no estimate at all.

Further qualities

Where accounting information is both relevant and faithfully represented, there are other qualities that, if present, can enhance its usefulness. These are comparability, verifiability, timeliness and understandability. Each of these qualities is now considered.

■ *Comparability.* When choosing between alternatives, users of accounting information seek to make comparisons. They may want to compare performance of the business over time (for example, the profit for this year compared to that for last year). They may also want to compare certain aspects of business performance (such as the level of sales achieved during the year) to those of similar businesses. To help users make comparisons, items that are alike should be treated in the same way – both over time and between businesses. Items that are not alike, on the other hand, should not be treated as though they are. Users must be able to detect both similarities and differences in items being compared.

■ *Verifiability.* This quality provides assurance to users that the accounting information provided faithfully portrays what it is supposed to portray. Accounting information is verifiable where different, independent experts can reach broad agreement, that it provides a faithful portrayal. Verification can be direct, such as checking a bank account balance, or indirect, such as checking the underlying assumptions and methods used to derive an estimate of a future cost.

■ *Timeliness.* Accounting information should be made available in time for users to make their decisions. A lack of timeliness undermines the usefulness of the information. Broadly speaking, the later accounting information is produced, the less useful it becomes.

■ *Understandability.* Accounting information should be presented in as clear and as concise a form as possible. Nevertheless, some accounting information may be too complex to be presented in an easily digestible form. This does not mean, however, that it should be ignored. To do so would result in reporting only a partial view of financial matters. (See Reference 1 at the end of the chapter.)

Activity 1.7

Accounting reports are aimed at users with a reasonable knowledge of accounting and business and who are prepared to invest time in studying them. Do you think, however, that accounting reports should be understandable to users without any knowledge of accounting or business?

It would be very helpful if everyone could understand accounting reports. This, however, is unrealistic as complex financial events and transactions cannot normally be expressed in simple terms. Any attempts to do so are likely to produce a very distorted picture of reality.

It is probably best that we regard accounting reports in the same way that we regard a report written in a foreign language. To understand either of these, we need to have had some preparation. When producing accounting reports, it is normally assumed that the user not only has a reasonable knowledge of business and accounting but is also prepared to invest some time in studying the reports. Nevertheless, the onus is clearly on accountants to provide information in a way that makes it as understandable as possible to non-accountants.

It is worth emphasising that the four additional qualities just discussed cannot make accounting information useful. They can only enhance the usefulness of information that is already relevant and faithfully represented.

WEIGHING UP THE COSTS AND BENEFITS

Even when an item of accounting information may have all the qualities described, this does not automatically mean that it should be collected and reported to users. There is still one more hurdle to jump. Consider Activity 1.8.

Activity 1.8

Suppose an item of information is capable of being provided. It is relevant to a particular decision and can be faithfully represented. It is also comparable, verifiable and timely, and can be understood by the decision maker.

   Can you think of the reason why, in practice, you might choose not to produce the information?

The reason is that you judge the cost of doing so to be greater than the potential benefit of having the information. This cost–benefit issue will limit the amount of accounting information provided.

In theory, a particular item of accounting information should only be produced if the costs of providing it are less than the benefits, or value, to be derived from its use. Figure 1.2 shows the relationship between the costs and value of providing additional accounting information.

The figure shows how the value of information received by the decision maker eventually begins to decline. This is, perhaps, because additional information becomes less relevant, or because of the problems that a decision maker may have in processing the sheer quantity of

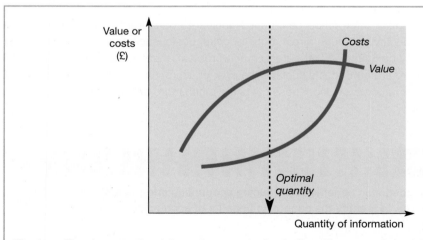

The benefits of accounting information eventually decline. The cost of providing information, however, will rise with each additional piece of information. The optimal level of information provision is where the gap between the value of the information and the cost of providing it is at its greatest.

Figure 1.2 Relationship between costs and the value of providing additional accounting information

information provided. The costs of providing the information, however, will increase with each additional piece of information. The broken line indicates the point at which the gap between the value of information and the cost of providing that information is at its greatest. This represents the optimal amount of information that can be provided. This theoretical model, however, poses a number of problems in practice.

To illustrate the practical problems of establishing the value of information, let us assume that we accidentally reversed our car into a wall in a car park. This resulted in a dented boot and scraped paintwork. We want to have the dent taken out and the paintwork re-sprayed at a local garage. We know that the nearest garage would charge £450 but we believe that other local garages may offer to do the job for a lower price. The only way of finding out the prices at other garages is to visit them, so that they can see the extent of the damage. Visiting the garages will involve using some fuel and will take up some of our time. Is it worth the cost of finding out the price for the job at the various local garages? The answer, as we have seen, is that if the cost of discovering the price is less than the potential benefit, it is worth having that information.

To identify the various prices for the job, there are several points to be considered, including:

- How many garages shall we visit?
- What is the cost of fuel to visit each garage?
- How long will it take to make all the garage visits?
- At what price do we value our time?

The economic benefit of having the information on the price of the job is probably even harder to assess. The following points need to be considered:

- What is the cheapest price that we might be quoted for the job?
- How likely is it that we shall be quoted a price cheaper than £450?

As we can imagine, the answers to these questions may be far from clear – remember that we have only contacted the local garage so far. When assessing the value of accounting information, we are confronted with similar problems.

Producing accounting information can incur significant costs. Furthermore, these costs can be difficult to identify. Although direct, out-of-pocket costs, such as salaries of accounting staff, can usually be identified without too much problem, these are only part of the total costs involved. There are other costs such as the cost of users' time spent on analysing and interpreting the information provided. These costs are much more difficult to identify and may vary between users.

Activity 1.9

What about the economic benefits of producing accounting information? Do you think it is easier, or harder, to identify the economic benefits of accounting information than the associated costs?

It is normally even harder to identify the benefits. We saw earlier that, even if we could accurately measure the economic benefits arising from a particular decision, accounting information will be only one factor influencing that decision. Furthermore, the benefits of accounting information, like the associated costs, can vary between users.

There are no easy answers to the problem of weighing costs and benefits. Although it is possible to apply some 'science' to the problem, a lot of subjective judgement is normally involved.

The qualities, or characteristics, influencing the usefulness of accounting information, which have been discussed above, are summarised in Figure 1.3.

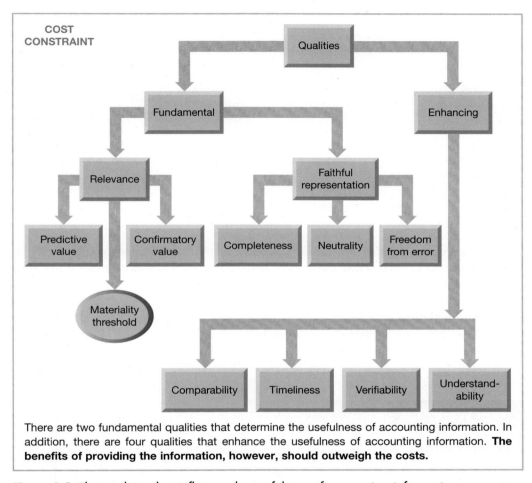

There are two fundamental qualities that determine the usefulness of accounting information. In addition, there are four qualities that enhance the usefulness of accounting information. **The benefits of providing the information, however, should outweigh the costs.**

Figure 1.3 The qualities that influence the usefulness of accounting information

ACCOUNTING AS AN INFORMATION SYSTEM

We have already seen that accounting can be seen as the provision of a service to 'clients'. Another way of viewing accounting is as a part of the business's total information system. Users, both inside and outside the business, have to make decisions concerning the allocation of scarce resources. To ensure that these resources are efficiently allocated, users often need financial information on which to base decisions. It is the role of the accounting system to provide this information.

The **accounting information system** should have certain features that are common to all information systems within a business. These are:

- identifying and capturing relevant information (in this case, financial information);
- recording, in a systematic way, the information collected;
- analysing and interpreting the information collected; and
- reporting the information in a manner that suits the needs of users.

The relationship between these features is set out in Figure 1.4.

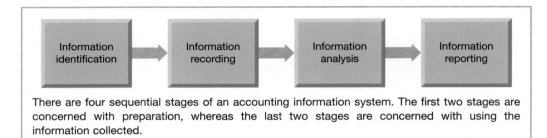

There are four sequential stages of an accounting information system. The first two stages are concerned with preparation, whereas the last two stages are concerned with using the information collected.

Figure 1.4 The accounting information system

Given the decision-making emphasis of this book, we shall be concerned primarily with the final two elements of the process: the analysis and reporting of financial information. We shall consider the way in which information is used by, and is useful to, users rather than the way in which it is identified and recorded.

Efficient accounting information systems are an essential ingredient of an efficient business. Where they contain errors, it can be both costly and disruptive. **Real World 1.1** describes how spreadsheets, which are widely used to prepare accounting and financial information, may introduce errors. This, in turn, can lead to poor financial decisions.

Real World 1.1

Systems error!

Almost one in five large businesses have suffered financial losses as a result of errors in spreadsheets, according to F1F9, which provides financial modelling and business forecasting to large businesses. It warns of looming financial disasters as 71 per cent of large British businesses always use spreadsheets for key financial decisions.

The company's new white paper entitled *Capitalism's Dirty Secret* showed that the abuse of the humble spreadsheet could have far-reaching consequences. Spreadsheets are used in the preparation of British company accounts worth up to £1.9 trillion and the UK manufacturing sector uses spreadsheets to make pricing decisions for up to £170 billion worth of business.

In total, spreadsheet calculations represent up to £38 billion of British private sector investment decisions per year, data harvested through YouGov found. Yet 16 per cent of large companies have admitted finding inaccurate information in spreadsheets more than 10 times in 2014.

Grenville Croll, a spreadsheet risk expert, said of the findings: 'Spreadsheets have been shown to be fallible yet they underpin the operation of the financial system. If the uncontrolled use of spreadsheets continues to occur in highly leveraged markets and companies, it is only a matter of time before another "Black Swan" event (an event that is highly unusual and difficult to predict) occurs causing catastrophic loss.'

The report warns that while 33 per cent of large businesses report poor decision-making as a result of spreadsheet problems, a third of the financial decision-makers using spreadsheets in large UK businesses are still given zero training.

Source: Adapted extract from: Burn-Callander, R. (2015) Stupid errors in spreadsheets could lead to Britain's next corporate disaster, *Daily Telegraph*, 7 April, www.telegraph.co.uk.

MANAGEMENT ACCOUNTING AND FINANCIAL ACCOUNTING

Accounting is usually seen as having two distinct strands. These are:

- **management accounting**, which seeks to meet the accounting needs of managers; and
- **financial accounting**, which seeks to meet the needs of owners and lenders. It should also, however, be useful to other users, identified earlier in the chapter , excluding the managers (see Figure 1.1).

The difference in their targeted user groups has led to each strand of accounting developing along different lines. The main areas of difference are as follows:

- *Nature of the reports produced.* Financial accounting reports tend to be general-purpose. As mentioned above, they are aimed primarily at providers of finance (owners and lenders) but contain financial information that should also be useful for a broad range of external users. Management accounting reports, on the other hand, are often specific-purpose reports. They are designed with a particular decision in mind and/or for a particular manager.
- *Level of detail.* Financial accounting reports provide users with a broad overview of the performance and position of the business for a period. As a result, information is aggregated (that is, added together) and detail is often lost. Management accounting reports, however, often provide managers with considerable detail to help them with a particular operational decision.
- *Regulations.* Financial accounting reports, for many businesses, are subject to accounting regulations imposed by the law and accounting rule makers. These regulations often require a standard content and, perhaps, a standard format to be adopted. Management accounting reports, on the other hand, are not subject to regulation and can be designed to meet the needs of particular managers.

Activity 1.10

Why do you think financial accounting reports are subject to regulation, whereas management accounting reports are not?

Financial accounting reports are for external publication. To protect external users, who depend on the quality of information provided by managers, they are subject to regulation. Management accounting reports, on the other hand, are produced exclusively for managers and so are for internal use only.

- *Reporting interval.* For most businesses, financial accounting reports are produced on an annual basis, although some large businesses produce half-yearly reports and a few produce quarterly ones. Management accounting reports will be produced as frequently as needed by managers. A sales manager, for example, may require routine sales reports on a daily, weekly or monthly basis, so as to monitor performance closely. Special-purpose reports can also be prepared when the occasion demands: for example, where an evaluation is required of a proposed investment in new equipment.
- *Time orientation.* Financial accounting reports reflect the performance and position of the business for the past period. In essence, they are backward looking. Management accounting reports, on the other hand, often provide information concerning future performance as well as past performance. It is an oversimplification, however, to suggest that financial accounting reports never incorporate expectations concerning the future. Occasionally, businesses will release projected information to other users in an attempt to raise funds or to fight off unwanted takeover bids. Even preparation of the routine financial accounting reports typically requires making some judgements about the future, as we shall see in Chapter 3.
- *Range and quality of information.* Two key points are worth mentioning. First, financial accounting reports concentrate on information that can be quantified in monetary terms. Management accounting also produces such reports, but is also more likely to produce reports that contain information of a non-financial nature, such as physical volume of inventories, number of sales orders received, number of new products launched, physical output per employee and so on. Second, financial accounting places greater emphasis on the use of objective, verifiable evidence when preparing reports. Management accounting reports may use information that is less objective and verifiable, but nevertheless provides managers with the information they need.

We can see from this that management accounting is less constrained than financial accounting. It may draw from a variety of sources and use information that has varying degrees of reliability. The only real test to be applied when assessing the value of the information produced for managers is whether or not it improves the quality of the decisions made.

The main differences between financial accounting and management accounting are summarised in Figure 1.5.

The differences between management accounting and financial accounting suggest that there are differences in the information needs of managers and those of other users. While differences undoubtedly exist, there is also a good deal of overlap between the needs of both.

Activity 1.11

Can you think of *two* areas of overlap between the information needs of managers and those of other users? (*Hint*: Think about the time orientation and the level of detail of accounting information.)

Two areas that spring to mind are:

- Managers will, at times, be interested in receiving a historical overview of business operations of the sort provided to other users.
- Other users would be interested in receiving detailed information relating to the future, such as the planned level of profits, and non-financial information, such as the state of the sales order book and the extent of product innovations.

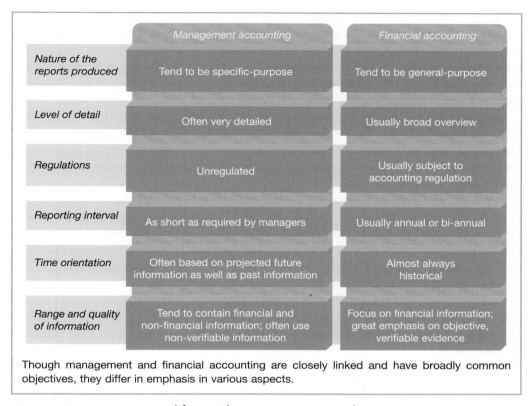

	Management accounting	Financial accounting
Nature of the reports produced	Tend to be specific-purpose	Tend to be general-purpose
Level of detail	Often very detailed	Usually broad overview
Regulations	Unregulated	Usually subject to accounting regulation
Reporting interval	As short as required by managers	Usually annual or bi-annual
Time orientation	Often based on projected future information as well as past information	Almost always historical
Range and quality of information	Tend to contain financial and non-financial information; often use non-verifiable information	Focus on financial information; great emphasis on objective, verifiable evidence

Though management and financial accounting are closely linked and have broadly common objectives, they differ in emphasis in various aspects.

Figure 1.5 Management and financial accounting compared

To some extent, differences between the two strands of accounting reflect differences in access to financial information. Managers have much more control over the form and content of the information that they receive. Other users have to rely on what managers are prepared to provide or what financial reporting regulations insist must be provided. Although the scope of financial accounting reports has increased over time, fears concerning loss of competitive advantage and user ignorance about the reliability of forecast data have resulted in other users not receiving the same detailed and wide-ranging information as that available to managers.

In the past, accounting systems tended to be primarily concerned with providing information for external users. Financial accounting requirements were the main priority and management accounting suffered as a result. Survey evidence suggests, however, that this is no longer the case. Modern management accounting systems usually provide managers with information that is relevant to their needs rather than that determined by external reporting requirements. External reporting cycles, however, retain some influence over management accounting. Managers tend to be aware of external users' expectations (see Reference 2 at the end of the chapter).

SCOPE OF THIS BOOK

This book is concerned with financial accounting rather than management accounting. In Chapter 2 we begin by introducing the three main financial statements:

- the statement of financial position;
- the income statement; and
- the statement of cash flows.

These statements are briefly reviewed before we go on to consider the statement of financial position in more detail. We shall see that the statement of financial position provides information concerning the wealth held by a business at a particular point in time and the claims against this wealth. Included in our consideration of the statement of financial position will be an introduction to the **conventions of accounting**. These are generally accepted rules that are followed when preparing financial statements.

Chapter 3 concentrates on the second of the major financial statements, the income statement. This statement provides information concerning the wealth (profit) created by a business during a period. We shall, therefore, be looking at such issues as how profit is measured, the point at which profit is recognised and the accounting conventions applied when preparing the income statement.

In the UK, and throughout much of the world, the limited company is the major form of business unit. In Chapter 4 we consider the accounting aspects of limited companies. Although these are, in essence, the same as for other types of business, some points of detail need to be considered. We shall continue our examination of limited companies in Chapter 5 and, in particular, consider the framework of rules governing the presentation of accounting reports to owners and external users.

Chapter 6 deals with the last of the three major financial statements, the statement of cash flows. This financial statement is important in identifying the financing and investing activities of the business over a period. It sets out how cash was generated and how cash was used during a period.

How financial reporting rules have developed to try to provide clear definitions and recognition criteria for key items appearing in the financial statements is developed in Chapter 7. The ultimate purpose of these rules is to enhance the comparability of financial statements between businesses. In an increasingly complex world, there is a need for rules to help both preparers and users of financial statements.

Chapters 8 and 9 consider the various techniques for analysing financial statements. To gain a deeper understanding about the financial health of a business, financial statements may be analysed using financial ratios and other techniques. Expressing two figures in the financial statements in the form of a ratio and then comparing it with a similar ratio for, say, another business, can often tell us much more than just reading the figures alone.

The typical large business in the UK operates as a group of companies rather than a single company. A group of companies exists where one company controls one or more other companies. In Chapter 10 we consider the reasons why groups exist and explore the accounting issues raised by combining companies into groups.

In Chapter 11 we shall see how the focus of financial reporting has changed over time to become more decision-oriented. We shall also look at possible ways in which the scope of financial reporting may be increased in order to meet the needs of users.

Finally, in Chapter 12, we consider the way in which larger businesses are managed. We examine the reasons why conflicts of interests may arise between owners and managers and how the behaviour of managers may be monitored and controlled.

THE CHANGING FACE OF ACCOUNTING

Over the past fifty years or so, the environment within which businesses operate has become increasingly turbulent and competitive. Various reasons have been identified to explain these changes, including:

- the increasing sophistication of customers;
- greatly improved speed and sophistication of communication (particularly with the Internet);
- the development of a global economy where national frontiers become less important;
- rapid changes in technology;
- the deregulation of domestic markets (for example, electricity, water and gas);
- increasing pressure from owners (shareholders) for competitive economic returns; and
- greater volatility of financial markets.

This new, more complex, environment has brought new challenges for managers and other users of accounting information. Their needs have changed and both financial accounting and management accounting have had to respond. To meet the changing needs of users, there has been a radical review of the kind of information to be reported.

The changed environment has given added impetus to the search for a clear conceptual framework, or framework of principles, upon which to base financial accounting reports. Various attempts have been made to clarify their purpose and to provide a more solid foundation for the development of accounting rules. Work on developing a conceptual framework tries to address fundamental questions such as:

- Who are the users of financial accounting information?
- What kinds of financial accounting reports should be prepared and what should they contain?
- How should items such as profit and assets be identified and measured?

The internationalisation of businesses has created a need for accounting rules to have an international reach. It can no longer be assumed that users of accounting information relating to a business are based in the country in which the business operates. Neither can it be assumed that the users are familiar with the accounting rules of that country. Thus, there has been increasing harmonisation of accounting rules across national frontiers.

Activity 1.12

How should the harmonisation of accounting rules benefit:

(a) an international investor?
(b) an international business?

(a) An international investor should benefit because the accounting definitions and policies used in preparing financial accounting reports will not vary across countries. This should make the comparison of performance between businesses operating in different countries much easier.
(b) An international business should benefit because the cost of producing accounting reports in order to comply with the rules of different countries can be expensive. Harmonisation can, therefore, lead to significant cost savings. It may also broaden the appeal of the business among international investors. Where there are common accounting rules, they may have greater confidence to invest.

In response to criticisms that the financial reports of some businesses are opaque and difficult for users to interpret, great efforts have been made to improve reporting rules. Accounting rule makers have tried to ensure that the accounting policies of businesses are more comparable and transparent and that the financial reports provide a more faithful portrayal of economic reality.

Management accounting has also changed by becoming more outward looking in its focus. In the past, information provided to managers has been largely restricted to that collected within the business. However, the attitude and behaviour of customers and rival businesses have now become the object of much information gathering. Increasingly, successful businesses are those that are able to secure and maintain competitive advantage over their rivals.

To obtain this advantage, businesses have become more 'customer driven' (that is, concerned with satisfying customer needs). This has led to the production of management accounting information that provides details of customers and the market, such as customer evaluation of services provided and market share. In addition, information about the costs and profits of rival businesses, which can be used as 'benchmarks' by which to gauge competitiveness, is gathered and reported.

To compete successfully, businesses must also find ways of managing costs. The cost base of modern businesses is under continual review and this, in turn, has led to the development of more sophisticated methods of measuring and controlling costs.

ACCOUNTING FOR BUSINESS

We have seen that the needs of the various user groups will determine the kind of accounting information to be provided. Those needs, however, will partly be shaped by the forms of business ownership and the ways in which a business is organised and structured. In the sections that follow, we shall consider the business environment within which accounting information is produced. This should help our understanding of points that crop up in later chapters.

WHAT IS THE PURPOSE OF A BUSINESS?

Peter Drucker, an eminent management thinker, has argued that 'the purpose of business is to create and keep a customer' (see Reference 3 at the end of the chapter). Drucker defined the purpose of a business in this way in 1967, at a time when most businesses did not adopt this strong customer focus. His view, therefore, represented a radical challenge to the accepted view of what businesses should do. More than fifty years on, however, his approach has become part of the conventional wisdom. It is now widely recognised that, in order to succeed, businesses must focus on satisfying the needs of the customer.

Although the customer has always provided the main source of revenue for a business, this has often been taken for granted. In the past, too many businesses have assumed that the customer would readily accept whatever services or products were on offer. When competition was weak and customers were passive, businesses could operate under this assumption and still make a profit. However, the era of weak competition has passed. Now, customers have much greater choice and are much more assertive concerning their needs. They now demand higher quality services and goods at cheaper prices. They also require that services and goods be delivered faster with an increasing emphasis on the product being tailored to their individual needs. If a business cannot meet these needs, a competitor often can. Thus, the business mantra for the current era is '*the customer is king*'. Most businesses recognise this fact and organise themselves accordingly.

Real World 1.2 describes how the Internet and social media have given added weight to this mantra. It points out that dissatisfied customers now have a powerful medium for broadcasting their complaints.

WHAT KINDS OF BUSINESS OWNERSHIP EXIST?

The particular form of business ownership has certain implications for financial accounting and so it is useful to be clear about the main forms of ownership that can arise. There are basically three arrangements for private-sector businesses:

- sole proprietorship;
- partnership; and
- limited company.

We shall now consider these.

Sole proprietorship

Sole proprietorship, as the name suggests, is where an individual is the sole owner of a business. This type of business is often quite small in terms of size (as measured, for example, by sales revenue generated or number of staff employed); however, the number of such businesses is very large indeed. Examples of sole-proprietor businesses can be found in most industrial sectors but particularly within the service sector. Hence, services such as electrical repairs, picture framing, photography, driving instruction, retail shops and hotels have a large proportion of sole-proprietor businesses.

The sole-proprietor business is easy to set up. No formal procedures are required and operations can often commence immediately (unless special permission is required because of the nature of the trade or service, such as running licensed premises (a pub)). The owner can decide the way in which the business is to be conducted and has the flexibility to restructure or dissolve the business whenever it suits. The law does not recognise the sole-proprietor business as being separate from the owner, so the business will cease on the death of the owner.

Although the owner must produce accounting information about the business to satisfy the taxation authorities, there is no legal requirement to provide it to other user groups. Some user groups, however, may demand accounting information about the business and may be in a position to enforce their demands (for example, a bank requiring accounting information on a regular basis as a condition of a loan). A sole proprietor has unlimited liability which means that no distinction is made between the proprietor's personal wealth and that of the business if there are business debts to be paid.

Partnership

A **partnership** exists where two or more individuals carry on a business together with the intention of making a profit. Partnerships have much in common with sole-proprietor businesses. They are usually quite small in size (although some, such as partnerships of accountants and solicitors, can be large). They are also easy to set up, as no formal procedures are required (and it is not even necessary to have a written agreement between the partners). The partners can agree whatever arrangements suit them concerning the financial and management aspects of the business. Similarly, the partnership can be restructured or dissolved by agreement between the partners.

Partnerships are not recognised in law as separate entities and so contracts with third parties must be entered into in the name of individual partners. The partners of a business usually have unlimited liability.

Activity 1.13

What do you think are the main advantages and disadvantages of a partnership compared to a sole-proprietor business?

The main advantages of a partnership over a sole-proprietor business are:

- sharing the burden of ownership;
- the opportunity to specialise rather than cover the whole range of services (for example, in a solicitors' practice each partner may specialise in a different aspect of the law); and
- the ability to raise capital where this is beyond the capacity of a single individual.

The main disadvantages of a partnership compared with a sole proprietorship are:

- the risks of sharing ownership of a business with unsuitable individuals; and
- the limits placed on individual decision making that a partnership will impose.

Limited company

A limited company can range in size from quite small to very large. There is no limit on the number of individuals who can subscribe capital and become the owners, which provides the opportunity to create a very large-scale business. The liability of owners, however, is limited (hence 'limited' company), which means that those individuals subscribing capital to the company are liable only for debts incurred by the company up to the amount that they have invested, or agreed to invest. This cap on the liability of the owners is designed to limit risk and to produce greater confidence to invest. Without such limits on owner liability, it is difficult to see how a modern capitalist economy could operate. In many cases, the owners of a limited company are not involved in the day-to-day running of the business and will, therefore, invest in a business only if there is a clear limit set on the level of investment risk.

Note that this 'limited liability' does not apply to sole proprietors and partners. These individuals have a legal obligation to meet all of their business debts, if necessary using, what they may have thought of as, private assets (for example, their private houses). The ability of the owners of limited companies to limit their liability can often make this type of type of business more attractive than either sole proprietorships or partnerships.

The benefit of limited liability, however, imposes certain obligations on such companies. To start up a limited company, documents of incorporation must be prepared that set out, among other things, the objectives of the business. Furthermore, a framework of regulations exists that places obligations on limited companies concerning the way in which they conduct their affairs. Part of this regulatory framework requires annual financial reports to be made available to owners and lenders and, usually, an annual general meeting of the owners has to be held to approve the reports. In addition, a copy of the annual financial reports must be lodged with the Registrar of Companies for public inspection. In this way, the financial affairs of a limited company enter the public domain.

With the exception of small companies, there is also a requirement for the annual financial reports to be subject to an audit. This involves an independent firm of accountants examining the annual reports and underlying records to see whether the reports provide a true and fair view of the financial health of the company and whether they comply with the relevant accounting rules established by law and by accounting rule makers. Limited companies are considered in more detail in Chapters 4 and 5.

All of the large household-name UK businesses (Marks and Spencer, Tesco, Shell, Sky, Rolls-Royce, BT, easyJet and so on) are limited companies.

Activity 1.14

What are the main advantages of forming a partnership business rather than a limited liability company? Try to think of at least three.

The main advantages are:

- the ease of setting up the business;
- the degree of flexibility concerning the way in which the business is conducted;
- the degree of flexibility concerning restructuring and dissolution of the business; and
- freedom from administrative burdens imposed by law (for example, the annual general meeting and the need for an independent audit).

As we saw earlier, the main disadvantage of a partnership compared with a limited company is that it is not normally possible to limit the liability of all of the partners. There is, however, a hybrid form of business ownership that is referred to as a Limited Liability Partnership (LLP). This has many of the attributes of a normal partnership but is different insofar that the LLP, rather than the individual partners, is responsible for any debts incurred. Accountants and solicitors often use this type of partnership.

This book concentrates on the accounting aspects of limited liability companies because they are, by far, the most important in economic terms. The early chapters will introduce accounting concepts through examples that do not draw a distinction between the different types of business. Once we have dealt with the basic accounting principles, which are precisely the same for all three types of business, we go on to see how they are applied to limited companies.

HOW ARE BUSINESSES ORGANISED?

Most businesses involving more than a few owners and/or employees are set up as limited companies. Finance will come from the owners (shareholders) both in the form of a direct cash investment to buy shares (in the ownership of the business) and through the shareholders allowing past profits, which belong to them, to be reinvested in the business. Finance will also come from lenders (banks, for example), who earn interest on their loans. Further finance will be provided through suppliers of goods and services being prepared to supply on credit.

In larger limited companies, the owners (shareholders) tend not to be involved in the daily running of the business; instead they appoint a board of directors to manage the business on their behalf. The board is charged with three major tasks:

1 setting the overall direction and strategy for the business;
2 monitoring and controlling the activities of the business; and
3 communicating with shareholders and others connected with the business.

Each board has a chairman, elected by the directors, who is responsible for running the board in an efficient manner. In addition, each board has a chief executive officer (CEO) who is responsible for running the business on a day-to-day basis. Occasionally, the roles of chairman and CEO are combined, although it is usually considered to be a good idea to separate them to prevent a single individual having excessive power. We shall consider the relationship between directors and shareholders in more detail in Chapters 4 and 12.

The board of directors represents the most senior level of management. Below this level, managers are employed, with each manager being given responsibility for a particular part of the business's operations.

THE QUEST FOR WEALTH CREATION

A business is normally created to enhance the wealth of its owners. This may come as a surprise, as there are other objectives that a business may pursue that would fulfil the needs of others with a stake in the business.

What other objectives might a business pursue? Try to think of at least two.

A business may seek:

- to provide well-paid jobs and good working conditions for its employees;
- to conserve the environment for the local community;
- to produce products or services that will benefit its customers; and/or
- to support local suppliers.

You may have thought of others.

Although a business may pursue other such objectives, it is normally set up primarily with a view to increasing the wealth of its owners. In practice, the behaviour of businesses over time appears to be consistent with this objective.

Within a market economy, there are strong competitive forces at work that ensure that failure to enhance owners' wealth will not be tolerated for long. Competition for the funds provided by the owners and competition for managers' jobs will normally mean that the owners' interests will prevail. If the managers do not provide the required increase in ownership wealth, the owners have the power to replace the existing management team with a new team that is more responsive to their needs.

MEETING THE NEEDS OF OTHER STAKEHOLDERS

The points made above do not mean that the needs of other groups with a stake in the business, such as employees, customers, suppliers, the community, are unimportant. In fact, the opposite is true, if the business wishes to survive and prosper over the longer term. For example, a business with disaffected customers may well find that they turn to another supplier, resulting in a loss of shareholder wealth. **Real World 1.3** provides examples of businesses that acknowledge the vital link between satisfying customers' needs and creating wealth (value) for their owners (shareholders).

Expressing its position

National Express plc, a leading transport provider, states its approach as follows:

> At National Express we believe our business model should start with our customers. By serving our customers with operational excellence, we are able to create profit and cash, thereby generating shareholder value.

Source: www.nationalexpress.com [accessed 2 January 2019].

Other stakeholders that contribute towards the wealth-creation process must also be considered. A dissatisfied workforce can result in low productivity and strikes while dissatisfied suppliers can withhold vital supplies or give lower priority to orders received. A discontented local community can withdraw access to community resources. In each case, the owners' wealth will suffer.

Real World 1.4 describes how one well-known business came to recognise that future success depended on the support of key stakeholder groups.

Real World 1.4

The price of clothes

Nike is a highly successful business with a globally-recognised brand. However, it was not so long ago that the business was mired in controversy. It had become a focal point for protesters who regarded the business as a byword for 'sweatshop' labour practices. In 1992, an article was published that exposed the low wages and poor working conditions of those producing Nike products in Indonesia. Subsequent protests and further revelations resulted in unwanted media attention to which the business was, at first, slow to properly respond. However, by 1998, weakening demand for its products meant that the issue could no longer be lightly dismissed. Nike publicly acknowledged the reputation it had gained for 'sweatshop' labour practices and the adverse effect this was having on customer attitudes.

Its management realised that, if nothing else, it was good business to improve the working lives of those producing Nike products in third world countries. This resulted in a commitment to better working conditions, higher wages and a minimum working age. A code of conduct for Nike suppliers concerning the treatment of their workforce was established and independent audits were implemented to monitor adherence to the code. The business also committed to greater transparency: it now publishes reports on its responsibilities and the ways in which these have been fulfilled.

Although Nike was not the only large business engaged in sweatshop practices, it took a lead in trying to eradicate them and, by doing so, removed the stain from its reputation. This has been rewarded by a continuing demand for its products.

Source: Based on information in Nisen, M. (2013) *How Nike Solved it Sweatshop Problem* Business Insider 9 May and Allarey, R. (2015) *This Is How Nike Managed to Clean Up Its Sweatshop Reputation* 8 June http://www.complex.com.

It is clear from the above that creating wealth for the owners is not the same as seeking to maximise the current year's profit. Wealth creation is concerned with the longer term. It relates not only to this year's profit but to that of future years as well. In the short term, corners can be cut and risks taken that improve current profit at the expense of future profit. **Real World 1.5** provides some examples of how emphasis on short-term profit can be very damaging.

Short-term gains, long-term problems

For many years, under the guise of defending capitalism, we have been allowing ourselves to degrade it. We have been poisoning the well from which we have drawn wealth. We have misunderstood the importance of values to capitalism. We have surrendered to the idea that success is pursued by making as much money as the law allowed without regard to how it was made.

Thirty years ago, retailers would be quite content to source the shoes they wanted to sell as cheaply as possible. The working conditions of those who produced them was not their concern. Then headlines and protests developed. Society started to hold them responsible for previously invisible working conditions. Companies like Nike went through a transformation. They realised they were polluting their brand. Global sourcing became visible. It was no longer viable to define success simply in terms of buying at the lowest price and selling at the highest.

Financial services and investment are today where footwear was thirty years ago. Public anger at the crisis will make visible what was previously hidden. Take the building up of huge portfolios of loans to poor people on US trailer parks. These loans were authorised without proper scrutiny of the circumstances of the borrowers. Somebody else then deemed them fit to be securitised and so on through credit default swaps and the rest without anyone seeing the transaction in terms of its ultimate human origin.

Each of the decision makers thought it okay to act like the thoughtless footwear buyer of the 1970s. The price was attractive. There was money to make on the deal. Was it responsible? Irrelevant. It was legal, and others were making money that way. And the consequences for the banking system if everybody did it? Not our problem.

The consumer has had a profound shock. Surely we could have expected the clever and wise people who invested our money to be better at risk management than they have shown themselves to be in the present crisis? How could they have been so gullible in not challenging the bankers whose lending proved so flaky? How could they have believed that the levels of bonuses that were, at least in part, coming out of their savings could have been justified in 'incentivising' a better performance? How could they have believed that a 'better' performance would be one that is achieved for one bank without regard to its effect on the whole banking system? Where was the stewardship from those exercising investment on their behalf?

The answer has been that very few of them do exercise that stewardship. Most have stood back and said it doesn't really pay them to do so. The failure of stewardship comes from the same mindset that created the irresponsible lending in the first place. We are back to the mindset that has allowed us to poison the well: never mind the health of the system as a whole, I'm making money out of it at the moment. Responsibility means awareness for the system consequences of our actions. It is not a luxury. It is the cornerstone of prudence.

BALANCING RISK AND RETURN

All decision making concerns the future and financial decision making is no exception. The only thing certain about the future, however, is that we cannot be sure what will happen. Things may not turn out as planned and this risk should be taken into account when making financial decisions.

As in other aspects of life, risk and return tend to be related. Evidence shows that returns relate to risk in something like the way shown in Figure 1.6.

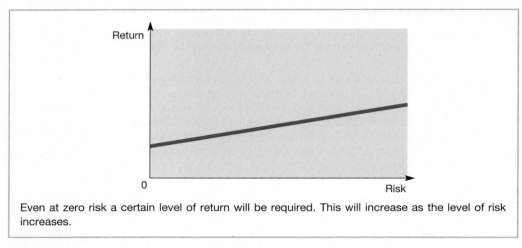

Even at zero risk a certain level of return will be required. This will increase as the level of risk increases.

Figure 1.6 Relationship between risk and return

This relationship between risk and return has important implications for setting financial objectives for a business. The owners will require a minimum return to induce them to invest at all, but will require an additional return to compensate for taking risks; the higher the risk, the higher the required return. Managers must be aware of this and must strike the appropriate balance between risk and return when setting objectives and pursuing particular courses of action.

The turmoil in the banking sector, earlier this century, has shown, however, that the right balance is not always struck. Some banks took on excessive risks in pursuit of higher returns and, as a consequence, incurred massive losses. They are now being kept afloat with taxpayers' money. **Real World 1.6** discusses the collapse of one leading bank, in which the UK government took a majority stake, and argues that the risk appetite of banks must now change.

REASONS TO BE ETHICAL

The way in which individual businesses operate in terms of the honesty, fairness and transparency with which they treat their stakeholders (customers, employees, suppliers, the community, the shareholders and so on) has become a key issue. There have been many examples of businesses, some of them very well known, acting in ways that most people would regard as unethical and unacceptable. Examples of such actions include:

■ paying bribes to encourage employees of other businesses to reveal information about the employee's business that could be useful;

■ oppressive treatment of suppliers, for example, making suppliers wait excessive periods before payment; and

■ manipulating the financial statements to mislead users of them, for example, to overstate profit so that senior managers become eligible for performance bonuses (known as 'creative accounting').

Despite the many examples of unethical acts that have attracted publicity over recent years, it would be very unfair to conclude that most businesses are involved in unethical activities. Nevertheless, revelations of unethical practice can be damaging to the entire business community. Lying, stealing and fraudulent behaviour can lead to a loss of confidence in business and the imposition of tighter regulatory burdens. In response to this threat, businesses often seek to demonstrate their commitment to acting in an honest and ethical way. One way of doing this is to develop, and adhere to, a code of ethics concerning business behaviour.

Accountants are likely to find themselves at the forefront with issues relating to business ethics. In the three examples of unethical business activity listed above, an accountant would probably have to be involved either in helping to commit the unethical act or in covering it up. Accountants are, therefore, particularly vulnerable to being put under pressure to engage in unethical acts. Some businesses acknowledge this risk and produce an ethical code for their accounting staff. **Real World 1.7** provides an example of one such code.

Real World 1.7

The only way is ethics

Vodafone plc, the telecommunications business, has a code of ethics for its chief executive and senior finance and accounting staff. The code states that they to have a duty to:

. . . act with integrity. Integrity requires, among other things, being honest and candid. Deceit, dishonesty and subordination of principle are inconsistent with integrity. Service to the Company should never be subordinated to personal gain and advantage.

The code specifically states that they must:

- act with integrity, including being honest and candid while still maintaining the confidentiality of Company information where required or in the Company's interests;
- observe, fully, applicable governmental laws, rules and regulations;
- comply with the requirements of applicable accounting and auditing standards and Company policies in the maintenance of a high standard of accuracy and completeness in the Company's financial records;
- adhere to a high standard of business ethics and not seek competitive advantage through unlawful or unethical business practices; and
- avoid conflicts of interest wherever possible. Anything that would be a conflict for a Relevant Officer will also be a conflict if it is related to a member of his or her family or a close relative.

Source: Code of Ethics Vodafone plc Accessed 13 February 2019 www.vodafone.com.

NOT-FOR-PROFIT ORGANISATIONS

Although the focus of this book is accounting as it relates to private-sector businesses, there are many organisations that do not exist mainly for the pursuit of profit.

All of these organisations need to produce accounting information for decision-making purposes. Once again, various user groups need this information to help them to make decisions. These user groups are often the same as, or similar to, those identified for private-sector businesses. They often have a stake in the future viability of the organisation and may use accounting information to check that the wealth of the organisation is being properly controlled and is used in a way that conforms to its objectives.

Can you think of at least four types of organisation that are not primarily concerned with making profits?

We thought of the following:

- charities
- clubs and associations
- universities
- local government authorities
- national government departments
- churches
- trade unions.

Nevertheless, certain types of not-for-profit organisation, such as charities, often suffer from inadequate accounting systems and a lack of financial skills among its managers. This can have disastrous consequences. **Real World 1.8** describes how one high-profile UK charity collapsed amid claims of weak accounting controls and financial mismanagement.

Real World 1.8

No kidding?

Senior directors at the charity Kids Company repeatedly warned trustees of the need to build up financial reserves or face going to the wall, the *Guardian* can reveal, as an analysis of the accounts show that its funding increased by more than 75% in five years.

Two finance directors at Kids Company left in less than three years because of their frustrations that no one – from the board of trustees, led by the BBC's Alan Yentob, to the chief executive, Camila Batmanghelidjh – heeded warnings of the need to build a financial cushion to protect the charity from catastrophe, the *Guardian* understands.

'If you keep building an organisation without building reserves, then it's a house of cards and it will fall down,' said one source who worked in a senior role at the charity for several years.

A *Guardian* analysis of five years of accounts show how the charity got itself into dire financial straits. Despite receiving millions of pounds in government funding, it lived hand to mouth, never built up any reserves, and spent almost all its income each year.

Analysis of the charity's accounts from 2009 to 2013 shows the organisation was receiving huge injections of funding, which included millions of pounds in government grants. Between 2009 and 2013, its income increased by 77% from £13m to £23m, but the charity was spending almost every penny it brought in. In the same period, its outgoings increased by 72%.

Despite repeated warnings on the accounts seen by trustees and presented to the Charity Commission, no consistent reserve was built up.

In March 2014, an audit of the charity was commissioned by the Cabinet Office and carried out by accountancy firm PKF Littlejohn. It noted that the charity was facing a 'serious cashflow' issue.

Historical note: The charity collapsed in August 2015.

Source: Laville S., Barr C. and Slawson, N. (2015) *Kids Company trustees accused of ignoring finance warnings*, www.theguardian.com, 6 August.

SUMMARY

The main points of this chapter may be summarised as follows:

What is accounting?

- Accounting provides financial information to help various user groups make better judgements and decisions.

Accounting and user needs

- For accounting to be useful, it must be clear *for whom* and *for what purpose* the information will be used.
- Owners, managers and lenders are important user groups, but there are several others.
- Conflicts of interest between users may arise over the ways in which business wealth is generated or distributed.
- The evidence suggests that accounting is both used and useful for decision-making purposes.

Providing a service

- Accounting can be viewed as a form of service as it involves providing financial information to various users.
- To provide a useful service, accounting information must possess certain qualities, or characteristics. The fundamental qualities are relevance and faithful representation. Other qualities that enhance the usefulness of accounting information are comparability, verifiability, timeliness and understandability.
- Providing a service to users can be costly and financial information should be produced only if the cost of providing the information is less than the benefits gained.

Accounting information

- Accounting is part of the total information system within a business. It shares the features that are common to all information systems within a business, which are the identification, recording, analysis and reporting of information.

Management accounting and financial accounting

- Accounting has two main strands – management accounting and financial accounting.
- Management accounting seeks to meet the needs of the business's managers, and financial accounting seeks to meet the needs of owners and lenders, but should also be of use to other user groups.
- These two strands differ in terms of the types of reports produced, the level of reporting detail, the time orientation, the degree of regulation and the range and quality of information provided.

The changing face of accounting

- Changes in the economic environment have led to changes in the nature and scope of accounting.

- Financial accounting has improved its framework of rules and there has been greater international harmonisation of accounting rules.
- Management accounting has become more outward looking, and new methods for managing costs have been developed to help a business gain competitive advantage.

What is the purpose of a business?

- The purpose of a business is to create and keep customers.

What kinds of business ownership exist?

There are three main forms of business unit:

- sole proprietorship – easy to set up and flexible to operate, but the owner has unlimited liability;
- partnership – easy to set up and spreads the burdens of ownership, but partners usually have unlimited liability and there are ownership risks if the partners are unsuitable;
- limited company – limited liability for owners, but obligations are imposed on how a company conducts its affairs.

How are businesses organised and managed?

- Most businesses of any size are set up as limited companies.
- A board of directors is appointed by owners (shareholders) to oversee the running of the business.

The quest for wealth creation

- The key financial objective of a business is to enhance the wealth of the owners.
- To achieve this objective, the needs of other groups connected with the business, such as employees, suppliers and the local community, cannot be ignored.
- When setting financial objectives, the right balance must be struck between risk and return.

Ethical behaviour

- Accounting staff may be put under pressure to commit unethical acts.
- Many businesses produce a code of ethical conduct to help protect accounting staff from this risk.

Not-for-profit organisations

- These organisations also produce accounting information for decision-making purposes.
- They have user groups that are similar to, or the same as, those of private-sector businesses.

REFERENCES

1. International Accounting Standards Board (2018) *Conceptual Framework for Financial Reporting*, pp. 14–20.
2. Dugdale, D., Jones, C. and Green, S. (2006) *Contemporary Management Accounting Practices in UK Manufacturing*, CIMA/Elsevier.
3. Drucker, P. (1967) *The Effective Executive*, Heinemann.

FURTHER READING

If you would like to explore the topics covered in this chapter in more depth, we recommend the following:

Alexander, D. and Nobes, C. (2016) *Financial Accounting: An International Introduction*, 6th edn, Pearson, Chapters 1 and 3.

Drury, C. (2018) *Management and Cost Accounting*, 10th edn, Cengage Learning EMEA, Chapter 1.

Elliott, B. and Elliott, J. (2017) *Financial Accounting and Reporting*, 18th edn, Pearson, Chapters 6 and 7.

Scott W. (2014) *Financial Accounting Theory*, 7th edn, Pearson, Chapters 1 and 3.

CRITICAL REVIEW QUESTIONS

Solutions to these questions can be found at the back of the book, starting on page 536.

1.1 Accounting is sometimes described as 'the language of business'. Why do you think this is the case? Is this an apt description of accounting?

1.2 Identify the main users of accounting information for a university. For what purposes would different user groups need information? Is there a major difference in the ways in which accounting information for a university would be used compared with that of a private-sector business?

1.3 'Not-for-profit organisations are not interested in making a profit.' Is this statement true? Does accounting and finance have a less important role to play in not-for-profit organisations than for businesses?

1.4 Financial accounting statements tend to reflect past events. In view of this, how can they be of any assistance to a user in making a decision when decisions, by their very nature, can only be made about future actions?

Chapter 2

MEASURING AND REPORTING FINANCIAL POSITION

INTRODUCTION

We saw in Chapter 1 that accounting has two distinct strands: financial accounting and management accounting. This chapter, along with Chapters 3 to 6, examines the three major financial statements that form the core of financial accounting. We start by taking an overview of these statements to see how each contributes towards an assessment of the overall financial position and performance of a business.

Following this overview, we begin a more detailed examination by turning our attention towards one of these financial statements: the statement of financial position. We identify the key elements of this statement and consider the interrelationships between them. We also consider the main accounting conventions, or rules, to be followed when preparing the statement of financial position.

Learning outcomes

When you have completed this chapter, you should be able to:

- explain the nature and purpose of the three major financial statements;
- prepare a simple statement of financial position and interpret the information that it contains;
- discuss the accounting conventions underpinning the statement of financial position; and
- discuss the uses and limitations of the statement of financial position for decision-making purposes.

THE MAJOR FINANCIAL STATEMENTS – AN OVERVIEW

The major financial accounting statements aim to provide a picture of the financial position and performance of a business. To achieve this, a business's accounting system will normally produce three financial statements on a regular, recurring basis. These three statements are concerned with answering the following questions relating to a particular period:

- What cash movements took place?
- How much wealth was generated?
- What is the accumulated wealth of the business at the end of the period and what form does it take?

To address each of these questions, there is a separate financial statement. The financial statements are:

- the statement of cash flows;
- the income statement (also known as the profit and loss account); and
- the statement of financial position (also known as the balance sheet).

Together they provide an overall picture of the financial health of the business.

Perhaps the best way to introduce these financial statements is to look at an example of a very simple business. From this we shall be able to see the sort of information that each of the statements can usefully provide. It is, however, worth pointing out that, while a simple business is our starting point, the principles for preparing the financial statements apply equally to the largest and most complex businesses. This means that we shall continually encounter these principles again in later chapters.

Example 2.1

Paul was unemployed and unable to find a job. He therefore decided to embark on a business venture. With Christmas approaching, he decided to buy gift wrapping paper from a local supplier and to sell it on the corner of his local high street. He felt that the price of wrapping paper in the high street shops was unreasonably high. This provided him with a useful business opportunity.

He began the venture with £40 of his own money, in cash. On Monday, Paul's first day of trading, he bought wrapping paper for £40 and sold three-quarters of it for £45 cash.

What cash movements took place in Paul's business during Monday?

For Monday, a *statement of cash flows* showing the cash movements (that is, cash in and cash out) for the day can be prepared as follows:

Statement of cash flows for Monday

	£
Cash introduced (by Paul)	40
Cash from sales of wrapping paper	45
Cash paid to buy wrapping paper	(40)
Closing balance of cash	**45**

The statement shows that Paul placed £40 cash into the business. The business received £45 cash from customers, but paid £40 cash to buy the wrapping paper. This left £45 of cash by Monday evening. Note that we are taking the standard approach found in financial statements of showing figures to be deducted (in this case the £40 paid out) in brackets. We shall take this approach consistently throughout the chapters dealing with financial statements.

How much wealth (that is, profit) was generated by the business during Monday?

An *income statement* can be prepared to show the wealth generated (profit) on Monday. The wealth generated arises from trading and will be the difference between the value of the sales made and the cost of the goods (that is, wrapping paper) sold.

Income statement for Monday

	£
Sales revenue	45
Cost of goods sold ($^3/_4$ of £40)	(30)
Profit	15

Note that it is only the cost of the wrapping paper *sold* that is matched against (and deducted from) the sales revenue in order to find the profit, not the whole of the cost of wrapping paper acquired. Any unsold inventories (also known as *stock*) will be charged against any future sales revenue that it generates. In this case the cost of the unsold inventories is $^1/_4$ of £40 = £10.

What is the accumulated wealth on Monday evening and what form does it take?

To establish the accumulated wealth at the end of Monday's trading, we can draw up a *statement of financial position* for Paul's business. This statement will also list the forms of wealth held at the end of that day.

Statement of financial position as at Monday evening

	£
Cash (closing balance)	45
Inventories of goods for resale ($^1/_4$ of 40)	10
Total assets	55
Equity	55

Note the terms 'assets' and 'equity' that appear in this statement. 'Assets' are business resources (things of value to the business) and include cash and inventories. 'Equity' is the word used in accounting to describe the investment, or stake, of the owner(s) – in this case Paul – in the business. Both of these terms will be discussed in some detail a little later in this chapter. Note that the equity on Monday evening was £55. This represented the £40 that Paul put in to start the business, plus Monday's profit (£15) – profits belong to the owner(s).

Let us now continue by looking at what happens on the following day.

On Tuesday, Paul bought more wrapping paper for £20 cash. He managed to sell all of the new inventories and all of the earlier inventories, for a total of £48.

The statement of cash flows for Tuesday will be as follows:

Statement of cash flows for Tuesday

	£
Opening balance (from Monday evening)	45
Cash from sales of wrapping paper	48
Cash paid to buy wrapping paper	(20)
Closing balance	**73**

The income statement for Tuesday will be as follows:

Income statement for Tuesday

	£
Sales revenue	48
Cost of goods sold (£20 + £10)	(30)
Profit	**18**

The statement of financial position as at Tuesday evening will be:

Statement of financial position as at Tuesday evening

	£
Cash (closing balance)	73
Inventories	–
Total assets	**73**
Equity	**73**

We can see that the total business wealth had increased to £73 by Tuesday evening. This represents an increase of £18 (that is, £73 − £55) over Monday's figure – which, of course, is the amount of profit made during Tuesday as shown on the income statement.

We can see from the financial statements in Example 2.1 that each statement provides part of a picture of the financial performance and position of the business. We begin by showing the cash movements. Cash is a vital resource that is needed for any business to function effectively. It is used to meet debts that become due and to acquire other resources (such as inventories). Cash has been described as the 'lifeblood' of a business.

Reporting cash movements alone, however, is not enough to portray the financial health of the business. To find out how much profit was generated, we need an income statement. It is important to recognise that cash and profits rarely move in unison. During Monday, for example, the cash balance increased by £5, but the profit generated, as shown in the income statement, was £15. The cash balance did not increase in line with profit because part of the wealth (£10) was held in the form of inventories.

The statement of financial position that was drawn up as at the end of Monday's trading provides an insight into the total wealth of the business. This wealth can be held in various forms. For Paul's business, wealth is held in the form of cash and inventories. This means that, when drawing up the statement of financial position, both forms will be listed. For a large business, many other forms of wealth may be held, such as property, equipment, motor vehicles and so on.

On Wednesday, Paul bought more wrapping paper for £46 cash. However, it was raining hard for much of the day and sales were slow. After Paul had sold half of his total inventories for £32, he decided to stop trading until Thursday morning.

Have a go at drawing up the three financial statements for Paul's business for Wednesday.

Statement of cash flows for Wednesday

	£
Opening balance (from Tuesday evening)	73
Cash from sales of wrapping paper	32
Cash paid to buy wrapping paper	(46)
Closing balance	59

Income statement for Wednesday

	£
Sales revenue	32
Cost of goods sold ($\frac{1}{2}$ of £46)	(23)
Profit	9

Statement of financial position as at Wednesday evening

	£
Cash (closing balance)	59
Inventories ($\frac{1}{2}$ of £46)	23
Total assets	82
Equity	82

Note that the total business wealth has increased by £9 (that is, the amount of Wednesday's profit) even though the cash balance has declined. This is because the business is holding more of its wealth in the form of inventories rather than cash, compared with the position on Tuesday evening.

By Wednesday evening, the equity stood at £82. This arose from Paul's initial investment of £40, plus his profits for Monday (£15), Tuesday (£18) and Wednesday (£9). This represents Paul's total investment in his business at that time. The equity of most businesses will similarly be made up of injections of funds by the owner(s) plus any accumulated profits.

We can see that the income statement and statement of cash flows are both concerned with measuring flows (of wealth and cash respectively) during a particular period. The statement of financial position, however, is concerned with the financial position at a particular moment in time. Figure 2.1 illustrates this point.

The three financial statements discussed are often referred to as the **final accounts** of the business.

For external users (that is, virtually all users except the managers of the business concerned), these statements are normally backward-looking because they are based on information concerning past events and transactions. This can be useful in providing feedback on past performance and in identifying trends that provide clues to future performance. However, the statements can also be prepared using projected data to help assess likely future profits, cash flows and so on. Normally, this is done only for management decision-making purposes.

Now that we have an overview of the financial statements, we shall consider each one in detail. The remainder of this chapter is devoted to the statement of financial position.

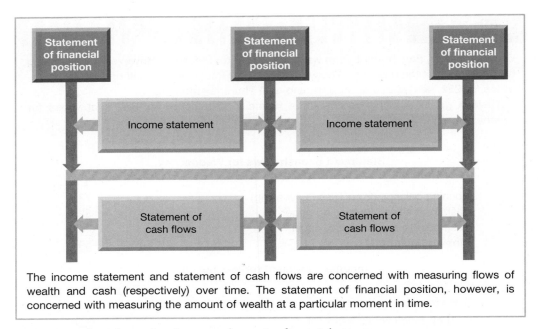

The income statement and statement of cash flows are concerned with measuring flows of wealth and cash (respectively) over time. The statement of financial position, however, is concerned with measuring the amount of wealth at a particular moment in time.

Figure 2.1 The relationship between the major financial statements

THE STATEMENT OF FINANCIAL POSITION

We saw a little earlier that this statement shows the forms in which the wealth of a business is held and how much wealth is held in each form. We can, however, be more specific about the nature of this statement by saying that it sets out the **assets** of a business, on the one hand, and the **claims** against the business, on the other. Before looking at the statement of financial position in more detail, we need to be clear about what these terms mean.

Assets

An asset is essentially a resource held by a business. To qualify as an asset for inclusion in the statement of financial position, however, a resource must possess the following characteristics:

■ *It must be an economic resource.* This type of resource provides a right to potential economic benefits. These benefits must not, however, be equally available to others. Take, for example, what economists refer to as *public goods.* These include resources such as the road system, GPS satellites or official statistics. Although these may provide economic benefits to a business, others can receive the same benefits at no great cost. A public good cannot, therefore, be regarded as an asset of a business. Economic benefits flowing from a resource can take various forms depending on how it is used by a business. Note that an economic resource need only have the *potential* to generate benefits. They need not be certain or even probable.

Activity 2.2

What forms might economic benefits take? Try to think of at least two.

These may include:

- cash generated from producing goods or services;
- cash received from the proceeds on selling the resource;
- the value received when exchanged for another economic resource;
- the value received when used to satisfy debts incurred by the business; and
- cash generated from renting or leasing it.

You may have thought of others.

■ *The economic resource must be under the control of the business*. This gives a business the exclusive right to decide how the resource is used as well as the right to any benefits that flow. Control is usually acquired by a business through legal ownership or through a contractual agreement (for example, leasing equipment). The event, or transaction, leading to control of the resource must have occurred in the past. In other words, the business must already exercise control over it. (See Reference 1 at the end of the chapter.)

Activity 2.3

Assume a business owns a 40 per cent stake in a gold mine. As this ownership stake will not give control over the whole of the gold mine, can this resource be regarded as an asset of the business?

In this case, the asset of the business will be the 40 per cent share of the mine that is under its control, rather than the whole of the gold mine.

■ *The economic resource must be capable of measurement in monetary terms*. Often, an economic resource cannot be measured with a great deal of certainty. Estimates may be used that ultimately prove to be inaccurate. Nevertheless, it can still be reported as an asset for inclusion in the statement of financial position as long as a sufficiently faithful representation of its measurement can be produced. There are cases, however, where uncertainty regarding measurement is so great that this cannot be done. Take for example, the title of a magazine (such as *Hello!* or *Vogue*) that has been created by its publisher. While it may be extremely valuable to the publishing business, any attempt to measure this resource would be extremely difficult: it would have to rely on arbitrary assumptions. As a result, any measurement produced is unlikely to be useful. The publishing title will not, therefore, appear as an asset in the statement of financial position.

Note that *all* the characteristics identified must exist if a resource is to qualify for recognition. This will strictly limit the resources that are regarded as an asset for inclusion in the statement of financial position. Once included, an asset will continue to be recognised until the economic benefits are exhausted, or the business disposes of it.

Figure 2.2 summarises the above discussion in the form of a decision chart.

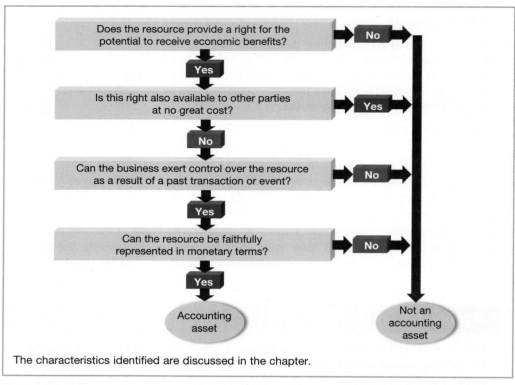

Figure 2.2 Identifying an asset for inclusion in the statement of financial position

---

Activity 2.4

Indicate which of the following items could appear as an asset on the statement of financial position of a business. Explain your reasoning in each case.

1 £1,000 owed to the business by a credit customer who is unable to pay.
2 A patent, bought from an inventor, that gives the business the right to produce a new product. Production of the new product is expected to increase profits over the period during which the patent is held.
3 A recently hired new marketing director who is confidently expected to increase profits by over 30 per cent during the next three years.
4 A recently purchased machine that will save the business £10,000 each year. It is already being used by the business but it has been acquired on credit and is not yet paid for.

Your answer should be along the following lines:

1 Under normal circumstances, a business would expect a customer to pay the amount owed. Such an amount is therefore typically shown as an asset under the heading 'trade receivables' (or 'debtors'). However, in this particular case, the customer is unable to pay. As a result, the item is not an economic resource and the £1,000 owing would not be regarded as an asset. Debts that are not paid are referred to as *bad debts*.
2 The patent would have all the characteristics identified and would, therefore, be regarded as an asset.

3 The new marketing director would not be considered as an asset. One argument in support of this position is that the business does not have rights of control over the director. Nevertheless, it may have control over the services that the director provides. Even if these services become the focus of attention, however, it is usually impossible to measure them in monetary terms with any degree of certainty.

4 The machine has the characteristics identified and so would be considered an asset even though it is not yet paid for. Once the business has contracted to buy the machine, and has accepted it, ownership will pass even though payment is still outstanding. (The amount outstanding would be shown as a claim, as we shall see shortly.)

The sorts of items that often appear as assets in the statement of financial position of a business include:

- property;
- plant and equipment;
- fixtures and fittings;
- patents and trademarks;
- trade receivables (debtors); and
- investments outside the business.

Activity 2.5

Can you think of two additional items that might appear as assets in the statement of financial position of a typical business?

You may be able to think of a number of other items. Two that we have met so far, because they were held by Paul's wrapping paper business (in Example 2.1), are inventories and cash.

Note that an asset does not have to be a physical item – it may be a non-physical one that gives a right to potential benefits. Assets that have a physical substance and can be touched (such as inventories) are referred to as tangible assets. Assets that have no physical substance but which, nevertheless, may provide future benefits (such as patents) are referred to as intangible assets.

Claims

A claim is an obligation of the business to provide cash, or some other form of benefit, to an outside party. It will normally arise as a result of the outside party providing assets for use by the business. There are essentially two types of claim against a business:

- Equity. This represents the claim of the owner(s) against the business. This claim is sometimes referred to as the *owner's capital*. Some find it hard to understand how the owner can have a claim against the business, particularly when we consider the example of a sole-proprietor-type business, like Paul's, where the owner *is*, in effect, the business. For accounting purposes, however, a clear distinction is made between the business and the owner(s). The business is viewed as being quite separate from the owner. It is seen as a separate entity with its own separate existence. This means that, when financial statements are prepared, they relate to the business rather than to the owner(s). Viewed from this perspective, any funds contributed by the owner will be seen as coming from outside the business and will appear as a claim against the business in its statement of financial position.

■ **Liabilities.** Liabilities represent the claims of other parties, apart from the owner (s). They involve an obligation to transfer economic resources (usually cash) as a result of past transactions or events. A liability incurred by a business cannot be avoided and so will remain a liability until it is settled.

Most liabilities arise for legal or contractual reasons, such as from acquiring goods or services or from borrowing funds. They can, however, arise from the policies and practices adopted by the business, such as 'no quibble' refunds.

Now that the meanings of the terms *assets*, *equity* and *liabilities* have been established, we can consider the relationship between them. This relationship is quite straightforward. If a business wishes to acquire assets, it must raise the necessary funds from somewhere. It may raise these funds from the owner(s), or from other outside parties, or from both. Example 2.2 illustrates this relationship.

Example 2.2

Jerry and Company is a new business that was created by depositing £20,000 in a bank account on 1 March. This amount was raised partly from the owner (£6,000) and partly from borrowing (£14,000). Raising funds in this way will give rise to a claim on the business by both the owner (equity) and the lender (liability). If a statement of financial position of Jerry and Company is prepared following these transactions, it will appear as follows:

Jerry and Company
Statement of financial position as at 1 March

	£
ASSETS	
Cash at bank	20,000
Total assets	20,000
EQUITY AND LIABILITIES	
Equity	6,000
Liabilities – borrowing	14,000
Total equity and liabilities	20,000

We can see from the statement of financial position that the total claims (equity and liabilities) are the same as the total assets. Thus:

$$\text{Assets} = \text{Equity} + \text{Liabilities}$$

This equation – which we shall refer to as the *accounting equation* – will always hold true. Whatever changes may occur to the assets of the business or the claims against it, there will be compensating changes elsewhere that will ensure that the statement of financial position always 'balances'. By way of illustration, consider the following transactions for Jerry and Company:

2 March	Bought a motor van for £5,000, paying by cheque.
3 March	Bought inventories (that is, goods to be sold) on one month's credit for £3,000. (This means that the inventories were bought on 3 March, but payment to the supplier will not be due until 3 April.)
4 March	Repaid £2,000 of the amount borrowed, to the lender, by cheque.
6 March	Owner introduced another £4,000 into the business bank account.

A statement of financial position may be drawn up after each day in which transactions have taken place. In this way, we can see the effect of each transaction on the assets and claims of the business. The statement of financial position as at 2 March will be:

Jerry and Company
Statement of financial position as at 2 March

	£
ASSETS	
Cash at bank (20,000 − 5,000)	15,000
Motor van	5,000
Total assets	20,000
EQUITY AND LIABILITIES	
Equity	6,000
Liabilities – borrowing	14,000
Total equity and liabilities	20,000

As we can see, the effect of buying the motor van is to decrease the balance at the bank by £5,000 and to introduce a new asset – a motor van – to the statement of financial position. The total assets remain unchanged. It is only the 'mix' of assets that has changed.

The claims against the business remain the same because there has been no change in the way in which the business has been funded.

The statement of financial position as at 3 March, following the purchase of inventories, will be:

Jerry and Company
Statement of financial position as at 3 March

	£
ASSETS	
Cash at bank	15,000
Motor van	5,000
Inventories	3,000
Total assets	23,000
EQUITY AND LIABILITIES	
Equity	6,000
Liabilities – borrowing	14,000
Liabilities – trade payable	3,000
Total equity and liabilities	23,000

The effect of buying inventories has been to introduce another new asset (inventories) to the statement of financial position. Furthermore, the fact that the goods have not yet been paid for means that the claims against the business will be increased by the £3,000 owed to the supplier, who is referred to as a **trade payable** (or trade creditor) on the statement of financial position.

Activity 2.6

Try drawing up a statement of financial position as at 4 March for Jerry and Company.

The statement of financial position as at 4 March, following the repayment of part of the borrowing, will be:

Jerry and Company
Statement of financial position as at 4 March

	£
ASSETS	
Cash at bank (15,000 − 2,000)	13,000
Motor van	5,000
Inventories	3,000
Total assets	21,000
EQUITY AND LIABILITIES	
Equity	6,000
Liabilities – borrowing (14,000 − 2,000)	12,000
Liabilities – trade payable	3,000
Total equity and liabilities	21,000

The repayment of £2,000 of the borrowing will result in a decrease in the balance at the bank of £2,000 and a decrease in the lender's claim against the business by the same amount.

Activity 2.7

Try drawing up a statement of financial position as at 6 March for Jerry and Company.

The statement of financial position as at 6 March, following the introduction of more funds, will be:

Jerry and Company
Statement of financial position as at 6 March

	£
ASSETS	
Cash at bank (13,000 + 4,000)	17,000
Motor van	5,000
Inventories	3,000
Total assets	25,000
EQUITY AND LIABILITIES	
Equity (6,000 + 4,000)	10,000
Liabilities – borrowing	12,000
Liabilities – trade payable	3,000
Total equity and liabilities	25,000

The introduction of more funds by the owner will result in an increase in the equity of £4,000 and an increase in the cash at bank by the same amount.

The example of Jerry and Company illustrates the point that the accounting equation (assets equals equity plus liabilities) will always hold true. It reflects the fact that, if a business wishes to acquire more assets, it must raise funds equal to the cost of those assets. The funds raised must be provided by the owners (equity), or by others (liabilities), or by a combination of the two. This means that the total cost of assets acquired should always equal the total equity plus liabilities. Similarly, if the business raises the funds by selling an existing asset, one asset replaces another, leaving the accounting equation holding true.

It is worth pointing out that businesses do not normally draw up a statement of financial position after each day, as shown in the example. We have done this to illustrate the effect on the statement of financial position of each transaction. In practice, a statement of financial position for a business is usually prepared at the end of a defined period. The period over which businesses measure their financial results is usually known as the reporting period, but it is sometimes called the 'accounting period' or 'financial period'.

Determining the length of the reporting period will involve weighing up the costs of producing the information against the perceived benefits of having that information for decision-making purposes. In practice, the reporting period will vary between businesses; it could be monthly, quarterly, half-yearly or annually. For external reporting purposes, an annual reporting period is the norm (although certain businesses, typically larger ones, report more frequently than this). For internal reporting purposes to managers, however, more frequent (perhaps monthly) financial statements are likely to be prepared.

THE EFFECT OF TRADING TRANSACTIONS

In the example (Jerry and Company), we showed how various types of transactions affected the statement of financial position. However, one very important type of transaction – trading transactions – has yet to be considered. To show how this type of transaction affects the statement of financial position, let us return to Jerry and Company.

Example 2.2 (continued)

The statement of financial position that we drew up for Jerry and Company as at 6 March was as follows:

Jerry and Company
Statement of financial position as at 6 March

	£
ASSETS	
Cash at bank	17,000
Motor van	5,000
Inventories	3,000
Total assets	25,000
EQUITY AND LIABILITIES	
Equity	10,000
Liabilities – borrowing	12,000
Liabilities – trade payable	3,000
Total equity and liabilities	25,000

→

On 7 March, the business managed to sell all of the inventories for £5,000 and received a cheque immediately from the customer for this amount. The statement of financial position on 7 March, after this transaction has taken place, will be:

Jerry and Company
Statement of financial position as at 7 March

	£
ASSETS	
Cash at bank (17,000 + 5,000)	22,000
Motor van	5,000
Inventories (3,000 − 3,000)	–
Total assets	27,000
EQUITY AND LIABILITIES	
Equity (10,000 + (5,000 − 3,000))	12,000
Liabilities – borrowing	12,000
Liabilities – trade payable	3,000
Total equity and liabilities	27,000

We can see that the inventories (£3,000) have now disappeared from the statement of financial position, but the cash at bank has increased by the selling price of the inventories (£5,000). The net effect has therefore been to increase assets by £2,000 (that is, £5,000 less £3,000). This increase represents the net increase in wealth (the profit) that has arisen from trading. Also note that the equity of the business has increased by £2,000, in line with the increase in assets. This increase in equity reflects the fact that wealth generated, as a result of trading or other operations, will be to the benefit of the owners and will increase their stake in the business.

Activity 2.8

What would have been the effect on the statement of financial position if the inventories had been sold on 7 March for £1,000 rather than £5,000?

The statement of financial position on 7 March would then have been:

Jerry and Company
Statement of financial position as at 7 March

	£
ASSETS	
Cash at bank (17,000 + 1,000)	18,000
Motor van	5,000
Inventories (3,000 − 3,000)	–
Total assets	23,000
EQUITY AND LIABILITIES	
Equity (10,000 + (1,000 − 3,000))	8,000
Liabilities – borrowing	12,000
Liabilities – trade payable	3,000
Total equity and liabilities	23,000

As we can see, the inventories (£3,000) will disappear from the statement of financial position, but the cash at bank will rise by only £1,000. This will mean a net reduction in assets of £2,000. This reduction represents a loss arising from trading and will be reflected in a reduction in the equity of the owners.

What we have just seen means that the accounting equation can be extended as follows:

Assets (at the end of the period) = Equity (amount at the start of the period)
+ Profit (or Loss) for the period)
+ Liabilities (at the end of the period)

(This is assuming that the owner makes no injections or withdrawals of equity during the period.)

Any funds introduced or withdrawn by the owners also affect equity. If the owners withdrew £1,500 for their own use, the equity of the owners would be reduced by £1,500. If these drawings were in cash, the cash balance would decrease by £1,500 in the statement of financial position.

Like all items in the statement of financial position, the amount of equity is cumulative. This means that any profit not taken out as drawings by the owner(s) remains in the business. These retained (or 'ploughed-back') earnings have the effect of expanding the business.

CLASSIFYING ASSETS

In the statement of financial position, assets and claims are usually grouped into categories. This is designed to help users, as a haphazard listing of these items could be confusing. Assets are usually categorised as being either current or non-current.

Current assets

Current assets are basically assets that are held for the short term. To be more precise, they are assets that meet any of the following conditions:

- they are held for sale or consumption during the business's normal operating cycle;
- they are expected to be sold within a year after the date of the relevant statement of financial position;
- they are held principally for trading; and
- they are cash, or near cash such as easily marketable, short-term investments.

The operating cycle of a business, mentioned above, is the time between buying and/or creating a product or service and receiving the cash on its sale. For most businesses, this will be less than a year. (It is worth mentioning that sales made by most businesses are made on credit. The customer pays some time after the goods are received or the service is rendered.)

The most common current assets are inventories, trade receivables (amounts owed by customers for goods or services supplied to them on credit) and cash. For businesses that sell goods, rather than render a service, the current assets of inventories, trade receivables and cash are interrelated. They circulate within a business as shown in Figure 2.3. We can see that cash can be used to buy inventories, which are then sold on credit. When the credit customers (trade receivables) pay, the business receives an injection of cash and so on.

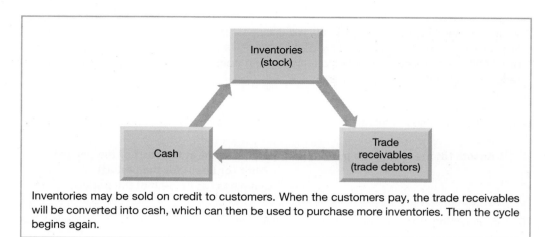

Inventories may be sold on credit to customers. When the customers pay, the trade receivables will be converted into cash, which can then be used to purchase more inventories. Then the cycle begins again.

Figure 2.3 The circulating nature of current assets

For purely service businesses, the situation is similar, except that inventories are not involved.

Non-current assets

Non-current assets (also called *fixed assets*) are simply assets that do not meet the definition of current assets. They tend to be held for long-term operations. Non-current assets may be either tangible or intangible. Tangible non-current assets normally consist of property, plant and equipment. We shall refer to them in this way from now on. This is a rather broad term that includes items such as land and buildings, machinery, motor vehicles and fixtures and fittings.

The distinction between those assets continuously circulating (current) and those used for long-term operations (non-current) may help readers of the statement of financial position when assessing the mix of assets held. Most businesses need a certain amount of both types of asset to operate effectively.

Activity 2.9

Can you think of two examples of assets that may be classified as non-current assets for an insurance business?

Examples of assets that may be defined as being non-current include:

- property;
- furniture;
- motor vehicles;
- computers;
- computer software; and
- reference books.

This is not an exhaustive list. You may have thought of others.

The way in which a particular asset is classified (that is, between current and non-current) may vary according to the nature of the business. This is because the *purpose* for which the asset is held may vary. For example, a motor van retailer will normally hold inventories of motor vans for sale; it would, therefore, classify them as part of the current assets. On the other hand, a business that buys one of these vans to use for delivering its goods to customers (that is, as part of its long-term operations) would classify it as a non-current asset.

Activity 2.10

The assets of Kunalun and Co., a large advertising agency, are as follows:

- cash at bank;
- fixtures and fittings;
- office equipment;
- motor vehicles;
- property;
- computers; and
- work in progress (that is, partly completed work for clients).

Which of these do you think should be defined as non-current assets and which should be defined as current assets?

Your answer should be as follows:

Non-current assets	Current assets
Fixtures and fittings	Cash at bank
Office equipment	Work in progress
Motor vehicles	
Property	
Computers	

CLASSIFYING CLAIMS

As we have already seen, claims are normally classified into equity (owner's claim) and liabilities (claims of outsiders). Liabilities are further classified as either current or non-current.

Current liabilities

Current liabilities are basically amounts due for settlement in the short term. To be more precise, they are liabilities that meet any of the following conditions:

- they are expected to be settled within the business's normal operating cycle;
- they arise principally as a result of trading;
- they are due to be settled within a year after the date of the relevant statement of financial position; and
- there is no right to defer settlement beyond a year after the date of the relevant statement of financial position.

Non-current liabilities

Non-current liabilities represent amounts due that do not meet the definition of current liabilities and so represent longer-term liabilities.

Activity 2.11

Can you think of one example of a current liability and one of a non-current liability?

An example of a current liability would be amounts owing to suppliers for goods supplied on credit (trade payables) or a bank overdraft (a form of short-term bank borrowing that is repayable on demand). An example of a non-current liability would be long-term borrowings.

It is quite common for non-current liabilities to become current liabilities. For example, borrowings to be repaid 18 months after the date of a particular statement of financial position will normally appear as a non-current liability. Those same borrowings will, however, appear as a current liability in the statement of financial position as at the end of the following year, by which time they would be due for repayment after six months.

This classification of liabilities between current and non-current helps to highlight those financial obligations that must shortly be met. It may be useful to compare the amount of current liabilities with the amount of current assets (that is, the assets that either are cash or will turn into cash within the normal operating cycle). This should reveal whether the business can cover its maturing obligations.

The classification of liabilities between current and non-current also helps to highlight the proportion of total long-term finance that is raised through borrowings rather than equity. Where a business relies on borrowings, rather than relying solely on funds provided by the owner(s), the financial risks increase. This is because borrowing brings a commitment to make periodic interest payments and capital repayments. The business may be forced to stop trading if this commitment cannot be fulfilled. Thus, when raising finance, a reasonable balance must be struck between borrowings and owners' equity. We shall consider this issue in more detail in Chapter 8.

STATEMENT LAYOUTS

Having looked at the classification of assets and liabilities, we shall now consider the layout of the statement of financial position. Although there is an almost infinite number of ways in which the same information on assets and claims could be presented, we shall consider two basic layouts. The first of these follows the style that we adopted with Jerry and Company earlier (see pages 42 to 47). A more comprehensive example of this style is shown in Example 2.3.

Example 2.3

Brie Manufacturing
Statement of financial position as at 31 December 2018

	£000
ASSETS	
Non-current assets	
Property	45
Plant and equipment	30
Motor vans	19
	94
Current assets	
Inventories	23
Trade receivables	18
Cash at bank	12
	53
Total assets	147
EQUITY AND LIABILITIES	
Equity	60
Non-current liabilities	
Long-term borrowings	50
Current liabilities	
Trade payables	37
Total equity and liabilities	147

The non-current assets have a total of £94,000 which, together with the current assets total of £53,000, gives a total of £147,000 for assets. Similarly, the equity totals £60,000 which, together with the £50,000 for non-current liabilities and £37,000 for current liabilities, gives a total for equity and liabilities of £147,000.

Within each category of asset (non-current and current) shown in Example 2.3, the items are listed in reverse order of liquidity (nearness to cash). Thus, the assets that are furthest from cash come first and the assets that are closest to cash come last. In the case of Brie manufacturing's non-current assets, property is listed first as this asset is tends to be the most difficult to turn into cash and motor vans are listed last as there is usually a ready market for them. In the case of current assets, we have already seen that inventories are converted to trade receivables and then trade receivables are converted to cash. As a result, under the heading of current assets, inventories are listed first, followed by trade receivables and finally cash itself. This ordering of assets will occur irrespective of the layout used.

Note that, in addition to a grand total for assets held, subtotals for non-current assets and current assets are shown. Subtotals are also used for non-current liabilities and current liabilities when more than one item appears within these categories.

A slight variation from the layout illustrated in Example 2.3 is as shown in Example 2.4.

Example 2.4

Brie Manufacturing
Statement of financial position as at 31 December 2018

	£000
ASSETS	
Non-current assets	
Property	45
Plant and equipment	30
Motor vans	19
	94
Current assets	
Inventories	23
Trade receivables	18
Cash at bank	12
	53
Total assets	147
LIABILITIES	
Non-current liabilities	
Long-term borrowings	(50)
Current liabilities	
Trade payables	(37)
Total liabilities	(87)
Net assets	60
EQUITY	60

We can see that the total liabilities are deducted from the total assets. This derives a figure for net assets – which is equal to equity. Using this format, the basic accounting equation is rearranged so that:

$$\text{Assets} - \text{Liabilities} = \text{Equity}$$

This rearranged equation highlights the fact that equity represents the residual interest of the owner(s) after deducting all liabilities of the business.

Figure 2.4 summarises the two types of layout discussed in this section.

The layout shown in Example 2.3 seems to be much the most popular in practice and so will be used throughout the book.

CAPTURING A MOMENT IN TIME

As we have already seen, the statement of financial position reflects the assets, equity and liabilities of a business at *a specified point in time.* It has been compared to a photograph. A photograph 'freezes' a particular moment in time and will represent the situation only at that moment. Hence, events may be quite different immediately before and immediately after the photograph was taken. When examining a statement of financial position, therefore, it is important to establish the date for which it has been drawn up. This information should be prominently displayed in the heading to the statement, as shown above in Example 2.4.

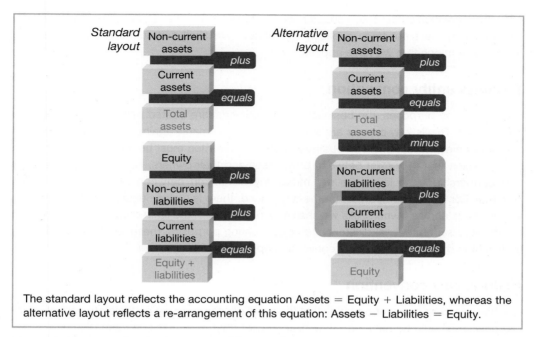

The standard layout reflects the accounting equation Assets = Equity + Liabilities, whereas the alternative layout reflects a re-arrangement of this equation: Assets − Liabilities = Equity.

Figure 2.4 Layouts for the statement of financial position

When we are trying to assess current financial position, the more recent the statement of financial position date, the more helpful it is likely to be.

A business will normally prepare a statement of financial position as at the close of business on the last day of its annual reporting period. In the UK, businesses are free to choose the date of the end of their reporting period and, once chosen, it will normally change only under exceptional circumstances. When making a decision on which year-end date to choose, commercial convenience can often be a deciding factor. For example, a business operating in the retail trade may choose to have a year-end date early in the calendar year (for example, 31 January) because trade tends to be slack during that period and more staff time is available to help with the tasks involved in the preparation of the annual financial statements (such as checking the amount of inventories held ('stocktaking')). Since trade is slack, the amount of inventories held by the retail business is likely to be unusually low compared with other times of the year.

Activity 2.12

Does this pose a problem for external users seeking to assess the business's financial health?

While the statement of financial position may provide a fair view of the inventories held at the time it was drawn up, it will not be typical of the position over the rest of the year.

THE ROLE OF ACCOUNTING CONVENTIONS

Accounting has a number of conventions, or rules, that have evolved over time. They have evolved as attempts to deal with practical problems experienced by preparers and users of financial statements, rather than to reflect some theoretical ideal. In preparing the statements of financial position earlier in this chapter, we have followed various accounting conventions, although they have not been explicitly mentioned. We shall now identify and discuss the major conventions that we have applied.

Business entity convention

For accounting purposes, the business and its owner(s) are treated as being quite separate and distinct. This is why owners are treated as being claimants against their own business in respect of their investment. The business entity convention must be distinguished from the legal position that may exist between businesses and their owners. For sole proprietorships and partnerships, the law does not make any distinction between the business and its owner(s). For limited companies, on the other hand, there is a clear legal distinction between the business and its owners. (As we shall see in Chapter 4, the limited company is regarded as having a separate legal existence.) For accounting purposes, these legal distinctions are irrelevant and the business entity convention applies to all businesses.

Historic cost convention

The historic cost convention holds that the value of assets shown on the statement of financial position should be based on their historic cost (that is, acquisition cost). The use of historic cost means that problems of measurement reliability are minimised, as the amount paid for a particular asset is often a matter of demonstrable fact. Reliance on opinion is avoided, or, at least reduced, which should enhance the credibility of the information in the eyes of users. A key problem, however, is that the information provided may not be relevant to user needs. Even quite early in the life of some assets, historic costs may become outdated compared to current market values. This can be misleading when assessing current financial position.

Many argue that recording assets at their current value would provide a more realistic view of financial position and would be relevant for a wide range of decisions. A system of measurement based on current value does, however, bring its own problems. The term 'current value' can be defined in different ways. It can be defined broadly, as either the current replacement cost or the current realisable value (selling price) of an asset. These two types of valuation may result in quite different figures being produced to represent the current value of an item. Furthermore, the broad terms 'replacement cost' and 'realisable value' can be defined in different ways. We must therefore be clear about what kind of current value accounting we wish to use.

Activity 2.13 illustrates some of the problems associated with current value accounting.

Activity 2.13

Plumber and Company has a fleet of motor vans that are used for making deliveries to customers. The owners want to show these vans on the statement of financial position at their current values rather than at their historic cost. They would like to use either current replacement cost (based on how much would have to be paid to buy vans of a similar type, age and condition) or current realisable value (based on how much a motor van dealer would pay for the vans, if the business sold them).

Why is the choice between the two current valuation methods important? Why would both current valuation methods present problems in establishing reliable values?

The choice between the two current valuation methods is important because the values derived under each method are likely to be quite different. Normally, replacement cost values for the motor vans will be higher than their current realisable values.

Establishing current values will usually rely on opinions, which may well vary from one dealer to another. Thus, instead of a single, unambiguous figure for, say, the current replacement cost for each van, a range of possible current replacement costs could be produced. The same problem will arise when trying to establish the current realisable value for each van.

We should bear in mind that the motor vans discussed in Activity 2.13 are less of a problem than are many other types of asset. There is a ready market for motor vans, which means that a value can be obtained by contacting a dealer. For a custom-built piece of equipment, however, identifying a replacement cost or, worse still, a selling price, could be very difficult.

Where the current values of assets are based on the opinion of managers of the business, there is a greater risk that they will lack credibility. Some form of independent valuation, or verification, may therefore be required to reassure users.

Despite the problems associated with current values, they are increasingly used when reporting assets in the statement of financial position. This has led to a steady erosion in the importance of the historic cost convention. Thus, many businesses now prepare financial statements on a modified historic cost basis. We shall consider the valuation of assets in more detail a little later in the chapter.

Prudence convention

In broad terms, the **prudence convention** holds that caution should be exercised when preparing financial statements. This may not seem to be a contentious issue: it would, after all, be difficult to argue that an incautious approach should be taken. Nevertheless, the prudence convention has excited much debate over the years. The root cause has been the way in which the convention is often applied. It can be used to support a bias towards the understatement of financial strength: that is, the understatement of assets and profit and the overstatement of liabilities.

Those who support this approach to prudence argue that it is better to understate than to overstate financial strength. They make the point that, by overstating financial strength, users of financial statements may be misled into making poor decisions.

Activity 2.14

What sort of poor decisions may be made as a result of overstating the financial strength of a business? Try to think of at least two.

Examples of poor decisions may include:

- excessive amounts being paid out of profit to the owners, thereby, depleting their equity and undermining the financial health of the business;
- excessive bonuses being paid to managers based on overstated profits;
- new owners paying more to acquire a part, or the whole, of a business than is justified; and
- lenders providing funds to a business based on a rosier picture of financial strength than is warranted by the facts.

You may have thought of others.

The bias towards the understatement of financial strength evolved in order to counteract the excessive optimism of managers. However, just as overstatement can lead to poor decisions, understatement can lead to the same. It may, for example, result in existing owners selling their business too cheaply, lenders refusing a loan application based on a distortedly pessimistic picture of financial strength and so on.

The systematic bias towards understatement just described clashes with the need for *neutrality* in preparing financial statements.

Activity 2.15

In Chapter 1 we discussed neutrality as a desirable element of one of the major qualitative characteristics of financial information. Can you remember which one?

Neutrality is one of three elements needed to ensure faithful representation. (The other two elements are completeness and freedom from error.)

Neutrality, by definition, requires that financial statements are not slanted or weighted so as to present either a favourable or unfavourable picture to users. To accommodate the concept of neutrality, therefore, prudence must be interpreted and applied in a different way than described above. Adopting a cautious approach to preparing financial statements should not result in the deliberate understatement of financial strength. In other words, assets and profit should not be understated and liabilities should not be overstated.

Going concern convention

Under the going concern convention, the financial statements should be prepared on the assumption that a business will continue operations for the foreseeable future, unless there is evidence to the contrary. In other words, it is assumed that there is no intention, or need, to sell off the non-current assets of the business.

Where a business is in financial difficulties, however, non-current assets may have to be sold to repay those with claims against the business. The realisable (sale) value of many non-current assets is often much lower than the values reported in the statement of financial position. In the event of a forced sale of assets, therefore, significant losses might arise. These losses must be anticipated and fully reported when, but only when, a business's going concern status is called into question.

Dual aspect convention

The dual aspect convention asserts that each transaction has two aspects, both of which will affect the statement of financial position. This means that, for example, the purchase of a computer for cash results in an increase in one asset (computer) and a decrease in another (cash). Similarly, the repayment of borrowings results in the decrease in a liability (borrowings) and the decrease in an asset (cash).

Recording the dual aspect of each transaction ensures that the statement of financial position will continue to balance, that is the accounting equation will continue to be valid.

Figure 2.5 summarises the main accounting conventions that exert an influence on the construction of the statement of financial position.

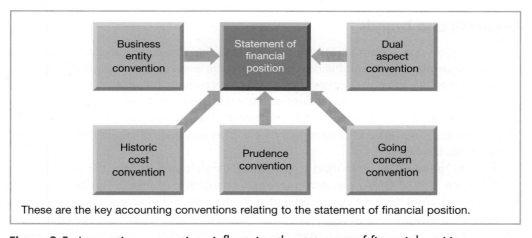

These are the key accounting conventions relating to the statement of financial position.

Figure 2.5 Accounting conventions influencing the statement of financial position

MONEY MEASUREMENT

We saw earlier that a resource will only be regarded as an asset and included on the statement of financial position where it is capable of being measured in monetary terms with a reasonable degree of certainty. Unless a measure can faithfully portray the resource, it is unlikely to be useful.

Various resources of a business fail to meet this criterion and so are excluded from the statement of financial position.

Activity 2.17

Can you identify any of these resources? Try to think of at least two.

They may include:

- human resources;
- business reputation;
- business location; and
- customer and supplier relationships.

From time to time, attempts are made to measure and report some of these resources in order to provide a more complete picture of financial position. However, these attempts usually attract little support. Measures with a high degree of uncertainty lead to inconsistency in reporting and create doubts in the minds of users. This, in turn, can undermine the integrity and credibility of the financial statement.

Let us now move on to discuss some key economic resources that normally pose measurement problems.

Goodwill and brands

Some intangible non-current assets are similar to tangible non-current assets: they have a clear and separate identity and the cost of acquiring the asset can be measured with a reasonable degree of certainty. Examples normally include patents, trademarks, copyrights and licences. Other intangible non-current assets, however, are quite different. They lack a clear and separate identity and reflect a hotch-potch of attributes, which are part of the essence of the business. Goodwill and product brands are often examples of assets that lack a clear and separate identity.

The term 'goodwill' is often used to cover various attributes such as the quality of the products, the skill of employees and the relationship with customers. The term 'product brands' is also used to cover various attributes, such as the brand image, the quality of the product, the trademark and so on. Where goodwill and product brands have been generated internally by the business, it is often difficult to determine their cost or to measure their current market value or even to be clear that they really exist. They are, therefore, excluded from the statement of financial position.

When such assets are acquired through an 'arm's-length transaction', however, the problems of uncertainty about their existence and measurement are resolved. (An arm's-length transaction is one that is undertaken between two unconnected parties.) If goodwill is acquired, when taking over another business, or if a business acquires a particular product brand, from another business, these items will be separately identified and a price agreed for them. Under these circumstances, they can be regarded as assets (for accounting purposes) by the business that acquired them and included in the statement of financial position.

To agree a price for acquiring goodwill or product brands means that some form of valuation must take place and this raises the question as to how it is done. Usually, the valuation will be based on estimates of future earnings from holding the asset – a process that is fraught with difficulties. Nevertheless, a number of specialist businesses now exist that are prepared to take on this challenge.

Human resources

Attempts have been made to place a monetary measurement on the human resources of a business, but without any real success. There are, however, certain limited circumstances in which human resources are measured and reported in the statement of financial position. Professional football clubs provide an example of where these circumstances normally arise. While football clubs cannot own players, they can own the rights to the players' services. Where these rights are acquired by compensating other clubs for releasing the players from their contracts with those other clubs, an arm's-length transaction arises and the amounts paid provide a reliable basis for measurement. This means that the rights to services can be regarded as an asset of the club for accounting purposes (assuming, of course, the player will bring benefits to the club).

Real World 2.2 describes how one leading club reports its investment in players on the statement of financial position.

Real World 2.1

United players appear on the team sheet and on the statement of financial position

Manchester United Football Club has acquired several key players as a result of paying transfer fees to other clubs. In common with most UK football clubs. The club reports the cost of acquiring the rights to the players' services on its statement of financial position. The club's statement as at 30 June 2017 shows the total cost of registering its squad of players at more than £645 million. A total of 70 players were under contract at the year end, which included reserve team and youth team players. The club treats a proportion of each player's transfer fee as an expense each year. The exact proportion depends on the length of the particular player's contract.

The £645 million does not include 'home-grown' players such as Jesse Lingard, because United did not pay a transfer fee for them and so no clear-cut value can be placed on their services. During the year to 30 June 2017, the club was active in the transfer market and spent more than £205 million on acquiring new players, including Paul Pogba from Juventus, Henrikh Mkhitaryan from Borussia Dortmund and Anthony Martial from AS Monaco. Some players also left the club during the year, including Angel Di Maria and Morgan Schneiderlin.

The item of players' registrations is shown as an intangible asset in the statement of financial position as it is the rights to services, not the players, that are the assets. It is shown net of depreciation (or *amortisation* as it is usually termed for intangible non-current assets). The net amount at 30 June 2017 was more than £290 million and represented almost 19 per cent of Manchester United's total assets, as shown in the statement of financial position.

Source: Manchester United plc, Annual Report 2017.

Monetary stability

When using money as the unit of measurement, we normally fail to recognise the fact that it will change in value over time, despite the fact that in the UK, and throughout much of the world, inflation has been a persistent problem. This has meant that the value of money has declined in relation to other assets. In past years, high rates of inflation have resulted in statements of financial position, which were prepared on a historic cost basis, reflecting figures for assets that were much lower than if current values were employed. Rates of inflation have been relatively low in recent years and so the disparity between historic cost values and current values has been less pronounced. Nevertheless, it can still be significant. The problem of inflation has added fuel to the more general debate concerning how to measure asset values in the statement of financial position. It is to the issue of valuing assets that we now turn.

VALUING ASSETS

We saw earlier that, when preparing the statement of financial position, the historic cost convention is normally applied for the reporting of assets. This point requires further explanation as, in practice, things are a little more complex than this. Large businesses throughout much of the world adhere to asset valuation rules set out in International Financial Reporting Standards. We shall now consider the key valuation rules.

Non-current assets

Non-current assets have useful lives that are either *finite* or *indefinite*. Those with a finite life provide benefits to a business for a limited period of time, whereas those with an indefinite life provide benefits without a foreseeable time limit. This distinction between the two types of non-current assets applies equally to both tangible and intangible assets.

Initially, non-current assets are recorded at their historic cost, which will include any amounts spent on getting them ready for use.

Non-current assets with finite lives

Benefits from assets with finite useful lives will be used up over time as a result of market changes, wear and tear and so on. The amount used up, which is referred to as *depreciation* (or *amortisation,* in the case of intangible non-current assets), must be measured for each reporting period for which the assets are held. Although we shall leave a detailed examination of depreciation until Chapter 3, we need to know that when an asset has been depreciated, this must be reflected in the statement of financial position.

The total depreciation that has accumulated over the period since the asset was acquired must be deducted from its cost. This net figure (that is, the cost of the asset less the total depreciation to date) is referred to as the carrying amount. It is sometimes also known as *net book value* or *written-down value.* The procedure just described is not really a contravention of the historic cost convention. It is simply recognition of the fact that a proportion of the historic cost of the non-current asset has been consumed in the process of generating, or attempting to generate, benefits for the business.

Non-current assets with indefinite useful lives

Benefits from assets with indefinite lives may, or may not, be used up over time. Property, in the form of land, is usually an example of a tangible non-current asset with an indefinite life. Purchased goodwill could be an example of an intangible one, although this is not always the case. These assets are not subject to routine depreciation each reporting period.

Fair values

Initially, non-current assets of all types (tangible and intangible) are recorded at cost. Subsequently, however, an alternative form of measurement may be allowed. Non-current assets may be recorded using **fair values** provided that these values can be measured with a reasonable degree of certainty. Fair values are market based. They represent the selling price that can be obtained in an orderly transaction under current market conditions. The use of fair values, rather than cost, provides users with more up-to-date information. This could well be more relevant to their needs. It may also place the business in a better light, as assets such as property may have increased significantly in value over time. Increasing the statement of financial position value of an asset does not, of course, make that asset more valuable. Perceptions of the business may, however, be altered by such a move.

One consequence of upwardly revaluing non-current assets with finite lives is that the depreciation charge will be increased. This is because the depreciation charge is based on the new (increased) value of the asset.

Real World 2.3 shows the effect of the revaluation of non-current assets on the financial position of one large business.

Real World 2.2

Rising asset levels

During the year to 31 March 2010, Veolia Water UK plc, which owns Thames Water, changed its policy on the valuation of certain types of non-current assets. These assets included land and buildings, infrastructure assets and vehicles, plant and machinery. The business switched from the use of historic cost to the use of fair values and a revaluation exercise was carried out by independent qualified valuers.

The effect of this policy change was to report a revaluation gain of more than £436 million during the year. There was a 40 per cent increase in owners' (shareholders') equity, which was largely due to this gain.

Source: Veolia Water UK plc, Annual Report 2009/10.

Activity 2.19

Refer to the statement of financial position of Brie Manufacturing shown earlier in Example 2.3 (page 51). What would be the effect of revaluing the property to a figure of £110,000 in the statement of financial position? Show the revised statement.

The effect on the statement of financial position would be to increase the figure for property to £110,000 and the gain on revaluation (that is, £110,000 − £45,000 = £65,000) would be added to equity, as it is the owner(s) who will have benefited from the gain. The revised statement of financial position would therefore be as follows:

Brie Manufacturing
Statement of financial position as at 31 December 2018

	£000
ASSETS	
Non-current assets	
Property	110
Plant and equipment	30
Motor vans	19
	159
Current assets	
Inventories	23
Trade receivables	18
Cash at bank	12
	53
Total assets	212
EQUITY AND LIABILITIES	
Equity (60 + 65)	125
Non-current liabilities	
Long-term borrowings	50
Current liabilities	
Trade payables	37
Total equity and liabilities	212

Once non-current assets are revalued, the frequency of revaluation becomes an important issue. Reporting assets on the statement of financial position at out-of-date revaluations is the worst of both worlds. It lacks the objectivity and verifiability of historic cost; it also lacks the realism of current values. Thus, where fair values are used, revaluations should be frequent enough to ensure that the carrying amount of the revalued asset does not differ materially from its fair value at the statement of financial position date.

When an item of property, plant or equipment (a tangible asset) is revalued on the basis of fair values, all assets within that particular group must be revalued. It is not therefore acceptable to revalue some items of property but not others. Although this rule provides some degree of consistency within a particular group of assets, it does not prevent the statement of financial position from containing a mixture of valuations.

Intangible assets are not usually revalued to fair values. This is because an active market is required to determine fair values. For most intangible assets, an active market does not exist. A few intangible assets, however, such as transferable taxi licences, fishing licences and production quotas, provide the exception.

It has been argued that recent emphasis on the use of fair values in accounting has resulted in the exercise of prudence becoming less important. **Real World 2.4** is an extract from an article by John Kay that explains why this change has taken place. The article, which is well worth reading in full, is highly critical of the change.

The impairment of non-current assets

All types of non-current asset are at risk of suffering a significant fall in value. This may be caused by changes in market conditions, technological obsolescence and so on. In some cases, this results in the carrying amount of the asset being higher than the amount that could be recovered from the asset; either through its continued use or through its sale. When this occurs, the asset value is said to be impaired and the general rule is to reduce the carrying amount on the statement of financial position to the recoverable amount. Unless this is done, the asset value will be overstated. The amount by which the asset value is reduced is known as an impairment loss. Note that this type of impairment in value should not be confused with routine depreciation of assets with finite lives. Routine depreciation arises from 'wear and tear' of the asset and/or the passage of time. Impairment results from a fundamental shift in market conditions or technological obsolescence.

Activity 2.20

With which one of the accounting conventions that we discussed earlier is this accounting treatment of impaired assets consistent?

The answer is prudence, which requires that we should adopt a cautious approach when preparing financial statements. The value of assets should not be overstated in the statement of financial position.

Real World 2.5 provides an example of where one large business incurred large impairment losses on the value of its assets.

Intangible non-current assets with indefinite useful lives must be tested for impairment as at the end of each reporting period. Other non-current assets, however, must also be tested where events suggest that impairment has taken place.

Activity 2.21

Why might it be a good idea to have impairment tests carried out by independent experts?

Impairment tests involve making judgements about the appropriate value to place on assets. Employing independent valuers to make these judgements will normally give users of the financial statements greater confidence in the information reported. There is always a risk that managers will manipulate impairment values to portray a picture that they would like users to see.

When a non-current asset with a finite useful life has its value impaired, the future, periodic, depreciation expense for that asset will be based on the new (lower) impaired value.

Inventories

It is not only non-current assets that run the risk of a significant fall in value. The inventories of a business could also suffer this fate as a result of changes in market taste, obsolescence, deterioration, damage and so on. Where a fall in value means that the amount likely to be recovered from the sale of the inventories will be lower than their cost, this loss must be reflected in the statement of financial position. Thus, if the net realisable value (that is, selling price less any selling costs) falls below the historic cost of inventories held, the former should be used as the basis of valuation. This reflects, once again, the influence of the prudence convention on the statement of financial position.

The published financial statements of large businesses will normally show the basis on which inventories are valued. **Real World 2.6** shows how one business reports this information.

Real World 2.5

Reporting inventories

The 2016/17 annual report of Ted Baker plc, a leading designer clothes brand, includes the following explanation concerning inventories:

> Inventories and work in progress are stated at the lower of cost and net realisable value. Cost includes materials, direct labour and inward transportation costs. Net realisable value is based on estimated selling price, less further costs expected to be incurred to completion and disposal. Provision is made for obsolete, slow moving or defective items where appropriate.

Source: Ted Baker plc, Annual Report and Accounts 2016/17, p. 90.

MEETING USER NEEDS

The statement of financial position is the oldest of the three main financial statements and may help users in the following ways:

- *It provides insights about how the business is financed and how its funds are deployed.* The statement of financial position shows how much finance the owners contribute and how much is contributed by outside lenders. It also shows the different kinds of assets acquired and how much is invested in each kind.

- *It can provide a basis for assessing the value of the business.* Since the statement of financial position lists, and places a value on, the various assets and claims, it can provide a starting point for assessing the value of the business. We have seen earlier, however, that accounting rules may result in assets being shown at their historic cost, which may vary quite considerably from the current valuation, and that the restrictive definition of assets may completely exclude certain business resources from the statement of financial position.

- *Relationships between assets and claims can be assessed.* It can be useful to look at relationships between various statement of financial position items, for example the relationship between how much wealth is tied up in current assets and how much is owed in the short term (current liabilities). From this relationship, we can see whether the business has sufficient short-term assets to cover its maturing obligations. We shall look at this and other relationships between statement of financial position items in some detail in Chapter 8.

- *Performance can be assessed.* The effectiveness of a business in generating wealth can usefully be assessed against the amount of investment that was involved. Thus, the relationship between profit earned during a period and the value of the net assets invested can be helpful to many users, particularly owners and managers. This and similar relationships will also be explored in detail in Chapter 8.

Once armed with the insights that a statement of financial position can provide, users are better placed to make investment and other decisions. **Real World 2.7** shows how a small business was able to obtain a loan because its bank was impressed by its strong statement of financial position.

Self-assessment question 2.1

The following information relates to Simonson Engineering as at 30 September 2018:

	£
Plant and equipment	25,000
Trade payables	18,000
Short-term borrowings	26,000
Inventories	45,000
Property	72,000

	£
Long-term borrowings	51,000
Trade receivables	48,000
Equity at 1 October 2017	117,500
Cash in hand	1,500
Motor vehicles	15,000
Fixtures and fittings	9,000
Profit for the year to 30 September 2018	18,000
Drawings for the year to 30 September 2018	15,000

Required:

(a) Prepare a statement of financial position for the business as at 30 September 2018 using the standard layout illustrated in Example 2.3.

(b) Comment on the financial position of the business based on the statement prepared in (a).

(c) Show the effect on the statement of financial position shown in (a) of a decision to revalue the property to £115,000 and to recognise that the net realisable value of inventories at the year end is £38,000.

The solution to this question can be found at the back of the book, on page 525.

SUMMARY

The main points of this chapter may be summarised as follows:

The major financial statements

- There are three major financial statements: the statement of cash flows, the income statement and the statement of financial position.
- The statement of cash flows shows the cash movements over a particular period.
- The income statement shows the wealth (profit) generated over a particular period.
- The statement of financial position shows the accumulated wealth at a particular point in time.

The statement of financial position

- The statement of financial position sets out the assets of the business, on the one hand, and the claims against those assets, on the other.
- Assets are resources of the business that have certain characteristics, such as the right to future economic benefits.
- Claims are obligations on the part of the business to provide cash, or some other benefit, to outside parties.
- Claims are of two types: equity and liabilities.
- Equity represents the claim(s) of the owner(s) and liabilities represent the claims of others.

- The statement of financial position reflects the accounting equation:

Assets = Equity + Liabilities

Classification of assets and liabilities

- Assets are normally categorised as being current or non-current.
- Current assets are cash, or near cash, or are held for sale or consumption in the normal course of business, or for trading, or for the short term.
- Non-current assets are assets that are not current assets. They are normally held for the long-term operations of the business.
- Liabilities are normally categorised as being current or non-current liabilities.
- Current liabilities represent amounts due in the normal course of the business's operating cycle, or are held for trading, or are to be settled within a year of, or cannot be deferred for at least a year after, the end of the reporting period.
- Non-current liabilities represent amounts due that are not current liabilities.

Statement of financial position layouts

- The standard layout begins with assets at the top of the statement of financial position and places equity and liabilities underneath.
- A variation of the standard layout also begins with the assets at the top of the statement of financial position, but then the non-current and current liabilities are deducted from the total assets figure to arrive at a net assets figure. Equity is placed underneath.

Accounting conventions

- Accounting conventions are the rules of accounting that have evolved to deal with practical problems experienced by those preparing financial statements.
- The main conventions relating to the statement of financial position include the business entity, historic cost, prudence, going concern and dual aspect conventions.

Money measurement

- Using money as the unit of measurement limits the scope of the statement of financial position.
- Certain resources such as goodwill, product brands and human resources are difficult to measure. An 'arm's-length transaction' is normally required before such assets can be measured reasonable certainty and reported on the statement of financial position.
- Money is not a stable unit of measurement – it changes in value over time.

Asset valuation

- The initial treatment is to show non-current assets at historic cost.
- Fair values may be used rather than historic cost, provided that they can be reliably obtained. This is rarely possible, however, for intangible non-current assets.
- Non-current assets with finite useful lives should be shown at cost (or fair value) less any accumulated depreciation (amortisation).

- Where the value of a non-current asset is impaired, it should be written down to its recoverable amount.
- Inventories are shown at the lower of cost or net realisable value.

The usefulness of the statement of financial position

- The statement of financial position shows how finance has been raised and how it has been deployed.
- It provides a basis for valuing the business, although it can only be a starting point.
- Relationships between various statement of financial position items can usefully be explored.
- Relationships between wealth generated and wealth invested can be helpful indicators of business effectiveness.

KEY TERMS

For definitions of these terms, see at the back of the book, starting on page 514.

statement of cash flows p. 34
income statement p. 34
statement of financial position p. 34
final accounts p. 37
asset p. 38
claim p. 38
trade receivable p. 40
tangible asset p. 41
intangible asset p. 41
equity p. 41
liability p. 42
trade payable p. 43
reporting period p. 45

current asset p. 47
non-current (fixed) asset p. 48
property, plant and equipment p. 48
current liability p. 49
non-current liability p. 50
accounting convention p. 54
business entity convention p. 54
historic cost convention p. 54
prudence convention p. 55
going concern convention p. 56
dual aspect convention p. 56
goodwill p. 58
fair value p. 61
impairment loss p. 63

REFERENCE

1. International Accounting Standards Board (2018) *Conceptual Framework for Financial Reporting*, pages 28 to 31.

FURTHER READING

If you would like to explore the topics covered in this chapter in more depth, we recommend the following:

Elliott, B. and Elliott, J. (2017) *Financial Accounting and Reporting*, 18th edn, Pearson, Chapters 17, 19 and 20.

International Accounting Standards Board (2016) *A Guide through IFRS Standards (Green Book)*, IAS 16 *Property, Plant and Equipment* and IAS 38 *Intangible Assets*.

The KPMG International Financial Reporting Group (2017) *Insights into IFRS*, 14th edn, Sweet and Maxwell, Sections 3.2, 3.3, 3.8 and 3.10 (a summarised version of this is available free at www.kpmg.com).

Melville, A. (2017) *International Financial Reporting: A Practical Guide*, 6th edn, Pearson, Chapters 5, 6, and 7.

CRITICAL REVIEW QUESTIONS

Solutions to these questions can be found at the back of the book, starting on page 536.

2.1 An accountant prepared a statement of financial position for a business. In this statement, the equity of the owner was shown next to the liabilities. This confused the owner, who argued 'My equity is my major asset and so should be shown as an asset on the statement of financial position.' How would you explain this misunderstanding to the owner?

2.2 'The statement of financial position shows how much a business is worth.' Do you agree with this statement? Explain the reasons for your response.

2.3 The statement of financial position is sometimes seen as the least important of the three major financial statements discussed in this chapter. Can you see why this might be the case?

2.4 From time to time, there have been attempts to place a value on the 'human assets' of a business in order to derive a figure that can be included on the statement of financial position. Do you think humans should be treated as assets? Would 'human assets' meet the conventional definition of an asset for inclusion on the statement of financial position?

EXERCISES

Solutions to exercises with coloured numbers **can be found at the back of the book, starting on page 545.**

Basic-level exercises

2.1 On Thursday, the fourth day of his business venture, Paul, the street trader in wrapping paper (see earlier in the chapter, pages 34 to 37), bought more inventories for £53 cash. During the day he sold inventories that had cost £33 for a total of £47.

Required:
Draw up the three financial statements for Paul's business venture for Thursday.

2.2 The equity of Paul's business belongs to him because he is the sole owner of the business. Can you explain how the figure for equity by Thursday evening has arisen? You will need to look back at the events of Monday, Tuesday and Wednesday (pages 34 to 37) to do this.

Intermediate-level exercises

2.3 While on holiday, Helen had her credit cards and purse stolen from the beach while she was swimming. She was left with only £40, which she had kept in her hotel room, but she had three days of her holiday remaining. She was determined to continue her holiday and decided to make some money to enable her to do so. She decided to sell orange juice to holiday-makers using the local beach. On the first day she bought 80 cartons of orange juice at £0.50 each for cash and sold 70 of these at £0.80 each. On the following day she bought 60 cartons at £0.50 each for cash and sold 65 at £0.80 each. On the third and final day she bought another 60 cartons at £0.50 each for cash. However, it rained and, as a result, business was poor. She managed to sell 20 at £0.80 each but sold off the rest of her inventories at £0.40 each.

Required:
Prepare an income statement and statement of cash flows for each day's trading and prepare a statement of financial position at the end of each day's trading.

2.4 On 1 March, Joe Conday started a new business. During March, he carried out the following transactions:

1 March	Deposited £20,000 in a newly opened business bank account.
2 March	Bought fixtures and fittings for £6,000 cash and inventories £8,000 on credit.
3 March	Borrowed £5,000 from a relative and deposited it in the bank.
4 March	Bought a motor car for £7,000 cash and withdrew £200 in cash for his own use.
5 March	Bought a further motor car costing £9,000. The motor car bought on 4 March was given in part exchange at a value of £6,500. The balance of the purchase price for the new car was paid in cash.
6 March	Conday won £2,000 in a lottery and paid the amount into the business bank account. He also repaid £1,000 of the borrowings.

Required:
Draw up a statement of financial position for the business at the end of each day.

2.5 The following is a list of assets and claims of a manufacturing business at a particular point in time:

	£
Short-term borrowings	22,000
Property	245,000
Inventories of raw materials	18,000
Trade payables	23,000
Plant and equipment	127,000
Loan from Manufacturing Finance Co. (long-term borrowing)	100,000
Inventories of finished goods	28,000
Delivery vans	54,000
Trade receivables	34,000

Required:
Write out a statement of financial position in the standard format incorporating these figures. (*Hint*: There is a missing item that needs to be deduced and inserted.)

2.6 You have been talking to someone who had read a few chapters of an accounting text some years ago. During your conversation, the person made the following statements:

(a) The income statement shows how much cash has come into and left the business during the accounting period and the resulting balance at the end of the period.

(b) In order to be included in the statement of financial position as an asset, an item must have a resale value – that is all.

(c) The accounting equation is:

$$\text{Assets} + \text{Equity} = \text{Liabilities}$$

(d) Non-current assets are things that cannot be moved.

(e) Goodwill has an indefinite life and so should not be amortised.

Required:

Comment critically on each of the above statements, going into as much detail as you can.

Advanced-level exercises

2.7 The following is a list of the assets and claims of Crafty Engineering as at 30 June last year:

	£000
Trade payables	86
Motor vehicles	38
Long-term borrowing (loan from Industrial Finance Company)	260
Equipment and tools	207
Short-term borrowings	116
Inventories	153
Property	320
Trade receivables	185

Required:

(a) Prepare the statement of financial position of the business as at 30 June last year from the information provided, using the standard layout. (*Hint*: There is a missing item that needs to be deduced and inserted.)

(b) Discuss the significant features revealed by this financial statement.

2.8 The statement of financial position of a business at the start of the week is as follows:

	£
ASSETS	
Property	145,000
Furniture and fittings	63,000
Inventories	28,000
Trade receivables	33,000
Total assets	269,000
EQUITY AND LIABILITIES	
Equity	203,000
Short-term borrowing (bank overdraft)	43,000
Trade payables	23,000
Total equity and liabilities	269,000

During the week, the following transactions took place:

(a) Sold inventories for £11,000 cash; these inventories had cost £8,000.

(b) Sold inventories for £23,000 on credit; these inventories had cost £17,000.

(c) Received cash from trade receivables totalling £18,000.

(d) The owners of the business introduced £100,000 of their own money, which was placed in the business bank account.

(e) The owners bought a motor van, valued at £10,000, into the business.

(f) Bought inventories on credit for £14,000.

(g) Paid trade payables £13,000.

Required:

Show the statement of financial position after all of these transactions have been reflected.

Chapter 3

MEASURING AND REPORTING FINANCIAL PERFORMANCE

INTRODUCTION

In this chapter, we shall continue our examination of the major financial statements by looking at the income statement. This statement was briefly considered in Chapter 2, but we shall now look at it in some detail. We shall see how it is prepared and how it links with the statement of financial position. We shall also consider some of the key measurement problems to be faced when preparing the income statement.

Learning outcomes

When you have completed this chapter, you should be able to:

- discuss the nature and purpose of the income statement;

- prepare an income statement from relevant financial information and interpret the information that it contains;

- discuss the main recognition and measurement issues to be considered when preparing the income statement; and

- explain the main accounting conventions underpinning the income statement.

THE INCOME STATEMENT

Businesses exist for the primary purpose of generating wealth, or **profit**. The income statement – or *profit and loss account*, as it is sometimes called – measures and reports how much profit a business has generated over a period. It is, therefore, an immensely important financial statement for many users.

To measure profit, the total **revenue** generated during a particular period must be identified. Revenue is simply a measure of the inflow of economic benefits arising from the ordinary operations of a business. These benefits will result in either an increase in assets (such as cash or amounts owed to the business by its customers) or a decrease in liabilities. Different forms of business enterprise will generate different forms of revenue. Some examples of the different forms that revenue can take include:

- sales of goods (for example, by a manufacturer);
- fees for services (for example, of a solicitor);
- subscriptions (for example, of a club); and
- interest received (for example, by an investment fund).

Real World 3.1 shows the various forms of revenue generated by a leading football club.

Real World 3.1

Gunning for revenue

Arsenal Football Club generated total revenue of £353 million for the year ended 31 May 2017. Like other leading clubs, it relies on various forms of revenue to sustain its success. Figure 3.1 shows the contribution of each form of revenue for the year.

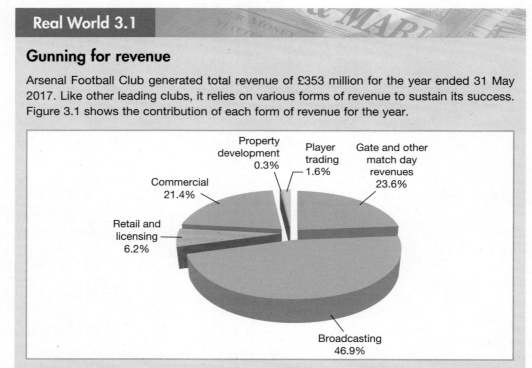

Figure 3.1 Arsenal's revenue for the year ended 31 May 2017

Source: Based on information in Arsenal Holdings plc, Annual Report 2016/2017, p. 47.

The total **expenses** relating to each period must also be identified. Expense is really the opposite of revenue. It represents the outflow of economic benefits arising from the ordinary operations of a business. This outflow results in either a decrease in assets (such as cash) or an increase in liabilities (such as amounts owed to suppliers). Expenses are incurred in the process of generating revenue or, at least, in attempting to generate it. The nature of the business will again determine the type of expenses that will be incurred. Examples of some of the more common types of expense include:

■ the cost of buying, or making, the goods sold during the period concerned – known as cost of sales or *cost of goods sold*;
■ salaries and wages;
■ rent;
■ motor vehicle running expenses;
■ insurance;
■ printing and stationery;
■ heat and light; and
■ telephone and postage.

The income statement simply shows the total revenue generated during a particular reporting period and deducts from this the total expenses incurred in generating that revenue. The difference between the total revenue and total expenses will represent either profit (if revenue exceeds expenses) or loss (if expenses exceed revenue). Therefore:

> **Profit (or loss) for the period = Total revenue for the period**
> **− Total expenses incurred in generating that revenue**

DIFFERENT ROLES

The income statement and the statement of financial position are not substitutes for one another. Rather, they perform different roles. The statement of financial position sets out the wealth held by the business at a single moment in time, whereas the income statement is concerned with the *flow* of wealth (profit) over a period of time. The two statements are, however, closely related.

The income statement for a reporting period links the statements of financial position at the beginning and the end of that period. At the start of a new reporting period, the statement of financial position shows the opening wealth position of the business. At the end of that reporting period, an income statement is prepared to show the wealth generated over that period. A statement of financial position is then prepared to show the new wealth position at the end of the period. It will reflect changes in wealth that have occurred since the previous statement of financial position was drawn up.

We saw in Chapter 2 (page 46) that the effect on the statement of financial position of making a profit (or loss) means that the accounting equation can be extended as follows:

> **Assets (at the end of the period) = Equity (amount at the start of the period**
> **+ Profit (or − Loss) for the period)**
> **+ Liabilities (at the end of the period)**

(This is assuming that the owner makes no injections or withdrawals of equity during the period.)

Can you recall from Chapter 2 how a profit, or loss, for a period is shown in the statement of financial position?

It is shown as an adjustment to owners' equity. Profit is added and a loss is subtracted.

The accounting equation can be further extended to:

**Assets (at the end of the period) = Equity (amount at the start of the period)
+ (Sales revenue − Expenses) (for the period)
+ Liabilities (at the end of the period)**

In theory, it is possible to calculate the profit (or loss) for the period by making all adjustments for revenue and expenses through the equity section of the statement of financial position. However, this would be rather cumbersome. A better solution is to have an 'appendix' to the equity section, in the form of an income statement. By deducting expenses from revenue for the period, the income statement derives the profit (or loss) by which the equity figure in the statement of financial position needs to be adjusted. This profit (or loss) figure represents the net effect of trading for the period. Through this 'appendix', users are presented with a detailed and more informative view of performance.

INCOME STATEMENT LAYOUT

The layout of the income statement will vary according to the type of business to which it relates. To illustrate an income statement, let us consider the case of a retail business (that is, a business that buys goods in their completed state and resells them).

Example 3.1 sets out a typical layout for the income statement of a retail business.

Example 3.1

Better-Price Stores
Income statement for the year ended 30 June 2018

	£
Sales revenue	232,000
Cost of sales	(154,000)
Gross profit	78,000
Salaries and wages	(24,500)
Rent	(14,200)
Heat and light	(7,500)
Telephone and postage	(1,200)
Insurance	(1,000)
Motor vehicle running expenses	(3,400)
Depreciation – fixtures and fittings	(1,000)
– motor van	(600)
Operating profit	24,600
Interest received from investments	2,000
Interest on borrowings	(1,100)
Profit for the period	25,500

We saw in Chapter 2 that brackets are used to denote when an item is to be deducted. This convention is used by accountants in preference to + or − signs and will be used throughout the text.

We can see from Example 3.1 that three measures of profit have been calculated. Let us now consider each of these in turn.

Gross profit

The first part of the income statement is concerned with calculating the **gross profit** for the period. We can see that revenue, which arises from selling the goods, is the first item to appear. Deducted from this item is the cost of sales figure (also called cost of goods sold) during the period. This gives the gross profit, which represents the profit from buying and selling goods, without taking into account any other revenues or expenses associated with the business.

Operating profit

Operating expenses (overheads) incurred in running the business (salaries and wages, rent, insurance and so on) are deducted from the gross profit. The resulting figure is known as the **operating profit**. This represents the wealth generated during the period from the normal activities of the business. It does not take account of income from other activities. Better-Price Stores in Example 3.1 is a retailer, so interest received on some spare cash that the business has invested is not part of its operating profit. Costs of financing the business are also ignored in the calculation of the operating profit.

Profit for the period

Having established the operating profit, we add any non-operating income (such as interest receivable) and deduct any interest payable on borrowings to arrive at the **profit for the period** (or *net profit*). This final measure of wealth generated represents the amount attributable to the owner(s) and will be added to the equity figure in the statement of financial position. It is a residual: that is, the amount remaining after deducting all expenses incurred in generating the sales revenue and taking account of non-operating income and expenses.

Activity 3.2

Look back to Example 3.1 and assume that a trainee accountant had prepared the income statement. Subsequent checking by the chief financial officer revealed the following errors:

1   Sales performance bonuses payable to staff amounting to £12,500 had been charged to cost of sales.
2   The depreciation charge for fixtures and fittings should be £10,000 not £1,000.
3   Stationery costing £500 had been treated as interest on borrowings.

What will be the gross profit, operating profit and profit for the period after these errors have been corrected?

Staff bonuses should be treated as part of the salaries and wages expense of the business. This means that cost of sales will decrease by £12,500 and gross profit will increase by a corresponding amount. The corrected gross profit is therefore £90,500 (that is, £78,000 + £12,500).

The operating profit and profit for the period, however, will not be affected by this correction. Although the operating expense salaries and wages will increase, this is offset by a compensating increase in gross profit.

The increase in the depreciation charge from £1,000 to £10,000 will decrease operating profit by £9,000. Furthermore, by treating stationery correctly, operating expenses will increase by £500, thereby decreasing operating profit by a corresponding amount. The corrected operating profit figure is, therefore, £15,100 (that is, £24,600 − £9,500).

Finally, the corrected profit for the period is calculated by taking the corrected operating profit £15,100, adding the interest received from investments, £2,000, and deducting the correct amount of interest on borrowing £600 (that is, £1,100 − £500) = £16,500.

FURTHER ISSUES

Having set out the main principles involved in preparing an income statement, let us consider some further points.

Cost of sales

The **cost of sales** (or cost of goods sold) figure for a period can be identified in different ways. In some businesses, it is identified for each individual item at the time of sale. By so doing, each item sold is matched with the relevant cost of that sale. Many large retailers (for example, supermarkets) have point-of-sale (checkout) systems that not only record each sale but also simultaneously pick up the cost of the goods that are the subject of the particular sale. Businesses that sell a relatively small number of high-value items (for example, an engineering business producing custom-made equipment) also tend to match sales revenue for each individual item with the cost of the goods sold at the time of sale. However, many businesses (for example, small retailers) may not find it practical to do this. Instead, they identify the cost of sales after the end of the reporting period.

To understand how this is done, we must remember that the cost of sales represents the cost of goods that were *sold* during the reporting period rather than the cost of goods that were *bought* during the period. Part of the goods bought during the period may remain, as inventories, at the end of the period. These will normally be sold in the next period. To derive the cost of sales, we need to know the amount of opening and closing inventories for the period and the cost of goods bought during the period. Example 3.2 illustrates how the cost of sales is derived.

Example 3.2

Better-Price Stores, which we considered in Example 3.1, began the year with unsold inventories of £40,000 and during that year bought inventories at a cost of £189,000. At the end of the year, unsold inventories of £75,000 were still held by the business.

The opening (beginning of the year) inventories *plus* the goods bought during the year represent the total goods available for resale, as follows:

	£
Opening inventories	40,000
Purchases (goods bought)	189,000
Goods available for resale	229,000

The closing inventories represent that portion of the total goods available for resale that remains unsold at the end of the year. This means that the cost of goods actually sold during the year must be the total goods available for resale *less* the inventories remaining at the end of the year. That is:

	£
Goods available for resale	229,000
Closing inventories	(75,000)
Cost of sales (or cost of goods sold)	154,000

These calculations are sometimes shown on the face of the income statement as in Example 3.3.

Example 3.3

	£	£
Sales revenue		232,000
Cost of sales:		
Opening inventories	40,000	
Purchases (goods bought)	189,000	
Closing inventories	(75,000)	(154,000)
Gross profit		78,000

This is just an expanded version of the first section of the income statement for Better-Price Stores, as set out in Example 3.1. We have simply included the additional information concerning inventories balances and purchases for the year, provided in Example 3.2.

Classifying expenses

The classification of expense items is often a matter of judgement. For example, the income statement set out in Example 3.1 could have included the insurance expense with the telephone and postage expense under a single heading – say, 'general expenses'. Such decisions are normally based on how useful a particular classification will be to users. This will usually mean that expense items of material size will be shown separately. For businesses that trade as limited companies, however, rules dictate the classification of expense items for external reporting purposes. These rules will be discussed in Chapter 5.

The following information relates to the activities of H & S Retailers for the year ended 30 April 2018:

	£
Motor vehicle running expenses	1,200
Closing inventories	3,000
Rent payable	5,000
Motor vans – cost less depreciation	6,300
Annual depreciation – motor vans	1,500
Heat and light	900
Telephone and postage	450
Sales revenue	97,400
Goods purchased	68,350
Insurance	750
Loan interest payable	620
Balance at bank	4,780
Salaries and wages	10,400
Opening inventories	4,000

Prepare an income statement for the year ended 30 April 2018. (*Hint*: Not all items listed should appear on this statement.)

Your answer should be as follows:

H & S Retailers
Income statement for the year ended 30 April 2018

	£	£
Sales revenue		97,400
Cost of sales:		
Opening inventories	4,000	
Purchases	68,350	
Closing inventories	(3,000)	(69,350)
Gross profit		28,050
Salaries and wages		(10,400)
Rent payable		(5,000)
Heat and light		(900)
Telephone and postage		(450)
Insurance		(750)
Motor vehicle running expenses		(1,200)
Depreciation – motor vans		(1,500)
Operating profit		7,850
Loan interest		(620)
Profit for the period		7,230

Note that neither the motor vans nor the bank balance are included in this statement. This is because they are both assets and so are neither revenues nor expenses.

Figure 3.2 shows the layout of the income statement.

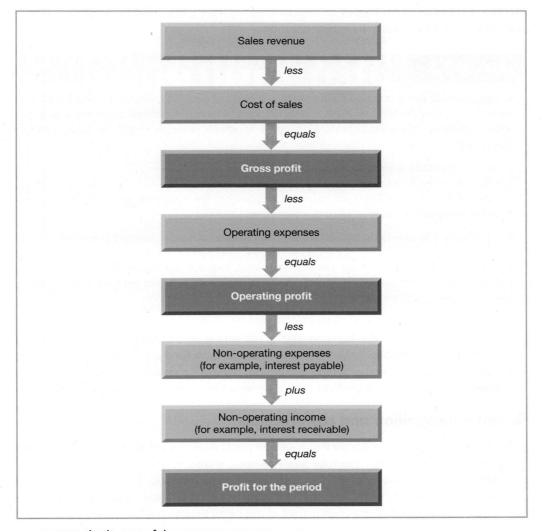

Figure 3.2 The layout of the income statement

RECOGNISING REVENUE

The financial amount to which a business is entitled for providing goods or services to a customer should be recognised as revenue. It should be recognised as soon as control of the goods or services is transferred to the customer. At this point, the business has satisfied its obligations towards the customer. To determine when control has passed, there are important indicators, such as when:

- physical possession passes to the customer;
- the business has the right to demand payment for the goods or services;
- the customer has accepted the goods or services;
- legal title passes to the customer; and
- significant risks and rewards of ownership passes to the customer.

If we take the example of a self-service store, where sales are for cash, the above indicators suggest that revenue can normally be recognised when the customer checks out. However, revenue recognition is not always so straightforward. Activity 3.4 provides the opportunity to apply the indicators to a slightly trickier situation.

The point at which revenue is recognised is not simply an academic issue. It can have a significant impact on reported revenues, and therefore profit, for a period. Where a credit sale transaction straddles the end of a reporting period, the point chosen for recognising revenue can determine whether it is included in an earlier reporting period or a later one.

Revenue recognition and cash receipts

We can see from Activity 3.4 above that a sale on credit is usually recognised *before* the cash is received. This means that the total sales revenue shown in the income statement may include sales transactions for which the cash has yet to be received. The total sales revenue will, therefore, often be different from the total cash received from sales during the period. For cash sales (that is, sales where cash is paid at the same time as the goods are transferred), there will be no difference in timing between reporting sales revenue and cash received.

Recognising revenue over time

Control of goods or services may be transferred to a customer over time rather than as a single 'one-off' event. When this occurs, the total revenue must be recognised over time. This situation may arise where:

- *the customer enjoys the benefits as the business carries out its obligations.* This can occur with service contracts, such as where an accounting firm undertakes employee payroll services for a large business or when an Internet service is being provided.
- *the business creates, or improves, an asset held by the customer.* This can occur with building contracts, such as where a builder undertakes the refurbishment of a shop owned by a retailer or when a shipbuilder carries out extensive repairs to a large ship.
- *the business creates an asset with no alternative use and the customer has agreed to pay for work carried out.* This can apply to special orders, such as where an engineering business produces specially-designed equipment for a manufacturer or where a furniture manufacturer makes customised furniture for a hotel chain.

Where control is transferred over time, the total revenue will be spread across the reporting periods covered by the contract. In other words, part of the total contract price will be treated as revenue in each reporting period. This is providing, however, it is possible to measure progress towards complete fulfilment of the business's obligations towards the customer. Otherwise, the amount of progress made during a particular period cannot really be determined.

To determine the appropriate revenue for each period, some method of measuring progress towards transferring the goods or services is needed. Various methods are available. Some are based on outputs, or achievements, such as particular 'milestones' reached in completing the contract, the number of units delivered, the number of services provided. Others are based on inputs, or effort expended, such as costs incurred, materials consumed, or hours worked. There is no single correct method: it depends on the particular circumstances. Nevertheless, methods based on output usually provide a more direct measure of the value of goods or services transferred to customers than those based on inputs. Hence, output-based measures are often preferred.

Activity 3.6

Why might a business choose input-based methods to measure progress if they are generally considered to be inferior?

Where methods based on output are unreliable, or unavailable, methods based on input may be the only real choice.

To illustrate one approach to recognising revenue over time, let us take the example of a builder entering into a contract with a manufacturer to build a factory. The work will be carried out on land owned by the manufacturer and will take three years to complete. The contract recognises that building the factory can be broken down into the following stages:

- Stage 1 – clearing and levelling the land and putting in the foundations.
- Stage 2 – building the walls.
- Stage 3 – putting on the roof.
- Stage 4 – putting in the windows and completing all the interior work.

It is expected that Stage 1 of the contract will be completed by the end of Year 1, Stages 2 and 3 will be completed by the end of Year 2 and Stage 4 by the end of Year 3.

Once the performance obligations for a particular stage are satisfied, the builder can recognise the agreed proportion of the total contract price for that stage as revenue. Thus, the agreed proportion for completing Stage 1 will be reported as revenue in the income statement for Year 1 and so on. Normally the contract would specify that the client would be required to pay the builder the appropriate proportion of the total contract price, following successful completion of each stage.

RECOGNISING EXPENSES

Having considered the recognition of revenue, let us now turn to the recognition of expenses. The matching convention provides guidance on this. This convention states that expenses should be matched to the revenue that they helped to generate. In other words, the expenses associated with a particular item of revenue must be taken into account in the same reporting period as that in which the item of revenue is included. We saw how this convention is applied with the costs of sales for Better-Price Stores in Example 3.2. The appropriate expense was the cost of inventories actually sold, rather than the total cost of inventories available for sale, during the period.

Applying this convention often means that an expense reported in the income statement for a period may not be the same as the cash paid for that item during the period. The expense reported might be either more or less than the cash paid during the period. Let us consider two examples that illustrate this point.

When the expense for the period is more than the cash paid during the period

Example 3.4

Domestic Ltd, a retailer, sells household electrical appliances. It pays its sales staff a commission of 2 per cent of sales revenue generated. Total sales revenue for last year amounted to £300,000. This means that the commission to be paid on sales for the year will be £6,000. However, by the end of the year, the amount of sales commission actually paid was only £5,000. If the business reported this amount as the sales commission expense, it would mean that the income statement would not reflect the full expense for the year. This would contravene the matching convention because not all of the expenses associated with the revenue of the year would have been matched with it in the income statement. This will be remedied as follows:

- Sales commission expense in the income statement will include the amount paid plus the amount outstanding (that is, £6,000 = £5,000 + £1,000).
- The amount outstanding (£1,000) represents an outstanding liability at the end of the year and will be included under the heading accrued expenses, or 'accruals', in the statement of financial position. As this item will have to be paid within twelve months of the year end, it will be treated as a current liability.
- The cash will already have been reduced to reflect the commission paid (£5,000) during the period.

These points are illustrated in Figure 3.3.

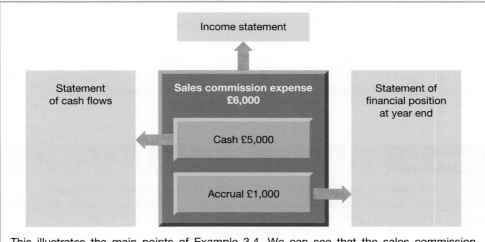

This illustrates the main points of Example 3.4. We can see that the sales commission expense of £6,000 (which appears in the income statement) is made up of a cash element of £5,000 and an accrued element of £1,000. The cash element appears in the statement of cash flows and the accrued.

Figure 3.3 Accounting for sales commission

In principle, all expenses should be matched to the period in which the sales revenue to which they relate is reported. It is sometimes difficult, however, to match certain expenses to sales revenue in the same precise way that we have matched sales commission to sales revenue. For example, electricity charges incurred often cannot be linked directly to particular sales in this way. As a result, the electricity charges incurred by, say, a retailer would be matched to the *period* to which they relate. Example 3.5 illustrates this.

Example 3.5

Domestic Ltd has reached the end of its reporting period and has only paid for electricity for the first three quarters of the year (amounting to £1,900). This is simply because the electricity company has yet to send out bills for the quarter that ends on the same date as Domestic Ltd's year end. The amount of Domestic Ltd's bill for the last quarter of the year is £500. In this situation, the amount of the electricity expense outstanding is dealt with as follows:

- Electricity expense in the income statement will include the amount paid, plus the amount of the bill for the last quarter of the year (that is, £1,900 + £500 = £2,400) in order to cover the whole year.
- The amount of the outstanding bill (£500) represents a liability at the end of the year and will be included under the heading 'accrued expenses' in the statement of financial position. This item would normally have to be paid within twelve months of the year end and will, therefore, be treated as a current liability.
- The cash will already have been reduced to reflect the amount (£1,900) paid for electricity during the period.

→

This treatment will mean that the correct figure for the electricity expense for the year will be included in the income statement. It will also have the effect of showing that, at the end of the reporting period, Domestic Ltd owed the amount of the last quarter's electricity bill. Dealing with the outstanding amount in this way reflects the dual aspect of the item and will ensure that the accounting equation is maintained.

Domestic Ltd may wish to draw up its income statement before it is able to discover how much it owes for the last quarter's electricity. In this case it is quite normal to make an estimate of the amount of the bill and to use this amount as described above.

Activity 3.7

How will the eventual payment of the outstanding sales commission (Example 3.4) and the electricity bill for the last quarter (Example 3.5) be dealt with in the accounting records of Domestic Ltd?

When these amounts are eventually paid, they will be dealt with as follows:

- Reduce cash by the amounts paid.
- Reduce the amount of the accrued expense as shown on the statement of financial position by the same amounts.

Other expenses, apart from electricity charges, may also be matched to the period to which they relate.

Activity 3.8

Can you think of other expenses for a retailer that cannot be linked directly to sales revenue and for which matching will therefore be done on a time basis? Try to think of at least two examples.

You may have thought of the following:

- rent payable;
- insurance;
- interest payable; and
- licence fees payable.

This is not an exhaustive list. You may have thought of others.

When the amount paid during the period is more than the full expense for the period

It is not unusual for a business to be in a situation where it has paid more during the year than the full expense for that year. Example 3.6 illustrates how we deal with this.

Example 3.6

Images Ltd, an advertising agency, normally pays rent for its premises quarterly in advance (on 1 January, 1 April, 1 July and 1 October). On the last day of the last reporting period (31 December), it paid the next quarter's rent (£4,000) to the following 31 March, which was a day earlier than required. This would mean that a total of five quarters' rent was paid during the year. If Images Ltd reports all of the cash paid as an expense in the income statement, this would be more than the full expense for the year. This would contravene the matching convention because a higher figure than the expenses associated with the revenue of the year would appear in the income statement.

The problem is overcome by dealing with the rental payment as follows:

- Show the rent for four quarters as the appropriate expense in the income statement (that is, 4 × £4,000 = £16,000).
- The cash (that is, 5 × £4,000 = £20,000) would already have been paid during the year.
- Show the quarter's rent paid in advance (£4,000) as a prepaid expense under assets in the statement of financial position. (The rent paid in advance will appear as a current asset in the statement of financial position, under the heading **prepaid expenses** or 'prepayments'.)

In the next reporting period, this prepayment will cease to be an asset and will become an expense in the income statement of that period. This is because the rent prepaid relates to the next period during which it will be 'used up'.

These points are illustrated in Figure 3.4.

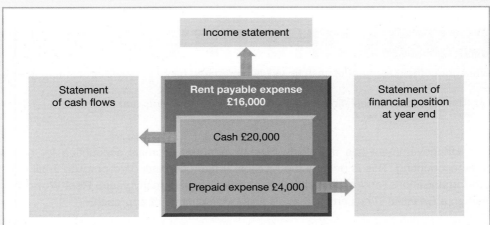

This illustrates the main points of Example 3.6. We can see that the rent expense of £16,000 (which appears in the income statement) is made up of four quarters' rent at £4,000 per quarter. This is the amount that relates to the period and is 'used up' during the period. The cash paid, £20,000 (which appears in the statement of cash flows), is made up of the cash paid during the period, which is five quarters at £4,000 per quarter. Finally, the prepayment of £4,000 (which appears on the statement of financial position) represents the payment made on 31 December and relates to the next reporting period.

Figure 3.4 Accounting for rent payable

In practice, the treatment of accruals and prepayments will be subject to the **materiality convention**. This convention states that, where the amounts involved are trivial, we should consider only what is expedient. This will usually mean treating an item as an expense in the period in which it is first recorded, rather than strictly matching it to the revenue to which it relates. For example, a large business may find that, at the end of a reporting period, it holds £20 worth of unused stationery. The time and effort taken to record this as a prepayment would outweigh the negligible effect on the measurement of profit or financial position. As a result, it would be treated as an expense of the current period and ignored in the following period.

PROFIT, CASH AND ACCRUALS ACCOUNTING

We have seen that, normally, for a particular reporting period, total revenue is not the same as total cash received and total expenses are not the same as total cash paid. As a result, the profit for the period (that is, total revenue minus total expenses) will not normally represent the net cash generated during that period. This reflects the difference between profit and liquidity. Profit is a measure of achievement, or productive effort, rather than a measure of cash generated. Although making a profit increases wealth, cash is only one possible form in which that wealth may be held.

These points are summarised in the **accruals convention**, which asserts that profit is the excess of revenue over expenses for a period, not the excess of cash receipts over cash payments. Leading on from this, the approach to accounting that is based on the accruals convention is frequently referred to as **accruals accounting**. The statement of financial position and the income statement are both prepared on the basis of accruals accounting.

Activity 3.9

What about the statement of cash flows? Is it prepared on an accruals accounting basis?

No. The statement of cash flows simply deals with cash receipts and payments.

The UK government has only fairly recently adopted accruals accounting for national income accounting. This is despite the fact that it has been standard practice in all private sector organisations, and many public sector ones, for very many years. **Real World 3.2** is based on a *Financial Times* article that discusses the change of approach.

Real World 3.2

Casting light on the UK economy

Only recently (2014) has the UK government started using accruals accounting principles in its assessment of national output, for example as measured by gross domestic product (GDP). Until then, it based its assessments of national economic effectiveness on a cash receipts and payments basis.

The main effect of the new, accruals, approach is that certain 'investments' will be recognised as such and not treated as 'expenses' as they tend to be with a cash-based approach.

Areas where a more logical approach to accounting for investments will have most effect are:

- research and development, that is the acquisition of economically valuable knowledge;
- expenditure on weapons systems; and
- cash invested in pension schemes.

It is estimated that the effect of introducing accrual accounting will raise the GDP value by between 3.5 per cent and 5 per cent. Similar changes in the accounting approach taken in the United States added 3.5 per cent to its GDP.

 Source: Based on Giles, C. (2014) Accounting rules unravel the mysteries of Britain's economy, ft.com, 23 April. © The Financial Times Limited 2014. All Rights Reserved.

DEPRECIATION

The expense of **depreciation**, which we have already come across, requires further examination. Most non-current assets do not have a perpetual existence, but have finite, or limited, lives. They are eventually 'used up' in the process of generating revenue for the business. This 'using up' may relate to physical deterioration (as with a motor vehicle). It may however be linked to obsolescence (as with some IT software that is no longer useful) or the mere passage of time (as with a purchased patent, which has a limited period of validity).

In essence, depreciation is an attempt to measure that portion of the cost (or fair value) of a non-current asset that has been depleted in generating the revenue recognised during a particular period. In the case of intangibles, we usually refer to the expense as **amortisation**, rather than *depreciation.*

Calculating the depreciation expense

To calculate a depreciation expense for a period, four factors have to be considered:

- the cost (or fair value) of the asset;
- the useful life of the asset;
- the residual value of the asset; and
- the depreciation method.

The cost (or fair value) of the asset

The cost of an asset will include all costs incurred by the business to bring the asset to its required location and to make it ready for use. This means that, in addition to the cost of acquiring the asset, any delivery costs, installation costs (for example, setting up a new machine) and legal costs incurred in the transfer of legal title (for example, in purchasing a lease on property) will be included as part of the total cost of the asset. Similarly, any costs incurred in improving or altering an asset to make it suitable for use will also be included as part of the total cost.

Andrew Wu (Engineering) Ltd bought a new motor car for its marketing director. The invoice received from the motor car supplier showed the following:

	£
New BMW 325i	29,350
Delivery charge	280
Alloy wheels	860
Sun roof	800
Petrol	80
Number plates	60
Road fund licence	150
	31,580
Part exchange – Reliant Robin	(1,000)
Amount outstanding	30,580

What is the total cost of the new car to be treated as part of the business's property, plant and equipment?

The cost of the new car will be as follows:

	£
New BMW 325i	29,350
Delivery charge	280
Alloy wheels	860
Sun roof	800
Number plates	60
	31,350

This cost includes delivery charges, which are necessary to bring the asset into use, and it includes number plates, as they are a necessary and integral part of the asset. Improvements (alloy wheels and sun roof) are also regarded as part of the total cost of the motor car. The petrol and road fund licence, however, are costs of operating the asset. These amounts will, therefore, be treated as expenses in the period in which they were incurred (although part of the cost of the licence may be regarded as a prepaid expense in the period in which it was incurred).

The part-exchange figure shown is part payment of the total amount outstanding and so is not relevant to a consideration of the total cost.

The fair value of an asset was defined in Chapter 2 as the selling price that could be obtained in an orderly transaction under market conditions. As we saw, assets may be revalued to fair value only if this can be measured reliably. Where fair values have been applied, the depreciation expense should be based on those fair values, rather than on the historic costs.

The useful life of the asset

A non-current asset has both a *physical life* and an *economic life.* The physical life will be exhausted through the effects of wear and tear and/or the passage of time. The economic life will be decided by the effects of technological progress, by changes in demand for the business's output or by changes in the way that the business operates. The benefits provided by the asset are eventually outweighed by the costs as it becomes unable to compete with newer assets, or becomes irrelevant to the needs of the business. The economic life of an asset may be much shorter than its physical life. For example, a computer may have a physical life of eight years and an economic life of three years.

The economic life determines the expected useful life of an asset for depreciation purposes. It is often difficult to estimate, however, as technological progress and shifts in consumer tastes can be swift and unpredictable.

Residual value (disposal value)

When a business disposes of a non-current asset that may still be of value to others, some payment may be received. This payment will represent the residual value, or *disposal value*, of the asset. To calculate the total amount to be depreciated, the residual value must be deducted from the cost (or fair value) of the asset. The likely amount to be received on disposal can, once again, be difficult to predict. The best guide is often past experience of similar assets sold.

Depreciation methods

Once the amount to be depreciated (that is, the cost, or fair value, of the asset less any residual value) has been estimated, the business must select a method of allocating this depreciable amount between the reporting periods covering the asset's useful life. Although there are various ways in which this may be done, there are only two methods that are commonly used in practice.

The first of these is known as the straight-line method. This method simply allocates the amount to be depreciated evenly over the useful life of the asset. In other words, there is an equal depreciation expense for each year that the asset is held.

Example 3.7

To illustrate the straight-line method of depreciation, consider the following information:

Cost of machine	£78,124
Estimated residual value at the end of its useful life	£2,000
Estimated useful life	4 years

To calculate the depreciation expense for each year, the total amount to be depreciated must be calculated. This will be the total cost less the estimated residual value: that is, £78,124 − £2,000 = £76,124. The annual depreciation expense can then be derived by dividing the amount to be depreciated by the estimated useful life of the asset of four years. The calculation is therefore:

$$\frac{£76,124}{4} = £19,031$$

This means that the annual depreciation expense that appears in the income statement in relation to this asset will be £19,031 for each of the four years of the asset's life.

The amount of depreciation relating to the asset will be accumulated for as long as the asset continues to be owned by the business or until the accumulated depreciation amounts to the cost less residual value. This accumulated depreciation figure will increase

$\rightarrow$

each year as a result of the annual depreciation expense in the income statement. This accumulated amount will be deducted from the cost of the asset in the statement of financial position. At the end of the second year, for example, the accumulated depreciation will be £19,031 × 2 = £38,062. The asset details will appear on the statement of financial position as follows:

	£
Machine at cost	78,124
Accumulated depreciation	(38,062)
	40,062

As we saw in Chapter 2, this balance of £40,062 is referred to as the **carrying amount** (sometimes also known as the **written-down value** or **net book value**) of the asset. It represents that portion of the cost (or fair value) of the asset that has still to be treated as an expense (written off) in future years plus the residual value. This carrying-amount figure does not, except by coincidence, represent the current market value, which may be quite different. The only point at which the carrying amount is intended to represent the market value of the asset is at the time of its disposal. In Example 3.7, at the end of the four-year life of the machine, the carrying amount would be £2,000 – its estimated disposal value.

The straight-line method derives its name from the fact that the carrying amount of the asset at the end of each year, when plotted against time, will result in a straight line, as shown in Figure 3.5.

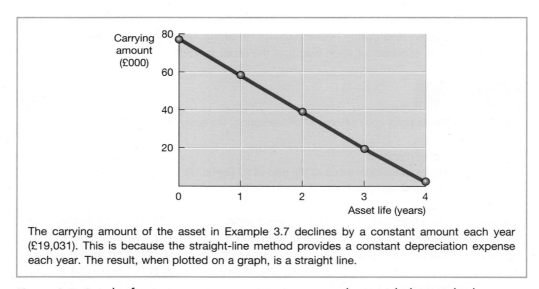

The carrying amount of the asset in Example 3.7 declines by a constant amount each year (£19,031). This is because the straight-line method provides a constant depreciation expense each year. The result, when plotted on a graph, is a straight line.

Figure 3.5 Graph of carrying amount against time using the straight-line method

The second approach to calculating the depreciation expense for a period is referred to as the **reducing-balance method**. This method applies a fixed percentage rate of depreciation to the carrying amount of the asset each year. The effect of this will be high annual depreciation expenses in the early years and lower expenses in the later years. To illustrate this method, let us take the same information that was used in Example 3.7. By using a fixed percentage of 60 per cent of the carrying amount to determine the annual depreciation expense, the effect will be to reduce the carrying amount to £2,000 after four years.

The calculations will be as follows:

	£
Cost of machine	78,124
Year 1 depreciation expense (60%* of cost)	(46,874)
Carrying amount	31,250
Year 2 depreciation expense (60% of carrying amount)	(18,750)
Carrying amount	12,500
Year 3 depreciation expense (60% of carrying amount)	(7,500)
Carrying amount	5,000
Year 4 depreciation expense (60% of carrying amount)	(3,000)
Residual value	2,000

* See the box below for an explanation of how to derive the fixed percentage.

Deriving the fixed percentage

Deriving the fixed percentage to be applied requires the use of the following formula:

$$P = (1 - \sqrt[n]{R/C} \times 100\%)$$

where:

P = the depreciation percentage
n = the useful life of the asset (in years)
R = the residual value of the asset
C = the cost, or fair value, of the asset.

The fixed percentage rate will, however, be given in all examples used in this book.

We can see that the pattern of depreciation is quite different between the two methods. If we plot against time the carrying amount of the asset, which has been derived using the reducing-balance method, the result will be as shown in Figure 3.6.

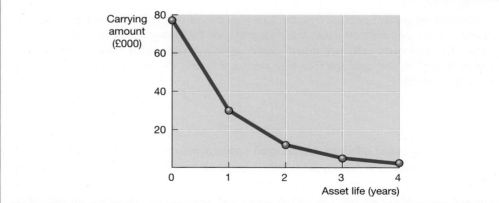

Under the reducing-balance method, the carrying amount of the asset in Example 3.7 falls by a larger amount in the earlier years than in the later years. This is because the depreciation expense is based on a fixed percentage of the carrying amount.

Figure 3.6 Graph of carrying amount against time using the reducing-balance method

Activity 3.11

Assume that the machine in Example 3.7 was owned by a business that made a profit before depreciation of £40,000 for each of the four years in which the asset was held.

Calculate the profit for the business for each year under each depreciation method, and comment on your findings.

Your answer should be as follows:

Straight-line method

	(a) Profit before depreciation £	(b) Depreciation £	(a − b) Profit £
Year 1	40,000	19,031	20,969
Year 2	40,000	19,031	20,969
Year 3	40,000	19,031	20,969
Year 4	40,000	19,031	20,969

Reducing-balance method

	(a) Profit before depreciation £	(b) Depreciation £	(a − b) Profit £
Year 1	40,000	46,874	(6,874)
Year 2	40,000	18,750	21,250
Year 3	40,000	7,500	32,500
Year 4	40,000	3,000	37,000

The straight-line method of depreciation results in the same profit figure for each year of the four-year period. This is because both the profit before depreciation and the depreciation expense are constant over the period. The reducing-balance method, however, results in very different profit figures for the four years, despite the fact that in this example the pre-depreciation profit is the same each year. In the first year a loss is reported and, thereafter, a rising profit.

Although the *pattern* of profit over the four-year period will be quite different, depending on the depreciation method used, the *total* profit for the period (£83,876) will remain the same. This is because both methods of depreciating will allocate the same amount of total depreciation (£76,124) over the four-year period. It is only the amount allocated *between years* that will differ.

In practice, the use of different depreciation methods may not have such a dramatic effect on profits as suggested in Activity 3.11. This is because businesses typically have more than one depreciating non-current asset. Where a business replaces some of its assets each year, the total depreciation expense calculated under the reducing-balance method will reflect a range of expenses (from high through to low), as assets will be at different points in their economic lives. This could mean that each year's total depreciation expense may not be significantly different from that which would have been derived under the straight-line method.

Selecting a depreciation method

The appropriate depreciation method to choose is the one that reflects the consumption of economic benefits provided by the asset. Where the economic benefits are consumed evenly over time (for example, with buildings), the straight-line method is usually appropriate. Where the economic benefits consumed decline over time (for example, with certain types of machinery that lose their efficiency), the reducing-balance method may be more appropriate.

There is an International Financial Reporting Standard (or International Accounting Standard) to deal with the depreciation of property, plant and equipment. As we shall see in Chapter 5, the purpose of financial reporting standards is to narrow areas of accounting difference and to ensure that information provided to users is transparent and comparable. The relevant standard endorses the view that the depreciation method chosen should reflect the pattern of consumption of economic benefits but does not specify particular methods to be used. It states that the useful life, depreciation method and residual values for property, plant and equipment should all be reviewed at least annually and adjustments made where appropriate. For intangible non-current assets with finite lives, there is a separate standard containing broadly similar rules. It does state, however, that the straight-line method must be chosen where the pattern of consumption of economic benefits is not clear.

Real World 3.3 sets out the depreciation policies of one large business.

Real World 3.3

Depreciating assets

Mothercare plc is a leading retailer that is focused on the needs of parents and young children. The annual report of the business for the 52 weeks ended 25 March 2017 set out the following depreciation policies.

Property, plant and equipment

Property, plant and equipment is carried at cost less accumulated depreciation and any recognised impairment losses. Depreciation is charged so as to write off the cost or valuation of assets, other than land and assets in the course of construction, over their estimated useful lives, using the straight-line method, on the following bases:

> Freehold buildings – 50 years
> Fixed equipment in freehold buildings – 20 years
> Leasehold improvements – the lease term
> Fixtures, fittings and equipment – 3 to 20 years

Intangible assets – software

Where computer software is not an integral part of a related item of computer hardware, the software is classified as an intangible asset. The capitalised costs of software for internal use include external direct costs of materials and services consumed in developing or obtaining the software and payroll and payroll-related costs for employees who are directly associated with and who devote substantial time to the project. These costs are amortised on a straight-line basis over their expected useful lives, which is normally five years.

Source: Extracts from Mothercare plc, Annual Report and Accounts 2017, p. 114, www.mothercare.com.

Mothercare plc is typical of most UK businesses in that it uses the straight-line method of depreciation. The reducing-balance method is very much less popular.

The approach taken to calculating depreciation is summarised in Figure 3.7.

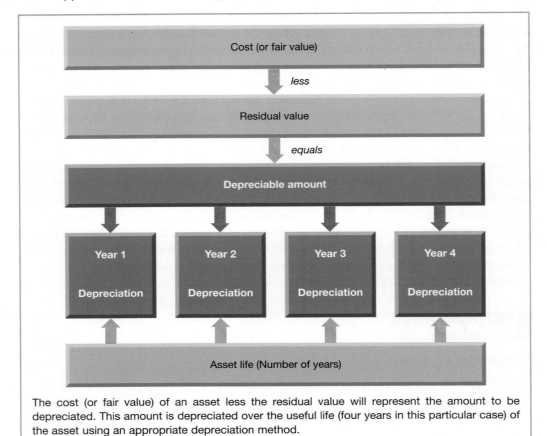

The cost (or fair value) of an asset less the residual value will represent the amount to be depreciated. This amount is depreciated over the useful life (four years in this particular case) of the asset using an appropriate depreciation method.

Figure 3.7 Calculating the annual depreciation expense

Impairment and depreciation

We saw in Chapter 2 that all non-current assets could be subjected to an impairment test. Where a non-current asset with a finite life has its carrying amount reduced following an impairment test, depreciation expenses for future reporting periods should be based on the impaired value.

Depreciation and asset replacement

Some appear to believe that the purpose of depreciation is to provide the funds for the replacement of a non-current asset when it reaches the end of its useful life. However, this is not the case. It was mentioned earlier that depreciation represents an attempt to allocate the cost or fair value (less any residual value) of a non-current asset over its expected useful life. The depreciation expense for a particular reporting period is used in calculating profit for that period. If a depreciation charge is excluded from the income statement, we shall not have a fair measure of financial performance. Whether or not the business intends to replace the asset in the future is irrelevant.

Where an asset is to be replaced, the depreciation expense in the income statement will not ensure that liquid funds are set aside specifically for this purpose. Although the depreciation expense will reduce profit, and therefore reduce the amount that the owners may decide to withdraw, the amounts retained within the business as a result may be invested in ways that are unrelated to the replacement of the asset.

Depreciation and judgement

From our discussions about depreciation, it is clear that accounting is not as precise and objective as it is sometimes portrayed as being. There are areas where subjective judgement is required.

Activity 3.12

What judgements must be made to calculate a depreciation expense for a period?

You may have thought of the following:

- the expected residual or disposal value of the asset;
- the expected useful life of the asset; and
- the choice of depreciation method.

Making different judgements on these matters would result in a different pattern of depreciation expenses over the life of the asset and, therefore, in a different pattern of reported profits. However, any underestimations or overestimations that are made will be adjusted for in the final year of an asset's life. As a result, the total depreciation expense (and total profit) over the asset's life will not be affected by estimation errors.

Real World 3.4 describes the effect on annual performance of extending the useful life of a non-current asset held by a well-known business.

Real World 3.4

Engineering an improvement?

BA reported a loss of £358 million for the 2008/09 financial year. This loss, however, would have been significantly higher had the business not changed its depreciation policies. The 2008/09 annual report of the business states:

> During the prior year, the Group changed the depreciation period for the RB211 engine, used on Boeing 747 and 767 fleets, from 54 months to 78 months. The change resulted in a £33 million decrease in the annual depreciation charge for this engine type.

Source: British Airways, Annual Report and Accounts 2008/09, Note 15, www.britishairways.com.

Activity 3.13

Sally Dalton (Packaging) Ltd bought a machine for £40,000. At the end of its useful life of four years, the amount received on sale was £4,000. When the asset was purchased the business received two estimates of the likely residual value of the asset. These were: (a) £8,000 and (b) zero.

Show the annual depreciation expenses over the four years and the total depreciation expenses for the asset under each of the two estimates. The straight-line method should be used to calculate the annual depreciation expenses.

The depreciation expense, assuming estimate (a), will be £8,000 a year (that is, (£40,000 − £8,000)/4)). The depreciation expense, assuming estimate (b), will be £10,000 a year (that is, £40,000/4). As the actual residual value is £4,000, estimate (a) will lead to under-depreciation of £4,000 (that is, £8,000 − £4,000) over the life of the asset and estimate (b) will lead to over-depreciation of £4,000 (that is, £0 − £4,000). These under- and overestimations will be dealt with in year 4.

The pattern of depreciation and total depreciation expenses will therefore be:

| | | Estimate | |
| | | (a) | (b) |
Year		£	£
1	Annual depreciation	8,000	10,000
2	Annual depreciation	8,000	10,000
3	Annual depreciation	8,000	10,000
4	Annual depreciation	8,000	10,000
		32,000	40,000
4	Under/(over)-depreciation	4,000	(4,000)
	Total depreciation	36,000	36,000

The final adjustment for under-depreciation of an asset is often referred to as 'loss (or deficit) on disposal of a non-current asset', as the amount actually received is less than the estimated residual value. Similarly, the adjustment for over-depreciation is often referred to as 'profit (or surplus) on disposal of a non-current asset'. These final adjustments are normally made as an addition to the expense (or a reduction in the expense) for depreciation in the reporting period during which the asset is disposed of.

Activity 3.14

In practice, would you expect it to be more likely that the amount of depreciation would be overestimated or underestimated? Why?

We might expect there to be systematic overestimations of the annual depreciation expense. Application of the prudence convention may lead to underestimating the lives and residual values of assets. Where this occurs, the result will be an overestimate for the annual depreciation charge.

COSTING INVENTORIES

The cost of inventories is important in determining financial performance and position. The cost of inventories sold during a reporting period will affect the calculation of profit and the cost of inventories held at the end of the reporting period will affect the portrayal of assets held.

To calculate the cost of inventories, an assumption must be made about the physical flow of inventories through the business. This assumption need not have anything to do with how inventories *actually* flow through the business. It is concerned only with identifying measures of performance and position that provide users of financial statements with useful information.

Three common assumptions used are:

- **first in, first out (FIFO)**, in which inventories are costed *as if* the earliest acquired inventories held are the first to be used;
- **last in, first out (LIFO)**, in which inventories are costed *as if* the latest acquired inventories held are the first to be used; and
- **weighted average cost (AVCO)**, in which inventories are costed *as if* inventories acquired lose their separate identity and go into a 'pool'. Any issues of inventories from this pool will reflect the weighted average cost of inventories held.

During a period of changing prices, the choice of assumption used in costing inventories can be important. Example 3.8 provides an illustration of how each assumption is applied and the effect of each on financial performance and position.

Example 3.8

A business that supplies grass seed to farmers and horticulturalists has the following transactions during a period:

		Tonnes	Cost/tonne £
1 May	Opening inventories	100	100
2 May	Bought	500	110
3 May	Bought	800	120
		1,400	
6 May	Sold	(900)	
	Closing inventories	500	

First in, first out (FIFO)

Using the FIFO approach, the first 900 tonnes of seed bought are treated *as if* these are the ones that are sold. This will consist of the opening inventories (100 tonnes), the purchases made on 2 May (500 tonnes) and some of the purchases made on 3 May (300 tonnes). The remainder of the 3 May purchases (500 tonnes) will comprise the closing inventories. This means that we have:

	Cost of sales			Closing inventories		
	Tonnes	Cost/tonne	Total	Tonnes	Cost/tonne	Total
		£	£000		£	£000
1 May	100	100	10.0			
2 May	500	110	55.0			
3 May	300	120	36.0	500	120	60.0
Cost of sales			101.0	Closing inventories		60.0

Last in, first out (LIFO)

Using the LIFO assumption, the later purchases will be treated *as if* these were the first to be sold. This is the 3 May purchases (800 tonnes) and some of the 2 May purchases (100 tonnes). The earlier purchases (the rest of the 2 May purchase and the opening inventories) will comprise the closing inventories. This can be set out as follows:

	Cost of sales			Closing inventories		
	Tonnes	Cost/tonne £	Total £000	Tonnes	Cost/tonne £	Total £000
3 May	800	120	96.0			
2 May	100	110	11.0	400	110	44.0
1 May			–	100	100	10.0
Cost of sales			107.0	Closing inventories		54.0

Figure 3.8 contrasts LIFO and FIFO.

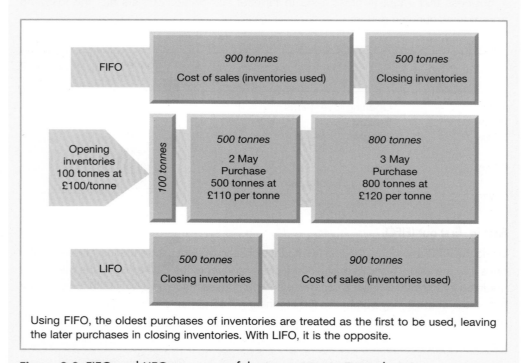

Using FIFO, the oldest purchases of inventories are treated as the first to be used, leaving the later purchases in closing inventories. With LIFO, it is the opposite.

Figure 3.8 FIFO and LIFO treatment of the inventories in Example 3.8

Weighted average cost (AVCO)

Using the AVCO assumption, a weighted average cost will be determined that will be used to derive both the cost of goods sold and the cost of the remaining inventories held. This simply means that the total cost of the opening inventories and the total cost of the 2 May and 3 May purchases are added together and divided by the total number of tonnes to obtain the weighted average cost per tonne. Both the cost of sales and closing inventories values are based on that average cost per tonne. This means that we have:

	Tonnes	Cost/tonne £	Total £000
1 May	100	100	10.0
2 May	500	110	55.0
3 May	800	120	96.0
	1,400		161.0

The average cost is £161,000/1,400 = £115 per tonne.

Cost of sales			Closing inventories		
Tonnes	Cost/tonne £	Total £000	Tonnes	Cost/tonne £	Total £000
900	115	103.5	500	115	57.5

Activity 3.15

Suppose the 900 tonnes of inventories in Example 3.8 were sold for £150 per tonne.

(a) Calculate the gross profit for this sale under each of the three methods.
(b) What observations concerning the portrayal of financial position and performance can you make about each method when prices are rising?

Your answer should be along the following lines:

(a) Gross profit calculation:

	FIFO £000	LIFO £000	AVCO £000
Sales revenue (900 @ £150)	135.0	135.0	135.0
Cost of sales	(101.0)	(107.0)	(103.5)
Gross profit	34.0	28.0	31.5
Closing inventories	60.0	54.0	57.5

(b) These figures show that FIFO will give the highest gross profit during a period of rising prices. This is because sales revenue is matched with the earlier (and cheaper) purchases. LIFO will give the lowest gross profit because sales revenue is matched against the more recent (and dearer) purchases. The AVCO method will normally give a figure that is between these two extremes.

  The closing inventories figure in the statement of financial position will be highest with the FIFO method. This is because the cost of goods still held will be based on the more recent (and dearer) purchases. LIFO will give the lowest closing inventories figure as the goods held will be based on the earlier (and cheaper) purchases. Once again, the AVCO method will normally give a figure that is between these two extremes.

Assume that prices are falling rather than rising. How would your observations concerning the portrayal of financial performance and position be different for the various costing methods?

When prices are falling, the positions of FIFO and LIFO are reversed. FIFO will give the lowest gross profit as sales revenue is matched against the earlier (and dearer) goods bought. LIFO will give the highest gross profit as sales revenue is matched against the more recent (and cheaper) goods bought. AVCO will give a cost of sales figure between these two extremes. The closing inventories figure in the statement of financial position will be lowest under FIFO as the cost of inventories will be based on the more recent (and cheaper) purchases. LIFO will provide the highest closing inventories figure and AVCO will provide a figure between the two extremes.

The different costing assumptions only have an effect on reported profit from one reporting period to the next. The figure derived for closing inventories will be carried forward and matched with sales revenue in a later period. If the cheaper purchases of inventories are matched to sales revenue in the current period, it will mean that the dearer purchases will be matched to sales revenue in a later period. Over the life of the business, therefore, total profit will be the same either way.

Inventories – some further issues

We saw in Chapter 2 that the convention of prudence requires that inventories be valued at the lower of cost and net realisable value. (The net realisable value of inventories is the estimated selling price less any further costs necessary to complete the goods and any costs involved in selling and distributing them.) In theory, this means that the valuation method applied to inventories could switch each year, depending on which of cost and net realisable value is the lower. In practice, however, the cost of the inventories held is usually below the current net realisable value – particularly during a period of rising prices. It is, therefore, the cost figure that will normally appear in the statement of financial position.

Activity 3.17

Can you think of any circumstances where the net realisable value will be lower than the cost of inventories held, even during a period of generally rising prices? Try to think of at least two.

The net realisable value may be lower where:

- goods have deteriorated or become obsolete;
- there has been a fall in the market price of the goods;
- the goods are being used as a 'loss leader', that is, they are deliberately going to be sold at a price lower than their cost; and/or
- bad buying decisions have been made.

There is also an International Financial Reporting Standard that deals with inventories. It states that, when preparing financial statements for external reporting, the cost of inventories should normally be determined using either FIFO or AVCO. The LIFO assumption is not acceptable for external reporting. (There is no reason, however, that a business should not apply LIFO when preparing financial statements for use by its own managers.) The standard also requires the 'lower of cost and net realisable value' rule to be used and so endorses the application of prudence.

Activity 3.18

Where inventories are written down (reduced) to their net realisable value, how do you think this should be treated in the financial statements?

The amount written down should be treated as an expense in the income statement of the period in which the write down occurs. The value of inventories shown in the statement of financial position should then report the inventories at their net realisable value rather than their cost.

Real World 3.5 sets out the inventories' costing methods used by some of the UK's leading businesses.

Real World 3.5

Counting the cost

Inventories costing methods used by some large UK businesses are as follows:

Name	Type of business	Costing method used
J Sainsbury plc	Supermarket	AVCO
Babcock International plc	Engineering support services	FIFO
British American Tobacco plc	Tobacco manufacturer	AVCO
Premier Foods plc	Food manufacturer	FIFO
Marks and Spencer plc	Food and clothing retailer	AVCO
Diageo plc	Alcoholic beverages	AVCO
Tate and Lyle plc	Food ingredients	FIFO or AVCO
AstraZeneca plc	Pharmaceuticals	FIFO or AVCO

Source: Annual reports of the relevant businesses for 2016 or 2017.

Note that Tate and Lyle plc and AstraZeneca plc employ more than one inventories' costing method. Tate and Lyle plc state that the choice of costing method will depend on the materials and production processes used. AstraZeneca plc does not state what determines the choice of costing method. However, it will probably vary according to location, production processes or some other key factor.

The table simply sets out a small, non-random sample of well-known businesses and so we cannot assess the relative popularity of the FIFO and LIFO methods in practice on the basis of this.

Costing inventories and depreciation provide two examples where the **consistency convention** should be applied. This convention holds that once a particular method of accounting is selected, it should be applied consistently over time. It would not be acceptable to switch from, say, FIFO to AVCO between periods (unless exceptional circumstances make it appropriate). The purpose of this convention is to help users make valid comparisons of performance and position from one period to the next. It, therefore, supports the qualitative characteristic of comparability that we considered in Chapter 1.

Activity 3.19

Reporting inventories in the financial statements provides a further example of the need to apply subjective judgement. For the inventories of a retail business, what are the main judgements that are required?

The main judgements are:

- the choice of costing method (FIFO, LIFO, AVCO); and
- deducing the net realisable value figure for inventories held.

One final point before leaving this topic. Costing inventories using FIFO, LIFO and AVCO applies to items that are interchangeable. Where they are not, as would be the case with custom-made items, the specific cost of the individual items must be used.

TRADE RECEIVABLES PROBLEMS

We have seen that, when businesses sell goods or services on credit, revenue will usually be recognised before the customer pays the amounts owing. Recording the dual aspect of a credit sale will involve increasing sales revenue and increasing trade receivables by the amount of the revenue from the credit sale.

With this type of sale there is always the risk that the customer will not pay the amount due. Where it becomes reasonably certain that the customer will not pay, the amount owed is considered to be a **bad debt**, which must be taken into account when preparing the financial statements.

Activity 3.20

What would be the effect on the income statement, and on the statement of financial position, of not taking into account the fact that a debt is bad?

The effect would be to overstate the assets (trade receivables) on the statement of financial position and to overstate profit in the income statement, as the revenue that has been recognised will not result in any future benefit.

To provide the users of the financial statements with a more realistic picture of financial performance and position, the bad debt must be 'written off'. This will involve reducing the trade receivables and increasing expenses (by creating an expense known as 'bad debts written off') by the amount of the bad debt. The matching convention requires that the bad debt is written off in the same period as the sale that gave rise to the debt is recognised.

Note that, when a debt is bad, the accounting response is not simply to cancel the original sale. If this were done, the income statement would not be so informative. Reporting the bad debts as an expense can be extremely useful in assessing management performance.

Real World 3.6 indicates the extent of the bad debts problem among small and medium size UK businesses.

Doubtful debts

At the end of a reporting period, it may not be possible to identify, with certainty, all bad debts incurred during the period. Doubts may surround certain trade receivables, but it may only be at a later date that the true position will become clear. Nevertheless, the possibility that some trade receivables will not be paid should not be ignored. It would not be prudent, nor would it comply with the need to match expenses to the period in which the associated revenue is recognised.

The business must try to determine the amount of trade receivables that, at the end of the period, are doubtful (that is, there is a possibility that they may eventually prove to be bad). This amount may be derived by examining individual trade receivables accounts or by taking a proportion (usually based on past experience) of the total trade receivables outstanding.

Once a figure has been derived, an expense known as an **allowance for trade receivables** should be recognised. This will be shown as an expense in the income statement and deducted from the total trade receivables figure in the statement of financial position. In this way, full account is taken, in the appropriate reporting period, of those trade receivables where there is a risk of non-payment. This accounting treatment of these 'doubtful' trade receivables will be in addition to the treatment of the more certain bad debts described above.

Example 3.9 illustrates the reporting of bad debts and allowances for trade receivables.

Example 3.9

Desai Enterprises, which began trading on 1 July 2017, had trade receivables of £350,000 outstanding at the end of the reporting period to 30 June 2018. Investigation of these trade receivables revealed that £10,000 would probably be irrecoverable and that there was doubt concerning the recoverability of a further £30,000.

Relevant extracts from the income statement for that year would be as follows:

Income statement (extracts) for the year ended 30 June 2018

	£
Bad debts written off	10,000
Allowances for trade receivables	30,000

Statement of financial position (extracts) as at 30 June 2018

	£
Trade receivables	340,000*
Allowances for trade receivables	(30,000)
	310,000

*That is, £350,000 less £10,000 irrecoverable trade receivables.

The allowances for trade receivables figure is, of course, an estimate; it is quite likely that the actual amount of trade receivables that prove to be bad will be different from the estimate. Let us say that, during the next reporting period, it was discovered that, in fact, £26,000 of the trade receivables considered doubtful proved to be irrecoverable. These trade receivables must now be written off as follows:

- reduce trade receivables by £26,000; and
- reduce allowances for trade receivables by £26,000.

However, allowances for trade receivables of £4,000 will remain. This amount represents an overestimate made when creating the allowance as at 30 June 2018. As the allowance is no longer needed, it should be eliminated. Remember that the allowance was made by creating an expense in the income statement for the year to 30 June 2018. As the expense was too high, the amount of the overestimate should be 'written back' in the next reporting period. In other words, it will be treated as revenue for the year to 30 June 2019. This will mean:

- reducing the allowances for trade receivables by £4,000; and
- increasing revenue by £4,000.

Ideally, of course, the amount should be written back to the 2018 income statement; however, it is too late to do this. At the end of the year to 30 June 2019, not only will 2018's overestimate be written back, but a new allowance should be created to take account of the trade receivables arising from 2019's credit sales that are considered doubtful.

Activity 3.21

Clayton Conglomerates had trade receivables of £870,000 outstanding at the end of the reporting period to 31 March 2017. The chief financial officer believed £40,000 of those trade receivables to be irrecoverable and a further £60,000 to be doubtful. In the subsequent year, it was found that a pessimistic estimate of those trade receivables considered doubtful had been made and that only a further £45,000 of trade receivables had actually proved to be bad.

Show the relevant income statement extracts for both 2017 and 2018 to report the bad debts written off and the allowances for trade receivables. Also show the relevant statement of financial position extract as at 31 March 2017.

Your answer should be as follows:

Income statement (extract) for the year ended 31 March 2017

	£
Bad debts written off	40,000
Allowances for trade receivables	60,000

Income statement (extract) for the year ended 31 March 2018

	£
Allowances for trade receivables written back (revenue)	15,000

(*Note*: This figure will usually be netted off against any allowances for trade receivables created in respect of 2018.)

Statement of financial position (extract) as at 31 March 2017

	£
Trade receivables (870,000 − 40,000)	830,000
Allowances for trade receivables	(60,000)
	770,000

The accounting treatment of bad debts and allowances for trade receivables are two further examples where judgement is needed to derive an appropriate expense figure.

What will be the effect of different judgements concerning the appropriate amount of bad debts expense and allowances for trade receivables expense on the profit for a particular period and on the total profit reported over the life of the business?

The judgement concerning whether to write off a debt as bad will affect the expenses for the period and, therefore, the reported profit. Over the life of the business, however, total reported profit would not be affected, as incorrect judgements made in one period will be adjusted for in a later period.

Suppose that a debt of £100 was written off in a period and that, in a later period, the amount owing was actually received. The increase in expenses of £100 in the period in which the bad debt was written off would be compensated for by an increase in revenue of £100 when the amount outstanding was finally received (bad debt recovered). If, on the other hand, the amount owing of £100 was never written off in the first place, the profit for the two periods would not be affected by the bad debt adjustment and would, therefore, be different – but the total profit for the two periods would be the same.

A similar situation would apply where there are differences in judgements concerning allowances for trade receivables.

USES AND USEFULNESS OF THE INCOME STATEMENT

The income statement may help in providing information on:

- *How effective the business has been in generating wealth.* Since wealth generation is the primary reason for most businesses to exist, assessing how much wealth has been created is an important issue. The income statement reveals the profit for the period, or *bottom line* as it is sometimes called. This provides a measure of the wealth created for the owners. Gross profit and operating profit are also useful measures of wealth creation.
- *How profit was derived.* In addition to providing various measures of profit, the income statement provides other information needed for a proper understanding of business performance. It reveals the level of sales revenue and the nature and amount of expenses incurred, which can help in understanding how profit was derived. The analysis of financial performance will be considered in detail in Chapters 8 and 9.

Self-assessment question 3.1

TT and Co. is a new business that started trading on 1 January 2017. The following is a summary of transactions that occurred during the first year of trading:

1 The owners introduced £50,000 of equity, which was paid into a bank account opened in the name of the business.
2 Premises were rented from 1 January 2017 at an annual rental of £20,000. During the year, rent of £25,000 was paid to the owner of the premises.

3 Rates (a tax on business premises) were paid during the year as follows:

For the period 1 January 2017 to 31 March 2017	£500
For the period 1 April 2017 to 31 March 2018	£1,200

4 A delivery van was bought on 1 January 2017 for £12,000. This is expected to be used in the business for four years and then to be sold for £2,000.
5 Wages totalling £33,500 were paid during the year. At the end of the year, the business owed £630 of wages for the last week of the year.
6 Electricity bills for the first three quarters of the year were paid totalling £1,650. After 31 December 2017, but before the financial statements had been finalised for the year, the bill for the last quarter arrived showing a charge of £620.
7 Inventories totalling £143,000 were bought on credit.
8 Inventories totalling £12,000 were bought for cash.
9 Sales revenue on credit totalled £152,000 (cost of sales £74,000).
10 Cash sales revenue totalled £35,000 (cost of sales £16,000).
11 Receipts from trade receivables totalled £132,000.
12 Payments of trade payables totalled £121,000.
13 Van running expenses paid totalled £9,400.

At the end of the year it was clear that a credit customer who owed £400 would not be able to pay any part of the debt. All of the other trade receivables were expected to be settled in full.

The business uses the straight-line method for depreciating non-current assets.

Required:
Prepare a statement of financial position as at 31 December 2017 and an income statement for the year to that date.

The solution to this question can be found at the back of the book, starting on page 525.

SUMMARY

The main points of this chapter may be summarised as follows:

The income statement (profit and loss account)

- The income statement reveals how much profit (or loss) has been generated over a period and links the statements of financial position at the beginning and end of a reporting period.
- Profit (or loss) is the difference between total revenue and total expenses for a period.
- There are three main measures of profit:
  - gross profit – which is calculated by deducting the cost of sales from the sales revenue;
  - operating profit – which is calculated by deducting overheads from the gross profit;
  - profit for the period – which is calculated by adding non-operating income and deducting non-operating expenses (such as finance costs) from the operating profit.

Expenses and revenue

■ Cost of sales may be identified by matching the cost of each sale to the particular sale or by adjusting the goods bought during a period by the opening and closing inventories.

■ Classifying expenses is often a matter of judgement, although there are rules for businesses that trade as limited companies.

■ Revenue is recognised when a business has performed its obligations, which is when control of the goods or services is passed to the customer.

■ Revenue can be recognised over a period of time or at a particular point in time.

■ The matching convention states that expenses should be matched to the revenue that they help generate.

■ An expense reported in the income statement may not be the same as the cash paid. This can result in accruals or prepayments appearing in the statement of financial position.

■ The materiality convention states that where the amounts are immaterial, we should consider only what is expedient.

■ The accruals convention states that:

$$\text{profit} = \text{revenue} - \text{expenses (not cash receipts} - \text{cash payments).}$$

Depreciation of non-current assets

■ Depreciation requires a consideration of the cost (or fair value), useful life and residual value of an asset. It also requires a consideration of the method of depreciation.

■ The straight-line method of depreciation allocates the amount to be depreciated evenly over the useful life of the asset.

■ The reducing-balance method applies a fixed percentage rate of depreciation to the carrying amount of an asset each year.

■ The depreciation method chosen should reflect the pattern of consumption of economic benefits of an asset.

■ Depreciation allocates the cost (or fair value), less the residual value, of an asset over its useful life. It does not provide funds for replacement of the asset.

Costing inventories

■ The way in which we derive the cost of inventories is important in the calculation of profit and the presentation of financial position.

■ The first in, first out (FIFO) assumption is that the earliest inventories held are the first to be used.

■ The last in, first out (LIFO) assumption is that the latest inventories are the first to be used.

■ The weighted average cost (AVCO) assumption applies an average cost to all inventories used.

■ When prices are rising, FIFO gives the lowest cost of sales figure and highest closing inventories figure and for LIFO it is the other way around. AVCO gives figures for cost of sales and closing inventories that lie between FIFO and LIFO.

■ When prices are falling, the positions of FIFO and LIFO are reversed.

■ Inventories are shown at the lower of cost and net realisable value.

■ When a particular method of accounting, such as a depreciation method, is selected, it should be applied consistently over time.

Bad debts

- Where it is reasonably certain that a credit customer will not pay, the debt is regarded as 'bad' and written off.

- Where it is doubtful that a credit customer will pay, an allowance for trade receivables expense should be created.

Uses of the income statement

- It provides measures of profit generated during a period.

- It provides information on how the profit was derived.

KEY TERMS

For definitions of these terms, see at the back of the book, starting on p 514.

profit p. 74
revenue p. 74
expense p. 75
gross profit p. 77
operating profit p. 77
profit for the period p. 77
cost of sales p. 78
matching convention p. 84
accrued expense p. 84
prepaid expense p. 87
materiality convention p. 88
accruals convention p. 88
accruals accounting p. 88

depreciation p. 89
amortisation p. 89
residual value p. 91
straight-line method p. 91
carrying amount p. 92
written-down value p. 92
net book value p. 92
reducing-balance method p. 92
first in, first out (FIFO) p. 99
last in, first out (LIFO) p. 99
weighted average cost (AVCO) p. 99
consistency convention p. 103
bad debt p. 104
allowance for trade receivables p. 106

FURTHER READING

If you would like to explore the topics covered in this chapter in more depth, we recommend the following:

Alexander, D. and Nobes, C. (2016) *Financial Accounting: An International Introduction*, 6th edn, Pearson, Chapters 2, 3, 9 and 10.

Elliott, B. and Elliott, J. (2017) *Financial Accounting and Reporting*, 18th edn, Pearson, Chapters 2, 11, 20 and 21.

International Accounting Standards Board (2017) *2017 A Guide through IFRS Standards (Green Book)*, IAS 2 *Inventories* and IFRS 15 *Revenue from Contracts with Customers*.

KPMG (2017) *Insights into IFRS*, 14th edn, Sweet and Maxwell, Sections 3.2, 3.3, 3.8, 3.10 and 4.2A (a summarised version of this is available free at www.kpmg.com).

CRITICAL REVIEW QUESTIONS

Solutions to these questions can be found at the back of the book, starting on page 536.

3.1 'Although the income statement is a record of past achievement, the calculations required for certain expenses involve estimates of the future.' What does this statement mean? Can you think of examples where estimates of the future are used?

3.2 'Depreciation is a process of allocation and not valuation.' What do you think is meant by this statement?

3.3 What is the convention of consistency? Does this convention help users in making a more valid comparison between businesses?

3.4 'An asset is similar to an expense.' In what ways is this true or untrue?

EXERCISES

Solutions to exercises with coloured numbers can be found at the back of the book, starting on page 545.

Basic-level exercises

3.1 You have heard the following statements made. Comment critically on them.

(a) 'Equity only increases or decreases as a result of the owners putting more cash into the business or taking some out.'
(b) 'An accrued expense is one that relates to next year.'
(c) 'Unless we depreciate this asset we shall be unable to provide for its replacement.'
(d) 'There is no point in depreciating the factory building. It is appreciating in value each year.'

3.2 Singh Enterprises, which started business on 1 January 2016, has a reporting period to 31 December and uses the straight-line method of depreciation. On 1 January 2016, the business bought a machine for £10,000. The machine had an expected useful life of four years and an estimated residual value of £2,000. On 1 January 2017, the business bought another machine for £15,000. This machine had an expected useful life of five years and an estimated residual value of £2,500. On 31 December 2018, the business sold the first machine bought for £3,000.

Required:
Show the relevant income statement extracts and statement of financial position extracts for the years 2016, 2017 and 2018.

3.3 The owner of a business is confused and comes to you for help. The financial statements for the business, prepared by an accountant, for the last reporting period revealed a profit of £50,000. However, during the reporting period the bank balance declined by £30,000. What reasons might explain this apparent discrepancy?

Intermediate-level exercises

3.4 Fill in the values (a) to (f) in the following table on the assumption that there were no opening balances involved.

| | Relating to period | | At end of period | |
	Paid/Received	Expense/revenue for period	Prepaid	Accruals/deferred revenues
	£	£	£	£
Rent payable	10,000	**(a)**	1,000	
Rates and insurance	5,000	**(b)**		1,000
General expenses	**(c)**	6,000	1,000	
Interest payable on borrowings	3,000	2,500	**(d)**	
Salaries	**(e)**	9,000		3,000
Rent receivable	**(f)**	1,500		1,500

3.5 Spratley Ltd is a builders' merchant. On 1 September the business had, as part of its inventories, 20 tonnes of sand at a cost of £18 per tonne and, therefore, at a total cost of £360. During the first week in September, the business bought the following amounts of sand:

	Tonnes	Cost per tonne £
2 September	48	20
4 September	15	24
6 September	10	25

On 7 September, the business sold 60 tonnes of sand to a local builder.

Required:
Calculate the cost of goods sold and of the remaining inventories using the following costing methods:

(a) first in, first out;
(b) last in, first out;
(c) weighted average cost.

Advanced-level exercises

3.6 The following is the statement of financial position of TT and Co. (see Self-Assessment Question 3.1 on page 108) at the end of its first year of trading:

Statement of financial position as at 31 December 2017

	£
ASSETS	
Non-current assets	
Property, plant and equipment	
Delivery van at cost	12,000
Depreciation	(2,500)
	9,500
Current assets	
Inventories	65,000
Trade receivables	19,600
Prepaid expenses*	5,300
Cash	750
	90,650
Total assets	100,150
EQUITY AND LIABILITIES	
Equity	
Original	50,000
Retained earnings	26,900
	76,900
Current liabilities	
Trade payables	22,000
Accrued expenses†	1,250
	23,250
Total equity and liabilities	100,150

* The prepaid expenses consisted of rates (£300) and rent (£5,000).
† The accrued expenses consisted of wages (£630) and electricity (£620).

During 2018, the following transactions took place:

1 The owners withdrew £20,000 of equity as cash.
2 Premises continued to be rented at an annual rental of £20,000. During the year, rent of £15,000 was paid to the owner of the premises.
3 Rates on the premises were paid during the year as follows: for the period 1 April 2018 to 31 March 2019, £1,300.
4 A second delivery van was bought on 1 January 2018 for £13,000. This is expected to be used in the business for four years and then to be sold for £3,000.
5 Wages totalling £36,700 were paid during the year. At the end of the year, the business owed £860 of wages for the last week of the year.
6 Electricity bills for the first three quarters of the year and £620 for the last quarter of the previous year were paid totalling £1,820. After 31 December 2018, but before the financial statements had been finalised for the year, the bill for the last quarter arrived showing a charge of £690.
7 Inventories totalling £67,000 were bought on credit.
8 Inventories totalling £8,000 were bought for cash.
9 Sales revenue on credit totalled £179,000 (cost £89,000).
10 Cash sales revenue totalled £54,000 (cost £25,000).
11 Receipts from trade receivables totalled £178,000.
12 Payments to trade payables totalled £71,000.
13 Van running expenses paid totalled £16,200.

The business uses the straight-line method for depreciating non-current assets.

Required:
Prepare a statement of financial position as at 31 December 2018 and an income statement for the year to that date.

3.7 The following is the statement of financial position of WW Associates as at 31 December 2017:

Statement of financial position as at 31 December 2017

	£
ASSETS	
Non-current assets	
Machinery	25,300
Current assets	
Inventories	12,200
Trade receivables	21,300
Prepaid expenses (rates)	400
Cash	8,300
	42,200
Total assets	67,500
EQUITY AND LIABILITIES	
Equity	
Original	25,000
Retained earnings	23,900
	48,900
Current liabilities	
Trade payables	16,900
Accrued expenses (wages)	1,700
	18,600
Total equity and liabilities	67,500

During 2018, the following transactions took place:

1 The owners withdrew £23,000 of equity in cash.
2 Premises were rented at an annual rental of £20,000. During the year, rent of £25,000 was paid to the owner of the premises.
3 Rates on the premises were paid during the year for the period 1 April 2018 to 31 March 2019 and amounted to £2,000.
4 Some machinery (a non-current asset), which was bought on 1 January 2017 for £13,000, has proved to be unsatisfactory. It was part-exchanged for some new machinery on 1 January 2018 and WW Associates paid a cash amount of £6,000. The new machinery would have cost £15,000 had the business bought it without the trade-in.
5 Wages totalling £23,800 were paid during the year. At the end of the year, the business owed £860 of wages.
6 Electricity bills for the four quarters of the year were paid totalling £2,700.
7 Inventories totalling £143,000 were bought on credit.
8 Inventories totalling £12,000 were bought for cash.
9 Sales revenue on credit totalled £211,000 (cost £127,000).
10 Cash sales revenue totalled £42,000 (cost £25,000).
11 Receipts from trade receivables totalled £198,000.
12 Payments to trade payables totalled £156,000.
13 Van running expenses paid totalled £17,500.

The business uses the reducing-balance method of depreciation for non-current assets at the rate of 30 per cent each year.

Required:
Prepare an income statement for the year ended 31 December 2018 and a statement of financial position as at that date.

3.8 The following is the income statement for Nikov and Co. for the year ended 31 December 2018, along with information relating to the preceding year.

Income statement for the year ended 31 December

	2018	2017
	£000	£000
Sales revenue	420.2	382.5
Cost of sales	(126.1)	(114.8)
Gross profit	294.1	267.7
Salaries and wages	(92.6)	(86.4)
Selling and distribution costs	(98.9)	(75.4)
Rent and rates	(22.0)	(22.0)
Bad debts written off	(19.7)	(4.0)
Telephone and postage	(4.8)	(4.4)
Insurance	(2.9)	(2.8)
Motor vehicle expenses	(10.3)	(8.6)
Depreciation – delivery van	(3.1)	(3.3)
– fixtures and fittings	(4.3)	(4.5)
Operating profit	35.5	56.3
Loan interest	(4.6)	(5.4)
Profit for the year	30.9	50.9

Required:
Analyse the performance of the business for the year to 31 December 2018 in so far as the information allows.

Chapter 4

ACCOUNTING FOR LIMITED COMPANIES (1)

INTRODUCTION

Most businesses in the UK, from the very largest to some of the very smallest, operate in the form of limited companies. Nearly four million limited companies now exist, accounting for the majority of business activity and employment. The economic significance of the limited liability company is not confined to the UK; it can be seen in virtually all of the world's developed countries.

In this chapter we shall examine the main features of a limited company and how this form of business differs from sole-proprietorship and partnership businesses. This expands on the discussion of various business forms contained in Chapter 1. We shall see that the nature of limited companies makes it necessary to distinguish between different aspects of equity finance, based on how each arose. These different aspects will be considered, along with the restrictions that owners face when seeking to withdraw part of their equity.

The financial statements of limited companies reflect several key features of this type of business. We shall discuss how the financial statements discussed in the previous two chapters are adapted to accommodate these. We shall see that the adaptations relate to matters of detail rather than of underlying principle.

Learning outcomes

When you have completed this chapter, you should be able to:

■ discuss the nature and financing of a limited company;

■ describe the different aspects of equity for a limited company;

■ explain the restrictions placed on owners seeking to withdraw part of their equity; and

■ describe how the income statement and statement of financial position of a limited company differ in detail from those of sole proprietorships and partnerships.

THE MAIN FEATURES OF LIMITED COMPANIES

Legal nature

Let us begin our examination of limited companies by discussing their legal nature. A *limited company* has been described as an artificial person that has been created by law. This means that a company has many of the rights and obligations that 'real' people have. It can, for example, enter into contracts in its own name. It can also sue other people (real or corporate) and it can be sued by them. This contrasts sharply with unincorporated businesses, such as sole proprietorships and partnerships, where it is the owner(s) rather than the business that must enter into contracts, sue and so on. This is because those businesses have no separate legal identity.

With the rare exceptions of those that are created by Act of Parliament or by Royal Charter, all UK companies are created (or *incorporated*) by registration. To create a company the person or persons wishing to create it (usually known as *promoters*) fill in a few simple forms and pay a modest registration fee. After having ensured that the necessary formalities have been met, the Registrar of Companies, a UK government official, enters the name of the new company on the Registry of Companies. Thus, in the UK, companies can be formed very easily and cheaply (for about £100).

All of the shares of a limited company may be owned by just one person, but most have more than one owner and some have many owners. The owners are usually known as *members* or *shareholders*. The ownership of a company is normally divided into a number of shares, each of equal size. Each owner, or shareholder, owns one or more shares in the company. Large companies typically have a very large number of shareholders. For example, at 31 March 2017, BT Group plc, the telecommunications business, had 791,000 different shareholders. These shareholders owned nearly 10 billion shares between them.

Since a limited company has its own legal identity, it is regarded as being quite separate from those that own and manage it. It is worth emphasising that this legal separateness of owners and the company has no connection with the business entity convention discussed in Chapter 2. This accounting convention applies equally to all business types, including sole proprietorships and partnerships where there is no legal distinction between the owner(s) and the business.

The legal separateness of the limited company and its shareholders leads to two important features of the limited company: perpetual life and limited liability. These are now explained.

Perpetual life

A company is normally granted a perpetual existence and so will continue even where an owner of some, or even all, of the shares in the company dies. The shares of the deceased person will simply pass to the beneficiary of his or her estate. The granting of perpetual existence means that the life of a company is quite separate from the lives of those individuals who own or manage it. It is not, therefore, affected by changes in ownership that arise when individuals buy and sell shares in the company.

Although a company may be granted a perpetual existence when it is first formed, it is possible for either the shareholders or the courts to bring this existence to an end. When this is done, the assets of the company are usually sold to generate cash to meet the outstanding liabilities. Any amounts remaining after all liabilities have been met will then be distributed between the shareholders. Shareholders may agree to end the life of a company where it has achieved the purpose for which it was formed or where they feel that the company has no real future. The courts may bring the life of a company to an end where creditors (those owed money by the company) have applied to the courts for this to be done because they have not been paid.

Where shareholders agree to end the life of a company, it is referred to as a 'voluntary liquidation'. **Real World 4.1** describes the demise of one company by this method.

Limited liability

Since the company is a legal person in its own right, it must take responsibility for its own debts and losses. This means that, once the shareholders have paid what they have agreed to pay for the shares, their obligation to the company, and to the company's creditors, is satisfied. Thus shareholders can limit their losses to the amount that they have paid, or agreed to pay, for their shares. This is of great practical importance to potential shareholders since they know that what they can lose, as part owners of the business, is limited.

Contrast this with the position of sole proprietors or partners. They cannot 'ring-fence' assets that they do not want to put into the business. If a sole-proprietorship or partnership business finds itself in a position where liabilities exceed the business assets, the law gives unsatisfied creditors the right to demand payment out of what the sole proprietor or partner may have regarded as 'non-business' assets. Thus the sole proprietor or partner could lose everything – house, car, the lot. This is because the law sees Jill, the sole proprietor, as being the same as Jill the private individual.

Real World 4.2 gives an example of a well-known case where the shareholders of a particular company were able to avoid any liability to those that had lost money as a result of dealing with the company.

Activity 4.1

The fact that shareholders can limit their losses to that which they have paid, or have agreed to pay, for their shares is of great practical importance to potential shareholders.

Can you think of any practical benefit to a private-sector economy, in general, of this ability of shareholders to limit losses?

Business is a risky venture – in some cases very risky. People will usually be happier to invest money when they know the limit of their liability. If investors are given limited liability, new businesses are more likely to be formed and existing ones are likely to find it easier to raise more finance. This is good for the private-sector economy and may ultimately lead to the generation of greater wealth for society as a whole.

Although limited liability has this advantage to the providers of equity finance (the shareholders), it is not necessarily to the advantage of all of the others who have a stake in the business, as we saw in the case of the Nationwide Football League clubs in Real World 4.2. Limited liability is attractive to shareholders because they can, in effect, walk away from the unpaid debts of the company if their committed contribution is not enough to cover those debts. As a consequence, individuals, or businesses, may be wary of entering into a contract with a limited company. This can be a real problem for smaller, less established companies. Suppliers may insist on cash payment before delivery of goods or the rendering of a service.

Alternatively, they may require a personal guarantee from a major shareholder that the debt will be paid before allowing trade credit. In this way, the supplier circumvents the company's limited liability status by demanding the personal liability of an individual. Larger, more established companies, on the other hand, find it easier to gain the confidence of suppliers.

LEGAL SAFEGUARDS

Various safeguards exist to protect individuals and businesses contemplating dealing with a limited company. They include the requirement to indicate limited liability status in the name of the company. This should alert prospective suppliers and lenders to the potential risks involved.

A further safeguard is the restrictions placed on the ability of shareholders to withdraw their equity from the company.

Activity 4.2

Can you think how these restrictions on the withdrawal of equity can act as a safeguard?

They are designed to prevent shareholders from protecting their own investment and, as a result, leaving lenders and suppliers in an exposed position.

We shall consider this point in more detail later in the chapter.

In addition, and importantly, limited companies are required to produce annual financial statements (income statements, statements of financial position and statements of cash flows) and make these publicly available. This means that anyone interested can gain an impression of the financial performance and position of the company. The form and content of the first two of these statements are considered in some detail later in the chapter and in Chapter 5. The statement of cash flows is considered in Chapter 6.

PUBLIC AND PRIVATE COMPANIES

When a company is registered with the Registrar of Companies, it must be registered either as a public or as a private company. The main practical difference between these is that a public limited company can offer its shares for sale to the general public, but a private limited company cannot. A public limited company must signal its status to all interested parties by having the words 'public limited company', or its abbreviation 'plc', in its name. For a private limited company, the word 'limited' or 'Ltd' must appear as part of its name.

Private limited companies tend to be smaller businesses where the ownership is divided among relatively few shareholders who are usually fairly close to one another – for example, a family company. There are vastly more private limited companies in the UK than public limited companies. Of the nearly four million UK limited companies now in existence, only around 6,900 (representing 0.19 per cent (that is, one in about 540) of the total) are public limited companies.

Real World 4.3 shows the trend in the numbers of public and private limited companies in recent years.

Company trends

Recent years have seen a steady decline in the number of public limited companies, yet at the same time the number of private ones has shown a steady increase. Figure 4.1 shows these trends.

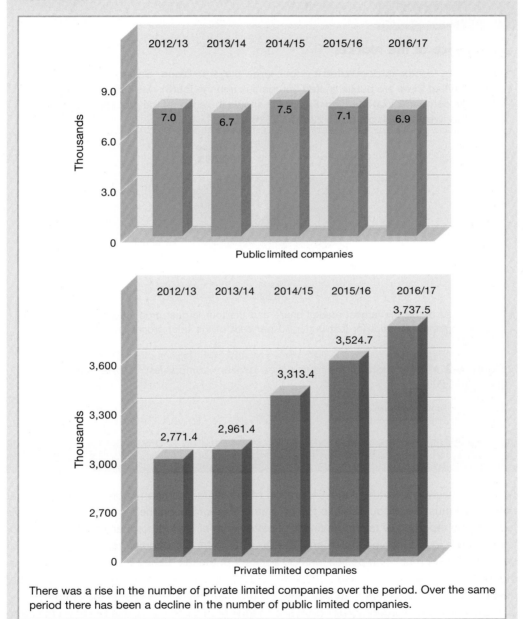

There was a rise in the number of private limited companies over the period. Over the same period there has been a decline in the number of public limited companies.

Figure 4.1 Numbers of public and private limited companies in the UK, 2012/13 to 2016/17

Source: Based on information in Companies Registration Activities 2012/13 to 2016/17, Table 1, www.companieshouse.gov.uk.

Since individual public companies tend to be larger, they are often economically more important. In some industry sectors, such as banking, insurance, oil refining and grocery retailing, they are completely dominant. Although some private limited companies are large, many are little more than the vehicle through which one-person businesses operate.

Real World 4.4 shows the extent of the market dominance of public limited companies in one particular business sector.

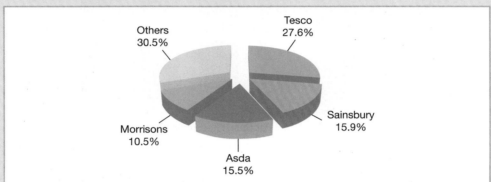

Real World 4.4

A big slice of the market

The grocery sector is dominated by four large players: Tesco, Sainsbury, Morrison and Asda. The first three are public limited companies and the fourth, Asda, is owned by a large US public company, Wal-Mart Inc. Figure 4.2 shows the share of the grocery market of each during the twelve-week period to 22 April 2018.

Others
30.5%

Tesco
27.6%

Sainsbury
15.9%

Asda
15.5%

Morrisons
10.5%

Tesco had by far the largest market share and the four largest grocery companies, when taken together, account for just under 70 per cent of the total grocery market during the period.

Figure 4.2 Market share of the four largest grocery companies, 12 weeks to 22 April 2018

Source: www.kantarworldpanel.com

TAXATION

Another consequence of the legal separation of the limited company from its owners is that companies must be accountable to the tax authorities for tax on their profits and gains. This leads to the reporting of tax in the financial statements of limited companies. The charge for tax is shown in the income statement. The tax charge for a particular year is based on that year's profit. For many companies, only 50 per cent of the tax liability is due for payment during the year concerned, so the other 50 per cent will appear on the end-of-year statement of financial position as a current liability. This will be illustrated a little later in the chapter.

Companies are charged corporation tax on their profits and gains. It is levied on the company's taxable profit, which may differ from the profit shown on the income statement. This is because tax law does not follow normal accounting rules in every respect. Generally, however, taxable profit and accounting profit are pretty close to one another. The percentage rate of corporation tax tends to vary over time. For the corporation tax year commencing 1 April 2018, the rate is set at 19 per cent and it will remain at this rate for the following tax year. For the tax year commencing 1 April 2020 the rate will be reduced to 18 per cent.

The tax position of companies contrasts with that of sole proprietorships and partnerships, where tax is levied not on the business but on the owner(s). This means that tax will not be reported in the financial statements of unincorporated businesses, as it is a matter between the owner(s) and the tax authorities. There can be tax advantages to trading as a limited company, rather than as a sole proprietor or partner. Although these advantages have been somewhat diminished by recent legislation, they may partly explain the rise in popularity of private limited companies over recent years.

THE ROLE OF THE STOCK EXCHANGE

A **Stock Exchange** typically acts as both an important *primary* and *secondary* capital market for companies. As a primary market, its function is to enable companies to raise new finance. As a secondary market its function is to enable investors to sell their securities (including shares and loan notes) with ease. We have already seen that shares in a company may be transferred from one owner to another. The wish of some investors to sell their shares, coupled with the wish of others to buy those shares, has led to the creation of a formal market in which shares are bought and sold.

As with most stock exchanges, only the shares of certain companies (*listed* companies) may be traded on the **London Stock Exchange**. As at 31 December 2017, just over 1,900 UK companies were listed, either on the 'Main Market' or the Alternative Investment Market (AIM – mainly, newer and smaller businesses). This represents only 1 in about 2,000 of all UK companies (public and private) and roughly 1 in 3.6 public limited companies. However, many of these listed companies are massive. Nearly all of the UK businesses that are 'household names' (for example, Tesco, Next, BT, Vodafone, BP, easyJet (all on Main Market) and Fever-tree, Asos, Boohoo (AIM)) are listed companies.

Activity 4.3

As mentioned earlier, the change in ownership of shares does not directly affect a particular company. Why, in that case, do many public companies seek to have their shares traded on a recognised Stock Exchange?

Investors are generally reluctant to pledge their money unless they can see some way of turning their investment back into cash (an 'exit route'). The shares of a particular company may be valuable because it has bright prospects. Unless this value can be turned into cash, however, the benefit to investors is dubious. After all, we cannot spend shares; we normally need cash. Thus, investors are more likely to buy new shares from a company where they can liquidate their investment (turn it into cash) as and when they wish. Stock Exchanges provide the means of liquidation and, by so doing, make it easier for a company to raise new share capital.

Disadvantages of a listing

A Stock Exchange listing can have certain disadvantages for a business. These include the following:

■ Strict rules are imposed on listed businesses, including requirements for levels of financial disclosure additional to those already imposed by International Financial Reporting

Standards (for example, the listing rules require that half-yearly financial reports are published).

■ Financial analysts, financial journalists and others tend to monitor closely the activities of listed businesses, especially larger ones. Such scrutiny may not be welcome, particularly if the business is dealing with sensitive issues or is experiencing operational problems.

■ It is often claimed that listed businesses are under pressure to perform well over the short term. This pressure may detract from undertaking projects that will yield benefits only in the longer term. If the market becomes disenchanted with the business, and the price of its shares falls, this may make it vulnerable to a takeover bid from another business.

■ The costs of obtaining and retaining a listing are high and this may be a real deterrent for some businesses.

Going private

Such are the disadvantages of a stock market listing that many businesses have 'delisted'. This has obviously denied them the advantages of a listing, but it has avoided the disadvantages.

CAPITAL MARKET EFFICIENCY

When share prices at all times rationally reflect all available, relevant information, the market in which they are traded is said to be an **efficient capital market**. This implies that any new information relating to a particular company and its share price will be taken into account quickly and rationally, in terms of size and direction of share price movement.

Activity 4.4

Can you suggest why a capital market like the Stock Exchange should be price efficient?

Many analysts study the performance of listed companies. Between them, they should make a valid assessment of the market value of those companies' shares.

Prices are set in capital markets by the forces of supply and demand. If the consensus view of those active in the market is that the shares of a particular business are underpriced, demand will force the price up.

In a secondary capital market such as the London Stock Exchange, share prices are observed by a large number of people, many of them skilled and experienced. Nearly all of them are incentivised by that great motivator – financial gain. They glean information relating to the business from a variety of sources, including the business itself. This information may include published financial statements, press releases and company 'leaks' as well as industry and economy reports.

Where observers spot what they consider to be an irrational price, they try to take advantage of it, or advise others to do so. For example, an investment analyst employed by a financial institution might assess the worth of a share in Tesco plc at £2.50 while the current share price is only £2.10. The analyst may then contact the investment manager to recommend buying Tesco shares because they are underpriced and there are gains to be made. The increase in demand from large-scale buying tends to increase the share price.

Price efficiency does not imply perfect powers of prediction on the part of investors. All it means is that the current price of a share is the best estimate of its future returns on the basis of the available evidence.

Evidence on capital market efficiency

An enormous amount of research has been undertaken on the pricing efficiency of most of the world's capital markets. Although there are some minor anomalies, the evidence on most capital markets (including the London Stock Exchange) is that:

1 the price of a share in any particular business fully, rationally and very rapidly takes account of all relevant *publicly* available information that bears on that business and its shares; and
2 any information that is only *privately* available is not necessarily taken into account in the share price.

This means that it is not possible for investors to make systematic gains from trading on the basis of any information that is publicly available. On the other hand, relevant information that is known only, say, to a director of a particular business, but will become publicly known later, may enable that person to gain from trading in the shares. In most jurisdictions, including the UK, such an action by a person in a privileged position would be illegal.

When we say that it is not possible for investors to make systematic gains from trading on the basis of any information that is publicly available, this is because in an efficient market, any relevant new information about the business will immediately be reflected in the price at which the business's shares are trading. For example, an investor notices that a particular business has just announced unexpectedly winning a contract that will significantly improve its profitability and value. However quickly our investor acts to buy shares in the business, in an attempt to benefit from the expected share price rise, it will be too late; the price will already have risen.

The fact that the market is efficient certainly does not mean that people who invest in shares do not make profits. Through a combination of capital appreciation (rises in share prices) and dividends received from the businesses, investors in UK businesses have earned, on average over the past 120 years, an annual return of the rate of inflation plus a little over 5 per cent. This is significantly higher than returns on lending, say to a building society or holding government bonds, or investing in property (real estate). During some periods, investing in shares would have yielded much higher returns. In other periods, very low (including negative) returns have been incurred.

Activity 4.6

If we look at a graph of the price of a share in a particular business plotted against time, we tend to find that it jumps up and down. This is similar to the effect that we get if we plot a graph of a series of random numbers.

Does this mean that share price movements are arbitrary?

No, it does not mean this. The share price movements mentioned above occur because new information does not arise in a gradual or systematic way but in a random, unexpected way. The share price movements will, however, be a rational and timely response to the new information coming to light.

MANAGING A COMPANY

A limited company may have a legal personality, but it is not a human being capable of making decisions and plans about the business and exercising control over it. People must undertake these management tasks. The most senior level of management of a company is the board of directors.

Directors are elected by shareholders to manage the company on a day-to-day basis on their behalf. By law there must be at least one director for a private limited company and two for a public limited company. In a small company, the board may be the only level of management and consist of all of the shareholders. In larger companies, the board may consist of ten or so directors out of many thousands of shareholders. (The directors are normally shareholders although they do not have to be.) Below the board of directors of the typical large company could be several layers of management comprising many thousands of people.

In recent years, the issue of corporate governance has generated much debate. The term is used to describe the ways in which companies are directed and controlled. The issue of corporate governance is important because, with larger companies, those who own the company (that is, the shareholders) are usually divorced from the day-to-day control of the business. The shareholders employ the directors to manage the company for them. Given this position, it may seem reasonable to assume that the best interests of shareholders will guide the directors' decisions. However, in practice this does not always seem to be the case. The directors may be more concerned with pursuing their own interests, such as increasing their pay and 'perks' (such as expensive motor cars, overseas visits and so on) and improving their job security and status. As a result, a conflict can occur between the interests of shareholders and the interests of directors.

The problems and issues associated with corporate governance will be explored in detail in Chapter 12.

FINANCING LIMITED COMPANIES

Equity (the owners' claim)

The equity of a sole proprietorship is normally encompassed in one figure on the statement of financial position. In the case of companies, things are a little more complicated, although the same broad principles apply. With companies, equity is divided between shares (for example, the original investment), on the one hand, and **reserves** (that is, profits and gains subsequently made), on the other. There is also the possibility that there will be more than one type of shares and of reserves. Thus, within the basic divisions of share capital and reserves, there will usually be further subdivisions. This might seem quite complicated, but we shall shortly consider the reasons for these subdivisions and all should become clearer.

The basic division

When a company is first formed, those who take steps to form it (the promoters) will decide how much needs to be raised from potential shareholders to set the company up with the necessary assets to operate. Example 4.1 illustrates this.

Example 4.1

Some friends decide to form a company to operate an office cleaning business. They estimate that the company will need £50,000 to obtain the necessary assets. Between them, they raise the cash, which they use to buy shares in the company, on 31 March 2017, with a **nominal value** (or **par value**) of £1 each.

At this point the statement of financial position of the company would be:

Statement of financial position as at 31 March 2017

	£
Net assets (all in cash)	50,000
Equity	
Share capital	
50,000 shares of £1 each	50,000

The company now buys the necessary non-current assets (vacuum cleaners and so on) and inventories (cleaning materials) and starts to trade. During the first year, the company makes a profit of £10,000 This, by definition, means that the equity expands by £10,000. During the year, the shareholders (owners) make no drawings of their equity, so at the end of the year the summarised statement of financial position looks like this:

Statement of financial position as at 31 March 2018

	£
Net assets (various assets less liabilities*)	60,000
Equity	
Share capital	
50,000 shares of £1 each	50,000
Reserves (revenue reserve)	10,000
Total equity	60,000

* We saw in Chapter 2 that Assets = Equity + Liabilities. We also saw that this can be rearranged to Assets − Liabilities = Equity.

The profit is shown as a reserve, known as a **revenue reserve**, because it arises from generating revenue (making sales). Note that we do not simply merge the profit with the share capital: we must keep the two amounts separate in order to satisfy company law. There is a legal restriction on the maximum drawings of the shareholders equity (for example, as a **dividend**) that can be made. This maximum is defined by the amount of revenue reserves and so it is helpful to show these separately. We shall look at why there is this restriction, and how it works, a little later in the chapter.

SHARE CAPITAL

Ordinary shares

Ordinary shares represent the basic units of ownership of a business. They are issued by all companies and are often known as *equities*. Ordinary shareholders are the primary risk takers as they share in the profits of the company only after other claims have been satisfied. There are no upper limits on the amount by which they may benefit. The potential rewards available to ordinary shareholders reflect the risks that they are prepared to take. Since ordinary shareholders take most of the risks, power normally rests in their hands. Usually, only the ordinary shareholders are able to vote on issues that affect the company, such as the appointment of directors.

The nominal value of such shares is at the discretion of those who start up the company. For example, if the initial share capital is to be £50,000 this could be two shares of £25,000 each, 5 million shares of one penny each or any other combination that gives a total of £50,000. All shares must have equal value.

Activity 4.7

The initial financial requirement for a new company is £50,000. There are to be two equal shareholders. Would you advise them to issue two shares of £25,000 each? Why?

Such large-denomination shares tend to be unwieldy and difficult to sell. If one of the shareholders wished to liquidate her shareholding, she would have to find a single buyer. Where, however, the shareholding consisted of shares of smaller denomination, the price per share would be lower and the whole shareholding could probably be sold more easily to various potential buyers. It would also be possible for the original shareholder to sell just part of the shareholding and retain a part.

In practice, £1 is the normal maximum nominal value for shares. Shares of 25 pence each and 50 pence each are among the more common. BT plc, the telecommunications business, has ordinary shares with a nominal value of 5 pence each (although their market value at 19 January 2018 was £2.67 per share).

Preference shares

In addition to ordinary shares, some companies issue preference shares. These shares guarantee that *if a dividend is paid*, the preference shareholders will be entitled to the first part of it up to a maximum value. This maximum is normally defined as a fixed percentage of the nominal value of the preference shares. If, for example, a company issues one million preference shares of £1 each with a dividend rate of 6 per cent, this means that the preference shareholders are entitled to receive the first £60,000 (that is, 6 per cent of £1 million) of any dividend that is paid by the company for a particular year. Any dividend payment in excess of £60,000 goes to the ordinary shareholders.

Real World 4.5 below describes the types of preference shares issued by one large company.

Real World 4.5

Having a preference

BP plc, the energy company, has two types of £1 preference share in issue, one with a dividend rate of 8 per cent and another with a dividend rate of 9 per cent. Both types of preference share are cumulative, which means that any unpaid dividends are carried forward for payment when a dividend is next declared. The unpaid dividends will be paid before ordinary shareholders receive a dividend. Not all preference shares are cumulative. Where non-cumulative preference shares are issued, any dividends not paid for a particular period are foregone.

Source: BP plc, Share information, www.bp.com [accessed 19 January 2018].

It is open to the company to issue shares of various classes – perhaps with some having unusual conditions – but in practice it is rare to find other than straightforward ordinary and preference shares. Even preference shares are not very common. Although a company may have different classes of shares with each class giving holders different rights, within each class all shares must have equal rights. The rights of the various classes of shareholders, as well as other matters relating to a particular company, are contained in that company's set of rules, known as the *memorandum and articles of association*. A copy of these rules must be lodged with the Registrar of Companies, who makes it available for inspection by the general public.

Altering the nominal value of shares

As we have already seen, the promoters of a new company may make their own choice of the nominal (par) value of the shares. This value need not be permanent. At a later date the shareholders can decide to change it.

Suppose that a company has 1 million ordinary shares of £1 each and a decision is made to change the nominal value of the shares from £1 to £0.50 - in other words to halve the value. To maintain the total nominal value of the share capital intact, the company would then issue each shareholder exactly twice as many shares, each with half the original nominal value. Thus, each shareholder would retain a holding of the same total nominal value as before. This process is known, not surprisingly, as **splitting** the shares. The opposite, reducing the number of shares and increasing their nominal value per share to compensate, is known as **consolidating**. Since each shareholder would be left, after a split or consolidation, with exactly the same proportion of ownership of the company's assets as before, the process should have no effect on the total value of the shares held.

Both splitting and consolidating may be used to help make the shares more marketable. Splitting may help avoid share prices becoming too high and consolidating may help avoid share prices becoming too low. It seems that investors do not like either extreme. In addition, some Stock Exchanges do not allow shares to be traded at too low a price.

Real World 4.6 provides an example of a share split by one business.

RESERVES

The shareholders' equity consists of share capital and reserves. As mentioned earlier, reserves are profits and gains that a company has made and which still form part of the shareholders' equity. One reason that past profits and gains may no longer continue to be part of equity is that they have been paid out to shareholders (as dividends and so on). Another reason is that reserves will be reduced by the amount of any losses that the company might suffer. In the same way that profits increase equity, losses reduce it.

Activity 4.8

Are reserves amounts of cash? Can you think of a reason why this is an odd question?

To deal with the second point first, it is an odd question because reserves are a claim, or part of one, on the assets of the company, whereas cash is an asset. So reserves cannot be cash.

Reserves are classified as either revenue reserves or **capital reserves**. In Example 4.1 we came across a revenue reserve. This reserve represents the company's retained trading profits as well as gains on the disposal of non-current assets. *Retained earnings*, as they are most often called, represent overwhelmingly the largest source of new finance for UK companies. Capital reserves arise for two main reasons:

- issuing shares at above their nominal value (for example, issuing £1 shares at £1.50);
- revaluing (upwards) non-current assets.

Where a company issues shares at above their nominal value, UK law requires that the excess of the issue price over the nominal value be shown separately.

Can you think why shares might be issued at above their nominal value? (*Hint*: This would not usually happen when a company is first formed and the initial shares are being issued.)

Once a company has traded and has been successful, the shares would normally be worth more than the nominal value at which they were issued. If additional shares are to be issued to new shareholders to raise finance for further expansion, unless they are issued at a value higher than the nominal value, the new shareholders will be gaining at the expense of the original ones.

Example 4.2 shows how this works.

Example 4.2

Based on future prospects, the net assets of a company are worth £1.5 million. There are currently 1 million ordinary shares in the company, each with a nominal value of £1. The company wishes to raise an additional £0.6 million of cash for expansion and has decided to raise it by issuing new shares. If the shares are issued for £1 each (that is 600,000 shares), the total number of shares will be:

$$1.0m + 0.6m = 1.6m$$

and their total value will be the value of the existing net assets plus the new injection of cash:

$$£1.5m + £0.6m = £2.1m$$

This means that the value of each share after the new issue will be:

$$£2.1m/1.6m = £1.3125$$

The current value of each share is:

$$£1.5m/1.0m = £1.50$$

so the original shareholders will lose:

$$£1.50 - £1.3125 = £0.1875 \text{ a share}$$

and the new shareholders will gain:

$$£1.3125 - £1.0 = £0.3125 \text{ a share}$$

The new shareholders will, no doubt, be delighted with this outcome; the original ones will not.

Things could be made fair between the two sets of shareholders described in Example 4.2 by issuing the new shares at £1.50 each. In this case, it would be necessary to issue 400,000 shares to raise the necessary £0.6 million. £1 a share of the £1.50 is the nominal value and will be included with share capital in the statement of financial position (£400,000 in total).

The remaining £0.50 is a share premium, which will be shown as a capital reserve known as the **share premium account** (£200,000 in total).

It is not clear why UK company law insists on the distinction between nominal share values and the premium. In some other countries (for example, the United States) with similar laws governing the corporate sector, there is not this distinction. Instead, the total value at which shares are issued is shown as one comprehensive figure on the company's statement of financial position.

Real World 4.7 shows the equity of one very well-known business.

Real World 4.7

Flying funds

Ryanair Holdings plc, the no-frills airline, had the following share capital and reserves as at 31 March 2017:

	€ million
Share capital (Ordinary shares)	7.3
Share premium	719.4
Retained earnings	3,456.8
Other reserves and capital	239.5
Total equity	**4,423.0**

Note how the nominal share capital figure is only a small fraction of the share premium account figure. This implies that Ryanair has issued shares at much higher prices than their nominal value. This reflects its trading success since the company was first formed. As at 31 March 2017, retained earnings (profits) made up nearly four fifths of the total for share capital and reserves.

Source: Information taken from Ryanair Holdings plc, Annual Report 2017, p. 137.

BONUS SHARES

It is always open to a company to take reserves of any kind (irrespective of whether they are capital or revenue) and turn them into share capital. This will involve transferring the desired amount from the reserve concerned to share capital and then distributing the appropriate number of new shares to the existing shareholders. New shares arising from such a conversion are known as **bonus shares**. Example 4.3 illustrates how bonus issues work.

A bonus issue simply takes one part of the equity (a reserve) and puts it into another part (share capital). The transaction has no effect on the company's assets or liabilities, so there is no effect on shareholders' wealth. Issues of bonus shares have become less common in recent years, perhaps because of the lack of business profitability during the recent past.

Note that a bonus issue is not the same as a share split. A split does not affect the reserves.

Example 4.3

The summary statement of financial position of a company at a particular point in time is as follows:

Statement of financial position

	£
Net assets (various assets less liabilities)	<u>128,000</u>
Equity	
Share capital	
50,000 shares of £1 each	50,000
Reserves	<u>78,000</u>
Total equity	<u>128,000</u>

The directors decide that the company will issue existing shareholders with one new share for every share currently owned by each shareholder. The statement of financial position immediately following this will appear as follows:

Statement of financial position

	£
Net assets (various assets less liabilities)	<u>128,000</u>
Equity	
Share capital	
100,000 shares of £1 each	100,000
Reserves	<u>28,000</u>
Total equity	<u>128,000</u>

We can see that the reserves have decreased by £50,000 and share capital has increased by the same amount. To complete the transaction, 50,000 new ordinary shares of £1 each, which have been created from reserves, will be issued to the existing shareholders.

Activity 4.10

A shareholder of the company in Example 4.3 owned 100 shares before the bonus issue. How will things change for this shareholder as regards the number of shares owned and the value of the shareholding?

The answer should be that the number of shares would double, from 100 to 200. Now the shareholder owns one five-hundredth of the company (that is, 200/100,000). Before the bonus issue, the shareholder also owned one five-hundredth of the company (that is, 100/50,000). The company's assets and liabilities have not changed as a result of the bonus issue and so, logically, one five-hundredth of the value of the company should be identical to what it was before. Thus, each share is worth half as much as it used to be.

Activity 4.11

Can you think of any reasons why a company might want to make a bonus issue if it has no economic consequence? Try to think of at least one reason.

We think that there are three possible reasons:

■ *Share price.* To lower the value of each share in order to make the shares more marketable. This has a similar effect to share splitting.
■ *Shareholder confidence.* To provide the shareholders with a 'feel-good factor'. It is believed that shareholders like bonus issues because they seem to make them better off, although in practice they should not affect their wealth.
■ *Lender confidence.* Where reserves arising from operating profits and/or realised gains on the sale of non-current assets (revenue reserves) are used to make the bonus issue, it has the effect of taking part of the shareholders' equity that could be withdrawn and locking it up. The amount transferred becomes part of the permanent equity base of the company. (We shall see a little later in this chapter that there are severe restrictions on the extent to which shareholders may make drawings from their equity.) An individual or business contemplating lending money to the company may insist that the extent to which shareholders can withdraw their funds is restricted as a condition of making the loan. This point will be explained shortly.

Real World 4.8 provides an example of a bonus share issue, where it seemed that the main motive was to make the share price more manageable. The 'feel-good' factor, however, also seems to play a part.

Real World 4.8

Is it really a bonus?

Medusa Mining is a gold producer that is listed on various international stock markets. In 2010, it announced a one-for-ten bonus issue of shares to all shareholders of the company.

In a statement, the company said that it had achieved several significant milestones in the last calendar year and that the bonus issue was in recognition of the invaluable support the company had received from its shareholders. The bonus issue was also designed to encourage greater liquidity in Medusa shares.

Geoff Davis, managing director of Medusa, said: 'The board is extremely pleased to be in a position to reward shareholders as a result of the company having rapidly expanded its production over the last 12 months and having met all targets on time.'

Source: Adapted from 'Medusa Mining', www.proactiveinvestors.co.uk, 8 March 2010.

SHARE CAPITAL JARGON

Before leaving our detailed discussion of share capital, it might be helpful to clarify some of the jargon relating to shares that is used in company financial statements.

Share capital that has been issued to shareholders is known as the issued share capital (or allotted share capital). Sometimes, but not very often, a company may not require shareholders to pay the whole amount that is due to be paid for the shares at the time of issue. This may happen where the company does not need the money all at once. Some money would normally be paid at the time of issue and the company would 'call' for further instalments until the shares were **fully paid shares**. That part of the total issue price that has been called is known as the **called-up share capital**. That part that has been called and paid is known as the **paid-up share capital**.

BORROWINGS

Most larger companies borrow money to supplement that raised from share issues and ploughed-back profits. Company borrowing is often on a long-term basis, perhaps on a ten-year contract. The contract, which is legally binding, will specify the rate of interest, the interest payments date and the repayment date for the amount borrowed. Lenders may be banks and other professional providers of loan finance, such as pension funds and insurance companies.

Many companies borrow in such a way that individual investors are able to lend only part of the total amount required. This is particularly the case with the larger, Stock Exchange listed, companies and involves them making an issue of **loan notes**. Although such an issue may be large, investors, whether individuals or institutions, can each take up a small slice of the issue. In some cases, these slices of loans can be bought and sold through the Stock Exchange. This means that investors do not have to wait the full term of their loan to obtain repayment. They can sell their slice of the loan to another would-be lender at some point during the loan term. This flexibility can make loan notes an attractive investment to certain investors. Loan notes are often known as **loan stock**, **bonds** or **debentures**.

Some of the features of financing by loan notes, particularly the possibility that the loan notes may be traded on the Stock Exchange, can lead to confusing loan notes with shares. We should be clear, however, that shares and loan notes are not the same thing.

Activity 4.12

What is the essential difference in status within a company between ordinary shareholders and a loan notes holders?

Ordinary shareholders are the owners of the company who share in the profits and losses of the company. We saw earlier that they are the main risk takers and are given voting rights. Holders of loan notes are simply lenders that receive interest on their investment. They have no ownership stake in the company.

Long-term loans are usually secured on assets of the company. This would give the lender the right, if the company fails to make the contractual payments, to seize the assets concerned, sell them and use the cash to rectify this failure. A mortgage granted to a private individual buying a house or an apartment is a very common example of a secured loan.

Long-term financing of companies can be depicted as in Figure 4.3.

It is important to the prosperity and stability of a company that it strikes a suitable balance between finance provided by the shareholders (equity) and from borrowing. This topic will be explored in Chapter 8.

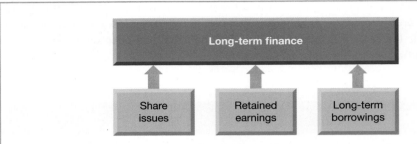

Companies derive their long-term finance from three sources: new share issues, retained earnings and long-term borrowings. For a typical company, the sum of the first two (jointly known as 'equity finance') exceeds the third. Retained earnings usually exceed either of the other two in terms of the amount of finance raised in most years.

Figure 4.3 Sources of long-term finance for a typical limited company

Real World 4.9 shows the long-term borrowings of Rolls-Royce Holdings plc, the engine-building business, at 31 December 2017.

Real World 4.9

Borrowing at Rolls-Royce

The following extract from the annual financial statements of Rolls-Royce plc sets out the sources of the company's long-term borrowings (non-current liabilities) as at 31 December 2017:

	£m
Unsecured	
Bank loans	572
6.75% notes 2019	519
2.375% notes 2020	362
2.125% notes 2021	701
3.625% notes 2025	726
3.375% notes 2026	412
Secured	
Obligations under finance leases	114
	3,406

Source: Rolls-Royce Holdings plc Annual Report and Accounts 2017 p. 148, note 15.

Note the large number of sources of the company's borrowings. This is typical of most large companies and probably reflects a desire to exploit all available means of raising finance, each of which may have advantages and disadvantages. Normally, a lender would accept a lower rate of interest where the loan is secured as there is less risk involved. It should be said that whether a loan to a company like Rolls-Royce is secured or unsecured is usually pretty academic. It is unlikely that such a large and profitable company would fail to meet its obligations.

RAISING SHARE CAPITAL

After an initial share issue, a company may decide to make further issues of new shares in order to finance its operations. These new share issues may be undertaken in various ways. They may involve direct appeals to investors or may employ the services of financial intermediaries. The most common methods of share issues are set out in Figure 4.4.

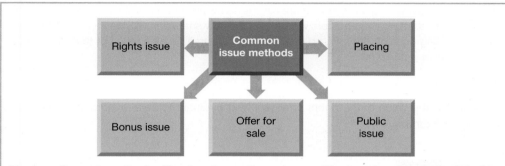

There are five main methods of issuing shares. Bonus issues differ from the other methods in that they do not lead to an injection of cash for the business. During the lifetime of a particular company, it may use all five of these approaches to issue new shares, though only public limited companies are allowed to make appeals to the general public.

Figure 4.4 Common methods of share issue

Let us now examine, in turn, each of the four methods of raising funds through a share issue that have been identified.

Rights issues

Rights issues are made by established companies wishing to raise additional funds by the issue of new shares to their existing shareholders. The new shares are offered to shareholders in proportion to their existing holding. Company law gives existing shareholders the first right of refusal to buy any new shares issued for cash by a company. Only where shareholders agree to waive this right can the shares be offered to outside investors.

The company (in effect, the existing shareholders) normally prefers existing shareholders to buy the shares through a rights issue, irrespective of the legal position. This is for two reasons:

1 Ownership (and, therefore, control) of the business remains in the same hands; there is no 'dilution' of control.
2 The costs of making the issue (advertising, complying with various company law requirements) tend to be lower if the shares are offered to existing shareholders. Fees incurred for rights issue are broadly 2 to 3 per cent of the total funds raised, depending on the size of the issue (see Reference 1 at the end of the chapter). Since much of the cost is fixed, the percentage tends to be higher for smaller rights issues.

To encourage existing shareholders to exercise their 'rights' to buy, the new shares are offered at a discount to the current market price of the existing shares.

The answer is that it does not matter *in these particular circumstances*, because, in a rights issue, the existing shareholders and the new shareholders are the same people. Moreover, the shareholders will hold the new shares in the same proportion as they currently hold the existing shares. Thus, shareholders will gain on the new shares exactly as much as they lose on the existing ones. In the end, no one is better or worse off as a result of the rights issue being made at a discount.

Calculating the value of the rights offer received by shareholders is quite straightforward, as shown in Example 4.4.

Example 4.4

Shaw Holdings plc has 20 million ordinary shares of 50p in issue. These shares are currently valued on the Stock Exchange at £1.60 per share. The directors have decided to make a one-for-four issue (that is, one new share for every four shares held) at £1.30 per share.

The first step in the valuation process is to calculate the price of a share following the rights issue. This is known as the *ex-rights price* and is simply a weighted average of the price of shares before the issue of rights and the price of the rights shares. In this example, we have a one-for-four rights issue. The theoretical ex-rights price is therefore calculated as follows:

	£
Price of four shares before the rights issue (4 × £1.60)	6.40
Price of taking up one rights share	1.30
	7.70
Theoretical ex-rights price = £7.70/5	= £1.54

As the price of each share, in theory, should be £1.54 following the rights issue and the price of a rights share is £1.30, the value per share of the rights offer will be the difference between the two:

$$£1.54 - £1.30 = £0.24 \text{ per share}$$

Market forces will usually ensure that the actual and theoretical price of rights shares will be fairly close.

The level of discount applied to rights shares will vary. In recent years, it has often been 30 to 40 per cent to the theoretical ex rights price (see Reference 2 at the end of the chapter). By offering a significant discount, the risk that the market price will fall below the rights price is reduced. This should increase the prospects of a successful issue. A significant discount may, however, convey the impression that the business is in distress and desperate for funds.

Activity 4.14

An investor with 2,000 shares in Shaw Holdings plc (see Example 4.4) has contacted you for investment advice. She is undecided whether to take up the rights issue, sell the rights or allow the rights offer to lapse.

Calculate the effect on the net wealth of the investor of each of the options being considered.

Before the rights issue the position of the investor was:

	£
Current value of shares (2,000 × £1.60)	3,200

If she takes up the rights issue, she will be in the following position:

	£
Value of holding after the rights issue ((2,000 + 500) × £1.54)	3,850
Cost of buying the rights shares (500 × £1.30)	(650)
	3,200

If the investor sells the rights, she will be in the following position:

	£
Value of holding after the rights issue (2,000 × £1.54)	3,080
Sale of the rights (500 × £0.24)	120
	3,200

If the investor lets the rights offer lapse, she will be in the following position:

	£
Value of holding after rights issue (2,000 × £1.54)	3,080

As we can see, the first two options should leave her in the same position concerning net wealth as before the rights issue. Before the rights issue she had 2,000 shares worth £1.60 each, or £3,200 in total. However, she will be worse off if she allows the rights offer to lapse than under the other two options.

In practice, businesses will typically sell the rights on behalf of those investors who allow them to lapse. The businesses will then pass on the proceeds to ensure that they are not worse off as a result of the issue.

When considering a rights issue, the directors must first think about the amount of funds to be raised. This will depend on the future plans and commitments of the business. The directors must then decide on the issue price of the rights shares. This decision is not normally of critical importance. In Example 4.4, the business made a one-for-four issue with the price of the rights shares set at £1.30. The same amount could have been raised, however, by making a one-for-two issue and setting the rights price at £0.65, a one-for-one issue and setting the price at £0.325, and so on. The issue price that is finally decided upon will not affect the value of the underlying assets of the business or the proportion of the underlying assets and earnings to which each shareholder is entitled. However, the directors must ensure that the issue price is not above the current market price of the shares.

Real World 4.10 describes how one large UK business, Cobham plc, made a rights issue to strengthen its financial position by reducing its level of borrowing. Cobham specialises in electronics, particularly relating to defence applications.

Offers for sale and public issues

When a business wishes to sell new shares to the general investing public, it may make an offer for sale or a public issue. In the former case, the shares are sold to an *issuing house* (in effect, a wholesaler of new shares), which then sells them on to potential investors. In the latter case, the shares are sold by the business making the share issue direct to potential investors. The advantage of an offer for sale, from the business's viewpoint, is that the sale proceeds of the shares are certain.

In practical terms, the net effect on the business is much the same whether there is an offer for sale or a public issue. As we have seen, the administrative costs of a public issue can be very large. Some share issues by Stock Exchange listed businesses arise from the initial listing of the business, often known as an *initial public offering (IPO)*. Other share issues are undertaken by businesses that are already listed and that are seeking additional finance from investors; usually such an issue is known as a *seasoned equity offering (SEO)*.

Private placings

A **private placing** does not involve an invitation to the public to subscribe for shares. Instead the shares are 'placed' with selected investors, such as large financial institutions. This can be a quick and relatively cheap form of raising funds, because savings can be made in advertising and legal costs. It can, however, result in the ownership of the business being concentrated in a few hands. Shares placed with investors may be offered at a discount to the current market price. This will normally be much lower than the discounts offered when a rights issue is made. For Stock Exchange listed businesses, a maximum discount of 10 per cent to the current market price is permitted.

Real World 4.11 describes how a placing was used by a well-known business to fund its activities.

Real World 4.11

Fashionably placed

Boohoo.com plc, the online fashion retailer raised around £50 million in June 2017, through a share placing. About £20 million of this was used to expand its warehousing capacity. The new warehousing was completed in January 2018.

Source: Boohoo.com plc (2017) Interim results for the six months ended 31 August 2017, 27 September.

Placings may be carried out in conjunction with a public offer or a rights issue. Where, for example, a public offer, or rights issue, is expected to raise less than is needed, a placing may be used to bridge the funding gap.

Placings are an extremely popular way of issuing shares among listed businesses. During 2017, they accounted for around 80 per cent of the total amount raised from shares issued by newly listed businesses (see Reference 1 at the end of the chapter). **Real World 4.12** indicates that they also account for a significant proportion of the total amount raised from shares issued by already-listed businesses.

Real World 4.12

Raising the issue

Table 4.1 reveals the percentage of the total amount raised from issuing shares, according to issuing method, by businesses already listed on the Main Market of the London Stock Exchange.

→

Table 4.1 Percentage of total funds raised through different issuing methods by already-listed businesses 2013–17

	2017	2016	2015	2014	2013
	%	%	%	%	%
Public offer	6.7	3.3	3.7	2.1	1.0
Placing	51.1	39.9	46.5	46.7	31.5
Public offer and placing	22.2	20.2	9.5	13.6	10.3
Rights issue	20.0	36.6	40.3	37.6	57.2
	100.0	100.0	100.0	100.0	100.0

We can see that, together, placings and rights issues account for a huge percentage of the total amount raised each year.

Source: Based on figures in: London Stock Exchange, Main Market Factsheet, Table 3, covering the five-year period ending 31 December 2017, www.londonstockexchange.com.

WITHDRAWING EQUITY

As we have seen, companies are legally obliged to distinguish, in the statement of financial position, between that part of the shareholders' equity that may be withdrawn and that part which may not. The withdrawable part consists of profits arising from trading and from the disposal of non-current assets. It is represented in the statement of financial position by *revenue reserves*.

Paying dividends is the most usual way of enabling shareholders to withdraw part of their equity. An alternative is for the company to buy its own shares from those shareholders wishing to sell them. This is usually known as a 'share repurchase'. The company would then normally cancel the shares concerned. Share repurchases usually involve only a small proportion of the shareholders, unlike a dividend which involves them all.

The total of revenue reserves appearing in the statement of financial position is rarely the total of all trading profits and profits on disposals of non-current assets generated since the company was first formed. This total will normally have been reduced by at least one of the following:

- corporation tax paid on those profits;
- any dividends paid or amounts paid to purchase the company's own shares; and
- any losses from trading and the disposal of non-current assets.

The non-withdrawable part consists of share capital plus profits arising from shareholders buying shares in the company and from upward revaluations of assets still held. It is represented in the statement of financial position by *share capital* and *capital reserves*.

Figure 4.5 shows the important division between the part of the shareholders' equity that can be withdrawn and the part that cannot.

The law does not specify the size of the non-withdrawable part of shareholders' equity. However, for a company to gain the confidence of prospective lenders and suppliers, the bigger the non-withdrawable part, the better.

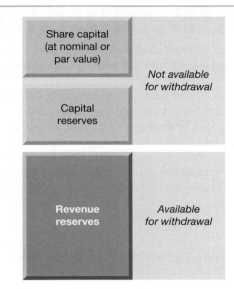

Total equity finance of limited companies consists of share capital, capital reserves and revenue reserves. Only the revenue reserves (which arise from realised profits and gains) can be used to fund a dividend or a share repurchase. In other words, the maximum legal withdrawal is the amount of the revenue reserves.

Figure 4.5 Availability for withdrawal of various parts of the shareholders' equity

Real World 4.13 describes how one company contravened the rules concerning the withdrawal of equity.

Why are limited companies required to distinguish different parts of their shareholders' equity, whereas sole-proprietorship and partnership businesses are not?

The reason stems from the limited liability that company shareholders enjoy but which owners of unincorporated businesses do not. If a sole proprietor or partner withdraws all of the equity, the position of the lenders and credit suppliers of the business is not weakened since they can legally enforce their claims against the sole proprietor or partner as an individual. With a limited company, however, the right to enforce claims against individual owners does not exist. To protect the company's lenders and credit suppliers, therefore, the law insists that the non-withdrawable part of shareholders' equity is clearly distinguished.

Let us now look at an example that illustrates how this protection of lenders and suppliers works.

Example 4.5

The summary statement of financial position of a company at a particular date is as follows:

Statement of financial position

	£
Total assets	<u>43,000</u>
Equity	
Share capital	
10,000 shares of £1 each	10,000
Reserves (revenue)	<u>33,000</u>
Total equity	<u>43,000</u>

A bank has been asked to make a £25,000 long-term loan to the company. If the loan is granted, the statement of financial position immediately following would appear as follows:

Statement of financial position (after the loan)

	£
Total assets	<u>68,000</u>
Equity	
Share capital	
10,000 shares of £1 each	10,000
Reserves (revenue)	<u>33,000</u>
	43,000
Non-current liability	
Borrowings – loan	<u>25,000</u>
Total equity and liabilities	<u>68,000</u>

As things stand, there are assets with a total carrying amount of £68,000 to meet the bank's claim of £25,000. It would be possible and perfectly legal, however, for the company to withdraw part of the shareholders' equity (through a dividend or share repurchase) equal to the total revenue reserves (£33,000). The statement of financial position would then appear as follows:

Statement of financial position (after withdrawal)

	£
Total assets (£68,000 − £33,000)	35,000
Equity	
Share capital	
10,000 shares of £1 each	10,000
Reserves [revenue (£33,000 − £33,000)]	–
	10,000
Non-current liabilities	
Borrowings – bank loan	25,000
Total equity and liabilities	35,000

This leaves the bank in a very much weaker position, in that there are now total assets with a carrying amount of £35,000 to meet a claim of £25,000 – bear in mind that the potential disposal proceeds of the assets may well fall far short of the carrying amount. Note that the difference between the amount of the borrowings (bank loan) and the total assets equals the equity (share capital and reserves) total. Thus, the equity represents a margin of safety for lenders and suppliers. The larger the amount of the equity that can be withdrawn by shareholders, the smaller the potential margin of safety for lenders and suppliers.

Activity 4.17

Can you recall the circumstances in which the non-withdrawable part of a company's capital could be reduced, without contravening the law? This was mentioned earlier in the chapter.

It can be reduced as a result of the company sustaining trading losses, or losses on disposal of non-current assets, which exceed the withdrawable amount of shareholders' equity.

THE MAIN FINANCIAL STATEMENTS

The financial statements of a limited company are, in essence, the same as those of a sole proprietor or partnership. There are, however, some differences of detail. We shall now consider these. Example 4.6 sets out the income statement and statement of financial position of a limited company.

Example 4.6

Da Silva plc
Income statement for the year ended 31 December 2018

	£m
Revenue	840
Cost of sales	(520)
Gross profit	320
Wages and salaries	(98)
Heat and light	(18)
Rent and rates	(24)
Motor vehicle expenses	(20)
Insurance	(4)
Printing and stationery	(12)
Depreciation	(45)
Audit fee	(4)
Operating profit	95
Interest payable	(10)
Profit before taxation	85
Taxation	(24)
Profit for the year	61

Statement of financial position as at 31 December 2018

	£m
ASSETS	
Non-current assets	
Property, plant and equipment	203
Intangible assets	100
	303
Current assets	
Inventories	65
Trade receivables	112
Cash	36
	213
Total assets	516
EQUITY AND LIABILITIES	
Equity	
Ordinary shares of £0.50 each	200
Share premium account	30
Other reserves	50
Retained earnings	25
	305
Non-current liabilities	
Borrowings	100
Current liabilities	
Trade payables	99
Taxation	12
	111
Total equity and liabilities	516

Let us now go through these statements and pick out those aspects that are unique to limited companies.

The income statement

The main points for consideration in the income statement are as follows:

Profit

We can see that, following the calculation of operating profit, two further measures of profit are shown:

- The first of these is the **profit before taxation**. Interest charges are deducted from the operating profit to derive this figure. In the case of a sole proprietor or partnership business, the income statement would end here.
- The second measure of profit is the profit for the reporting period (usually a year). As the company is a separate legal entity, it is liable to pay tax (known as corporation tax) on the profits generated. This measure of profit represents the amount that is available for the shareholders.

Audit fee

Companies beyond a certain size are required to have their financial statements audited by an independent firm of accountants, for which a fee is charged. As we shall see in Chapter 5, the purpose of the audit is to lend credibility to the financial statements. Although it is also open to sole proprietorships and partnerships to have their financial statements audited, relatively few do so. Audit fee is, therefore, an expense that is most often seen in the income statement of a company.

Figure 4.6 shows an outline of the income statement for a limited company.

The statement of financial position

The main points for consideration in the statement of financial position are as follows:

Taxation

For many companies, the amount that appears as part of the current liabilities represents 50 per cent of the tax on the profit for the year 2017. It is, therefore, 50 per cent (£12 million) of the charge that appears in the income statement (£24 million) the other 50 per cent will already have been paid. The unpaid 50 per cent will be paid shortly after the statement of financial position date. These payment dates are set down by law.

Other reserves

This will include any reserves that are not separately identified on the face of the statement of financial position. It may include a *general reserve*, which normally consists of trading profits that have been transferred to this separate reserve for reinvestment ('ploughing back') into the operations of the company. It is not necessary to set up a separate reserve for this purpose. The trading profits could remain unallocated and still swell the retained earnings of the company. It is not entirely clear why directors decide to make transfers to general reserves, since the profits concerned remain part of the revenue reserves, and as such they still remain available for dividend.

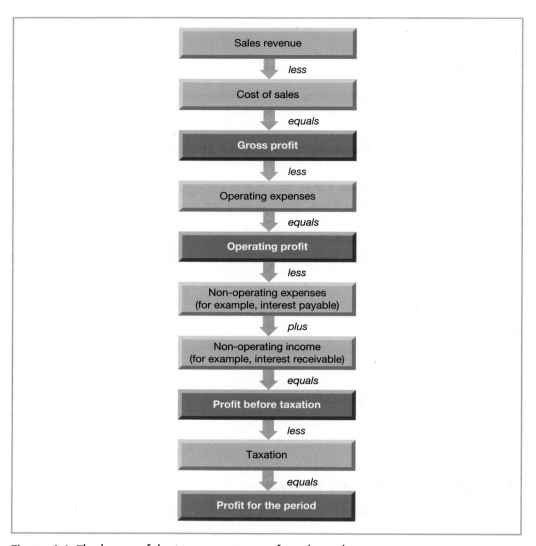

Figure 4.6 The layout of the income statement for a limited company

Retained earnings appearing on the statement of financial position are, of course, also a reserve, but that fact is not indicated in its title.

DIVIDENDS

Although most companies pay dividends to shareholders, they are under no legal obligation to do so. The decision whether to pay dividends will be influenced by commercial factors such as the financial resources of the company, future commitments and shareholder expectations. It must also take account of the legal restraints on the withdrawal of equity, as discussed earlier.

Dividends are paid out of the revenue reserves and should be deducted from these reserves (usually retained earnings) when preparing the statement of financial position. Shareholders are often paid an annual dividend, perhaps in two parts. An 'interim' dividend may be paid part way through the year and a 'final' dividend shortly after the year end.

Dividends declared by the directors during the year but still unpaid at the year end *may* appear as a liability in the statement of financial position. To be recognised as a liability, however, they must be properly authorised before the year-end date. This normally means that the shareholders must approve the dividend by that date.

Large businesses tend to have a clear and consistent policy towards the payment of dividends. Any change in the policy provokes considerable interest and is usually interpreted by shareholders as a signal of the directors' views concerning the future. For example, an increase in dividends may be taken as a signal from the directors that future prospects are bright: a higher dividend is seen as tangible evidence of their confidence.

Real World 4.14 provides an example of one well-known business that restored its dividend after a difficult period.

Real World 4.14

Sending a signal

Tesco chief Dave Lewis will this week attempt to confirm the supermarket giant's comeback by restoring its dividend, even as the alleged 'colossal fraud' that blew a hole in its finances is laid bare in court.

Mr Lewis, who was drafted in to lead a salvage operation at Tesco three years ago after investigators uncovered hundreds of millions of pounds of missing profits, scrapped the dividend months into his reign to help repair the balance sheet.

Its expected return as part of Tesco's half-year results on Wednesday comes as investor nerves are tested by the high-profile trial of three former senior executives accused of masterminding a scheme to 'cook the books'. The trial of Christopher Bush, Tesco UK's former managing director, Carl Rogberg, the company's former UK finance director, and John Scouler, former food commercial director, began on Friday.

Bruno Monteyne, an analyst at Bernstein, has said that, while the size of any dividend may be small, it will be 'important symbolically, signalling the next stage of the Tesco recovery to the market'.

Source: Extract from Armstrong, A. (2017) "Tesco to signal comeback with return to dividend", *Daily Telegraph*, 30 September.

Dividend policy

The fact that directors of profitable businesses can decide the amount of dividends to be paid to shareholders raises the question of how large each year's dividend should be. The traditional view is that dividend payments should be maximised. The belief is that the higher the dividend payments, the more attractive the ordinary shares will become. This, in turn, will lead to higher share prices and more wealthy shareholders. Since the 1950s, however, this traditional view has been subject to increasing challenge.

The main thrust of the critics' argument is that, since the shareholders own the business, why should transferring some of the business's assets to shareholders through a cash dividend make them better off? What shareholders are gaining, through the dividend, they are losing through their business being less well off. Funds handed to shareholders as dividends means less being retained within the business for investment in wealth-generating projects.

An alternative, more modern, view is that the interests of shareholders are best served by the directors retaining, and investing, the funds that the shareholders might otherwise receive as dividends, provided that those funds would generate higher returns than the shareholders could individually achieve by reinvesting them. Where the directors cannot generate higher returns, however, the shareholders would be worse off. This means that the directors should only retain earnings where they can be invested at a rate at least as high as the shareholders' opportunity cost of funds. The residue should be paid as a dividend.

Not all businesses follow the modern view on dividend policy. One that does is Asos plc (the online fashion and beauty retailer). Asos was formed in 2004, but has yet to pay a dividend, despite being profitable for every year up to the time of writing. This is because it needed the funds to expand. **Real World 4.15**, an extract from the business's 2017 annual report, explains the situation.

Real World 4.15

Dividends out of fashion

The Board has again decided not to declare a dividend. We generate a significant return on invested capital, and we firmly believe the right thing for the business and our shareholders is to invest in the opportunities that lie ahead.

Source: Asos plc, 2017 Annual report, p. 19.

Self-assessment question 4.1

The summarised statement of financial position of Dev Ltd at a particular point in time is as follows:

Statement of financial position

	£
Net assets (various assets less liabilities)	235,000
Equity	
Share capital: 100,000 shares of £1 each	100,000
Share premium account	30,000
Revaluation reserve	37,000
Retained earnings	68,000
Total equity	235,000

Required:

(a) Without any other transactions occurring at the same time, the company made a one-for-five rights share issue at £2 per share payable in cash. This means that each shareholder was offered one share for every five already held. All shareholders took up their rights. Immediately afterwards, the company made a one-for-two bonus issue. Show the statement of financial position immediately following the bonus issue, assuming that the directors wanted to retain the maximum dividend payment potential for the future.

(b) Explain what external influence might cause the directors to choose not to retain the maximum dividend payment possibilities.

(c) Show the statement of financial position immediately following the bonus issue, assuming that the directors wanted to retain the *minimum* dividend payment potential for the future.

(d) What is the maximum dividend that could be paid before and after the events described in (a) if the minimum dividend payment potential is achieved?

(e) Lee owns 100 shares in Dev Ltd before the events described in (a). Assuming that the net assets of the company have a value equal to their carrying amount on the statement of financial position, show how these events will affect Lee's wealth.

(f) Looking at the original statement of financial position of Dev Ltd, shown above, what four things do we know about the company's status and history that are not specifically stated on the statement of financial position?

The solution to this question can be found at the back of the book, starting on page 525.

SUMMARY

The main points of this chapter may be summarised as follows:

Main features of a limited company

- It is an artificial person that has been created by law.
- It has a separate life to its owners and is granted a perpetual existence.
- It must take responsibility for its own debts and losses but its owners are granted limited liability.
- To safeguard those dealing with a limited company, limited liability status is included as part of the business name, restrictions are placed on the ability of owners to withdraw equity and annual financial statements are made publicly available.
- A public company can offer its shares for sale to the public; a private company cannot.
- A limited company is governed by a board of directors elected by the shareholders.

The Stock Exchange

- The Stock Exchange is an important primary and secondary market in capital for large businesses. However, a Stock Exchange listing can have certain drawbacks for a business.
- The Stock Exchange is broadly seen as an *efficient capital market*. New information that becomes publicly available is quickly and rationally reflected in share prices. This leads to share prices representing the best estimate of the 'true' value of shares, on the basis of publicly known information.

Financing a limited company

- The share capital of a company can be of two main types: ordinary shares and preference shares.
- Holders of ordinary shares (equities) are the main risk-takers and are given voting rights; they form the backbone of the company.
- Holders of preference shares are given a right to a fixed dividend before ordinary shareholders receive a dividend.

- Reserves are profits and gains made by the company and form part of the ordinary shareholders' claim.
- Borrowings provide another major source of finance.

Share issues

- Share issues that involve the payment of cash by investors can take the form of a rights issue, public issue, offer for sale or a private placing.
- A rights issue is made to existing shareholders. Most share issues are of this type as the law requires that shares that are to be issued for cash must first be offered to existing shareholders. Rights issue costs are relatively low.
- A public issue involves a direct issue to the public and an offer for sale involves an indirect issue to the public.
- A private placing is an issue of shares to selected investors.
- A bonus issue does not involve the receipt of cash in exchange for shares issued.

Withdrawing equity

- Reserves are of two types: revenue reserves and capital reserves.
- Revenue reserves arise from trading profits and from realised profits on the sale of non-current assets.
- Capital reserves arise from the issue of shares above their nominal value or from the upward revaluation of non-current assets.
- Revenue reserves can be withdrawn as dividends by the shareholders whereas capital reserves normally cannot.

Financial statements of limited companies

- The financial statements of limited companies are based on the same principles as those of sole-proprietorship and partnership businesses. However, there are some differences in detail.
- The income statement has two measures of profit displayed after the operating profit figure: profit before taxation and profit for the year.
- The income statement also shows audit fees and tax on profits for the year.
- The statement of financial position will show any unpaid tax and any unpaid, but authorised, dividends as current liabilities.
- The share capital plus the reserves make up 'equity'.

KEY TERMS

For definitions of these terms, see at the back of the book, starting on page 514.

limited liability p. 119
public limited company p. 120
private limited company p. 120
corporation tax p. 122
Stock Exchange p. 123

London Stock Exchange p. 123
efficient capital market p. 124
directors p. 126
corporate governance p. 126
reserves p. 127
nominal value p. 127
par value p. 127

REFERENCES

1 London Stock Exchange (2017) *Main Market Factsheet*, December, Table 3.
2 Association of British Insurers (2013) *Encouraging Equity Investment*, July, p. 32.

FURTHER READING

If you would like to explore the topics covered in this chapter in more depth, we recommend the following:

Alexander D., Britton A., Jorissen, A., Hoogendorn M. and Van Mourik C. (2017) *International Financial Reporting and Analysis*, Cengage Learning EMEA, 7th edn, Chapter 10.

Elliott, B. and Elliott, J. (2017) *Financial Accounting and Reporting*, 18th edn, Pearson, Chapters 3, 12 and 22.

Melville, A. (2017) *International Financial Reporting: A Practical Guide*, 6th edn, Pearson, Chapter 1.

Thomas, A. and Ward, A.M. (2015) *Introduction to Financial Accounting*, 8th edn, McGraw-Hill Education, Chapters 28 and 29.

CRITICAL REVIEW QUESTIONS

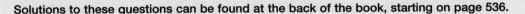

Solutions to these questions can be found at the back of the book, starting on page 536.

4.1 You and a friend have decided to set up in business offering a bicycle delivery service in your local area. You feel that you can raise enough funds from your own resources to get the business going. You have calculated that you can finance your planned future expansion from profits. You intend to create a limited company to own the business. Would a public limited company or a private one be more appropriate? Explain your reasons.

4.2 The London Stock Exchange has the power to suspend dealing in shares of businesses that have failed to comply with particular regulations. Why is this seen as a punishment for the business concerned?

4.3 'For a capital market to be efficient requires that there are certain individuals that have superior powers of prediction.' Is this statement true?

4.4 Issues of new preference shares are extremely rare these days. Suggest reasons why this is the case.

Solutions to exercises with coloured numbers can be found at the back of the book, starting on page 545.

Basic-level exercises

4.1 Comment on the following quote:

'Limited companies can set a limit on the amount of debts that they will meet. They tend to have reserves of cash as well as share capital, and they can use these reserves to pay dividends to the shareholders. Many companies have preference shares as well as ordinary shares. The preference shares give a guaranteed dividend. The shares of many companies can be bought and sold on the Stock Exchange. Shareholders selling their shares can represent a useful source of new finance to the company.'

4.2 Comment on the following quotes:

(a) 'Bonus shares increase the shareholders' wealth because, after the issue, they have more shares, but each one of the same nominal value as they had before.'

(b) 'By law, once shares have been issued at a particular nominal value, they must always be issued at that value in any future share issues.'

(c) 'By law, companies can pay as much as they like by way of dividends on their shares, provided that they have sufficient cash to do so.'

(d) 'Companies do not have to pay tax on their profits because the shareholders have to pay tax on their dividends.'

4.3 Briefly explain each of the following expressions that you have seen in the financial statements of a limited company:

(a) dividend
(b) audit fee
(c) share premium account.

Intermediate-level exercises

4.4 Iqbal Ltd started trading on 1 July 2013. During the first five years of trading, the following occurred:

Year ended 30 June	Trading profit/(loss)	Profit/(loss) on sale of non-current assets	Upward revaluation of non-current assets
	£	£	£
2014	(15,000)	–	–
2015	8,000	–	10,000
2016	15,000	5,000	–
2017	20,000	(6,000)	–
2018	22,000	–	–

Required:

Assume that the company paid the maximum legal dividend each year. Under normal circumstances, how much would each year's dividend be?

4.5 Hudson plc's outline statement of financial position as at a particular date was as follows:

	£m
Net assets (assets less liabilities)	72
Equity	
£1 Ordinary shares	40
General reserve	32
Total equity	72

The directors made a one-for-four bonus issue, immediately followed by a one-for-four rights issue at a price of £1.80 per share.

Required:
Show the statement of financial position of Hudson plc immediately following the two share issues.

Advanced-level exercises

4.6 The following is a draft set of simplified financial statements for Pear Limited for the year ended 30 September 2018:

Income statement for the year ended 30 September 2018

	£000
Revenue	1,456
Cost of sales	(768)
Gross profit	688
Salaries	(220)
Depreciation	(249)
Other operating costs	(131)
Operating profit	88
Interest payable	(15)
Profit before taxation	73
Taxation at 30%	(22)
Profit for the year	51

Statement of financial position as at 30 September 2018

	£000
ASSETS	
Non-current assets	
Property, plant and equipment	
Cost	1,570
Depreciation	(690)
	880
Current assets	
Inventories	207
Trade receivables	182
Cash at bank	21
	410
Total assets	1,290

	£000
EQUITY AND LIABILITIES	
Equity	
Share capital	300
Share premium account	300
Retained earnings at beginning of year	104
Profit for year	51
	755
Non-current liabilities	
Borrowings (10% loan notes repayable 2020)	300
Current liabilities	
Trade payables	88
Other payables	20
Taxation	22
Borrowings (bank overdraft)	105
	235
Total equity and liabilities	1,290

The following information is available:

1 Depreciation has not been charged on office equipment with a carrying amount of £100,000. This class of assets is depreciated at 12 per cent a year using the reducing-balance method.

2 A new machine was purchased, on credit, for £30,000 and delivered on 29 September 2018 but has not been included in the financial statements. (Ignore depreciation.)

3 A sales invoice to the value of £18,000 for September 2018 has been omitted from the financial statements. (The cost of sales figure is stated correctly.)

4 A dividend of £25,000 had been approved by the shareholders before 30 September 2018, but was unpaid at that date. This is not reflected in the financial statements.

5 The interest payable on the loan notes for the second half-year was not paid until 1 October 2018 and has not been included in the financial statements.

6 An allowance for trade receivables is to be made at the level of 2 per cent of trade receivables.

7 An invoice for electricity to the value of £2,000 for the quarter ended 30 September 2018 arrived on 4 October 2018 and has not been included in the financial statements.

8 The charge for taxation will have to be revised to take account of any amendments to the taxable profit arising from items 1 to 7. Make the simplifying assumption that tax is payable shortly after the end of the year, at the rate of 30 per cent of the profit before tax.

Required:
Prepare a revised set of financial statements for the year ended 30 September 2018 incorporating the additional information in 1 to 8 above. (Work to the nearest £1,000.)

4.7 Presented below is a draft set of financial statements for Chips Limited.

Income statement for the year ended 30 June 2018

	£000
Revenue	1,850
Cost of sales	(1,040)
Gross profit	810
Depreciation	(220)
Other operating costs	(375)
Operating profit	215
Interest payable	(35)
Profit before taxation	180
Taxation	(60)
Profit for the year	120

Statement of financial position as at 30 June 2018

	Cost £000	Depreciation £000	£000
ASSETS			
Non-current assets			
Property, plant and equipment			
Buildings	800	(112)	688
Plant and equipment	650	(367)	283
Motor vehicles	102	(53)	49
	1,552	(532)	1,020
Current assets			
Inventories			950
Trade receivables			420
Cash at bank			16
			1,386
Total assets			2,406
EQUITY AND LIABILITIES			
Equity			
Ordinary shares of £1, fully paid			800
Reserves at beginning of the year			248
Profit for the year			120
			1,168
Non-current liabilities			
Borrowings (secured 10% loan notes)			700
Current liabilities			
Trade payables			361
Other payables			117
Taxation			60
			538
Total equity and liabilities			2,406

The following additional information is available:

1   Purchase invoices for goods received on 29 June 2018 amounting to £23,000 have not been included. This means that the cost of sales figure in the income statement has been understated.

2   A motor vehicle costing £8,000 with depreciation amounting to £5,000 was sold on 30 June 2018 for £2,000, paid by cheque. This transaction has not been included in the company's records.

3   No depreciation on motor vehicles has been charged. The annual rate is 20 per cent of cost at the year end.

4   A sale on credit for £16,000 made on 1 July 2018 has been included in the financial statements in error. The cost of sales figure is not affected.

5   A half-yearly payment of interest on the secured loan due on 30 June 2018 has not been paid.

6   The tax charge should be 30 per cent of the reported profit before taxation. Assume that it is payable, in full, shortly after the year end.

Required:
Prepare a revised set of financial statements incorporating the additional information in 1 to 6 above. (Work to the nearest £1,000.)

4.8   Rose Limited is a wholesaler and retailer of high-quality teas and coffees. Approximately half of sales are on credit. Abbreviated and unaudited financial statements are as follows:

Rose Limited
Income statement for the year ended 31 March 2018

	£000
Revenue	12,080
Cost of sales	(6,282)
Gross profit	5,798
Labour costs	(2,658)
Depreciation	(625)
Other operating costs	(1,003)
Operating profit	1,512
Interest payable	(66)
Profit before taxation	1,446
Taxation	(434)
Profit for the year	1,012

Statement of financial position as at 31 March 2018

	£000
ASSETS	
Non-current assets	2,728
Current assets	
Inventories	1,583
Trade receivables	996
Cash	26
	2,605
Total assets	5,333
EQUITY AND LIABILITIES	
Equity	
Share capital (50p shares, fully paid)	750
Share premium	250
Retained earnings	1,468
	2,468
Non-current liabilities	
Borrowings – secured loan notes	300
Current liabilities	
Trade payables	1,118
Other payables	417
Tax	434
Borrowings – overdraft	596
	2,565
Total equity and liabilities	5,333

Since the unaudited financial statements for Rose Limited were prepared, the following information has become available:

1   An additional £74,000 of depreciation should have been charged on fixtures and fittings.
2   Invoices for credit sales on 31 March 2018 amounting to £34,000 have not been included; cost of sales is not affected.
3   Trade receivables totalling £21,000 are recognised as having gone bad, but they have not yet been written off.
4   Inventories which had been purchased for £2,000 have been damaged and are unsaleable. This is not reflected in the financial statements.
5   Fixtures and fittings to the value of £16,000 were delivered just before 31 March 2018, but these assets were not included in the financial statements and the purchase invoice had not been processed.
6   Wages for Saturday-only staff, amounting to £1,000 have not been paid for the final Saturday of the year. This is not reflected in the financial statements.
7   Tax is payable at 30 per cent of profit before taxation. Assume that it is payable shortly after the year end.

Required:
Prepare revised financial statements for Rose Limited for the year ended 31 March 2018, incorporating the information in 1 to 7 above. (Work to the nearest £1,000.)

Chapter 5

ACCOUNTING FOR LIMITED COMPANIES (2)

INTRODUCTION

This chapter continues our examination of the financial statements of limited companies. We begin by considering the importance of accounting rules in preparing financial statements and the main sources of these rules. The accounting rules in place enjoy widespread support and are generally considered to have had a beneficial effect on the quality of financial information provided to users. There are, however, potential problems with imposing accounting rules. In this chapter, we shall consider these problems and how they might affect the financial statements. We shall also consider the efforts made to ensure that a coherent conceptual framework underpins the accounting rules.

Over the years, the published annual financial reports of larger companies have greatly increased in scope. They now include a comprehensive set of financial statements for users. A detailed consideration of the various rules relating to these statements is beyond the scope of this book; however, we shall take a look at the key rules that shape their form and content. To accompany the financial statements, the directors must provide comments, and supplementary information, concerning the performance and position of the company. In this chapter, we outline the key topics that the directors must address.

Despite the proliferation of accounting rules and the increasing supply of financial information to users, concerns have been expressed over the quality of some published financial reports. We end the chapter by looking at some well-publicised accounting scandals and the problem of creative accounting.

Learning outcomes

When you have completed this chapter, you should be able to:

- discuss the case for and against a rule-based approach to the preparation of financial statements;

- prepare a statement of financial position, statement of comprehensive income and statement of changes in equity in accordance with International Financial Reporting Standards;

- describe the role and content of the directors' report and the strategic report; and

- discuss the threat posed by creative accounting and describe the main methods used to distort the fair presentation of position and performance.

THE DIRECTORS' DUTY TO ACCOUNT

For all companies, except the very small ones, it is not practical for all shareholders to be involved in the management of the company. Instead, they appoint directors to act on their behalf. This separation of ownership from day-to-day control creates a need for directors to be accountable for their stewardship (management) of the company's assets. To fulfil this need, the directors must prepare financial statements that fairly represent the financial position and performance of the business. Fair representation involves selecting appropriate accounting policies, making reasonable accounting estimates and keeping to the relevant accounting rules when preparing the statements. To avoid mistaken, or deliberately misleading, statements appearing in the financial statements appropriate internal control systems must be maintained.

Activity 5.1

Do you think that, in practice, the directors will undertake the task of preparing the financial statements themselves?

Probably not – they will normally delegate this task to the accounting staff. Nevertheless, they will retain responsibility for the financial statements and must monitor the work done.

Each of the company's shareholders has the right to be sent a copy of the financial statements produced by the directors. A copy must also be sent to the Registrar of Companies, which is then made available for public inspection. A Stock Exchange listed company has the additional obligation to publish its financial statements on its website.

Activity 5.2

It can be argued that the publication of financial statements is vital to a well-functioning private sector. Why might this be the case? Try to think of at least one reason.

There are at least two reasons:

■ Unless shareholders receive regular information about the performance and position of a business they will encounter problems in evaluating their investment. As a result, they would probably be reluctant to invest.
■ Suppliers of labour, goods, services and loans need information about the financial health of a business. They would probably be reluctant to engage in commercial relationships where a company does not provide this information. The fact that a company has limited liability increases the risks involved in dealing with it.

In both cases, the functioning of the private sector of the economy will be adversely affected by the absence of financial statements.

THE NEED FOR ACCOUNTING RULES

The obligation on directors to prepare and publish financial statements has led to the creation of a framework of rules concerning their form and content. Without rules, there is a much greater risk that unscrupulous directors will employ accounting policies and practices that portray an unrealistic view of financial health. There is also a much greater risk that the financial statements will not be comparable over time, or with those of other businesses. Accounting rules can narrow areas of differences and reduce the variety of accounting methods. This should help ensure that businesses treat similar transactions in a similar way.

Example 5.1 illustrates the problems that may arise where businesses can exercise choice over the accounting policies used.

Example 5.1

Rila plc and Pirin plc are both wholesalers of electrical goods. Both commenced trading on 1 March 2018 with an identical share capital. Both acquired identical property, plant and equipment on 1 March and both achieved identical trading results during the first year of trading. The following financial information relating to both businesses is available:

	£m
Ordinary £1 shares fully paid on 1 March 2018	60
Non-current assets (at cost) acquired on 1 March 2018	40
Revenue for the year to 28 February 2019	100
Purchases of inventories during the year to 28 February 2019	70
Expenses for the year to 28 February 2019 (excluding depreciation)	20
Trade receivables as at 28 February 2019	37
Trade payables as at 28 February 2019	12
Cash as at 28 February 2019	5

The non-current assets held by both businesses are leasehold buildings that have five years left to run on the lease. Inventories for both businesses have been valued at the year end at £16 million on a FIFO basis and £12 million on a LIFO basis.

When preparing their financial statements for the first year of trading,

■ Rila plc decided to write off the cost of the leasehold buildings at the end of the lease period. Pirin plc adopted the straight-line basis of depreciation for the leasehold buildings.

■ Rila plc adopted the FIFO method of inventories valuation and Pirin plc adopted the LIFO method.

The income statements and the statements of financial position for the two businesses, ignoring taxation, will be as follows:

Income statements for the year to 28 February 2019

	Rila plc £m	Pirin plc £m
Revenue	100	100
Cost of sales		
Rila plc (£70m − £16m)	(54)	
Pirin plc (£70m − £12m)		(58)
Gross profit	46	42
Expenses (excluding depreciation)	(20)	(20)
Depreciation		
Rila plc	(−)	
Pirin plc (£40m/5)		(8)
Profit for the year	26	14

Statements of financial position as at 28 February 2019

	Rila plc £m	Pirin plc £m
ASSETS		
Non-current assets		
Property, plant and equipment at cost	40	40
Accumulated depreciation	(−)	(8)
	40	32
Current assets		
Inventories	16	12
Trade receivables	37	37
Cash	5	5
	58	54
Total assets	98	86
EQUITY AND LIABILITIES		
Equity		
Share capital	60	60
Retained earnings	26	14
	86	74
Current liabilities		
Trade payables	12	12
Total equity and liabilities	98	86

Although the two businesses are identical in terms of funding and underlying trading performance, the financial statements create an impression that the financial health of each business is quite different. The accounting policies selected by Rila plc help to portray a much rosier picture. We can see that Rila plc reports a significantly higher profit for the year and higher assets at the year end.

Depreciation and inventories valuation are not the only areas where choices might be exercised. Nevertheless, they illustrate the potential impact of different accounting choices over the short term.

Accounting rules should help to create greater confidence in the integrity of financial statements. This should make it easier to raise funds from investors and to build stronger relationships with customers and suppliers. We must be realistic, however, about what can be achieved through regulation. Problems of manipulation and of concealment can still occur even within a highly regulated environment (and examples of both will be considered later in the chapter). Nevertheless, the scale of these problems should be reduced where accounting rules are in place.

Problems of comparability between businesses can also still occur. Accounting is not a precise science. Even within a regulated environment, estimates and judgements must be made and these may vary according to who makes them. Furthermore, no two businesses are identical (unlike those in Example 5.1). Different accounting policies may therefore be applied to fit different circumstances.

SOURCES OF ACCOUNTING RULES

In recent years, there has been an increasing trend towards both the internationalisation of business and the integration of financial markets. This has helped to strengthen the case for the international harmonisation of accounting rules. By adopting a common set of rules, users of financial statements are better placed to compare the financial health of companies based in different countries. It can also relieve international companies of some of the burden of preparing financial statements. Different financial statements are no longer needed to comply with the rules of the particular countries in which these companies operate.

The International Accounting Standards Board (IASB) is an independent body that is at the forefront of the move towards harmonisation. The Board, which is based in the UK, is dedicated to developing a single set of high-quality, globally accepted, accounting rules. These aim to provide transparent and comparable information in financial statements. The rules, which are known as International Accounting Standards (IASs) or International Financial Reporting Standards (IFRSs), deal with key issues such as:

■ what information should be disclosed;
■ how information should be presented;
■ how assets should be valued; and
■ how profit should be measured.

Activity 5.3

We have already come across some IASs and IFRSs in earlier chapters. Try to recall at least two topics where financial reporting standards were mentioned.

We came across financial reporting standards when considering:

1 the valuation and impairment of assets (Chapter 2);
2 depreciation and impairment of non-current assets (Chapter 3); and
3 the valuation of inventories (Chapter 3).

The growing authority of the IASB

Over recent years the authority of the IASB has gone from strength to strength. The first major boost came when the European Commission required nearly all companies listed on the stock exchanges of European Union member states to adopt IFRSs for reporting periods commencing on or after 1 January 2005. As a result, nearly 7,000 companies in 25 different countries switched to IFRSs. Since this landmark development, the authority of the IASB has continued to grow. Of the 166 countries that the IASB profiles, 144 (87 per cent) require the use of IFRS Standards for all, or most, public companies and financial institutions listed in their capital markets (such as stock exchanges). (See Reference 1 at the end of the chapter.)

Non-listed UK companies are not required to adopt IFRSs but have the option to do so. It is possible, however, that IFRSs will eventually become a requirement for all UK companies.

Adopting IFRSs

The EU requirement to adopt IFRSs, mentioned earlier, overrides any laws in force in member states that could either hinder or restrict compliance with them. The ultimate aim is to achieve a single framework of accounting rules for companies from all member states. The EU recognises that this will be achieved only if individual governments do not add to the requirements imposed by the various IFRSs. Thus, it seems that accounting rules developed within individual EU member countries will eventually disappear. For the time being, however, the EU accepts that the governments of member states may need to impose additional disclosures for some corporate governance matters and regulatory requirements.

In the UK, company law requires disclosure relating to various corporate governance issues. There is, for example, a requirement to disclose details of directors' remuneration in the published financial statements, which goes beyond anything required by IFRSs. Furthermore, the Financial Conduct Authority (FCA), in its role as the UK listing authority, imposes rules on Stock Exchange listed companies. These include the requirement to publish a condensed set of interim (half-yearly) financial statements in addition to the annual financial statements. (Interim statements are not required by the IASB although, if prepared, there is an appropriate standard.)

Figure 5.1 sets out the main sources of accounting rules for Stock Exchange listed companies.

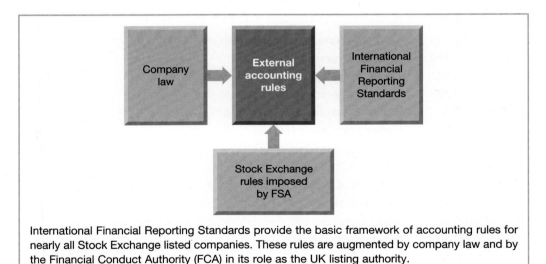

International Financial Reporting Standards provide the basic framework of accounting rules for nearly all Stock Exchange listed companies. These rules are augmented by company law and by the Financial Conduct Authority (FCA) in its role as the UK listing authority.

Figure 5.1 Sources of external accounting rules for a UK public limited company listed on the London Stock Exchange

Real World 5.1 provides a list of IASB standards that were in force as at 5 February 2018. It gives some idea of the range of topics that are covered. The IASB continues its work and so changes to this list will occur over time.

International standards

The following is a list of the International Accounting Standards (IASs) and International Financial Reporting Standards (IFRSs) in force as at 5 February 2018. (The latter term is used for standards issued from 2003 onwards.) Several standards have been issued and subsequently withdrawn, which explains the gaps in the numerical sequence. In addition, several have been revised and reissued.

IAS 1	*Presentation of Financial Statements*
IAS 2	*Inventories*
IAS 7	*Statement of Cash Flows*
IAS 8	*Accounting Policies, Changes in Accounting Estimates and Errors*
IAS 10	*Events after the Reporting Period*
IAS 11	*Construction Contracts*
IAS 12	*Income Taxes*
IAS 16	*Property, Plant and Equipment*
IAS 17	*Leases*[1]
IAS 18	*Revenue*[2]
IAS 19	*Employee Benefits*
IAS 20	*Accounting for Government Grants and Disclosure of Government Assistance*
IAS 21	*The Effects of Changes in Foreign Exchange Rates*
IAS 23	*Borrowing Costs*
IAS 24	*Related Party Disclosures*
IAS 26	*Accounting and Reporting by Retirement Benefit Plans*
IAS 27	*Separate Financial Statements*
IAS 28	*Investments in Associates*
IAS 29	*Financial Reporting in Hyperinflationary Economies*
IAS 32	*Financial Instruments: Presentation*
IAS 33	*Earnings per Share*
IAS 34	*Interim Financial Reporting*
IAS 36	*Impairment of Assets*
IAS 37	*Provisions, Contingent Liabilities and Contingent Assets*
IAS 38	*Intangible Assets*
IAS 39	*Financial Instruments: Recognition and Measurement*
IAS 40	*Investment Property*
IAS 41	*Agriculture*
IFRS 1	*First-time Adoption of International Financial Reporting Standards*
IFRS 2	*Share-based Payment*
IFRS 3	*Business Combinations*
IFRS 4	*Insurance Contracts*

IFRS 5	Non-current Assets Held for Sale and Discontinued Operations
IFRS 6	Exploration for and Evaluation of Mineral Resources
IFRS 7	Financial Instruments: Disclosures
IFRS 8	Operating Segments
IFRS 9	Financial Instruments[1]
IFRS 10	Consolidated Financial Statements
IFRS 11	Joint Arrangements
IFRS 12	Disclosure of Interests in Other Entities
IFRS 13	Fair Value Measurement
IFRS 14	Regulatory Deferral Accounts
IFRS 15	Revenue from Contracts with Customers
IFRS 16	Leases
IFRS 17	Insurance Contracts

1   Will be superseded by IFRS 16
2   Will be superseded by IFRS 15

PROBLEMS WITH STANDARDS

There is broad agreement that financial reporting standards have improved the quality of financial statements. Nevertheless, we should be alert to the potential problems associated with their use. These include the following:

Standards may inhibit change

By setting out rigid procedures to be followed, the development of new and better procedures may be stifled. Progress in financial reporting may, therefore, depend on businesses having the freedom to experiment and innovate. Unless this happens, accounting practice may become ossified.

Although this argument has some appeal, history has shown that financial reporting standards are changed when they prove to be ineffective or inadequate. Over the years, numerous standards have been either modified or withdrawn. Furthermore, developing a new standard involves wide consultation with interested parties and much debate about what constitutes best practice. Thus, financial reporting standards can provide the stimulus for new thinking.

Standards may impose false conformity

No two businesses are identical: each will have its own characteristics and operating methods. When common standards are imposed, there is a risk that the unique aspects of each business will be obscured.

Again, this argument has some appeal, but it can be taken too far. Differences between businesses can be overstated while their common features are understated. Furthermore, there is nothing to prevent standards from offering a limited choice between accounting methods. This may help in reflecting individual characteristics.

Activity 5.4

Can you think of a financial reporting standard that allows some choice of accounting method? (*Hint*: Think back to Chapter 3).

The inventories standard permits some choice over inventories costing methods and the depreciation standard permits some choice over depreciation methods.

Finally, a business can, in exceptional circumstances, depart from a financial reporting standard where it conflicts with the overriding requirement to provide a fair presentation of financial health. Businesses do not, therefore, have to comply with unreasonable rules.

Standards involve consensus seeking

Financial reporting standards affect particular interest groups who must be prepared to accept them. Unless this occurs, standards cannot be implemented effectively. The development of standards may, therefore, be influenced more by the need to achieve consensus than by technical considerations of what is the best approach to adopt. Where this occurs, the quality of financial statements will suffer.

To date, there is no evidence to suggest that this has been a major problem. In order to command authority, standard setters must be responsive to the groups affected. In a democracy, this is how authority is legitimised. The goal that they must seek to achieve, however, is to make rules that are both technically sound and broadly acceptable.

Standards can be costly

There is now an intricate web of financial reporting standards surrounding large businesses. The costs of complying with these rules are high and are borne by shareholders. Each additional standard that incurs costs for businesses means that less is available for distribution to shareholders. There is an assumption that the benefits of standards outweigh their costs, but what if this is not the case? Before adding to the burden of rules, the likely costs and benefits should be assessed.

Standards can be complex

There is a concern that international financial reporting standards have made financial statements far too complex. They have lost sight of their original purpose and have made financial statements less, rather than more, useful to users. This has led to calls for better regulation. To avoid excessive complexity, international financial reporting standards are meant to be based on principles, rather than on legalistic rules. The concern raised suggests that a principles-based approach has not been implemented properly.

Real World 5.2 gives an indication of the type of criticism levelled at the annual financial reports of financial institutions.

Complexity is standard practice

Banks and other financial companies are publishing annual reports that are overly compli-cated and indigestible, prompted in part by regulatory requirements that have swelled the numbers of disclosures, analysts have complained. Nearly two-thirds of analysts ques-tioned by accountancy firm EY said they found annual reports and accounts to be 'too complex', while a similar proportion indicated the tomes being published by firms are hard to digest.

Reports from big lenders for 2013 confirmed the scale of the paper mountain, with HSBC publishing an annual report weighing in at nearly 600 pages while Barclays produced a document that was 444 pages. A decade ago HSBC's annual report was half the current length.

The gripes about the tsunami of paperwork come as the UK's Financial Reporting Coun-cil attempts to foster more clarity and concision in corporate reporting.

A fifth of the analysts went so far as saying the reports are not 'fit for purpose'. The companies' governance report was ranked as the least useful section, closely followed by the chairman's statement to shareholders.

Isabelle Santenac, EY's head of financial services audit for Europe, the Middle East, India and Africa, said: 'The IFRS accounting standards both made the accounts more complex and significantly increased the disclosures. Regulators regularly ask for more information with an objective of greater transparency. But there is a need to find the right balance between giving very detailed information and being as clear and concise as possible.'

ACCOUNTING RULES OR ACCOUNTING CHOICE?

The alternative to a rule-based approach is to give businesses the freedom to choose their accounting methods. Rather than creating standards for all to follow, the shareholders of each business should decide how much and what kind of information they need. Competi-tive forces, so it is argued, should ensure that managers are responsive to shareholders' needs.

Activity 5.5

What sort of competitive forces should ensure that managers are responsive as suggested?

These include competition for investors' funds and competition for managers' jobs.

It would be nice to think that the supply of financial information could be left to competitive forces. There are times, however, when these forces are weak. There are also times when managers have an incentive to conceal relevant information from shareholders.

What sort of information might managers have an incentive to conceal?

Managers may wish to conceal information that would cast doubt on their ability or integrity or might prevent the business from obtaining funds. This may include information relating to excessive management rewards, poor business performance or weak financial health.

Managers also have an incentive to select accounting methods and policies that enhance profits, particularly if they are linked to managerial rewards. This point will be considered further when we discuss creative accounting later in the chapter.

Given the management incentives described, there is a risk that shareholders will not receive the information they need. Financial reporting standards combat this risk by imposing discipline on managers when preparing financial statements. This disciplinary role was an important impetus to the creation of standards.

With freedom of choice comes the problem of comparability. Differences in shareholder needs and the strength of competitive forces between businesses can lead to differences in both the quantity and quality of information disclosed. This, of course, leads us back to the central purpose of financial reporting standards.

THE NEED FOR A CONCEPTUAL FRAMEWORK

In Chapters 2 and 3 we came across various accounting conventions such as the prudence, historic cost and going concern conventions. These were developed as a practical response to particular problems that were confronted when preparing financial statements. They have stood the test of time and are still of value to preparers today. However, they do not provide, and were never designed to provide, a conceptual framework, or framework of principles, to guide the development of financial statements. As we grapple with increasingly complex financial reporting problems, the need to have a sound understanding of *why* we account for things in a particular way becomes more pressing. Knowing *why* we account, rather than simply *how* we account, is vital if we are to improve the quality of financial statements.

In recent years, much effort has been expended in trying to develop a clear conceptual framework to guide us in the future development of accounting. This framework should provide clear answers to such fundamental questions as:

- Who are the main users of financial statements?
- What is the purpose of financial statements?
- What qualities should financial information possess?
- What are the main elements of financial statements?
- How should these elements be defined, recognised and measured?

If these questions can be answered, accounting rule makers, such as the IASB, will be in a stronger position to identify best practice and to develop more coherent and consistent rules. This should, in turn, increase the credibility of financial reports in the eyes of users. It may even help reduce the possible number of rules.

THE IASB FRAMEWORK

The quest for a conceptual framework began in earnest in the 1970s when the Financial Accounting Standards Board (FASB) in the US devoted a large amount of time and resources to this task. This resulted in a broad framework, which other rule-making bodies, including the IASB, then drew upon to develop their own frameworks. The main aim of the IASB conceptual framework is to provide a firm foundation for the development of International Financial Reporting Standards (IFRSs). It seeks to ensure that IFRSs are underpinned by a clear set of principles. These principles, however, should also provide guidance to preparers when reporting events not covered by a particular IFRS and should help both users and preparers in the interpretation of current IFRSs.

History shows that the IASB conceptual framework is not set in stone. It is revised over time to take account of developments in accounting and the changing business environment. In 2018, the IASB produced its latest version of the *Conceptual Framework for Financial Reporting*. This states that the objective of general purpose financial reporting is '*to provide financial information about the reporting entity that is useful to existing and potential investors, lenders and other creditors in making decisions relating to providing resources to the entity*'. Note that it is the providers of finance that are seen as the primary users of general-purpose financial reports. This is because investors, lenders and other creditors largely rely on these reports to make their investment decisions. Although other users may find general-purpose financial reports useful, the reports are not particularly aimed at them.

The IASB framework sets out the qualitative characteristics that make financial statements useful. These are the same as those discussed in Chapter 1.

The IASB conceptual framework also recognises that producing financial information incurs costs, which should be justified by the benefits provided.

The framework discusses three important accounting conventions that were covered in earlier chapters: going concern, prudence and accruals. It states that financial statements should normally be prepared on the assumption that a business is a going concern. Where, however, this assumption cannot be applied, a different basis for preparation must be used. This basis should then be described in the financial statements. The framework defines prudence as the exercise of caution when making judgements under conditions of uncertainty. More controversially, prudence is viewed, as supporting the concept of neutrality, a component of faithful representation. This is a point to which we shall return later. The IASB framework supports the accruals convention as a better means of assessing past and future performance than a system based on cash inflows and outflows. Nevertheless, information regarding cash flows is seen as useful when assessing financing and investing activities, liquidity and solvency.

The IASB conceptual framework goes on to identify the main elements of financial statements. Those relating to the measurement of financial position are assets, liabilities and equity. Those relating to the measurement of performance are income and expense. Each of these elements is defined and corresponds to those discussed in Chapters 2 and 3. The procedure for recognising each of the main elements, as well as the way in which they should be presented and disclosed in the financial statements, is also discussed.

Finally, the IASB conceptual framework discusses different measurement bases for assets and liabilities. These include historic cost and current value measures, such as current cost and fair value. No attempt is made to support a particular measurement basis. Instead, the framework states that, when selecting a particular measurement basis, the nature of the information produced must be considered. This information must be useful to users, which means that it must possess the qualitative characteristics of relevance, faithful representation and so on. Furthermore, the cost constraint should be applied when selecting an appropriate measurement basis. (See Reference 2 at the end of the chapter.)

Activity 5.9

Which do you think is likely to be the less costly measurement basis to employ: one based on historic cost or one based on current values?

A measurement basis that employs historic cost will normally prove to be far less costly. Establishing the cost of acquisition is usually fairly straightforward, assuming proper records are kept. Establishing current value, on the other hand, can be time consuming and can involve out-of-pocket search costs. (Similar search costs, however, can be incurred under historic cost when calculating impairment and depreciation charges for an asset.)

The general approach to developing a conceptual framework has attracted some criticism. It has been suggested, for example, that the IASB framework is too broad in nature to provide useful guidance for the development of financial reporting standards, or to help deal with emerging accounting issues. It has also been suggested that the framework is merely descriptive and fails to provide theoretical underpinning to the financial statements.

There has also been criticism of specific issues covered. The recent version of the conceptual framework, for example, has sparked controversy for asserting that prudence supports the concept of neutrality. This runs counter to traditional practice, where prudence and neutrality are not seen as comfortable bedfellows. Rather, prudence is taken to mean that more convincing evidence is required for recognising assets and income than for liabilities and expenses. Despite such criticism, however, IASB's efforts in developing a principles-led approach to standard setting are widely supported.

THE AUDITORS' ROLE

Shareholders are required to elect a qualified and independent person or, more usually, a firm to act as **auditors**. The auditors' main duty is to report whether, in their opinion, the financial statements do what they are supposed to do, namely to show a true and fair view of the financial performance, position and cash flows of the company. To form an opinion, auditors must carefully scrutinise the financial statements and the underlying evidence upon which those statements are based. This will involve an examination of the accounting principles followed, the accounting estimates made and the robustness of the company's internal control systems. Following this examination, the auditors should be able to assess the risks of misstatements arising from either fraud or error. Their opinion must accompany the financial statements provided for shareholders and the Registrar of Companies.

The relationship between the shareholders, the directors and the auditors is illustrated in Figure 5.2. This shows that the shareholders elect the directors to act on their behalf, in the day-to-day running of the company. The directors are then required to 'account' to the shareholders on the performance, position and cash flows of the company, on an annual basis. The shareholders also elect the auditors, who then report back to the shareholders.

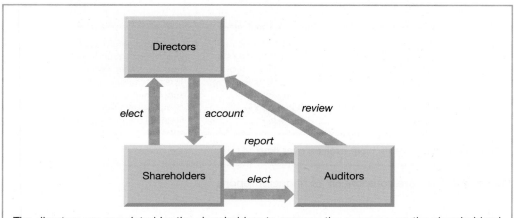

The directors are appointed by the shareholders to manage the company on the shareholders' behalf. The directors are required to report each year to the shareholders, principally by means of financial statements, on the company's performance, position and cash flows. To give greater confidence in the statements, the shareholders also appoint auditors to investigate the reports and to express an opinion on their reliability.

Figure 5.2 The relationship between the shareholders, the directors and the auditors

The audit and its relationship to the management of the company will be discussed in more detail in Chapter 12.

THE FRAMEWORK OF ANNUAL FINANCIAL REPORTS

Over the years, there has been a trend towards greater disclosure in the published annual financial reports of limited companies. Various reasons have been put forward to explain this trend. They include the increasing complexity of business, the increasing sophistication of users and a growing recognition that other groups with a stake in the business, apart from shareholders, require information.

The content of annual financial reports now ventures way beyond the main financial statements. A wide range of information is provided and the reporting boundaries are ill defined. As well as financial information, annual reports often contain information concerning social matters (such as community involvement) and environmental matters (such as carbon emissions). This has led to a growing debate as to whether this kind of information should be included. Questions raised include: 'Does this information fit with the objectives of financial reporting? Should more appropriate forms of reporting be devised to convey this information?'

Whatever the outcome of this debate, it has exposed the need for a more coherent reporting framework. A useful starting point in developing this framework is to identify the core components of annual financial reports. It has been argued that three core components have evolved over time (see Reference 3 at the end of the chapter). These are set out in Figure 5.3.

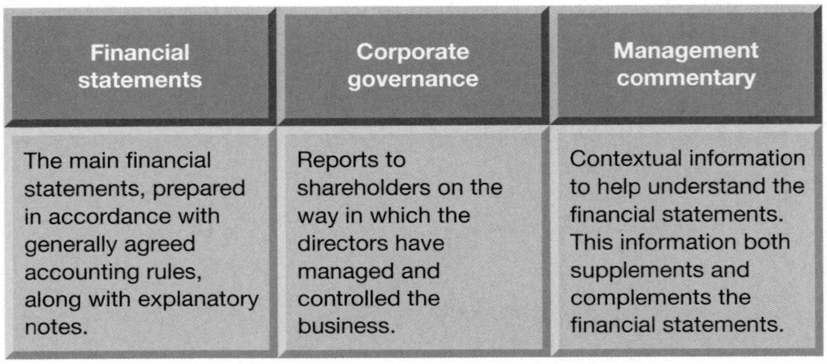

Financial statements	Corporate governance	Management commentary
The main financial statements, prepared in accordance with generally agreed accounting rules, along with explanatory notes.	Reports to shareholders on the way in which the directors have managed and controlled the business.	Contextual information to help understand the financial statements. This information both supplements and complements the financial statements.

Three core components have evolved over time.

Figure 5.3 The core components of financial reports

In the sections that follow, we turn our attention to two of these three components: the main financial statements and management commentary. The third component, corporate governance, will be considered in detail in Chapter 12.

PRESENTING THE FINANCIAL STATEMENTS

Let us begin by examining the main financial statements and the rules that surround them. In doing so, our main focus will be on the IASB rules and, in particular, those contained in IAS 1 *Presentation of Financial Statements*. This standard is very important as it sets out the structure and content of the main financial statements and the principles to be followed in their preparation.

It might be helpful to have a set of the most recent financial statements of a Stock Exchange listed company available as you work through this section. They should all be available on the Internet. Select a listed company that interests you and go to its website.

The financial statements identified in IAS 1 are as set out in Figure 5.4.

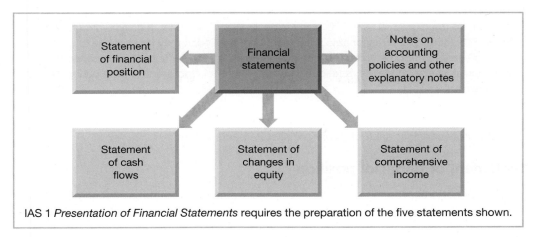

IAS 1 *Presentation of Financial Statements* requires the preparation of the five statements shown.

Figure 5.4 Financial statements required under IAS 1

Each of the financial statements identified in Figure 5.4 should be presented with equal prominence.

According to the standard, these financial statements should normally cover a one-year period and should be accompanied by comparative information for the previous year. Thus, at the end of each reporting period companies should normally produce two of each of the statements, plus the related notes. In practice, virtually all companies satisfy this requirement by showing the equivalent figures for the previous year in a separate column in the current year's statements.

Comparative narrative information should also be provided if needed for a better grasp of current period results – for example, as background to an ongoing legal dispute.

Fair representation

Before considering the various financial statements, it is important to note that IAS 1 contains an overriding requirement that these statements provide a *fair representation* of a company's financial position, financial performance and cash flows. There is a presumption that this will occur as long as they are drawn up in accordance with current IASB standards. Only in very rare circumstances would this not be the case. Where the financial statements have applied all relevant IASB standards, this fact should be clearly stated in the notes.

Activity 5.10

IAS 1 says that the financial statements are required to show a 'fair representation' of financial health. It does not say that the statements should show a 'correct' or an 'accurate' representation of financial health. Why, in your opinion, does it not use those words? (*Hint*: Think of depreciation of non-current assets.)

Accounting can never really be said to be 'correct' or 'accurate' as these words imply that there is a precise value that an asset, claim, revenue or expense could have. This is simply not true in many, if not most, cases.

Depreciation provides a good example of where 'correct' or 'accurate' would not be appropriate. The annual depreciation expense is based on judgements about the future concerning the expected useful life and residual value of an asset. If all relevant factors are taken into account and reasonable judgements are applied, it may be possible to achieve a fair representation of the amount of the cost or fair value of the asset that is consumed for a particular period. However, a uniquely correct figure for depreciation for a period cannot be achieved.

Let us now consider each of the financial statements in turn.

Statement of financial position

IAS 1 does not prescribe the layout for this financial statement but does set out the *minimum* information that should be presented on the face of the statement of financial position. This includes the following:

- property, plant and equipment;
- investment property;
- intangible assets;
- financial assets (such as shares and loan notes of other companies held as assets);
- inventories;
- trade and other receivables;
- cash and cash equivalents;
- trade and other payables;
- provisions (a provision is a liability that is of uncertain timing or amount – such as a possible obligation arising from a legal case against the company that has yet to be determined – we shall consider them in detail in Chapter 7);
- financial liabilities (other than payables and provisions shown above);
- tax liabilities; and
- issued share capital and reserves (equity).

Additional information should also be shown where it is relevant to an understanding of the financial position of the business.

The standard requires that, on the statement of financial position, a distinction is normally made between current assets and non-current assets and between current liabilities and non-current liabilities. However, for certain types of business, such as financial institutions (such as banks), the standard accepts that it may be more appropriate to order items according to their liquidity (that is, their nearness to cash).

Some of the assets and claims listed above may have to be sub-classified to comply with particular standards or because of their size or nature. This means that, sub-classifications are required for assets such as property, plant and equipment, trade receivables and inventories as well as for claims such as provisions and reserves. Certain details relating to share capital, such as the number of issued shares and their nominal value, must also be shown. To avoid cluttering up the statement of financial position, however, this additional information can be shown in the notes. In practice, most companies use notes for this purpose.

Statement of comprehensive income

This statement extends the conventional income statement to include certain other gains and losses that affect shareholders' equity. It may be presented either in the form of a single statement or as two separate statements, comprising an income statement (such as we have considered so far) and a **statement of comprehensive income**. This choice of presentation, however, may be a transitional arrangement as the IASB's preference is for a single statement.

Again, the layout of the statement of comprehensive income is not prescribed, but IAS 1 sets out the *minimum* information to be presented on the face of the statement. This includes:

- revenue;
- finance costs;
- impairment losses;
- profits or losses arising from discontinued operations;
- share of the profits or losses of associates or joint ventures;
- tax expense;
- profit or loss;
- total other comprehensive income (as well as certain items such as the share of other comprehensive income from associate and joint ventures); and
- total comprehensive income (profit or loss plus other comprehensive income).

As a further aid to understanding, all material expenses should be separately disclosed. However, they need not be shown on the face of the income statement, they can appear in the notes to the financial statements. The kind of material items that may require separate disclosure include:

- write-down of inventories to net realisable value;
- write-down of property, plant and equipment;
- disposals of investments;
- restructuring costs;
- discontinued operations; and
- litigation settlements.

This is not an exhaustive list and, in practice, other material expenses may require separate disclosure.

The standard suggests two possible ways in which expenses can be presented on the face of the income statement. Expenses can be presented either:

- according to their nature, for example as depreciation, employee expenses and so on; or
- according to business functions, such as administrative activities and distribution (where, for example, depreciation of delivery lorries will be included in distribution expenses).

The choice between the two possible ways of presenting expenses will depend on which one the directors believe will provide the more relevant and reliable information.

To understand what additional information must be presented, apart from that already in a conventional income statement, we should remember that, broadly, the conventional income statement shows all *realised* gains and losses for the period. It also includes some unrealised losses (that is, losses relating to assets still held).

Activity 5.11

Identify two types of unrealised loss that may appear in the conventional income statement. (*Hint*: Think back to Chapter 3.)

Unrealised losses may include:

- impairment losses following the revaluation of non-current assets; and
- inventories written down to net realisable value.

Unrealised gains and some unrealised losses, however, do not pass through the conventional income statement, but, instead, go directly to equity. In the case of limited companies, a separate revaluation reserve (forming part of total equity) is created for each type of revaluation. In an earlier chapter, we came across an example of an unrealised gain that did not pass through the conventional income statement.

Activity 5.12

Can you think of this example? (*Hint*: Think back to Chapter 2.)

The example that we met earlier is where a business revalues its land and buildings. The gain arising is not shown in the conventional income statement, but is transferred directly to the equity of the owners. (See Activity 2.18 on page 61.) For a limited company, this gain is transferred to a separate revaluation reserve.

Land and buildings are not the only assets to which this rule relates, but these types of asset, in practice, provide the most common example of unrealised gains.

An example of unrealised gains, or losses, that has not been mentioned so far, arises from those arising from holding marketable equity shares. Any such gains, or losses, will bypass the income statement and be taken directly to a reserve.

A weakness of conventional accounting is that no robust principle can be applied in order to determine precisely what should, and what should not, be included in the income statement. Losses arising from the impairment of property, plant and equipment, as we have seen, appear in the income statement. However, losses arising from holding marketable equity shares that are available for sale do not. In principle, there is no significant difference between these two types of loss, but the difference in treatment is ingrained in conventional accounting practice.

The statement of comprehensive income attempts to overcome the deficiencies mentioned by taking into account unrealised gains as well as any unrealised losses not reported in the conventional income statement. It extends the conventional income statement by including these items immediately beneath the profit for the year figure. An illustration of this statement is shown in Example 5.2. Here, expenses are presented according to business function and comparative figures for the previous year are shown alongside the figures for the current year.

Example 5.2

Malik plc
Statement of comprehensive income for the year ended 30 June

	2018 £m	2017 £m
Revenue	100.6	97.2
Cost of sales	(60.4)	(59.1)
Gross profit	40.2	38.1
Other income	4.0	3.5
Distribution expenses	(18.2)	(16.5)

	2018 £m	2017 £m
Administration expenses	(10.3)	(11.2)
Other expenses	(2.1)	(2.4)
Operating profit	13.6	11.5
Finance charges	(2.0)	(1.8)
Profit before tax	11.6	9.7
Tax	(2.9)	(2.4)
Profit for the year	8.7	7.3
Other comprehensive income		
Revaluation of property, plant and equipment	20.3	6.6
Gains on holding equity investments available for sale	12.5	4.0
Tax related to other comprehensive income	(6.0)	(2.0)
Other comprehensive income net of tax	26.8	8.6
Total comprehensive income for the year	35.5	15.9

This example adopts a single-statement approach to presenting comprehensive income. The alternative two-statement approach simply divides the information shown into two separate parts. The income statement, which is the first statement, begins with the revenue and ends with the profit for the reporting period. The statement of comprehensive income, which is the second statement, begins with the profit for the reporting period and ends with the total comprehensive income.

Statement of changes in equity

The statement of changes in equity reveals the changes in share capital and reserves that took place during the reporting period. It reconciles the figures for these items at the beginning of the period with those at the end. This is achieved by showing the effect of the total comprehensive income for the reporting period on the share capital and reserves as well as share issues and redemptions during the period. The effect of dividends during the period may also be shown in this statement, although dividends can be shown in the notes instead.

To see how a statement of changes in equity may be prepared, let us consider Example 5.3.

Example 5.3

At 1 January 2018 Miro plc had the following equity:

Miro plc

	£m
Share capital (£1 ordinary shares)	100
Revaluation reserve	20
Translation reserve	40
Retained earnings	150
Total equity	310

→

During 2018, the company made a profit for the year from normal business operations of £42 million and reported an upward revaluation of property, plant and equipment of £120 million (net of any tax payable if the unrealised gains were realised). A loss on exchange differences on translating the results of foreign operations of £10 million was also reported under 'Other comprehensive income'. To strengthen its financial position, the company issued 50 million ordinary shares during the year at a premium of £0.40. Dividends for the year were £27 million.

This information for 2018 can be set out in a statement of changes in equity as follows:

Statement of changes in equity for the year ended 31 December 2018

	Share capital £m	Share premium £m	Revaluation reserve £m	Translation reserve £m	Retained earnings £m	Total £m
Balance as at 1 January 2018	100	–	20	40	150	310
Changes in equity for 2018						
Profit for the period[1]					42	42
Other comprehensive income for the year[2]			120	(10)		110
Issue of ordinary shares[3]	50	20	–	–	–	70
Dividends[4]	–	–	–	–	(27)	(27)
Balance at 31 December 2018	150	20	140	30	165	505

Notes:
1 The profit for the year is added to retained earnings.
2 The effect of each component of comprehensive income on the various elements of shareholders' equity must be separately disclosed. The revaluation gain and the loss on translating foreign operations are each allocated to a specific reserve.
3 The premium on the share price is transferred to a specific reserve.
4 We have chosen to show dividends in the statement of changes in equity rather than in the notes. They represent an appropriation of equity and are deducted from retained earnings.

Statement of cash flows

The statement of cash flows should help users to assess the ability of a company to generate cash and to assess the company's need for cash. The presentation requirements for this statement are set out in IAS 7 *Statement of Cash Flows,* which we shall consider in some detail in the next chapter.

Notes

The notes play an important role in helping users to understand the financial statements. They will normally contain the following:

■ a declaration that the financial statements comply with relevant financial reporting standards;
■ a summary of the measurement bases used and other significant accounting policies applied (for example, the basis of inventories valuation);
■ any dividends proposed;
■ information concerning the objectives and policies for managing capital;

- information relevant to an understanding of the financial statements but not presented elsewhere;
- information required by accounting standards but not presented elsewhere; and
- key assumptions made concerning the future and major sources of estimation uncertainty.

These notes to accompany the financial statements must be presented in a systematic manner.

General points

The standard provides support for three key accounting conventions when preparing the financial statements. These are:

- the going concern convention;
- the accruals convention (except for the statement of cash flows); and
- the consistency convention.

These conventions were discussed in Chapters 2 and 3.

Finally, to improve the transparency of financial statements, the standard states that:

- offsetting liabilities against assets, or expenses against income, is not allowed unless specifically permitted by a particular accounting standard. It is not acceptable, for example, to offset a bank overdraft against a positive bank balance (where a company has both); and
- material items must be shown separately.

MANAGEMENT COMMENTARY

Many businesses create complex organisational structures, operating systems and financing methods. These features must be accommodated within the financial statements if those statements are to faithfully portray financial position and performance. The statements, as a consequence, can become lengthy, detailed and difficult to understand. To provide a clearer picture, a management commentary can be very helpful. It involves a review of the results and the disclosure of any further information relevant to an understanding of financial health.

Activity 5.13

What do you think are the main qualitative characteristics that information contained in a management commentary should possess? (*Hint*: Think back to Chapter 1.)

To be useful, the information should exhibit the characteristics for accounting information in general, which we identified in Chapter 1. Thus, the information should be relevant and faithfully represented. It should also be comparable, verifiable, timely and understandable. The fact that we may be dealing with narrative information does not alter the need for these characteristics to be present.

In the UK, a management commentary has become part of the financial reporting landscape. We shall now consider two narrative reports, the directors' report and the strategic report, which both supplement and complement the main financial statements. Each of these forms part of the management commentary.

DIRECTORS' REPORT

For many years, the directors have been required to prepare a report to shareholders relating to each reporting period. The content of the **directors' report** is prescribed by law and includes assorted topics such as financing decisions, business activities, future prospects and broader social aspects. For larger companies the report must cover, among other things, the following matters:

- the names of those who were directors during the reporting period;
- any recommended dividend;
- the acquisition by a public listed company of its own shares;
- the involvement of employees in the affairs of the company;
- the employment and training of disabled persons;
- important events affecting the company since the year end;
- financial risk management objectives and policies;
- greenhouse gas emissions by a public listed company;
- likely future developments in the business; and
- research and development activities.

In addition to disclosing the information mentioned above, the directors' report must contain a declaration that the directors are not aware of any other information that the auditors might need in preparing their audit report. There must also be a declaration that the directors have taken steps to ensure that the auditors are aware of all relevant information. The auditors do not carry out an audit of the directors' report. However, they do check to see that the information in the report is consistent with that contained in the audited financial statements.

While this report provides useful information, there is a strong case for revising its role, form and content. It contains a disjointed collection of items that lacks an underlying theme. It seems little more than a repository for miscellaneous items. The structure and presentation of the report is not tightly prescribed and so, in practice, comparisons between companies can be difficult. Furthermore, its relationship with the strategic report, which also provides additional information about the business and which is discussed below, is not clear.

STRATEGIC REPORT

The overall aim of the **strategic report** is to provide context for the financial statements and so help shareholders assess how well the directors have performed in promoting the success of the company. The content of the report has five main themes, which are summarised in Figure 5.5.

Directors of all but the smallest companies are legally obliged to produce a strategic report. The report produced should be fair, balanced and understandable. This means that both positive and negative aspects of performance, position and future prospects should be covered. The report must not be biased and there should be no omissions of important information. Although the report should be concise, it should also be comprehensive. This means that it must convey all information relevant to an understanding of business performance and position.

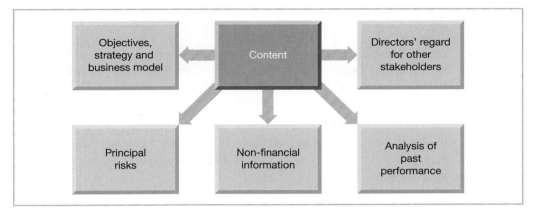

Figure 5.5 Strategic report: content themes

The strategic reports prepared by Stock Exchange listed companies must disclose more than those of other companies, including disclosures concerning its strategy and business model. Figure 5.6 summarises their main features.

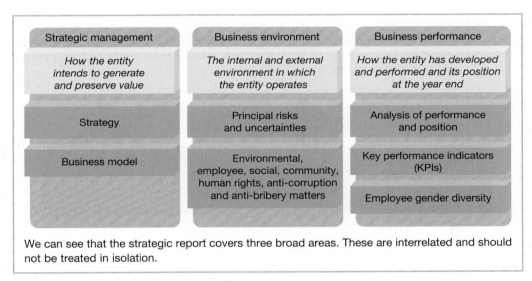

Figure 5.6 The main features of the strategic report

Source: Guidance on the Strategic Report, Financial Reporting Council, July 2018, p. 40.

Activity 5.14

Stock Exchange listed companies are required to disclose more information about their business than other companies? Try to think of at least one reason for this requirement.

Various arguments can be made in favour of greater accountability from such companies. They include:

■ Greater transparency concerning the companies' business operations should help investors make more informed decisions. This is particularly important with Stock Exchange listed companies since their shares are frequently traded. Share prices may, therefore, be set in a more efficient manner, which can contribute towards the smooth functioning of capital markets.

■ Stock Exchange listed companies tend to be larger, have more economic power and have more stakeholders than other companies. Their impact on the economy and society as a whole, therefore, tends to be greater. This, in turn, creates an obligation for them to account more fully for their operations and actions.

We saw earlier that Stock Exchange listed companies must, along with other matters, report on their strategy and business model. **Real World 5.3** illustrates how one listed company reports these elements.

Real World 5.3

Equipped for the future

VP plc is a specialist equipment rental group operating in the UK, Ireland and mainland Europe. It offers products and services to a diverse range of markets including rail, transmission, water, civil engineering, construction, house building, oil and gas. The business has summed up its strategy and business model as follows:

> Our aim is to generate sustainable value creation for shareholders and other stakeholders through our expertise in asset management, by exceeding customer expectations, maintaining and utilising our financial strength and retaining and attracting the best people.

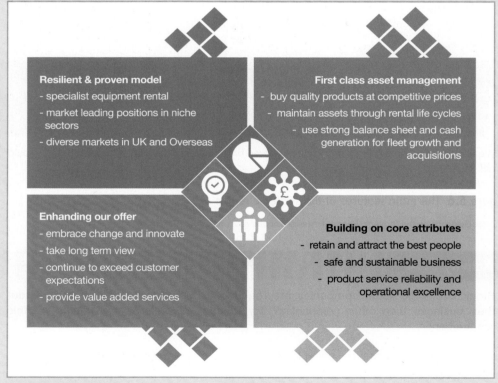

Resilient & proven model
- specialist equipment rental
- market leading positions in niche sectors
- diverse markets in UK and Overseas

First class asset management
- buy quality products at competitive prices
- maintain assets through rental life cycles
- use strong balance sheet and cash generation for fleet growth and acquisitions

Enhanding our offer
- embrace change and innovate
- take long term view
- continue to exceed customer expectations
- provide value added services

Building on core attributes
- retain and attract the best people
- safe and sustainable business
- product service reliability and operational excellence

Figure 5.7 VP plc business model

Source: Business Model and Strategy © Vp plc 2018 www.vpplc.com/investors/business-model-and-strategy [accessed 2 January 2019].

The auditors have the same duty towards the strategic report as that of the directors' report. They must give an opinion as to whether the information it contains is consistent with the financial statements and complies with legal requirements. Where there are any material misstatements they must be disclosed. Both narrative reports are, therefore, subject to independent scrutiny.

ACCOUNTING STANDARDS AND ACCOUNTING POLICIES

In earlier chapters, we have considered a number of financial reporting standards, for example those relating to depreciation and to the valuation of inventories. We shall now discuss two other important standards. Both of these have a broad application and relate to general accounting policies that should be followed.

IAS 8 *Accounting Policies, Changes in Accounting Estimates and Errors*

IAS 8 sets out the criteria for selecting and changing accounting policies and the appropriate treatment for disclosing these policies. It also sets out the treatment for disclosing changes in accounting estimates and for the correction of errors. A key aim of the standard is to improve the comparability of financial statements both over time and between different businesses.

Accounting policies

Accounting policies are the principles, rules and conventions used to prepare the financial statements. Wherever possible, they should be determined by reference to appropriate financial reporting standards. (The standard on inventories, for example, will provide policies to be followed in this area.) In the absence of an appropriate standard, managers must make suitable judgements to ensure that users receive relevant and reliable information.

The general rule is that, once a particular policy has been selected and applied, it should not be changed. This is designed to ensure consistency in approach. However, an accounting policy may be changed where:

1 it is required by a new financial reporting standard; or
2 it will result in more relevant and reliable information being provided to users.

If a new financial reporting standard requires changes to be made, the name of the standard, and any transitional arrangements, should be disclosed. If it is a voluntary change, the reasons why it will result in more relevant and reliable information should be disclosed. In both cases, the nature of the change in policy and the amount of the adjustment on relevant items and on earnings per share for both the current and the prior period should be disclosed.

Changes in accounting estimates

Managers are normally required to make various estimates when preparing financial statements.

Activity 5.15

What estimates will normally be required? Try to think of at least three. (*Hint*: Think back to Chapter 3.)

They will normally include estimates of:

- the amount of bad debts incurred;
- the net realisable value of inventories;
- the useful life of non-current assets;
- the fair value of non-current assets;
- the residual value of non-current assets; and
- the amount of accrued expenses (such as electricity) incurred.

These estimates may need revision in the light of new information. If a revised estimate affects assets, liabilities or equity, it should be adjusted in the period of the change. If it affects profit, it should be revised in the period affected. This may be in the period of change and/or in future periods.

Activity 5.16

Try to think of an example of an estimate that will normally affect only the period of change and an example of one that will normally affect the period of change and future periods.

Normally, estimates of bad debts will only affect the period of change whereas a change in the estimated useful life of a non-current asset will affect the period of change and future periods.

Both the nature and amount of a change in estimate affecting the current period or future periods should be disclosed. If it is impracticable to estimate the amount, this fact must be disclosed.

Errors

Errors are omissions or misstatements in the financial statements. They may arise for a variety of reasons, which include arithmetical mistakes, oversights, misinterpretation of facts and fraud. Sometimes these errors are significant in nature and/or size and are not discovered until a later period. In such a situation, the general rule is that the relevant figures for the earlier period(s) in which the errors occurred should be restated for comparison purposes. If the errors occurred before the prior periods presented for comparison, then the opening balances of assets, liabilities and equity for the earliest prior period presented should be restated. The nature of the errors and their effect on relevant items and on earnings per share for the current and the prior period(s) should also be disclosed.

IAS 10 *Events After the Reporting Period*

The main aim of IAS 10 is to clarify the circumstances in which financial statements should be adjusted for events that took place after the reporting period (or accounting period). The standard deals with events that occur between the end of the reporting period and the date when the financial statements are authorised to be issued both to the shareholders and to the general public. Two types of events are identified:

1 those providing evidence of conditions that existed before the end of the reporting period (adjusting events); and
2 those indicating conditions arising after the end of the reporting period (non-adjusting events).

The standard requires that financial statements should incorporate only the adjusting events.

Activity 5.17

Vorta plc received the following information between the end of the reporting period and the date at which the financial statements were authorised for issue:

1 Inventories which were reported in the statement of financial position at an estimated net realisable value of £250,000 were sold immediately after the year end for £200,000.
2 There was a decline of £150,000 in the market value of investments after the end of the reporting period.
3 An error was discovered which indicated that the trade receivables figure on the statement of financial position was understated by £220,000.

Which of the above are adjusting events?

Items 1 and 3 meet the definition of an adjusting event whereas item 2 meets the definition of a non-adjusting event. This is because, with items 1 and 3, we have received additional information on the position at the year end. With item 2, a change has occurred *after the* year end.

The standard clarifies two important points concerning events after the reporting period. First, if a dividend is declared for equity shareholders after the reporting period, it should not be treated as a liability in the financial statements. In other words, it is a non-adjusting event. In the past, it had been normal practice to treat such dividends as liabilities. Secondly, if it becomes clear after the reporting period that the business will cease trading, the going concern assumption will not apply. As a result, the financial statements must be prepared using a different basis for valuation. Assets, for example, would normally have to be shown at their estimated realisable values.

The date at which the financial statements were authorised for issue to shareholders and to others must be disclosed. This is important to understanding what events should and should not be included. There should also be disclosure of who authorised the issue.

Activity 5.18

Who do you think will normally authorise the issue of the financial statements?

It is normally the board of directors.

Where non-adjusting events are significant, they are capable of influencing users' decisions. The standard therefore requires significant non-adjusting events to be disclosed by way of a note. A major restructuring, a plan to discontinue an operation and the proposed purchase of a major asset are examples of non-adjusting events that might be disclosed. The standard requires the nature of the event and its likely financial effect be disclosed. If the financial effect cannot be reliably estimated, this fact should be disclosed.

Real World 5.4 sets out two transactions described in the notes to the financial statements of A G Barr plc, makers of the well-known drink IRN-BRU. They deal with non-adjusting events occurring between the statement of financial position date and the date of issue of the financial statements.

Real World 5.4

Non-adjusting events

In February 2017, the Group entered into three revolving credit facilities over periods of 3 to 5 years with Royal Bank of Scotland plc, Bank of Scotland plc and HSBC Bank plc. These facilities provide £60m of Sterling debt facilities to 2019/20, reducing to £20m for the period to 2021/22.

On 1 February 2017, the Group completed on the sale of the Walthamstow distribution site. The asset was held for sale at 28 January 2017. Total proceeds of £3.8m were received against a net book value of £1.3m, giving rise to a gain on sale of £2.5m, which will be recognised in the year to 27 January 2018. The Group has entered into a 3-year operating lease to continue to operate from the site for the short term.

Source: A G Barr plc, Annual Report and Accounts 2017 p.128.

Figure 5.8 summarises the main points to be considered when applying IAS 10.

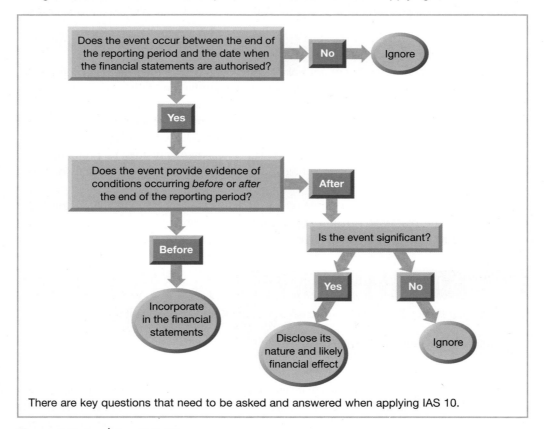

There are key questions that need to be asked and answered when applying IAS 10.

Figure 5.8 Applying IAS 10

CREATIVE ACCOUNTING

Despite the proliferation of accounting rules and the independent checks that are imposed, concerns over the quality of published financial statements surface from time to time. There are occasions when directors apply particular accounting policies, or structure particular transactions, in such a way as to portray a picture of financial health that is in line with what they want users to see, rather than what is a true and fair view of financial position and performance. Misrepresenting the performance and position of a business in this way is often called creative accounting and it poses a major problem for accounting rule makers and for society generally.

Activity 5.19

Why might the directors of a company engage in creative accounting? Try to think of at least two reasons.

There are many reasons, including:

- to get around restrictions (for example, to report sufficient profit to pay a dividend);
- to avoid government action (for example, the taxation of profits);
- to hide poor management decisions;
- to achieve sales revenue or profit targets, thereby ensuring that performance bonuses are paid to the directors;
- to attract new share capital or long-term borrowing by showing an apparently healthy financial position; and
- to satisfy the demands of major investors concerning levels of return.

Creative accounting methods

There are many ways in which unscrupulous directors can manipulate the financial statements. They usually involve adopting novel or unorthodox practices for reporting key elements of the financial statements, such as revenue, expenses, assets and liabilities. They may also involve the use of complicated or obscure transactions in an attempt to hide the underlying economic reality. The manipulation carried out may be designed either to bend the rules or to break them.

   We shall now consider some of the more important ways in which rules may be bent or broken.

Misstating revenue

Some creative accounting methods are designed to overstate the revenue for a period. These methods often involve the early recognition of sales revenue or the reporting of sales transactions that have no real substance. **Real World 5.5** provides examples of both types of revenue manipulation.

The manipulation of revenue has been at the heart of many of the accounting scandals recently exposed. Given its critical role in the measurement of performance, this is, perhaps, not surprising. **Real World 5.6** discusses how the reported revenues of one UK software business have been hotly disputed. It was acquired by a US computer giant, which concluded that, as a result of this and other alleged irregularities, the price paid was far too much. It, therefore, reported a huge impairment charge soon after the acquisition.

deals later fell through, while another was completed for less than the amount Autonomy recorded.

Under one of the contracts, Autonomy was said to have booked $11 million in revenue at the end of March 2010 on a transaction involving MicroTech and an unnamed end customer. The final sale failed to materialise, with Autonomy only receiving $500,000 on the contract. After an auditor queried the large uncollected debt from MicroTech at the end of the year, according to the claims, Autonomy made a payment of $9.6 million to the contractor under the heading 'Advanced technology innovation centre' and MicroTech wired back the same amount to cover some of the money it owed Autonomy.

Autonomy booked a further $15.7 million of revenue in two instalments on the final days of March and June the following year on a separate deal involving Capax, even though the ultimate sales transactions had not been completed, according to the Air Force document. The deal was later completed for $14.1 million.

In the third case, a $1.95 million sale was booked in December 2010, six months before it was finalised.

In November 2018, Mike Lynch was charged with fraud by a federal court in Los Angeles.

Massaging expenses

Some creative accounting methods focus on the manipulation of expenses. Those expenses that rely on directors' estimates of the future or their choice of accounting policy are particularly vulnerable to manipulation.

Activity 5.20

Can you identify the kind of expenses where the directors make estimates or choices in the ways described? Think back to Chapter 3 and try to identify at least two.

These include certain expenses that we discussed in Chapter 3, such as:

- depreciation of property, plant and equipment;
- amortisation of intangible assets, such as goodwill;
- inventories (cost of sales); and
- allowances for trade receivables.

By changing estimates about the future (for example, the useful life or residual value of an asset), or by changing accounting policies (for example, switching from FIFO to AVCO), it may be possible to derive an expense figure and, consequently, a profit figure, that suits the directors.

The incorrect 'capitalisation' of expenses may also be used as a means of manipulation. This involves treating expenses as if they were amounts incurred to acquire or develop non-current assets, rather than amounts consumed during the period. Businesses that build their own assets are often best placed to undertake this form of malpractice.

Real World 5.7 provides an example of one business that capitalised expenses on a huge scale.

Real World 5.7

Sorry – wrong numbers

One particularly notorious case of capitalising expenses is alleged to have occurred in the financial statements of WorldCom (now renamed MCI). This company, which is a large US telecommunications business, is alleged to have overstated profits by treating certain operating expenses, such as basic network maintenance, as capital expenditure. This happened over a fifteen-month period during 2001 and 2002. To correct for this overstatement, profits had to be reduced by a massive $3.8 billion.

Source: Based on two personal views on WorldCom posted on the ft.com site, 27 June 2002.
© The Financial Times Limited 2002. All rights reserved.

Concealing 'bad news'

Some creative accounting methods focus on the concealment of losses or liabilities. The financial statements can look much healthier if these can somehow be eliminated. One way of doing this is to create a 'separate' entity that will take over the losses or liabilities.

Real World 5.8 describes how one large business concealed losses and liabilities.

Real World 5.8

For a very special purpose

Perhaps the most well-known case of concealment of losses and liabilities concerned the Enron Corporation. This was a large US energy business that used 'special purpose entities' (SPEs) as a means of concealment. SPEs were used by Enron to rid itself of problem assets that were falling in value, such as its broadband operations. In addition, liabilities were transferred to these entities to help Enron's statement of financial position look healthier. The company had to keep its gearing ratios (the relationship between borrowing and equity) within particular limits to satisfy credit-rating agencies and SPEs were used to achieve this. The SPEs used for concealment purposes were not independent of the company and should have been consolidated in the statement of financial position of Enron, along with their losses and liabilities.

When these, and other accounting irregularities, were discovered in 2001, there was a restatement of Enron's financial performance and position to reflect the consolidation of the SPEs, which had previously been omitted. As a result of this restatement, the company recognised $591 million in losses over the preceding four years and an additional $628 million worth of liabilities at the end of 2000.

The company collapsed at the end of 2001.

Source: William Thomas, C. (2002) The rise and fall of Enron, *Journal of Accountancy,* vol. 194, no. 3. This article represents the opinions of the author, which are not necessarily those of the Texas Society of Certified Public Accountants.

Misstating assets

There are various ways in which assets may be misstated. These include:

- using asset values that are higher than the assets' fair market values;
- capitalising costs that should have been written off as expenses, as described earlier; and
- recording assets that are not owned, or which do not exist.

Real World 5.9 describes how one large business is alleged to have overstated some of its assets.

Real World 5.9

It's worth . . . less

Anglo-Australian mining giant Rio Tinto has been charged with fraud in the US and fined £27.4 million in the UK after being accused of overstating the value of African coal assets. The FTSE 100 company and two of its top former executives were charged in the US of hiding losses by inflating the value of assets in Mozambique, which Rio bought in 2011 for $3.7 billion and sold a few years later for $50 million.

America's financial regulator, the Securities and Exchange Commission, filed a complaint in federal court in Manhattan. It alleges that Rio Tinto, its former chief executive, Tom Albanese, and its former chief financial officer, Guy Elliott, failed to follow accounting standards and company policies to accurately value and record its assets.

As the project began to suffer setbacks, resulting in the rapid decline of the value of the coal assets, Albanese and Elliott sought to hide or delay disclosure of the nature and extent of the adverse developments from Rio Tinto's board of directors, auditors, and investors, the SEC alleges.

'Rio Tinto and its top executives allegedly failed to come clean about an unsuccessful deal that was made under their watch. They tried to save their own careers at the expense of investors by hiding the truth,' said Steven Peikin, co-director of the SEC's enforcement division.

The miner said it intends to 'vigorously defend itself' against the allegations.

Source: Extract from: Rio Tinto charged with fraud in US and fined £27.4m in UK, www.theguardian.com, 18 October 2017.

Inadequate disclosure

Directors may misrepresent or try to conceal certain information. This may relate to commitments made, illegal behaviour, key changes in accounting policies or estimates, significant events and so on. **Real World 5.10** reveals how one large bank allegedly tried to conceal its actions in order to avoid the legal consequences.

Figure 5.9 summarises the main methods of creative accounting.

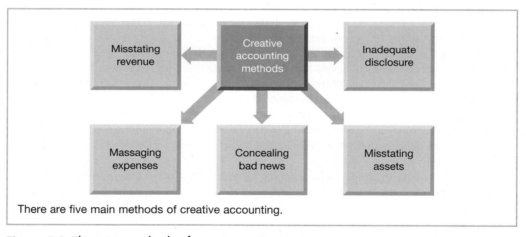

There are five main methods of creative accounting.

Figure 5.9 The main methods of creative accounting

Checking for creative accounting

When the financial statements of a business are being examined, a number of checks may be carried out to help gain a feel for their reliability. These can include checks to see whether:

■ the reported profits are significantly higher than the operating cash flows for the period (as shown in the business's statement of cash flows), which may suggest that profits have been overstated;

- the tax charge is low in relation to reported profits, which may suggest, again, that profits are overstated, although there may be other, more innocent, explanations;
- the valuation methods used for assets held are based on historic cost or fair values, and, if the latter approach has been used, why and how the fair values were determined;
- there have been changes in accounting policies over the period, particularly in key areas such as revenue recognition, inventories valuation and depreciation;
- the accounting policies adopted are in line with those adopted by the rest of the industry;
- the auditors' report gives a 'clean bill of health' to the financial statements; and
- the 'small print' (that is the notes to the financial statements) is being used to hide significant events or changes.

Real World 5.11 describes the emphasis that one analyst places on this last check.

Real World 5.11

Taking note

Alistair Hodgson, investment manager at private client stockbroker Pilling and Co, says 'I almost look at the notes more than I look at the main figures at first. The notes tend to hold the key to anything that looks strange. I look to pick out things that the auditor has told the company to declare – the kind of thing they might not want to declare, but they have got to do so in order to make the accounts honest.'

 Source: Smith, S. (2005) It pays to read between the lines, *Financial Times,* 17 September.

Checks may also be carried out to provide confirmation of positive financial health. These may include checks to see whether:

- the business is paying increased dividends; and/or
- the directors are buying shares in the business.

Although the various checks described are useful, they cannot be used to guarantee the reliability of the financial statements. Some creative accounting practices may be very deeply seated and may go undetected for years.

Creative accounting and economic growth

Some years ago, there was a wave of creative accounting scandals, particularly in the US but also in Europe. It seems, however, that this wave has now subsided. As a result of action taken by various regulatory bodies, the behaviour of companies is now subject to stricter controls. Corporate governance procedures have been strengthened and tighter financial reporting rules have been imposed. Creative accounting has now become a more risky and difficult process for those who attempt it. However, it will never disappear completely and a further wave of creative accounting scandals may occur in the future.

The wave of creative accounting scandals coincided with a period of strong economic growth. During good economic times, investors and auditors become less vigilant, making it easier to manipulate the figures. We must not, therefore, become too complacent. Things may change again when we next experience a period of strong growth.

Real World 5.12 concludes this chapter by identifying some key features of businesses that engage in creative accounting.

Self-assessment question 5.1

You have overheard the following statements:

(a) 'Dividends announced between the end of the reporting period and the date at which the financial reports are authorised for publication, which relate to the reporting period just ended, should be treated as a liability in the statement of financial position at the end of that period.'

(b) 'IAS 1 provides support for three key accounting conventions – accruals, historic cost and consistency.'

(c) 'IAS 1 permits bank overdrafts to be offset against positive bank balances when preparing the statement of financial position.'

(d) 'Accounting policies can only be changed if it is required by a new financial reporting standard.'

(e) 'All non-adjusting events occurring between the end of the reporting period and the date at which the financial statements are authorised for issue should be ignored.'

(f) 'The strategic report should be prepared by the company's auditors rather than by the directors of the company.'

Required:
Critically comment on each of the statements.

The solution to this question can be found at the back of the book, starting on page 525.

SUMMARY

The main points of this chapter may be summarised as follows:

Directors' duty

- Separation of ownership from day-to-day control creates a need for directors to be accountable.
- To fulfil this need, the directors have a duty to prepare and publish financial statements.
- Shareholders have a right to receive a copy of the published financial statements.

The need for accounting rules

- Accounting rules are necessary in order to avoid unacceptable accounting practices and to improve the comparability of financial statements.
- This should give greater confidence in the integrity of financial statements.

Source of accounting rules

- The International Accounting Standards Board (IASB) has become an important source of rules.
- Company law and the London Stock Exchange are also sources of rules for UK companies.

Problems with standards

- Various problems may arise from using financial reporting standards:
  - they may inhibit change
  - they may impose false conformity
  - they involve consensus seeking
  - they can be costly
  - they can introduce complexity.
- The alternative is to allow accounting choice. This, however, leads to the risk of manipulation, inadequate disclosure and lack of comparability.

Conceptual framework

- This helps to underpin financial reporting standards.
- The IASB framework sets out the objective of general purpose financial reports, the primary user groups, the qualitative characteristics, the elements of financial statements and the different measurement bases that may be used.

The role of auditors

- Auditors are required to report to shareholders whether, in their opinion, the financial statements provide a true and fair view of the financial health of a business.

- They are elected by the shareholders.

Financial reporting framework

- Company reports consist of three core components: the main financial statements, corporate governance disclosure and a management commentary.

Presenting financial statements

- IAS 1 sets out the structure and content of financial statements.

- It requires preparation of a statement of financial position, a statement of comprehensive income, a statement of changes in equity and a statement of cash flows. In addition, explanatory notes are required.

- The financial statements must provide a fair representation of the financial health of a company, which will only normally be achieved by sticking to relevant IASB standards.

- IAS 1 sets out information to be shown in the various financial statements and some of the accounting conventions and principles to be followed in preparing the statements.

Management commentary

- A management commentary reviews the financial results. It aims to complement and supplement the financial statements.

- The directors' report contains information of a financial and non-financial nature. It includes such diverse matters as any recommended dividend, the involvement of employees in company affairs and important events since the year end. It lacks any underlying theme.

- The strategic report aims to provide context for the financial statements and so help shareholders assess how well the directors have performed in promoting the success of the company. It should be fair, balanced and understandable.

- The strategic report of Stock Exchange listed companies must provide additional information, including the strategy and business model adopted.

Accounting standards and accounting policies

- IAS 8 sets out the criteria for selecting and changing accounting policies.

- It also sets out the treatment for disclosing changes in accounting estimates and for the correction of errors.

- IAS 10 aims to clarify when financial statements should be adjusted for events that took place after the reporting period.

- Only events that provide evidence of conditions before the end of the reporting period lead to adjustments to the financial statements.

Creative accounting

- This involves using accounting practices to show what the directors would like users to see rather than what is a fair representation of reality.

- The main forms of creative accounting involve misstating revenues, massaging expenses, concealing bad news, misstating assets and inadequate disclosure.

REFERENCES

1 *Analysis of the IFRS jurisdiction profiles,* www.ifrs.org [accessed 2 January 2019].
2 International Accounting Standards Board (2018) *Conceptual Framework for Financial Reporting,* pp. 28–31.
3 FRC (2012). *Thinking about disclosures in a broader context: A roadmap for a disclosure framework,* Discussion paper, Financial Reporting Council, www.frc.org.uk, October.

FURTHER READING

If you would like to explore the topics covered in this chapter in more depth, we recommend the following:

Alexander, D., Britton, A., Jorissen, A. Hoogendoorn and Van Mourik C. (2017) *International Financial Reporting and Analysis,* 7th edn, Cengage Learning EMEA, Chapters 2, 3, and 8.

Elliott, B. and Elliott, J. (2017) *Financial Accounting and Reporting,* 18th edn, Pearson, Chapters 3, 6 and 7.

International Accounting Standards Board, *The Conceptual Framework for Financial Reporting,* March 2018.

International Accounting Standards Board, *2017 A Guide through IFRS (Green Book),* IAS 1 *Presentation of Financial Statements.*

CRITICAL REVIEW QUESTIONS

Solutions to these questions can be found at the back of the book, starting on page 536.

5.1 There is a risk that managers will be inhibited from providing meaningful management commentaries. Instead, their commentaries may be uninformative and written in a bland form. Can you think why managers may feel inhibited? What might be done to overcome any concerns they may have?

5.2 'Searching for an agreed conceptual framework for accounting rules is likely to be a journey without an ending.' Discuss.

5.3 Why are accounting rules needed when preparing financial statements? Can you see any difficulties arising from harmonising accounting rules between different countries?

5.4 What are the main methods of creative accounting? How might the problem of creative accounting in developing countries be mitigated by harmonising accounting rules across national boundaries?

Solutions to exercises with coloured numbers can be found at the back of the book, starting on page 545.

Basic-level exercises

5.1 'Financial reporting standards eliminate the need for accountants to make judgements and so lower their professional status.' Do you agree?

5.2 The size of annual financial reports published by limited companies has increased steadily over the years. Can you think of any reasons, apart from the increasing volume of accounting regulation, why this has occurred?

Intermediate-level exercises

5.3 Thor plc has the following events occurring between the end of the reporting period and the date the financial statements were authorised for issue:

1 The discovery that, during the reporting period, an employee had defrauded the business of £120,000.
2 The bankruptcy of a customer who owes the business £280,000. This sum was outstanding at the end of the reporting period.
3 A fire occurring after the reporting period that destroyed a large factory owned by Thor plc.
4 An increase in the value of land held by Thor plc by £10 million that occurred as a result of a change in the planning laws, which occurred after the end of the reporting period.

According to IAS 10 *Events After the Reporting Period,* how should each of these events be treated?

5.4 What are the potential benefits arising from developing a conceptual framework for accounting? What are the possible drawbacks?

Advanced-level exercises

5.5 The following information was extracted from the financial statements of I. Ching (Booksellers) plc for the year to 31 May 2018:

	£000
Finance charges	40
Cost of sales	460
Distribution expenses	110
Revenue	943
Administrative expenses	212
Other expenses	25
Gain on revaluation of property, plant and equipment	20
Loss on foreign currency translations on foreign operations	15
Tax on profit for the year	24
Tax on other components of comprehensive income	1

Required:

Prepare a statement of comprehensive income for the year ended 31 May 2018 that is set out in accordance with the requirements of IAS 1 *Presentation of Financial Statements*.

5.6 Manet plc had the following share capital and reserves as at 1 June 2017:

	£m
Share capital (£0.25 ordinary shares)	250
Share premium account	50
Revaluation reserve	120
Currency translation reserve	15
Retained earnings	380
Total equity	815

During the year to 31 May 2018, the company revalued property, plant and equipment upwards by £30 million and made a loss on foreign exchange translation of foreign operations of £5 million (and which is treated as other comprehensive income.). The company made a profit for the year from normal operations of £160 million and the dividend for the year to 31 May 2018 was £80 million.

Required:

Prepare a statement of changes in equity for the year ended 31 May 2018 in accordance with the requirements of IAS 1 *Presentation of Financial Statements*.

5.7 Professor Myddleton argues that financial reporting standards should be limited to disclosure requirements and should not impose rules on companies as to how to measure particular items in the financial statements. He states:

> *The volume of accounting instructions is already high. If things go on like this, where will we be in 20 or 30 years' time? On balance I conclude we would be better off without any standards on accounting measurement. There could still be some disclosure requirements for listed companies, though probably less than now.*

Do you agree with this idea? Discuss.

5.8 You have overheard the following statements:

(a) 'The role of independent auditors is to prepare the financial statements of the company.'

(b) 'International Accounting Standards (IASs) apply to all UK companies, but London Stock Exchange listed companies must also adhere to International Financial Reporting Standards (IFRSs).'

(c) 'All listed companies in the European Union states must follow IASs and IFRS Standards.'

(d) 'According to IAS 1, companies' financial statements must show an "accurate representation" of what they purport to show.'

(e) 'IAS 1 leaves it to individual companies to decide the format that they use in the statement of financial position.'

(f) 'The statement of changes in equity deals with unrealised profits and gains, for example an upward revaluation of a non-current asset.'

Critically comment on each of these statements.

Chapter 6

MEASURING AND REPORTING CASH FLOWS

INTRODUCTION

This chapter is devoted to the first major financial statement identified in Chapter 2: the statement of cash flows. This statement reports the movements of cash during a period and the effect of these movements on the cash position of the business. It is an important statement because cash is vital to the survival of a business. Without cash, a business cannot operate.

In this chapter, we shall see how the statement of cash flows is prepared and how the information that it contains may be interpreted. We shall also see why the inability of the income statement, to identify and explain cash flows, makes a separate statement necessary.

The statement of cash flows is being considered after the chapters on limited companies because the format of the statement requires an understanding of this type of business.

Learning outcomes

When you have completed this chapter, you should be able to:

- discuss the crucial importance of cash to a business;
- explain the nature of the statement of cash flows and discuss how it can be helpful in identifying cash flow problems;
- prepare a statement of cash flows; and
- interpret a statement of cash flows.

THE STATEMENT OF CASH FLOWS

The statement of cash flows is a fairly late addition to the annual published financial statements. At one time, companies were only required to publish an income statement and a statement of financial position. It seems the prevailing view was that all the financial information needed by users would be contained within these two statements. This view may have been based partly on the assumption that, if a business is profitable, it will also have plenty of cash. While in the long run this is likely to be true, it is not necessarily true in the short to medium term.

We saw in Chapter 3 that the income statement sets out the revenue and expenses, for the period, rather than the cash inflows and outflows. This means that the profit (or loss), which represents the difference between the revenue and expenses for the period, may have little or no relation to the cash generated for the period.

To illustrate this point, let us take the example of a business making a sale (generating revenue). This may well lead to an increase in wealth that will be reflected in the income statement. However, if the sale is made on credit, no cash changes hands – at least not at the time of the sale. Instead, the increase in wealth is reflected in another asset: trade receivables. Furthermore, if an item of inventories is the subject of the sale, wealth is lost to the business through the reduction in inventories. This means that an expense is incurred in making the sale, which will also be shown in the income statement. Once again, however, no cash changes hands at the time of sale. For such reasons, profit and cash generated during a period rarely go hand in hand.

Activity 6.1 helps to underline how particular transactions and events can affect profit and cash for a period differently.

Activity 6.1

The following is a list of business/accounting events. In each case, state the immediate effect (increase, decrease or none) on both profit and cash:

	Effect on profit	on cash
1 Repayment of borrowings	_____	_____
2 Making a profitable sale on credit	_____	_____
3 Buying a non-current asset on credit	_____	_____
4 Receiving cash from a credit customer (trade receivable)	_____	_____
5 Depreciating a non-current asset	_____	_____
6 Buying some inventories for cash	_____	_____
7 Making a share issue for cash	_____	_____

You should have come up with the following:

	Effect on profit	on cash
1 Repayment of borrowings	none	decrease
2 Making a profitable sale on credit	increase	none
3 Buying a non-current asset on credit	none	none

	Effect	
	on profit	*on cash*
4 Receiving cash from a credit customer (trade receivable)	none	increase
5 Depreciating a non-current asset	decrease	none
6 Buying some inventories for cash	none	decrease
7 Making a share issue for cash	none	increase

The reasons for these answers are as follows:

1 Repaying borrowings requires that cash be paid to the lender. This means that two figures in the statement of financial position will be affected, but none in the income statement.
2 Making a profitable sale on credit will increase the sales revenue and profit figures. No cash will change hands at this point, however.
3 Buying a non-current asset on credit affects neither the cash balance nor the profit figure.
4 Receiving cash from a credit customer increases the cash balance and reduces the credit customer's balance. Both of these figures are on the statement of financial position. The income statement is unaffected.
5 Depreciating a non-current asset means that an expense is recognised. This causes a decrease in profit. No cash is paid or received.
6 Buying some inventories for cash means that the value of the inventories will increase and the cash balance will decrease by a similar amount. Profit is not affected.
7 Making a share issue for cash increases the shareholders' equity and increases the cash balance. Profit is not affected.

From what we have seen so far, it is clear that the income statement is not the place to look if we are to gain insights about cash movements over time. We need a separate financial statement.

WHY IS CASH SO IMPORTANT?

It is worth asking why cash is so important. In one sense, it is just another asset that the business needs to enable it to function. Hence, it is no different from inventories or non-current assets.

The importance of cash lies in the fact that people will only normally accept cash in settlement of their claims. If a business wants to employ people, it must pay them in cash. If it wants to buy a new non-current asset, it must normally pay the seller in cash (perhaps after a short period of credit). When businesses fail, it is the lack of cash to pay amounts owed that really pushes them under. Cash generation is vital for businesses to survive and to exploit commercial opportunities. This is what makes cash the pre-eminent business asset. During an economic downturn, the ability to generate cash takes on even greater importance. Banks become more cautious in their lending and businesses with weak cash flows often find it difficult to obtain finance.

Real World 6.1 is taken from an article by Luke Johnson, who is a 'serial entrepreneur'. Among other things, he was closely involved with taking Pizza Express from a business that owned just 12 restaurants to over 250 and, at the same time, increasing its share price from 40 pence to over £9. In the article he highlights the importance of cash flow in managing a business.

Real World 6.2 is taken from a column written by John Timpson, which appeared in the *Daily Telegraph*. Timpson is the chief executive of the successful, high street shoe repairing and key cutting business that bears his name. In the column he highlights the importance of cash reporting in managing the business.

Real World 6.2

Cash is key

Everyday the figure I look for is our bank balance. By concentrating on the cash, I can stay in control of the business.

Keeping a close eye on the cash not only gives peace of mind, it also provides the best measure of your company's performance.

The aim of the game is to make money – in other words, to create cash. The trick is to compare your bank balance with exactly the same date last year and be able to explain the difference.

My daily cash flow email compares the bank balance with the figure we forecast yesterday. I don't like surprises, but if things go awry, I want the surprise spotted straight away.

Source: Timpson, J. (2016) Ask John, *The Daily Telegraph Business*, 29 August.

Real World 6.3 reveals how small and medium-sized UK businesses often suffer from acute cash flow problems. This can arise for various reasons, including a lack the financial expertise, a weak bargaining position when negotiating with large customers and underfunding.

Real World 6.3

Big problems for small businesses

Four-in-ten (38%) small and medium-sized businesses (SMEs) have suffered cashflow problems over the past two years, according to new research by Amicus Commercial Finance, the specialist lender of flexible working capital to SMEs. The figure rises to two-thirds (65%) among medium-sized firms with between 50 and 250 staff.

According to the study conducted among 500 small businesses owners, over the past two years one-in-seven (15%) are still suffering liquidity problems and 12% either came close to or became insolvent. Small businesses recognise the threat cashflow problems can pose; nearly three-quarters (71%) say it is the biggest risk they face.

On a sector basis, 35% of finance and accounting firms report that are affected by cash-flow problems. Regionally, companies in the North East have been the worst hit by cashflow shortages.

The biggest challenge caused by cashflow shortages is paying suppliers, cited by 41% of business owners. This is followed by meeting debt repayments (30%), buying inventory (29%) and paying staff (24%). One-in-five (18%) said they had lost contracts due to cashflow problems.

Source: Amicus plc (2016) Cashflow problems undermine four in ten small firms, https://amicusplc.co.uk, 7 December.

Having established that cash is of the utmost importance to businesses of all sizes, let us now go on to examine the financial statement that deals with movements in this asset.

THE MAIN FEATURES OF THE STATEMENT OF CASH FLOWS

The statement of cash flows summarises the inflows and outflows of cash (and cash equivalents) for a business over a period. To help user understanding, these cash flows are divided into categories (for example, those relating to investments in non-current assets). Cash inflows and outflows falling within each category are added together and the totals for each category are reported on the statement of cash flows. By adding the totals for each category together, an overall total is achieved that reveals the net increase or decrease in cash (and cash equivalents) over the period.

When describing in detail how this statement is prepared and presented, we shall follow the requirements of International Accounting Standard (IAS) 7 *Statement of Cash Flows*. This standard applies to Stock Exchange listed companies.

A DEFINITION OF CASH AND CASH EQUIVALENTS

IAS 7 defines cash as notes and coins in hand and deposits in banks and similar institutions that are accessible to the business on demand. Cash equivalents are short-term, highly liquid investments that can be readily convertible to known amounts of cash. They are also subject to an insignificant risk of changes of value. Figure 6.1 sets out this definition of cash equivalents in the form of a decision chart.

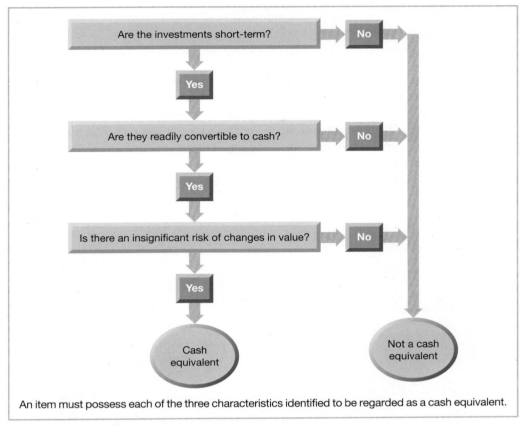

An item must possess each of the three characteristics identified to be regarded as a cash equivalent.

Figure 6.1 Decision chart for identifying cash equivalents

Activity 6.2 should clarify the types of items that fall within the definition of 'cash equivalents'.

Activity 6.2

At the end of its reporting period, Zeneb plc's statement of financial position included the following items:

1 A bank deposit account where one month's notice of withdrawal is required.
2 Ordinary shares in Jones plc (a Stock Exchange listed business).
3 A high-interest bank deposit account that requires six months' notice of withdrawal.
4 An overdraft on the business's bank current account.

Which (if any) of these four items would be included in the figure for cash and cash equivalents?

Your response should have been as follows:

1 A cash equivalent. It is readily withdrawable and there is no risk of a change of value.
2 Not a cash equivalent. It can be converted into cash because it is Stock Exchange listed. There is, however, a significant risk that the amount expected (hoped for!) when the shares are sold may not actually be forthcoming.
3 Not a cash equivalent because it is not readily convertible into liquid cash.
4 This is cash itself, though a negative amount of it. The only exception to this classification would be where the business is financed in the longer term by an overdraft, when it would be part of the financing of the business, rather than negative cash.

THE RELATIONSHIP BETWEEN THE MAIN FINANCIAL STATEMENTS

The statement of cash flows is, along with the income statement and the statement of financial position, a major financial statement. The relationship between the three statements is shown in Figure 6.2. The statement of financial position shows the various assets (including cash) and claims (including the shareholders' equity) of the business *at a particular point in time*. The statement of cash flows and the income statement explain the *changes over a period* to two of the items in the statement of financial position. The statement of cash flows explains the changes to cash. The income statement explains changes to equity, arising from trading operations.

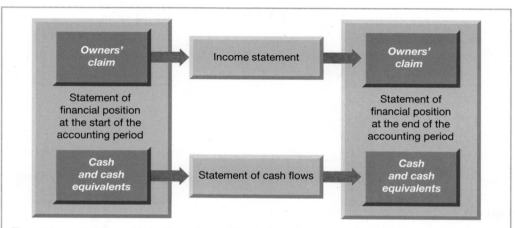

The statement of financial position shows the relationship, at a particular point in time, between the business's assets and claims. The income statement explains how, over the period between two statements of financial position, the equity figure in the first statement of financial position has altered as a result of trading operations. The statement of cash flows also looks at changes over the reporting period, but this statement explains the alteration in the cash (and cash equivalent) balances from the first to the second of the two consecutive statements of financial position.

Figure 6.2 The relationship between the statement of financial position, the income statement and the statement of cash flows

THE LAYOUT OF THE STATEMENT OF CASH FLOWS

As mentioned earlier, the cash flows of a business are divided into categories. The various categories, and the way in which they are presented in the statement of cash flows, are shown in Figure 6.3.

Let us now consider each of the categories that have been identified.

Cash flows from operating activities

These represent the cash inflows and outflows arising from normal day-to-day trading activities, after taking account of the tax paid and financing costs (equity and borrowings) relating to these activities. The cash inflows for the period are the amounts received from trade

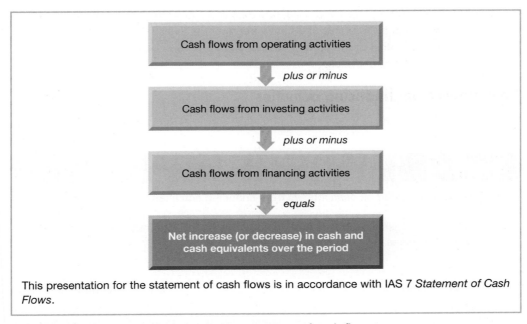

This presentation for the statement of cash flows is in accordance with IAS 7 *Statement of Cash Flows*.

Figure 6.3 Standard presentation for the statement of cash flows

receivables (credit customers settling their accounts) and from cash sales for the period. The cash outflows for the period are the amounts paid for inventories, operating expenses (such as rent and wages) corporation tax, interest and dividends.

Note that it is the cash inflows and outflows during a period that appear in the statement of cash flows, not revenue and expenses for that period. Similarly, tax and dividends that appear in the statement of cash flows are those actually paid during the period. Many companies pay tax on their annual profits in four equal instalments. Two of these are paid during the year concerned and the other two are paid during the following year. Thus, by the end of each year, half of the tax will have been paid and the remaining half will still be outstanding, to be paid during the following year. This means that the tax payment during a year is normally equal to half of the previous year's tax charge and half of that of the current year and it is this total that should appear in the current year's statement of cash flows.

Cash flows from investing activities

These include cash outflows to acquire non-current assets and cash inflows from their disposal. In addition to items, such as property, plant and equipment, non-current assets might include financial investments made in loans or shares in another business.

These cash flows also include cash inflows *arising from* financial investments (loans and shares).

Activity 6.3

What might be included as cash inflows from financial investments?

This can include interest received from loans that have been made and dividends received from shares that are held in other businesses. It would also include any cash received as proceeds from the disposal of a financial asset.

Under IAS 7, interest received and dividends received could also be classified under *Cash flows from operating activities*. This alternative treatment is available as these items appear in the calculation of profit. For the purpose of this chapter, however, we shall include them in *Cash flows from investing activities*.

Cash flows from financing activities

These represent cash inflows and outflows relating to the long-term financing of the business.

Activity 6.4

What might be included as cash inflows from financing activities?

This would include cash movements relating to the raising and redemption of both long-term borrowings and shares.

Under IAS 7, interest and dividend paid by the business could also appear under this heading as outflows. This alternative to including them in *Cash flows from operating activities* is available as they represent a cost of raising finance. For the purpose of this chapter, however, we shall not use this alternative treatment.

Whichever treatment for interest and dividends (both paid and received) is chosen, it should be applied consistently.

Net increase or decrease in cash and cash equivalents

The final total shown on the statement will be the net increase or decrease in cash and cash equivalents over the period. It is calculated by simply adding together the totals from each of the three categories mentioned above.

Real World 6.4 shows a summarised statement of cash flows of Tesco plc, the UK-based supermarket company.

Real World 6.4

Cashing in

A summary of the statement of cash flows for Tesco plc for the year ended 24 February 2018 shows the cash flows of the business under each of the headings described above.

Summary group statement of cash flows
Year ended 24 February 2018

	£m
Cash generated from operations	3,309
Interest paid	(351)
Corporation tax paid	(176)
Net cash generated from operating activities	2,782
Net cash generated from investing activities	666
Net cash used in financing activities	(3,236)
Net increase in cash and cash equivalents	212

Source: Adapted from: Tesco plc, Annual Report and Financial Statements 2018, p. 78 www.tescoplc.com.

As we shall see shortly, more detailed information under each of the main categories is provided in the statement of cash flows presented to shareholders and other users.

THE NORMAL DIRECTION OF CASH FLOWS

The effect on a business's cash and cash equivalents of activities relating to each category is shown in Figure 6.4. The arrows show the *normal* direction of cash flow for the typical, profitable, business during a reporting period.

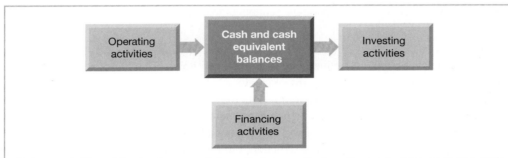

Various activities of the business each have their own effect on the total of the cash and cash equivalents, either positive (increasing the total) or negative (reducing it). The net increase or decrease in the cash and cash equivalents over a period will be the sum of these individual effects, taking account of the direction (cash in or cash out) of each activity.

Note that the direction of the arrow shows the *normal* direction of the cash flow in respect of each activity. In certain circumstances, each of these arrows could be reversed in direction.

Figure 6.4 Diagrammatical representation of the statement of cash flows

Normally, *operating activities* provide positive cash flows and, therefore, increase the business's cash resources. For most UK businesses, cash generated from day-to-day trading, even after deducting tax, interest and dividends, is by far the most important source of new finance.

Activity 6.5

Last year's statement of cash flows for Angus plc showed a negative cash flow from operating activities. What could be the reason for this and should the business's management be alarmed by it? (*Hint*: We think that there are two broad possible reasons for a negative cash flow.)

The two reasons are:

1 *The business is unprofitable*. This leads to more cash being paid out to employees, to suppliers of goods and services, for interest and so on, than is received from trade receivables. This should be of concern as a major expense for most businesses is depreciation. Since depreciation does not lead to a cash flow, it is not considered in *net cash inflows from operating activities*. A negative operating cash flow might well indicate, therefore, a much larger trading loss – in other words, a significant loss of the business's wealth.

2   *The business is expanding its activities (level of sales revenue).* Although the business may be profitable, it may be spending more cash than is being generated from sales. Cash will be spent on acquiring more assets, non-current and current, to accommodate increased demand. For example, a business may need to have inventories in place before additional sales can be made. Similarly, staff will have to be employed and paid. Even when additional sales are made, they would normally be made on credit, with the cash inflow lagging behind the sales. This means that there would be no immediate cash benefit.

Expansion often causes cash flow strains for new businesses, which will be expanding inventories and other assets from zero. They would also need to employ and pay staff. To add to this problem, increased profitability may encourage a feeling of optimism, leading to a lack of attention being paid to the cash flows. Although the cause of the cash flow problem is less disturbing than a lack of profitability, the effect could be a severe strain on cash resource and the consequent dangers of this.

Investing activities typically cause net negative cash flows. This is because many non-current assets either wear out or become obsolete and need to be replaced. Businesses may also expand their asset base. Non-current assets may, of course, be sold, which would give rise to positive cash flows. In net terms, however, the cash flows are normally negative, with cash spent on new assets far outweighing that received from the sale of old ones.

Financing activities can go in either direction, depending on the financing strategy at the time. Since businesses seek to expand, however, there is a tendency for these activities to result in cash inflows rather than cash outflows.

Before leaving this section let us consider **Real World 6.5**. It explains how, in recent years, many US businesses have experienced cash outflows that exceed their cash flows from operating activities. This has resulted in a need for greater borrowing. It also points out that the cash outflows were often not incurred for re-investment purposes.

Real World 6.5

Spend, spend, spend!

Corporate America is swimming in cash. There is no great news about this, and no great mystery about where it came from. Seven years of historically low interest rates will prompt companies to borrow. A new development, however, is that investors are starting to ask in more detail what companies are doing with their cash. And they are starting to revolt against signs of over-borrowing. That over-borrowing has grown most blatant in the last year, as earnings growth has petered out and, in many cases, turned negative. This has made the sharp increases in corporate debt look far harder to sustain.

Perhaps the most alarming illustration of the problem compares annual changes in net debt with the annual change in earnings before interest, tax, depreciation and amortization (EBITDA), which is a decent approximation for the operating cash flow from which they can expect to repay that debt. As the chart shows, debt has grown at almost 30 per cent over the past year; the cash flow to pay it has fallen slightly.

According to Andrew Lapthorne of Société Générale, the reality is that 'US corporates appear to be spending way too much (over 35 per cent more than their gross operating cash flow, the biggest deficit in over 20 years of data) and are using debt issuance to make up the difference'. The decline in earnings and cash flows in the past year has accentuated the problem, and brought it to the top of investors' consciousness.

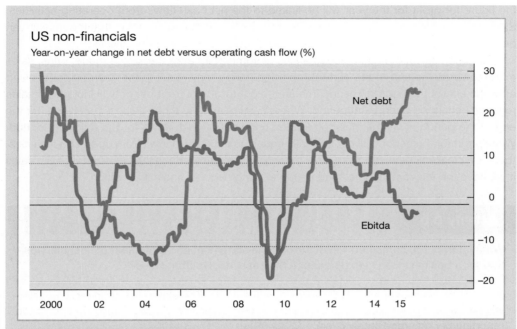

US non-financials
Year-on-year change in net debt versus operating cash flow (%)

Figure 6.5 Year-on-year change in net debt of US (non-financial) businesses versus operating cash flow (percentage)

Source: Société Générale.

A further issue is the uses to which the debt has been put. As pointed out many times in the post-crisis years, it has generally not gone into capital expenditures (property, plant and equipment), which might arguably be expected to boost the economy. It has instead been deployed to pay dividends, or to buy back shares – or to buy other companies.

 Source: Adapted extract from Authers, J. (2016) Alarm over corporate debt and stalled earnings, ft.com, 27 April. © The Financial Times Limited 2016. All rights reserved.

PREPARING THE STATEMENT OF CASH FLOWS

Deducing net cash flows from operating activities

As we have seen, the first category within the statement of cash flows is the *Cash flows from operating activities*. There are two approaches that can be taken to deriving this figure: the direct method and the indirect method.

The direct method

The direct method involves an analysis of the cash records of the business for the period, identifying all payments and receipts relating to operating activities. These receipts and payments are then summarised to provide the total figures for inclusion in the statement of cash flows. Since accounting records are normally computerised, this is a fairly simple matter. Nevertheless, very few businesses adopt the direct method.

The indirect method

The indirect method is a much more popular approach. It relies on the fact that, sooner or later, sales revenue gives rise to cash inflows and expenses give rise to outflows. This means that the figure for profit for the year will be linked to the net cash flows from operating activities. Since businesses have to produce an income statement, the information that it contains can be used as a starting point to deduce the cash flows from operating activities.

With credit sales, the cash receipt arises at some point after the sale is made. Thus, sales made towards the end of the current reporting period may result in the cash being received after the end of the period. The income statement for the current period will include all sales revenue generated during that period. Where cash relating to those sales is received after the end of the period, it will be included in the statement of cash flows for the following period. While profit for the period will not normally equal the net cash inflows from operating activities, there is a clear link between them. This means that we can deduce the cash inflows from sales if we have the relevant income statement and statements of financial position.

Activity 6.6

What information contained within the income statement and statement of financial position for a business can help us deduce the cash inflows from sales?

The income statement tells us the sales revenue figure. The statement of financial position will tell us how much was owed in respect of credit sales at the beginning and end of the reporting period (trade receivables).

If we adjust the sales revenue figure by the increase or decrease in trade receivables over the period, we deduce the cash from sales for the period. Example 6.1 shows how this is done.

Example 6.1

The sales revenue figure for a business for the year was £34 million. The trade receivables totalled £4 million at the beginning of the year, but had increased to £5 million by the end of the year.

Basically, the trade receivables figure is dictated by sales revenue and cash receipts. It is increased when a sale is made and decreased when cash is received from a credit customer. If, over the year, the sales revenue and the cash receipts had been equal, the beginning-of-year and end-of-year trade receivables figures would have been equal. Since the trade receivables figure increased, it must mean that less cash was received than sales revenues were made. In fact, the cash receipts from sales must have been £33 million (that is, $34 - (5 - 4)$).

Put slightly differently, we can say that as a result of sales, assets of £34 million flowed into the business. If £1 million of this went to increasing the asset of trade receivables, this leaves only £33 million that went to increase cash.

The same general point is true in respect of nearly all of the other items that are taken into account in deducing the operating profit figure. The main exception is depreciation. This expense is not normally associated with any movement in cash during that same period.

All of this means that we can take the *profit before taxation* (that is, the profit after interest but before taxation) for the year, add back the depreciation and interest expense charged in arriving at that profit, and adjust this total by movements in inventories, trade (and other) receivables and payables. If we then go on to deduct payments made during the reporting period for taxation, interest on borrowings and dividends, we have the net cash from operating activities. Example 6.2 illustrates this process.

Example 6.2

The relevant information from the financial statements of Dido plc for last year is as follows:

	£m
Profit before taxation (after interest)	122
Depreciation charged in arriving at profit before taxation	34
Interest expense	6
At the beginning of the year:	
Inventories	15
Trade receivables	24
Trade payables	18
At the end of the year:	
Inventories	17
Trade receivables	21
Trade payables	19

The following further information is available about payments during last year:

	£m
Taxation paid	32
Interest paid	5
Dividends paid	9

The cash flow from operating activities is derived as follows:

	£m
Profit before taxation (after interest)	122
Depreciation	34
Interest expense	6
Increase in inventories (17 − 15)	(2)
Decrease in trade receivables (21 − 24)	3
Increase in trade payables (19 − 18)	1
Cash generated from operations	164
Interest paid	(5)
Taxation paid	(32)
Dividends paid	(9)
Net cash from operating activities	118

As we can see, the net increase in **working capital*** (that is, current assets less current liabilities) as a result of trading was £162 million (that is, 122 + 34 + 6). Of this, £2 million went into increased inventories. More cash was received from trade receivables than sales revenue was made. Similarly, less cash was paid to trade payables than purchases of goods and services on credit. Both of these had a favourable effect on cash. Over the year, therefore, cash increased by £164 million. When account was taken of the payments for interest, tax and dividends, the net cash from operating activities was £118 million (inflow).

Note that we needed to adjust the profit before taxation (after interest) by the depreciation and interest expenses to derive the profit before depreciation, interest and taxation.

* Working capital is a term widely used in accounting and finance, not just in the context of the statement of cash flows. We shall encounter it several times in later chapters.

In deriving the cash generated from operations, we add the depreciation expense for the period to the profit before taxation. Does this mean that depreciation is a source of cash?

No. Depreciation is a not source of cash. The periodic depreciation expense is irrelevant to cash flow. Since the profit before taxation is derived *after* deducting the depreciation expense for the period, we need to eliminate the impact of depreciation by adding it back to the profit figure. This will give us the profit before tax *and before* depreciation, which is what we need.

We should be clear why we add back an amount for interest at the start of the derivation of cash flow from operating activities only to deduct an amount for interest further down. The reason is that the first is the *interest expense* for the reporting period, whereas the second is the amount of *cash paid out for interest* during that period. These may well be different amounts, as was the case in Example 6.2.

The relevant information from the financial statements of Pluto plc for last year is as follows:

	£m
Profit before taxation (after interest)	165
Depreciation charged in arriving at operating profit	41
Interest expense	21
At the beginning of the year:	
Inventories	22
Trade receivables	18
Trade payables	15
At the end of the year:	
Inventories	23
Trade receivables	21
Trade payables	17

The following further information is available about payments during last year:

	£m
Taxation paid	49
Interest paid	25
Dividends paid	28

What figure should appear in the statement of cash flows for *Net cash from operating activities*?

Cash flow from operating activities:

	£m
Profit before taxation (after interest)	165
Depreciation	41
Interest expense	21
Increase in inventories (23 − 22)	(1)
Increase in trade receivables (21 − 18)	(3)
Increase in trade payables (17 − 15)	2
Cash generated from operations	225
Interest paid	(25)
Taxation paid	(49)
Dividends paid	(28)
Net cash from operating activities	123

The indirect method of deducing the net cash flow from operating activities is summarised in Figure 6.6.

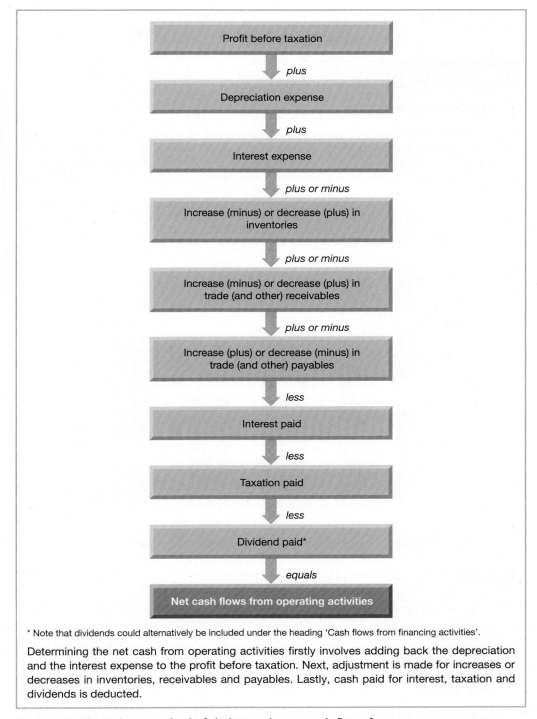

* Note that dividends could alternatively be included under the heading 'Cash flows from financing activities'.

Determining the net cash from operating activities firstly involves adding back the depreciation and the interest expense to the profit before taxation. Next, adjustment is made for increases or decreases in inventories, receivables and payables. Lastly, cash paid for interest, taxation and dividends is deducted.

Figure 6.6 The indirect method of deducing the net cash flows from operating activities

Real World 6.6 explains how, like many other businesses, one well-known business uses cash flow from operating activities as a key performance indicator.

Turning energy into cash

Royal Dutch Shell plc, the energy business, employs cash flow from operating activities as one of its key indicators of financial performance. It points out that this measure indicates the ability of the business to pay its debts, undertake investments and make cash distributions to shareholders. Performance over the four years ending 31 December 2017 is set out in Figure 6.7.

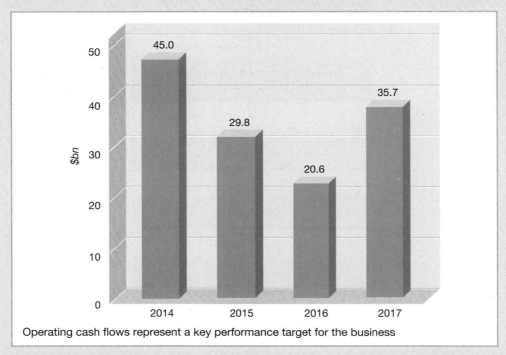

Operating cash flows represent a key performance target for the business

Figure 6.7 Royal Dutch Shell plc: Cash flows from operating activities 2012–16

In its 2017 annual report, the business explained the increase in this key performance indicator over time as follows:

> Cash flow from operating activities in 2017 was an inflow of $35.7 billion. The increase from $20.6 billion in 2016 was mainly due to higher earnings. The decrease in cash flow from operating activities in 2016 compared with $29.8 billion in 2015 mainly reflected unfavourable working capital impacts.

Shell bases part of the remuneration of senior staff on its various key performance indicators, including cash flow from operating activities.

Source: Graph produced from information in Shell 2017 Annual Report, p. 22. Quote from p. 55 of the report.

Before moving on to consider other areas of the statement of cash flows, it is useful to emphasise an important point. The fact that we can work from the profit before taxation to derive the net cash flows from operating activities, should not lead us to conclude that these two figures are broadly in line. Typically, adjustments made to the profit figure to derive net cash flows from operating activities are significant in size.

Deducing the other areas of the statement of cash flows

Deriving the cash flows from investing and financing activities is much easier than deriving *Net cash flows from operating activities*. It largely involves a comparison of the opening and closing statements of financial position to detect movements in non-current assets, non-current liabilities and equity over the period. We show how this is done in Example 6.3, which prepares a complete statement of cash flows.

Example 6.3

Torbryan plc's income statement for the year ended 31 December 2018 and the statements of financial position as at 31 December 2017 and 2018 are as follows:

Income statement for the year ended 31 December 2018

	£m
Revenue	576
Cost of sales	(307)
Gross profit	269
Distribution expenses	(65)
Administrative expenses	(26)
	178
Other operating income	21
Operating profit	199
Interest receivable	17
Interest payable	(23)
Profit before taxation	193
Taxation	(46)
Profit for the year	147

Statements of financial position as at 31 December 2017 and 2018

	2017 £m	2018 £m
ASSETS		
Non-current assets		
Property, plant and equipment		
Land and buildings	241	241
Plant and machinery	309	325
	550	566
Current assets		
Inventories	44	41
Trade receivables	121	139
	165	180
Total assets	715	746

	2017 £m	2018 £m
EQUITY AND LIABILITIES		
Equity		
Called-up ordinary share capital	150	200
Share premium account	–	40
Retained earnings	26	123
	176	363
Non-current liabilities		
Borrowings – loan notes	400	250
Current liabilities		
Borrowings (all bank overdraft)	68	56
Trade payables	55	54
Taxation	16	23
	139	133
Total equity and liabilities	715	746

During 2018, the business spent £95 million on additional plant and machinery. There were no other non-current-asset acquisitions or disposals. A dividend of £50 million was paid on ordinary shares during the year. The interest receivable revenue and the interest payable expense for the year were each equal to the cash inflow and outflow respectively. £150 million of loan notes were redeemed at their nominal (par) value.

The statement of cash flows would be:

Torbryan plc
Statement of cash flows for the year ended 31 December 2018

	£m
Cash flows from operating activities	
Profit before taxation (after interest) (see Note 1 below)	193
Adjustments for:	
Depreciation (Note 2)	79
Interest receivable (Note 3)	(17)
Interest payable (Note 4)	23
Increase in trade receivables (139 − 121)	(18)
Decrease in trade payables (55 − 54)	(1)
Decrease in inventories (44 − 41)	3
Cash generated from operations	262
Interest paid	(23)
Taxation paid (Note 5)	(39)
Dividend paid	(50)
Net cash from operating activities	150
Cash flows from investing activities	
Payments to acquire tangible non-current assets	(95)
Interest received (Note 3)	17
Net cash used in investing activities	(78)
Cash flows from financing activities	
Repayments of loan notes	(150)
Issue of ordinary shares (Note 6)	90
Net cash used in financing activities	(60)
Net increase in cash and cash equivalents	12
Cash and cash equivalents at 1 January 2018 (Note 7)	(68)
Cash and cash equivalents at 31 December 2018	(56)

We can see that a reconciliation of the cash of the business at the beginning and end of the year is provided at the end of the statement.

Notes:
1 This is simply taken from the income statement for the year.
2 Since there were no disposals, the depreciation charges must be the difference between the start and end of the year's plant and machinery (non-current assets) values, adjusted by the cost of any additions.

	£m
Carrying amount at 1 January 2018	309
Additions	95
	404
Depreciation (balancing figure)	(79)
Carrying amount at 31 December 2018	325

3 Interest receivable must be deducted to work towards what the profit would have been before it was added in the income statement, because it is not part of operations but of investing activities. The cash inflow from this source appears under the *Cash flows from investing activities* heading.
4 The interest payable expense must be taken out, by adding it back to the profit figure. We subsequently deduct the cash paid for interest payable during the year. In this case the two figures are identical.
5 Taxation is paid by many companies in two instalments: 50 per cent during their reporting year and 50 per cent in the following year. As a result, the 2018 payment would have been half the tax on the 2017 profit (that is, the figure that would have appeared in the current liabilities at the end of 2017), plus half of the 2018 taxation charge (that is, $16 + (^1/_2 \times 46) = 39$). Probably the easiest way to deduce the amount paid during the year to 31 December 2018 is by following this approach:

	£m
Taxation owed at start of the year (from the statement of financial position as at 31 December 2017)	16
Taxation charge for the year (from the income statement)	46
	62
Taxation owed at the end of the year (from the statement of financial position as at 31 December 2018)	(23)
Taxation paid during the year	39

This follows the logic that if we start with what the business owed at the beginning of the year, add what was owed as a result of the current year's taxation charge and then deduct what was owed at the end, the resulting figure must be what was paid during the year.
6 The share issue raised £90 million, of which £50 million went into the share capital total on the statement of financial position and £40 million into share premium.
7 There were no 'cash equivalents', just cash (though negative).

RECONCILIATION OF LIABILITIES FROM FINANCING ACTIVITIES

IAS 7 requires businesses to provide a reconciliation that shows the link between liabilities at the beginning and end of reporting period that relate to *Cash flows from financing activities* in the statement of cash flows. This reconciliation sets out movements in liabilities, such as long-term borrowings and lease liabilities, over the reporting period. A separate reconciliation is required for each type of liability.

The reconciliation appears as a note to the statement of cash flows and is designed to help users track changes occurring in the liabilities of the business. Example 6.4 illustrates how this reconciliation may be presented.

Example 6.4

Based on the information set out in the financial statements of Torbryan plc for the financial years ended 31 December 2017 and 2018 (see Example 6.3), the following reconciliation of long-term liabilities for the year to 31 December 2018 can be carried out:

Reconciliation of liabilities from financing activities for the year to 31 December 2018

	£m
Loan notes outstanding at 1 January 2018	400
Cash paid to redeem loan notes	(150)
Loan notes outstanding at 31 December 2018	250

Activity 6.9

IAS 7 requires a statement reconciling movements in liabilities, for the reporting period, but does not require a reconciliation of movements of equity. Can you suggest why this is?

The reason is that such a statement (statement of changes in equity) is required under IAS 1 *Presentation of Financial Statements*, as we saw in Chapter 5.

WHAT DOES THE STATEMENT OF CASH FLOWS TELL US?

The statement of cash flows tells us how the business has generated cash during the period and how that cash was used. This is potentially very useful information. Tracking the sources and uses of cash over time may reveal trends that may help users to assess likely future cash movements for the business.

Looking specifically at the statement of cash flows for Torbryan plc, in Example 6.3, we can see the following:

- Net cash flow from operations seems strong, much larger than the profit for the year, after taking account of the dividend paid. This might be expected as depreciation is deducted in arriving at profit.
- Working capital has absorbed some cash, which may indicate an expansion of activity (sales revenue) over the year. As we have only one year's income statement, however, we cannot tell whether this has occurred.

- There were net outflows of cash for investing activities, but this would not be unusual. Many types of non-current assets have limited lives and need to be replaced. Expenditure during the year was not out of line with the depreciation expense for the year, which is to be expected for a business with a regular replacement programme for its non-current assets.
- There was a major outflow of cash to redeem borrowings, which was partly offset by the proceeds of a share issue. This may well represent a change of financing strategy.

Activity 6.10

Why might this be the case? What has been the impact of these changes on the long-term financing of the business?

The financing changes, together with the retained earnings for the year, have led to a significant shift in the equity/borrowings balance.

Real World 6.7 identifies the important changes in the cash flows of Ryanair plc during the year ended 31 March 2017.

Real World 6.7

Flying high

Ryanair's summarised statement of cash flows for the year ended 31 March 2017

	€m
Net cash provided by operating activities	1,927.2
Net cash from (used in) investing activities	(1,290.8)
Net cash from (used in) financing activities	(671.6)
Net decrease in cash and cash equivalents	(35.2)

We can see that there was a net decrease in cash and cash equivalents of €35.2 million during the year. Cash and cash equivalents decreased from €1,259.2 million at 31 March 2016 to €1,224.0 million at 31 March 2017. Both, however, are very large balances and represent 11 per cent and 10 per cent respectively of total assets held.

The net cash inflow from operating activities during the year to 31 March 2017 was €1,927.2 million. This was higher than the previous year's figure of €1,846.3 million. The increase was largely due to an increase in profit after tax of €74.3 million over 2016. There were also changes in working capital.

The net cash outflow from investing activities during the year totalled €1,290.8 million, which is a significant increase from the previous year's figure of €283.6 million. This was due to an outflow of €1,449.8 million for the purchase of property, plant and equipment (mostly new aircraft and related equipment), which was partly offset by a decrease of €157.8 million in financial investments with a maturity of more than three months.

The net cash outflow from financing activities was €671.6 million. This outflow was made up of repayments of long-term borrowings of €447.1 million and share repurchases of a massive €1,017.9 million. These outflows were partly offset by the issue of additional borrowings of €750.0 million.

Source: Information taken from Ryanair plc Annual Report 2017, pp. 97, 137 and 142.

Real World 6.8 is an article that discusses the usefulness of the statement of cash flows.

Using the statement of cash flows

The City cheered results from oil majors BP and Royal Dutch Shell this week, despite a slump in profitability. It's all down to cash – or, rather, better cash management. This is the ultimate test of a company's ability to create real value out of its assets.

For investors, cash really is king. Keeping an eye on what a business is doing with its money can give you a good handle on its prospects. So, it is vital investors are comfortable looking at how a company uses its cash – and use this information to inform their investment decisions.

Many ignore cash flow and focus on profits and revenues alone. This is a mistake. The cash flow statement is just as important as the balance sheet or income statement in a company's accounts.

With the majority of investors owning shares in oil companies for their income, good cash management is vital to keep the dividend pipe flowing. Free cash flow is very important as it is from this pot that dividends are paid.

A quick and easy way of working out an approximate free cash flow figure is to take the operating cash flow number from the cash flow statement and subtract capital expenditures. You will then have a figure which is roughly the cash generated by the company after it has invested in maintaining and growing its business.

Following a profit warning in January, Shell's new chief executive Ben van Beurden unveiled a strategy that aimed to boost its cash by managing its business better, by making investments and disposing of non-core assets.

The group's cash flow hit $14 billion (£8.3bn) in the first quarter, up 21 per cent from a year ago and more than double the $6 billion seen in the fourth quarter of 2013. This was ahead of market expectations. BP also said it was on track to meet its target of $30 billion–$31 billion in operating cash flow for the year, compared with $22 billion in 2013. Both these statements cheered City analysts.

Investors had been critical of the returns both companies have generated from their invested capital over the last few years. A similar situation has been seen in mining – a sector arguably ahead of the game when compared with oil majors. BHP reported a £7.8 billion increase in free cash flow at the interim stage, by employing a similar strategy to BP and Shell. But the oil groups' cash strategy could end up having more of an impact, because oil prices have held up significantly better than the price of metals in the last few years.

Looking at cash flows can also identify companies where the dividend outlook is negative. For example, rail and bus operator FirstGroup is expected to have negative free cash flow for a number of years. Morgan Stanley is forecasting a negative free cash flow of £82.3 million this year, rising to £90.5 million in 2015. The company cancelled its dividend last year, as it needs to use its cash to service its debt pile. It did not make an interim payment but hinted that it may make a payment alongside its final results, due to be issued on May 21.

FirstGroup's board 'expects to propose a final dividend of up to £50 million for the year to 31 March 2014, as a transition to a progressive dividend policy thereafter', it said in November. However, some in the City think that, given the state of its free cash flow, it should reconsider making any payment until it becomes cash generative.

'A significant part of FirstGroup's cash flow pressure comes from servicing debt,' broker Jefferies said last month. 'For us, dividends look inappropriate for now.'

Of course, it is too simplistic to say that a fall in free cash flow is always a bad thing. A company may be making large investments that will provide a significant return in the future. A good recent example of this is Deutsche Telekom, which slashed its guidance for

2015 free cash flow in March. Management lowered its target of €6 billion (£4.9bn) of free cash flow next year to €4.2 billion, down from €4.6 billion in 2013.

'We could achieve our original ambition level for 2015 if we were to slam the door in the face of the customer rush in the US. That's not what we want,' said Thomas Dannenfeldt, Deutsche Telekom's chief financial officer. 'The market is offering us the opportunity to achieve a different ambition: value-driven customer growth in the US that translates into an increase in the value of the company.'

And if a company is stopping investment in its business merely to make cash flows look better this could store up problems further down the line. There is always a judgment call for an investor to make when looking at cash movements and the market has judged that BP and Shell are now spending their money much more wisely.

Both BP and Shell – the most significant dividend payers in the FTSE 100 – appear to be taking steps in the right direction to return to sustainable dividend growth. But one swallow does not a summer make. This needs to be sustained – for the sake of income seekers across the UK and beyond.

Source: White, G. (2014) Cash flow is king when judging a company's prospects, *Sunday Telegraph Business*, 3 May.

PROBLEMS WITH IAS 7

IAS 7 *Statement of Cash Flows* does not enjoy universal acclaim. Its critics argue that the standard is too permissive in the description and classification of important items.

Some believe that the standard would inspire greater confidence among users if it insisted that only the direct method be used to calculate cash flows from operating activities. Supporters of the direct method argue that, being cash based, it provides greater clarity by setting out operating cash receipts and payments. No accrual-based adjustments are made, which means that it is less susceptible to manipulation than the indirect approach. This greater transparency 'would enable the market to distinguish between the weak and the strong – the better companies would be safe, and the worse would be more exposed' (see Reference 1 at the end of the chapter). In its defence, however, it should be said that the indirect approach may help to shed light on the quality of reported profits by reconciling profit with the net cash from operating activities for a period. A business must demonstrate an ability to convert profits into cash. Revealing the link between profits and cash is, therefore, very helpful.

Self-assessment question 6.1

Touchstone plc's income statements for the years ended 31 December 2017 and 2018 and statements of financial position as at 31 December 2017 and 2018 are as follows:

Income statements for the years ended 2017 and 2018

	2017 £m	2018 £m
Revenue	173	207
Cost of sales	(96)	(101)
Gross profit	77	106

→

	2017	2018
	£m	£m
Distribution expenses	(18)	(20)
Administrative expenses	(24)	(26)
Other operating income	3	4
Operating profit	38	64
Interest payable	(2)	(4)
Profit before taxation	36	60
Taxation	(8)	(16)
Profit for the year	28	44

Statements of financial position as at 31 December 2017 and 2018

	2017	2018
	£m	£m
ASSETS		
Non-current assets		
Property, plant and equipment		
Land and buildings	94	110
Plant and machinery	53	62
	147	172
Current assets		
Inventories	25	24
Treasury bills (short-term investments)	–	15
Trade receivables	16	26
Cash at bank and in hand	4	4
	45	69
Total assets	192	241
EQUITY AND LIABILITIES		
Equity		
Called-up ordinary share capital	100	100
Retained earnings	30	56
	130	156
Non-current liabilities		
Borrowings – loan notes (10%)	20	40
Current liabilities		
Trade payables	38	37
Taxation	4	8
	42	45
Total equity and liabilities	192	241

Included in 'cost of sales', 'distribution expenses' and 'administrative expenses', depreciation was as follows:

	2017	2018
	£m	£m
Land and buildings	5	6
Plant and machinery	6	10

There were no non-current asset disposals in either year.

The interest payable expense equalled the cash payment made during each of the years.

The business paid dividends on ordinary shares of £14 million during 2017 and £18 million during 2018.

The Treasury bills represent a short-term investment of funds that will be used shortly in operations. There is insignificant risk that this investment will lose value.

Required:
Prepare a statement of cash flows for the business for 2018.

The solution to this question can be found at the back of the book, starting on page 525.

SUMMARY

The main points of this chapter may be summarised as follows:

The need for a statement of cash flows

- Cash is important because no business can operate without it.
- The statement of cash flows is specifically designed to reveal movements in cash over a period.
- Cash movements cannot be readily detected from the income statement, which focuses on revenue and expenses rather than on cash inflows and outflows.
- Profit (or loss) and cash generated for the period are rarely equal.
- The statement of cash flows is a major financial statement, along with the income statement and the statement of financial position.

Preparing the statement of cash flows

- The statement of cash flows has three major categories of cash flows: cash flows from operating activities, cash flows from investing activities and cash flows from financing activities.
- The total of the cash movements under these three categories will provide the net increase or decrease in cash and cash equivalents for the period.
- A reconciliation can be undertaken to check that the opening balance of cash and cash equivalents plus the net increase (or decrease) for the period equals the closing balance.

Calculating the cash generated from operations

- The net cash flows from operating activities can be derived by either the direct method or the indirect method.
- The direct method is based on an analysis of the cash records for the period, whereas the indirect method uses information contained within the income statement and statements of financial position.
- The indirect method takes the profit before taxation (after interest) for the period, adds back any depreciation charge and then adjusts for changes in inventories, receivables and payables during the period.

KEY TERMS

For definitions of these terms, see at the back of the book, starting on page 514.

direct method p. 213

indirect method p. 213
working capital p. 215

REFERENCE

1 Clacher, D. (2013) 'Why the numbers add up for direct cash flow statements', *Financial Director*, 17 December.

FURTHER READING

If you would like to explore the topics covered in this chapter in more depth, we recommend the following:

Alexander, D. and Nobes, C. (2016) *Financial Accounting: An International Introduction*, 6th edn, Pearson, Chapter 13.

Elliott, B. and Elliott, J. (2017) *Financial Accounting and Reporting*, 18th edn, Pearson, Chapter 5.

International Accounting Standards Board, *2016 A Guide Through IFRS* (Green Book), 2016, IAS 7 *Statement of Cash Flows*.

KPMG (2017) *Insights into IFRS*, 14th edn, Sweet and Maxwell, Section 2.3 (a summary of this book is available free at www.kpmg.com).

Solutions to these questions can be found at the back of the book, starting on page 536.

6.1 The typical business outside the service sector has about 50 per cent more of its resources tied up in inventories than in cash, yet there is no call for a 'statement of inventories flows' to be prepared. Why is cash regarded as more important than inventories?

6.2 What is the difference between the direct and indirect methods of deducing cash generated from operations? Can you see an advantage of using the indirect method rather than the direct method from the perspective of an external user of financial statements?

6.3 IAS 7 carefully defines cash (and cash equivalents). Can you explain why the authors of this standard were so careful and precise in their definition?

6.4 'Profit should more or less equal the net cash inflow for a period?' Do you agree? Explain your reasoning.

EXERCISES

Solutions to exercises with coloured numbers can be found at the back of the book, starting on page 545.

Basic-level exercises

6.1 How will each of the following events ultimately affect the amount of cash?

(a) An increase in the level of inventories
(b) A rights issue of ordinary shares
(c) A bonus issue of ordinary shares
(d) Writing off part of the value of some inventories
(e) The disposal of a large number of the business's shares by a major shareholder
(f) Depreciating a non-current asset.

6.2 The following information has been taken from the financial statements of Juno plc for last year and the year before last:

	Year before last £m	Last year £m
Operating profit	156	187
Depreciation charged in arriving at operating profit	47	55
Inventories held at end of year	27	31
Trade receivables at end of year	24	23
Trade payables at end of year	15	17

Required:
What is the figure for cash generated from the operations for Juno plc for last year?

Intermediate-level exercises

6.3 Torrent plc's income statement for the year ended 31 December 2018 and the statements of financial position as at 31 December 2017 and 2018 are as follows:

Income statement for the year ended 31 December 2018

	£m
Revenue	623
Cost of sales	(353)
Gross profit	270
Distribution expenses	(44)
Administrative expenses	(30)
Operating profit	196
Interest payable	(26)
Profit before taxation	170
Taxation	(36)
Profit for the year	134

Statements of financial position as at 31 December 2017 and 2018

	2017 £m	2018 £m
ASSETS		
Non-current assets		
Property, plant and equipment		
Land and buildings	310	310
Plant and machinery	325	314
	635	624
Current assets		
Inventories	41	35
Trade receivables	139	145
	180	180
Total assets	815	804
EQUITY AND LIABILITIES		
Equity		
Called-up ordinary share capital	200	300
Share premium account	40	–
Revaluation reserve	69	9
Retained earnings	123	197
	432	506
Non-current liabilities		
Borrowings – loan notes	250	150
Current liabilities		
Borrowings (all bank overdraft)	56	89
Trade payables	54	41
Taxation	23	18
	133	148
Total equity and liabilities	815	804

During 2018, the business spent £67 million on additional plant and machinery. There were no other non-current asset acquisitions or disposals.

There was no share issue for cash during the year. The interest payable expense was equal in amount to the cash outflow. A dividend of £60 million was paid.

Required:

Prepare the statement of cash flows for Torrent plc for the year ended 31 December 2018.

6.4 Chen plc's income statements for the years ended 31 December 2017 and 2018 and the statements of financial position as at 31 December 2017 and 2018 are as follows:

Income statements for the years ended 31 December 2017 and 2018

	2017 £m	2018 £m
Revenue	207	153
Cost of sales	(101)	(76)
Gross profit	106	77
Distribution expenses	(22)	(20)
Administrative expenses	(20)	(28)
Operating profit	64	29
Interest payable	(4)	(4)
Profit before taxation	60	25
Taxation	(16)	(6)
Profit for the year	44	19

Statements of financial position as at 31 December 2017 and 2018

	2017 £m	2018 £m
ASSETS		
Non-current assets		
Property, plant and equipment		
Land and buildings	110	130
Plant and machinery	62	56
	172	186
Current assets		
Inventories	24	25
Trade receivables	26	25
Cash at bank and in hand	19	–
	69	50
Total assets	241	236
EQUITY AND LIABILITIES		
Equity		
Called-up ordinary share capital	100	100
Retained earnings	56	57
	156	157
Non-current liabilities		
Borrowings – loan notes (10%)	40	40
Current liabilities		
Borrowings (all bank overdraft)	–	2
Trade payables	37	34
Taxation	8	3
	45	39
Total equity and liabilities	241	236

Included in 'cost of sales', 'distribution expenses' and 'administrative expenses', depreciation was as follows:

	2017	2018
	£m	£m
Land and buildings	6	10
Plant and machinery	10	12

There were no non-current asset disposals in either year. The amount of cash paid for interest equalled the expense in each year. Dividends were paid totalling £18 million in each year.

Required:
Prepare a statement of cash flows for the business for 2018.

6.5 The following are the financial statements for Nailsea plc for the years ended 30 June 2017 and 2018:

Income statement for years ended 30 June

	2017	2018
	£m	£m
Revenue	1,230	2,280
Operating expenses	(722)	(1,618)
Depreciation	(270)	(320)
Operating profit	238	342
Interest payable	–	(27)
Profit before taxation	238	315
Taxation	(110)	(140)
Profit for the year	128	175

Statements of financial position as at 30 June

	2017	2018
	£m	£m
ASSETS		
Non-current assets		
Property, plant and equipment (at carrying amount)		
Land and buildings	1,500	1,900
Plant and machinery	810	740
	2,310	2,640
Current assets		
Inventories	275	450
Trade receivables	100	250
Bank	–	118
	375	818
Total assets	2,685	3,458
EQUITY AND LIABILITIES		
Equity		
Share capital (fully paid £1 shares)	1,400	1,600
Share premium account	200	300
Retained earnings	828	958
	2,428	2,858
Non-current liabilities		
Borrowings – 9% loan notes (repayable 2022)	–	300
Current liabilities		
Borrowings (all bank overdraft)	32	–
Trade payables	170	230
Taxation	55	70
	257	300
Total equity and liabilities	2,685	3,458

There were no disposals of non-current assets in either year. Dividends were paid in 2017 and 2018 of £40 million and £45 million, respectively.

Required:

Prepare a statement of cash flows for Nailsea plc for the year ended 30 June 2018.

Advanced-level exercises

6.6 The following financial statements for Blackstone plc are a slightly simplified set of published accounts. Blackstone plc is an engineering business that developed a new range of products in 2013. These products now account for 60 per cent of its sales revenue.

Income statement for the years ended 31 March

	Notes	2017 £m	2018 £m
Revenue		7,003	11,205
Cost of sales		(3,748)	(5,809)
Gross profit		3,255	5,396
Operating expenses		(2,205)	(3,087)
Operating profit		1,050	2,309
Interest payable	1	(216)	(456)
Profit before taxation		834	1,853
Taxation		(210)	(390)
Profit for the year		624	1,463

Statements of financial position as at 31 March

	Notes	2017 £m	2018 £m
ASSETS			
Non-current assets			
Property, plant and equipment	2	4,300	7,535
Intangible assets	3	–	700
		4,300	8,235
Current assets			
Inventories		1,209	2,410
Trade receivables		641	1,173
Cash at bank		123	–
		1,973	3,583
Total assets		6,273	11,818
EQUITY AND LIABILITIES			
Equity			
Share capital		1,800	1,800
Share premium		600	600
Capital reserves		352	352
Retained earnings		685	1,748
		3,437	4,500
Non-current liabilities			
Borrowings – bank loan (repayable 2021)		1,800	3,800
Current liabilities			
Trade payables		931	1,507
Taxation		105	195
Borrowings (all bank overdraft)		–	1,816
		1,036	3,518
Total equity and liabilities		6,273	11,818

Notes:
1 The expense and the cash outflow for interest payable are equal for each year.
2 The movements in property, plant and equipment during the year are:

	Land and buildings £m	Plant and machinery £m	Fixtures and fittings £m	Total £m
Cost				
At 1 April 2017	4,500	3,850	2,120	10,470
Additions	–	2,970	1,608	4,578
Disposals	–	(365)	(216)	(581)
At 31 March 2018	4,500	6,455	3,512	14,467
Depreciation				
At 1 April 2017	1,275	3,080	1,815	6,170
Charge for year	225	745	281	1,251
Disposals	–	(305)	(184)	(489)
At 31 March 2018	1,500	3,520	1,912	6,932
Carrying amount				
At 31 March 2018	3,000	2,935	1,600	7,535

3 Intangible assets represent the amounts paid for the goodwill of another engineering business acquired during the year.
4 Proceeds from the sale of non-current assets in the year ended 31 March 2018 amounted to £54 million.
5 £300 million was paid in dividends on ordinary shares in 2017, and £400 million in 2018.

Required:
Prepare a statement of cash flows for Blackstone plc for the year ended 31 March 2018. (*Hint*: A loss (deficit) on disposal of non-current assets is simply an additional amount of depreciation and should be dealt with as such in preparing the statement of cash flows.)

6.7 Simplified financial statements for York plc are:

Income statement for the year ended 30 September 2018

	£m
Revenue	290.0
Cost of sales	(215.0)
Gross profit	75.0
Operating expenses (Note 1)	(62.0)
Operating profit	13.0
Interest payable (Note 2)	(3.0)
Profit before taxation	10.0
Taxation	(2.6)
Profit for the year	7.4

Statement of financial position as at 30 September

	2017 £m	2018 £m
ASSETS		
Non-current assets (Note 4)	80.0	85.0
Current assets		
Inventories and trade receivables	119.8	122.1
Cash at bank	9.2	16.6
	129.0	138.7
Total assets	209.0	223.7
EQUITY AND LIABILITIES		
Equity		
Share capital	35.0	40.0
Share premium account	30.0	30.0
Reserves	31.0	34.9
	96.0	104.9
Non-current liabilities		
Borrowings	32.0	35.0
Current liabilities		
Trade payables	80.0	82.5
Taxation	1.0	1.3
	81.0	83.8
Total equity and liabilities	209.0	223.7

Notes:

1 Operating expenses include depreciation of £13 million and a surplus of £3.2 million on the sale of non-current assets.
2 The expense and the cash outflow for interest payable are equal.
3 A dividend of £3.5 million was paid during 2018.
4 Non-current asset costs and depreciation:

	Cost £m	Accumulated depreciation £m	Carrying amount £m
At 1 October 2017	120.0	40.0	80.0
Disposals	(10.0)	(8.0)	(2.0)
Additions	20.0	–	20.0
Depreciation	–	13.0	(13.0)
At 30 September 2018	130.0	45.0	85.0

Required:

Prepare a statement of cash flows for York plc for the year ended 30 September 2018.

6.8 The statements of financial position of Axis plc as at 31 December 2017 and 2018 and the income statement for the year ended 31 December 2018 were as follows:

Statements of financial position as at 31 December

	2017		2018	
	£m	£m	£m	£m
ASSETS				
Non-current assets				
Property, plant and equipment				
Land and building at cost	130		130	
Accumulated depreciation	(30)	100	(32)	98
Plant and machinery at cost	70		80	
Accumulated depreciation	(17)	53	(23)	57
		153		155
Current assets				
Inventories		25		24
Trade receivables		16		26
Short-term investments		–		12
Cash at bank and in hand		–		7
		41		69
Total assets		194		224
EQUITY AND LIABILITIES				
Equity				
Share capital		100		100
Retained earnings		36		40
		136		140
Non-current liabilities				
Borrowings – 10% loan notes		20		40
Current liabilities				
Trade payables		31		36
Taxation		7		8
		38		44
Total equity and liabilities		194		224

Income statement for the year ended 31 December 2018

	£m
Revenue	173
Cost of sales	(96)
Gross profit	77
Sundry operating expenses	(24)
Deficit on sale of non-current asset	(1)
Depreciation – buildings	(2)
– plant	(16)
Operating profit	34
Interest receivable	2
Interest payable	(2)
Profit before taxation	34
Taxation	(16)
Profit for the year	18

Notes:

1 During the year, plant (a non-current asset) costing £15 million and with accumulated depreciation of £10 million was sold.
2 The short-term investments were government securities, where there was little or no risk of loss of value.
3 The expense and the cash outflow for interest payable were equal.
4 During 2018 a dividend of £14 million was paid.

Required:

1 Prepare a statement of cash flows for Axis plc for the year ended 31 December 2018.
2 Prepare a reconciliation of liabilities from financing activities for the year ended 31 December 2018.

Chapter 7

RECOGNISING AND REPORTING ASSETS AND LIABILITIES

INTRODUCTION

In Chapter 2, we discussed the broad definitions of assets and liabilities and the criteria for recognising these items in financial statements. However, the definitions and recognition criteria discussed provide more questions than answers. In an increasingly complex world, the treatment of certain assets and liabilities in the financial statements can create headaches for both their preparers and users. Various international financial reporting (or accounting) standards have been issued to provide clearer definitions and recognition criteria for these items. Enhancing the comparability of financial statements is the ultimate purpose of these standards.

In this chapter, we consider the reporting rules set out in key international financial reporting standards. We shall see how certain items are defined and what recognition criteria should be applied. We shall also see why some of these standards have attracted criticism.

The chapter contains a short appendix, which deals with the concept of present value. This is relevant to our examination of assets and liabilities arising under lease contracts.

Learning outcomes

When you have completed this chapter, you should be able to:

- discuss the main recognition criteria for provisions, contingent liabilities and contingent assets and explain the main reporting requirements for each;

- discuss the main recognition criteria and reporting requirements for internally-generated intangible assets;

- discuss the main recognition criteria for leases and describe their treatment in the financial statements; and

- explain the circumstances under which borrowing costs may be capitalised.

PROVISIONS, CONTINGENT LIABILITIES AND CONTINGENT ASSETS

In this first section, we shall examine the main features of IAS 37 *Provisions, Contingent Liabilities and Contingent Assets*. We shall begin by looking at the nature of provisions and at the way in which they should be reported. We then go on to consider contingent liabilities and contingent assets. We shall see that uncertainty concerning future events provides a common thread for these items.

PROVISIONS

Businesses often report provisions in their financial statements. To understand what a **provision** is, let us begin by recalling how a liability is defined.

Activity 7.1

Can you recall (from Chapter 2) how we define a liability?

It is an obligation by a business to an outside party, which arises from past events and which is settled through an outflow of resources (usually cash).

A provision is simply a form of liability. To be more precise, it is a liability where the timing or amount involved is uncertain. Although other liabilities, such as accruals, may suffer from uncertainty, the degree of uncertainty is higher for a provision.

According to IAS 37, a provision should be recognised where *all* of the following criteria have been met:

- there is an obligation arising from a past event;
- an outflow of resources is probably needed to settle the obligation; and
- a reliable estimate of the obligation can be made.

The amount of the provision should be the best estimate of the sum needed to settle the obligation. A reliable estimate is assumed to be possible in all but exceptional cases.

A few points about the nature of the obligation which leads to the recognition of a provision should be noted:

1 The obligation need not always arise from legal requirements. It may arise from particular business practices. (This is known as a *constructive obligation*.) This will occur where practices, or policies, lead others to form expectations as to how the business will discharge its responsibilities.
2 The obligation does not have to be established with perfect certainty. It is enough for the evidence to suggest that it probably exists (that there is a greater than 50 per cent chance that it exists).
3 The obligation must be unavoidable. If a business can take action to avoid a future outflow of resources, the obligation cannot lead to the recognition of a provision.

Activity 7.2 should help to clarify the kind of situations where a provision should be recognised and reported in the financial statements. Use the points that we have just covered to guide your thoughts.

Activity 7.2

Consider the following:

1 A coach operated by a transport business was involved in a major accident in which a number of people were seriously injured. The business is being sued for gross negligence and the court will soon make a decision on this matter. Lawyers for the business have advised that the business is unlikely (less than 50 per cent chance) to be found liable for the accident.

2 A travel business has expanded its operations and its current offices are no longer suitable for use. As a result, the business is relocating to larger offices on the opposite side of the city. The current offices are leased and another two years remain before the lease period ends. There is no real likelihood that these offices can be sub-let to another business and cancellation of the lease is not possible.

3 A retail business operates a well-established and well-known refunds policy. If a customer is unhappy with goods purchased for any reason, a full refund is provided. Past experience shows that 2 per cent of customers seek a refund.

4 A manufacturing business is expected to make a large operating loss next year as a result of a fall in demand for its goods.

5 A mining business, when carrying out its operations over a number of years, has caused contamination to some land. New environmental legislation is about to be enacted that will create an obligation for businesses to clean up the contaminated land.

Which of these should lead to the recognition of a provision? Give your reasons.

Your answer should be along the following lines:

1 On the basis of the lawyers' opinion, there is no probable obligation arising from the accident. It therefore fails the first criterion and so a provision should not be recognised.

2 A provision should be recognised because:
   – there is an obligation under the lease; and
   – the obligation will probably give rise to future outflows of resources.

3 A provision should normally be recognised because:
   – the sale of goods will result in a constructive obligation because of the refunds policy of the business; and
   – a proportion of the goods sold will probably be returned (based on past experience), leading to an outflow of resources.

4 A provision should not be recognised. There is no obligation arising from a past event and so it fails to meet the first criterion.

5 A provision should be recognised because:
   – the contamination of the land will produce an obligation because of impending legislation; and
   – an outflow of resources will probably be needed to decontaminate the land.

Where a provision is recognised, it has been assumed in each case that a reliable estimate of the outflow of resources can be made.

Provisions and business restructuring

An important form of provision is where a business decides to restructure its operations. Restructuring may involve selling a division, relocating business operations, changing the management hierarchy and so on. This can give rise to future outflows of resources and so a provision may be recognised.

IAS 37 states, however, that a constructive obligation will only exist where there is a formal, detailed restructuring plan. Furthermore, this plan must either have been communicated to those affected by it or started to be implemented by the end of the reporting period. In these circumstances, the obligation to restructure is considered unavoidable. Where restructuring involves the sale of a business operation, an obligation arises only where there is a binding sale agreement.

Only the direct costs associated with restructuring must be included in the amount of the provision. These are the necessary costs of restructuring rather than those associated with ongoing business operations. Thus, costs incurred as a result of retraining employees, marketing and investment in new systems must not be included in any restructuring provision as they relate to future operations of the business.

Recognising and reporting provisions

Recognising a provision is fairly straightforward. The income statement is charged with the amount of the provision and this amount then appears as a liability in the statement of financial position. Thus, profit will decrease and liabilities will increase by the amount of the provision. Where costs relating to the provision are subsequently incurred, they will be charged against the provision rather than to the income statement.

A provision, once recognised, should be reviewed at the end of each reporting period and, if necessary, adjusted to reflect the current best estimate of the obligation. Where it is probable that an outflow of resources will no longer arise, the provision must be reversed.

Activity 7.3

Can you think how this reversal should be shown in the financial statements?

The provision will be added back to the income statement and eliminated from the liabilities.

IAS 37 sets out disclosure requirements for provisions. For each type of provision, the amounts at the beginning and end of the reporting period, increases or decreases in the provision and amounts charged against the provision during the period must be shown. The following must also be shown:

- the nature and timing of any obligation;
- the uncertainties surrounding the amount or timing of any outflow of resources; and
- where necessary, any major assumptions used concerning future events must be revealed.

Real World 7.1 explains how a major bank was forced to create a provision for potential claims from 'misselling' payment protection insurance to its customers.

Provisions and creative accounting

There is a risk that unscrupulous directors will misuse provisions. Excessive provisions may be recognised in one period (thereby reducing that period's profit), only to be eliminated, or decreased, in a subsequent period (thereby increasing that period's profit). The purpose may be to smooth profits from one year to the next. Investors are often assumed to prefer a smooth, upward trend in profits rather than an erratic pattern. Where provisions are created and then reversed, in this way, investors may be misled over the degree of profit volatility.

IAS 37 has made this type of misuse of provisions much more difficult. Various rules are now in place to restrict the opportunity for creative accounting. Three such rules are:

- An obligation must be unavoidable before a provision can be recognised.
- A provision can only be used for the purpose for which it was created. Thus, unrelated expenditure cannot be offset against a particular provision.
- Excessive provisions cannot be created. Prudence must not be used as an excuse for treating an adverse future outcome as more probable than is likely to be the case.

CONTINGENT LIABILITIES

IAS 37 *Provisions, Contingent Liabilities and Contingent Assets* defines a contingent liability as:

1 a possible obligation arising from past events, the existence of which will only be confirmed by future events not wholly within the control of the business; or
2 a present obligation arising from past events, where either it is not probable that an outflow of resources is needed, or the amount of the obligation cannot be reliably measured.

It is the uncertainty surrounding the timing, or amount, of both provisions and contingent liabilities, that has led to them both being dealt with in the same standard. The degree of uncertainty, however, differs. Where, for example, a present obligation leads to a probable (more than 50 per cent chance) outflow of resources, a provision is normally recognised. Where a future outflow is possible, but not probable (less than 50 per cent chance), a contingent liability arises.

Activity 7.4 should help to identify the kind of situations where a contingent liability arises.

Consider the following:

1 A pharmaceutical manufacturing business is being sued by a rival for infringement of patent rights. The court case has begun, but a decision is not expected until after the end of the reporting period. Lawyers representing the business believe that it is probable that the court will find in favour of the rival.

2 A football club acquired a new player by a transfer from another club during its current reporting period. The terms of the transfer agreement state that, in addition to the £10 million fee already paid, a further £2 million will be paid if the player is selected for the national team within the next three years. It is possible that this will happen.

3 A manufacturer undertakes to guarantee a bank loan of £3 million borrowed by the supplier of raw materials that are vitally important to the manufacturer. The supplier has experienced some financial difficulties lately, but it is not probable that it will default on its loan obligations.

4 A chemical business has accidentally contaminated a river by releasing dangerous chemicals into it. The business is legally obliged to pay to decontaminate the river; it will also be liable to pay fines. The accident occurred near the end of the reporting period and it is too early to derive a reliable estimate of the likely future costs incurred.

Which of these should be regarded as a contingent liability? Give your reasons.

Your answers should be as follows:

1 As it is likely that the court will find in favour of the rival business, this should be regarded as a present obligation where an outflow of resources is probably needed. This meets the criteria for recognition of a provision (provided a reasonable estimate of the amount can be made). It is not, therefore, a contingent liability.

2 This is a possible obligation arising from past events that is not wholly within the control of the football club. It should, therefore, be regarded as a contingent liability.

3 The loan guarantee is, again, a possible obligation arising from past events that is not wholly within the control of the business. It should, therefore, be regarded as a contingent liability.

4 This is a present obligation which, if the amount of the obligation could be reliably estimated, would give rise to a provision. As no reliable estimate can be made, it should be regarded as a contingent liability.

Reporting contingent liabilities

A contingent liability is not recognised in the financial statements. Given the degree of uncertainty associated with such an item, this should not come as a surprise. We have seen that, for an item to be classified as a contingent liability, it must be less than probable that:

1 a present obligation exists: or
2 an outflow of resources is required; or
3 the amount of the obligation can be reliably measured.

Nevertheless, information concerning this type of liability may still be relevant to user needs.

IAS 37 states that contingent liabilities should be disclosed in the notes to the financial statements, unless the possibility of an outflow of resources is remote. For each class of contingent liability, there should be a brief description of its nature. Where practicable, there should also be some indication of its financial effect, the uncertainties surrounding the timing and amount of the outflow and the possibility of reimbursement.

Figure 7.1 summarises the recognition requirements for provisions and contingent liabilities.

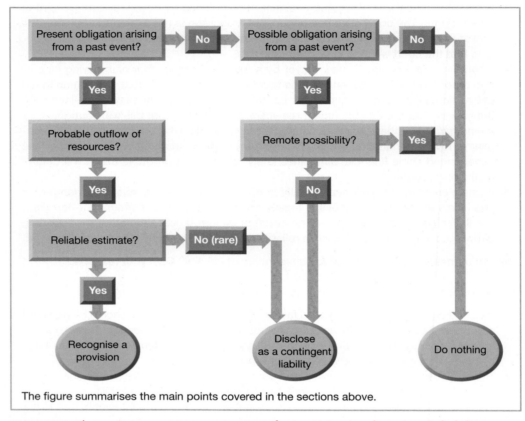

The figure summarises the main points covered in the sections above.

Figure 7.1 The main recognition requirements for provisions and contingent liabilities

Source: Adapted from diagram in IAS 37 *Provisions, Contingent Liabilities and Contingent Assets*, Appendix B.

Real World 7.2 is an extract from the 2017 annual report of Vodafone Group plc, the telecommunications business. It had a number of contingent liabilities outstanding at the end of its reporting period, one of which is described.

Real World 7.2

Patent dispute

Vodafone Group Plc has been sued in Spain by TOT Power Control ('TOT'), an affiliate of Top Optimized Technologies. The claim makes a number of allegations including patent infringement, with TOT seeking over €500 million from Vodafone Group Plc as well as an injunction against using the technology in question. Vodafone's challenge of the appropriateness of Spain as a venue for this dispute has been denied. Vodafone Group Plc will appeal the denial. A hearing on TOT's application for an injunction has taken place, and a decision is expected shortly.

Source: Vodafone Group plc, Annual Report 2017, p. 165.

CONTINGENT ASSETS

IAS 37 defines a **contingent asset** as a possible asset arising from past events, the existence of which will only be confirmed by future events not wholly within the control of the business.

Contingent assets are not recognised in the financial statements since they may not lead to an inflow of resources. Where, however, a future inflow of resources is probable, they should be disclosed by way of a note. This will involve a brief description of the nature of the contingent assets and, where practicable, an estimate of their financial effect.

Note the difference in disclosure requirements for a contingent liability and for a contingent asset. A contingent liability should be disclosed, unless the possibility of an outflow of resources is remote. A contingent asset, on the other hand, should only be disclosed where an inflow of resources is probable.

Activity 7.5

With which accounting convention is this difference in disclosure requirements consistent?

We saw in Chapter 2 that the prudence convention holds that caution should be exercised when making accounting judgements. Application of this convention normally requires recognition of anticipated losses and liabilities in the financial statements. Profits and assets, however, receive recognition only when they actually arise. A similarly cautious approach underpins these disclosure requirements.

Contingent assets should be reviewed continually to ensure that there has been no change in circumstances. Where it becomes virtually certain that the business will benefit from an inflow of resources, the asset is no longer treated as a contingent asset. It is recognised as an asset and will, therefore, be shown in the financial statements.

Figure 7.2 sets out the choices available where a contingent asset is being reviewed at the end of the reporting period.

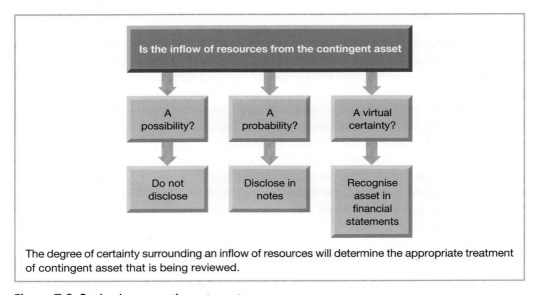

The degree of certainty surrounding an inflow of resources will determine the appropriate treatment of contingent asset that is being reviewed.

Figure 7.2 Reviewing a contingent asset

The following activity should help to identify the kind of situations where a contingent asset arises.

INTERNALLY-GENERATED INTANGIBLE ASSETS

A business may spend large amounts in developing an intangible asset. Examples may include developing computer software, creating a patented product, producing a film and so on. In some cases, the intangible asset that has been developed may have a tangible element. One example would be a compact disc (CD) for storing computer software. Where, however, the intangible element is considered the more significant, the asset will be regarded as intangible. In the case of the CD storing software, the cost of the CD is likely to be a matter of pence, whereas the software development cost could be vast.

Internally-generated intangible assets can create recognition problems. IAS 38 *Intangible Assets* makes it clear that intangible assets should be recognised only if their cost can be reliably measured and it is probable that expected future benefits will flow to the business. Where intangible assets are internally generated, however, it can be difficult to demonstrate that these conditions are met.

The research phase and the development phase

To deal with the recognition problems, IAS 38 classifies the generation of an intangible asset into two phases: a research phase and a development phase. The research phase precedes the development phase and may have no direct connection to the development of a particular product or service. It can cover activities such as:

- obtaining new knowledge;
- searching for, evaluating and applying research findings;
- searching for new materials, devices, processes and services; and
- designing and evaluating new materials, devices, processes and services.

Amounts spent during the research phase are regarded as an expense of the reporting period during which they are incurred and are, therefore, charged to the income statement for that period. They are not treated as part of the cost of an intangible asset as they cannot be directly related to any future economic benefits.

The development phase is further advanced than the research phase and covers activities such as:

- the design, construction and testing of prototypes and models;
- the design of tools, jigs, moulds and dies;
- the design, construction and operation of a pilot plant to test the feasibility of commercial operations; and
- the design, construction and testing of new materials, devices, processes and services.

For such activities, it may be possible to demonstrate that future economic benefits will flow from any amounts spent.

IAS 38 requires that, for an intangible asset arising from the development phase to be recognised, *all* of the following must be demonstrated:

- the technical feasibility of completing the intangible asset for use or sale;
- the intention to complete the intangible asset for use or sale;
- the ability to use or sell the intangible asset;
- how the intangible asset will generate probable future economic benefits;
- the availability of adequate technical, financial and other resources to complete the intangible asset for use or sale; and
- the ability to measure expenditure, attributable to the intangible asset, reliably.

These demanding conditions severely restrict the opportunities to carry forward development expenditure as an asset rather than to charge it as an expense. (This carrying forward of expenditure as an asset is often referred to as capitalisation.)

Activity 7.7

Consider the conditions for capitalisation mentioned above. How might a business demonstrate:

1 that the intangible asset will generate probable future economic benefits; and
2 its ability to measure reliably the expenditure attributable to the intangible asset?

Future economic benefits may be demonstrated by the existence of a market for whatever the asset produces. If the asset is used for internal purposes, its contribution to business processes must be demonstrated.

Reliable measurement of expenditure may be demonstrated by having efficient accounting systems that are able to identify the salaries, materials, services and fees that are incurred in relation to that particular intangible asset.

In some cases, it will not be possible to distinguish between a research phase and a development phase for expenditure on an intangible asset. Under these circumstances, all expenditure will be treated as though it were incurred during the research phase. That is, it will be charged to the income statement as it is incurred.

Capitalising development costs

Only development costs incurred after the intangible asset has met the conditions mentioned earlier should be capitalised. These costs, which are restricted to those directly attributable to producing the asset or getting it ready for use, may include:

■ materials and services consumed in creating the asset;
■ employee costs;
■ legal fees; and
■ depreciation (amortisation) of patents and licences.

They will not include selling, administrative or general overhead costs.

Research and development expenditure in practice

Many UK businesses spend considerable sums on researching and developing new products and services. During 2016, for example, the total came to £22.2 billion. Figure 7.3 shows the amount spent, both in real terms (that is, after adjusting for inflation) and in cash terms, over the period 1992 to 2016.

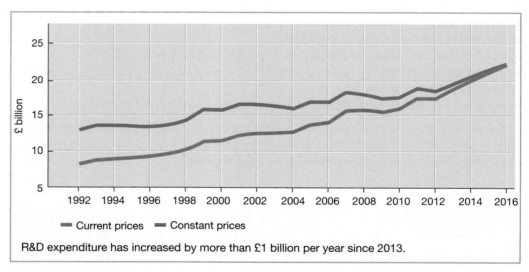

Figure 7.3 Research and development expenditure by UK businesses 1992–2016

Source: UK Business Enterprise Research and Development 2016, Office for National Statistics, www.ons.gov.uk, Office for National Statistics licensed under the Open Government Licence v.3.0, www.nationalarchives.gov.uk/doc/open-government-licence/version/3/.

Expenditure on research and development (R&D) varies between industries. The pharmaceutical, aerospace and car manufacturing industries tend to be particularly heavy spenders. **Real World 7.3** gives an insight into the R&D expenditure and policies of one large pharmaceutical business.

Real World 7.3

Hey big spender!

During 2016, AstraZeneca plc charged $5,890 million against revenue for research and development. For recent years, this R&D expense represented the following percentages of the business's annual sales revenue:

	Per cent
2011	16
2012	19
2013	19
2014	21
2015	24
2016	26

Looking back at Figure 7.3, it seems that, in 2016, AstraZeneca plc accounted for a large proportion of all R&D expenditure by UK businesses.

The accounting policies adopted by AstraZeneca plc for R&D expenditure are explained in its 2016 annual report as follows:

> Internal development expenditure is capitalised only if it meets the recognition criteria of IAS 38 'Intangible Assets'. Where regulatory and other uncertainties are such that the criteria are not met, the expenditure is recognised in profit and this is almost invariably the case prior to approval of the drug by the relevant regulatory authority. Where, however, recognition criteria are met, intangible assets are capitalised and amortised on a straight-line basis over their useful economic lives from product launch. At 31 December 2016, no amounts have met recognition criteria.

Source: AstraZeneca plc, Annual Report 2016, p. 143.

The case of AstraZeneca plc provides an insight into the practical effect of IAS 38. Despite the huge amount spent on R&D during 2016, the business did not capitalise a single penny. This was also the case in the previous year.

Activity 7.8

Why might managers prefer to capitalise both research costs and development costs? Try to think of at least one reason.

Managers may view these costs as a form of strategic investment, which is vital to the future survival and prosperity of the business. Capitalisation may, therefore, be considered the appropriate treatment.

They may, however, wish to capitalise for less worthy reasons. Capitalisation involves the transfer of costs incurred during a reporting period to the statement of financial position rather than to the income statement. This will result in higher reported profit and asset figures. They may well prefer to report this rosier picture of the business's financial health.

Recognition issues

IAS 38 specifically excludes certain types of internally-generated assets from recognition. Internally-generated brands, mastheads (the name or logo of newspapers or magazines) and customer lists cannot be recognised as intangible assets. The argument against their recognition is that it is not possible to distinguish the development of intangible assets from the development of the business as a whole. Internally-generated goodwill cannot be recognised as an intangible asset for a similar reason. It is not a separately identifiable resource.

Reporting internally-generated intangible assets

In cases where internally-generated intangible assets are recognised, they are reported in the financial statements in the same way as externally-acquired intangible assets. As we saw in Chapter 2, intangible assets are initially recognised at cost but, where there is an active market, they may subsequently be shown at fair value. Where an intangible asset is shown at its fair value, other assets of the same class must also be shown at their fair value, providing there is an active market.

An intangible asset may have a finite or indefinite life. If it is the former, the asset must be depreciated (amortised) over its useful life. When calculating the depreciation charge, the residual value of the asset is normally assumed to be zero. The useful life and depreciation method must be reviewed at least annually and changes made where necessary. Where an intangible asset has an indefinite life, there is no depreciation charge but impairment tests must be carried out at least annually. There must also be an annual review to determine whether the asset still has an indefinite life.

IAS 38 requires that internally-generated intangible assets be disclosed separately from other intangible assets. The disclosure requirements for all intangible assets are extensive and require information relating to carrying amounts, revaluations, impairment losses, depreciation methods and useful life.

Finally, total research and development expenditure charged to the income statement for the period must be separately disclosed.

LEASES

When a business needs a particular asset, such as a piece of equipment, instead of buying it direct from a supplier, the business may arrange for a financier (a bank or other provider of finance) to buy the asset and then lease it to the business. The lease arrangement will give the business the right to use the asset for a period in exchange for a payment or, much more likely, a series of payments. The financier is known as a 'lessor' (of the asset). The business that leases the asset from the financier and then uses it is known as the 'lessee'.

A finance lease, as such an arrangement is known, is in essence a form of lending. This is because, had the lessee borrowed the funds and then used them to buy the asset itself, the effect would be much the same. The lessee would have use of the asset but would also have a financial obligation to the lender – just as with a leasing arrangement.

With finance leasing, legal ownership of the asset remains with the lessor but the lease agreement transfers to the lessee virtually all the rewards and risks associated with the leased item. The finance lease agreement will usually cover a substantial part of the life of the leased item and may not be capable of being cancelled.

A lease that does not fit the description of a finance lease is known as an operating lease. For such leases, the rewards and risks of ownership do not transfer to the lessee. In practice, the operating lease period tends to be fairly short in relation to the life of the asset. An example of an operating lease is where a builder hires earth-moving equipment for three months to carry out a particular job.

Real World 7.4 provides an indication of the use of leasing by a well-known airline.

Leased assets take off

The fleet of aircraft held by easyJet plc as at 30 September 2017 is shown below. The table reveals that more than a quarter of the aircraft are held through some form of leasing arrangement, but only a small percentage under finance leases.

Aircraft	Owned	Operating leases	Finance leases	Total
A319	89	54	–	143
A320	111	18	5	134
A320neo	2	–	–	2
Total	202	72	5	279

Source: easyJet plc, Annual Report and Accounts 2017, p. 16.

Finance leases

Over the years, some important benefits associated with finance leasing have disappeared. Changes in the tax laws mean that it is no longer such a tax-efficient form of financing, and changes in disclosure requirements rule out concealing this form of 'borrowing' from investors. Nevertheless, the popularity of finance leases has continued. Other reasons must, therefore, exist for businesses to adopt this form of financing. These reasons are said to include the following:

- *Ease of borrowing.* Leasing may be obtained more easily than other forms of long-term finance. Lenders normally require some form of security and a profitable track record before making advances to a business. However, a lessor may be prepared to lease assets to a new business without a track record and to use the leased assets as security for the amounts owing.
- *Cost.* Leasing agreements may be offered at reasonable cost. As the asset leased is used as security, standard lease arrangements can be applied and detailed credit checking of lessees may be unnecessary. This can reduce administration costs for the lessor and, thereby, help in providing competitive lease rentals.
- *Flexibility.* Leasing can help provide flexibility where there are rapid changes in technology. If an option to cancel can be incorporated into the lease, the business may be able to exercise this option and invest in new technology as it becomes available. This will help the business to avoid the risk of obsolescence.
- *Cash flows.* Leasing, rather than buying an asset outright, means that large cash outflows can be avoided. The leasing option allows cash outflows to be smoothed out over the asset's life. In some cases, it is possible to arrange for low lease payments to be made in the early years of the asset's life, when cash inflows may be low, and for these to increase over time as the asset generates positive cash flows.

These benefits are summarised in diagrammatic form in Figure 7.4.

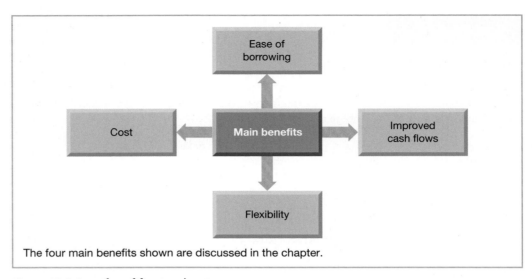

The four main benefits shown are discussed in the chapter.

Figure 7.4 Benefits of finance leasing

Real World 7.5 provides some impression of the importance of finance leasing over recent years.

Figure 7.5 charts the changes in the value of asset finance in the UK over the years 2012 to 2016.

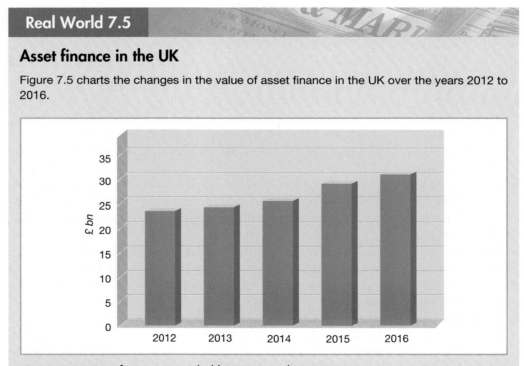

Figure 7.5 Asset finance provided by FLA members, 2012–16

In recent years, there has been a steady increase in the use of this form of finance by businesses. For 2016, it accounted for 32.3 per cent of the total UK investment in machinery, equipment and purchased software.

Source: Finance and Leasing Association (FLA), Annual Review 2017, p. 19.

Recognising leases

We have just seen that a lessee under a finance lease is not granted legal ownership of the leased asset. However, under the terms of a normal lease contract, it is granted the right to control its use. This provides the right to substantially all the economic benefits from the leased asset as well as the right to direct how, and for what purpose, it is used during the lease period. In exchange for this right to control, the lease contract imposes an obligation on the lessee to make payments. In substance, therefore, a lease gives rise to both an asset and a liability. It is this substance, rather than any legal form, that determines the accounting treatment of the lease in the financial statements of the lessee.

Activity 7.9

What problems would arise by *not* treating an asset acquired through a lease in the way described?

If assets acquired through a lease were not dealt with as mentioned, the economic resources and the financial obligations of the business would be understated. Users of the lessee's financial statements could, therefore, be misled about the financial position of the business.

IFRS 16 Leases

IFRS 16 *Leases* covers most forms of lease contracts. It makes no distinction between finance leases and operating leases: both are seen as giving the lessee the right to control the use of an asset and to a lease liability. The few exemptions under the standard include leases to explore mineral rights or to use biological assets, licenses of intellectual property and service concessions. There are also opt-out elections for leases for a year or less and for leases of low-value assets. These last two types of lease contracts may be treated as an expense and written off over the lease period. Where an election is made, therefore, they will not usually appear on the statement of financial position.

The standard requires that, at the commencement date of the lease, the lessee should recognise both an asset and a liability. Initially, the leased asset will be valued at cost. This will normally comprise the amount of the lease liability plus any lease payments made before, or at, the commencement date. It will also include any initial direct costs incurred in negotiating and securing the lease agreement and any estimated costs to be incurred for the eventual removal of the leased asset and restoration of the site where it is to be used.

The lease liability is initially measured at the **present value** of the lease payments outstanding at the commencement date. The term 'present value' refers to the value in today's terms of the future lease payments using a specified discount rate. (This concept of present value is explained in more detail in a short appendix to be found at the end of the chapter, which you should read if you are not familiar with the concept. If you are already familiar with this concept, please go straight on to the next section.)

Calculating the lease liability

We have just seen that, at the commencement date of the finance lease, a lessee should recognise both an asset and a liability in the statement of financial position. To measure both, the present value of the lease payments outstanding at the commencement date must be determined. This is done by calculating the present value figure for each of the future lease payments and then adding them together.

The discount rate to be used when determining the present value of future lease payments is the interest rate implicit in the lease or, where this cannot be determined, the incremental borrowing rate of the business. One way to determine this latter figure is to use the rate of interest that the business would have to pay on a similar lease. **Example 7.1** illustrates the discounting process where there are fixed lease payments.

Example 7.1

On 1 January 2019, Platina plc takes out a lease for robotic equipment. Details of the lease are as follows:

Annual lease payments	£1 million
Lease period	4 years
Lease payment date	31 December (in arrears)
Implicit interest rate	10 per cent per year

At the commencement of the lease, the present value of the lease payments is calculated as follows:

	£000	Present value £000
One year's time	$1,000 \times 1/(1 + 0.10)^1$	909
Two years' time	$1,000 \times 1/(1 + 0.10)^2$	826
Three years' time	$1,000 \times 1/(1 + 0.10)^3$	751
Four years' time	$1,000 \times 1/(1 + 0.10)^4$	683
Lease liability at commencement date		3,169

After the commencement date, the lease liability may be reassessed under certain circumstances, such as a change in the lease period. Any reassessment will, of course, have an effect on both the leased asset and the lease liability figures.

The lease period is the non-cancellable period during which the lessee has the right to control the asset. It will also include any period covered by an option to:

1 extend the lease, where it is reasonably certain the lessee will exercise this option; and
2 terminate the lease, where it is reasonably certain the lessee will not exercise this option.

We can see that the lease period may not always be clear cut. The lessee may have to exercise judgement when deciding upon the appropriate lease period.

Accounting for leases

An asset held through a lease contract is reported in the financial statements of a lessee in the same way as if it were owned. Thus, where the asset depreciates over time, it is depreciated in accordance with the requirements set out in IAS 16 *Property, Plant and Equipment*. There will be annual depreciation charges and the carrying amount of the leased asset will reflect their cumulative effect. Where it is reasonably certain that the lessee will take ownership of the asset by the end of the lease term, the asset will be depreciated over its useful life. Otherwise, the depreciation period will be the shorter of the asset's useful life and the lease term. Impairment tests will also be carried out as if the asset were owned.

After initial recognition, the carrying amount of the lease liability will be increased to reflect interest charges and reduced to reflect any lease payments made. A constant rate of interest should be charged over the lease period and should be applied to the carrying amount of the lease liability. Interest payable relating to the lease contract is normally included in the income statement.

Some lease contracts incorporate a requirement for the lessee to purchase certain goods or services, such as maintenance services, from the lessor. Where this arises, the non-lease component should be identified and accounted for separately. As a practical expedient, however, the lessee can elect to treat both the lease and non-lease components as a single lease component.

Presentation and disclosure of lease arrangements

Presentation and disclosure requirements for leases, in the financial statements of the lessee, are extensive and we shall not consider them in detail. However, they include:

■ separate presentation in the statement of financial position, or separate disclosure in the notes, of both leased assets and lease liabilities;
■ separate presentation in the income statement of both the interest expense relating to lease liabilities and of depreciation of the leased assets;
■ cash payments relating to the principal portion of the lease payments classified separately under 'cash flows from financing activities' in the statement of cash flows; and
■ cash payments relating to the interest portion of lease payments classified in the statement of cash flows under either 'cash flows from operating activities' or 'cash flows from financing activities' in accordance with IAS 7.

IFRS 16 replaces an earlier standard that made a distinction between finance leases and operating leases. In the earlier accounting standard, it was only finance leases that gave rise to both an asset and a liability as described above. Assets acquired under an operating lease were exempt from these requirements and so did not appear on the statement of financial position. This led to much criticism of the earlier standard and IFRS 16 was introduced to correct this perceived anomaly.

Real World 7.6 describes the likely impact of IFRS 16 on the financial statements of companies in certain industries, such as the airline industry, where operating leases are widely used.

Real World 7.6

No hiding place

When Sir David Tweedie was chairman of the International Accounting Standards Board [IASB], he joked his life-long ambition was to fly in an aircraft that actually existed on an airline's balance sheet (statement of financial position). Now, some six years later, his hope is becoming a reality. A new IASB financial reporting standard will force companies, including airlines, to include leasing obligations in annual statements of assets and liabilities, from 2019.

It ends a practice that investors claim has hidden assets and liabilities from plain sight. At present, all kinds of companies have operating leases for some equipment and property, but they do not bill them as assets and liabilities on their balance sheets (statement of financial position). They only record them as footnotes and include payments for the assets in

→

income statements. Now, operating leases will appear alongside financial leases on balance sheets – with only short-term leases and small ticket items excluded.

According to the IASB, the new IFRS 16 standard will affect one in two quoted companies globally, forcing them to put about $3 trillion of leasing obligations on to their balance sheets. It will bear upon the companies' credit scores and debt covenants based on ratios of obligations to cash, assets or profits. Retailers, hoteliers and airlines will be the most affected by the new requirement. For these companies, off balance sheet leases represent close to 30 per cent of assets, according to the IASB. Investors and analysts have largely welcomed the new standard. While IFRS 16 will add to a company's liabilities, they say it will bring offshore financing into the open, make accounts more transparent and improve comparisons of return on capital.

Vincent Papa, director of financial reporting policy for Chartered Financial Analysts, says IFRS 16 will standardise the currently varied disclosure of leasing costs in footnotes. He argues that, too often, a company's reported leverage (gearing) understates reality and IFRS 16 will improve calculations of default risk. Some accountants have warned that companies might try to change their lease terms to sidestep the new rules. However, analysts point out that the effect has been well flagged to investors. 'The stock market impact of this is going to be minimal because analysts [already] capitalise leases,' notes Stephen Furlong, an airline analyst at Davy Research. Credit rating agencies have for some time used the information disclosed in accounting footnotes to adjust credit scores to include operating leases. Moody's says it already adds about $1.7 trillion in debt to its numbers for global non-financial rated companies.

Many companies have already accepted the inevitability of change, and changed their models. In the airline industry, for example, off balance sheet leasing has been diminishing. Fewer than 10 of Ryanair's aircraft will be leased by 2019, when the changes take effect. Already, less than a third of easyJet's fleet is leased. Tesco's headline debt will more than double to £17 billion under the new rules, but it already discloses all lease obligations, so analysts say they are unlikely to change the view of the company. This has caused some to complain about the cost of the new rules. 'It's going to be a lot of messing for not much gain in my view,' says Mr Furlong. But given the pace of accounting change, the IASB may deem it a triumph that Sir David will realise his lifetime ambition only a few years into retirement.

 Source: Extracts from Burgess, K. and Agnew, H. (2016) Accounting's big shake-up to bring more transparency, ft.com. 20 January.

BORROWING COSTS

Suppose that a business borrows money to finance the construction of an asset. The asset takes some time to complete and, during the construction period, the business pays interest on the amounts borrowed. A key question that arises is whether the interest payable should be charged against income in the period incurred or capitalised as part of the cost of the asset.

The general rule is that the cost of an asset should include all costs required to get it ready for use or for sale. The case for capitalisation is that borrowing costs, which include interest payable and finance charges relating to finance leases, can be properly regarded as part of these costs. IAS 23 *Borrowing Costs* adopts this view. It argues that the cost of the asset will not be faithfully represented unless borrowing costs are included.

The core principle set out in IAS 23 is that borrowing costs which are directly attributable to the acquisition, production or construction of a qualifying asset should be included as part of its cost. All other borrowing costs are treated as an expense in the period incurred.

Two practical problems arise in applying this core principle. The first is that it is not always easy to identify a direct link between particular borrowings and a qualifying asset. It may be, for example, that a business borrows from various sources, at various rates of interest, to create a general pool of funds. It then draws on this pool to finance the construction of a qualifying asset. IAS 23 states that, in such a situation, a capitalisation rate based on the weighted average cost of the pool of borrowing should be applied.

The second problem concerns the definition of a 'qualifying asset'. IAS 23 states that it is an asset that takes a substantial period of time to get ready for use or for resale. It may include:

■ inventories (excluding those taking a short period to produce);
■ manufacturing plants;
■ power-generation facilities;
■ intangible assets; and
■ investment properties.

This is a rather broad definition that could benefit from further clarification.

IAS 23 states that capitalisation of borrowing costs can begin only when:

1 borrowing costs are incurred;
2 expenditure for the asset is incurred; and
3 activities to prepare the asset for use or sale are in progress.

Capitalisation ends when active development of the asset is suspended or when the asset is substantially completed.

The disclosure requirements set out in the standard are quite straightforward. The borrowing costs capitalised during the period and the capitalisation rate used to determine any capitalised borrowing costs must be specified.

The amount of interest capitalised can be very significant. **Real World 7.7** illustrates how much interest one large business capitalised.

Real World 7.7

Quite a lot of interest

Severn River Crossing plc ordered the construction of a second bridge crossing for the River Severn between England and Wales. The six-lane motorway bridge was opened in June 1996. The total cost of the Second Severn Crossing was £464 million, which included £387.4 million payable to John Laing Construction Ltd/GTM-Europe Joint Venture and £76.6 million in capitalised interest. The interest element relates to funds borrowed for the design and construction of the bridge and represents around one sixth of the total cost.

Source: Severn Bridge Crossing plc, Annual Report 2016, pp. 17 and.22.

Criticisms of IAS 23

The capitalisation of borrowing costs has attracted some criticism. It has been argued that measuring and monitoring capitalised borrowing costs is time consuming, cumbersome and costly. It has also been argued that the benefits, to users of financial statements, of capitalising interest are unclear. It has been claimed, for example, that, when examining the income statement to assess the degree of financial risks arising from interest charges, financial analysts reverse any capitalised interest. There is no strong evidence, however, of widespread dissatisfaction with the standard.

Some critics of IAS 23 would like businesses to be given a choice over whether to capitalise borrowing costs or to charge them to the period incurred. This choice was permitted in an earlier version of IAS 23.

Activity 7.10

What problems arise from giving businesses a choice over the treatment of borrowing costs?

One problem is that a quite different portrayal of financial performance and position may occur, according to whether interest charges are capitalised or whether they are charged to the current period. Providing a choice can, therefore, undermine comparability between different businesses or between different time periods.

A further problem is that, by offering a choice, the question as to what should be included in the cost of an asset is effectively avoided. This is an important question, to which the IASB should have a clear answer.

The following self-assessment question brings together some of the points contained within the chapter.

Self-assessment question 7.1

Prentaxia plc produced a draft income statement for the year just ended that reported a profit before tax of £87.2 million. An investigation of the underlying records produced the following information:

1 During the year, the business entered into a lease agreement to acquire a machine. The lease period is five years with an annual lease payment, payable in arrears, of £5 million. The first lease payment, which was paid at the end of the financial year, was charged in full as an expense in the draft income statement. This was the only transaction reported concerning the lease agreement. The interest element of the lease payment was £2 million. The cost of the machine at the commencement date of the lease agreement was £19 million and the residual value is estimated to be nil. All non-current assets are depreciated using the straight-line method.

2 Two years ago, the business began the construction of a new factory. Borrowing costs of £2 million relating to factory construction were incurred during the current year. These costs were charged to the draft income statement.

3 In the previous financial year, a provision was recognised for £10 million for cleaning up contaminated land near a factory owned by the business. The clean up of the land is due to take place in two years' time. At the end of the current year, it was found that the contamination was more extensive than first estimated and that the total clean-up cost was now expected to be £12.6 million. No action has so far been taken.

4 One of the factories owned by the business has a large furnace. The lining of the furnace must be replaced every four years in order for it to remain in working order. A replacement lining is due next year. The existing lining, which cost £1.0 million, is being depreciated over its life. The directors decided to recognise a provision of £1.4 million during the current year to replace the lining.

5 During the year, a court case was brought against the business for infringement of patent rights. A rival business is claiming £4.5 million as compensation. The business is defending the action but its lawyers believe that it will probably not succeed in its defence. A contingent liability for the full amount claimed has been disclosed in the draft financial statements.

6 During the year, the business spent £1.3 million in a search for new materials to replace materials that are currently used in its range of products. This amount was capitalised.

7 The law requires the business to fit smoke alarms throughout its offices and factories by next year. The estimated cost of doing so is £0.4 million. To date, no action has been taken in respect of this.

Required:

Show the revised profit before tax for the current year of Prentaxia plc after taking account of the above information, briefly stating the reasons for any adjustments that have been made.

The solution to this question can be found at the back of the book, starting on page 525.

SUMMARY

The main points of this chapter may be summarised as follows:

Provisions, contingent liabilities and contingent assets (IAS 37)

■ A provision is a form of liability where the timing or amount involved is uncertain.

■ A provision is recognised where all of the following criteria are met:
  – there is an obligation arising from a past event;
  – an outflow of resources is probably needed to settle the obligation; and
  – a reliable estimate of the obligation can be made.

■ The amount of the provision should be the best estimate of the amount needed to settle the obligation.

■ A provision is created by charging the income statement with the amount of the provision. This amount then appears on the statement of financial position.

■ In the past, provisions have been used for creative accounting purposes.

■ A contingent liability is defined as:
  – a possible obligation arising from past events, the existence of which will only be confirmed by future events not wholly within the control of the business; or
  – a present obligation arising from past events, where it is either not probable that an outflow of resources is needed, or the amount of the obligation cannot be reliably measured.

■ Contingent liabilities are disclosed in the notes to financial statements, unless the possibility of an outflow of resources is remote.

■ A contingent asset is defined as a possible asset arising from past events, the existence of which will only be confirmed by future events not wholly within the control of the business.

- Contingent assets are not recognised in the financial statements. Where, however, a future inflow of resources is probable, they should be disclosed by way of a note.

Internally-generated intangible assets (IAS 38)

- The generation process is divided into two phases: a research phase and a development phase.
- The research phase precedes the development phase and may have no direct connection to the development of a particular product or service.
- Research expenditure is regarded as an expense when incurred as it cannot be directly related to future economic benefits.
- The development phase is further advanced than the research phase and is related to the development of a product or service.
- Development expenditure should be capitalised provided it meets strict conditions including the ability to demonstrate probable future economic benefits.
- Only development costs arising after the internally-generated asset has been recognised and which are directly attributable to creating the asset or getting it ready for use can be capitalised.
- Certain internally-generated assets, such as goodwill, brands, mastheads, customer lists and publishing titles, cannot be recognised.

Leases (IFRS 16)

- A lease does not grant legal ownership of the leased asset to the lessee. However, under the terms of a lease contract, the lessee is granted the right to control its use.
- The substance, rather than the legal form, of a finance lease agreement is that it gives rise to both an asset and a liability in the financial statements of the lessee.
- Initially, the leased asset will be valued at cost.
- The leased asset is reported in the financial statements in the same way as if it were owned.
- The lease liability is initially measured at the present value of the lease payments outstanding at the commencement date.
- After initial recognition, the carrying amount of the lease liability will be increased to reflect interest charges and reduced to reflect any lease payments made.
- The non-lease component within a lease contract should be identified and normally accounted for separately.

Borrowing costs (IAS 23)

- Borrowing costs that are directly attributable to the acquisition, production or construction of a qualifying asset form part of its cost.
- All other borrowing costs are treated as an expense in the period in which they are incurred.
- A qualifying asset is an asset that takes a substantial period of time to get ready for use or for resale.

FURTHER READING

If you would like to explore the topics covered in this chapter in more depth, we recommend the following:

Alexander, D., Britton, A., Jorissen, A., Hoogendorn, M. and Van Mourik, C. (2017) *International Financial Reporting and Analysis*, 7th edn, Cengage Learning, Chapters 13, 15 and 19.

Elliott, B. and Elliott, J. (2017) *Financial Accounting and Reporting*, 18th edn, Pearson, Chapters 18 and 19.

International Accounting Standards Board (2018) *IFRS Standards – Required 1 January 2018 (Blue Book)*, IFRS Foundation, IAS 23, 37 and 38.

Melville, A. (2017) *International Financial Reporting: A Practical Guide*, 6th edn, Pearson, Chapters 9 and 12.

CRITICAL REVIEW QUESTIONS

Solutions to these questions can be found at the back of the book, starting on page 536.

7.1 The threshold for disclosure for contingent assets differs from that for contingent liabilities. Why is this the case? Can you see a problem with this difference in thresholds in the context of a lawsuit?

7.2 A provision is recognised when it is more likely than not (greater than 50 per cent chance) that an outflow of economic benefits will be needed to satisfy the obligation. This threshold established in IAS 37 represents a lower recognition threshold than is required by the equivalent US accounting standard. When considering a lawsuit in which the company is the defendant, can you see a potential problem having to adopt this lower threshold?

7.3 'The treatment of research and development expenditure set out in IAS 38 *Intangible Assets* reflects the tension between the prudence convention and the accruals convention in accounting.' Explain.

7.4 In the past, operating lease payments were treated as an expense in the period incurred. Critics claimed, however, that this treatment could be used for creative accounting purposes. Explain how this could be the case.

Solutions to exercises with coloured numbers can be found in at the back of the book, starting on page 545.

Basic-level exercises

7.1 Consider the following:

1 A motor car manufacturer offers a three-year warranty on all cars that it produces. The warranty undertakes to make good any defects arising from the manufacturing process. On past experience, 0.5 per cent of car owners make claims under the terms of the warranty.

2 A cruise ship suffered an outbreak of food poisoning that affected most of its passengers. Legal proceedings have been brought against the cruise ship company and a court case has just commenced. The lawyers for the company believe that it is probable that the cruise ship company will be found liable.

3 An airline company has just commenced operations and has acquired three new aircraft. The law requires that these aircraft be subject to a rigorous overhaul after two years of flying.

Required:
State for which of these should a provision be recognised. Give your reasons.

Intermediate-level exercises

7.2 On 1 January 2019, Markon plc took out a finance lease for new plant. Details of the lease are as follows:

Annual lease payments	£2.0m
Lease period	4 years
Lease payment date	31 December (in arrears)

The business has a reporting-year-end date of 31 December. The non-cancellable part of the lease covers the four annual lease payments. The implicit interest rate in the lease is 12 per cent per year.

The business incurred £0.2 million in preparing the site for the new plant and expects to incur a further £0.3 million in removing the plant at the end of the lease period and making good the site. A deposit of £1.0 million was paid to the lessor at the commencement of the lease and of £0.1 million was spent in securing and negotiating the lease.

Required:
Calculate at the commencement date of the lease:

(a) the lease liability;
(b) the cost of the plant.

7.3 Consider the following:

1 Under new legislation, a retail business will be obliged to fit handrails to the staircases used in its stores. The law will come into force six months after the end of its current reporting period. So far the business has done nothing to respond to this change in the law. The cost of fitting the handrails is expected to be £2 million.

2 The board of directors of a manufacturing business has decided to close down its motor cycle division. The board has charged the chief executive with the task of drawing up a

formal detailed plan for the closure. The costs of closure have been estimated as £4.5 million.

3 An energy business operates a nuclear power station. In 50 years' time, the power station will be decommissioned and the law requires the business to incur the costs of decommissioning. Decommissioning costs of £80 million are expected.

4 New health and safety rules have been introduced by the government, which apply to manufacturing businesses. A large manufacturer will need to retrain its managers to ensure compliance with the new rules. The cost of the retraining programme is estimated at £1 million. At the end of the reporting period, no retraining has taken place.

5 An energy business operates an oilfield in the North Sea. The licensing agreement with the UK government requires the business to remove its oil rigs when oil production ceases and to restore the sea bed. An additional oil rig has just been constructed, but so far it has not commenced operations and so no oil has been extracted. It is estimated that 80 per cent of the restoration cost will arise from removal of the additional oil rig and 20 per cent from damage created from oil extraction. Total restoration costs, associated with the additional oil rig, are estimated to be £10 million.

Required:
State for which of these should a provision be recognised. Give your reasons.

7.4 Ondamin plc produced a draft income statement that revealed a profit before tax of £65.5 million. Subsequent checking of the underlying records revealed the following:

1 A licence costing £10 million was acquired at the beginning of the year, which has a remaining legal life of 10 years. The licence has been amortised, on a straight-line basis for the year. The commercial director believes, however, that the licence could be sold in the market for £15 million. The board of directors has, therefore, decided to switch to using the fair value of the asset from the current year onwards.

2 A masthead has been developed during the year at an estimated cost of £6.0 million. The business has decided to write-off this amount evenly over the next 10 years and so an appropriate charge was included in the current year's income statement. However, the commercial director believes that the masthead has an indefinite life.

3 Research expenditure of £2.0 million was incurred during the year. The business wishes to write this off over the next five years, using the straight-line method, and an appropriate charge was included in the current year's income statement.

4 Development costs incurred during the year relating to a new product were as follows:

	£m
Legal fees	0.4
Payments to development engineers	1.2
Materials consumed in developing the product	0.6
General overhead costs	1.0

These amounts are to be written off evenly over a five-year period. An appropriate charge was, therefore, included in the current year's income statement.

Required:
Recalculate the profit before tax for the current year. Explain any adjustments and any assumptions that you make in doing so.

Advanced-level exercises

7.5 The draft income statement for the most recent reporting period of Barchester United Football Club plc has reported a profit before tax of £48.8 million. An examination of the underlying records, however, shows that the following items need to be taken into account during the current period:

1 A provision for £15 million for restructuring the club was recognised in the preceding year. During the current year, the first phase of the restructuring was carried out and restructuring costs of £5.4 million were incurred. This amount has been charged to the current income statement.

2 A provision for a legal action against the club for unfair dismissal of the previous manager for £2.2 million was recognised in the preceding year. During the current year, the manager lost his case at an industrial tribunal and does not intend to appeal.

3 During the previous reporting period, a contingent asset was reported. This relates to an agreement to allow a television channel exclusive rights to televise reserve team matches. The agreement includes a formula for payment to Barchester United based on the number of television viewers per match (as measured by an independent body). A dispute over the precise interpretation of this formula led Barchester United to sue the television channel for £2 million in underpaid income. The court case to decide the issue recently ended abruptly when the television channel finally accepted (on the advice of its lawyers) that its interpretation of the formula had been incorrect.

4 The club spent £1 million during the year to help fund research studies on the main causes of football injuries among professional football players. This amount was capitalised and shown on the statement of financial position.

5 The club is building new training facilities for its players. The facilities are currently being constructed and will take three years to complete. During the current year, the club incurred £3.3 million in interest charges on the construction of the facilities. These were charged to the current income statement.

6 At the beginning of the year, the club took out a finance lease to acquire a new type of plastic all-weather turf for its new training ground. Annual lease payments, which are payable in arrears, are £1.5 million per year in each of the four years. The interest charge appearing in the draft income statement has been calculated on the basis that the total interest charge for the lease is allocated evenly over the lease period. The total interest charges should, however, be allocated as follows:

Year	Interest £m
1	0.8
2	0.6
3	0.4
4	0.2

Required:

Calculate a revised profit before tax for the current reporting period, after taking account of the information shown above, and write brief notes to explain each adjustment that you have made to the draft profit before tax.

We do not normally see an amount paid out today as being equivalent in value to the same amount being received in the future. Thus, if offered £1,000 in one year's time in exchange for £1,000 now, we would not normally be interested. This is because we are aware that, by being deprived of the opportunity to spend our money for a year, we are unable to invest it in a way that would earn interest. To put it another way, we are aware that money has a *time value*.

The time value of money can be seen from two perspectives: future value and present value. We shall now consider each of these in turn.

Future value

The *future value* of an investment is the amount to which its present value will grow in the future. Suppose that you want to invest £1,000 today at an interest rate of 20 per cent per year. Over a five-year period, the future value of your investment would build up as follows:

		Future value £
Initial investment	$£1,000 \times (1 + 0.20)^0$	1,000
One year's time	$£1,000 \times (1 + 0.20)^1$	1,200
Two years' time	$£1,000 \times (1 + 0.20)^2$	1,440
Three years' time	$£1,000 \times (1 + 0.20)^3$	1,728
Four years' time	$£1,000 \times (1 + 0.20)^4$	2,074
Five years' time	$£1,000 \times (1 + 0.20)^5$	2,488

The principles of compound interest are applied to determine the future value. Thus, interest earned is reinvested and then added to the initial investment to derive the future value. Reading from the table, we can see that the future value of the £1,000 investment, when invested at a compound interest rate of 20 per cent over five years, is £2,488.

The formula for deriving the future value of an investment for a given period is:

$$FV = PV (1 + r)^n$$

where:
FV = Future value of the investment
PV = Initial sum invested (also known as the present value)
r = Rate of return per year from the investment (expressed as a proportion rather than a percentage)
n = Number of years of the investment.

This formula is being applied in the second column of the above table to reveal the future value of the investment in one year's time, two years' time and so on.

Present value

We have just seen that future value of an investment is the amount to which its present value will grow at some future point in time. As an alternative, we can take the future value of a sum of money and express it in terms of its *present value*. In other words, we can bring the future sum of money back to today's value.

Suppose that you are given an opportunity to receive £1,000 in one year's time by investing a sum of money today. You are told that similar investments provide a rate of return of 20 per cent. The maximum that you should be prepared to invest is the sum that would grow to £1,000 if invested at 20 per cent over one year. This maximum figure will represent the present value of the future sum of money.

Taking the example just mentioned, we can say of the present value (PV) figure that:

$$PV + (PV \times 20\%) = £1,000$$

or, to put it another way, that the amount plus income from investing the amount for the year must equal £1,000.

If we rearrange this equation, we find:

$$PV \times (1 + 0.20) = £1,000$$

Further rearranging gives:

$$PV = £1,000/(1 + 0.20) = £833 \text{ (to nearest £1)}$$

These calculations shown can be expressed more formally as

$$\mathbf{PV = FV\,(1/1 + \mathit{r})^\mathit{n}}$$

Activity 7.11

Complete the table below to show the present value of £1,000 to be received in each year over a five-year period, assuming a rate of return of 20 per cent. (We already know the present value for today and for one year's time.)

		Present value £
Immediate receipt	$£1,000 \times 1/(1 + 0.20)^0$	1,000
One year's time	$£1,000 \times 1/(1 + 0.20)^1$	833
Two years' time	_____	____
Three years' time	_____	____
Four years' time	_____	____
Five years' time	_____	____

Your answer should be as follows:

		Present value £
Immediate receipt	$£1,000 \times 1/(1 + 0.20)^0$	1,000
One year's time	$£1,000 \times 1/(1 + 0.20)^1$	833
Two years' time	$£1,000 \times 1/(1 + 0.20)^2$	694
Three years' time	$£1,000 \times 1/(1 + 0.20)^3$	579
Four years' time	$£1,000 \times 1/(1 + 0.20)^4$	482
Five years' time	$£1.000 \times 1/(1 + 0.20)^5$	402

The rate of return that is used to determine the present value of future receipts is referred to as the *discount rate*.

The answer to Activity 7.11 shows how the value of £1,000 diminishes as its receipt, or payment, goes further into the future. This is shown in diagrammatic form in Figure 7.6.

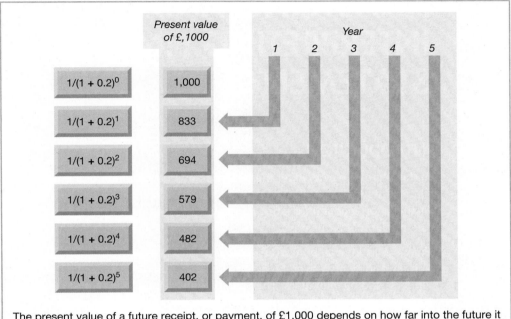

The present value of a future receipt, or payment, of £1,000 depends on how far into the future it will occur. Those that occur in the near future will have a larger present value than those occurring at a more distant point in time.

Figure 7.6 Present value of £1,000 receivable at various points in the future at an annual rate of return of 20 per cent

Once you feel that you have grasped the concept of present value please read the section on 'Calculating the lease liability' (page 253).

Chapter 8

ANALYSING AND INTERPRETING FINANCIAL STATEMENTS (1)

INTRODUCTION

In this chapter we consider the analysis and interpretation of the financial statements discussed in Chapters 2, 3 and 6. We shall see how the use of financial (or accounting) ratios can help to assess the financial performance and position of a business.

Financial ratios can be used to examine various aspects of financial health and are widely employed by external users, such as shareholders and lenders, and by managers. They can be very helpful to managers in a wide variety of decision areas, such as profit planning, pricing, working capital management and financial structure.

We shall continue our examination of the analysis and interpretation of financial statements in Chapter 9.

Learning outcomes

When you have completed this chapter, you should be able to:

- explain how ratios can be used to assess the position, performance and cash flows of a business;
- identify the major categories of ratios that can be used for analysing financial statements;
- calculate key ratios for assessing the profitability, efficiency, liquidity and gearing of a business; and
- explain the significance of the ratios calculated.

FINANCIAL RATIOS

Financial ratios provide a quick and relatively simple means of assessing the financial health of a business. A ratio simply relates one figure appearing in the financial statements to another figure appearing there (for example, operating profit in relation to sales revenue) or, perhaps, to some non-financial resource of the business (for example, operating profit per employee).

Ratios can be very helpful when comparing the financial health of different businesses. Differences may exist between businesses in the scale of operations. As a result, a direct comparison of, say, the operating profit generated by each business may be misleading. By expressing operating profit in relation to some other measure (for example, capital employed), the problem of scale is eliminated. This means that a business with an operating profit of £10,000 and capital employed of £100,000 can be compared with a much larger business with an operating profit of £80,000 and capital employed of £1,000,000 by the use of a simple ratio. The operating profit to capital employed ratio for the smaller business is 10 per cent (that is, (10,000/100,000) × 100%) and the same ratio for the larger business is 8 per cent (that is, (80,000/1,000,000) × 100%). These ratios can be directly compared, whereas a comparison of the absolute operating profit figures might be much less meaningful. The need to eliminate differences in scale through the use of ratios can also apply when comparing the performance of the same business from one time period to another.

By calculating a small number of ratios it is often possible to build up a revealing picture of the position and performance of a business. It is not surprising, therefore, that ratios are widely used by those who have an interest in businesses and business performance. Ratios are not difficult to calculate but they can be difficult to interpret.

Ratios help us to identify which questions to ask, rather than provide the answers. They help to highlight the financial strengths and weaknesses of a business, but cannot explain why those strengths or weaknesses exist or why certain changes have occurred. They provide a starting point for further analysis. Only a detailed investigation will reveal the underlying reasons.

Ratios can be expressed in various forms, for example as a percentage or as a proportion. The way that a particular ratio is presented will depend on the needs of those who will use the information. Although it is possible to calculate a large number of ratios, only a few, based on key relationships, tend to be helpful to a particular user. Many ratios that could be calculated from the financial statements (for example, rent payable in relation to current assets) may not be considered because there is not usually any clear or meaningful relationship between the two items.

There is no generally accepted list of ratios that can be applied to the financial statements, nor is there a standard method of calculating many ratios. Variations in both the choice of ratios and their calculation will be found in practice. It is important, therefore, to be consistent in the way in which ratios are calculated for comparison purposes. The ratios that we shall discuss are very popular – presumably because they are seen as useful for decision-making purposes.

FINANCIAL RATIO CLASSIFICATIONS

Ratios tend to be grouped into categories, with each category relating to a particular aspect of financial performance or position. The following broad categories are those that are usually found in practice. There are five of them:

- *Profitability.* Businesses generally exist with the primary purpose of creating wealth for their owners. Profitability ratios provide some indication of the degree of success in achieving this. These ratios express the profit made in relation to other key figures in the financial statements or to some business resource.
- *Efficiency.* Ratios may be used to measure the efficiency with which particular resources, such as inventories or employees, have been used within the business. These ratios are also referred to as *activity* ratios.
- *Liquidity.* It is vital to the survival of a business that there are sufficient liquid resources available to meet maturing obligations (that is, amounts owing that must be paid in the near future). Liquidity ratios examine the relationship between liquid resources, or cash generated, and amounts due for payment in the near future.
- *Financial gearing.* This is the relationship between the contribution to financing a business made by the owners and the contribution made by others, in the form of loans. This relationship is important because the level of gearing has an important effect on the level of risk associated with a business. Gearing ratios help to reveal the extent to which loan finance is utilised and the consequent effect on the level of risk borne by a business.
- *Investment.* Certain ratios are concerned with assessing the returns and performance of shares in a particular business from the perspective of shareholders who are not involved with the management of the business.

These five key aspects of financial health that ratios seek to examine are summarised in Figure 8.1.

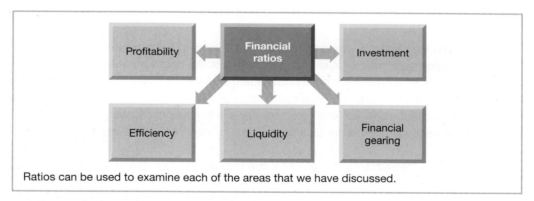

Ratios can be used to examine each of the areas that we have discussed.

Figure 8.1 The key aspects of financial health

The analyst must be clear *who* the target users are and *why* they need the information. Different users of financial information are likely to have different information needs. This will, in turn, determine the ratios that they find useful. Shareholders, for example, are likely to be interested in their returns in relation to the level of risk associated with their investment. Profitability, investment and gearing ratios should, therefore, be of particular interest. Long-term lenders are likely to be concerned with the long-term viability of the business and, to assess this, profitability and gearing ratios should be of interest. Short-term lenders, such as suppliers of goods and services on credit, are likely to be interested in the ability of the business to repay the amounts owing in the short term. Liquidity ratios should, therefore, be of particular interest.

THE NEED FOR COMPARISON

Merely calculating a ratio will not tell us very much about the position or performance of a business. For example, if a ratio revealed that a retail business was generating £100 in sales revenue per square metre of floor space, it would not be possible to deduce from this information alone whether this particular level of performance was good, bad or indifferent. It is only when we compare this ratio with some 'benchmark' that the information can be interpreted and evaluated.

Activity 8.1

Can you think of any bases that could be used to compare a ratio that you have calculated from the financial statements of your business for a particular period? (*Hint*: There are three main possibilities.)

You may have thought of the following bases:

- past periods for the same business;
- similar businesses for the same or past periods; and/or
- planned performance for the business.

We shall now take a closer look at these three in turn.

Past periods

By comparing the ratio that we have calculated with the same ratio, but for a previous period, it is possible to detect whether there has been an improvement or deterioration in performance. Indeed, it is often useful to track particular ratios over time (say, five or ten years) to see whether it is possible to detect trends. The comparison of ratios from different periods brings certain problems, however. In particular, there is always the possibility that trading conditions were quite different in the periods being compared. There is the further problem that, when comparing the performance of a single business over time, operating inefficiencies may not be clearly exposed. For example, the fact that sales revenue per employee has risen by 10 per cent over the previous period may at first sight appear to be satisfactory. This may not be the case, however, if similar businesses have shown an improvement of 50 per cent for the same period or had much better sales revenue per employee ratios to start with. Finally, there is the problem that inflation may have distorted the figures on which the ratios are based. Inflation can lead to an overstatement of profit and an understatement of asset values, as will be discussed later (in Chapters 9 and 11).

Similar businesses

In a competitive environment, a business must consider its performance in relation to that of other businesses operating in the same industry. Survival may depend on its ability to achieve comparable levels of performance. A useful basis for comparing a particular ratio, therefore, is the ratio achieved by similar businesses during the same period. This basis is not, however, without its problems. Competitors may have different year ends and so trading conditions may not be identical. They may also have different accounting policies, which can have a significant effect on reported profits and asset values (for example, different methods of calculating depreciation or valuing inventories). Crucially, it may be difficult to obtain the financial statements of competitor businesses. Sole proprietorships and partnerships, for example, are not obliged to make their financial statements available to the public. In the case of limited companies, there is a legal obligation to do so. However, a diversified business may not provide a breakdown of activities that is sufficiently detailed to enable comparisons with other businesses. This is despite the requirement for diversified businesses to report certain information on their different segments, as we shall discuss later in the book in Chapter 11.

Planned performance

Planned performance often provides the most valuable benchmark against which managers may assess their own business. Ratios based on the actual results may be compared with targets that management developed before the start of the period under review. This comparison can be a useful way of assessing the level of achievement attained. However, planned performance must be based on realistic assumptions if it is to be worthwhile for comparison purposes.

Planned, or target, ratios may be prepared for each aspect of the business's activities. When developing these ratios, account will normally be taken of past performance and the performance of other businesses. This does not mean, however, that the business should seek to achieve either of these levels of performance. Neither may provide an appropriate target.

We should bear in mind that those outside the business do not normally have access to the business's plans. For such people, past performance and the performances of other, similar, businesses may provide the only practical benchmarks.

The three most used bases of comparison for financial ratios are shown in Figure 8.2.

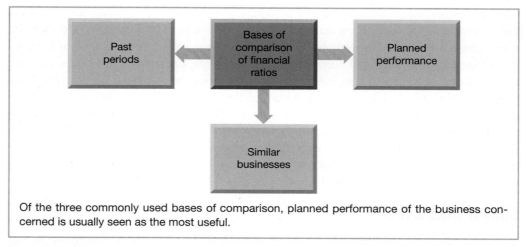

Of the three commonly used bases of comparison, planned performance of the business concerned is usually seen as the most useful.

Figure 8.2 The commonly used bases of comparison for financial ratios

CALCULATING THE RATIOS

Probably the best way to explain financial ratios is through an example. Example 8.1 provides a set of financial statements from which we can calculate important ratios.

Example 8.1

The following financial statements relate to Alexis plc, which operates a wholesale carpet business:

Statements of financial position (balance sheets) as at 31 December

	2017 £m	2018 £m
ASSETS		
Non-current assets		
Property, plant and equipment (at cost less depreciation)		
Land and buildings	381	427
Fixtures and fittings	129	160
	510	587
Current assets		
Inventories	300	406
Trade receivables	240	273
Cash at bank	4	–
	544	679
Total assets	1,054	1,266
EQUITY AND LIABILITIES		
Equity		
£0.50 ordinary shares (Note 1)	300	300
Retained earnings	263	234
	563	534
Non-current liabilities		
Borrowings – 9% loan notes (secured)	200	300
Current liabilities		
Trade payables	261	354
Taxation	30	2
Short-term borrowings (all bank overdraft)	–	76
	291	432
Total equity and liabilities	1,054	1,266

Income statements for the year ended 31 December

	2017 £m	2018 £m
Revenue (Note 2)	2,240	2,681
Cost of sales (Note 3)	(1,745)	(2,272)
Gross profit	495	409
Operating expenses	(252)	(362)
Operating profit	243	47
Interest payable	(18)	(32)
Profit before taxation	225	15
Taxation	(60)	(4)
Profit for the year	165	11

Statement of cash flows for the year ended 31 December

	2017 £m	2018 £m
Cash flows from operating activities		
Profit, after interest, before taxation	225	15
Adjustments for:		
Depreciation	26	33
Interest expense	18	32
	269	80
Increase in inventories	(59)	(106)
Increase in trade receivables	(17)	(33)
Increase in trade payables	58	93
Cash generated from operations	251	34
Interest paid	(18)	(32)
Taxation paid	(63)	(32)
Dividend paid	(40)	(40)
Net cash from/(used in) operating activities	130	(70)
Cash flows from investing activities		
Payments to acquire property, plant and equipment	(77)	(110)
Net cash used in investing activities	(77)	(110)
Cash flows from financing activities		
Issue of loan notes	–	100
Net cash from financing activities	–	100
Net increase in cash and cash equivalents	53	(80)
Cash and cash equivalents at start of year		
Cash/(overdraft)	(49)	4
Cash and cash equivalents at end of year		
Cash/(overdraft)	4	(76)

Notes:

1. The market value of the shares of the business at the end of the reporting period was £2.50 for 2017 and £1.50 for 2018.
2. All sales and purchases are made on credit.
3. The cost of sales figure can be analysed as follows:

	2017 £m	2018 £m
Opening inventories	241	300
Purchases (Note 2)	1,804	2,378
	2,045	2,678
Closing inventories	(300)	(406)
Cost of sales	1,745	2,272

4. At 31 December 2016, the trade receivables stood at £223 million and the trade payables at £183 million.
5. A dividend of £40 million had been paid to the shareholders in respect of each of the years.
6. The business employed 13,995 staff at 31 December 2017 and 18,623 at 31 December 2018.
7. The business expanded its capacity during the year to 31 December 2018 by setting up a new warehouse and distribution centre.
8. At 1 January 2017, the total of equity stood at £438 million and the total of equity and non-current liabilities stood at £638 million.

A BRIEF OVERVIEW

Before we start our detailed look at the ratios for Alexis plc (see Example 8.1), it is helpful to take a quick look, before calculating any ratios, at what information is obvious from the financial statements. This will usually pick up some issues that ratios may not be able to identify. It may also highlight some points that could help us in our interpretation of the ratios. Starting at the top of the statement of financial position, the following points can be noted:

- *Expansion of non-current assets.* These have increased by about 15 per cent (from £510 million to £587 million). Note 7 mentions a new warehouse and distribution centre, which may account for much of the additional investment in non-current assets. We are not told when this new facility was established, but it is quite possible that it was well into the year. This could mean that not much benefit was reflected in terms of additional sales revenue or cost saving during 2018. Sales revenue, in fact, expanded by about 20 per cent (from £2,240 million to £2,681 million); this is greater than the expansion in non-current assets.
- *Major expansion in the elements of working capital.* Inventories increased by about 35 per cent, trade receivables by about 14 per cent and trade payables by about 36 per cent between 2017 and 2018. These are major increases, particularly in inventories and payables (which are linked because the inventories are all bought on credit – see Reference 2).
- *Reduction in the cash balance.* The cash balance fell from £4 million (in funds) to a £76 million overdraft between 2017 and 2018. The bank may be putting the business under pressure to reverse this, which could create difficulties.
- *Apparent debt capacity.* Comparing the non-current assets with the long-term borrowings implies that the business may well be able to offer security on further borrowing. This is because potential lenders usually look at the value of assets that can be offered as security when assessing loan requests. Lenders seem particularly attracted to land and buildings as security. For example, at 31 December 2018, non-current assets had a carrying amount (the value at which they appeared in the statement of financial position) of £587 million, but long-term borrowing was only £300 million (though there was also an overdraft of £76 million). Carrying amounts are not normally, of course, market values. On the other hand, land and buildings tend to have a market value higher than their value as shown on the statement of financial position due to a general tendency to inflation in property values.
- *Lower operating profit.* Though sales revenue expanded by 20 per cent between 2017 and 2018, both cost of sales and operating expenses rose by a greater percentage, leaving both gross profit and, particularly, operating profit massively reduced. The level of staffing, which increased by about 33 per cent (from 13,995 to 18,623 employees – see Note 6), may have greatly affected the operating expenses. (Without knowing when the additional employees were recruited during 2018, we cannot be sure of the effect on operating expenses.) Increasing staffing by 33 per cent must put an enormous strain on management, at least in the short term. It is not surprising, therefore, that the year to 31 December 2018 was not successful for the business – not, at least, in immediate profit terms.

Having had a quick look at what is fairly obvious, without calculating any financial ratios, we shall now go on to calculate and interpret those relating to profitability, efficiency, liquidity, gearing and investment.

The following ratios may be used to evaluate the profitability of the business:

- return on ordinary shareholders' funds;
- return on capital employed;
- operating profit margin;
- gross profit margin.

We shall now look at each of these in turn.

Return on ordinary shareholders' funds (ROSF)

The **return on ordinary shareholders' funds ratio** compares the amount of profit for the period available to owners with their average investment in the business during that same period. The ratio (which is normally expressed in percentage terms) is as follows:

$$\text{ROSF} = \frac{\text{Profit for the year (less any preference dividend)}}{\text{Ordinary share capital} + \text{Reserves}} \times 100$$

The profit for the year (less any preference dividend) is used in calculating the ratio, because this figure represents the amount of profit that accrues to the owners.

In the case of Alexis plc, the ratio for the year ended 31 December 2017 is:

$$\text{ROSF} = \frac{165}{(438 + 563)/2} \times 100 = 33.0\%$$

Note that, when calculating the ROSF, the average of the figures for ordinary shareholders' funds as at the beginning and at the end of the year has been used. This is because an average figure is normally more representative. The amount of shareholders' funds was not constant throughout the year, yet we want to compare it with the profit earned during the whole period. We know, from Note 8, that the amount of shareholders' funds at 1 January 2017 was £438 million. By a year later, however, it had risen to £563 million, according to the statement of financial position as at 31 December 2017.

The easiest approach to calculating the average amount of shareholders' funds is to take a simple average based on the opening and closing figures for the year. This is often the only information available, as is the case with Example 8.1. Averaging is normally appropriate for all ratios that combine a figure for a period (such as profit for the year) with one taken at a point in time (such as shareholders' funds).

The average shareholders' funds for the period can be calculated as a simple average of the opening and closing figures. If there has not been a smooth increase or decrease in the figure over the period, however, a monthly average would be more appropriate. Such information may not, however, be available, as in the present case. This point concerning monthly averaging is equally relevant to any asset or claim that varies over the reporting period.

Where not even the beginning-of-year figure is available, it will be necessary to rely on just the year-end figure. This is not ideal but, when this approach is consistently applied, it can still produce useful ratios.

Calculate the ROSF for Alexis plc for the year to 31 December 2018.

The ratio for 2018 is:

$$\text{ROSF} = \frac{11}{(563 + 534)/2} \times 100 = 2.0\%$$

Broadly, businesses seek to generate as high a value as possible for this ratio. This is provided that it is not achieved at the expense of jeopardising future returns by, for example, taking on more risky activities. In view of this, the 2018 ratio is very poor by any standards; a bank deposit account can often yield a better return. We need to find out why things went so badly wrong in the year to 31 December 2018. As we look at other ratios, we should find some clues.

Return on capital employed (ROCE)

The **return on capital employed ratio (ROCE)** is a fundamental measure of business performance. This ratio expresses the relationship between the operating profit generated during a period and the average long-term capital invested in the business.

The ratio is expressed in percentage terms and is as follows:

$$\text{ROCE} = \frac{\textbf{Operating profit}}{\textbf{Share capital + Reserves + Non-current liabilities}} \times 100$$

Note, in this case, that the profit figure used is the operating profit (that is, the profit *before* interest and taxation), because the ratio attempts to measure the returns to all suppliers of long-term finance before any deductions for interest payable on borrowings, or payments of dividends to shareholders, are made.

For the year to 31 December 2017, the ratio for Alexis plc is:

$$\text{ROCE} = \frac{243}{(638 + 763)/2} \times 100 = 34.7\%$$

(The capital employed figure, which is the total equity plus non-current liabilities, at 1 January 2017 is given in Reference 8.)

ROCE is considered by many to be a primary measure of profitability. It compares inputs (capital invested) with outputs (operating profit) so as to reveal the effectiveness with which funds have been deployed. Once again, an average figure for capital employed should be used where the information is available.

Calculate the ROCE for Alexis plc for the year to 31 December 2018.

The ratio for 2018 is:

$$\text{ROCE} = \frac{47}{(763 + 834)/2} \times 100 = 5.9\%$$

This ratio tells much the same story as ROSF; namely a poor performance, with the return on the assets being less than the rate that the business pays for most of its borrowed funds (that is, 9 per cent for the loan notes).

Real World 8.1 shows how financial ratios are used by businesses as a basis for setting profitability targets.

Targeting profitability

The ROCE ratio is widely used by businesses when establishing targets for profitability. These targets are sometimes made public and here are some examples:

- Barratt Developments plc, the builder, has a target ROCE on all new land acquisitions of 25 per cent.
- Greene King plc, the brewing, pub and hotel business has a target ROCE of 9.6 per cent.
- J Sainsbury plc, the supermarket business, has a minimum target ROCE of 8 per cent.
- Tate and Lyle plc, the sugar and associated products producer, has a target ROCE of between 12.6 and 15.6 per cent.
- ■˙ Bovis Homes Group plc, the house builder, has a target ROCE of 25 per cent.

Sources: Information taken from Barratt Developments plc, Key performance indicators, www.barrattdevelopments. com [accessed 30 January 2018]; Greene King plc, Annual Report 2017, p. 64; J Sainsbury plc, Annual Report 2017, p. 77; Tate and Lyle plc, Annual Report 2017, p. 75; and Bovis Homes Group plc, Half year results for the six months ended 30 June 2017.

Real World 8.2 provides some indication of the levels of ROCE achieved by businesses in a selection of European countries.

Comparing profitability

Average ROCE ratios for non-financial businesses in different European countries for the five-year period ending in 2016 are shown in Figure 8.3.

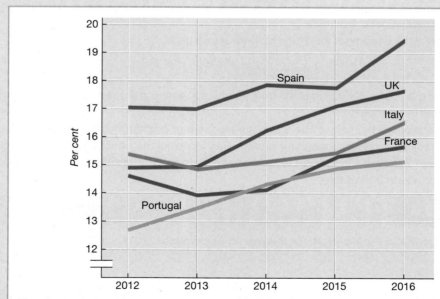

The chart reveals a steady improvement in average ROCE for businesses in three of the five different countries over the period. For Italy and France, there has also been an improvement but it has been less steady over time.

Figure 8.3 The average ROCE of companies in different European countries

Source: Eurostat database (2017) Gross return on capital employed, before taxes, of non-financial corporations, October, http://ec.europa.eu/eurostat/tgm/.

Operating profit margin

The operating profit margin ratio relates the operating profit for the period to the sales revenue. The ratio is expressed as follows:

$$\text{Operating profit margin} = \frac{\text{Operating profit}}{\text{Sales revenue}} \times 100$$

Operating profit (that is, profit before interest and taxation) is used in this ratio as it represents the profit from trading operations before interest payable is taken into account. It is normally the most appropriate measure of operational performance, when making comparisons. This is because differences arising from the way in which the business is financed will not influence the measure.

For the year ended 31 December 2017, Alexis plc's operating profit margin ratio is:

$$\text{Operating profit margin} = \frac{243}{2{,}240} \times 100 = 10.8\%$$

This ratio compares one output of the business (operating profit) with another output (sales revenue). The ratio can vary considerably between types of business. Supermarkets, for example, tend to operate on low prices and, therefore, low operating profit margins. This is done in an attempt to stimulate sales and thereby increase the total amount of operating profit generated. Jewellers, on the other hand, tend to have high operating profit margins but have much lower levels of sales volume. Factors such as the degree of competition, the type of customer, the economic climate and industry characteristics (such as the level of risk) will influence the operating profit margin of a business. This point is picked up again later in the chapter.

Activity 8.4

Calculate the operating profit margin for Alexis plc for the year to 31 December 2018.

The ratio for 2018 is:

$$\text{Operating profit margin} = \frac{47}{2{,}681} \times 100 = 1.8\%$$

Once again, this indicates a very weak performance compared with that of 2017. In 2017, for every £1 of sales revenue an average of 10.8p (that is, 10.8 per cent) was left as operating profit, after paying the cost of the carpets sold and other expenses of operating the business. By 2018, however, this had fallen to only 1.8p for every £1. The reason for the poor ROSF and ROCE ratios appears to have been partially, if not wholly, due to a high level of other expenses relative to sales revenue. The next ratio should provide us with a clue as to how the sharp decline in this ratio occurred.

Before looking at this ratio, however, let us consider **Real World 8.3**. This sets out the target operating profit margins for some well-known car manufacturers.

Gross profit margin

The **gross profit margin ratio** relates the gross profit of the business to the sales revenue generated for the same period. Gross profit represents the difference between sales revenue and the cost of sales. The ratio is therefore a measure of profitability in buying (or producing) and selling goods or services before any other expenses are taken into account. As cost of sales represents a major expense for many businesses, a change in this ratio can have a significant effect on the 'bottom line' (that is, the profit for the year). The gross profit margin ratio is calculated as follows:

$$\text{Gross profit margin} = \frac{\text{Gross profit}}{\text{Sales revenue}} \times 100$$

For the year to 31 December 2017, the ratio for Alexis plc is:

$$\text{Gross profit margin} = \frac{495}{2{,}240} \times 100 = 22.1\%$$

Activity 8.5

Calculate the gross profit margin for Alexis plc for the year to 31 December 2018.

The ratio for 2018 is:

$$\text{Gross profit margin} = \frac{409}{2{,}681} \times 100 = 15.3\%$$

The decline in this ratio means that gross profit was lower *relative* to sales revenue in 2018 than it had been in 2017. Bearing in mind that:

> **Gross profit = Sales revenue − Cost of sales (or cost of goods sold)**

this means that cost of sales was higher *relative* to sales revenue in 2018 than in 2017. This could mean that sales prices were lower and/or that the purchase price of carpets had increased. It is possible that both sales prices and purchase prices had reduced, but the former at a greater rate than the latter. Similarly they may both have increased, but with sales prices having increased at a lesser rate than purchase prices.

Clearly, part of the decline in the operating profit margin ratio is linked to the dramatic decline in the gross profit margin ratio. Whereas, after paying for the carpets sold, for each £1 of sales revenue, 22.1p was left to cover other operating expenses in 2017, this was only 15.3p in 2018.

Real World 8.4 sets out the gross profit margin and operating profit margin of four large UK food producers.

Real World 8.4

Food for thought

The gross profit margin and operating profit margin for four large food producers for 2017 are set out in Figure 8.4.

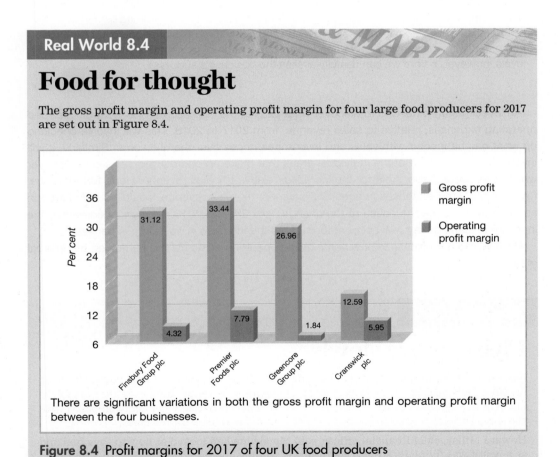

There are significant variations in both the gross profit margin and operating profit margin between the four businesses.

Figure 8.4 Profit margins for 2017 of four UK food producers

FT *Source*: Chart constructed from information in https://markets.ft.com/data/equities/tearsheet/financials, *Financial Times* [accessed 1 February 2018]. © The Financial Times Limited 2018. All rights reserved.

The profitability ratios for the business over the two years can be set out as follows:

	2017 %	2018 %
ROSF	33.0	2.0
ROCE	34.7	5.9
Operating profit margin	10.8	1.8
Gross profit margin	22.1	15.3

Activity 8.6

What do you deduce from a comparison of the declines in the operating profit and gross profit margin ratios?

We can see that the difference in the operating profit margin was 9 percentage points (that is, 10.8 per cent to 1.8 per cent), whereas that of the gross profit margin was only 6.8 percentage points (that is, from 22.1 per cent to 15.3 per cent). This can only mean that operating expenses were greater compared with sales revenue in 2018 than they had been in 2017. The decline in both ROSF and ROCE was caused partly, therefore, by the business incurring higher inventories purchasing costs relative to sales revenue and partly through higher operating expenses compared with sales revenue. We need to compare each of these ratios with their planned levels, however, before we can usefully assess the business's success.

An investigation is needed to discover what caused the increases in both cost of sales and operating expenses, relative to sales revenue, from 2017 to 2018. This will involve checking on what has happened with sales and inventories prices over the two years. Similarly, it will involve looking at each of the individual areas that make up operating expenses to discover which ones were responsible for the increase, relative to sales revenue. Here, further ratios, for example, staff expenses (wages and salaries) to sales revenue, could be calculated in an attempt to isolate the cause of the change from 2017 to 2018. As mentioned earlier, the increase in staffing may well account for most of the increase in operating expenses.

Real World 8.5 discusses how some airline operating costs can be controlled by unusual means.

Real World 8.5

Flying more slowly

Ryanair's profits dropped sharply in the first quarter of its reporting year largely because of rising fuel costs. Europe's largest low-cost carrier by revenue said profit after tax fell 21 per cent to €78 million, in line with its forecasts. Fuel costs rose 6 per cent compared with the same period last year to make up 47 per cent of its total operating costs.

Howard Millar, chief financial officer, said the airline had looked at how to save fuel and as a result was flying its aircraft more slowly, adding about two minutes to an hour of flying time. 'We're flying slightly slower, but what we're seeing is we're burning less fuel,' Mr Millar said. 'Fuel is our single biggest cost, so we have a proportionally bigger problem than everybody else from these higher fuel prices.'

Having a fly in

McKinsey and Company, the international management consultancy, reports that one of its clients, an airline, saves on operating expenses in an unusual way. Some of the planes operated by the airline have seats that could go flat to make it easier for passengers to sleep on overnight flights. It was the policy of the airline to leave the cabin lights off as late in the morning as possible to avoid passengers demand for – and cost of – breakfast.

 Sources: Wild, J. (2013) Ryanair sees sharp fall in profits due to higher fuel costs, ft.com, 29 July; and information contained in Dichter, A., Sorensen, A and Saxon, S. (2017) Buying and flying: next generation airline procurement, McKinsey and Company, www.mckinsey.com, April.

The profitability ratios discussed above are summarised in Figure 8.5.

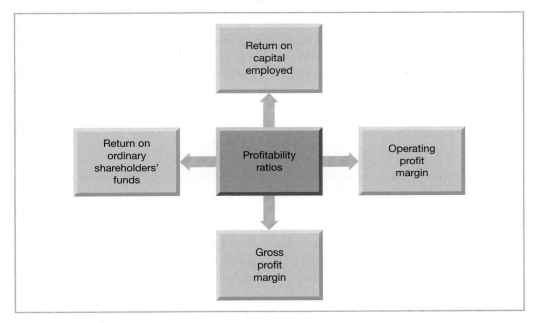

Figure 8.5 Profitability ratios

EFFICIENCY

Efficiency ratios are used to try to assess how successfully the various resources of the business are managed. The following ratios consider some of the more important aspects of resource management:

- average inventories turnover period;
- average settlement period for trade receivables;
- average settlement period for trade payables;
- sales revenue to capital employed;
- sales revenue per employee.

We shall now look at each of these in turn.

Average inventories turnover period

Inventories often represent a significant investment for a business. For some types of business (for example, manufacturers and certain retailers), inventories may account for a substantial proportion of the total assets held (see Real World 9.5 on page 000). The average inventories turnover period ratio measures the average period for which inventories are being held. The ratio is calculated as follows:

$$\text{Average inventories turnover period} = \frac{\text{Average inventories held}}{\text{Cost of sales}} \times 365$$

The average inventories for the period can be calculated as a simple average of the opening and closing inventories levels for the year. In the case of a highly seasonal business, however, where inventories levels vary considerably over the year, a monthly average would be more appropriate. Such information may not, however, be available. This point concerning monthly averaging is, as we saw earlier in the chapter, equally relevant to any asset or claim that varies over the reporting period, including trade receivables and trade payables.

In the case of Alexis plc, the inventories turnover period for the year ended 31 December 2017 is:

$$\text{Average inventories turnover period} = \frac{(241 + 300)/2}{1,745} \times 365 = 56.6 \text{ days}$$

(The opening inventories figure was taken from Note 3 to the financial statements.)

This means that, on average, the inventories held are being 'turned over' every 56.6 days. So, a carpet bought by the business on a particular day would, on average, have been sold about eight weeks later. A business will normally prefer a short inventories turnover period to a long one, because holding inventories has costs, for example the opportunity cost of the funds tied up. When judging the amount of inventories to carry, the business must consider such things as the likely demand for them, the possibility of supply shortages, the likelihood of price rises, the amount of storage space available, their perishability and susceptibility to obsolescence.

This ratio is sometimes expressed in terms of weeks or months rather than days: multiplying by 52 or 12, rather than 365, will achieve this.

Activity 8.7

Calculate the average inventories turnover period for Alexis plc for the year ended 31 December 2018.

The ratio for 2018 is:

$$\text{Average inventories turnover period} = \frac{(300 + 406)/2}{2,272} \times 365 = 56.7 \text{ days}$$

The inventories turnover period is virtually the same in both years.

Average settlement period for trade receivables

Selling on credit is the norm for most businesses, except for retailers, and so trade receivables tend to be a necessary evil. A business will naturally be concerned with the amount of funds tied up in trade receivables and try to keep this to a minimum. The speed of payment can have a significant effect on the business's cash flow. The average settlement period for trade receivables ratio indicates how long, on average, credit customers take to pay the amounts that they owe to the business. The ratio is as follows:

$$\text{Average settlement period for trade receivables} = \frac{\text{Average trade receivables}}{\text{Credit sales revenue}} \times 365$$

A business will normally prefer a shorter average settlement period to a longer one as, once again, funds are being tied up that may be used for more profitable purposes. Although this ratio can be useful, it is important to remember that it produces an *average* figure for the number of days for which debts are outstanding. This average may be badly distorted by, for example, a few large customers who are very slow, or very fast, payers.

Since all sales made by Alexis plc are on credit, the average settlement period for trade receivables for the year ended 31 December 2017 is:

$$\text{Average settlement period for trade receivables} = \frac{(223 + 240)/2}{2,240} \times 365 = 37.7 \text{ days}$$

(The opening trade receivables figure was taken from Note 4 to the financial statements.)

Activity 8.8

Calculate the average settlement period for Alexis plc's trade receivables for the year ended 31 December 2018.

The ratio for 2018 is:

$$\text{Average settlement period for trade receivables} = \frac{(240 + 273)/2}{2,681} \times 365 = 34.9 \text{ days}$$

On the face of it, this reduction in the settlement period is welcome. It means that less cash was tied up in trade receivables for each £1 of sales revenue in 2018 than in 2017. Only if the reduction were achieved at the expense of customer goodwill or through high out-of-pocket cost might its desirability be questioned. For example, the reduction may have been due to chasing customers too vigorously or by giving large discounts to customers for prompt payment.

Average settlement period for trade payables

The average settlement period for trade payables ratio measures how long, on average, the business takes to pay those who have supplied goods and services on credit. The ratio is calculated as follows:

$$\text{Average settlement period for trade payables} = \frac{\text{Average trade payables}}{\text{Credit purchases}} \times 365$$

This ratio provides an average figure, which, like the average settlement period for trade receivables ratio, can be distorted by the payment period for one or two large suppliers.

As trade payables provide a free source of finance for the business, it is perhaps not surprising that some businesses attempt to increase their average settlement period for trade payables. Such a policy can be taken too far, however, and can result in a loss of goodwill of suppliers.

For the year ended 31 December 2017, Alexis plc's average settlement period for trade payables is:

$$\text{Average settlement period for trade payables} = \frac{(183 + 261)/2}{1,804} \times 365 = 44.9 \text{ days}$$

(The opening trade payables figure was taken from Note 4 to the financial statements and the purchases figure from Note 3.)

Activity 8.9

Calculate the average settlement period for trade payables for Alexis plc for the year ended 31 December 2018.

The ratio for 2018 is:

$$\text{Average settlement period for trade payables} = \frac{(261 + 354)/2}{2,378} \times 365 = 47.2 \text{ days}$$

There was an increase between 2017 and 2018 in the average length of time that elapsed between buying goods and services and paying for them. On the face of it, this is beneficial because the business is using free finance provided by suppliers. This may not be so, however, where it results in a loss of supplier goodwill and Alexis plc suffers adverse consequences.

Small businesses often suffer acute cash flow problems because large business customers refuse to pay within a reasonable period. This has led the UK government to introduce a Prompt Payment Code, which sets standards for the payment practices of large businesses. **Real World 8.6** describes how the Code is aimed at improving matters.

Real World 8.6

Better late than never – new rules for late payers

Large businesses paying their suppliers late is a serious problem for smaller businesses. The Federation of Small Businesses claims that late payment causes 50,000 businesses (presumably mainly small ones) a year to close.

In an attempt to address this problem, the UK government introduced the Prompt Payment Code, in April 2017. The objective of the Code was to apply pressure on businesses, buying from other businesses on credit (as is the case with nearly all business-to-business transactions), to pay within a reasonable time.

Under the new code, large businesses will have to have to report twice yearly, on a publicly accessible government website, prescribed information concerning their payment practices. These businesses will be required to specify how long they take to pay invoices, the percentage of invoices paid late, plus some other information.

It is hoped that the transparency that this provision will cause will apply pressure on businesses to treat their suppliers more reasonably or risk the opprobrium of the pubic and media exposure. It is expected that businesses, who are contemplating supplying a large business on credit, will use the website to check the payment record of the potential customer. It could also lead to the contract between the two businesses specifying the payment terms in detail.

Source: Information taken from: GT News (2017) *Are you ready for the Prompt Payment Code?* www.gtnews.com, 11 September.

Sales revenue to capital employed ratio

The **sales revenue to capital employed ratio** (or net asset turnover ratio) examines how effectively the assets of the business are being used to generate sales revenue. It is calculated as follows:

$$\text{Sales revenue to capital employed ratio} = \frac{\text{Sales revenue}}{\text{Share capital} + \text{Reserves} + \text{Non-current liabilities}}$$

Normally, a higher sales revenue to capital employed ratio is preferred to a lower one. A higher ratio tends to suggest that assets are being used more productively in the generation of revenue. However, a very high ratio may suggest that the business is 'overtrading' on its assets. In other words, it has insufficient assets to sustain the level of sales revenue achieved. We shall take a closer look at overtrading in Chapter 9.

When comparing the sales revenue to capital employed ratio for different businesses, factors such as the age and condition of assets held, the valuation bases for assets and whether assets are leased or owned outright can complicate interpretation.

A variation of this formula is to use the total assets less current liabilities (which is equivalent to long-term capital employed) in the denominator (lower part of the fraction). The same result is obtained.

For the year ended 31 December 2017, this ratio for Alexis plc is:

$$\text{Sales revenue to capital employed} = \frac{2{,}240}{(638 + 763)/2} = 3.20 \text{ times}$$

Activity 8.10

Calculate the sales revenue to capital employed ratio for Alexis plc for the year ended 31 December 2018.

The ratio for 2018 is:

$$\text{Sales revenue to capital employed} = \frac{2{,}681}{(763 + 834)/2} = 3.36 \text{ times}$$

This seems to be an improvement, since, in 2018, more sales revenue was being generated for each £1 of capital employed (£3.36) than was the case in 2017 (£3.20). Provided that overtrading is not an issue, and that the additional sales generate an acceptable profit, this is to be welcomed.

Sales revenue per employee

The sales revenue per employee ratio relates sales revenue generated during a reporting period to a particular business resource – labour. It provides a measure of the productivity of the workforce. The ratio is:

$$\text{Sales revenue per employee} = \frac{\text{Sales revenue}}{\text{Number of employees}}$$

Generally, businesses would prefer a high value for this ratio, implying that they are deploying their staff efficiently.

For the year ended 31 December 2017, the ratio for Alexis plc is:

$$\text{Sales revenue per employee} = \frac{£2,240m}{13,995} = £160,057$$

Activity 8.11

Calculate the sales revenue per employee for Alexis plc for the year ended 31 December 2018.

The ratio for 2018 is:

$$\text{Sales revenue per employee} = \frac{£2,681m}{18,623} = £143,962$$

This represents a fairly significant decline, which merits further investigation. As already mentioned, the number of employees increased quite notably (by about 33 per cent) during 2018. We need to know why this had not generated additional sales revenue sufficient to maintain the ratio at its 2017 level. It may be because the extra employees were not appointed until late in the year ended 31 December 2018.

The efficiency, or activity, ratios may be summarised as follows:

	2017	2018
Average inventories turnover period	56.6 days	56.7 days
Average settlement period for trade receivables	37.7 days	34.9 days
Average settlement period for trade payables	44.9 days	47.2 days
Sales revenue to capital employed (net asset turnover)	3.20 times	3.36 times
Sales revenue per employee	£160,057	£143,962

Activity 8.12

What do you deduce from a comparison of the efficiency ratios over the two years?

Maintaining the inventories turnover period at the 2017 level may be reasonable, though to assess whether this is a satisfactory period we need to know the planned inventories turnover period. The inventories turnover period for other businesses operating in carpet retailing, particularly those regarded as the market leaders, may have been helpful in formulating the plans. On the face of things, a shorter trade receivables settlement period and a longer trade payables settlement period are both desirable. These may, however, have been achieved at the cost of a loss of the goodwill of customers and suppliers, respectively. The increased sales revenue to capital employed ratio seems beneficial, provided the business can manage this increase. The decline in the sales revenue per employee ratio is undesirable but is probably related to the dramatic increase in the number of employees. As with the inventories turnover period, these other ratios need to be compared with planned, or target, ratios.

Figure 8.6 summaries the efficiency ratios that we have discussed.

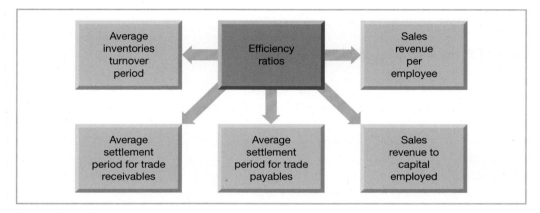

Figure 8.6 Efficiency ratios

RELATIONSHIP BETWEEN PROFITABILITY AND EFFICIENCY

In our earlier discussions concerning profitability ratios, we saw that return on capital employed (ROCE) is regarded as a key ratio by many businesses. The ratio is:

$$\text{ROCE} = \frac{\text{Operating profit}}{\text{Long-term capital employed}} \times 100$$

where long-term capital comprises share capital plus reserves plus long-term borrowings. This ratio can be broken down into two elements, as shown in Figure 8.7. The first ratio is the operating profit margin ratio and the second is the sales revenue to capital employed (net asset turnover) ratio, both of which we discussed earlier. By breaking down the ROCE ratio in this manner, we highlight the fact that the overall return on funds employed within the business will be determined both by the profitability of sales and by efficiency in the use of capital.

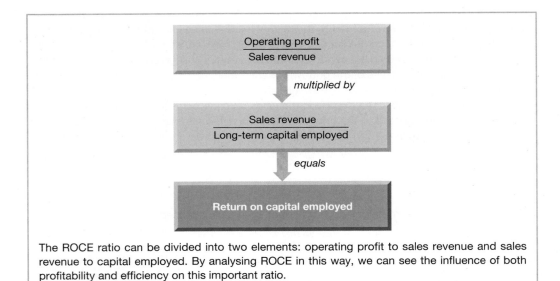

The ROCE ratio can be divided into two elements: operating profit to sales revenue and sales revenue to capital employed. By analysing ROCE in this way, we can see the influence of both profitability and efficiency on this important ratio.

Figure 8.7 The main elements of the ROCE ratio

Example 8.2 looks at ROCE for two different businesses operating in the same industry.

Example 8.2

Consider the following information, for last year, Antler plc and Baker plc:

	Antler plc £m	Baker plc £m
Operating profit	20	15
Average long-term capital employed	100	75
Sales revenue	200	300

The ROCE for each business is identical (20 per cent). However, the manner in which that return was achieved by each business is quite different. In the case of Antler plc, the operating profit margin is 10 per cent and the sales revenue to capital employed ratio is 2 times (so, ROCE = 10% × 2 = 20%). In the case of Baker plc, the operating profit margin is 5 per cent and the sales revenue to capital employed ratio is 4 times (and so, ROCE = 5% × 4 = 20%).

Example 8.2 demonstrates that a relatively high sales revenue to capital employed ratio can compensate for a relatively low operating profit margin. Similarly, a relatively low sales revenue to capital employed ratio can be overcome by a relatively high operating profit margin. In many areas of retail and distribution (for example, supermarkets and delivery services), operating profit margins are quite low, but the ROCE can be high, provided that assets are used productively (that is, low margin, high sales revenue to capital employed).

Show how the ROCE ratio for Alexis plc can be analysed into the two elements for each of the years 2017 and 2018. What conclusions can you draw from your figures?

	ROCE	=	Operating profit margin	×	Sales revenue to capital employed
2017	34.7%		10.8%		3.20
2018	5.9%		1.8%		3.36

As we can see, the relationship between the three ratios holds for Alexis plc for both years. The small apparent differences arise because the three ratios are stated here only to one or two decimal places.

In the year to 31 December 2018, the business was more effective at generating sales revenue (sales revenue to capital employed ratio increased). However, it fell well below the level needed to compensate for the sharp decline in the profitability of sales (operating profit margin). As a result, the 2018 ROCE was well below the 2017 value.

LIQUIDITY

Liquidity ratios are concerned with the ability of the business to meet its short-term financial obligations. The following ratios are widely used:

- current ratio;
- acid test ratio;
- cash generated from operations to maturing obligations ratio.

These ratios will now be considered.

Current ratio

The current ratio compares the 'liquid' assets (that is, cash and those assets held that will soon be turned into cash) of the business with the current liabilities. The ratio is calculated as follows:

$$\text{Current ratio} = \frac{\text{Current assets}}{\text{Current liabilities}}$$

It seems that some believe there is an 'ideal' current ratio (usually 2 times or 2:1) for all businesses. However, this is not the case. Different types of business tend to have different current ratios. A manufacturing business, for example, will normally have a relatively high current ratio because it will tend to hold inventories of finished goods, raw materials and work in progress. It will also normally sell goods on credit, thereby giving rise to trade receivables. A supermarket chain, on the other hand, will have a relatively low ratio, as it will hold only fast-moving inventories of finished goods and its sales will be for cash rather than on credit (see Real World 9.5 on page 326).

The higher the current ratio, the more liquid the business is considered to be. As liquidity is vital to the survival of a business, a higher current ratio might be thought to be preferable to a lower one. If a business has a very high ratio, however, it may be that excessive funds are tied up in cash or other liquid assets and are not, therefore, being used as productively as they might otherwise be.

As at 31 December 2017, the current ratio of Alexis plc is:

$$\text{Current ratio} = \frac{544}{291} = 1.9 \text{ times (or 1.9:1)}$$

Activity 8.14

Calculate the current ratio for Alexis plc as at 31 December 2018.

The ratio as at 31 December 2018 is:

$$\text{Current ratio} = \frac{679}{432} = 1.6 \text{ times (or 1.6:1)}$$

Although this is a decline from 2017 to 2018, it may not be a matter for concern. The next ratio may provide a clue as to whether there seems to be a problem.

Acid test ratio

The **acid test ratio** is similar to the current ratio, but represents a more stringent test of liquidity. For many businesses, inventories cannot be converted into cash quickly. (Note that, in the case of Alexis plc, the inventories turnover period was about 57 days in both years (see page 284).) As a result, there is a good case for excluding this particular asset.

The acid test ratio is calculated as follows:

$$\text{Acid test ratio} = \frac{\text{Current assets (excluding inventories)}}{\text{Current liabilities}}$$

The acid test ratio for Alexis plc as at 31 December 2017 is:

$$\text{Acid test ratio} = \frac{544 - 300}{291} = 0.8 \text{ times (or 0.8:1)}$$

We can see that the 'liquid' current assets do not quite cover the current liabilities, so the business may be experiencing some liquidity problems.

The minimum level for this ratio is often stated as 1.0 times (or 1:1; that is, current assets (excluding inventories) equal current liabilities). However, for many highly successful businesses, it is not unusual for the acid test ratio to be below 1.0 without causing liquidity problems. (Again, see Real World 9.5 on page 326.)

Calculate the acid test ratio for Alexis plc as at 31 December 2018.

The ratio as at 31 December 2018 is:

$$\text{Acid test ratio} = \frac{679 - 406}{432} = 0.6 \text{ times}$$

The 2018 ratio is significantly below that for 2017 and may well be a cause for concern. The underlying reasons for the rapid decline in the ratio should be investigated and, if necessary, steps taken to prevent any further deterioration.

Cash generated from operations to maturing obligations ratio

The cash generated from operations to maturing obligations ratio compares the cash generated from operations (taken from the statement of cash flows) with the current liabilities of the business. It provides a further indication of the ability of the business to meet its maturing obligations. The ratio is expressed as:

$$\frac{\text{Cash generated from operations}}{\text{to maturing obligations ratio}} = \frac{\text{Cash generated from operations}}{\text{Current liabilities}}$$

The higher this ratio is, the better the liquidity of the business. This ratio has the advantage over the current ratio that the operating cash flows for a period usually provide a more reliable guide to the liquidity of a business than current assets held at the statement of financial position date. Alexis plc's ratio for the year ended 31 December 2017 is:

$$\text{Cash generated from operations to maturing obligations ratio} = \frac{251}{291} = 0.9 \text{ times}$$

This indicates that the operating cash flows for the year are not quite sufficient to cover the current liabilities at the end of the year.

Calculate the cash generated from operations to maturing obligations ratio for Alexis plc for the year ended 31 December 2018.

The ratio for 2018 is:

$$\text{Cash generated from operations to maturing obligations ratio} = \frac{34}{432} = 0.1 \text{ times}$$

This shows an alarming decline in the ability of the business to meet its maturing obligations from its operating cash flows. This confirms that liquidity is a real cause for concern. **Real World 8.7** shows the liquidity ratios for four leading UK supermarkets.

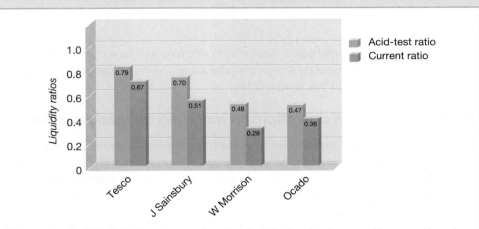

Real World 8.7

Checking out liquidity

Figure 8.8 shows the current ratio and acid-test ratio for the financial year ending in 2017 for four leading supermarkets.

Legend:
- Acid-test ratio
- Current ratio

Tesco: 0.79, 0.67
J Sainsbury: 0.70, 0.51
W Morrison: 0.48, 0.28
Ocado: 0.47, 0.36

Liquidity ratios (y-axis: 0, 0.2, 0.4, 0.6, 0.8, 1.0)

We can see that the liquidity ratios are low for all of the four businesses. However, there is a clear difference between the liquidity ratios of Tesco plc and J. Sainsbury plc, on the one hand, and those of Wm. Morrison plc and Ocado Group plc, on the other. Ocado Group plc differs from the other three supermarkets insofar that it operates exclusively online.

Figure 8.8 Liquidity ratios for 2017 of four UK supermarkets

 Source: Chart constructed from information in https://markets.ft.com/data/equities/tearsheet/financials, *Financial Times* [accessed 1 February 2018]. © The Financial Times Limited 2018. All rights reserved.

The liquidity ratios for the two-year period may be summarised as follows:

	2017	2018
Current ratio	1.9	1.6
Acid test ratio	0.8	0.6
Cash generated from operations to maturing obligations ratio	0.9	0.1

Activity 8.17

What do you deduce from these liquidity ratios?

There has clearly been a decline in liquidity from 2017 to 2018. This is indicated by all three ratios. The most worrying is the decline in the last ratio as it reveals the ability to generate cash from trading operations has declined significantly in relation to short-term obligations. The apparent liquidity problem may, however, be linked to the increase in non-current assets and number of employees, planned and short-term. When the benefits of the expansion come on stream, liquidity may improve. On the other hand, short-term lenders and suppliers may become anxious by the decline in liquidity. This could lead them to press for payment, which could well cause further problems.

The liquidity ratios that we have considered are summarised in Figure 8.9.

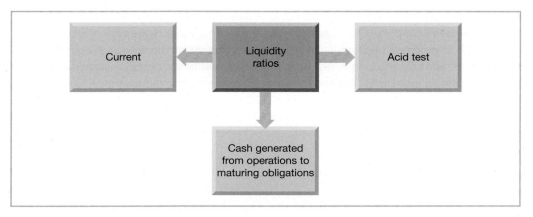

Figure 8.9 Liquidity ratios

OPERATING CASH CYCLE

When managing cash, it is important to be aware of the **operating cash cycle (OCC)** of the business. For a business that purchases goods on credit for subsequent resale on credit, such as a wholesaler, it represents the period between the outlay of cash for the purchase of inventories and the ultimate receipt of cash from their sale. The OCC for this type of business is as shown in Figure 8.10.

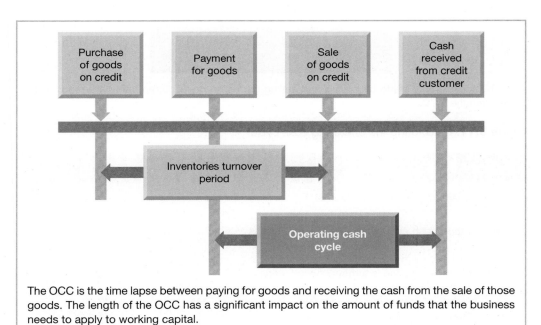

The OCC is the time lapse between paying for goods and receiving the cash from the sale of those goods. The length of the OCC has a significant impact on the amount of funds that the business needs to apply to working capital.

Figure 8.10 The operating cash cycle

Figure 8.10 shows that payment for inventories acquired on credit occurs some time after those inventories have been purchased. Therefore, no immediate cash outflow arises from the purchase. Similarly, cash receipts from credit customers will occur some time after the sale is made so there will be no immediate cash inflow as a result of the sale. The OCC is the period between the payment made to the supplier, for the goods concerned, and the cash received from the credit customer. Although Figure 8.10 depicts the position for a wholesaling business, the precise definition of the OCC can easily be adapted for other types of business.

The OCC is important because it has a significant influence on the financing requirements of the business. Broadly, the longer the cycle, the greater will be the financing requirements and the greater the financial risks. The business may therefore wish to reduce the OCC to the minimum period possible. A business with a short OCC is said to have 'good (or strong) cash flow'.

For businesses that trade by buying and selling goods on credit, the OCC can be deduced from their financial statements through the use of certain ratios. The calculations required are as shown in Figure 8.11.

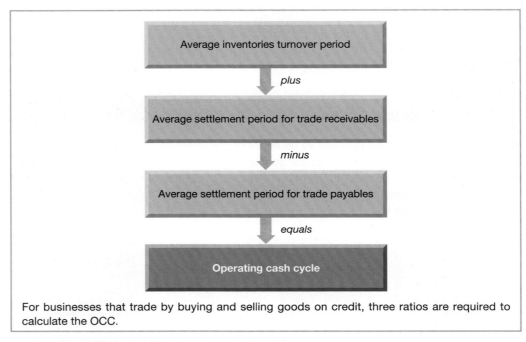

For businesses that trade by buying and selling goods on credit, three ratios are required to calculate the OCC.

Figure 8.11 Calculating the operating cash cycle

Activity 8.18

Calculate Alexis plc's OCC for 2018.

The operating cash cycle for Alexis plc for 2018 is:

	Days
Average inventories turnover period (page 284)	56.7
Average settlement period for trade receivables (page 285)	34.9
Average settlement period for trade payables (page 285)	(47.2)
Operating cash cycle	44.4

We can see from the formula above that, if a business wishes to reduce the OCC, it should do one or more of the following:

■ reduce the average inventories turnover period;
■ reduce the average settlement period for trade receivables; and/or
■ increase the average settlement period for trade payables.

An objective of working capital management may be to maintain the OCC at a particular target level or within certain limits each side of the target. A problem with this objective is that not all days in the OCC are equally valuable. Take, for example, Alexis plc's 2018 OCC (Activity 8.18), where the operating cycle is 44.4 days. If both trade receivables and trade payables were increased by seven days (by allowing customers longer to pay and by Alexis plc taking longer to pay suppliers), the OCC would be unchanged at 44.4 days. This would not, however, leave the amount tied up in working capital unchanged. Trade receivables would increase by £51.4 million (that is, 7 × £2,681m/365) whereas, trade payables would increase by only £45.6 million (that is, 7 × £2,378m/365). This would mean a net increase of £5.8 million in working capital.

Real World 8.8 shows the average operating cash cycle for large European businesses.

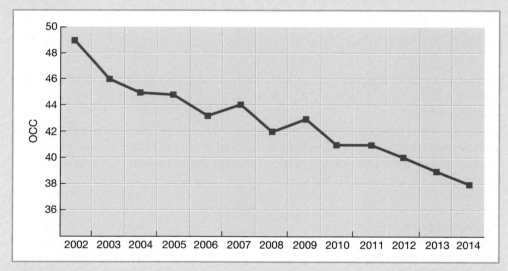

Real World 8.8

Cycling along

A survey of working capital management by Ernst and Young calculated the average operating cash cycle for the top 1,000 US and top 1,000 European businesses (excluding financial and auto manufacturing businesses). The results for the period 2002 to 2015 are set out in Figure 8.12.

Figure 8.12 The average OCC of large US and European businesses from 2002 to 2015

The average operating cash cycle has reduced by 12 per cent for US businesses and 21 per cent for European businesses over the period. For US businesses, the inventories turnover period increased by 3 per cent and the trade receivables settlement period fell by 9 per cent, while the trade payables settlement period increased by 7 per cent. For European businesses, the inventories turnover period fell by 2 per cent and the trade receivables settlement period fell by 12 per cent, while the trade payables settlement period increased by 7 per cent.

We can see from the figure that the average operating cash cycles for US and European businesses are now very similar.

Source: Ernst and Young (2016) *All Tied Up: Working Capital Management Report 2016*, p. 6, www.ey.com.

FINANCIAL GEARING

Financial gearing occurs when a business is financed, at least in part, by borrowing rather than by owners' equity. The extent to which a business is geared (that is, financed from borrowing) is an important factor in assessing risk. Borrowing involves taking on a commitment to pay interest charges and to make capital repayments. Where the borrowing is heavy, this can be a significant financial burden; it can increase the risk of the business becoming insolvent. Nevertheless, virtually all businesses, except some of the very smallest, are geared to some extent.

Given the risks involved, we may wonder why a business would want to take on gearing. One reason is that the owners have insufficient funds, so the only way to finance the business adequately is to borrow. Another reason is that gearing can be used to increase the returns to owners. This is possible provided the returns generated from borrowed funds exceed the cost of paying interest. Example 8.3 illustrates this point.

Example 8.3

The long-term capital structures of two new businesses, Lee Ltd and Nova Ltd, are as follows:

	Lee Ltd £	Nova Ltd £
£1 ordinary shares	100,000	200,000
10% loan notes	200,000	100,000
	300,000	300,000

In their first year of operations, they each make an operating profit (that is, profit before interest and taxation) of £50,000. The tax rate is 20 per cent of the profit before taxation (but after interest).

Lee Ltd would probably be considered relatively highly geared, as it has a high proportion of borrowed funds in its long-term capital structure. Nova Ltd is much lower geared. The profit available to the shareholders of each business in the first year of operations will be:

	Lee Ltd £	Nova Ltd £
Operating profit	50,000	50,000
Interest payable	(20,000)	(10,000)
Profit before taxation	30,000	40,000
Taxation (20%)	(6,000)	(8,000)
Profit for the year (available to ordinary shareholders)	24,000	32,000

The return on ordinary shareholders' funds (ROSF) for each business will be:

$$\text{Lee Ltd} \qquad\qquad \text{Nova Ltd}$$
$$\frac{24,000}{100,000} \times 100 = 24\% \qquad \frac{32,000}{200,000} \times 100 = 16\%$$

We can see that Lee Ltd, the more highly geared business, has generated a higher ROSF than Nova Ltd. This is despite the fact that the ROCE (return on capital employed) is identical for both businesses (that is, (£50,000/£300,000) × 100 = 16.7%).

Note that at the £50,000 level of operating profit, the shareholders of both businesses have generated higher returns as a result of gearing. If both businesses were totally financed by equity, the profit for the year (that is, after taxation) would be £40,000 (that is, £50,000 less 20 per cent taxation), giving an ROSF of 13.3 per cent (that is, £40,000/£300,000).

An effect of gearing is that returns to shareholders become more sensitive to changes in operating profits. For a highly geared business, a change in operating profits will lead to a proportionately greater change in the ROSF ratio.

Activity 8.19

Assume that the operating profit is £70,000 rather than £50,000. What would be the effect of this on ROSF?

The revised profit available to the shareholders of each business in the first year of operations will be:

	Lee Ltd £	Nova Ltd £
Operating profit	70,000	70,000
Interest payable	(20,000)	(10,000)
Profit before taxation	50,000	60,000
Taxation (20%)	(10,000)	(12,000)
Profit for the year (available to ordinary shareholders)	40,000	48,000

The ROSF for each business will now be:

Lee Ltd

$$\frac{40,000}{100,000} \times 100 = 40\%$$

Nova Ltd

$$\frac{48,000}{200,000} \times 100 = 24\%$$

We can see that for Lee Ltd, the higher-geared business, the returns to shareholders have increased by two thirds (from 24 per cent to 40 per cent), whereas for the lower-geared business, Nova Ltd, the benefits of gearing are less pronounced, increasing by only half (from 16 per cent to 24 per cent). The effect of gearing can, of course, work in both directions. So, for a highly geared business, a small decline in operating profit will bring about a much greater decline in the returns to shareholders.

The reason that gearing seems to be beneficial to shareholders is that, in practice, interest rates for borrowings tend to be low by comparison with the returns that the typical business can earn. On top of this, interest expenses are tax-deductible, in the way shown in Example 8.3 and Activity 8.19. This makes the apparent cost of borrowing quite cheap. It is debatable, however, whether low interest rates really are beneficial to shareholders. Since borrowing increases the risk to shareholders, there is a hidden cost involved. Many argue that this cost is precisely compensated by the higher returns, giving no net benefit to shareholders. In other words, the apparent benefits of higher returns from gearing are illusory. What are not illusory, however, are the benefits to shareholders from the tax-deductibility of interest payments.

The effect of gearing is like that of two intermeshing cogwheels of unequal size (see Figure 8.13). The circular movement in the larger cog (operating profit) causes a more than proportionate movement in the smaller cog (returns to ordinary shareholders).

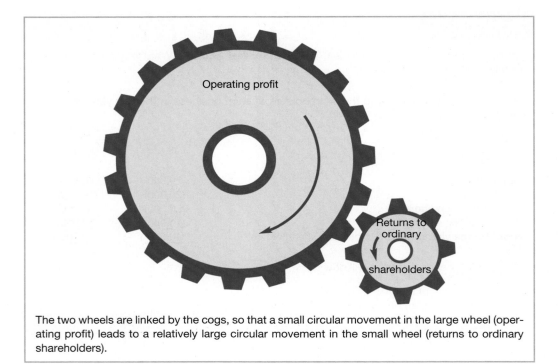

The two wheels are linked by the cogs, so that a small circular movement in the large wheel (operating profit) leads to a relatively large circular movement in the small wheel (returns to ordinary shareholders).

Figure 8.13 The effect of financial gearing

Two ratios are widely used to assess gearing:

■ gearing ratio;
■ interest cover ratio.

Gearing ratio

The **gearing ratio** measures the contribution of long-term lenders to the long-term capital structure of a business:

$$\text{Gearing ratio} = \frac{\text{Long-term (non-current) liabilities}}{\text{Share capital} + \text{Reserves} + \text{Long-term (non-current) liabilities}} \times 100$$

The gearing ratio for Alexis plc, as at 31 December 2017, is:

$$\text{Gearing ratio} = \frac{200}{(563 + 200)} \times 100 = 26.2\%$$

This is a level of gearing that would not normally be considered to be very high.

Activity 8.21

Calculate the gearing ratio of Alexis plc as at 31 December 2018.

The ratio as at 31 December 2018 is:

$$\text{Gearing ratio} = \frac{300}{(534 + 300)} \times 100 = 36.0\%$$

This is a substantial increase in the level of gearing over the year.

Interest cover ratio

The interest cover ratio measures the amount of operating profit available to cover interest payable. The ratio may be calculated as follows:

$$\text{Interest cover ratio} = \frac{\text{Operating profit}}{\text{Interest payable}}$$

The ratio for Alexis plc for the year ended 31 December 2017 is:

$$\text{Interest cover ratio} = \frac{243}{18} = 13.5 \text{ times}$$

This ratio shows that the level of operating profit is considerably higher than the level of interest payable. This means that a large fall in operating profit could occur before operating profit levels failed to cover interest payable. The lower the level of operating profit coverage, the greater the risk to lenders that interest payments will not be met. There will also be a greater risk to the shareholders that the lenders will take action against the business to recover the interest due.

Activity 8.22

Calculate the interest cover ratio of Alexis plc for the year ended 31 December 2018.

The ratio for the year ended 31 December 2018 is:

$$\text{Interest cover ratio} = \frac{47}{32} = 1.5 \text{ times}$$

Alexis plc's gearing ratios are:

	2017	2018
Gearing ratio	26.2%	36.0%
Interest cover ratio	13.5 times	1.5 times

What do you deduce from a comparison of Alexis plc's gearing ratios over the two years?

The gearing ratio has changed significantly. This is mainly due to the substantial increase in the contribution of long-term lenders to financing the business. The gearing ratio at 31 December 2018 would not be considered very high for a business that is trading successfully. It is the low profitability that is the problem. The interest cover ratio has declined dramatically from 13.5 times in 2017 to 1.5 times in 2018. This was partly caused by the increase in borrowings in 2018, but mainly caused by the dramatic decline in profitability in that year. The situation in 2018 looks hazardous. Only a small decline in future operating profits would result in the profit being unable to cover interest payments.

Without knowledge of the planned ratios, it is not possible to reach a valid conclusion on Alexis plc's gearing.

Figure 8.14 shows the gearing ratios that we considered.

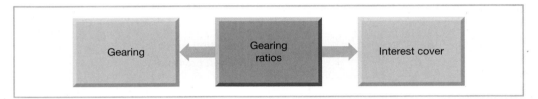

Figure 8.14 Gearing ratios

Both Ali plc and Bhaskar plc operate wholesale electrical stores throughout the UK. The financial statements of each business for the year ended 30 June 2018 are as follows:

Statements of financial position as at 30 June 2018

	Ali plc £m	Bhaskar plc £m
ASSETS		
Non-current assets		
Property, plant and equipment (cost less depreciation)		
Land and buildings	360.0	510.0
Fixtures and fittings	87.0	91.2
	447.0	601.2
Current assets		
Inventories	592.0	403.0
Trade receivables	176.4	321.9
Cash at bank	84.6	91.6
	853.0	816.5
Total assets	1,300.0	1,417.7

	Ali plc £m	Bhaskar plc £m
EQUITY AND LIABILITIES		
Equity		
£1 ordinary shares	320.0	250.0
Retained earnings	367.6	624.6
	687.6	874.6
Non-current liabilities		
Borrowings – loan notes	190.0	250.0
Current liabilities		
Trade payables	406.4	275.7
Taxation	16.0	17.4
	422.4	293.1
Total equity and liabilities	1,300.0	1,417.7

Income statements for the year ended 30 June 2018

	Ali plc £m	Bhaskar plc £m
Revenue	1,478.1	1,790.4
Cost of sales	(1,018.3)	(1,214.9)
Gross profit	459.8	575.5
Operating expenses	(308.5)	(408.6)
Operating profit	151.3	166.9
Interest payable	(19.4)	(27.5)
Profit before taxation	131.9	139.4
Taxation	(32.0)	(34.8)
Profit for the year	99.9	104.6

All purchases and sales were on credit.

Required:
For each business, calculate two ratios that are concerned with each of the following aspects:

- profitability
- efficiency
- liquidity
- gearing

(eight ratios in total).
  What can you conclude from the ratios that you have calculated?

The solution to this question can be found at the back of the book, starting on page 525.

The main points of this chapter may be summarised as follows:

Ratio analysis

- Compares two related figures, usually both from the same set of financial statements.
- Is an aid to understanding what the financial statements really mean.
- Is an inexact science so results must be interpreted cautiously.
- Usually requires the performance for past periods, similar businesses and/or planned performance as benchmark ratios.
- Can often benefit from a brief overview of the financial statements to provide insights that may not be revealed by ratios and/or may help in the interpretation of them.

Profitability ratios

- Are concerned with effectiveness at generating profit.
- Most commonly found in practice are the return on ordinary shareholders' funds (ROSF), return on capital employed (ROCE), operating profit margin and gross profit margin.

Efficiency ratios

- Are concerned with efficiency of using assets/resources.
- Most commonly found in practice are the average inventories turnover period, average settlement period for trade receivables, average settlement period for trade payables, sales revenue to capital employed and sales revenue per employee.

Liquidity ratios

- Are concerned with the ability to meet short-term obligations.
- Most commonly found in practice are the current ratio, the acid test ratio and the cash generated to maturing obligations ratio.
- Operating cash cycle (for a wholesaler) = Average inventories' turnover period + Average settlement period for trade receivables − Average settlement period for trade payables.
- An objective of working capital management is to limit the length of the operating cash cycle (OCC), subject to any risks that this may cause.

Gearing ratios

- Are concerned with relationship between equity and debt financing.
- Most commonly found in practice are the gearing ratio and the interest cover ratio.

For definitions of these terms, see at the back of the book, starting on page 514.

return on ordinary shareholders' funds ratio (ROSF) p. 276

return on capital employed ratio (ROCE) p. 277

operating profit margin ratio p. 279

gross profit margin ratio p. 280

average inventories turnover period ratio p. 284

average settlement period for trade receivables ratio p. 285

FURTHER READING

If you would like to explore the topics covered in this chapter in more depth, we recommend the following:

Alexander D., Britton, A., Jorissen, A., Hoogendoorn, M., and Van Mourik, C. (2017) *International Financial Reporting and Analysis*, Cengage Learning, 7th edn, Chapters 29–31.

Elliott, B. and Elliott, J. (2017) *Financial Accounting and Reporting*, 18th edn, Pearson, Chapters 28 and 29.

Robinson, T., Henry, E., Pirie, W. and Broihahn, M. (2015) *International Financial Statement Analysis*, 3rd edn, CFA Institute, Chapter 7.

Subramanyam, K and Wild, J. (2015) *Financial Statement Analysis*, 11th edn, McGraw-Hill Higher Education, Chapters 6 and 8.

CRITICAL REVIEW QUESTIONS

Solutions to these questions can be foundat the back of the book, starting on page 536.

8.1 Some businesses (for example, supermarket chains) operate on a low operating profit margin. Does this mean that the return on capital employed from the business will also be low?

8.2 For the current year, the average settlement period for trade receivables at Arkle plc was 60 days. This figure is much higher than in previous years. What factors may have contributed to this change of ratio?

8.3 Two businesses operate in the same industry. One has an inventories turnover period that is longer than the industry average. The other has an inventories turnover period that is shorter than the industry average. Give three possible explanations for each business's inventories turnover period ratio.

8.4 In the chapter it was mentioned that ratios help to eliminate some of the problems of comparing businesses of different sizes. Does this mean that size is irrelevant when interpreting and analysing the position and performance of different businesses?

Solutions to exercises with coloured numbers can be found at the back of the book, starting on page 545.

Basic-level exercises

8.1 Set out below are ratios relating to three different businesses. Each business operates within a different industrial sector.

Ratio	A plc	B plc	C plc
Operating profit margin	3.6%	9.7%	6.8%
Sales to capital employed	2.4 times	3.1 times	1.7 times
Average inventories turnover period	18 days	N/A	44 days
Average settlement period for trade receivables	2 days	12 days	26 days
Current ratio	0.8 times	0.6 times	1.5 times

Required:
State, with reasons, which one of the three businesses is:

(a) a holiday tour operator;
(b) a supermarket chain;
(c) a food manufacturer.

8.2 I. Jiang (Western) Ltd has recently produced its financial statements for the current year. The directors are concerned that the return on capital employed (ROCE) has decreased from 14 per cent last year to 12 per cent for the current year.

The following reasons were suggested as to why this reduction in ROCE has occurred:

1 an increase in the gross profit margin;
2 a reduction in sales revenue;
3 an increase in overhead expenses;
4 an increase in amount of inventories held;
5 the repayment of some borrowings at the year end; and
6 an increase in the time taken for trade receivables (credit customers) to pay.

Required:
Taking each of these six suggested reasons in turn, state, with reasons, whether each of them could lead to a reduction in ROCE.

8.3 Amsterdam Ltd and Berlin Ltd are both engaged in retailing, but they seem to take a different approach to it according to the following information:

Ratio	Amsterdam Ltd	Berlin Ltd
Return on capital employed (ROCE)	20%	17%
Return on ordinary shareholders' funds (ROSF)	30%	18%
Average settlement period for trade receivables	63 days	21 days
Average settlement period for trade payables	50 days	45 days
Gross profit margin	40%	15%
Operating profit margin	10%	10%
Average inventories turnover period	52 days	25 days

Required:
Describe what this information indicates about the differences in approach between the two businesses. If one of them prides itself on personal service and one of them on competitive prices, which do you think is which and why?

Intermediate-level exercises

8.4 The directors of Helena Beauty Products Ltd have been presented with the following abridged financial statements:

Helena Beauty Products Ltd
Income statement for the year ended 30 September

	2017		2018	
	£000	£000	£000	£000
Sales revenue		3,600		3,840
Cost of sales				
Opening inventories	320		400	
Purchases	2,240		2,350	
	2,560		2,750	
Closing inventories	(400)	(2,160)	(500)	(2,250)
Gross profit		1,440		1,590
Expenses		(1,360)		(1,500)
Profit		80		90

Statement of financial position as at 30 September

	2017	2018
	£000	£000
ASSETS		
Non-current assets		
Property, plant and equipment	1,900	1,860
Current assets		
Inventories	400	500
Trade receivables	750	960
Cash at bank	8	4
	1,158	1,464
Total assets	3,058	3,324
EQUITY AND LIABILITIES		
Equity		
£1 ordinary shares	1,650	1,766
Retained earnings	1,018	1,108
	2,668	2,874
Current liabilities	390	450
Total equity and liabilities	3,058	3,324

Required:
Using six ratios, comment on the profitability (three ratios) and efficiency (three ratios) of the business.

8.5 Conday and Co. Ltd has been in operation for three years and produces antique repro-
duction furniture for the export market. The most recent set of financial statements for the
business is set out as follows:

Statement of financial position as at 30 November

	£000
ASSETS	
Non-current assets	
Property, plant and equipment (cost less depreciation)	
Land and buildings	228
Plant and machinery	762
	990
Current assets	
Inventories	600
Trade receivables	820
	1,420
Total assets	2,410
EQUITY AND LIABILITIES	
Equity	
Ordinary shares of £1 each	700
Retained earnings	365
	1,065
Non-current liabilities	
Borrowings – 9% loan notes (Note 1)	200
Current liabilities	
Trade payables	665
Taxation	48
Short-term borrowings (all bank overdraft)	432
	1,145
Total equity and liabilities	2,410

Income statement for the year ended 30 November

	£000
Revenue	2,600
Cost of sales	(1,620)
Gross profit	980
Selling and distribution expenses (Note 2)	(408)
Administration expenses	(194)
Operating profit	378
Finance expenses	(58)
Profit before taxation	320
Taxation	(95)
Profit for the year	225

Notes:
1 The loan notes are secured on the land and buildings.
2 Selling and distribution expenses include £170,000 in respect of bad debts.
3 A dividend of £160,000 was paid on the ordinary shares during the year.
4 The directors have invited an investor to take up a new issue of ordinary shares in the business at
£6.40 each making a total investment of £200,000. The directors wish to use the funds to finance
a programme of further expansion.

Required:

(a) Analyse the financial position and performance of the business and comment on any features that you consider significant.

(b) State, with reasons, whether or not the investor should invest in the business on the terms outlined.

Advanced-level exercises

8.6 Threads Limited manufactures nuts and bolts, which are sold to industrial users. The abbreviated financial statements for 2017 and 2018 are as follows:

Income statements for the year ended 30 June

	2017	2018
	£000	£000
Revenue	1,180	1,200
Cost of sales	(680)	(750)
Gross profit	500	450
Operating expenses	(200)	(208)
Depreciation	(66)	(75)
Operating profit	234	167
Interest	(–)	(8)
Profit before taxation	234	159
Taxation	(80)	(48)
Profit for the year	154	111

Statements of financial position as at 30 June

	2017	2018
	£000	£000
ASSETS		
Non-current assets		
Property, plant and equipment	702	687
Current assets		
Inventories	148	236
Trade receivables	102	156
Cash	3	4
	253	396
Total assets	955	1,083
EQUITY AND LIABILITIES		
Equity		
Ordinary share capital (£1 shares, fully paid)	500	500
Retained earnings	256	295
	756	795
Non-current liabilities		
Borrowings – bank loan	–	50
Current liabilities		
Trade payables	60	76
Other payables and accruals	18	16
Taxation	40	24
Short-term borrowings (all bank overdraft)	81	122
	199	238
Total equity and liabilities	955	1,083

Dividends were paid on ordinary shares of £70,000 and £72,000 for 2017 and 2018, respectively.

Required:

(a) Calculate the following financial ratios for *both* 2017 and 2018 (using year-end figures for statement of financial position items):

1 return on capital employed
2 operating profit margin
3 gross profit margin
4 current ratio
5 acid test ratio
6 settlement period for trade receivables
7 settlement period for trade payables
8 inventories turnover period.

(b) Comment on the performance of Threads Limited from the viewpoint of a business considering supplying a substantial amount of goods to Threads Limited on usual trade credit terms.

8.7 Broadbury Ltd is a family-owned clothes manufacturer. For a number of years the chairman and managing director was David Broadbury. During his period of office, sales revenue had grown steadily at a rate of 2 to 3 per cent each year. David Broadbury retired on 30 November 2016 and was succeeded by his son Simon. Soon after taking office, Simon decided to expand the business. Within weeks he had successfully negotiated a five-year contract with a large clothes retailer to make a range of sports and leisurewear items. The contract will result in an additional £2 million in sales revenue during each year of the contract. To fulfil the contract, Broadbury Ltd acquired new equipment and premises.

Financial information concerning the business is given below:

Income statements for the years ended 30 November

	2016	2017
	£000	£000
Revenue	9,482	11,365
Operating profit	914	1,042
Interest charges	(22)	(81)
Profit before taxation	892	961
Taxation	(358)	(386)
Profit for the year	534	575

Statements of financial position as at 30 November

	2016	2017
	£000	£000
ASSETS		
Non-current assets		
Property, plant and equipment		
Premises at cost	5,240	7,360
Plant and equipment (net)	2,375	4,057
	7,615	11,417
Current assets		
Inventories	2,386	3,420
Trade receivables	2,540	4,280
	4,926	7,700
Total assets	12,541	19,117

	2016 £000	2017 £000
EQUITY AND LIABILITIES		
Equity		
Share capital	2,000	2,000
Reserves	7,813	8,268
	9,813	10,268
Non-current liabilities		
Borrowing – loans	1,220	3,675
Current liabilities		
Trade payables	1,157	2,245
Taxation	179	193
Short-term borrowings (all bank overdraft)	172	2,736
	1,508	5,174
Total equity and liabilities	12,541	19,117

Dividends of £120,000 were paid on ordinary shares in respect of each of the two years.

Required:

(a) Calculate, for each year (using year-end figures for statement of financial position items), the following ratios:
1 operating profit margin
2 return on capital employed
3 current ratio
4 gearing ratio
5 trade receivables settlement period
6 sales revenue to capital employed.

(b) Using the above ratios, and any other ratios or information you consider relevant, comment on the results of the expansion programme.

8.8 The financial statements for Harridges Ltd are given below for the two years ended 30 June 2017 and 2018. Harridges Limited operates a department store in the centre of a small town.

Income statements for the years ended 30 June

	2017 £000	2018 £000
Sales revenue	2,600	3,500
Cost of sales	(1,560)	(2,350)
Gross profit	1,040	1,150
Wages and salaries	(320)	(350)
Overheads	(260)	(200)
Depreciation	(150)	(250)
Operating profit	310	350
Interest payable	(50)	(50)
Profit before taxation	260	300
Taxation	(105)	(125)
Profit for the year	155	175

Statement of financial position as at 30 June

	2017 £000	2018 £000
ASSETS		
Non-current assets		
Property, plant and equipment	1,265	1,525
Current assets		
Inventories	250	400
Trade receivables	105	145
Cash at bank	380	115
	735	660
Total assets	2,000	2,185
EQUITY AND LIABILITIES		
Equity		
Share capital: £1 shares fully paid	490	490
Share premium	260	260
Retained earnings	350	450
	1,100	1,200
Non-current liabilities		
Borrowings – 10% loan notes	500	500
Current liabilities		
Trade payables	300	375
Other payables	100	110
	400	485
Total equity and liabilities	2,000	2,185

Dividends were paid on ordinary shares of £65,000 and £75,000 for 2017 and 2018, respectively.

Required:

(a) Choose and calculate eight ratios that would be helpful in assessing the performance of Harridges Ltd. Use end-of-year values and calculate ratios for both 2017 and 2018.

(b) Using the ratios calculated in (a) and any others you consider helpful, comment on the business's performance from the viewpoint of a prospective purchaser of a majority of shares.

Chapter 9

ANALYSING AND INTERPRETING FINANCIAL STATEMENTS (2)

INTRODUCTION

In this chapter we shall continue our examination of the analysis and interpretation of financial statements. We begin by taking a detailed look at investment ratios. These ratios consider business performance from the perspective of a shareholder. After a brief consideration of overtrading, and the problems that it brings, we go on to look at common-size financial statements. This technique presents the financial statements in the form of ratios and can offer useful insights to performance and position.

Decision-making involves making predictions about the future. In this chapter we shall also see how ratios may be of value in one important area, the prediction of financial collapse. Finally, we shall consider the problems encountered when undertaking ratio analysis. Although ratios can be of very useful in assessing financial health, it is important to be aware of their limitations.

Learning outcomes

When you have completed this chapter, you should be able to:

- calculate and interpret key investment ratios;
- prepare and interpret common-size financial statements;
- evaluate the use of ratios in helping to predict financial failure; and
- discuss the limitations of ratios as a tool of financial analysis.

To demonstrate how particular ratios are calculated and interpreted, we shall continue to refer to Alexis plc, whose financial statements and other information are set out in Example 8.1 on pages 273 to 274.

INVESTMENT RATIOS

Various ratios are available that are designed to help shareholders assess the returns on their investment. The following are widely used:

- dividend payout ratio;
- dividend yield ratio;
- earnings per share;
- cash generated from operations per share;
- price/earnings ratio.

Dividend payout ratio

The dividend payout ratio measures the proportion of earnings paid out to shareholders in the form of dividends. The ratio is calculated as follows:

$$\text{Dividend payout ratio} = \frac{\text{Dividends announced for the year}}{\text{Earnings for the year available for dividends}} \times 100$$

In the case of ordinary shares, the earnings available for dividends will normally be the profit for the year (that is, the profit after taxation) less any preference dividends relating to the year. This ratio is normally expressed as a percentage.

The dividend payout ratio for Alexis plc for the year ended 31 December 2017 is:

$$\text{Dividend payout ratio} = \frac{40}{165} \times 100 = 24.2\%$$

Activity 9.1

Calculate the dividend payout ratio of Alexis plc for the year ended 31 December 2018.

The ratio for 2018 is:

$$\text{Dividend payout ratio} = \frac{40}{11} \times 100 = 363.6\%$$

This would normally be regarded as an alarming increase in the ratio over the two years. At first sight, paying a dividend of £40 million in 2018 would seem to be very imprudent.

The information provided by the above ratio is often expressed slightly differently as the dividend cover ratio. Here, the calculation is:

$$\text{Dividend cover ratio} = \frac{\text{Earnings for the year available for dividend}}{\text{Dividends announced for the year}}$$

For 2017, the ratio for Alexis plc would be 165/40 = 4.1 times. That is to say, the earnings available for dividend cover the actual dividend paid by just over four times. For 2018, the ratio is 11/40 = 0.3 times.

Dividend yield ratio

The dividend yield ratio relates the cash return from a share to its current market value. This can help investors to assess the cash return on their investment in the business. The ratio, expressed as a percentage, is:

$$\text{Dividend yield} = \frac{\text{Dividend per share}}{\text{Market value per share}} \times 100$$

The dividend yield for Alexis plc for the year ended 31 December 2017, therefore, is:

$$\text{Dividend yield} = \frac{0.067^*}{2.50} \times 100 = 2.7\%$$

The shares' market value is given in Note 1 to Example 8.1 (page 274).

*Dividend proposed/number of shares = 40/(300 × 2) = £0.067 dividend per share (the 300 is multiplied by 2 because they are £0.50 shares).

Activity 9.2

Calculate the dividend yield for Alexis plc for the year ended 31 December 2018.

The ratio for 2018 is:

$$\text{Dividend yield} = \frac{0.067^*}{1.50} \times 100 = 4.5\%$$

*40/(300 × 2) = £0.067.

Earnings per share

The earnings per share (EPS) ratio relates the earnings generated by the business, and available to shareholders, during a period to the number of shares in issue. For equity (ordinary) shareholders, the amount available will be represented by the profit for the year (profit after taxation) less any preference dividend, where applicable. The ratio for equity shareholders is calculated as follows:

$$\text{Earnings per share} = \frac{\text{Earnings available to ordinary shareholders}}{\text{Number of ordinary shares in issue}}$$

In the case of Alexis plc, the earnings per share for the year ended 31 December 2017 is:

$$\text{EPS} = \frac{£165m}{600m} = 27.5p$$

Many investment analysts regard the EPS ratio as a fundamental measure of share performance. The trend in earnings per share over time is used to help assess the investment potential of a business's shares. Although it is possible to make total profit increase through ordinary shareholders investing more in the business, this will not necessarily lead to an increase in the profitability *per share*.

Real World 9.1 points out the danger of placing too much emphasis on this ratio. The equity fund manager, Terry Smith, argues that, had more attention been paid to ROCE rather than EPS, investors would have spotted that all was not well with Tesco plc, the supermarket giant, which went through a difficult period early in this century. He also takes to task, Warren Buffett, the legendary investor, for ignoring his own advice and investing heavily in the business.

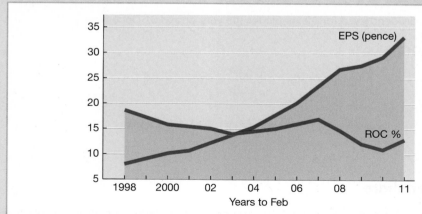

Real World 9.1

A trolley load of problems

In his 1979 letter to shareholders, Mr Buffett stated: 'The primary test of managerial economic performance is the achievement of a high earnings rate on equity capital employed (without undue leverage, accounting gimmickry, etc.) and not the achievement of consistent gains in earnings per share.'

This makes it all the more surprising to me that both Mr Buffett and the many acolytes who have seemingly followed him to the gates of hell in Tesco, ignored this chart:

While Tesco's EPS figures were rising from around 8 pence to 30, the more telling ROCE figures were dropping from 19 per cent to 10 per cent.

Figure 9.1 Tesco: the Leahy years. EPS and ROCE

This is not the first such chart that I have come across in which a company reports steadily rising earnings per share (EPS), on which most analysts and 'investors' focus. For them, the rise in EPS seems to have a mesmeric effect like Kaa the snake in *The Jungle Book*. But they ignore the point that more capital is being employed to generate those earnings at ever lower returns. Add in the fact that Tesco has changed its definition of return on capital employed (ROCE) eight times during those years, and there's more than enough material to send investors running for cover – even those who have less aversion than I do to retailers.

Yet much of the commentary about what has gone wrong at Tesco focuses on Philip Clarke, who took over as chief executive from Sir Terry Leahy in 2011, as if everything was going swimmingly until then. Looking at the ROCE line in the chart it is clear that this was not the case.

Moreover, one thing to bear in mind is that if Tesco's ROCE during the Leahy years fell from a very good 19 per cent to a less than adequate 10 per cent, this is an average of returns on capital employed, which includes both capital invested years ago and more recent commitments. To drag the average ROCE down so dramatically it is likely that returns on new investments in those years were not just inadequate, but in some cases negative – as the ill-starred US expansion proved to be.

Even if return on capital employed does not have the same importance for you as it does for me, or Mr Buffett (at least in 1979), consider this: in 14 of the past 18 years (taking us back to 1997 when Sir Terry became chief executive) Tesco's free cash flow less its dividend (with free cash defined as operating cash flow less gross capital expenditure) was a negative number. In plain English, Tesco was not generating enough cash both to invest and to pay its dividend. In half of those 14 years, the proceeds of fixed asset disposals took the numbers back into the black, but that is not exactly a sustainable source of financing.

So guess what they did instead? Yes, they borrowed it. Tesco's gross debt, which was £894 million when Sir Terry took over, peaked at nearly £15.9 billion in 2009. The company spent much of its free cash on fixed-asset investment and raised debt to help pay the dividend. This is neither healthy nor sustainable, as investors in Tesco have now come to realise.

The concept that this might not be sustainable hardly requires much thought. Neither does charting the ROCE versus the growth in EPS. Yet it is evident that many investors, including it seems Mr Buffet (who has been trimming his Tesco stake in recent years) either didn't do this or ignored the results if they did. It makes me wonder what else they are ignoring.

It is not usually very helpful to compare the EPS of one business with that of another. Differences in financing arrangements (for example, in the nominal value of shares issued) can render any such comparison meaningless. However, it can be useful to monitor changes that occur in this ratio for a particular business over time.

Activity 9.3

Calculate the earnings per share of Alexis plc for the year ended 31 December 2018.

The ratio for 2018 is:

$$\text{EPS} = \frac{£11\text{m}}{600\text{m}} = 1.8\text{p}$$

Cash generated from operations per share

In the short term at least, cash generated from operations (found in the statement of cash flows) can provide a good guide to the ability of a business to pay dividends and to undertake planned expenditures. Many see a cash generation measure as more useful in this context than the earnings per share figure. The **cash generated from operations (CGO) per ordinary share ratio** is calculated as follows:

$$\text{Cash generated from operations per share} = \frac{\text{Cash generated from operations less preference dividend (if any)}}{\text{Number of ordinary shares in issue}}$$

The ratio for Alexis plc for the year ended 31 December 2017 is:

$$\text{CGO per share} = \frac{£251m}{600m} = 41.8p$$

Activity 9.4

Calculate the CGO per ordinary share for Alexis plc for the year ended 31 December 2018.

The ratio for 2018 is:

$$\text{CGO per share} = \frac{£34m}{600m} = 5.7p$$

There has been a dramatic decrease in this ratio over the two-year period.

Note that, for both years, the CGO per share for Alexis plc is higher than the earnings per share. This is not unusual. The effect of adding back depreciation to derive the CGO figures will often ensure that a higher figure is derived.

Price/earnings (P/E) ratio

The **price/earnings (P/E) ratio** relates the market value of a share to the earnings per share. This ratio can be calculated as follows:

$$\text{P/E ratio} = \frac{\text{Market value per share}}{\text{Earnings per share}}$$

The P/E ratio for Alexis plc as at 31 December 2017 is:

$$\text{P/E ratio} = \frac{£2.50}{27.5p^*} = 9.1 \text{ times}$$

*The EPS figure (27.5p) was calculated on page 316.

This ratio indicates that the market value of the share is 9.1 times the current level of earnings. It is a measure of market confidence in the future of a business. The higher the P/E ratio, the greater the confidence in the future earning power of the business and, consequently, the more investors are prepared to pay in relation to that current earning power.

Calculate the P/E ratio of Alexis plc as at 31 December 2018.

The ratio for 2018 is:

$$\text{P/E ratio} = \frac{£1.50}{1.8\text{p}} = 83.3 \text{ times}$$

As P/E ratios provide a useful guide to market confidence about the future, they can be helpful when comparing different businesses. However, differences in accounting policies between businesses can lead to different profit and earnings per share figures. This can distort comparisons.

The investment ratios for Alexis plc over the two-year period are as follows:

	2017	2018
Dividend payout ratio	24.2%	363.6%
Dividend yield ratio	2.7%	4.5%
Earnings per share	27.5p	1.8p
Cash generated from operations per share	41.8p	5.7p
P/E ratio	9.1 times	83.3 times

What do you deduce from the investment ratios set out above? Can you offer an explanation why the share price has not fallen as much as it might have done, bearing in mind the much poorer trading performance in 2018?

Although the EPS has fallen dramatically and the dividend payment for 2018 seems very imprudent, the share price has held up reasonably well (fallen from £2.50 to £1.50). Moreover, the dividend yield and P/E ratios have improved in 2018. This is an anomaly of these two ratios, which stems from using a forward-looking value (the share price) in conjunction with historic data (dividends and earnings). Share prices are based on investors' assessments of the business's future. It seems that the 'market' was less happy with Alexis plc at the end of 2018 than at the end of 2017. This is evidenced by the fact that the share price had fallen by £1 a share. The decline in share price, however, was less dramatic than the decline in profit for the year. This suggests that investors believe the business will perform better in the future. Perhaps they are confident that the large increase in assets and employee numbers occurring during the year to 31 December 2018 will yield benefits in the future; benefits that the business has not yet been able to generate.

The investment ratios that we have discussed are summarised in Figure 9.2.

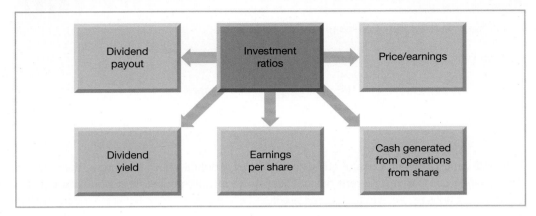

Figure 9.2 Investment ratios

Real World 9.2 provides information about the share performance of a selection of large, well-known UK businesses. This type of information is provided on a daily basis by some newspapers, notably the *Financial Times*.

So, for example, for the retail business Marks and Spencer plc,

- the shares had a mid-market price of 297.50 pence each at the close of Stock Exchange trading on 19 February 2018;
- the shares had decreased in price by 1.30 pence during trading on 19 February 2018;
- the shares had highest and lowest prices during the previous 52 weeks of 397.80 pence and 282.00 pence, respectively;
- the shares had a dividend yield, based on the 19 February 2018 closing price (and the dividend for the most recent year), of 6.29 per cent;
- the shares had a P/E ratio, based on the 19 February 2018 closing price (and the after-taxation earnings per share for the most recent year), of 26.10;
- during trading on 19 February 2018, 3,774,100 of the business's shares changed hands between buyers and sellers.

Real World 9.3 shows how investment ratios can vary between different industry sectors.

Real World 9.3

Yielding dividends

Investment ratios can vary significantly between businesses and between industries. To give some indication of the range of variations that occur, the average dividend yield ratios and average P/E ratios for listed businesses in twelve different industries are shown in Figures 9.3 and 9.4, respectively.

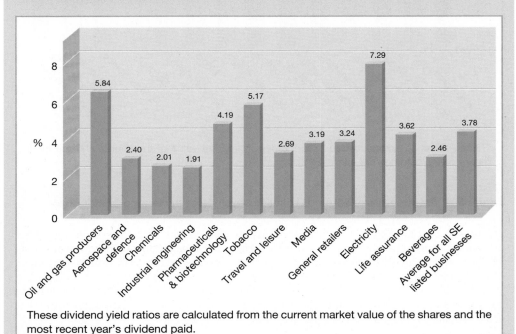

These dividend yield ratios are calculated from the current market value of the shares and the most recent year's dividend paid.

Figure 9.3 Average dividend yield ratios for businesses in a range of industries

Some industries tend to pay out lower dividends than others, leading to lower dividend yield ratios. The average for all Stock Exchange listed businesses was 3.78 per cent (as is shown in Figure 9.3), but there is a wide variation, with industrial engineering at 1.91 per cent and electricity at 7.29 per cent.

Some types of businesses tend to invest heavily in developing new products, hence their tendency to pay low dividends compared with their share prices. Some of the inter-industry differences in the dividend yield ratio can be explained by the nature of the calculation of the ratio. The prices of shares at any given moment are based on expectations of their economic futures; dividends are actual past events. A business that had a good trading year recently may have paid a dividend that, in the light of investors' assessment of the business's economic future, may be high (a high dividend yield).

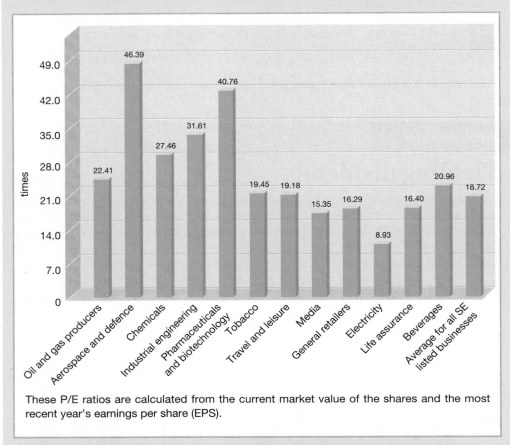

These P/E ratios are calculated from the current market value of the shares and the most recent year's earnings per share (EPS).

Figure 9.4 Average price/earnings ratios for businesses in a range of industries

Businesses that have a high share price relative to their recent historic earnings have high P/E ratios. This may be because their future is regarded as economically bright, which may be the result of investing heavily in the future at the expense of recent profits (earnings). On the other hand, high P/Es also arise where businesses have recent low earnings, but investors believe that their future is brighter. The average P/E for all Stock Exchange listed businesses was 18.72 times, but the average for electricity was as low as 8.93 times and that for aerospace and defence as high as 46.39 times.

 Source: Both figures are constructed from data appearing in the *Financial Times*, 20 February 2018, p. 18. © The Financial Times Limited 2018. All rights reserved.

FINANCIAL RATIOS AND THE PROBLEM OF OVERTRADING

Overtrading occurs where a business is operating at a level of activity that cannot be supported by the amount of finance that has been committed. This situation is often due to poor financial control over the business by its managers. The underlying reasons for overtrading are varied. It may occur:

- in young, expanding businesses that fail to prepare adequately for the rapid increase in demand for their goods or services. This often leads to insufficient finance to fund the level of trade receivables and inventories needed to support the level of sales revenue generated;
- in businesses where the managers may have misjudged the level of expected sales demand or have failed to control escalating project costs;
- as a result of a fall in the value of money (inflation), causing more finance to have to be committed to inventories and trade receivables, even where there is no expansion in the real volume of trade; and
- where the owners are unable to inject further funds into the business themselves and/or they cannot persuade others to invest in the business.

Whatever the reason, the problems that it brings must be dealt with if the business is to survive over the longer term.

Overtrading results in liquidity problems such as exceeding borrowing limits, or slow repayment of borrowings and trade payables. The last of these can result in suppliers withholding supplies, thereby making it difficult to meet customer needs. The managers of the business might be forced to direct all of their efforts to dealing with immediate and pressing problems, such as finding cash to meet interest charges due or paying wages. Longer-term planning becomes difficult as managers spend their time going from crisis to crisis. Ultimately, the business may fail because it cannot meet its maturing obligations – it runs out of cash.

Activity 9.7

If a business is overtrading, do you think the following ratios would be higher or lower than normally expected?

1 Current ratio
2 Average inventories turnover period
3 Average settlement period for trade receivables
4 Average settlement period for trade payables

Your answer should be along the following lines:

1 The current ratio would be lower than normally expected. This ratio is a measure of liquidity, and lack of liquidity is a typical symptom of overtrading.
2 The average inventories turnover period would be lower than normally expected. Where a business is overtrading, the level of inventories held will be low because of the problems of financing them. In the short term, sales revenue may not be badly affected by the low inventories levels, and therefore inventories will be turned over more quickly.

3   The average settlement period for trade receivables may be lower than normally expected. Where a business is suffering from liquidity problems it may chase credit customers more vigorously in an attempt to improve cash flows.
4   The average settlement period for trade payables may be higher than normally expected. The business may try to delay payments to its suppliers because of the liquidity problems arising.

To deal with the overtrading problem, a business must ensure that the finance available is consistent with the level of operations. Thus, if a business that is overtrading is unable to raise new finance, it should cut back its level of operations in line with the finance available. Although this may mean lost sales and lost profits in the short term, cutting back may be necessary to ensure survival over the longer term.

KEY PERFORMANCE INDICATORS

Many businesses use **key performance indicators (KPIs)** to help measure the degree of success achieved in carrying out their operations. These KPIs often include financial ratios such as those that we have encountered. They may also, however, include other measures of performance. They may, for example, include ratios that compare a figure on the financial statements with a particular business resource. They may also include non-financial measures of performance.

easyJet plc, the well-known budget airline operator, has developed various KPIs, through which it monitors its own performance. Some are non-financial indicators, such as customer satisfaction and employee turnover, but others are based on financial ratios. Not only does easyJet calculate and, presumably, use various KPIs, it also publishes them in its annual report. **Real World 9.4** shows extracts from the table of the business's financial KPIs. Results over a five-year period are provided to help assess progress over time.

Real World 9.4

Key performance measures of easyJet plc

	2013	2014	2015	2016	2017
Return on capital employed (%)	17.4	20.5	22.2	15.0	11.9
Profit before tax per seat (£)	7.03	8.12	9.15	6.35	4.45
Revenue per seat (£)	62.58	63.31	62.48	58.46	58.23
Cost per seat (£)	55.55	55.19	53.33	52.11	53.78
Cost per seat excluding fuel (£)	38.17	37.70	37.55	38.16	41.53

After having grown steadily since 2009, easyJet's ROCE peaked in 2015 and then declined in the next two years. This must be a worry to management since, unsurprisingly, ROCE is seen by the business as an important indicator. This is evidenced not only by the fact that easyJet states it to be a KPI, but also because it is the basis of a major component of bonuses paid to senior managers.

Source: easyJet plc, Annual Report 2017, p. 131.

COMMON-SIZE FINANCIAL STATEMENTS

Common-size financial statements are financial statements (such as the income statement, statement of financial position and statement of cash flows) that are expressed in terms of some base figure. Presenting financial statements in this way can help in making comparisons. Differences and trends can often be easier to detect than when examining the original statements. We shall now discuss the two main approaches to preparing common-size statements.

Vertical analysis

The first approach to preparing common-size statements is to express all the figures in a particular financial statement in terms of one of the figures contained within it. This 'base' figure is typically a key figure in the statement, such as sales revenue in an income statement, total long-term funds in a statement of financial position and the cash flow from operating activities in the statement of cash flows.

Example 9.1 is a common-size income statement that uses sales revenue as the base figure. Note that the base figure is set at 100 and all other figures are expressed as a percentage of this.

Example 9.1

The common-size income statement of Alexis plc (see Example 8.1 on pages 273 to 274) for 2018, in abbreviated form and using revenue as the base figure, will be as follows:

Common-size income statement for the year ended 31 December 2018

		Calculation of figures
Revenue	100.0	Base figure
Cost of sales	(77.9)	$(1{,}745/2{,}240) \times 100\%$
Gross profit	22.1	$(495/2{,}240) \times 100\%$
Operating expenses	(11.3)	$(252/2{,}240) \times 100\%$
Operating profit	10.8	$(243/2{,}240) \times 100\%$
Interest payable	(0.8)	$(18/2{,}240) \times 100\%$
Profit before taxation	10.0	$(225/2{,}240) \times 100\%$
Taxation	(2.7)	$(60/2{,}240) \times 100\%$
Profit for the year	7.3	$(165/2{,}240) \times 100\%$

Each of the figures in the income statement is simply the original financial figure divided by the revenue figure and then expressed as a percentage. Since the revised values have been expressed to only one decimal place, which gave rise to rounding errors, it was necessary to make adjustments so that the income statement 'adds up'.

Not much, of course, can be discerned from looking at just one common-size statement. We need some benchmark for comparison. This could be other accounting periods for the same business.

The following is a set of common-size income statements for a major high street depart-ment store for five consecutive accounting periods:

	Year 1	Year 2	Year 3	Year 4	Year 5
Revenue	100.0	100.0	100.0	100.0	100.0
Cost of sales	(68.9)	(68.5)	(67.2)	(66.5)	(66.3)
Gross profit	31.1	31.5	32.8	33.5	33.7
Operating expenses	(28.1)	(28.4)	(27.6)	(29.2)	(30.2)
Operating profit	3.0	3.1	5.2	4.3	3.5
Interest payable	(1.1)	(1.2)	(1.6)	(2.1)	(1.3)
Profit before taxation	1.9	1.9	3.6	2.2	2.2

What significant features are revealed by the common-size income statements?

Operating profit, relative to revenue, rose in Year 3 but fell back again in Years 4 and 5 to end the five-year period at a higher level than it had been in Years 1 and 2. Although the gross profit margin rose steadily over the five-year period, so did the operating expenses, with the exception of Year 3. Clearly, the fall in operating expenses to revenue in Year 3 led to the improvement in operating profit to revenue.

Common-size financial statements being compared do not have to be for the same busi-ness. They can be for different businesses. **Real World 9.5** sets out common-size statements of financial position for five UK businesses whose name, or whose products, are very well-known. These businesses were randomly selected, except that each one is high profile and from a different industry. For each business, the statement of financial position items are expressed as a percentage of the total investment by the providers of long-term finance (equity and non-current liabilities).

A summary of the statements of financial position of five UK businesses

Business:	Next plc	Ryanair Holdings plc	Babcock Int Group plc	Tesco plc	Severn Trent plc
Statement of financial position date:	27.1.17	31.3.18	31.3.18	24.2.18	31.3.18
ASSETS					
Non-current assets	46	91	99	121	103
Current assets					
Inventories	30	–	3	9	–
Trade and other receivables	76	1	22	6	5
Other current assets	–	5	1	19	–
Cash and near cash	3	41	6	20	1
	109	47	32	54	6
Total assets	155	138	131	175	109

EQUITY AND LIABILITIES

Equity and non-current liabilities	<u>100</u>	<u>100</u>	<u>100</u>	<u>100</u>	<u>100</u>
Current liabilities					
Trade and other payables	35	31	29	35	5
Other short-term liabilities	9	7	1	34	–
Overdrafts and short-term borrowings	<u>11</u>	<u>–</u>	<u>1</u>	<u>6</u>	<u>4</u>
	<u>55</u>	<u>38</u>	<u>31</u>	<u>75</u>	<u>9</u>
Total equity and non-current liabilities	<u>155</u>	<u>138</u>	<u>131</u>	<u>175</u>	<u>109</u>

The non-current assets, current assets and current liabilities are expressed as a percentage of the total long-term investment (equity plus non-current liabilities) of the business concerned. Next plc is a major retail and home shopping business. Ryanair is a leading airline. Babcock International Group plc is a large engineering and support business. Tesco plc is one of the UK's leading supermarkets. Severn Trent plc is an important supplier of water, sewerage services and waste management, mainly in the UK.

Source: Table constructed from information appearing in the financial statements for the year ended during 2018 for each of the five businesses concerned.

Real World 9.5 reveals quite striking differences in the make-up of the statement of financial position from one business to another. Take, for example, the current assets and current liabilities. Although the totals for current assets are pretty large when compared with the total long-term investment, these percentages vary considerably between businesses. When looking at the mix of current assets, we can see that only Next, Babcock and Tesco, which produce and/or sell goods, hold some inventories. The other two businesses are service providers and so inventories are an insignificant item. We can also see that very few of the sales of Tesco, Ryanair and Severn Trent are on credit, as they have relatively little invested in trade receivables.

Note that Tesco's trade payables are very much higher than its inventories. Since trade payables represent amounts due to suppliers of inventories, it means that Tesco receives the cash from a typical trolley load of groceries well in advance of paying for them. The relatively large 'Other current assets' and 'Other short-term liabilities' for Tesco arises from advances to and deposits from customers, respectively, that arise from the business's involvement in banking.

So far we have been considering what is known as **vertical analysis**. That is, we have been treating all of the figures in each statement as a percentage of a figure in that statement. This 'baseline' figure has been the sales revenue figure, in the case of the income statement, and the total long-term investment, with the statement of financial position. Note that common-size statements do not have to be expressed in terms of any particular factor; it all depends on the purpose of the analysis.

Horizontal analysis

Horizontal analysis is an alternative to the vertical analysis that we have just considered. Here all of the figures appearing in a particular financial statement are expressed as a base figure (that is 100) and the equivalent figures appearing in similar statements are expressed as a percentage of this base figure. When analysing the same business over time, the 'base' statement would normally be the earliest (or latest) of a set of financial statements. Thus, the inventories figure appearing in a particular statement of financial position can be set as the base figure (that is, set at 100) and inventories figures appearing in successive statements will each be expressed as a percentage of this figure. When analysing the financial statements of different businesses, as in Real World 9.5 above, a 'base' business must be selected. This would be the one that is of most interest.

Example 9.2 shows a horizontally analysed common-size income statement for the business, a department store, which was the subject of Activity 9.8.

Example 9.2

The following is a set of common-size income statements for a major high street department store for five consecutive accounting periods, using horizontal analysis and making Year 1 the base year:

	Year 1	Year 2	Year 3	Year 4	Year 5
Revenue	100.0	104.3	108.4	106.5	108.9
Cost of sales	(100.0)	(103.7)	(105.7)	(102.9)	(104.8)
Gross profit	100.0	105.5	114.4	114.5	118.0
Operating expenses	(100.0)	(105.4)	(106.7)	(110.4)	(117.2)
Operating profit	100.0	106.6	105.9	113.3	125.6
Interest payable	(100.0)	(111.9)	(157.1)	(202.4)	(127.4)
Profit before taxation	100.0	103.5	102.8	104.5	124.5

Year 1 is the base year so all of the figures in the Year 1 income statement are 100.0. All of the figures for the other years are that year's figure divided by the Year 1 figure for the same item and then expressed as a percentage. For example, the Year 4 profit before taxation, divided by the profit before taxation for Year 1 was 104.5. This tells us that the profit was 4.5 per cent greater in Year 4 than it had been for Year 1.

Activity 9.9

What are the significant features revealed by the common-size income statement in Example 9.2?

Revenue did not show much of an increase over the five years, particularly if these figures are not adjusted for inflation. Years 2 and 3 saw increases, but Years 4 and 5 were less impressive. The rate of increase in the cost of sales was less than that for revenue and, therefore, the gross profit growth was greater, than the rate of increase of revenue. Operating expenses showed growth over the years. Interest payable increased strongly during the first four years of the period, but then fell back significantly in Year 5.

Activity 9.10

The vertical approach to common-size financial statements (see Real World 9.5, for example) has the advantage of enabling the analyst to see each figure expressed in terms of the same item (revenue, long-term finance and so on).

■ What are the disadvantages of this approach?
■ How do horizontally analysed common-size statements overcome any problems?
■ What problems do horizontally analysed statements bring?

The problem with the horizontal approach is that it is not possible to see, for example, that revenue values are different from one year or business to the next. Normally a vertically analysed common-size income statement shows the revenue figure as 100 for all years or businesses. This is, of course, a problem of all approaches to ratio analysis.

Horizontally analysed common-size statements overcome this problem because, say, revenue figures are expressed in terms of one year or one particular business. This makes differences in revenue levels crystal clear. Unfortunately, such an approach makes comparison within each year's, or within a particular business's, statement rather difficult.

Perhaps the answer is to produce two sets of common-size statements, one analysed vertically and the other horizontally.

TREND ANALYSIS

It is often helpful to see whether ratios are indicating trends. Key ratios can be plotted on a graph to provide a simple visual display of changes occurring over time. The trends occurring within a business may, for example, be plotted against trends for rival businesses or for the industry as a whole for comparison purposes. An example of trend analysis is shown in **Real World 9.6**.

Real World 9.6

Trend setting

In Figure 9.5, the current ratio of three of the UK's leading supermarkets is plotted over time. Tesco plc was lower than that of its two main rivals, until 2005, when it overtook Morrison, and 2009, when it overtook Sainsbury's. Since then, however, the ratios of Tesco and Sainsbury's have been fairly close. Morrison has maintained the lowest current ratio over time.

With well-managed businesses like these, it is highly likely that any changes are the result of deliberate policy.

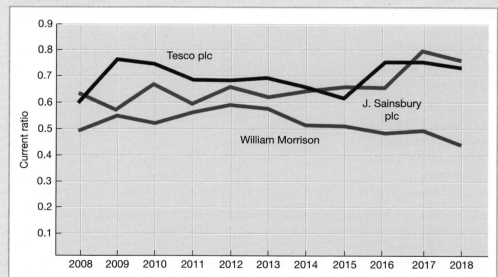

The current ratio for three leading UK supermarket businesses is plotted for the financial years ended during 2008 to 2018. This enables comparison to be made regarding the ratio, both for each of the three businesses over time and between the businesses.

Figure 9.5 Current ratio of three leading businesses

Source: Ratios calculated from information in the annual reports of the three businesses for each of the years 2008–2018.

Source: Annual reports of the three businesses 2008–18.

USING RATIOS TO PREDICT FINANCIAL FAILURE

Financial ratios, based on current or past performance, are often used to help predict the future. However, both the choice of ratios and the interpretation of results are normally dependent on the judgement and opinion of the analyst. Attempts have been made, however, to develop a more rigorous and systematic approach to the use of ratios for prediction purposes. In particular, there has been an interest in the ability of ratios to predict the financial failure of a business.

By financial failure, we mean a business either being forced out of business or being severely adversely affected by its inability to meet its financial obligations. It is often referred to as 'going bust' or 'going bankrupt'. This is, of course, a likely area of concern for all those connected with the business.

Using single ratios

Various approaches have been developed that attempt to use ratios to predict future financial failure. Early research focused on the examination of individual ratios to see whether one was a good or bad predictor of financial failure. Here, the past financial statements of a particular business that had actually failed were examined to try to see whether the information contained in those statements might have offered warning signs that the business might be in difficulties. In doing this, a particular ratio (for example the current ratio) for the failed business might be tracked over several years leading up to the date of the failure.

Beaver (see Reference 1 at the end of the chapter) carried out the first published research in this area. He identified 79 businesses that had failed. He then calculated the average (mean) of various ratios for these 79 businesses, going back over the financial statements of each business for each of the ten years leading up to each business's failure. Beaver then compared these average ratios with similarly derived ratios for a sample of 79 businesses that did not fail over this period. (The research used a matched-pair design, where each failed business was matched with a non-failed business of similar size and industry type.) Beaver found that certain ratios exhibited a marked difference between the failed and non-failed businesses for up to five years prior to failure. These ratios were:

- Cash flow/Total debt
- Net income (profit)/Total assets
- Total debt/Total assets
- Working capital/Total assets
- Current ratio
- No credit interval (that is, cash generated from operations to maturing obligations).

To illustrate Beaver's findings, the average current ratio of failed businesses for five years prior to failure, along with the average current ratio of non-failed businesses for the same period, is shown in Figure 9.6.

Similar research by Zmijewski (see Reference 2 at the end of the chapter), using a sample of 72 failed and 3,573 non-failed businesses over a six-year period, found that businesses that ultimately went on to fail were characterised by lower rates of return, higher levels of gearing, lower levels of coverage for their fixed interest payments and more variable returns on shares. While we may not find these results very surprising, it is interesting to note that Zmijewski, like a number of other researchers in this area, did not find liquidity ratios particularly useful in predicting financial failure. As already mentioned, however, Beaver found the current ratio to be a useful predictor.

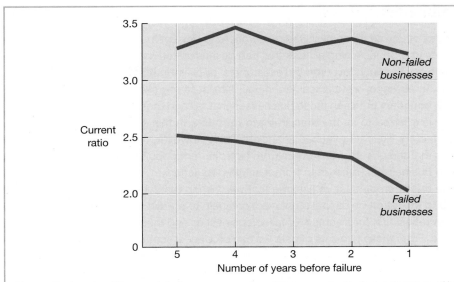

The vertical scale of the graph is the average value of the current ratio for each group of businesses (failed and non-failed). The horizontal axis is the number of years before failure. Thus, Year 1 is the most recent year and Year 5 the earliest year. We can see that a clear difference between the average for the failed and non-failed businesses can be detected five years prior to the failure of the former group.

Figure 9.6 Average (mean) current ratio of failed and non-failed businesses

The approach adopted by Beaver and Zmijewski is referred to as univariate analysis because it looks at one ratio at a time. It can produce interesting results but there are practical problems with its use.

Activity 9.11

Let us assume that research indicates that a particular ratio is shown to be a good predictor of failure. Can you think of a practical problem that may arise when using this ratio to predict financial failure for a particular business?

Where a particular ratio for a business differs from the average value for that same ratio for non-failed businesses, the analyst must rely on judgement to interpret whether this difference is significant. There is no clear decision rule that can be applied. Different analysts may, therefore, come to different conclusions about the likelihood of failure.

A further problem arises where more than one ratio is used to predict failure. Let us say, for example, that past research has identified two ratios as being good predictors of financial failure. When applied to a particular business, however, it may be that one ratio predicts financial failure, whereas the other does not. Given these conflicting signals, how should the analyst interpret the results?

Using combinations of ratios

The weaknesses of univariate analysis led researchers to develop models that combine ratios in such a way as to produce a single index that can be interpreted more clearly. One approach to model development, much favoured by researchers, applies **multiple discriminate analysis (MDA)**. This is, in essence, a statistical technique, similar to regression analysis, that can be used to draw a boundary between those businesses that fail and those businesses that do not. This boundary is referred to as the **discriminate function**. In this context, MDA attempts to identify those factors likely to influence financial failure. However, unlike regression analysis, MDA assumes that the observations come from two different populations (for example, failed and non-failed businesses) rather than from a single population.

To illustrate this approach, let us assume that we wish to test whether two ratios (say, the current ratio and the return on capital employed) can help to predict failure. To do this, we can calculate these ratios, first for a sample of failed businesses and then for a matched sample of non-failed ones. From these two sets of data we can produce a scatter diagram that plots each business according to these two ratios to produce a single coordinate. Figure 9.7 illustrates this approach.

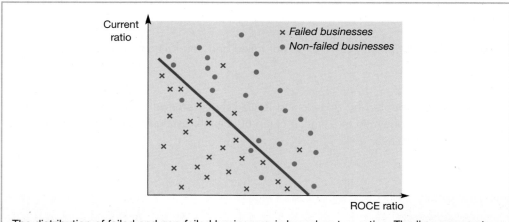

The distribution of failed and non-failed businesses is based on two ratios. The line represents a boundary between the samples of failed and non-failed businesses. Although there is some crossing of the boundary, the boundary represents the line that minimises the problem of misclassifying particular businesses.

Figure 9.7 Scatter diagram showing the distribution of failed and non-failed businesses

Using the observations plotted on the diagram, we try to identify the boundary between the failed and the non-failed businesses. This is the diagonal line in Figure 9.7.

We can see that those businesses that fall below and to the left of the line are predominantly failed ones and those that fall to the right are predominantly non-failed ones. Note that there is some overlap between the two populations. In practice, the boundary produced is unlikely, therefore, to eliminate all errors. Some businesses that fail may fall on the non-failed businesses side of the boundary. The opposite also happens. However, the analysis will tend to *minimise* the misclassification errors.

The boundary shown in Figure 9.7 can be expressed in the form:

$$Z = a + (b \times \text{Current ratio}) + (c \times \text{ROCE})$$

where a, b and c are all constants and b and c are weights to be attached to each ratio. A weighted average or total score (Z) is then derived. By 'constants' we mean that the same values are used for assessing each individual business. The weights given to the two ratios will depend on the slope of the line and its absolute position (that is, they will depend on the values of a, b and c). Using this model to assess a particular business's health, we would deduce the current and ROCE ratios for that business and use them in the equation above. If the resulting Z-score were to come out below a certain value, we should view that business as being at risk.

Note that this example, using the current and ROCE ratios, is purely hypothetical and only intended to illustrate the approach.

Z-score models

Altman (see Reference 3 at the end of the chapter) was the first to develop a model (in 1968), using financial ratios, that was able to predict financial failure in practice. In 2000 he updated the model by making some minor revisions. Altman's revised model, the Z-score model, is based on five financial ratios and is as follows:

$$Z = 0.717a + 0.847b + 3.107c + 0.420d + 0.998e$$

where $a =$ Working capital/Total assets
$b =$ Accumulated retained profits/Total assets
$c =$ Operating profit/Total assets
$d =$ Book (statement of financial position) value of ordinary and preference shares/ Total liabilities at book (statement of financial position) value
$e =$ Sales revenue/Total assets.

The coefficients (the numbers) in the above model are constants that reflect the importance to the Z-score of each of the ingredients (a to e).

In developing and revising this model, Altman carried out experiments using a paired sample of failed businesses and non-failed businesses and collected relevant data for each business for five years prior to failure. He found that the model represented by the formula shown above was able to predict failure for up to two years before it occurred. But as we might expect, however, the predictive accuracy of the model became weaker the longer the time before the date of the actual failure.

The ratios used in this model were identified by Altman through a process of trial and error, as there is no underlying theory of financial failure to help guide researchers in their selection of appropriate ratios. According to Altman, those businesses with a Z-score of less than 1.23 tend to fail. The lower the score, the greater is the probability of failure. Those with a Z-score greater than 4.14 tend not to fail. Those businesses with a Z-score between 1.23 and 4.14 occupied a 'zone of ignorance' and were difficult to classify. However, the model was able overall to classify 91 per cent of the businesses correctly; only 9 per cent fell into the 'zone of ignorance'. Altman based his model on US businesses.

In recent years, other models, using a similar approach, have been developed throughout the world. In the UK, for example, Taffler has developed separate Z-score models for different types of business. (See Reference 4 at the end of the chapter for a discussion of the work of Taffler and others.)

The prediction of financial failure is not the only area where research into the predictive ability of ratios has taken place. Researchers have also developed ratio-based models that claim to assess the vulnerability of a business to takeover by another. This is another area that is of vital importance to all those connected with the business.

Real World 9.7 discusses some research that showed that investing in shares in businesses with very low Z-scores is unsuccessful compared with investing in businesses with fairly high Z-scores. This is what we might expect to happen and provides support for the use of Z-scores in assessing the health of businesses. The research did not show, however, that the higher the Z-score, the more successful the investment. In other words, the businesses with the very highest Z-scores did not necessarily provide the very highest returns.

Real World 9.7

From A to Z

Investors looking to profit during a recession should be targeting stocks [shares] with strong fundamentals, according to research by Morgan Stanley. This 'value investing' approach – buying into companies where fundamental measures, such as book value and earnings, are not yet reflected in their share prices – is not new. But Morgan Stanley's analysis has found that the ability of this approach to deliver returns in downturns depends on the financial strength of the companies – in particular, the importance attached to the balance sheet [statement of financial position] by investors. 'If a stock's balance sheet is weak, the valuation multiple will be of little importance at this stage in the economic cycle,' says Graham Secker, Morgan Stanley strategy analyst.

He ranked a basket of European companies by their Altman Z-score – a measure of financial strength devised by US academic Edward Altman. A Z-score can be calculated for all non-financial companies and the lower the score, the greater the risk of the company falling into financial distress. When Secker compared the companies' Z-scores with their share price movements, he discovered that the companies with weaker balance sheets underperformed the market more than two thirds of the time.

Morgan Stanley also found that a company with an Altman Z-score of less than 1 tends to underperform the wider market by more than 4 per cent over the year with an associated probability of 72 per cent. 'Given the poor performance over the last year by stocks with a low Altman Z-score, the results of our backtest are now even more compelling than they were 12 months ago,' argues Secker. 'We calculate that the median stock with an Altman Z-score of 1 or less has underperformed the wider market by 5 to 6 per cent per annum between 1990 and 2008.'

Secker sees this as logical. In a recession, companies with balance sheets that are perceived to be weak are deemed a higher risk by lenders and face a higher cost of capital. This turns market sentiment against them and will generally lead to their share prices falling below their peers.

In 2008, the share price performance for stocks with an Altman Z-score of less than 1 was the worst since Morgan Stanley's analysis began in 1991. Under the Morgan Stanley methodology, the 2008 score is calculated using 2007 company financials. Of all the companies with a 2008 Z-score of less than 1, the median share price performance was a loss of 49 per cent, compared with a wider market fall of 42 per cent.

When compound annual growth rates since 1991 are analysed, the results are more dramatic. On average, companies with Z-scores of less than 1 saw their shares fall 4.4 per cent, compared with an average rise of 1.3 per cent for their peers. In only five of the last 18 years has a stock with an Altman score of 1 or less outperformed the market. These were generally years of strong economic growth. However, companies with the highest Z-scores aren't necessarily the best performers. During the bear market of 2000 to 2002, companies that had a Z-score above 3 fell almost twice as much as the market.

Analysts say the 2009 Z-scores, based on 2008 balance sheets, are far lower than in previous years as companies absorb the strain of the downturn in their accounts. 'There's been a lot of change between 2007 and 2008 [accounting years], tightening of credit and a vast deterioration in corporate balance sheets,' says Secker. 'I'd expect 2009 [Z-scores] to be much worse.'

Analysis by the Financial Times and Capital IQ, the data provider, corroborates this – showing that the 2009 scores have been badly affected by the crisis. Some 8 per cent of global companies with a market capitalisation of more than $500 million have Altman scores below 1 for 2009 – based on 2008 company financials. This is the highest percentage since 2002 and the largest annual increase since 2001 – showing the impact of the recession on the balance sheets of even the largest companies. If smaller companies were included, the results would be worse – as their earnings and market capitalisations have been affected far more.

European balance sheets were hit the hardest, with companies averaging a Z-score of 2.8, compared with 4.0 for Asia and the US, according to Capital IQ. This suggests the scores are not due to chance. A similar differential was recorded in 2001 during the last recession. On this evidence, US companies appear more resilient than their global peers in a downturn.

On a sector basis, healthcare and IT companies have the highest Z-scores. In 2008, their scores were more than three times higher than the average for the lowest scoring sector: utilities. A similar pattern was found in 2001 – suggesting that investors may want to think twice before buying into 'defensive' utilities in a downturn.

 Source: Mathurin, P. (2009) New study re-writes the A to Z of value investing, ft.com, 14 August.

It seems clear that the Z-score approach to assessing the riskiness of individual businesses to financial failure is very widely used.

LIMITATIONS OF RATIO ANALYSIS

Although ratios offer a quick and useful method of analysing the position and performance of a business, they are not without their problems and limitations. We shall now turn our attention to some of these.

Quality of financial statements

It must always be remembered that ratios are based on financial statements. The results of ratio analysis are, therefore, dependent on the quality of these underlying statements. Ratios will inherit the limitations of the financial statements on which they are based. In Chapter 2 we saw that one important limitation of financial statements is their failure to include all resources controlled by the business. Internally generated goodwill and brands, for example, are excluded from the statement of financial position because they fail to meet the strict definition of an asset. This means that, even though these resources may be of considerable value, key ratios such as ROSF, ROCE and the gearing ratio will fail to acknowledge their presence.

Assume that a business has internally generated goodwill that had been created in earlier years. If this resource were introduced as a non-current asset with an indefinite life in the current statement of financial position, what would be the effect on ROSF, ROCE and the gearing ratio?

The effect of introducing internally generated goodwill will be similar to that of an asset revaluation, which we considered in Chapter 2. Total assets will increase and equity will also increase. An increase in equity will increase the denominator (lower part of the fraction) for all three ratios. This will, in turn, lead to lower ratios than would be the case if the goodwill were not introduced.

There is also the problem of deliberate attempts to make the financial statements misleading. We discussed this problem of 'creative accounting' in Chapter 5.

Inflation

A persistent, though recently less severe, problem, in most countries is that the financial results of businesses can be distorted as a result of inflation. One effect of inflation is that the reported value of assets held for any length of time may bear little relation to current values. Generally speaking, the reported value of assets will be understated in current terms during a period of inflation as they are usually reported at their original cost (less any amounts written off for depreciation). This means that comparisons, either between businesses or between periods, will be hindered. A difference in, say, ROCE may occur simply because assets shown in one of the statements of financial position being compared were acquired more recently (ignoring the effect of depreciation on the asset values). Another effect of inflation is to distort the measurement of profit. In the calculation of profit, sales revenue is often matched with costs incurred at an earlier time. This is because there is often a time lag between acquiring a particular resource and using it to help generate sales revenue. For example, inventories may well be acquired several months before they are sold. During a period of inflation, this will mean that the expense does not reflect prices that are current at the time of the sale. The cost of sales figure is usually based on the historic cost of the inventories concerned. As a result, expenses will be understated in the income statement and this, in turn, means that profit will be overstated. One effect of this will be to distort the profitability ratios discussed earlier. We shall take a look at attempts to correct for inflation in financial statements in Chapter 11.

The restricted view of ratios

It is important not to rely exclusively on ratios, thereby losing sight of information contained in the underlying financial statements. As we saw in Chapter 8, and earlier in this chapter, some items reported in these statements can be vital in assessing position and performance. For example, the total sales revenue, capital employed and profit figures may be useful in assessing changes in absolute size that occur over time, or in assessing differences in scale between businesses. Ratios do not provide such information. When comparing one figure with another, ratios measure *relative* performance and position and, therefore, provide only part of the picture. When comparing two businesses, therefore, it will often be useful to assess the absolute size of profits, as well as the relative profitability of each business. For example, Business A may generate £1 million operating profit and have a ROCE of 15 per cent and Business B may generate £100,000 operating profit and have a ROCE of 20 per cent. Although Business B has a higher level of *profitability*, as measured by ROCE, it generates lower total operating profits.

The basis for comparison

We saw earlier that, if ratios are to be useful, they require a basis for comparison. Moreover, it is important that the analyst compares like with like. Where the comparison is with another business, there can be difficulties. No two businesses are identical: the greater the differences between the businesses being compared, the greater are the limitations of ratio analysis. Furthermore, any differences in accounting policies, financing methods (gearing levels) and financial year ends will add to the problems of making comparisons between businesses.

Ratios relating to the statement of financial position

The statement of financial position is only a 'snapshot' of the business at a particular moment in time. This means that certain ratios, such as the liquidity ratios, that are based on figures from this statement may not be representative of the position of the business for the year as a whole. It is common, for example, for a seasonal business to have a financial year end that coincides with a low point in business activity. Inventories and trade receivables may therefore be low at the year end. As a result, the liquidity ratios may also be low. A more representative picture of liquidity can only really be gained by taking additional measurements at other points in the year.

Finally, **Real World 9.8** points out another way in which ratios are limited.

Real World 9.8

Remember, it's people that really count . . .

Lord Weinstock (1924–2002) was an influential industrialist whose management style and philosophy helped to shape management practice in many UK businesses. During his long and successful reign at GEC plc, a major engineering business, Lord Weinstock relied heavily on financial ratios to assess performance and to exercise control. In particular, he relied on ratios relating to sales revenue, expenses, trade receivables, profit margins and inventories turnover. However, he was keenly aware of the limitations of ratios and recognised that, ultimately, people produce profits.

In a memo written to GEC managers, he pointed out that ratios are an aid to good management rather than a substitute for it. He wrote:

> The operating ratios are of great value as measures of efficiency but they are only the measures and not efficiency itself. Statistics will not design a product better, make it for a lower cost or increase sales. If ill-used, they may so guide action as to diminish resources for the sake of apparent but false signs of improvement.
>
> Management remains a matter of judgement, of knowledge of products and processes and of understanding and skill in dealing with people. The ratios will indicate how well all these things are being done and will show comparison with how they are done elsewhere. But they will tell us nothing about how to do them. That is what you are meant to do.

Source: Extract from *Arnold Weinstock and the Making of GEC*, published by Aurum Press (Aris, S. 1998). Thanks to the author, Stephen Aris, for permission to reproduce this extract. Published in *The Sunday Times*, 22 February, 1998, p. 3.

The income statement and statement of financial position of Achilles plc are as follows:

Income statement for the year ended 31 December 2018

	£ million
Revenue	701
Cost of sales	(394)
Gross profit	307
Distribution costs	(106)
Administrative expenses	(104)
Operating profit	97
Interest payable	(33)
Profit before taxation	64
Taxation	(18)
Profit for the year	46

Statement of financial position as at 31 December 2018

	£ million
ASSETS	
Non-current assets	
Property, plant and equipment	
Land and buildings	550
Plant and machinery	34
Motor vehicles	69
	653
Current assets	
Inventories	41
Trade receivables	108
Prepaid expenses	10
	159
Total assets	812
EQUITY AND LIABILITIES	
Equity	
Ordinary share capital	
200 million shares of £1 each	200
Retained earnings	151
	351
Non-current liabilities	
10% secured loan notes	300
Current liabilities	
Bank overdraft	86
Trade payables	43
Accrued expenses	14
Taxation	18
	161
Total equity and liabilities	812

The market price of the ordinary £1 shares was £3.49 each at 31 December 2018. During 2018 the company paid a dividend on the ordinary shares totalling £15 million.

Required:

(a) Calculate the following ratios for Achilles plc for 2018:
- dividend payout ratio;
- dividend yield ratio;
- earnings per share;
- P/E ratio.

What can you conclude from the ratios that you have calculated?

(b) Calculate the Z-score for Achilles plc (using the equation given in the text) and comment on it.

The solution to this question can be found at the back of the book, starting on page 525.

SUMMARY

The main points of this chapter may be summarised as follows:

Investment ratios

- Investment ratios are concerned with returns to shareholders.
- The investment ratios covered are the dividend payout ratio, the dividend yield ratio, earnings per share (EPS), cash generated from operations per share, and the price/earnings ratio.

Uses of ratios

- Can be used to identify signs of overtrading.
- Individual ratios can be tracked to detect trends, for example by plotting them on a graph.
- Predicting financial distress
- Ratios can be used to predict financial failure.
- Univariate analysis looks at just one ratio over time in an attempt to predict financial failure.
- Multiple discriminate analysis (that is, looking at several ratios, combined in a model) can produce Z-scores that can also be used to predict financial failure.
- Various Z-score models, particularly Altman's, seem to be very widely used.

Limitations of ratio analysis

- Ratios are only as reliable as the financial statements from which they derive.
- Inflation can distort the information.
- Ratios give a restricted view.
- It can be difficult to find a suitable benchmark (for example, another business) to compare with.
- Some ratios could mislead due to the 'snapshot' nature of the statement of financial position.
- The key issue in the use of ratios is their intelligent and perceptive interpretation by human beings.

REFERENCES

1 Beaver, W.H. (1966) Financial ratios as predictors of failure, in *Empirical Research in Accounting: Selected Studies*, pp. 71–111.

2 Zmijewski, M.E. (1983) Predicting corporate bankruptcy: An empirical comparison of the extent of financial distress models, Research Paper, State University of New York.

3 Altman, E.I. (2000) Predicting financial distress of companies: Revisiting the Z-score and Zeta models, New York University Working Paper, June.

4 Neophytou, E., Charitou, A. and Charalamnous, C. (2001) Predicting corporate failure: Empirical evidence for the UK, University of Southampton Department of Accounting and Management Science Working Paper 01-173.

FURTHER READING

If you would like to explore the topics covered in this chapter in more depth, we recommend the following:

Alexander D., Britton, A., Jorissen, A., Hoogendoorn, M., and Van Mourik, C. (2017) *International Financial Reporting and Analysis*, 7th edn, Cengage Learning, Chapters 29–31

Elliott, B. and Elliott, J. (2017) *Financial Accounting and Reporting*, 18th edn, Pearson, Chapter 29.

Robinson, T., Henry, E., Pirie, W. and Broihahn, M. (2015) *International Financial Statement Analysis*, 3rd edn, CFA Institute, Chapters 4, 5, 7 and 17.

Subramanyam, K and Wild, J. (2015) *Financial Statement Analysis*, 11th edn, McGraw-Hill Higher Education, Chapters 10 and 11.

CRITICAL REVIEW QUESTIONS

Solutions to these questions can be found at the back of the book, starting on page 536.

9.1 Why might a business prefer not to have its Z-score made public?

9.2 Real World 9.3 shows that the average dividend yield for businesses in electricity supply is nearly four times that of businesses in the industrial engineering sector. Why might this be the case?

9.3 Identify and discuss three reasons why the P/E ratio of two businesses operating within the same industry may differ.

9.4 Identify and discuss three ratios that are likely to be affected by a business overtrading.

Solutions to exercises with coloured numbers can be found at the back of the book, starting on page 545.

Basic-level exercises

9.1 At the close of share trading on 19 February 2018, investment ratios for Next plc, the UK fashion and textiles retailer, and the averages for the 'general retailers' section, were as follows:

	Next plc	General retailers section
Dividend yield (%)	3.21	3.24
P/E ratio (times)	11.51	16.29
Dividend cover (times)	3.58	1.90

Source: Financial Times, 20 February 2018, pages 18 and 20 and Next plc 2017 annual report.

Required:

Comment on what can be deduced about Next plc, relative to the general retailers' sector, from an equity investor's point of view.

9.2 Telford Industrial Services plc is a medium-sized business. Extracts from the business's financial statements appear below.

Summary of statements of financial position at 31 December

	2015 £m	2016 £m	2017 £m	2018 £m
ASSETS				
Non-current assets	48	51	65	64
Current assets				
Inventories	21	22	23	26
Trade receivables	34	42	34	29
Cash	–	3	–	–
	55	67	57	55
Total assets	103	118	122	119
EQUITY AND LIABILITIES				
Equity	48	61	61	63
Non-current liabilities	30	30	30	30
Current liabilities				
Trade payables	20	27	25	18
Short-term borrowings	5	–	6	8
	25	27	31	26
Total equity and liabilities	103	118	122	119

Summary of income statements for years ended 31 December

	2015 £m	2016 £m	2017 £m	2018 £m
Sales revenue	152	170	110	145
Operating profit	28	40	7	15
Interest payable	(4)	(3)	(4)	(5)
Profit before taxation	24	37	3	10
Taxation	(12)	(16)	–	(4)
Profit for the year	12	21	3	6

Required:

Prepare a set of common-size statements of financial position and common-size income statements, on a vertical basis, using equity as the base figure for the statements of financial position and sales revenue as the base figure for the income statements.

9.3 Delta plc is a listed business in the 'general retailers' section of the market. Its most recent income statement and statement of financial position are outlined as follows:

Income statement for the year

	£m
Revenue	224
Profit before taxation	81
Taxation	(16)
Profit for the year	65

A dividend totalling £30 million was paid to shareholders in respect of the year.

Statement of financial position at the end of the year

	£m
NET ASSETS (total assets less current liabilities)	122
EQUITY AND NON-CURRENT LIABILITIES	
Equity	
200 million ordinary shares of 25p each	50
Reserves	57
	107
Non-current liabilities	
10% loan notes	15
Total equity and non-current liabilities	122

At the end of the year the ordinary shares were quoted on the London Stock Exchange at £2.50 each.

Required:

Calculate, and comment on, each of the following ratios for Delta plc:

1 dividend payout;
2 dividend yield;
3 earnings per share;
4 price/earnings ratio.

Where relevant, compare these ratios with the averages for general retailers, given in Exercise 9.1.

Intermediate-level exercises

9.4 Ali plc and Bhaskar plc both operate electrical stores throughout the UK. The financial statements of each business for the year ended 30 June 2018 are as follows:

Statements of financial position as at 30 June 2018

	Ali plc £m	Bhaskar plc £m
ASSETS		
Non-current assets		
Property, plant and equipment (cost less depreciation)		
Land and buildings	360.0	510.0
Fixtures and fittings	87.0	91.2
	447.0	601.2
Current assets		
Inventories	592.0	403.0
Trade receivables	176.4	321.9
Cash at bank	84.6	91.6
	853.0	816.5
Total assets	1,300.0	1,417.7
EQUITY AND LIABILITIES		
Equity		
£1 ordinary shares	320.0	250.0
Retained earnings	367.6	624.6
	687.6	874.6
Non-current liabilities		
Borrowings – loan notes	190.0	250.0
Current liabilities		
Trade payables	406.4	275.7
Taxation	16.0	17.4
	422.4	293.1
Total equity and liabilities	1,300.0	1,417.7

Income statements for the year ended 30 June 2018

	Ali plc £m	Bhaskar plc £m
Revenue	1,478.1	1,790.4
Cost of sales	(1,018.3)	(1,214.9)
Gross profit	459.8	575.5
Operating expenses	(308.5)	(408.6)
Operating profit	151.3	166.9
Interest payable	(19.4)	(27.5)
Profit before taxation	131.9	139.4
Taxation	(32.0)	(34.8)
Profit for the year	99.9	104.6

Ali plc paid a dividend of £135 million and Bhaskar plc £95 million during the year. The market values of a share in Ali plc and Bhaskar plc at the end of the year were £6.50 and £8.20 respectively.

Required:

(a) Calculate the Z-scores for Ali plc and Bhaskar plc using the Altman model given in the text.

(b) Comment on the Z-scores calculated and on the validity of using this particular model to assess these businesses.

9.5 Diversified Industries plc (DI) is a business that has interests in engineering, caravan manufacturing and a chain of shops selling car accessories. DI has recently been approached by the directors of Automobile Care plc (AC), a smaller chain of accessory shops, who wish to negotiate the sale of their business to DI. The following information, which has been extracted from AC's financial statements, is available:

	Years ended 31 December		
	2016	*2017*	*2018*
	£m	*£m*	*£m*
Revenue	18.1	28.2	36.9
Profit before taxation	3.2	4.1	7.3
Taxation	(1.0)	(1.7)	(3.1)
Profit for the year	2.2	2.4	4.2
Dividend paid for the year	0.9	1.1	1.3
Issued share capital			
16 million shares of 25p each	4.0	4.0	4.0
Reserves	8.0	9.3	12.2

AC's market price per share at 31 December 2018 was £3.15.

Required:

(a) Calculate the following items for AC for 2018 and explain the use of each one:
1 earnings per share;
2 price/earnings ratio;
3 dividend yield;
4 dividend payout ratio.

(b) Write some short notes on the factors the directors of DI should take into account when considering the possible purchase of AC. You should use the income statement details together with the figures that you calculated in your answer to part (a).

9.6 As with many businesses, Marks and Spencer plc (M&S), the retailer, has identified a number of key performance indicators (KPIs). Typical of such businesses, M&S publishes the results for each of these in its annual report. It also shows how these KPIs have scored over the recent years before each annual report date.

In its 2017 annual report, M&S set out the following information:

	2014	*2015*	*2016*	*2017*
Group revenue (£ billion)	10.3	10.3	10.4	10.6
Group profit before tax (£ billion)	622.9	661.2	684.1	613.8
Return on capital employed (per cent)	14.8	14.7	15.0	13.7
Earnings per share (pence)	32.2	33.1	34.8	30.4
Dividend per share (pence)	17.0	18.0	18.7	18.7
Net cash generated before dividends (£ million)	427.9	524.2	539.3	585.4

Required:
Discuss what M&S's KPIs seem to suggest about the business's progress over the four years.

Advanced-level exercises

9.7 SeaSwift plc builds luxury yachts for the international market. The most recently published income statement and statement of financial position are set out below. Since the business builds the yachts specifically to customers' requirements, it carries no inventories of finished yachts.

Income statement for the year ended 31 December 2018

	£ million
Revenue	837
Cost of sales (including raw materials inventories usage £253 million)	
(Note: Raw material purchases totalled £255 million)	(478)
Gross profit	359
Operating costs	(224)
Operating profit	135
Interest payable	(30)
Profit before taxation	105
Taxation	(27)
Profit for the year	78

Statement of financial position as at 31 December 2018

	£ million Cost	£ million Depreciation	£ million
ASSETS			
Non-current assets			
Property, plant and equipment			
Land	550	–	550
Plant and machinery	253	(226)	27
Motor vehicles	102	(56)	46
	905	(282)	623
Current assets			
Inventories			43
Trade receivables			96
Prepaid expenses			12
Cash			25
			176
Total assets			799
EQUITY AND LIABILITIES			
Equity			
Ordinary share capital – 200,000 shares of £1 each			200
Retained earnings			209
Non-current liabilities			409
10% secured loan notes			300
Current liabilities			
Trade payables			45
Accrued expenses			18
Taxation			27
			90
Total equity and liabilities			799

A dividend totalling £20 million was paid on ordinary shares for the year.

SeaSwift plc's ordinary shares had a market value of £5.10 each on 31 December 2018.

Following the publication of the 2017 financial statements, SeaSwift plc's finance director carried out a ratio analysis of the business's financial performance and position and derived the following ratios:

Accounting ratios for the year ended 31 December 2017

Profitability ratios

Return on capital employed (%)	14.9
Return on ordinary shareholders' funds (%)	13.1
Gross profit margin (%)	43.8
Operating profit margin (%)	13.8

Activity ratios

Sales revenue to capital employed (times)	1.08
Inventories turnover period (days)	78.8
Trade receivables settlement period (days)	56.2
Trade payables settlement period (days)	83.9

Liquidity ratios

Current	0.99:1
Acid-test	0.73:1

Gearing ratios

Gearing (%)	52.4
Interest cover (times)	2.9

Investors' ratios

Earnings per share (£)	0.23
Price/earnings (times)	15.2
Dividend yield (%)	2.4
Dividend cover (times)	3.1

Required:

Calculate the same ratios for 2018 as are given above for 2017 then go on to discuss changes that have taken place over the two years. Note that the 2017 ratios were calculated using the 2017 statement of financial position figures, where relevant, rather than an average. This means that to enable a valid comparison the 2018 ratios need to be calculated using the 2018 year-end figures.

9.8 Genesis Ltd was incorporated three years ago and has grown rapidly since then. The rapid rate of growth has created problems for the business, which the directors have found difficult to deal with. Recently, a firm of management consultants has been asked to help the directors to overcome these problems.

In a preliminary report to the board of directors, the management consultants state: 'Most of the difficulties faced by the business are symptoms of an underlying problem of overtrading.' The most recent financial statements of the business are set out below:

Statement of financial position as at 31 October

	£000	£000
ASSETS		
Non-current assets		
Property, plant and equipment		
Land and buildings at cost	530	
Accumulated depreciation	(88)	442
Fixtures and fittings at cost	168	
Accumulated depreciation	(52)	116
Motor vans at cost	118	
Accumulated depreciation	(54)	64
		622

Statement of financial position as at 31 October

	£000	£000
Current assets		
Inventories		128
Trade receivables		104
		232
Total assets		854
EQUITY AND LIABILITIES		
Equity		
Ordinary £0.50 shares		60
General reserve		50
Retained earnings		74
		184
Non-current liabilities		
Borrowings – 10% loan notes (secured)		120
Current liabilities		
Trade payables		184
Taxation		8
Short-term borrowings (all bank overdraft)		358
		550
Total equity and liabilities		854

Income statement for the year ended 31 October

	£000	£000
Revenue		1,640
Cost of sales		
Opening inventories	116	
Purchases	1,260	
	1,376	
Closing inventories	(128)	(1,248)
Gross profit		392
Selling and distribution expenses		(204)
Administration expenses		(92)
Operating profit		96
Interest payable		(44)
Profit before taxation		52
Taxation		(16)
Profit for the year		36

All purchases and sales were on credit.

A dividend was paid during the year on ordinary shares totalling £4,000.

Required:

(a) Calculate and discuss five financial ratios that might be used to establish whether the business is overtrading. Do these five ratios suggest that the business is overtrading?

(b) State the ways in which a business may overcome the problem of overtrading.

Chapter 10

REPORTING THE FINANCIAL RESULTS OF GROUPS OF COMPANIES

INTRODUCTION

Many larger businesses, including virtually all of those that are household names in the UK, consist of a group of companies rather than just a single company. Here one company (the parent company) controls one or more other companies (the subsidiary companies). This usually arises because the parent company owns more than 50 per cent of the ordinary shares of the subsidiary companies.

In this chapter we shall look at the accounting treatment of groups of companies. This will draw heavily on what we have covered so far, particularly in Chapters 2 to 6. We shall also consider the accounting treatment of associate companies. An associate company relationship exists where one company has a substantial, but not a controlling, influence in another company.

Learning outcomes

When you have completed this chapter, you should be able to:

- discuss the nature of groups, and explain why they exist and how they are formed;

- prepare a group statement of financial position and income statement;

- explain the nature of associate company status and its accounting implications; and

- explain and interpret the contents of a set of group financial statements.

WHAT IS A GROUP OF COMPANIES?

It is quite common for one company to be able to exercise control over the activities of another. Control typically arises because the first company (the **parent company**) owns more than 50 per cent of the ordinary (voting) shares of the second company (the **subsidiary company**). This leads to the directors of the parent company having the power to appoint the directors of the subsidiary company and, therefore, being able to dictate its policies. Where this relationship arises, a **group (of companies)** is said to exist.

Where there is a group, the relevant International Financial Reporting Standards (IAS 27 *Consolidated and Separate Financial Statements* and IFRS 3 *Business Combinations*) normally require that a set of financial statements is drawn up annually not only for each individual company, but also for the group taken as a whole. Before we go on to consider how the **group financial statements** (that is, the financial statements of a group of companies) are prepared, we shall look at why groups exist at all and at the types of group relationships that may arise.

It is very common for large businesses to be made up of a number of individual companies. These companies are controlled by a *parent company*, sometimes known as the **holding company**. In some cases, the only assets of the parent company are the shares that it owns in the subsidiary companies. Although the subsidiary companies own the land, buildings, machinery, inventories and so on, since the parent owns the subsidiaries, it effectively controls the productive assets of those companies. **Real World 10.1** looks at Associated British Foods plc, the major UK food manufacturer and retailer.

Real World 10.1

Food for thought

Under the heading 'Non-current assets' in the statement of financial position of Associated British Foods plc, there is no property, plant and equipment, just 'goodwill' and 'investment in subsidiaries'. The productive assets of the group are owned by more than 80 subsidiary companies. These include such well-known names as:

- British Sugar plc
- R. Twining and Company Limited (tea producers)
- Primark Stores Limited (high street fashion retailer).

Source: Associated British Foods plc, Annual report 2017, p. 158.

Activity 10.1

Why do think that so many businesses operate through subsidiaries? To put it another way, why do the parent companies not own all of the assets of the business directly, instead of them being owned by the subsidiaries? We feel that there are broadly three reasons.

Three reasons are:

1 to gain limited liability for each individual subsidiary, so that, should one subsidiary get into financial difficulties, this will not impact on fellow subsidiaries;
2 to try to create, or continue, the apparent independence of each business within the group; and
3 to gain a possible tax advantage.

Let us expand on these points:

■ *Limited liability.* Each individual company has limited liability. This means that, in the event of the financial failure of a subsidiary, the assets of other subsidiaries, or those of the parent, would not be legally accessible to unsatisfied claimants (lenders, trade payables and so on). In other words, the parent can 'ring-fence' each part of the business by having separate companies, each with its own limited liability.

■ *Individual identity.* A sense of independence and autonomy may be created that could, in turn, increase levels of commitment among staff. It may also help to develop, or perpetuate, a market image of a smaller, independent business. Customers, as well as staff, may prefer to deal with what they see as a smaller, specialist business than with a division of a large diversified business.

■ *Tax advantage.* When a company makes a trading loss, it can normally offset this loss, for tax purposes, against either past or future profits and so pay less tax on those profits. Where the loss-making company is a member of a group of companies, any loss can be transferred to another company within the group. This means that, where the loss-making company has insufficient past profits, the group can still gain immediate tax relief for the loss. Where the loss-making subsidiary never makes a future profit, the tax relief would be lost if it were not a member of a group.

HOW DO GROUPS ARISE?

Parent companies have subsidiaries where:

1 it creates a new company to operate some part of its business, perhaps a new activity;
2 it buys a majority, or perhaps all, of the shares of an existing company – that is, a **takeover**.

Many parent companies have subsidiaries for both of these reasons.

Newly created companies

To create a subsidiary, the would-be parent may simply form a new company in the normal way. The new company would then issue shares to the parent, in exchange for some asset, or assets, of the parent. Where the new subsidiary has been formed to undertake a completely new activity, the asset may well be cash. If the subsidiary is created to carry on an activity previously undertaken by the parent company, the assets are likely to be the non-current and current assets associated with the particular activity.

Example 10.1

The summarised statement of financial position of Baxter plc is as follows:

Statement of financial position

	£m
ASSETS	
Non-current assets	
Property, plant and equipment	
Land	43
Plant	15
Vehicles	8
	66
Current assets	
Inventories	15
Trade receivables	23
Cash	13
	51
Total assets	117
EQUITY AND LIABILITIES	
Equity	
Called-up share capital:	
ordinary shares of £1 each, fully paid	50
Retained earnings	16
	66
Non-current liabilities	
Borrowings – loan notes	40
Current liabilities	
Trade payables	11
Total equity and liabilities	117

Baxter plc has recently formed a new company, Nova Ltd, which is to undertake the work that has previously been done by the industrial fibres division of Baxter plc. The following assets are to be transferred to Nova Ltd at the values that currently are shown in the statement of financial position of Baxter plc:

	£m
Land	10
Plant	5
Vehicles	3
Inventories	6
Cash	3
	27

Nova Ltd is to issue £1 ordinary shares at their nominal value to Baxter plc in exchange for these assets.

→

Baxter plc's statement of financial position immediately after these transfers will be:

Statement of financial position

	£m
ASSETS	
Non-current assets	
Property, plant and equipment	
Land (43 − 10)	33
Plant (15 − 5)	10
Vehicles (8 − 3)	5
	48
Investments	
27 million ordinary £1 shares of Nova Ltd	27
	75
Current assets	
Inventories (15 − 6)	9
Trade receivables	23
Cash (13 − 3)	10
	42
Total assets	117
EQUITY AND LIABILITIES	
Equity	
Called-up share capital:	
ordinary shares of £1 each, fully paid	50
Retained earnings	16
	66
Non-current liabilities	
Borrowings – loan notes	40
Current liabilities	
Trade payables	11
Total equity and liabilities	117

As you have probably noted, the asset of shares in Nova Ltd has simply replaced the individual productive assets.

Activity 10.2

Try to prepare the statement of financial position of Nova Ltd, immediately following the transfers of the assets and the shares being issued.

It should look something like this:

Statement of financial position

	£m
ASSETS	
Non-current assets	
Property, plant and equipment (at transfer value)	
Land	10
Plant	5
Vehicles	3
	18
Current assets	
Inventories	6
Cash	3
	9
Total assets	27
EQUITY AND LIABILITIES	
Equity	
Called-up share capital:	
ordinary shares of £1 each, fully paid	27
Total equity and liabilities	27

Real World 10.2 discusses how BT, the telecommunications business, created a new subsidiary. The reason for doing so was unusual as it was not one of the three discussed earlier.

Real World 10.2

Subsidiary broadband

During 2017, a new company was formed to take over the role of Openreach, BT's division that was responsible for providing and maintaining all of the 'land line' telephone connections throughout the UK. Openreach-BT plc is now a wholly owned subsidiary of BT Group plc.

Moving the staff and assets of Openreach to a new subsidiary was at the insistence of Ofcom, the UK government agency that regulates telecommunications. The objective was to make the activity more independent of BT. Openreach is responsible for providing the infrastructure used by other landline telephone and broadband service providers, such as Sky, Talktalk and Vodafone as well as by BT.

Source: Information taken from: Curry, R. and Yeomans, J. (2017) What is Openreach and why is it being spun off from BT? *The Telegraph*, 10 March.

Takeovers

A would-be parent company may also create a subsidiary by taking over an existing company. Here it acquires more than 50 per cent of the shares of a target company to enable it to exercise control, thereby making the target company a subsidiary. The shares are, of course, acquired from the existing shareholders of the target company.

The bid consideration in a takeover will normally take the form of cash, or shares in the parent company, or some combination of the two. Where shares are offered as all, or part, of the bid consideration, the target company shareholders that accept the offer will exchange their shares for shares in the parent company. They therefore cease to be shareholders of the target company and become shareholders in the parent.

Real World 10.3 outlines a recent 'share-for-share' takeover involving Tesco plc, the well-known supermarket business, and Booker plc, a grocery wholesaler, both of which were listed on the London Stock Exchange.

Real World 10.3

Wholesale changes

When Tesco took over Booker in March 2018, the latter's shareholders were given, for each Booker share, 0.861 Tesco shares plus 42.6p in cash. The value of the entire new business is estimated at around £20 billion.

Source: Information taken from: Reuters News Agency (2018) Tesco completes £4 billion takeover of Booker, *The Telegraph*, 5 March.

Example 10.2 below illustrates the effect of a takeover involving a share-for-share exchange on the statement of financial position of the parent company.

Example 10.2

The summarised statement of financial position of Adams plc is as follows:

Statement of financial position

	£m
ASSETS	
Non-current assets	
Property, plant and equipment	
Land	35
Plant	21
Vehicles	12
	68
Current assets	
Inventories	25
Trade receivables	28
Cash	22
	75
Total assets	143
EQUITY AND LIABILITIES	
Equity	
Called-up share capital:	
ordinary shares of £1 each, fully paid	60
Share premium account	5
Retained earnings	5
	70
Non-current liabilities	
Borrowings – loan notes	50
Current liabilities	
Trade payables	23
Total equity and liabilities	143

Adams plc has recently made an offer of £1 a share for all the share capital of Beta Ltd. Beta Ltd's issued share capital is 20 million shares of 50p each. Adams plc will 'pay' for this by issuing the appropriate number of new ordinary shares of Adams plc at an issue value of £2 a share.

All the Beta Ltd shareholders accepted the offer. This means that Adams plc will need to issue shares to the value of £20 million (that is, 20 million × £1). Since the Adams plc shares are to be issued at £2 each, 10 million shares will need to be issued, at a share premium of £1 each.

Following the takeover, the statement of financial position of Adams plc will look as follows:

Statement of financial position

	£m
ASSETS	
Non-current assets	
Property, plant and equipment	
Land	35
Plant	21
Vehicles	12
	68
Investments	
Shares in Beta Ltd	20
	88
Current assets	
Inventories	25
Trade receivables	28
Cash	22
	75
Total assets	163
EQUITY AND LIABILITIES	
Equity	
Called-up share capital:	
ordinary shares of £1 each, fully paid (60 + 10)	70
Share premium account (5 + 10)	15
Retained earnings	5
	90
Non-current liabilities	
Borrowings – loan notes	50
Current liabilities	
Trade payables	23
Total equity and liabilities	163

Note that the assets have increased by £20 million and that this is balanced by the value of the shares issued (£10 million share capital and £10 million share premium).

If, instead of the consideration offered being all in shares, the offer had been 50 per cent in cash and 50 per cent in Adams plc shares, what would the statement of financial position of Adams plc have looked like after the takeover?

The total offer value would still be £20 million, but this would be met by paying cash totalling £10 million and issuing shares worth £10 million (£5 million share capital and £5 million share premium). So the statement of financial position would be:

Statement of financial position

	£m
ASSETS	
Non-current assets	
Property, plant and equipment	
Land	35
Plant	21
Vehicles	12
	68
Investments	
Shares in Beta Ltd	20
	88
Current assets	
Inventories	25
Trade receivables	28
Cash (22 − 10)	12
	65
Total assets	153
EQUITY AND LIABILITIES	
Equity	
Called-up share capital:	
ordinary shares of £1 each, fully paid (60 + 5)	65
Share premium account (5 + 5)	10
Retained earnings	5
	80
Non-current liabilities	
Borrowings – loan notes	50
Current liabilities	
Trade payables	23
Total equity and liabilities	153

How would the takeover affect the statement of financial position of Beta Ltd?

The statement of financial position of Beta Ltd would not be affected at all. A change of shareholders does not affect the financial statements of a company.

It is not necessary for the parent company to retain the target/subsidiary as a separate company after the takeover. The subsidiary could be wound up and its assets owned directly by the parent. However, this would not usually happen for reasons, such as limited liability and individual identity, that were considered earlier. The latter reason may be particularly important where the new subsidiary boasts a strong brand image.

TYPES OF GROUP RELATIONSHIP

So far we have considered a situation where there is a simple relationship between a parent and its subsidiary or subsidiaries such as that shown in Figure 10.1.

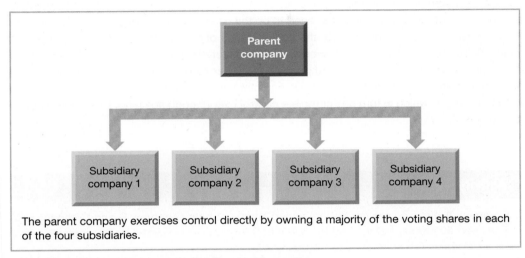

The parent company exercises control directly by owning a majority of the voting shares in each of the four subsidiaries.

Figure 10.1 A simple parent/subsidiaries relationship

A slightly more complex relationship is shown in Figure 10.2.

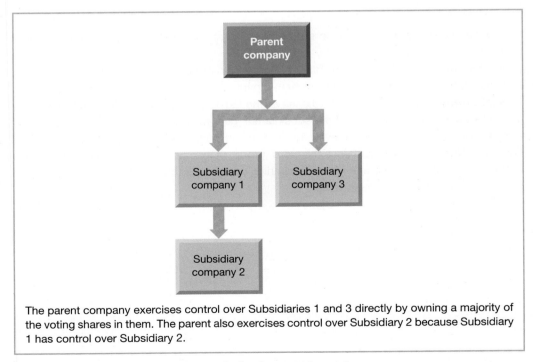

The parent company exercises control over Subsidiaries 1 and 3 directly by owning a majority of the voting shares in them. The parent also exercises control over Subsidiary 2 because Subsidiary 1 has control over Subsidiary 2.

Figure 10.2 A more complex parent/subsidiaries relationship

Here Subsidiary 2 is a subsidiary by virtue of being controlled by another company (Subsidiary 1) that is, in turn, a subsidiary of the parent. In these circumstances, Subsidiary 2 is usually called a 'sub-subsidiary' of the parent. In this case, the parent company is sometimes known as the 'ultimate' parent company of Subsidiary 2. Subsidiaries 1 and 3 are straightforward subsidiaries.

Earlier, it was pointed out that one company is a subsidiary of another because the latter *controls* the former. This is usually as a result of the parent owning a majority of the voting shares of the other, but this does not need to be the case. Consider Figure 10.2 and suppose that the parent owns 60 per cent of the voting shares of Subsidiary 1 and that Subsidiary 1 owns 60 per cent of the shares of Subsidiary 2. In effect, the parent only owns 36 per cent of the shares of Subsidiary 2 (that is, 60 per cent of 60 per cent), yet the latter is a subsidiary of the former. This is because the parent has complete control over (though not total ownership of) Subsidiary 1, which in turn has complete control over (though again not total ownership of) Subsidiary 2.

Activity 10.5

Company A owns 40 per cent of the voting shares of both Company B and Company C. The other 60 per cent of the voting shares of Company C are owned by Company B.
  Is Company C a subsidiary of Company A?

The answer is no. This is despite the fact that Company A can be seen to own 64 per cent of the shares of Company C; 40 per cent directly and 24 per cent (that is, 40 per cent × 60 per cent) through Company B. Since A does not control B, it cannot control B's shares in C.

Though ownership and control do not necessarily go hand-in-hand, in practice they tend to do so.

Whether one company is a subsidiary of another is, of course, important because group financial statements must be prepared where a parent/subsidiary relationship exists.

Real World 10.4 shows the subsidiaries of the Go-Ahead Group plc. Most UK residents use the services of at least one of the subsidiaries, perhaps on a daily basis. The majority of the group's productive assets are owned by the subsidiaries, rather than directly by the parent company. Note that Go-Ahead uses the word 'group' in its official name. This is not unusual, but it is not a legal requirement. Many companies operating through subsidiaries do not indicate the group structure in their name.

Going ahead with subsidiaries

Go-Ahead Group plc: Principal subsidiaries

Name	Country of incorporation	Percentage of shares owned
Go-Ahead Holding Limited	UK	100
Go North East Limited	UK	100
London General Transport Services Limited	UK	100
UK Go-Ahead London Rail Replacement Services Limited	UK	100
Go-Ahead Brighton and Hove Bus and Coach Company Limited	UK	100
The City of Oxford Motor Services Limited	UK	100
Go South Coast Limited	UK	100
Plymouth Citibus Limited	UK	100
Konectbus Limited	UK	100
Thames Travel (Wallingford) Limited	UK	100
Carousel Buses limited	UK	100
Hedingham and District Omnibuses Limited	UK	100
Anglian Bus Limited	UK	100
HC Chambers and Son Limited	UK	100
Aviance UK Limited	UK	100
New Southern Railway Limited	UK	65
London and South Eastern Railway Limited	UK	65
London and Birmingham Railway Limited	UK	65
Southern Railway Limited	UK	65
Govia Limited	UK	65
Go-Ahead Scotland Limited	UK	100
Thamesdown Transport Limited	UK	100
Excelsior Coaches Limited	UK	100
Excelsior Transport Limited	UK	100
Excelsior Travel Limited	UK	100
Go-Ahead Verkehrsgesellschaft Deutschland GmbH	Germany	100
Go-Ahead Baden Württemberg GmbH	Germany	100
Go-Ahead Facility GmbH Germany	Germany	100
Go-Ahead Seletar PTE Ltd	Singapore	100
Go-Ahead Loyang PTE Ltd	Singapore	100

Source: Go-Ahead Group plc, Annual Report 2017, p. 156.

PREPARING A GROUP STATEMENT OF FINANCIAL POSITION

We shall now look at the preparation of a group statement of financial position. We can do this by considering a series of examples, starting with the simplest possible case and gradually building in more and more complexities found in real life.

Each company within the group will prepare its own statement of financial position. In addition, however, the parent company will produce a statement of financial position that reflects the assets and claims of the group as a whole. In effect, the group statement of financial position looks at the group as if the parent company owns the assets and is, therefore, responsible for the outside liabilities of all the group members. This means, among other things, that whereas the *parent company* statement of financial position will include the investments made in the shares of the subsidiary companies, in the *group* statement of financial position, these investments will be replaced by the net assets of the subsidiaries. In other words, the group statement of financial position looks behind the subsidiary company shares to see what they represent, in terms of assets and liabilities. The assets and liabilities of subsidiaries are consolidated into the statement of financial position of the parent company. This point should become clearer as we look at some examples. (Group financial statements are often known as **consolidated financial statements**.)

Example 10.3

The statements of financial position of Parent plc and of Subsidiary Ltd, on the date that the former bought all the shares in the latter, were as follows:

Statements of financial position

	Parent plc £m	Subsidiary Ltd £m
ASSETS		
Non-current assets		
Property, plant and equipment		
Land	40	5
Plant	30	2
Vehicles	20	2
	90	9
Investment		
5 million shares of Subsidiary Ltd	10	–
	100	9
Current assets		
Inventories	20	3
Trade receivables	30	2
Cash	10	2
	60	7
Total assets	160	16
EQUITY AND LIABILITIES		
Equity		
Called-up share capital:		
ordinary shares of £1 each, fully paid	70	5
Share premium account	10	–
Retained earnings	30	5
	110	10
Non-current liabilities		
Borrowings – loan notes	30	–
Current liabilities		
Trade payables	20	6
Total equity and liabilities	160	16

To derive the group statement of financial position, we simply combine each of the like items by adding them together. For example, the group investment in land is £45 million, representing £40 million invested by Parent plc and £5 million invested by Subsidiary Ltd.

The only exceptions to the rule that we simply add like items together lies with the investment in the shares of Subsidiary Ltd in the statement of financial position of Parent plc, and with the equity (share capital plus reserves) in the statement of financial position of Subsidiary Ltd. In effect, these are two sides of the same coin, since Parent plc is the owner of Subsidiary Ltd. For this reason, it is logical simply to add these two items together and since one is an asset and the other is a claim and they are equal in amount, they will cancel each other out.

The group statement of financial position will be as follows:

Statement of financial position

	£m
ASSETS	
Non-current assets	
Property, plant and equipment	
Land (40 + 5)	45
Plant (30 + 2)	32
Vehicles (20 + 2)	22
	99
Current assets	
Inventories (20 + 3)	23
Trade receivables (30 + 2)	32
Cash (10 + 2)	12
	67
Total assets	166
EQUITY AND LIABILITIES	
Equity	
Called-up share capital:	
ordinary shares of £1 each, fully paid	70
Share premium account	10
Retained earnings	30
	110
Non-current liabilities	
Borrowings – loan notes (30 + 0)	30
Current liabilities	
Trade payables (20 + 6)	26
Total equity and liabilities	166

The 'Equity' section of the group statement of financial position is simply that of Parent plc. The £10 million equity for Subsidiary Ltd cancels out with the £10 million that relates to '5 million shares of Subsidiary Ltd' in the non-current assets section of the parent company's statement of financial position. Since Parent owns all of Subsidiary's shares, all of Subsidiary's equity is attributable to Parent.

The statements of financial position of Large plc and of Small plc, on the date that Large plc bought all the shares in Small plc, were as follows:

Statements of financial position

	Large plc £m	Small plc £m
ASSETS		
Non-current assets		
Property, plant and equipment		
Land	55	–
Plant	43	21
Vehicles	25	17
	123	38
Investment		
20 million shares of Small plc	32	–
	155	38
Current assets		
Inventories	42	18
Trade receivables	18	13
Cash	24	13
	84	44
Total assets	239	82
EQUITY AND LIABILITIES		
Equity		
Called-up share capital:		
ordinary shares of £1 each, fully paid	100	20
Share premium account	–	5
Retained earnings	64	7
	164	32
Non-current liabilities		
Borrowings – loan notes	50	30
Current liabilities		
Trade payables	25	20
Total equity and liabilities	239	82

Have a try at deducing the group statement of financial position.

The group statement of financial position will be as follows:

Statement of financial position

	£m
ASSETS	
Non-current assets	
Property, plant and equipment	
Land (55 + 0)	55
Plant (43 + 21)	64
Vehicles (25 + 17)	42
	161
Current assets	
Inventories (42 + 18)	60
Trade receivables (18 + 13)	31
Cash (24 + 13)	37
	128
Total assets	289
EQUITY AND LIABILITIES	
Equity	
Called-up share capital:	
ordinary shares of £1 each, fully paid	100
Retained earnings	64
	164
Non-current liabilities	
Borrowings – loan notes (50 + 30)	80
Current liabilities	
Trade payables (25 + 20)	45
Total equity and liabilities	289

The 'equity' section of the group statement of financial position is simply that of Large plc. The £32 million for the equity (share capital and reserves) of Small plc cancels out with the £32 million relating to 'Investment in 20 million shares of Small plc' in the non-current assets section of the statement of financial position of Large plc.

The example and the activity represent the simplest case because:

1 the parent owns all of the shares of the subsidiary;
2 the price paid for the shares (£10 million and £32 million, respectively) exactly equals the 'carrying amount', or 'book value', of the net assets of the subsidiary (that is the values at which they appear in the subsidiary's statement of financial position); and
3 no trading has taken place since the shares were acquired.

In practice, things are usually more complex. We shall now look at various 'complications' that may arise, both one by one and together.

Complication 1: Less than 100 per cent ownership of the subsidiary by the parent

The problem here is that when setting the asset of 'shares of subsidiary', in the statement of financial position of the parent, against the 'equity' (owners' claim) in the statement of financial position of the subsidiary, they do not completely cancel one another out.

Example 10.4

The statements of financial position of Parent plc and of Subsidiary Ltd, on the date that the former bought the shares in the latter, are the same as in the previous example (Example 10.3) except that Parent plc owns only 4 million (of the 5 million) shares of Subsidiary Ltd. Thus the investment is only £8 million, instead of £10 million. As a result, Parent plc's cash balance is £2 million greater than in the previous example.

The two statements of financial position were as follows:

Statements of financial position

	Parent plc £m	Subsidiary Ltd £m
ASSETS		
Non-current assets		
Property, plant and equipment		
Land	40	5
Plant	30	2
Vehicles	20	2
	90	9
Investment		
4 million shares of Subsidiary Ltd	8	–
	98	9
Current assets		
Inventories	20	3
Trade receivables	30	2
Cash	12	2
	62	7
Total assets	160	16
EQUITY AND LIABILITIES		
Equity		
Called-up share capital:		
ordinary shares of £1 each, fully paid	70	5
Share premium account	10	–
Retained earnings	30	5
	110	10
Non-current liabilities		
Borrowings – loan notes	30	–
Current liabilities		
Trade payables	20	6
Total equity and liabilities	160	16

As before, to prepare the group statement of financial position, we simply add like items together. The problem is that when we come to set the £8 million investment made by Parent plc against the £10 million equity of Subsidiary Ltd, they do not cancel. There is an owners' claim of £2 million in the statement of financial position of Subsidiary Ltd that has not been cancelled out.

Can you figure out what the £2 million represents?

It represents the extent to which Parent plc does not own all of the shares of Subsidiary Ltd. Parent plc only owns 80 per cent of the shares and, therefore, other investors must own the rest. Since we are including all of the assets and liabilities of Subsidiary Ltd as being those of the group, the group statement of financial position must acknowledge that there is another source of equity finance, as well as Parent plc.

This £2 million owners' claim is known as non-controlling interests (or minority interests). It is shown in the group statement of financial position as an addition to, but not part of, the equity.

The group statement of financial position will be as follows:

Statement of financial position

	£m
ASSETS	
Non-current assets	
Property, plant and equipment	
Land (40 + 5)	45
Plant (30 + 2)	32
Vehicles (20 + 2)	22
	99
Current assets	
Inventories (20 + 3)	23
Trade receivables (30 + 2)	32
Cash (12 + 2)	14
	69
Total assets	168
EQUITY AND LIABILITIES	
Equity	
Called-up share capital:	
ordinary shares of £1 each, fully paid	70
Share premium account	10
Retained earnings	30
	110
Non-controlling interests	2
	112
Non-current liabilities	
Borrowings – loan notes (30 + 0)	30
Current liabilities	
Trade payables (20 + 6)	26
Total equity and liabilities	168

This statement of financial position reflects the fact that the group has control over net assets totalling £112 million (at statement of financial position values). Of this amount, £110 million is financed by shareholders of the parent company and £2 million by others.

It may have occurred to you that an alternative approach to dealing with less than 100 per cent ownership is to scale down the assets and liabilities to reflect this, before carrying out the consolidation of the two sets of financial statements. Since Parent plc only owns 80 per cent of Subsidiary Ltd, we could multiply all of the figures in Subsidiary Ltd's statement of financial position by 0.8 before preparing the group financial statements. If we did this, the owners' claim would be reduced to £8 million, which would exactly cancel with the asset (shares of Subsidiary Ltd) in the statement of financial position of Parent plc.

Activity 10.8

Can you think why we do not 'scale down' for less than 100 per cent owned subsidiaries when preparing the group statement of financial position?

The reason why the whole of the carrying amounts of the assets and liabilities of the subsidiary are included in the group statement of financial position is that the parent company *controls* all of the subsidiaries' assets, even though it may not strictly own them all. Control is the key issue in group financial statements.

Activity 10.9

The statements of financial position of Large plc and of Small plc, on the date that Large plc bought the shares in Small plc, were as follows:

Statements of financial position

	Large plc £m	Small plc £m
ASSETS		
Non-current assets		
Property, plant and equipment		
Land	55	–
Plant	43	21
Vehicles	25	17
	123	38
Investment		
15 million shares of Small plc	24	–
	147	38
Current assets		
Inventories	42	18
Trade receivables	18	13
Cash	32	13
	92	44
Total assets	239	82
EQUITY AND LIABILITIES		
Equity		
Called-up share capital:		
ordinary shares of £1 each, fully paid	100	20
Share premium account	–	5
Retained earnings	64	7
	164	32
Non-current liabilities		
Borrowings – loan notes	50	30
Current liabilities		
Trade payables	25	20
Total equity and liabilities	239	82

Have a go at preparing the group statement of financial position.

The group statement of financial position will be as follows:

Statement of financial position

	£m
ASSETS	
Non-current assets	
Property, plant and equipment	
Land (55 + 0)	55
Plant (43 + 21)	64
Vehicles (25 + 17)	42
	161
Current assets	
Inventories (42 + 18)	60
Trade receivables (18 + 13)	31
Cash (32 + 13)	45
	136
Total assets	297
EQUITY AND LIABILITIES	
Equity	
Called-up share capital:	
ordinary shares of £1 each, fully paid	100
Retained earnings	64
	164
Non-controlling interests	8
	172
Non-current liabilities	
Borrowings – loan notes (50 + 30)	80
Current liabilities	
Trade payables (25 + 20)	45
Total equity and liabilities	297

Large plc owns 75 per cent of the shares, costing £24 million. The £8 million for non-controlling interests represents the remaining 25 per cent of the Small plc shares owned by the 'outside' shareholders (that is, 25 per cent of £32 million).

Complication 2: Paying more or less than the underlying net asset value for the shares

Here the problem is that, even where the subsidiary is 100 per cent owned, the asset of 'shares of the subsidiary', in the statement of financial position of the parent, will not exactly cancel against the equity figure in the statement of financial position of the subsidiary. Anything paid in excess of the underlying net asset value of the subsidiary's shares must represent an undisclosed asset, which is normally referred to as goodwill arising on consolidation. Any amount paid below the underlying net asset value is normally referred to as negative goodwill arising on consolidation. This situation will only normally arise where there is a takeover of an existing business rather than where a parent company creates a new subsidiary.

For the sake of simplicity, we shall assume that the statement of financial position of a subsidiary reflects all of its assets and liabilities and that these are recorded at their fair values. We shall, however, consider the situation where this is not the case later in the chapter.

Example 10.5

We are returning to the original statements of financial position of Parent plc and Subsidiary Ltd as shown in Example 10.3, on the date that Parent plc bought the shares in Subsidiary Ltd. So Parent plc owns all of the shares in Subsidiary Ltd, but we shall assume that they were bought for £15 million rather than £10 million. Parent plc's cash balance reflects the higher amount paid. The statements of financial position are as follows:

Statements of financial position

	Parent plc £m	Subsidiary Ltd £m
ASSETS		
Non-current assets		
Property, plant and equipment		
Land	40	5
Plant	30	2
Vehicles	20	2
	90	9
Investment		
5 million shares of Subsidiary Ltd	15	–
	105	9
Current assets		
Inventories	20	3
Trade receivables	30	2
Cash	5	2
	55	7
Total assets	160	16
EQUITY AND LIABILITIES		
Equity		
Called-up share capital:		
ordinary shares of £1 each, fully paid	70	5
Share premium account	10	–
Retained earnings	30	5
	110	10
Non-current liabilities		
Borrowings – loan notes	30	–
Current liabilities		
Trade payables	20	6
Total equity and liabilities	160	16

The normal routine of adding like items together and cancelling the investment in Subsidiary Ltd shares against the equity of that company is followed, except that the last two do not exactly cancel. The difference is, of course, goodwill arising on consolidation.

The group statement of financial position will be as follows:

Statement of financial position

	£m
Non-current assets	
Property, plant and equipment	
Land (40 + 5)	45
Plant (30 + 2)	32
Vehicles (20 + 2)	22
	99
Intangible assets	
Goodwill arising on consolidation (15 − 10)	5
	104
Current assets	
Inventories (20 + 3)	23
Trade receivables (30 + 2)	32
Cash (5 + 2)	7
	62
Total assets	166
EQUITY AND LIABILITIES	
Equity	
Called-up share capital:	
ordinary shares of £1 each, fully paid	70
Share premium account	10
Retained earnings	30
	110
Non-current liabilities	
Borrowings – loan notes (30 + 0)	30
Current liabilities	
Trade payables (20 + 6)	26
Total equity and liabilities	166

The goodwill represents the excess of what was paid by Parent plc for the shares over the fair value of their underlying net assets, at the time of the takeover.

The statements of financial position of Large plc and of Small plc, on the date that Large plc bought all the shares in Small plc, were as follows:

Statements of financial position

	Large plc £m	Small plc £m
ASSETS		
Non-current assets		
Property, plant and equipment		
Land	48	–
Plant	43	21
Vehicles	25	17
	116	38
Investment		
20 million shares of Small plc	35	–
	151	38
Current assets		
Inventories	42	18
Trade receivables	18	13
Cash	28	13
	88	44
Total assets	239	82
EQUITY AND LIABILITIES		
Equity		
Called-up share capital:		
ordinary shares of £1 each, fully paid	100	20
Share premium account	–	5
Retained earnings	64	7
	164	32
Non-current liabilities		
Borrowings – loan notes	50	30
Current liabilities		
Trade payables	25	20
Total equity and liabilities	239	82

Have a go at preparing the group statement of financial position.

The group statement of financial position will be as follows:

Statement of financial position

	£m
ASSETS	
Non-current assets	
Property, plant and equipment	
Land (48 + 0)	48
Plant (43 + 21)	64
Vehicles (25 + 17)	_42_
	154
Intangible asset	
Goodwill arising on consolidation (35 − 32)	_3_
	157
Current assets	
Inventories (42 + 18)	60
Trade receivables (18 + 13)	31
Cash (28 + 13)	_41_
	132
Total assets	289
EQUITY AND LIABILITIES	
Equity	
Called-up share capital:	
ordinary shares of £1 each, fully paid	100
Retained earnings	_64_
	164
Non-current liabilities	
Borrowings – loan notes (50 + 30)	_80_
Current liabilities	
Trade payables (25 + 20)	_45_
Total equity and liabilities	289

Later we shall see that a slightly different approach can be taken in the valuation of goodwill arising on consolidation in the group statement of financial position. In practice, however, most businesses take the approach just described.

Complications 1 and 2 taken together

Let us now take a look at how we deal with a situation where the parent owns less than all of the shares of its subsidiary *and* it has paid more, or less, than the underlying net asset value of the shares.

Example 10.6

Again, we shall look at the statements of financial position of Parent plc and Subsidiary Ltd, on the date that the former bought the shares in the latter. This time we shall combine both of the 'complications' already met. Here, Parent plc now only owns 80 per cent of the shares of Subsidiary Ltd, for which it paid £3 a share, that is, £1 above their underlying net asset value.

Statements of financial position

	Parent plc £m	Subsidiary Ltd £m
ASSETS		
Non-current assets		
Property, plant and equipment		
Land	40	5
Plant	30	2
Vehicles	20	2
	90	9
Investment		
4 million shares of Subsidiary Ltd	12	–
	102	9
Current assets		
Inventories	20	3
Trade receivables	30	2
Cash	8	2
	58	7
Total assets	160	16
EQUITY AND LIABILITIES		
Equity		
Called-up share capital:		
ordinary shares of £1 each, fully paid	70	5
Share premium account	10	–
Retained earnings	30	5
	110	10
Non-current liabilities		
Borrowings – loan notes	30	–
Current liabilities		
Trade payables	20	6
Total equity and liabilities	160	16

The normal routine still applies. This means adding like items together and cancelling the investment in Subsidiary Ltd shares against the equity of that company. Again, they will not cancel, but this time for a combination of two reasons; non-controlling interests *and* goodwill arising on consolidation.

We need to separate out these two issues before we go on to prepare the group financial statements.

To establish the non-controlling interests element, we need simply to calculate the part of the owners' claim of Subsidiary Ltd that is not owned by Parent plc. Parent plc owns 80 per cent of the shares, so others own the remaining 20 per cent. Twenty per cent of the equity of Subsidiary Ltd is £2 million (that is, 20 per cent × £10 million).

To discover the appropriate goodwill figure, we need to compare what Parent plc paid and what it received, in terms of the fair values reflected in the statement of financial position. It paid £12 million and received net assets with a fair value of £8 million (that is, 80 per cent × £10 million). Thus, goodwill is £4 million (that is, 12 − 8).

The group statement of financial position will be as follows:

Statement of financial position

	£m
ASSETS	
Non-current assets	
Property, plant and equipment	
Land (40 + 5)	45
Plant (30 + 2)	32
Vehicles (20 + 2)	22
	99
Intangible assets	
Goodwill arising on consolidation (12 − (80% × 10))	4
	103
Current assets	
Inventories (20 + 3)	23
Trade receivables (30 + 2)	32
Cash (8 + 2)	10
	65
Total assets	168
EQUITY AND LIABILITIES	
Equity	
Called-up share capital:	
ordinary shares of £1 each, fully paid	70
Share premium account	10
Retained earnings	30
	110
Non-controlling interests	2
	112
Non-current liabilities	
Borrowings – loan notes (30 + 0)	30
Current liabilities	
Trade payables (20 + 6)	26
Total equity and liabilities	168

The statements of financial position of Large plc and Small plc, on the date that Large plc bought the shares in Small plc, were as follows:

Statements of financial position

	Large plc £m	Small plc £m
ASSETS		
Non-current assets		
Property, plant and equipment		
Land	49	–
Plant	43	21
Vehicles	25	17
	117	38
Investment		
15 million shares of Small plc	27	–
	144	38
Current assets		
Inventories	42	18
Trade receivables	18	13
Cash	35	13
	95	44
Total assets	239	82
EQUITY AND LIABILITIES		
Equity		
Called-up share capital:		
ordinary shares of £1 each, fully paid	100	20
Share premium account	–	5
Retained earnings	64	7
	164	32
Non-current liabilities		
Borrowings – loan notes	50	30
Current liabilities		
Trade payables	25	20
Total equity and liabilities	239	82

Have a go at preparing the group statement of financial position.

The non-controlling interests will be £8 million (that is, 25 per cent of £32 million).

To determine goodwill, we must compare what was paid (£27 million) with what was received (75 per cent of £32 million = £24 million). Thus, the goodwill is £3 million.

The group statement of financial position will be as follows:

Statement of financial position

	£m
ASSETS	
Non-current assets	
Property, plant and equipment	
Land (49 + 0)	49
Plant (43 + 21)	64
Vehicles (25 + 17)	42
	155
Intangible assets	
Goodwill arising on consolidation	3
	158
Current assets	
Inventories (42 + 18)	60
Trade receivables (18 + 13)	31
Cash (35 + 13)	48
	139
Total assets	297
EQUITY AND LIABILITIES	
Equity	
Called-up share capital:	
ordinary shares of £1 each, fully paid	100
Retained earnings	64
	164
Non-controlling interests (25% × 32)	8
	172
Non-current liabilities	
Borrowings – loan notes (50 + 30)	80
Current liabilities	
Trade payables (25 + 20)	45
Total equity and liabilities	297

Complication 3: Trading has taken place since the shares were acquired

Most group statements of financial position will be prepared some time after the date that the parent company acquired the shares in the subsidiary. This time lapse does not raise major difficulties, but we need to backtrack to the time of acquisition in order to establish the goodwill figure.

Let us now look at another example. In this case, all three of our 'complications' exist.

The statements of financial position of Mega plc and Micro plc, as at 31 December, are set out below. Mega plc bought its shares in Micro plc some time ago, at a time at which the latter's share capital was exactly as shown below and the retained earnings balance stood at £30 million.

Statements of financial position as at 31 December

	Mega plc £m	Micro plc £m
ASSETS		
Non-current assets		
Property, plant and equipment		
Land	53	18
Plant	34	11
Vehicles	24	9
	111	38
Investment		
6 million shares of Micro plc	33	–
	144	38
Current assets		
Inventories	27	10
Trade receivables	29	11
Cash	11	1
	67	22
Total assets	211	60
EQUITY AND LIABILITIES		
Equity		
Called-up share capital:		
ordinary shares of £1 each, fully paid	100	10
Retained earnings	38	35
	138	45
Non-current liabilities		
Borrowings – loan notes	50	10
Current liabilities		
Trade payables	23	5
Total equity and liabilities	211	60

We can see that the investment in Micro plc, as shown in the statement of financial position of Mega plc (£33 million), comes nowhere near cancelling with the £45 million owners' claim of Micro plc. We need to separate out the elements.

Let us start with non-controlling interests. Here, we are not concerned with the position at the date of the takeover. If the equity of Micro plc totals £45 million at the statement of financial position date and the minorities own 4 million of the 10 million shares, their contribution to the financing of the group's assets must be £18 million (that is, 40 per cent × £45 million).

Next let us ask ourselves what Mega plc received when it paid £33 million for the shares. At that time, the equity part of Micro plc's statement of financial position looked like this:

	£m
Called-up share capital:	
ordinary shares of £1 each, fully paid	10
Retained earnings	30
	40

This means that the net assets of Micro plc must have also been worth (in terms of fair values reflected in the statement of financial position) £40 million; otherwise the statement of financial position, drawn up at the time that the takeover occurred, would not have balanced. Since Mega plc bought 6 million of 10 million of Micro plc's shares (60 per cent), it paid £33 million for net assets worth £24 million (that is, 60 per cent of £40 million). Thus, there is goodwill arising on consolidation of £9 million (that is, £33m − £24m).

We shall assume that no steps have been taken since the takeover to alter this goodwill figure. However, we shall consider why such steps may have been taken a little later.

In dealing with non-controlling interests and goodwill we have, in effect, picked up the following parts of the owners' claim of Micro plc at 31 December:

- the minorities' share of the equity (as non-controlling interests);
- Mega plc's share of the share capital and its share of the reserves as they stood at the date of the takeover (in the calculation of the goodwill figure).

The only remaining part of the owners' claim of Micro plc at 31 December is Mega plc's share of Micro plc's reserves that have built up since the takeover, in other words its share of the £5 million (that is, £35 million − £30 million). This share is £3 million (that is, 60 per cent of £5 million). This is Mega plc's share of the profits earned by its subsidiary since the takeover, after any dividends have been paid. As such, it is logical for this £3 million to be added to the retained earnings balance of the parent company in arriving at the group reserves.

This treatment of the equity of Micro plc can be represented in a tabular form as shown in Figure 10.3.

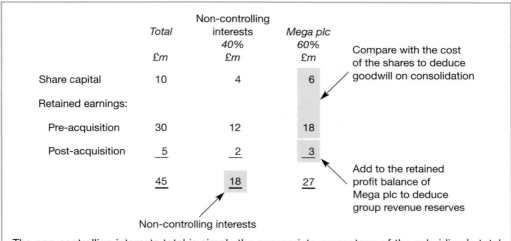

The non-controlling interests total is simply the appropriate percentage of the subsidiary's total equity, without reference to when the reserves arose. The parent's share of the subsidiary's total of equity, at the date of the takeover, is compared with the price paid by the parent to deduce the goodwill arising on consolidation. The parent's share of the subsidiary's post-acquisition reserves is added to the parent's reserves to find the total reserves.

Figure 10.3 The treatment of the share equity of Micro plc in producing the group statement of financial position

The group statement of financial position will be as follows:

Statement of financial position as at 31 December

	£m
ASSETS	
Non-current assets	
Property, plant and equipment	
Land (53 + 18)	71
Plant (34 + 11)	45
Vehicles (24 + 9)	33
	149
Intangible assets	
Goodwill arising on consolidation (33 − (6 + 18))	9
	158
Current assets	
Inventories (27 + 10)	37
Trade receivables (29 + 11)	40
Cash (11 + 1)	12
	89
Total assets	247
EQUITY AND LIABILITIES	
Equity	
Called-up share capital:	
ordinary shares of £1 each, fully paid	100
Retained earnings (38 + 3)	41
	141
Non-controlling interests (40% × 45)	18
	159
Non-current liabilities	
Borrowings – loan notes (50 + 10)	60
Current liabilities	
Trade payables (23 + 5)	28
Total equity and liabilities	247

The statements of financial position of Grand plc and Petit Ltd, as at 30 June, are set out below. Grand plc bought its shares in Petit Ltd at a time when the latter's share capital was the same as it is currently and the retained earnings balance stood at £14 million.

Statements of financial position as at 30 June

	Grand plc £m	Petit Ltd £m
ASSETS		
Non-current assets		
Property, plant and equipment		
Land	12	10
Plant	14	8
Vehicles	3	6
	29	24
Investment		
7.5 million shares of Petit Ltd	21	–
	50	24
Current assets		
Inventories	10	5
Trade receivables	9	4
Cash	2	2
	21	11
Total assets	71	35
EQUITY AND LIABILITIES		
Equity		
Called-up share capital:		
ordinary shares of £1 each, fully paid	30	10
Retained earnings	14	22
	44	32
Non-current liabilities		
Borrowings – loan notes	20	–
Current liabilities		
Trade payables	7	3
Total equity and liabilities	71	35

Prepare the statement of financial position for the group as at 30 June.

Your answer should be something like this:

Non-controlling interests:

$$25\% \times £32 \text{ million} = £8 \text{ million}$$

Goodwill arising on consolidation:

$$£21 \text{ million} - (75\% \times (£10 \text{ million} + £14 \text{ million})) = £3 \text{ million}$$

Grand plc's share of Petit Ltd's post-acquisition reserves:

$$75\% \times (£22 \text{ million} - £14 \text{ million}) = £6 \text{ million}$$

Assuming that no steps have been taken since the takeover to alter the goodwill figure, the group statement of financial position will be as follows:

→

Statement of financial position as at 30 June

	£m
ASSETS	
Non-current assets	
Property, plant and equipment	
Land (12 + 10)	22
Plant (14 + 8)	22
Vehicles (3 + 6)	9
	53
Intangible assets	
Goodwill arising on consolidation	3
	56
Current assets	
Inventories (10 + 5)	15
Trade receivables (9 + 4)	13
Cash (2 + 2)	4
	32
Total assets	88
EQUITY AND LIABILITIES	
Equity	
Called-up share capital:	
ordinary shares of £1 each, fully paid	30
Retained earnings (14 + 6)	20
	50
Non-controlling interests	8
	58
Non-current liabilities	
Borrowings – loan notes (20 + 0)	20
Current liabilities	
Trade payables (7 + 3)	10
Total equity and liabilities	88

INTER-COMPANY ASSETS AND CLAIMS

Although each subsidiary is a separate legal entity, the control exercised by the parent, and close relations between subsidiaries, often lead to inter-company trading and other inter-company transactions. As a result, a particular asset in one company's statement of financial position could relate to an equal-sized liability in the statement of financial position of another company within the same group.

The principle underlying the group statement of financial position is that it should represent the situation as if all the assets and claims of individual subsidiaries were directly the assets and claims of the parent company. Since the parent company cannot owe itself money, where there are inter-company balances these must be eliminated when preparing the group statement of financial position.

Delta plc and its subsidiary Gamma plc are the only members of a group. Delta plc sells goods on credit to Gamma plc. At the statement of financial position date, in other words the following balances existed in the books of the companies:

	Trade receivables £m	Trade payables £m
Delta plc	34	26
Gamma plc	23	18

Included in the trade receivables of Delta plc, and the trade payables of Gamma plc, is £5 million in respect of some recent inter-company trading.

In deducing the figures to be included in the group statement of financial position, we have to eliminate the inter-company balance, as follows:

$$\text{Trade receivables} = 34 - 5 + 23 = £52 \text{ million}$$
$$\text{Trade payables} = 26 + 18 - 5 = £39 \text{ million}$$

Note that the consolidated trade receivables and trade payables figures represent what is owed by, and owed to, individuals and organisations *outside* the group. This is in accordance with the principles of group accounting.

GOODWILL ARISING ON CONSOLIDATION AND ASSET CARRYING AMOUNTS

Goodwill arising on consolidation represents the difference between the cost of acquiring the shares in a subsidiary and the fair value of the net assets acquired. In the examples considered so far, we have assumed that the values at which a subsidiary's assets appear in its statement of financial position are the same as the fair values of those assets. Thus, it has been possible to deduce goodwill by making a comparison of the cost of acquiring the subsidiary with the values appearing in the subsidiary's statement of financial position. Unfortunately, things are not usually that simple!

Carrying amounts often differ from the fair values of assets. Generally speaking, the values at which assets are shown in the statement of financial position are lower because accounting conventions such as prudence and historic cost conspire to produce a conservative bias. As a result, not only do assets tend to be shown on the statement of financial position at less than their fair value, but some assets are completely omitted from the normal statement of financial position. This is particularly true of intangible assets, such as brand values. This means that, to calculate goodwill arising on consolidation, we cannot rely on statement of financial position values. We must find out what the fair values of the assets acquired really are. This must include those assets that appear on the statement of financial position of the subsidiary as well as those that do not (such as brand values).

Example 10.9 illustrates this point.

Example 10.9

The statements of financial position of Parent plc and of Subsidiary Ltd (which we last met in Example 10.6), on the date that the former bought the shares in the latter, were as follows:

Statements of financial position

	Parent plc £m	Subsidiary Ltd £m
ASSETS		
Non-current assets		
Property, plant and equipment		
Land	40	5
Plant	30	2
Vehicles	20	2
	90	9
Investment		
5 million shares of Subsidiary Ltd	15	–
	105	9
Current assets		
Inventories	20	3
Trade receivables	30	2
Cash	5	2
	55	7
Total assets	160	16
EQUITY AND LIABILITIES		
Equity		
Called-up share capital:		
ordinary shares of £1 each, fully paid	70	5
Share premium account	10	–
Retained earnings	30	5
	110	10
Non-current liabilities		
Borrowings – loan notes	30	–
Current liabilities		
Trade payables	20	6
Total equity and liabilities	160	16

When Parent plc was valuing the shares of Subsidiary Ltd, it was judged that most of the statement of financial position values were in line with the fair values. However, the following fair values should be applied to the three categories of property, plant and equipment of the subsidiary:

	£m
Land	7
Plant	3
Vehicles	3

In addition, it was judged that the subsidiary has goodwill valued at £1 million. When these fair values are incorporated into the group statement of financial position, it will be as follows:

Statement of financial position

	£m
ASSETS	
Non-current assets	
Property, plant and equipment	
Land (40 + 7)	47
Plant (30 + 3)	33
Vehicles (20 + 3)	23
	103
Intangible assets	
Goodwill	1
	104
Current assets	
Inventories (20 + 3)	23
Trade receivables (30 + 2)	32
Cash (5 + 2)	7
	62
Total assets	166
EQUITY AND LIABILITIES	
Equity	
Called-up share capital:	
ordinary shares of £1 each, fully paid	70
Share premium account	10
Retained earnings	30
	110
Non-current liabilities	
Borrowings – loan notes (30 + 0)	30
Current liabilities	
Trade payables (20 + 6)	26
Total equity and liabilities	166

This example takes the simple case of no outside shareholdings in the subsidiary (that is, the subsidiary is 100 per cent owned by the parent) and no post-acquisition trading (the statements of financial position are at the date of acquisition), but these 'complications' would not alter the principles.

There is no need for the statement of financial position of the subsidiary to be adjusted for fair values, only the group statement of financial position. As far as the subsidiary is concerned, no change occurs with the takeover except a change in the names on the list of shareholders.

The financial reporting standard that deals with this aspect of group financial statements (IFRS 3) is clear that intangible assets of the subsidiary, at the date of the takeover, such as brand values and patent rights, must be separately identified at their fair value. These assets must then be incorporated at those values in the group statement of financial position.

The non-current assets of the subsidiary that have finite lives should have a depreciation (or amortisation) charge, based on their fair values, in the group income statement. This charge may well be different to that shown in the financial statements of the subsidiary. This is because the value, at which an asset appears in the subsidiary's statement of financial position, may well differ from its value in the group statement.

Goodwill arising on consolidation is simply the excess of what the parent company paid for the subsidiary company's shares over their fair value, based on all of the identifiable assets (tangible and intangible) of the subsidiary. This means that what is identified as goodwill arising on consolidation tends to represent only the value of:

- having a workforce in place;
- cost synergies – arising from the fact that the combined business can make cost savings by, say, having just one head office instead of two; and
- sales synergies – arising, for example, from group members trading with one another.

These attributes representing goodwill could be enduring, but could also be lost, either partially or completely. Thus, IFRS 3 requires that the value of goodwill be reviewed annually, or even more frequently if circumstances dictate. Where its value has been impaired, it must be reduced accordingly in the group financial statements. It should be noted that goodwill arising on consolidation does not appear in the statements of financial position of either the parent or the subsidiary. It only appears on the group statement of financial position.

We saw earlier the requirement of IFRS 3 that all subsidiary company assets, whether they appear on the subsidiary's statement of financial position, whether they are tangible or intangible, should be reflected at their fair value in the group statement of financial position. These requirements, however, do not always seem to be followed. **Real World 10.5** describes an investigation into how some large, well-known businesses do not appear to adhere to the spirit of IFRS 3.

Real World 10.5

Where there's goodwill . . .

Since the first year that IFRS 3 applied (2005), there have been two surveys conducted to find out how businesses treated the acquisition cost following a takeover. The first involved the largest 100 businesses listed on the London Stock Exchange that took over other businesses during 2005. The other involved over 200 businesses operating in a range of countries where IFRS 3 was relevant and related to takeovers during 2010.

Acquisition costs were treated as follows in the group statements of financial position:

	2005	2010
	%	%
Tangible assets	17	7
Goodwill arising on consolidation	53	54
Other intangible assets	30	39

Forbes, the author of the 2005 study, concluded that this treatment was counter to the spirit of IFRS 3. It seems implausible that such a large proportion of the total should be treated as goodwill, when IFRS 3 limits what should be treated as goodwill quite severely.

Forbes identified some examples including the takeover of RAC plc (the UK motoring organisation) by Aviva plc (the UK-based insurance business) in March 2005. Aviva paid £1.1 billion, of which the majority was treated as goodwill. RAC had 7 million customers and is one of the most trusted brands in the UK, yet these were valued at only £260 million and £132 million respectively.

Forbes identified four possible reasons for the apparent misapplications of IFRS 3. These are:

1 *To reduce depreciation charges and increase profits.* Since goodwill cannot be depreciated and intangible assets with finite lives should be, reported profit will tend to be enhanced by treating as much of the purchase price as possible as goodwill.
2 *To minimise impairment charges.* Though both intangible assets without finite lives and goodwill are subject to impairment tests and a possible charge against profits as a result, the tests for goodwill are less stringent. This means that other intangible assets are more likely to lead to an impairment charge than goodwill.
3 *Lack of skills.* Having to value intangibles following a takeover was a new requirement and so the skills to do so may not have been available.
4 *Failure to see the big picture.* Businesses may get too bogged down with the regulations and so fail to consider the key issues and effects of the takeover.

Forbes went on to say:

> The implications of this inadequate reporting are far reaching. It renders annual reports more useless than they currently are, it makes a standard ineffective when applied and the financial bodies that govern them, it sets a dangerous precedent for future years and it opens a new era of creative accounting that distances shareholders and investors further from reality.

The position had not improved greatly by 2009. The Financial Reporting Council looked at the financial reporting of twenty takeovers that had occurred in 2008 and reported in the financial statements of the relevant parent company during 2009. The Council concluded that 'there is a need for improved compliance with the disclosure requirements of IFRS'.

According to the table above, the situation in 2010 remained a cause for concern. The proportion of the total amount allocated to goodwill was only marginally higher, at 54 per cent, than in it had been in 2005.

Sources: Forbes, T. (2007) Technical update – inadequate IFRS 3, *Finance Week*, 30 January, www.financeweek.co.uk; Forbes, T. (2008) Intangibles and IFRS 3: Seen but not heard, *Thayne Forbes*, www.intangiblebusiness.com, 8 February; Financial Reporting Council, *Accounting for Acquisitions*, January 2010, p. 3; and Tsalavoutas, I., Andre, P. and Dionysiou, D. (2014) Worldwide application of IFRS 3, IAS 38 and IAS 36, related disclosures, and determinants of non-compliance, *ACCA Research Report* 134, pp. 21 and 22.

The main issue that Real World 10.5 addresses is the allocation of the total for intangible assets between 'Goodwill' and 'Other intangible assets'. Another striking aspect of what is revealed is the very small percentage allocated to 'Tangible assets' (7 per cent in 2010). There is, however, no suggestion that this tangible/intangible split is improper. The value of many modern businesses lies principally in attributes such as intellectual property, reputation, trade names and so on. Relatively little value resides in assets like such as buildings and machinery.

Negative goodwill

In the cases considered so far, goodwill arising on consolidation has always been a positive value (that is, more was paid for the parent's share of the net assets of the subsidiary than their fair values). It is, however, possible for goodwill to be negative. This is where the parent pays less than the fair values. Where negative goodwill on consolidation arises, IFRS 3 says that fair values of all assets and liabilities of the subsidiary concerned should be reassessed. This reassessment is to try to ensure that no assets have been overstated, or liabilities understated or omitted. Where this reassessment still results in negative goodwill, the amount should be treated as a gain and transferred immediately to the group income statement in the year of acquisition. In practice, negative goodwill is pretty rare.

Goodwill arising on consolidation: an alternative approach

IFRS 3 *Business Combinations* allows an alternative approach to identifying the value of goodwill to that described above. Although, in practice, the approach used so far is the most common way of arriving at the goodwill figure, the alternative approach appears to be more logical, as we shall now see.

Activity 10.13

Can you figure out why the most common approach can be seen as being illogical? (*Hint*: It is concerned with the fact that goodwill arising on consolidation is treated differently from all other assets of the subsidiary that appear in the group statement of financial position.)

The point is that goodwill is the only asset relating to the subsidiary company that is not shown in full; it is scaled down according to the proportion of the subsidiary's shares that are owned by the parent. All other assets of the subsidiary are included in full, irrespective of the parent's proportion of the ownership.

We saw earlier that a basic principle of preparing group financial statements is that, if the parent controls the assets of the subsidiary, even if it does not own them 100 per cent, *all* of their value should be included. The alternative approach allows for goodwill be shown in the statement of financial position at its full value.

Our Example 10.10 returns to Example 10.6, which included two of our 'complications' (the parent owning less than 100 per cent of the subsidiary and paying more than the fair value for them).

Example 10.10

The group statement of financial position for Parent plc and its subsidiary applying the 'old' IFRS 3 approach is as follows:

Statement of financial position

	£m
ASSETS	
Non-current assets	
Property, plant and equipment	
Land	45
Plant	32
Vehicles	22
	99
Intangible assets	
Goodwill arising on consolidation (12 − (80% × 10))	4
	103
Current assets	
Inventories	23
Trade receivables	32
Cash	10
	65
Total assets	168
EQUITY AND LIABILITIES	
Equity	
Called-up share capital:	
ordinary shares of £1 each, fully paid	70
Share premium account	10
Retained earnings	30
	110
Non-controlling interests	2
	112
Non-current liabilities	
Borrowings – loan notes	30
Current liabilities	
Trade payables	26
Total equity and liabilities	168

The goodwill (£4 million) represents the excess of what was paid by Parent plc for the shares (£12 million) over the fair value of its proportion of the underlying net assets at the time of the takeover (£8 million).

Logically, if Parent's share of the goodwill is £4 million, the total value of it is £5 million. Including this total value in the group statement of financial position would be more in line with the general approach to preparing group financial statements.

If the goodwill figure in the statement of financial position in Example 10.10 is to be increased by £1 million, something else on the statement will also need to be adjusted to maintain equality between total assets and total claims (equity and liabilities). What would this adjustment logically be?

The answer is that the figure for non-controlling interests will need to be increased by that amount. This is because £1 million of the value of the goodwill belongs to outside share-holders, which needs to be reflected in their claim, as it appears in the group statement of financial position.

The alternative approach to valuing goodwill arising on consolidation does not seem to be widely used in practice. It appears to have more support among academics than among businesses.

In view of the limited use of the alternative approach, we shall continue to use the approach described earlier in all subsequent examples and exercises.

PREPARING A GROUP INCOME STATEMENT

The **group income statement** follows very similar principles to those that apply to the group statement of financial position. These are:

- Like items are added together. For example, the revenue of each subsidiary is added to that of the parent company to discover group revenue.
- All the amounts appearing under each heading in the income statements of subsidiaries are included in the total, even where they are not wholly owned subsidiaries. For example, the revenue of a subsidiary that is 60 per cent owned by the parent is included in full.
- The interests of outside shareholders (non-controlling interests) are separately identified towards the bottom of the income statement.

Example 10.11

Holder plc owns 75 per cent of the ordinary shares of Sub Ltd. The outline income statements of the two companies for the year ended on 31 December are as follows:

Income statements for the year ended 31 December

	Holder plc £m	Sub Ltd £m
Revenue	83	40
Cost of sales	(41)	(15)
Gross profit	42	25
Administration expenses	(16)	(9)
Distribution expenses	(6)	(3)
Operating profit	20	13
Interest payable	(2)	(1)
Profit before taxation	18	12
Taxation	(8)	(4)
Profit for the year	10	8

Preparing the group income statement is a simple matter of adding like items together, except that not all of the profit for the year of the subsidiary 'belongs' to the group. Twenty-five per cent (£2 million) of it belongs to outside shareholders. We recognise this in the group income statement by deducting the 25 per cent of the subsidiary's profit for the year from the combined profit for the year.

The group income statement will be as follows:

Income statement for the year ended 31 December

	£m
Revenue (83 + 40)	123
Cost of sales (41 + 15)	(56)
Gross profit	67
Administration expenses (16 + 9)	(25)
Distribution expenses (6 + 3)	(9)
Operating profit	33
Interest payable (2 + 1)	(3)
Profit before taxation	30
Taxation (8 + 4)	(12)
Profit for the year	18
Attributable to non-controlling interests	(2)
Profit for the year attributable to Holder plc shareholders	16

This statement says that the assets under the control of the group generated profit for the year of £18 million. Of this, £2 million is the share of the 'outside' shareholders of Sub Ltd. This follows the normal approach of group financial statements of treating all assets, claims, revenues, expenses and cash flows of group companies as if they were those of the group. Where the subsidiaries are not 100 per cent owned by the parent, this fact is acknowledged by making an adjustment to reflect the non-controlling interests.

Activity 10.15

Ajax plc owns 60 per cent of the ordinary shares of Exeter plc. The outline income statements of the two companies for the year ended on 31 December are as follows:

Income statements for the year ended 31 December

	Ajax plc £m	Exeter plc £m
Revenue	120	80
Cost of sales	(60)	(40)
Gross profit	60	40
Administration expenses	(17)	(4)
Distribution expenses	(10)	(15)
Operating profit	33	21
Interest payable	(3)	(1)
Profit before taxation	30	20
Taxation	(12)	(10)
Profit for the year	18	10

Have a try at preparing a consolidated (group) income statement.

→

Your answer should look something like this:

Group income statement for the year ended 31 December

	£m
Revenue (120 + 80)	200
Cost of sales (60 + 40)	(100)
Gross profit	100
Administration expenses (17 + 4)	(21)
Distribution expenses (10 + 15)	(25)
Operating profit	54
Interest payable (3 + 1)	(4)
Profit before taxation	50
Taxation (12 + 10)	(22)
Profit for the year	28
Attributable to non-controlling interests (40% × 10)	(4)
Profit for the year attributable to Ajax plc shareholders	24

THE STATEMENT OF COMPREHENSIVE INCOME

As we saw in Chapter 5, IAS 1 *Presentation of Financial Statements* requires listed companies to provide a statement of comprehensive income, which extends the conventional income statement to include certain other gains and losses affecting shareholders' equity. It may be presented either as a single statement or as two separate statements, an income statement and a statement of comprehensive income. IAS 1 requires that, in the group's statement of comprehensive income, both the profit (or loss) for the period and the comprehensive income for the period distinguish between that which is attributable to non-controlling interests and that attributable to the shareholders of the parent company.

INTER-COMPANY TRADING

As we saw earlier, it is common for members of the group to trade with one another. As far as each member of the group is concerned, such trading should be dealt with in the accounting records, including the income statement, in exactly the same way as trading with any other party. For the group income statement, however, trading between group members must be eliminated. The principles of group accounting require that the group income statement should recognise only trading with parties outside of the group. The group is considered to be, in effect, a single entity.

GROUP STATEMENT OF CASH FLOWS

Groups must normally prepare a statement of cash flows that follows the same logic as the statement of financial position and income statement – that is, it has to show the movements in all of the cash that is in the control of the group, for the period under review.

The preparation of a **group statement of cash flows** follows the same rules as those that apply to the preparation of the statement for individual companies. In view of this, we need not spend time looking separately at statements of cash flows in a group context.

Cash transfers between group members should not be reflected in the group statement of cash flows. It is only cash transfers with parties outside of the group that must be taken into account.

ACCOUNTING FOR LESS THAN A CONTROLLING INTEREST – ASSOCIATE COMPANIES

What happens when one company makes a substantial investment in another company but this does not provide the investing company with a controlling interest? In other words, the company whose shares have been acquired does not become a subsidiary of the investing company. One approach would simply be to include the investment of shares in the company at cost in the investing company's statement of financial position. Assuming that the shares are held on a long-term basis, they would be treated as a non-current asset. Any dividends received from the investment would be treated as income in the investing company's income statement.

The problem with this approach, however, is that companies normally pay dividends of much less than the profits earned for the period. The profits that are not distributed, but are ploughed back to help to generate more profits for the future, still belong to the shareholders. From the perspective of the investing company, the accounting treatment described would not, therefore, fully reflect the benefits from the investment made. Where the investment does not involve the purchase of a substantial shareholding in the company, this problem is overlooked and so the treatment of the investment described above (that is, showing the investment, at cost, as a non-current asset and taking account only of any dividends received) is applied. Where, however, the investment involves the purchase of a significant number of voting shares in the company, a different kind of accounting treatment is more appropriate.

To deal with the problem identified above, a particular type of relationship between the two companies has been defined. An **associate company** is one in which an investing company or group has a substantial, but not controlling, interest. To be more precise, it is a company over which another company can exercise significant influence regarding its operating and financial policies. If a company holds 20 per cent or more of the voting shares of another company it is presumed to be able to exercise significant influence. This influence is usually demonstrated by the investing company being represented on the board of directors of the associate company or by participation in policy making. The relevant international accounting standard (IAS 28 *Investments in Associates*) provides detailed guidelines concerning what constitutes an associate company.

The accounting treatment of an associate company falls somewhere between full consolidation, as with group financial statements, and the treatment of small share investments, as described at the beginning of this section. Let us assume that a company invests in another company, so that the latter becomes an associate of the former. The accounting treatment will be as follows:

■ The investing company will be required to produce consolidated financial statements that reflect not only its own performance and position, but also those of its associate company.
■ In the consolidated income statement, the investing company's share of the operating profit of the associate company will be shown and will be added to the operating profit of the

investing company. As operating profit represents the profit before interest and taxation, the investing company's share of any interest payable and tax relating to the associate company will also be shown. These will be deducted in deriving the profit for the year for the investing company and its associate company.

- In the consolidated statement of financial position, the investment made in the associate company will be shown and the investing company's share of any post-acquisition reserves will be added to the investment. In this way, profits of the associate that have not been paid to the investing company will be recognised in the investing company's statement of financial position. This will have the effect of showing more fully the investment in the associate company.

- Dividends received by the investing company from the associate company will not be included in the consolidated income statement. This is because the investing company's share of the associate company's profit will already be fully reflected in the consolidated income statement.

- If the investing company also has subsidiaries, their financial statements must also be incorporated, in the way that we saw for groups earlier. Thus, a company that has both subsidiary companies and associate companies will prepare just one set of consolidated financial statements reflecting all of these, irrespective of how many subsidiaries and associates it may have.

To illustrate these points, let us take a simple example.

Example 10.12

Antrim plc owns 25 per cent of the ordinary shares of Buxor plc. The price paid for the shares was £26 million. Antrim plc bought its shares in Buxor plc when the latter's reserves stood at £24 million. The reserves of Buxor plc have increased to £40 million by 31 March last year.

The income statements for Antrim plc and Buxor plc for the year ended 31 March this year are as follows:

Income statements for the year ended 31 March this year

	Antrim plc £m	Buxor plc £m
Revenues	800	100
Cost of sales	(500)	(60)
Gross profit	300	40
Operating expenses	(120)	(12)
Operating profit	180	28
Interest payable	(30)	(8)
Profit before taxation	150	20
Taxation	(40)	(4)
Profit for the year	110	16

To comply with the relevant standard (IAS 28), Antrim plc's share of the operating profit of Buxor plc, as well as its share of interest payable and taxation relating to Buxor plc, will be incorporated within Antrim plc's consolidated income statement. Antrim plc's consolidated income statement will, therefore, be as follows:

Antrim plc – Consolidated income statement

	£m	
Revenues	800	
Cost of sales	(500)	
Gross profit	300	
Operating expenses	(120)	
	180	
Share of operating profit of associate – Buxor plc	7	(25% × £28m)
Operating profit	187	
Interest payable:		
Antrim plc	(30)	
Associate – Buxor plc	(2)	(25% × £8m)
Profit before taxation	155	
Taxation:		
Antrim plc	(40)	
Associate – Buxor plc	(1)	(25% × £4m)
Profit for the year	114	

The consolidated statement of financial position of Antrim plc, treating Buxor plc as an associate company, would include an amount for the investment in Buxor plc that is calculated as follows:

Extract from Antrim plc's consolidated statement of financial position as at 31 March this year

	£m	
Cost of investment in associate company	26	
Share of post-acquisition reserves	4	(that is, 25% × (40 − 24))
	30	

Activity 10.16

What is the crucial difference between the approach taken when consolidating subsidiary company results and incorporating the results of associate companies, as far as the statement of financial position and income statement are concerned?

In preparing group financial statements, all of the items in the statements are added together, as if the parent owned them all, even when the subsidiary is less than 100 per cent owned. For example, the revenue figure in the consolidated income statement is the sum of all the revenues made by group companies; the inventories figure in the statement of financial position is the sum of all the inventories held by all members of the group.

When dealing with associate companies, we only deal with the shareholding company's share of the profit of the associate and its effect on the value of the shareholding.

Real World 10.6 looks at an associate of Associated British Foods plc.

THE ARGUMENT AGAINST CONSOLIDATION

There seems to be a compelling logic for consolidating the results of subsidiaries controlled by a parent company, to reflect the fact that the shareholders of the parent company effectively control all of the assets of all of the companies within the group. There is also, however, a fairly strong argument against doing so.

Anyone reading the consolidated financial statements of a group of companies could be misled into believing that trading with any member of the group would, in effect, be the same as trading with the group as a whole. It might be imagined that all of the group's assets could be called upon to meet any amounts owed by any member of the group. This, however, is not the case. Only assets owned by the particular group member are available to creditors of that group member. The reason for this is, of course, the legal separateness of the limited company from its shareholder(s), which in turn leads to limited liability of individual group members. There is no legal obligation on a parent company, or a fellow subsidiary, to meet the financial obligations of a struggling subsidiary. In fact, this is why some businesses operate through a series of subsidiaries, as mentioned earlier.

Despite this criticism of consolidation, the requirement to prepare group financial statements is a very popular legal requirement throughout the world.

Self-assessment question 10.1

The statements of financial position, as at 31 December last year, and income statements, for the year ended last 31 December, of Great plc and Small plc are set out below. Great plc bought its shares in Small plc on 1 January last year at which time the latter's share capital was the same as it is currently and the retained earnings balance stood at £35 million.

At the time of the acquisition, the fair value of all the assets of Small plc was thought to be the same as that shown in their statement of financial position, except for land whose fair value was thought to be £5 million more than the statement of financial position value. It is believed that there has been no impairment in the value of the goodwill arising on consolidation since 1 January last year.

Statements of financial position as at 31 December last year

	Great plc £m	Small plc £m
ASSETS		
Non-current assets		
Property, plant and equipment		
Land	80	14
Plant	33	20
Vehicles	20	11
	133	45
Investment		
16 million shares of Small plc	53	–
	186	45
Current assets		
Inventories	20	9
Trade receivables	21	6
Cash	17	5
	58	20
Total assets	244	65
EQUITY AND LIABILITIES		
Equity		
Called-up share capital:		
ordinary shares of £1 each, fully paid	100	20
Retained earnings	77	40
	177	60
Non-current liabilities		
Borrowings – loan notes	50	–
Current liabilities		
Trade payables	17	5
Total equity and liabilities	244	65

Income statements for the year ended 31 December last year

	Great plc £m	Small plc £m
Revenue	91	27
Cost of sales	(46)	(13)
Gross profit	45	14
Administration expenses	(8)	(3)
Distribution expenses	(6)	(2)
Operating profit	31	9
Interest payable	(3)	–
Profit before taxation	28	9
Taxation	(12)	(4)
Profit for the year	16	5

Required:

Prepare the statement of financial position and income statement for the group.

The solution to this question can be found at the back of the book, starting on page 525.

SUMMARY

The main points of this chapter may be summarised as follows:

Groups

- A group exists where one company (parent) can exercise control over another (subsidiary), usually by owning more than 50% of the voting shares.
- Groups arise by a parent setting up a new company or taking over an existing one.
- Businesses operate as groups in order to have limited liability for each part of the business, to give each an individual identity and to take advantage of tax relief on trading losses.
- Normally, parent companies are required to produce financial statements for the group as a whole, as if all group members' assets, liabilities, revenues, expenses and cash flows were those of the parent company directly.

Group statements of financial position

- Group statements of financial position are derived by adding like items (assets and liabilities) together and setting the equity of each subsidiary (in the subsidiary's statement of financial position) against the 'investment in subsidiary' figure (in the parent's statement of financial position).
- Inter-group company balances (receivables and payables) must be eliminated from the group statement of financial position.
- Where the equity of the subsidiary does not cancel the investment in subsidiary, it will be for three possible reasons:
  1 more (or less) was paid for the subsidiary shares than their fair value, leading to either goodwill arising on consolidation (an intangible non-current asset) or negative goodwill arising on consolidation.
  2 the parent does not own all of the shares of the subsidiary, leading to non-controlling (or minority) interests reflecting the fact that the parent's shareholders do not supply all of the equity finance to fund the group's net assets;
  3 the subsidiary has made profits or losses since it became a subsidiary.
- 'Goodwill arising on consolidation' represents the value of the ability of the subsidiary to generate additional profits as a result of an established workforce, cost synergies or sales synergies.
- Goodwill remains on the group statement of financial position, but is subject to impairment review annually and will be written down in value if it its value has diminished.
- Genuine negative goodwill should be immediately credited to the group income statement.
- It is permissible for a company to show the entire value of the goodwill of its subsidiaries, not just the parent's share of that value.
- Inter-group company balances (receivables and payables) must be eliminated from the group statement of financial position.

Group income statement

- Group income statements are derived by adding like items (revenues and expenses).

- The non-controlling (minority) shareholders' share of the after-tax profit is deducted from the group total to reflect the fact that not all of the subsidiary's profit belongs to the parent company's shareholders.

- Inter-group company trading transactions (revenues and expenses) must be eliminated from the group income statement.

Group statement of comprehensive income

- Group statements of comprehensive income are derived by adding like items.

- The statement must distinguish between comprehensive income that is attributable to non-controlling interests and that which is attributable to the shareholders of the parent company.

Group statement of cash flows

- Group statements of cash flows are derived by adding like items (cash flows).

- Inter-group company cash transfers must be eliminated from the group statement of cash flows.

Associate companies

- An 'associate company' is one in which a company has less than a controlling interest, but yet is able to exert significant influence over it, often indicated by representation on the board of directors.

- The investing company will be required to produce consolidated financial statements that reflect not only its own performance and position, and those of its subsidiaries, but also those of its associate companies.

- In the consolidated income statement, the investing company's share of the operating profit of the associate company is added to the operating profit of the investing company. Any interest payable and tax relating to the associate company will also be shown.

- In the consolidated statement of financial position, the investment made in the associate company will be shown and the investing company's share of any post-acquisition reserves will be added to the investment.

- Dividends received by the investing company from the associate company are not included in the consolidated income statement.

KEY TERMS

FURTHER READING

If you would like to explore the topics covered in this chapter in more depth, we recommend the following:

Alexander D., Britton A., Jorissen, A., Hoogendorn M. and Van Mourik C. (2017) *International Financial Reporting and Analysis*, Cengage Learning, 7th edn, Chapters 25–28.

Elliott, B. and Elliott, J. (2017) *Financial Accounting and Reporting*, 18th edn, Pearson, Chapters 22–26.

Melville, A. (2017) *International Financial Reporting: A Practical Guide*, 6th edn, Pearson, Chapters 18 to 20.

Thomas, A. and Ward, A.M. (2015) *Introduction to Financial Accounting*, 8th edn, McGraw-Hill Education, Chapter 34.

CRITICAL REVIEW QUESTIONS

Solutions to these questions can be found at the back of the book, starting on page 536.

10.1 Why is the amount for 'non-controlling interests' recalculated each time we prepare a statement of financial position, but 'goodwill arising on consolidation' is calculated just once?

10.2 There are two different approaches to calculating goodwill arising on consolidation. What factors might influence a particular company to choose one basis rather than another?

10.3 Quite often, when an existing company wishes to start a new venture, perhaps to produce a new product or render a new service, it will form a subsidiary company as a vehicle for the new venture. In other cases, however, the existing company chooses to undertake the new activity itself using the original company name. Why might it choose to do the latter?

10.4 An associate company is one over which the investing company has sufficient shares to enable it to exercise significant influence, but not control. Sufficient shares, in this context, is defined as 20 per cent or more of the shares. How can such a low percentage be regarded as giving significant influence?

EXERCISES

Solutions to exercises with coloured numbers can be found at the back of the book, starting on page 545.

Basic-level exercises

10.1 An abridged set of consolidated financial statements for Toggles plc is given below.

Toggles plc
Consolidated income statement for the year ended 30 June

	£m
Revenue	172.0
Operating profit	21.2
Taxation	(6.4)
Profit after taxation	14.8
Non-controlling interests	(2.4)
Profit for the year	12.4

Consolidated statement of financial position as at 30 June

ASSETS	£m
Non-current assets	
Property, plant and equipment	85.6
Intangible assets	
Goodwill arising on consolidation	7.2
	92.8
Current assets	
Inventories	21.8
Trade receivables	16.4
Cash	1.7
	39.9
Total assets	132.7
EQUITY AND LIABILITIES	
Equity	
Share capital	100.0
Retained earnings	16.1
	116.1
Non-controlling interests	1.3
	117.4
Current liabilities	
Trade payables	15.3
Total equity and liabilities	132.7

Required:

(a) Answer, briefly, the following questions:

1 What is meant by 'non-controlling interests' in both the income statement and the statement of financial position?

2 What is meant by 'goodwill arising on consolidation'?

3 Why will the 'retained earnings' figure on the consolidated statement of financial position usually be different from the 'retained earnings' as shown in the parent company's statement of financial position?

(b) Explain the purposes and advantages in preparing consolidated financial statements for the parent company's shareholders.

10.2 Arnold plc owns 75 per cent of the ordinary shares of Baker plc. The outline income statements of the two companies for the year ended on 31 December are as follows:

Income statements for the year ended 31 December

	Arnold plc	Baker plc
	£m	£m
Revenue	83	47
Cost of sales	(36)	(19)
Gross profit	47	28
Administration expenses	(14)	(7)
Distribution expenses	(21)	(10)
Profit before taxation	12	11
Taxation	(4)	(3)
Profit for the year	8	8

Required:

Prepare the consolidated (group) income statement for Arnold plc and its subsidiary for the year ended 31 December.

Intermediate-level exercises

10.3 Giant plc bought a majority shareholding in Jack Ltd, on 31 March. On that date, the statements of financial position of the two companies were as follows:

Statements of financial position as at 31 March

	Giant plc £m	Jack Ltd £m
ASSETS		
Non-current assets		
Property, plant and equipment		
Land	27	12
Plant	55	8
Vehicles	18	7
	100	27
Investment		
10 million shares of Jack Ltd	30	–
	130	27
Current assets		
Inventories	33	13
Trade receivables	42	17
Cash	22	5
	97	35
Total assets	227	62
EQUITY AND LIABILITIES		
Equity		
Called-up share capital:		
ordinary shares of £1 each, fully paid	50	10
Share premium account	40	5
Revaluation reserve	–	8
Retained earnings	46	7
	136	30
Non-current liabilities		
Borrowings – loan notes	50	13
Current liabilities		
Trade payables	41	19
Total equity and liabilities	227	62

Required:

Assume that the statement of financial position values of Jack Ltd's assets represent 'fair' values. Prepare the group statement of financial position immediately following the takeover.

10.4 The statements of financial position of Jumbo plc and of Nipper plc, on the date that Jumbo plc bought the shares in Nipper plc, were as follows:

Statements of financial position as at 31 March

	Jumbo plc £m	Nipper plc £m
ASSETS		
Non-current assets		
Property, plant and equipment		
Land	84	18
Plant	34	33
Vehicles	45	12
	163	63
Investment		
12 million shares of Nipper plc	24	–
	187	63
Current assets		
Inventories	55	32
Trade receivables	26	44
Cash	14	10
	95	86
Total assets	282	149
EQUITY AND LIABILITIES		
Equity		
Called-up share capital:		
ordinary shares of £1 each, fully paid	100	20
Share premium account	–	12
Retained earnings	41	8
	141	40
Non-current assets		
Borrowings – loan notes	100	70
Current liabilities		
Trade payables	41	39
Total equity and liabilities	282	149

Required:

Assume that the statement of financial position values of Nipper plc's assets represent fair values. Prepare the group statement of financial position immediately following the share acquisition.

10.5 The summary statements of financial position for Apple plc and Pear Limited are set out below.

Statements of financial position as at 30 September

	Apple Limited £000	Pear Limited £000
ASSETS		
Non-current assets		
Property, plant and equipment	950	320
Investment		
Shares in Pear Limited	240	–
	1,190	320
Current assets		
Inventories	320	160
Trade receivables	180	95
Cash at bank	41	15
	541	270
Total assets	1,731	590
EQUITY AND LIABILITIES		
Equity		
£1 fully paid ordinary shares	700	200
Reserves	307	88
	1,007	288
Non-current liabilities		
Loan notes	500	160
Current assets		
Trade payables	170	87
Taxation	54	55
	224	142
Total equity and liabilities	1,731	590

Apple plc purchased 150,000 shares in Pear Ltd at a price of £1.60 per share on 30 September (the above statement of financial position date). The statement of financial position of Pear Ltd reflects all of the assets of the company, net of liabilities, stated at their fair values.

Required:
Prepare a consolidated statement of financial position for Apple plc as at 30 September.

Advanced-level exercises

10.6 Abridged financial statements for Harvest plc and Wheat Limited as at 30 June this year are set out below. On 1 July last year Harvest Limited acquired 800,000 ordinary shares in Wheat Limited for a payment of £3,500,000. Wheat Ltd's share capital and share premium were the same throughout. Similarly, the assets in the statement of financial position of Wheat Limited were shown at fair market values throughout.

Statements of financial position as at 30 June this year

	Harvest plc £000	Wheat Limited £000
ASSETS		
Non-current assets		
Property, plant and equipment	10,850	4,375
Investment		
Shares of Wheat Limited	3,500	–
	14,350	4,375
Current assets	3,775	1,470
Total assets	18,125	5,845
EQUITY AND LIABILITIES		
Equity		
Share capital (£1 shares)	2,000	1,000
Share premium account	3,000	500
Revenue reserves at 1 July last year	2,800	375
Profit for the current year	399	75
	8,199	1,950
Non-current liabilities		
Bank loans	7,000	2,500
Current liabilities	2,926	1,395
Total equity and liabilities	18,125	5,845

Required:

Prepare the consolidated statement of financial position for Harvest plc as at 30 June this year, using the data given above.

10.7 A year ago Pod plc bought 225,000 £1 fully paid ordinary shares of Pea Limited for a consideration of £500,000. Pea Limited's share capital and share premium were the same as at today's date. Simplified statements of financial position for both companies as at today's date, after having traded as a group for a year, are set out below. The statement of financial position of Pea Ltd reflects all of the assets of the company, net of liabilities, stated at their fair values.

Statements of financial position as at today

	Pod plc £	Pea Limited £
ASSETS		
Non-current assets		
Property, plant and equipment	1,104,570	982,769
Investment		
Shares in Pea Limited	500,000	–
	1,604,570	982,769
Current assets		
Inventories	672,471	294,713
Trade receivables	216,811	164,517
Amounts due from subsidiary company	76,000	–
Cash	2,412	1,361
	967,694	460,591
Total assets	2,572,264	1,443,360
EQUITY AND LIABILITIES		
Equity		
Share capital: £1 ordinary shares	750,000	300,000
Share premium	250,000	50,000
Reserves as at a year ago	449,612	86,220
Profit for year	69,504	17,532
	1,519,116	453,752
Non-current liabilities		
Bank loan	800,000	750,000
Current liabilities		
Trade payables	184,719	137,927
Amounts owing to holding company	–	76,000
Borrowings – overdraft	68,429	25,681
	253,148	239,608
Total equity and liabilities	2,572,264	1,443,360

Required:
Prepare a consolidated statement of financial position for Pod plc and its subsidiary company as at today's date.

10.8 The statements of financial position for Maxi plc and Mini Limited are set out below:

Statements of financial position as at 31 March this year

	Maxi plc £000	Mini Limited £000
ASSETS		
Non-current assets		
Property, plant and equipment	23,000	17,800
Investment		
1,500,000 shares in Mini Limited	5,000	–
	28,000	17,800
Current assets		
Inventories	5,000	2,400
Trade receivables	4,280	1,682
Amounts owed by Maxi plc	–	390
Cash at bank	76	1,570
	9,356	6,042
Total assets	37,356	23,842
EQUITY AND LIABILITIES		
Equity		
10,000,000 £1 ordinary shares, fully paid	10,000	
2,000,000 50p ordinary shares, fully paid		1,000
Share premium account	3,000	2,000
Retained earnings at beginning of year	3,100	2,080
Profit for the year	713	400
	16,813	5,480
Non-current liabilities		
Bank loans	13,000	14,000
Current liabilities		
Trade payables	3,656	2,400
Other payables	1,047	1,962
Amounts owed to Mini Limited	390	–
Short-term borrowings – overdraft	2,450	–
	7,543	4,362
Total equity and liabilities	37,356	23,842

On 1 April last year, Maxi plc bought 1,500,000 shares of Mini Limited for a total consideration of £5 million. At that date Mini Limited's share capital and share premium were each the same as shown above. The statement of financial position of Mini Ltd reflects all of the assets of the company, net of liabilities stated at their fair values.

Required:
Prepare a consolidated statement of financial position for Maxi plc at 31 March this year.

Chapter 11

INCREASING THE SCOPE OF FINANCIAL REPORTING

INTRODUCTION

In Chapter 5, we examined the main financial statements published by large businesses. In this chapter, we shall go on to consider other financial statements that may be published. We begin by taking a look at segmental reports, which are prepared by larger businesses with more than one type of business activity. We shall see that these reports provide a more detailed breakdown of key information already contained within the main financial statements.

We continue by discussing the nature and role of summary financial statements. These financial statements reflect a contrary philosophy to that of segmental reports. Rather than providing more information than is contained within the main financial statements, they provide less. The form and content of summary financial statements will be discussed, along with the issues that this form of reporting raises.

Interim financial reports were developed to help investors track the progress of businesses more frequently than on an annual basis. We shall take a look at what financial statements and other information is provided within these reports. We shall also consider the key measurement issues that arise from preparing financial statements for a period shorter than one year.

The value added statement is concerned with measuring the wealth created by a business over a period. In this sense, it is similar to the income statement. Although once a popular element within the annual financial reports, it has since become less popular. It is, nevertheless, still worth examining as it provides a different perspective on how business performance may be defined and measured.

Finally we consider the impact of inflation on the financial statements. We shall see that inflation can seriously distort the measurement of both financial performance and position. We shall examine the two main schools of thought as to how to take account of inflation in the financial reports. We shall see that each school reflects a particular view concerning how equity should be maintained.

Learning outcomes

When you have completed this chapter, you should be able to:

■ explain the purpose of segmental reports and describe their main features;

■ set out the advantages and disadvantages of publishing summary financial statements

■ discuss the role of interim financial statements and outline the key measurement and reporting requirements of IAS 34;

■ explain the purpose of the value added statement and prepare a simple value added statement from available information;

■ describe the impact of inflation on the measurement of financial position and performance and outline the two main approaches to dealing with inflation in financial statements.

THE DEVELOPMENT OF FINANCIAL REPORTING

Let us begin by placing the additional financial reports to be discussed in historical context. Financial reporting has been around for many hundreds of years. It seems to have emerged as a result of one or more persons having custody and management of assets belonging to one or more others. Examples might include a farm manager looking after land owned by another person, or a merchant ship's captain taking goods, owned by someone else, overseas and selling them. In circumstances like these, the owners would normally require that the steward (that is, the person looking after the assets) report on how the assets were deployed and the degree of success achieved. These reports were often expressed in financial terms and gave rise to what is known as 'stewardship accounting'.

Limited liability companies first came into being during the middle of the nineteenth century. Their introduction increased a tendency for assets, that were owned by one group of people (the shareholders), to be managed by another group (the directors). In the early days of the limited liability company there was no stringent requirement to publish financial statements and to have them audited. Nevertheless, many companies did so.

Activity 11.1

Why do you think many companies did so?

It was largely in response to pressure from investors who were reluctant to part with their money without relevant feedback, in the form of periodic financial reports, from the directors.

The published financial statements reduced uncertainty in the minds of investors. Not only did this make them more willing to invest their money, but they were also prepared to do so for expectations of a lower rate of return. There is quite strong evidence to suggest that greater disclosure of financial information tends to lower a company's cost of capital (that is, the required rate of return for shareholders and other providers of finance) (see Reference 1 at the end of the chapter). Thus, directors may have an incentive to disclose financial information in order to lower the cost of capital and, in turn, generate greater wealth.

Relying on market forces to determine the form and content of financial reports is, however, a risky business. Directors control access to financial information about their companies and it is not always in their interests to ensure that the truth is revealed in a timely and accurate way. Furthermore, investors may be widely dispersed and find it difficult to act collectively. Shareholders may, therefore, be in a weak position to exert pressure on the directors. Given these problems, it is not surprising that the 'market model', as it is called, resulted in abuses and led, inevitably, to calls for regulation.

The past century and a half has been characterised by a movement away from market-led financial reporting towards a highly elaborate regulatory environment. The UK government started the ball rolling with the Companies Act 1862, which recommended the preparation of a rudimentary income statement and statement of financial position each year (as well as an audit of the latter). This was followed by a succession of Companies Acts, with each requiring greater financial disclosure. Since the 1970s accounting standard-setting bodies have been created in various countries. In addition, the IASB has been brought into being to produce global accounting standards. The IASB now represents a major source of financial reporting regulation and has contributed considerably towards the mountain of rules. It has more than 40 standards currently in existence (see Chapter 5, page 166).

The relentless increase in reporting requirements has created some disquiet. Doubts have been raised as to whether the growing complexity of financial statements has led to an improvement in their usefulness. There is concern that both accounting regulators and businesses have lost a sense of focus and forgotten the purpose for which financial statements are prepared. Thus, a major challenge for the future is to produce better regulation, rather than simply more of it. The quality of financial statements is dependent on regulators ensuring that rules are clearly targeted and are proportionate to the problems that they address. It is also dependent on businesses providing financial statements that are as clear, open and understandable as possible within the rules that exist.

FROM STEWARDSHIP TO DECISION MAKING

We have seen that, in the early days of financial reporting, stewardship was the key issue. It was concerned with recounting what had happened so as to make stewards (managers) accountable and, hopefully, more careful in deploying the assets of the owner. Over time, however, the focus of interest among users changed towards its decision-making potential. This has resulted in regulation becoming more targeted on making financial statements useful as decision-making tools. This change raises the question as to how this should be done.

Decision making involves making predictions about the future. To help users, financial reporting should therefore have a *predictive role*. That is to say, it should enable users to make reliable predictions about future profits and cash flows. However, it should also have a *confirmatory role*. That is, it should also enable users to confirm whether past predictions turned out to be reliable. In the sections that follow we consider a number of additional financial reports. In evaluating their usefulness, their predictive value or confirmatory value for users is, therefore, a critical factor.

Let us now turn our attention to segmental financial reports. Preparing these reports is obligatory for many larger businesses.

SEGMENTAL FINANCIAL REPORTS

Most large businesses are engaged in a number of different operations, with each having its own levels of risk, growth and profitability. Information relating to each type of business operation, however, is normally aggregated (added together) in the financial statements so as to provide an overall picture of financial performance and position for the business as a whole. For example, the revenue figure at the top of the income statement represents all of the business's revenues. This will be true even where the revenues come from quite different activities. Although this aggregation of information can help to provide a clearer broad picture, it can make it difficult to undertake comparisons over time or between businesses. Some idea of the range and scale of the various types of operation must be gained for a proper assessment of financial health. Thus, to undertake any meaningful analysis of financial performance and position, it is usually necessary to disaggregate the information contained within the financial statements. This disaggregated information is disclosed in segmental financial reports.

By breaking down the financial information according to each type of business operation, or operating segment, we can evaluate the relative risks and profitability of each segment and make useful comparisons with other businesses or other business operating segments. We can also see the trend of performance for each operating segment over time and so determine more accurately the likely growth prospects for the business as a whole. We should also be able to assess more easily the impact on the overall business of changes in market conditions relating to particular operating segments.

Disclosure of information relating to the performance of each segment may also help to improve the efficiency of the business.

Activity 11.2

Can you think why this may be the case?

Operating segments that are performing poorly will be revealed, which should put pressure on managers to take corrective action.

Where an operating segment has been sold, the shareholders will be better placed to assess the wisdom of the managers' decision to sell it.

Segmental reporting rules

An IASB standard (IFRS 8 *Operating Segments*) requires listed companies to disclose information about their various operating segments. Defining an operating segment, however, can be a tricky business. The IASB has opted for a 'management approach', which means that an operating segment is defined by reference to how management has segmented the business for internal reporting and monitoring purposes. An operating segment is, therefore, defined as a part of the business that:

- generates revenues and expenses,
- has its own separate financial statements, and
- has its results regularly reviewed for resource-allocation and assessment purposes by management.

Not all parts of the business will meet the criteria identified. The headquarters of the business ('head office'), for example, is unlikely to do so.

Activity 11.3

What do you think are the main advantages of adopting the management approach? Try to think of at least one.

Three advantages spring to mind:

1 Shareholders will receive similar reports to the internal reports produced for management, which means that they can assess business performance from the same viewpoint as management.
2 There will no delays in reporting the information to shareholders as the information has already been produced.
3 Additional, perhaps significant, reporting costs will be avoided for the same reason as mentioned in 2 above.

There are, of course, other ways of identifying an operating segment. One approach would be to define a segment according to the industry to which it relates. This, however, may lead to endless definition and classification problems.

To be reported separately, an operating segment must be of significant size. This normally means that it must account for 10 per cent or more of the combined revenue, profits or assets of all operating segments. A segment that does not meet this size threshold may be combined with other similar segments to produce a reportable segment, or separately reported despite its size, at the directors' discretion. If neither of these options is chosen, it should be reported with other segments under a separate category of 'all other segments'.

Segmental disclosure

Financial information to be disclosed includes some profit (or loss) measure (for example, operating profit) for each segment, along with the following income statement items, provided that they are regularly reported to management:

■ revenue, distinguishing between revenue from external customers and revenue from other segments of the business;
■ interest revenue and interest expense;
■ depreciation and other material non-cash items;
■ material items of income and expense;
■ any profit (loss) from associate companies or joint ventures; and
■ income tax (where it is separately reported for a segment).

The business must also disclose the total assets and the total liabilities for each segment, along with any additions to non-current assets during the period, if these are regularly reported to management. Where these items are not regularly reported to management, they need not be included in the segmental report that appears in the business's annual report.

Example 11.1 provides an illustrative segmental financial report for a business.

Example 11.1

Goya plc
Segmental report for the year ended 31 December 2018

	Publishing £m	Film-making £m	All other £m	Totals £m
Revenue from external customers	150	200	25	375
Inter-segment revenue	20	10	–	30
Interest revenue	10	–	–	10
Interest expense	–	15	–	15
Depreciation	40	20	5	65
Reportable segment profit	15	19	4	38
Other material non-cash items:				
Impairment of assets	–	10	–	10
Reportable segment assets	60	80	12	152
Expenditures for reportable				
segment non-current assets	12	18	2	32
Reportable segment liabilities	25	32	4	61

We can see that information relating to each segment, as well as a combined total for all operating segments, is shown.

Key items, which include revenues, profits, assets, and liabilities, must be reconciled with the corresponding amounts for the business as a whole. For example, Goya plc's income statement should show revenue of £375 million for the business as a whole. When carrying out a reconciliation, we should bear in mind that:

- inter-segment revenues should be eliminated as no transaction with external parties occurs;
- any profit arising from inter-segment transfers should also be eliminated; and
- assets and liabilities that have not been allocated to a particular segment should be taken into account.

The last item normally refers to assets and liabilities relating to business-wide activities. Thus, head office buildings may provide an example of unallocated assets, and staff pension liabilities may provide an example of unallocated liabilities.

IFRS 8 requires certain non-financial information concerning segments to be disclosed, including the basis for identifying operating segments and the types of products and services that each segment provides. It also requires business-wide information, such as geographical areas of operations and reliance on major customers, to be disclosed.

Segmental reporting problems

Various problems arise when preparing segmental reports, not least of which is identifying a segment. We have already seen that the relevant IFRS identifies operating segments according to the internal reporting and monitoring procedures of the business. While this may be the most sensible course of action, comparisons between segments in other businesses may be impossible because of the different ways in which they are defined.

Another problem may arise where there is a significant amount of sales between operating segments. Where this occurs, the **transfer price** of the goods or services between segments can have a substantial impact on the reported profits of each segment. (The transfer price is the price at which sales are made between different segments of the business.) A potential risk is that revenues and profits will be manipulated for each segment through the use of particular transfer pricing policies.

Real World 11.1 indicates the extent of the use of transfer pricing by multinational businesses to avoid UK tax.

Real World 11.1

A taxing issue

Multinationals avoided paying as much as £5.8 billion in UK corporate taxes last year by booking profits in overseas entities, a 50 per cent increase over previous government forecasts, according to newly published estimates from British tax authorities.

'The standards of what is acceptable in transfer pricing have changed,' said Sanjay Mehta, a partner at law firm Katten Muchin Rosenman. 'HMRC has invested heavily in the area of transfer pricing as this is an area of growing complexity and there is a recognition of historic underpayment of tax by some large corporates.' Transfer pricing now represents almost a quarter of the total £25 billion tax potentially underpaid by large businesses last year – up from 17 per cent the previous year, according to Pinsent Masons, the law firm.

 Source: Extracts from Marriage, M. (2017) Multinationals avoid up to £5.8bn in UK tax, HMRC finds, ft.com, 24 October. © The Financial Times Limited 2017. All rights reserved.

IFRS 8 recognises the impact of transfer pricing policies on segmental revenues and profit by stating that the basis for accounting for transactions between segments must be disclosed.

A final problem is that some expenses and assets may relate to more than one operating segment and their allocation between segments may vary between businesses. Again, this may hinder comparisons of segmental profits and profitability between businesses.

Should segmental results be published?

It has been argued that, despite the benefits mentioned, the publication of segmental results can damage a business. Information is revealed that would otherwise be hidden. This may undermine the competitive position of a business and may attract new entrants into the industry. Revealing the segmental results may also inhibit managers from taking risks. Losses incurred in one operating segment cannot be obscured by profits generated in others.

Although these arguments carry some truth, they do not build a case for non-disclosure of segmental results. If a single operating unit is set up as a separate company, rather than as a segment of a large business, the financial disclosure requirements become even more demanding. On the grounds of equity, therefore, there is an argument for greater disclosure of segmental results rather than less.

Real World 11.2 is the segmental report for Asos plc, the online fashion retailer. Note how Asos defines a segment on the basis of geography. Unlike many businesses, Asos is largely focused on a single activity.

Real World 11.2

Dividing up the world: segmental analysis

IFRS 8 'Operating Segments' requires operating segments to be determined based on the Group's internal reporting to the Chief Operating Decision Maker. The Chief Operating Decision Maker has been determined to be the Executive Board who receive information on the basis of the Group's operations in key geographical territories, based on the Group's management and internal reporting structure. The Executive Board assesses the performance of each segment based on revenue and gross profit after distribution expenses, which excludes administrative expenses.

Year to 31 August 2017

	UK	US	EU	RoW	Total
	£m	£m	£m	£m	£m
Retail sales	698.2	261.6	544.1	372.6	1,876.5
Delivery receipts	16.1	6.3	10.8	7.6	40.8
Third-party revenues	6.0	0.2	0.1	–	6.3
Total revenues	720.3	268.1	555.0	380.2	1,923.6
Cost of sales	(389.7)	(103.5)	(292.4)	(179.7)	(965.3)
Gross profit	330.6	164.6	262.6	200.5	958.3
Distribution expenses	(81.9)	(69.2)	(89.8)	(58.3)	(299.2)
Segment result	248.7	95.4	172.8	142.2	659.1
Administrative expenses					(579.5)
Operating profit					79.6
Finance income					0.4
Profit before tax					80.0

Note: RoW = rest of world.
Source: Asos plc, 2017 Annual report, p. 85.

SUMMARY FINANCIAL STATEMENTS

We saw in Chapter 5 that each shareholder has the right to receive a copy of the annual financial statements. These financial statements can be extremely detailed and complicated. Along with accompanying notes, they may extend over many pages. Some shareholders, however, may not want to receive such detailed information. They may not have the time, interest or skill necessary to be able to gain much from it. Reproducing and posting copies of the full annual financial statements is expensive. It can therefore be argued that it is a waste of resources where shareholders are unlikely to benefit.

Until some years ago in the UK, the directors had the option to provide a summarised version of the full financial statements to shareholders who agreed to this. This option did not, however, interfere with the shareholders' right to receive the full version of the financial statements if they so wished. It became common practice for large businesses to send shareholders, who were private individuals, a copy of the summary financial statements. These were accompanied with a clear message that a copy of the full version was available on request. Institutional investors (insurance companies, pension funds and so on) still received a full version as a matter of routine.

Legal regulations relating to summary financial statements set out the following minimum information requirements:

- a summary income statement, showing corresponding amounts for the previous period;
- any dividends recognised and proposed;
- a summary statement of financial position, showing corresponding amounts for the previous period;
- a summary directors' remuneration report (for listed businesses only); and
- any other information needed to ensure the summary financial statements were consistent with the full version of the financial statements.

In addition, independent auditors were required to provide an opinion as to whether the summary financial statements were consistent with the full annual financial statements.

To alert shareholders to the limitations of summary financial reports, a 'health warning' had to be included. This was a statement to the effect they did not contain information for as complete an understanding of the results and state of affairs of the business as provided by the full financial statements.

Should summary financial statements be published?

The option for shareholders to receive a summary financial statements in place of the full version has now been revoked. Some mourn their passing. They argue that these statements met the needs of less financially-sophisticated shareholders. As a result, communication between directors and shareholders was enhanced. Critics of summary financial statements, however, take a different view.

Activity 11.5

What is the main reason why shareholders require financial information about the business? (*Hint*: Think back to Chapter 1.)

Shareholders require financial information in order to make decisions concerning whether to buy, hold or sell shares in the business.

When making investment decisions, summary financial statements provide a poor substitute for the full financial statements. Despite the 'health warning' mentioned earlier, shareholders may, nevertheless, rely on them for this purpose. By doing so, they place themselves at a distinct disadvantage, to those who rely on the full statements.

Summary financial statements attempt to simplify complexity. This runs the risk of discarding important information and distorting the message. If a shareholder is unwilling or unable to develop the necessary accounting skills, or to spend the necessary time, to examine the full version of the financial statements, the appropriate response is either to seek expert advice or to invest in mutual funds managed by experts. When considered from this viewpoint, the best thing that a business can do to help such shareholders is to provide more detailed information to experts, such as investment analysts.

Finally, summary financial statements may impede efforts to improve the quality of financial reporting. It was argued in an earlier section that both regulators and businesses must rise to the challenge of providing clear and understandable financial statements. The excessive complexity contained within the full annual statements needs to be tackled. There may be less incentive to do so, however, where summarised reports are provided for less financially-sophisticated users.

The option to provide summary financial statements was replaced by an option to provide a strategic report, along with certain supplementary information, in place of the full annual report. Where this option is exercised, the strategic report must be the same as that contained within the annual report. The supplementary material must include information relating to the audit report that appears in the annual report and, for Stock Exchange listed companies, extracts from the directors' remuneration report. There is nothing, however, to stop the directors going beyond the minimum legal requirements and providing further information, such as extracts from the annual reports or summarised versions of information within the annual report. Any further information provided will normally depend on the perceived information needs of share-holders and so will vary from company to company.

It can be argued that the problems discussed in relation to summary financial reports are not resolved where shareholders exercise this option. There is no real substitute for the full annual report when making investment decisions.

And finally . . .

Summary financial statements have not entirely disappeared from the financial reporting land-scape. To accord with good practice, they may be used by a listed company when providing a five-year financial summary of performance and position. In this context, they do not provide a substitute for the full financial statements but rather a supplement to them. **Real World 11.3** illustrates how a summary income statement and statement of financial position (balance sheet) can be used to present trends over time.

Real World 11.3

To summarise . . .

FirstGroup plc, the passenger transport business, provides a summary income statement and statement of financial position (balance sheet) as part of its five-year financial summary. In its 2017 annual report, they were presented as follows:

Consolidated balance sheet

	2017 £m	2016 £m	2015 £m	2014 £m	2013 £m
Non-current assets	4,524.9	4,201.3	4,025.1	3,686.7	4,060.3
Net current liabilities	(153.0)	(239.3)	(160.9)	(78.4)	(320.4)
Non-current liabilities	(2,011.8)	(2,066.5)	(2,141.3)	(2,123.7)	(2,602.3)
Provisions	(284.2)	(262.3)	(236.7)	(261.6)	(323.1)
Net assets	2,075.9	1,633.2	1,486.2	1,223.0	814.5

Consolidated income statement

	2017 £m	2016 £m	2015 £m	2014 £m	2013 £m
Group revenue	5,653.3	5,218.1	6,050.7	6,717.4	6,900.9
Operating profit before amortisation charges and other adjustments	339.0	300.7	303.6	268.0	254.1
Amortisation charges	(60.2)	(51.9)	(54.3)	(53.4)	(52.0)
Other adjustments	4.8	(2.5)	(3.5)	17.6	(62.3)
Operating profit	283.6	246.3	245.8	232.2	139.8
Net finance cost	(132.0)	(132.4)	(139.7)	(156.1)	(163.2)
Ineffectiveness on financial derivatives	1.0	(0.4)	(0.3)	(17.6)	(5.5)
Profit/(loss) before tax	152.6	113.5	105.8	58.5	(28.9)
Tax	(36.5)	(17.1)	(20.3)	5.7	23.9
Profit/(loss) for the year	116.1	96.4	85.5	64.2	(5.0)

The presentation and content of the five-year financial summary are not tightly prescribed and so can vary considerably between companies.

Source: Extracts from Group Financial Summary, FirstGroup plc, Annual Report and Accounts 2017, p. 142.

INTERIM FINANCIAL STATEMENTS

Interim financial statements were first published in the US at the turn of the last century and began to appear in the UK in the 1950s. The main impetus for their publication came from progressive managers who felt that the interval between annual financial statements is too long for users to be without information. Now, interim financial statements are an integral part of the financial reporting cycle of most large businesses. Regulatory authorities, particularly Stock Exchanges, have been the major reason for this. Producing half-yearly or quarterly interim financial statements is usually an important listing requirement.

Activity 11.6

The London Stock Exchange requires listed businesses to produce half-yearly interim financial statements. The US Securities and Exchange Commission (SEC), on the other hand, requires listed businesses to produce quarterly financial statements.

What are the advantages and disadvantages of producing interim financial statements on a quarterly, rather than a half-yearly, basis?

Quarterly statements will track more closely financial progress throughout the year and will provide more timely information to users than half-yearly statements. This may, however, be achieved at the expense of reliability. The shorter the reporting period, the greater the need for estimates as there is not enough time for events to unfold. This leads to a greater risk of inaccuracy and error. The costs of quarterly reporting will also be greater.

The precise role of interim financial statements has proved to be a source of contention. Some believe that they are simply a supplement to the annual financial statements, their purpose being to provide timely information that can help in predicting annual profits or losses.

This is to say that they are seen as early indicators of the full-year's results. Others, however, believe that they should not focus simply on helping to predict the future. They should also help to confirm the results of earlier predictions. Like annual financial statements, they could have both a predictive and a confirmatory role and there is no reason why they should not. A year, after all, is an arbitrary reporting period and annual financial statements rarely cover the operational cycle of a business.

Measuring interim profit

How the role of interim financial statements is viewed has important implications for the measurement of interim profit. Two methods of measuring interim profit have been proposed, with each reflecting one side of the debate. The **integral method** of profit measurement sees the interim period as being simply part of the annual reporting period. It seeks to provide a measure of interim profit that can be used to help predict the annual profit. To do this, annual expenses are predicted and then a proportion of these are allocated to the interim period based on the proportion of annual sales revenue generated in that period. Under this approach, interim and annual profit margins are maintained at a fairly consistent level. The **discrete method** of profit measurement, on the other hand, treats the interim period as quite separate and distinct from the annual period. It is not primarily concerned with predicting annual profit and adopts accounting methods and policies for measuring interim profit that are the same as those used to measure annual profit. In other words, it treats the interim period as a freestanding one, in much the same way that the measurement of profit in the annual report does.

Example 11.2 should make the differences between the two methods clear.

Example 11.2

Varna plc is a large retailer that produces interim financial statements on a half-yearly basis. The business has produced the following estimates for the forthcoming year:

1 Revenue will be £40 million for the first half-year and £100 million for the whole year.
2 Cost of sales will be 50 per cent of sales revenue.
3 Administration expenses will be fixed at £1.5 million per month for the first six months of the year and £2.5 million per month thereafter.
4 The business will sponsor a sports event at a total cost of £5 million in the first half year. The benefits from the sponsorship deal are expected to benefit the whole year.

The estimated interim profit for the first half year, calculated using the integral and discrete methods, will be as follows:

	Estimated interim profit	
	Integral	Discrete
	£m	£m
Revenue	40.0	40.0
Cost of sales (50%)	(20.0)	(20.0)
Administration − (40/100 × £24m)	(9.6)	
− (6 × £1.5m)		(9.0)
Sponsorship − (40/100 × £5m)	(2.0)	
	−	(5.0)
Interim profit	**8.4**	**6.0**

Notes:

1 The discrete method uses the same approach to profit measurement as for the annual period. Expenses are assigned to the particular period in which they are incurred. The sponsorship cost will be written off in the first half year even though the benefits are expected to extend into the second half year. This cost would not meet the definition of an asset at the year end and so is not deferred at the end of an interim period.

2 The integral method apportions the total annual expenses between the two half-year periods based on the level of activity. Thus, the first half year is charged with 40% (that is, £40m/£100m) of the total expenses for the year.

Let us now calculate annual profit to see how interim profit, when derived using the integral method, may be helpful for prediction purposes.

	Estimated annual profit
	£m
Revenue	100.0
Cost of sales (50%)	(50.0)
Administration ((6 × £1.5m) + (6 × £2.5m))	(24.0)
Sponsorship	(5.0)
Profit for the year	21.0

Interim profit, based on the integral method, represents 40 per cent of the annual profit (£8.4m/£21m = 40%). This, of course, is the same as the percentage of interim sales to annual sales (£40m/£100m = 40%). In other words, (interim sales/annual sales)% = (interim profit/annual profit)%. (See Reference 2 at the end of the chapter.) If users can predict sales for the second half of the year, this should provide a good basis for predicting profit. (Having ploughed through this example, you may wonder whether, instead of adopting the integral approach, it would be better simply to provide external users with a profit forecast for the year.)

The International Accounting Standards Board (IASB) has produced a standard for interim financial statements (IAS 34 *Interim Financial Reporting*). It applies to all businesses that either are required, or wish, to prepare these statements in line with international standards. The standard favours the discrete approach to income measurement and states that accounting policies and methods adopted at the interim stage should be in line with those adopted at the annual stage. One problem, however, is that certain items, such as tax, can only be considered in the context of the year as a whole. The standard deals with the tax problem by stating that the tax rate applied to interim profit should be based on the average effective tax rate for the year as a whole.

Interim financial disclosure

There is nothing to stop a business producing a comprehensive set of financial statements for the interim period, although cost and timeliness considerations will usually make this impractical. IAS 34 recognises that a full reporting option is available to businesses and therefore sets out the *minimum* components of interim financial statements. The standard requires:

- a condensed statement of financial position;
- a condensed statement of comprehensive income (either as a single statement or as a separate income statement plus a statement of comprehensive income);
- a condensed statement of changes in equity;
- a condensed statement of cash flows; and
- selected explanatory notes.

Headings and subtotals appearing in the condensed (summarised) financial statements should be in line with those appearing in the most recent annual financial statements. This should help users to track events occurring since the annual statements were published.

Activity 11.7

What do you think is the main risk of preparing condensed interim financial statements? (*Hint*: Think back to the earlier section where we considered summary financial statements.)

The main risk is that, if an attempt is made to simplify complex reality, important information may be lost and the message may become distorted.

The standard assumes that users will have access to the most recent annual report and so explanatory notes focus on issues relating specifically to the interim reporting period. These include:

- confirmation that the interim financial statements use the same accounting policies and methods as those used for the annual financial statements;
- suitable explanations concerning the seasonality and cyclicality of business operations;
- the nature and amount of any unusual items affecting assets, liabilities, income and cash flows;
- details of the issue/redemption of loans or share capital and dividends paid;
- information relating to business segments; and
- details of significant events, including changes in the composition of the business, changes in contingent assets or liabilities, and material events affecting the business after the end of the interim period.

These disclosure requirements should enable users to glean a fair amount of information concerning the financial progress of the business.

Interim reports and short-termism

Interim financial statements are generally regarded as a valuable contribution to financial reporting. Nevertheless, they have attracted criticism. It is claimed that they encourage investors to focus on short-term fluctuations in the fortunes of a business. This, in turn, can lead managers to strive for good results in the short-term, even though this could damage long-term competitiveness.

Activity 11.8

Can you think of two examples where, in an effort to boost short-term profits, managers may make decisions that undermine long-term performance?

The following examples spring to mind:

- cutting back on training programmes for employees;
- reducing expenditure on research and development;
- investing in projects with an immediate return at the expense of projects with a slower, but higher, return; and
- cancelling, or delaying, marketing campaigns or refurbishment programmes.

You may have thought of others.

We should not, however, overstate the extent to which publishing interim statements can influence management behaviour. Much will depend on the way in which management remuneration is structured. To ensure that managers retain a long-term focus, their pay and incentives should be designed accordingly.

Let us now turn our attention to a financial statement that offers a different perspective on how financial performance may be measured.

THE VALUE ADDED STATEMENT

The **value added statement (VAS)** came to prominence in the mid 1970s following publication of an influential discussion document entitled *The Corporate Report* (see Reference 3 at the end of the chapter). This report argued for the inclusion of the VAS within the annual report. It regarded the VAS as an important financial statement and went so far as to suggest that the VAS might one day become more important than the income statement. Following publication of *The Corporate Report*, two government reports lent further support for the inclusion of the VAS within the annual reports of large businesses.

The VAS is similar to the income statement insofar that they are both concerned with measuring wealth created by a business over time. The key difference between the two, however, is the way in which wealth is defined and measured. The VAS measures *value added* whereas the income statement measures *profit earned*.

What is value added?

Value added is an alternative measure of the wealth generated by a business over time. A business can be seen as buying in goods and/or services to which it then 'adds value'. Taking the total output of the business and then deducting the cost of total inputs provides the amount of value added. This is shown diagrammatically in Figure 11.1.

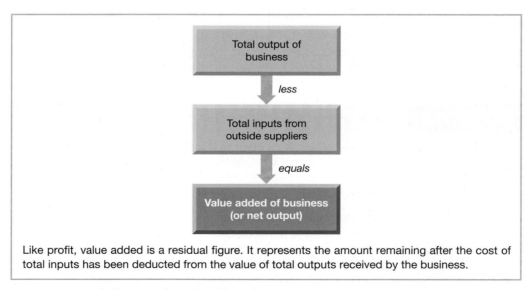

Like profit, value added is a residual figure. It represents the amount remaining after the cost of total inputs has been deducted from the value of total outputs received by the business.

Figure 11.1 Calculating value added by a business

The total output of the business will normally be the sales revenue for the period. The total inputs will be the bought-in materials and services such as the purchase of inventories, rent, rates, electricity, telephone, postage and so on. The difference between total outputs and total inputs, which is the value added, represents the wealth generated from the collective effort of those with a stake in the business – that is, employees, suppliers of capital and government.

Value added is a broader measure of wealth than profit. It recognises that various groups contribute to, and have a stake in, the wealth generated by a business and it seeks to measure how much wealth is attributable to these 'stakeholders'. This is in contrast to the measure of profit, which is concerned only with the wealth attributable to the owners (that is, the shareholders).

Preparing a value added statement

The VAS begins by measuring the value added by a business and then goes on to show how it is distributed among the key 'stakeholders'. Example 11.3 shows the layout for a value added statement.

Example 11.3

Value added statement for the year ended 30 June

	£m
Revenue	130.6
Bought-in materials and services	(88.4)
Value added	42.2
Applied in the following way:	
To employees	
Wages, pensions and fringe benefits	28.1
To suppliers of capital	
Interest payable on loans	2.6
Dividends to shareholders	3.8
	6.4
To pay government	
Tax payable	3.2
To provide for maintenance and expansion of assets	
Depreciation of non-current assets	3.0
Retained earnings	1.5
	4.5
	42.2

We can see that, in the first part of the VAS, valued added is derived by deducting the cost of bought-in materials and services from sales revenue. The second part then shows how much value added is divided between the various stakeholder groups and how much is retained within the business. (Depreciation and retained earnings represent amounts reinvested to maintain and expand the asset base.)

The VAS does not provide any information that is not already contained within the conventional income statement. It is simply a rearrangement of the income statement. It is claimed, however, that through this rearrangement new insights concerning the performance of the business may be gained.

Ray Cathode (Lighting Supplies) plc has produced the following income statement for the year to 31 December:

Income statement for the year ended 31 December

	£m
Revenue	198
Cost of sales	(90)
Gross profit	108
Salaries and wages	(35)
Rent and rates	(18)
Insurance	(3)
Light and heat	(10)
Postage and stationery	(1)
Advertising	(4)
Depreciation	(19)
Operating profit	18
Interest payable	(6)
Profit before taxation	12
Taxation	(4)
Profit for the year	8

During the year a dividend of £3 million was announced and paid.

From the above information, see if you can produce a value added statement for the year to 31 December. (Use the format in Example 11.3 above to guide you.)

Your answer should be as follows:

Value added statement for the year ended 31 December

	£m
Revenue	198
Bought-in materials and services (90 + 18 + 3 + 10 + 1 + 4)	(126)
Value added	72
Applied in the following way:	
To employees	
Salaries and wages	35
To suppliers of capital	
Interest payable on loans	6
Dividends to shareholders	3
	9
To pay government	
Tax payable	4
To provide for maintenance and expansion of assets	
Depreciation of non-current assets	19
Retained profits (8 − 3)	5
	24
	72

What useful information can you glean from the VAS in Activity 11.9?

The VAS reveals that nearly half of the value added generated by the business during the year was distributed to employees in the form of salaries and wages. This proportion is much higher than that distributed to suppliers of capital. A relatively high proportion of value added being distributed to employees is not unusual. The business retained one-third of the value added to replace and expand the assets. A high proportion of value added retained may suggest a concern for growth to be financed through internally generated sources. The proportion of value added required to pay tax is relatively small.

Benefits of the VAS

The VAS helps to promote the message that a business is a coalition of interests and that business success depends on co-operation between the various stakeholders. It may even foster better relations by encouraging a team spirit among those with a stake in the business. If employees are identified as important stakeholders, they may feel more part of the business team and respond by showing greater co-operation and commitment. The VAS may also help managers to appreciate that employees are team members and not simply an expense, as portrayed in the conventional income statement.

A further benefit claimed for the VAS is that some useful ratios can be derived from this statement. These include:

- value added to sales revenue (per cent);
- value added per £1 of wages and salaries (£);
- dividends to value added (per cent);
- tax to value added (per cent);
- depreciation and retentions to value added (per cent); and
- value added to capital employed (per cent).

Calculate each of the above ratios using the information contained in the solution to Activity 11.9 above. How could these ratios be useful? (For purposes of calculation, assume that the business's capital employed is £80 million.)

Your answer should be as follows:

$$\text{Value added to sales revenue} = \frac{72}{198} \times 100\% = 36.4\%$$

The lower this ratio is, the greater will be the reliance on outside sources of materials and services. For example, a wine retailer that purchases its wine from a wholesaler will have a lower ratio than a wine retailer that owns its own vineyards and bottling facilities. A low ratio may indicate vulnerability to difficulties caused by external suppliers.

$$\text{Value added per £1 of wages} = \frac{72}{35} = £2.06$$

$\rightarrow$

This ratio is a measure of labour productivity. In this case, the employees are generating £2.06 of value added for every £1 of wages expended: the higher the ratio, the higher the level of productivity. Normally, the ratio would be higher than 1.0. A ratio of less than 1.0 would indicate that employees are being paid more than the value of their output.

$$\text{Dividends to value added} = \frac{3}{72} \times 100\% = 4.2\%$$

This ratio shows the portion of value added that will be received in cash, more or less immediately, by shareholders. The trend of this ratio may provide an insight into the distribution policy of the business over time. It is important to remember, however, that shareholders also benefit, in the form of capital growth, from amounts reinvested in the business. Thus, the ratio is only a partial measure of the benefits received by shareholders.

$$\text{Tax to value added} = \frac{4}{72} \times 100\% = 5.6\%$$

This ratio indicates that portion of the value added which is payable to government in the form of taxes. It may be useful in assessing whether the business has an unfair burden of taxation.

$$\text{Depreciation and retentions to value added} = \frac{24}{72} \times 100\% = 33.3\%$$

This ratio provides some indication of the way that finance is raised. A high ratio may indicate that finance for new investment tends to be raised from internal sources rather than from external sources, such as borrowing or new share issues.

$$\text{Value added to capital employed} = \frac{72}{80} \times 100\% = 90\%$$

This ratio is a measure of the productivity of capital employed. A high ratio is, therefore, normally preferred to a low ratio.

Value added is an important measure in preparing the UK National Accounts. **Real World 11.4** provides a measure of gross value added for the UK, broken down into different industrial sectors.

Real World 11.4

Value added by UK plc

Analysis of broad industrial groups shows that in 2015 the 'government, health and education' and 'distribution, transport, hotel and restaurant' industries provided the largest contributions to gross value added at current basic prices, with values of £306.7 billion and £306.1 billion, respectively, out of a total of £1,685 billion (about 18 per cent in each case).

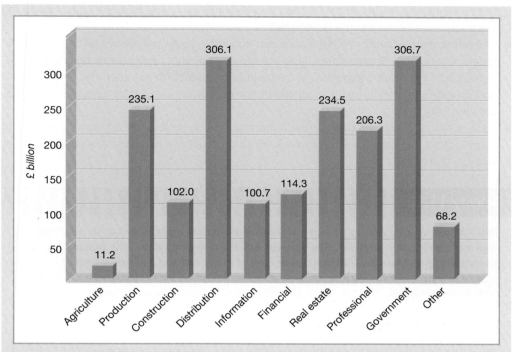

Figure 11.2 Breakdown of gross value added at basic prices by industry 2015

Source: Office for National Statistics (2017) Explanation of industry analysis, www.ons.gov.uk, 31 October.

Problems of the VAS

The proposal to include a VAS as part of the annual report was initially greeted with enthusiasm. At the peak of its popularity, it was included in the annual reports of almost one-third of the hundred largest listed businesses. This peak has long passed, however, and now the VAS has become a rare sighting in financial reports.

Although the VAS simply rearranges information contained in the conventional income statement, the effect of this rearrangement is to raise a number of thorny theoretical and practical problems. Many of these problems remain unresolved, leaving doubts over its usefulness. The more important of these problems are:

- *The team concept.* Some dismiss the idea of a business being a team of stakeholders working together as no more than a public relations exercise. It is seen as a misguided attempt to obscure the underlying conflict between suppliers of capital and employees.
- *Team membership.* Even if the team concept is accepted, there is room for debate about the nature and composition of the team. Suppliers, for example, may work closely with a business to ensure the timely flow of goods and services, yet cannot be treated as team members because of the way in which value added is calculated. They may, however, have a stronger case for being considered team members than, say, government, which may have little contact with a business, apart from when collecting taxes.
- *The classification of items.* The VAS is beset with classification problems. For example, gross payments to employees (that is, wages before tax and national insurance payments are deducted) are normally shown under the heading 'To employees'. Yet it is the government that receives the taxation and National Insurance payments. Employees will receive

their salaries and wages net of taxation and National Insurance, with the employer paying the deductions directly to the government.

- *The importance of profit.* Within a capitalist economy, profit will always be at the heart of financial reporting. Shareholders, who are the owners and principal risk takers, are concerned with the returns from their investment. If managers do not keep this firmly in mind and provide shareholders with acceptable returns, they are likely to be replaced by managers who will.
- *Loss of focus.* There is a danger that if managers become too concerned with increasing value added this may have an adverse effect on profit. To illustrate this point, consider Activity 11.12.

Activity 11.12

Ray Von plc is considering whether to make a particular component or to purchase the item from an outside supplier. Ray Von can sell the component for £40. Making the component would involve Ray Von in a labour cost of £12 a unit and a material cost of £18. The cost of buying the item from an outside supplier would be £26. Calculate both the value added and profit arising from one unit of the component under each option.

Your answer should be as follows:

	Buy-in £	Make £
Selling price	40	40
Bought-in materials	(26)	(18)
Value added	14	22
Labour costs	(–)	(12)
Profit	14	10

We can see that making the item will provide a higher value added but a lower profit than buying in. Thus, a decision to maximise value added would be at the expense of profit.

Finally, it is worth making the point that the profit generated by a business is likely to be important to various stakeholders and not simply to shareholders. Lenders will be interested in the profit generated to enable them to assess the riskiness of their loan; governments will be interested for taxation purposes; and employees will be interested for the assessment of likely future pay increases and job security. So far, there has been a failure to demonstrate that value added is as useful for decision-making purposes as profit.

Reporting value added

Although the VAS now rarely appears in the annual reports of UK businesses, some of them still use this statement when reporting business performance to employees. It may then be portrayed in diagrammatic form for ease of understanding. For example, the application of total value added of Ray Cathode (Lighting Supplies) plc that we met earlier in Activity 11.9 can be represented in the form of a pie chart, as in Figure 11.3.

Reporting value added only to employees, however, raises an issue of credibility. Employees may well ask why a financial report that is not regarded as being important to other users is being provided to them. They may feel it is mainly to demonstrate the extent to which value

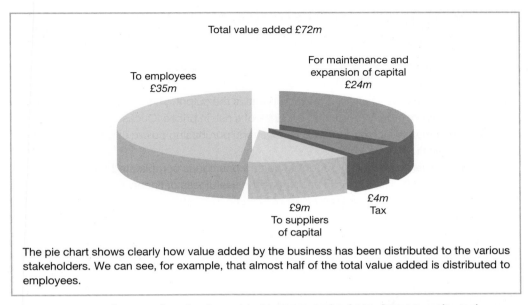

Total value added £72m

For maintenance and expansion of capital £24m

To employees £35m

£9m To suppliers of capital

£4m Tax

The pie chart shows clearly how value added by the business has been distributed to the various stakeholders. We can see, for example, that almost half of the total value added is distributed to employees.

Figure 11.3 Distribution of total value added by Ray Cathode (Lighting Supplies) plc

added is absorbed by salaries and wages. As mentioned earlier, a sizeable proportion of total value added is usually distributed to employees.

Although UK businesses rarely include a VAS with their annual reports, elsewhere in the world they seem to be more popular. Sri Lanka appears to be an example of where the VAS is found. **Real World 11.5** sets out the VAS of one business, Nestle Lanka plc. This business is the Sri Lanka branch of the Swiss business whose many branded products tend to be in the areas of food and confectionery.

Real World 11.5

Something of value

Value added statement for the year ended 31 March 2017

	Rs 000s	%
Direct economic value generated		
Revenue	36,461,695	
Bought out goods and services	(22,362,679)	
Value added	14,099,016	
To government as taxes/duties	6,841,153	48.5
To employees as remuneration and other benefits	2,190,313	15.5
To lenders as interest	43,732	0.3
To shareholders as dividends	4,298,037	30.5
Retained with business (including depreciation)	725,781	5.2
	14,099,016	100.0

Source: Nestle Lanka plc, Annual Report 2016, p. 111.

INFLATION ACCOUNTING AND REPORTING

We saw in Chapter 2 that there is an assumption in accounting that money, which is the unit of measurement, will remain stable over time. This, however, is an unrealistic assumption as the value of money changes. Usually, it is inflation that is the culprit. This occurs when the general purchasing power of money is reduced because of a rise in prices. Occasionally, however, it is because of deflation, which occurs when the general purchasing power of money is increased because of a fall in prices.

The measurement of financial performance and position is complicated by changes in the value of money and this, in turn, can undermine the usefulness of financial statements. We are now going to consider the distorting effect of inflation in financial reporting as it is this, rather than deflation, that has been the more persistent problem over the years. We shall see that inflation results in an overstatement of profit and an inadequate portrayal of financial position. We shall also consider two broad approaches that attempt to correct for the distorting effects of inflation in the financial statements.

Inflation and profit measurement

During a period of inflation, profit tends to be overstated. This is because time elapses between buying a particular resource and its subsequent use. Inventories are a good example of this problem, as illustrated in Example 11.4.

Example 11.4

Kostova Car Sales Ltd acquired a new Mercedes motor car for £25,000 as part of its showroom inventories. The car was held for three months before being sold to a customer for £30,000. The cost of replacing the vehicle from the manufacturer increased during the three-month inventories holding period to £26,250. This was in line with the general rate of inflation for that period. What is the profit made on the sale of the motor car?

The conventional approach to measuring profit is to match the selling price of the vehicle with the original cost of acquisition. Thus, the conventionally derived profit will be £5,000:

	£
Sale of motor car	30,000
Cost of acquisition	(25,000)
Profit	5,000

Where the value of money is constant, this approach can produce a valid result. Where, however, prices are rising, there is a problem. The original acquisition cost will understate the resources consumed. During the inventories holding period, the cost of replacing the car increased in line with the rate of inflation. (This is to say that the *average* purchasing power of money, as measured by the general rate of inflation, and the *specific* purchasing power of money, as measured by changes in the cost of the car, decreased by the same amount during the inventories holding period.) Given this loss of purchasing power, the original cost of the car is no longer a meaningful measure of the resources consumed during the period. It would be more realistic to calculate the profit for the period by taking the difference between the selling price and cost of the new car *expressed in current terms*.

This means the inflation-adjusted profit will be £3,750:

	£
Sale of motor car	30,000
Current purchase cost of car	(26,250)
Profit	3,750

We can see that, if the current purchase cost of the car is substituted for the original cost, the profit for the period is lower. It can be argued that, unless this is done, profits will be overstated.

The problem of time elapsing between the acquisition of a resource and its ultimate use is even more acute in the case of non-current assets. A non-current asset, such as a building, may be held for many years and the income statement for each of these years will be charged with its depreciation. Where this charge is based on the acquisition (historic) cost of the asset, it will become increasingly out of date and so will not reflect the resources consumed during the period. Unless revenues are matched with depreciation charges expressed in current terms, profits will be overstated.

Inflation and financial position

During a period of rising prices, financial statements based on historic cost do not adequately portray financial position. There are three potentially serious problems:

- an erosion of the equity base may not be clearly recognised;
- the assets of the business will tend to be understated; and
- any gains and losses from holding monetary items will not be recognised.

Let us now consider each of these problems.

Maintaining the equity base

If the owners are to maintain the purchasing power of their investment and the business is to maintain its scale of operations, the equity base of the business must be kept intact. There is a risk, however, that inflation will erode this base and that the statement of financial position will fail to indicate that this erosion has occurred. To illustrate this point, let us consider Example 11.5.

Example 11.5

Habbad Enterprises sells software packages to small businesses. The statement of financial position of the business at the beginning of a period is:

Statement of financial position at beginning of the period

	£
ASSETS	
Inventories (20 packages @ £100)	2,000
EQUITY	
Opening equity	2,000

$\rightarrow$

During the period, the business managed to sell all of the software packages for cash for £150 each. The conventionally derived profit for the period would be £1,000 (that is, 20 × £(150 − 100)) and the statement of financial position at the end of the period would be:

Statement of financial position at the end of the period

		£
ASSETS		
Cash (20 × £150)		3,000
EQUITY		
Opening equity		2,000
Profit for the period		1,000
		3,000

When prices are constant, it would be possible for Habbad Enterprises to distribute the whole of the reported profit for the period to the owners and still retain the equity base intact. That is, the distribution would not have an adverse effect on the purchasing power of the owners' investment in the business, or the ability of the business to maintain its scale of operations. Following the distribution of profits, £2,000 would still remain, representing the equity at the start of the period.

Let us assume, however, that the general rate of inflation during the period was 10 per cent and the cost of the software packages increased in line with this rate. To ensure that the owners' investment in the business is kept intact and the business is able to continue its current scale of operations, it would not now be possible to distribute all of the profits as conventionally measured.

Activity 11.13

What amount of profit do you think could be distributed to the owners of Habbad Enterprises without any adverse effect on the equity base?

As the general rate of inflation was 10 per cent during the period, and the cost of software packages increased in line with this rate, the equity base must be increased by this amount to preserve the owners' investment and to ensure that the existing scale of operations can be maintained. The equity at the end of the period should, therefore, be:

$$£2,000 + (10\% × £2,000) = £2,200$$

As the equity at the end of the period is £3,000, the amount that can be distributed will be:

$$£3,000 − £2,200 = £800$$

Calculating profit by matching revenue with the cost of purchases expressed in current terms will also provide a measure of the amount that can be safely distributed to owners. Hence:

	£
Sales revenue (20 @ £150)	3,000
Cost of packages in current terms (20 @ £110)	(2,200)
Profit	800

Maintaining the equity base and profit measurement are really two sides of the same coin. Profit can be defined as the amount that may be distributed to the owners without eroding the equity base.

Reporting assets

During a period of rising prices, the acquisition (historic) cost of assets acquired becomes outdated. Current values will be higher and so reporting assets using their original costs will tend to understate the financial position: the higher the rate of inflation, the greater this understatement.

It is worth remembering that assets held at the end of a reporting period will normally be acquired at different dates. Consider an example involving equipment (a non-current asset), where the total amount held at the end of a particular reporting period was acquired at various times, as follows:

Equipment at cost

	£
Acquired 31 March 2013	48,000
Acquired 30 June 2016	64,000
Acquired 20 September 2018	82,000
	194,000

During a period of inflation, the purchasing power of the pound will be quite different at each acquisition date. The total cost of this group of assets (£194,000) appearing on the statement of financial position will, therefore, be meaningless. In effect, the pounds spent at the various dates represent different currencies, each with different purchasing power.

Activity 11.14

What will be the effect of inflation on the calculation of key profitability ratios such as the operating profit margin and return on capital employed (ROCE)?

As profit is normally overstated during a period of inflation, profitability ratios will tend to be higher. Where profit is related to capital employed (net assets), such as in the ROCE ratio, this problem is compounded. This is because the capital employed (net assets) of the business tends to be understated.

Monetary items

Some items appearing on a statement of financial position have a fixed number of pounds assigned to them. The particular amount may be fixed by contract or by statute and will not change as a result of inflation. These are known as monetary items.

Activity 11.15

Can you think of any monetary assets or monetary liabilities that would appear on a statement of financial position? Try to think of at least one of each.

Examples of monetary assets would be trade receivables and cash. Examples of monetary liabilities would be borrowings, bank overdrafts, trade payables and tax owing.

It is important to identify monetary items. This is because holding monetary assets during a period of inflation will result in a loss of purchasing power. Holding monetary liabilities, on the other hand, will lead to a gain. Example 11.6 illustrates this point.

Example 11.6

A business holds a constant £1,000 in cash during a year when inflation is at the rate of 20 per cent. As a result, the purchasing power of the cash held will be lower at the end of the year than at the beginning. Those goods and services, which would have cost £1,000 at the beginning of the period, would, on average, cost £1,200 by the end of the period. This represents a loss of purchasing power of £200 (in terms of end-of-period £s) over the period.

This loss of purchasing power will have a real effect on the business's ability to preserve the capital invested by the owners and on its ability to maintain its scale of operations.

The reverse situation will apply where a monetary liability is held during a period of inflation. The liability will be reduced, in real terms, and so the owners will make a gain at the expense of the lenders. These monetary gains and losses may be significant but will not be reported in the conventional financial statements. This is because money is the unit of measurement and it cannot measure changes in its own purchasing power.

Reporting the effects of inflation

The distorting effects of inflation on the conventional financial statements can be severe. Even relatively low inflation rates can have a significant cumulative effect over time. To combat the problem, various methods of accounting for inflation have been proposed and there has been much debate as to which should be adopted. At the heart of the debate lies the problem of equity maintenance and, in particular, how equity maintenance should be defined. If this problem is resolved, other problems, such as the way in which profit is measured and how assets should be reported, can then be resolved.

Approaches to equity maintenance

Two broad approaches to equity maintenance have competed for acceptance. We shall now discuss both of them.

Maintaining the owners' investment

The first approach is concerned with ensuring that the *general purchasing power of the owners' investment in the business* is maintained during a period of inflation. To do this, a general price index, such as the Retail Price Index (RPI), is used to measure changes in the purchasing power of the pound. (A general price index is constructed by taking a basket of goods and services at a particular point in time and expressing their total cost at a base value of 100. The prices of these goods and services are then measured regularly over time and any changes are expressed in relation to the base value.) A set of financial statements is then prepared using the price index measures for different dates.

Financial transactions occurring at different dates will be expressed in terms of their purchasing power at a single, common date – normally the end of the reporting period. This is done by adjusting for the change in the price index between the date of the transaction and the end of the reporting period. Profit available for distribution will be derived by expressing both the revenue received and the cost of the goods sold for the period in terms of their current (end-of-reporting-period) purchasing power. The cost of assets acquired will also be expressed in terms of their current purchasing power.

To illustrate how **current (or constant) purchasing power (CPP) accounting** works, let us look at Example 11.7.

Example 11.7

Konides and Co. commenced trading on 1 August when the RPI stood at 110. The conventional financial statements of the business showed the opening statement of financial position as follows:

Statement of financial position as at 1 August

	£
ASSETS	
Cash	<u>280,000</u>
EQUITY	
Opening equity	<u>280,000</u>

On 1 August, inventories were purchased for cash at a cost of £200,000 and land was acquired at a cost of £80,000. The inventories were sold on 31 August for £250,000 cash when the RPI stood at 121. No other transactions took place during the month.

The CPP profit for the period is calculated by matching revenues and costs of goods sold *after* the amounts have been expressed in terms of their purchasing power at the end of August. Thus, the CPP income statement will be as follows:

CPP income statement for the period to 31 August

	CPP £
Sales revenue (250,000 × 121/121) (Note 1)	250,000
Cost of sales (200,000 × 121/110) (Note 2)	(220,000)
Profit for the period	<u>30,000</u>

Notes:

1 The sales revenue is already expressed in terms of current purchasing power as the sale of inventories took place on the last day of the reporting period.

2 The cost of sales figure is adjusted as the inventories were acquired at an earlier date. [Note that where there are lots of sales and purchases that accrue evenly over the period, an average index for the period tends to be used as the denominator (bottom figure) when making adjustments.]

The CPP statement of financial position at the end of August will be as follows:

CPP statement of financial position as at 31 August

	CPP £
ASSETS	
Non-current assets	
Land (£80,000 × 121/110) (Note 1)	88,000
Current assets	
Cash (Note 2)	250,000
Total assets	338,000
EQUITY	
Equity (£280,000 × 121/110) (Note 3)	308,000
Retained earnings	30,000
Total equity	338,000

Notes:

1 The value for land has been adjusted to reflect changes in the purchasing power of the pound since the date of acquisition.

2 Cash has not been adjusted as it is a monetary item that stays fixed irrespective of changes in the purchasing power of the pound. (There is no loss on holding cash during the period as it was received at the end of the period.)

3 To maintain the equity base, the opening equity will have to be increased by £280,000 × 121/110 = CPP £308,000. This has been achieved and so the owners' investment in the business has been maintained.

Activity 11.16

We have seen that maintaining the owners' investment relies on the use of a *general* price index. From the owners perspective, can you think of a problem with this?

The main problem is that a general price index may not reflect the particular cost of goods and services for individual owners.

Maintaining business operations

The second approach to maintaining equity intact is concerned with ensuring that the business is able to maintain its scale of operations. To do this, the specific price changes that affect the business must be taken into account when preparing the financial statements. **Current cost accounting (CCA)** is an important method of accounting for specific price changes. It is mainly, but not exclusively, based on the current cost of replacing an item. Thus, the current cost rather than the historic cost of items are reported.

Under CCA, the profit available for distribution is normally calculated by matching revenue with the cost of replacing the goods that were sold. In many cases, price changes that affect a business will not correspond to general price changes occurring within the economy (although, for the sake of convenience, we assumed in earlier examples that the specific price of goods changed in line with the general rate of inflation).

Example 11.8

Referring to Konides and Co. (see Example 11.7), let us assume that the cost of replacing the inventories sold rose by 20 per cent and the value of the land rose by 5 per cent during August. Using the specific purchasing power approach to accounting for inflation, the profit for the period would be:

CCA income statement for the period to 31 August

	£
Sales revenue	250,000
Cost of sales (£200,000 + (20% × £200,000))	(240,000)
Profit for the period	10,000

We can see that the cost of sales is increased by 20 per cent to reflect the current replacement cost of the goods sold.

CCA statement of financial position as at 31 August

	£
ASSETS	
Non-current assets	
Land (£80,000 + (5% × £80,000)) (Note 1)	84,000
Current assets	
Cash (Note 2)	250,000
Total assets	334,000
EQUITY	
Equity (£280,000 + £4,000 + £40,000) (Note 3)	324,000
Retained earnings	10,000
Total equity	334,000

Notes:

1 The value for land has been adjusted to reflect changes in replacement cost since the date of acquisition.

2 Cash has not been adjusted as it is already shown at replacement cost.

3 To maintain the equity base, the opening equity must be increased to reflect the increase in the replacement cost of the land (£4,000) and inventories (£40,000), giving (£280,000 + £4,000 + £40,000) = £324,000. This allows the business to maintain its scale of operations. Konides and Co. could pay out £10,000 to its owners and still be left with £240,000 to replace the inventories just sold. Thus it would be able to maintain the same level of operations.

We have seen that CCA regards maintaining the operating capacity of the business as important. Can you think of any circumstances where it would not be important?

There would be no point in maintaining operating capacity if demand for the goods or services produced by the business was falling.

Which method is better?

There is a clear philosophical divide between the two approaches regarding the issue of equity maintenance. We have seen that the CPP approach seeks to protect the general purchasing power of the owners' investment, so that the owners would still have the same command over goods and services generally. The CCA approach, on the other hand, seeks to maintain the scale of business operations, so that the business can continue operating at the same level. Choosing between the two approaches will inevitably involve a value judgement as to whether it is the owners' investment or the business entity that is of paramount importance.

It could be argued that the two approaches are not mutually exclusive and that annual financial reports could incorporate both. In other words, the business could produce CPP, CCA and historic cost financial statements. This would provide users with a fuller picture. It, however, ignores, or at least underplays, the reporting costs involved and problems of interpreting the various statements for less sophisticated users.

The two approaches (CPP and CCA) reflect, to some extent, the familiar tension in accounting between verifiability and relevance. The CPP approach is often commended for its verifiability. The historic cost of items is normally used as the basis for making adjustments and the adjustments are made using a generally-accepted index. The relevance of some of the CPP information produced, however, is questionable. In Example 11.7 above, we saw that the value for land had been adjusted to take account of the general rise in prices. We also saw, however, that the current value (replacement cost) of the land did not rise in line with the general rate of inflation. We may well ask, therefore, what is the point of reporting the CPP figure relating to the land? How can it be used for decision-making purposes?

The CCA approach is often commended for its relevance. The current value of land appearing on the statement of financial position, for example, may help in decisions as to whether to hold or to sell this item. The verifiability of the information, however, may be an issue, particularly where assets are unique and where there is no market for them. Sometimes, the spectre is raised of unscrupulous directors manipulating CCA figures to portray a picture of financial health that they would like users to see. Hiring independent, professional valuers to provide the CCA information may, however, mitigate this risk.

CPP and CCA differ in their choice of measurement unit. The CPP approach abandons 'real' money as the unit of measurement and replaces it with a synthetic measure; pounds of current purchasing power. Many users, however, may find this measurement unit difficult to understand and so may struggle to interpret the significance of CPP financial statements. The CCA approach, on the other hand, continues to use money as the unit of measurement. (A consequence of using different measurement units is that the profit calculated under each approach cannot be easily compared.)

The vital importance of money for business transactions, and for accounting measurement, cannot be overstated. It is, after all, money that is received from customers and that is used to pay dividends, suppliers, taxes and so on. This means that, if the CPP approach is adopted, it can only provide information in the form of supplementary reports. The conventional financial statements, on which the CPP adjustments are based, will remain the centrepiece of financial reporting. CCA financial statements, on the other hand, could replace, rather than be supplementary to, the conventional financial statements.

The future

The inflation accounting debate has lost its intensity in recent years as most of the industrialised world has enjoyed relatively low rates of inflation. Preparers and users display little enthusiasm for including inflation accounting statements within the financial reports. Furthermore, accounting regulators have given the issue low priority and have, instead, grappled with issues that they see as more pressing. For the moment, therefore, historic cost still provides the foundation upon which financial reports are prepared.

Activity 11.18

Can you think of any arguments in favour of sticking with historic cost financial statements and excluding inflation-adjusted statements from the annual reports? Try to think of at least three.

Various arguments exist, including the following:

- Historic cost accounting is a 'tried and tested' approach with which users are familiar.
- It provides objective, verifiable information that can help reassure users of the integrity of the financial statements.
- It is based on actual transactions that have been carried out.
- It avoids some of the key weaknesses of CPP and CCA. (For example, it uses money as the unit of measurement and does not rely on valuations that may prove to be incorrect.)
- There is a lack of agreement concerning which of the two approaches to dealing with inflation should be adopted.

You may have thought of others.

The weaknesses of the historic cost approach, however, are widely recognised. This has led to a number of international accounting standards either allowing, or requiring, current values to be used rather than historic costs. Thus, a form of modified historic cost accounting is already being employed by many businesses. In the future, it is possible that current values will take centre stage in the measurement of profit and the portrayal of financial position. This may be as a result of further progress in developing a conceptual framework for accounting and/or a less benign inflationary environment.

Self-assessment question 11.1

You have overheard the following comments:

(a) 'Stewardship accounting is concerned with determining the profit earned in the various bars on cruise ships.'
(b) 'The market model of financial reporting deals with the accounts of street traders.'
(c) 'IFRS 8 requires that businesses produce segmental accounts on a geographical basis, with each region being treated as a separate segment. Any segment with less than 10 per cent of a business's combined revenue can aggregate that segment's results with those of other, similar, segments.'
(d) 'In a segmental report, segmental revenues must not include revenues for transfers between segments.'
(e) 'Interim financial statements are the first draft of the annual financial statements which are adjusted for events that occur after the year-end date to derive the final version that is sent to the shareholders.'
(f) 'A business's value added is generally taken to be its sales revenue.'
(g) 'CPP financial statements are based on the historic cost statements.'
(h) 'In inflation accounting, monetary items are those aspects of the business that appear in the financial statements with a monetary value.'
(i) 'CCA is particularly concerned with maintaining the spending power of the shareholders' investment over a range of goods and services.'

Required:
Discuss each of the statements pointing out any errors and explaining them fully.

The solution to this question can be found at the back of the book, starting on page 525.

SUMMARY

The main points of this chapter may be summarised as follows:

Developments in financial reporting

- Initially, financial reports were unregulated and only prepared in response to investors' demands for information.
- Stewardship accounting is the reporting by the custodians of assets, to their owners, as to how effectively the assets have been deployed. Company directors can be viewed as a steward in this context.
- Abuses arising from the provision of unregulated reports led to financial reporting regulation and the need for independent audit.
- Financial reporting regulation from government, and more recently from standard setters, has increased dramatically over the past 150 years.
- In the future the challenge is to provide better, rather than more, regulation.

Segmental reports

- Segmental reports disaggregate information on the financial statements to help users to achieve a better understanding of financial health.
- An operating segment is defined by the IASB using the 'management approach'.
- IFRS 8 requires certain information relating to each segment to be shown.
- The way in which an operating segment is defined can hinder comparisons of segments between businesses.

Summary financial statements

- Summary financial statements offer a condensed version of the full financial statements.
- They aim to improve communication between the directors and those shareholders with less sophisticated information needs.
- Critics argue, however, that it is dangerous to try to simplify complexity.

Interim financial statements

- Interim financial statements may be seen as supplements to the annual financial statements or as separate financial statements in their own right.
- The integral method of interim profit measurement reflects the predictive role of interim financial statements. It aims to smooth out annual expenses between interim periods in order to enhance the ability of interim statements to help users to predict annual profit.
- The discrete method of interim profit measurement reflects the role of interim financial statements in both confirming past predictions and predicting the future. It uses the same accounting policies and methods as those used for annual financial statements.
- IAS 34 favours the discrete method but requires the tax rate applied to interim profit to reflect the average effective tax rate for the year.
- IAS 34 sets out minimum disclosure requirements for interim reports. These consist of condensed financial statements and explanatory notes.

Value added statements (VAS)

- Value added = Total outputs − Total inputs.
- The VAS consists of two parts: a calculation of value added and a description of how value added was applied.

- The VAS has a number of problems, including the team concept, team membership and the classification of items.
- Within a capitalist economy, value added has only limited usefulness as a measure of wealth creation.

Inflation accounting and reporting

- Inflation can lead to an overstatement of profit.
- Inflation can also undermine the portrayal of financial position. Problems include obscuring erosion of the equity base, understatement of asset values, and failure to show gains and losses on holding monetary items.
- Two broad approaches to accounting for inflation have been proposed. Each reflects a different view about how equity is maintained.
- Current purchasing power (CPP) accounting focuses on the general purchasing power of the owners' investment.
- Current cost accounting (CCA) focuses on maintaining a business's scale of operations.

KEY TERMS

For definitions of these terms, see at the back of the book, starting on page 514.

REFERENCES

1 Mangena, M., Jing, Li, and Tauringana, V. (2016) Disentangling the effects of corporate disclosure on the cost of equity capital: A study of the role of intellectual capital disclosure, *Journal of Accounting, Auditing & Finance*, Vol. 31(1), pp. 3–27.
2 Green, D. (1964) Towards a theory of interim reports, *Journal of Accounting Research,* Spring, pp. 35–49. (Note: Variations to this integral model can be found in the literature.)
3 Accounting Standards Committee (1975) *The Corporate Report*, ASC.

FURTHER READING

If you would like to explore the topics covered in this chapter in more depth, we recommend the following:

Alexander, D., Britton, A., Jorissen, A., Hoogendorn, M. and Van Mourik, C. (2017) *International Financial Reporting and Analysis*, Cengage Learning, 7th edn, Chapters 4–7.

Elliot, B. and Elliot, J. (2017) *Financial Accounting and Reporting*, 18th edn, Pearson, Chapters 6 and 7.

IASC Foundation Education (2016) *A Guide through International Financial Reporting Standards*, IFRS 8 and IAS 34.

Morley, M. (1978) *The Value Added Statement*, Gee Publishing.

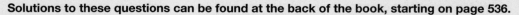
Solutions to these questions can be found at the back of the book, starting on page 536.

11.1 'Including a VAS as part of the annual financial reports will undermine their credibility.' What might be the basis for such criticism and do you think that it is valid?

11.2 'CCA is not a method of accounting for inflation. There is really only one method and that is CPP.' What might be the justification for such a statement?

11.3 Can you think of any drawbacks in providing interim financial statements for users?

11.4 What problems does a user of segmental financial statements face when seeking to make comparisons between businesses?

EXERCISES

Solutions to exercises with coloured numbers can be found the back of the book, starting on page 545.

Basic-level exercises

11.1 It has been suggested that too much information might be as bad as too little information for users of annual reports. Explain.

11.2 'The value added statement simply rearranges information contained within the conventional income statement. As a result it is of little value to users.' Discuss the validity of this statement.

Intermediate-level exercises

11.3 What problems are likely to be encountered when preparing summary financial statements for shareholders?

11.4 The following information has been taken from the accounts of Buttons Ltd for the year ended 30 September:

	£
Revenue	950,000
Materials	(220,000)
Wages and salaries	(160,000)
Other expenses	(95,000)
Depreciation	(80,000)
Operating profit	395,000
Interest	(45,000)
Profit before taxation	350,000
Taxation	(110,000)
Profit for the year	240,000

During the year a dividend of £120,000 was announced and paid.

Required:
(a) Prepare a value added statement for Buttons Ltd for the year ended 30 September.
(b) State and comment upon the reasons why a business may present a value added statement to its shareholders in addition to an income statement.

11.5 Refer to your answer to Exercise 11.4 above. Calculate ratios that you believe could be used to interpret the VAS for Buttons Ltd. Explain the purpose of each ratio.

Advanced-level exercises

11.6 Segmental information relating to Dali plc for the year to 31 December 2018 is shown below:

	Car parts £m	Aircraft parts £m	Boat parts £m	Total £m
Revenues from external customers	360	210	85	655
Inter-segment revenues	95	40	–	135
Interest revenue	34	–	–	34
Interest expense	–	28	8	36
Depreciation	80	55	15	150
Reportable segment profit	20	24	18	62
Other material non-cash items:				
Impairment of assets	–	39	–	39
Reportable segment assets	170	125	44	339
Expenditures for reportable segment:				
Non-current assets	28	23	26	77
Reportable segment liabilities	85	67	22	174

Required:
Analyse the performance of each of the three main business segments for the year and comment on your results.

11.7 Alkrom plc, an oil trader, commenced trading on 1 January and had the following opening statement of financial position:

Statement of financial position as at 1 January

	£m
ASSETS	
Cash	20.0
EQUITY	
Opening equity	20.0

On 1 January Alkrom plc acquired offices at a cost of £4m, and 320,000 barrels of oil at £50 per barrel; both acquisitions were paid for immediately. The company held on to the oil as oil prices were expected to rise in the following months. On 31 March all the oil was sold on credit for £60 per barrel.

The RPI stood at 115 on 1 January and 120 on 31 March.

Required:
Prepare a CPP income statement for the three-month period to 31 March and a CPP statement of financial position as at 31 March. (Ignore taxation and depreciation and work to one decimal place.)

11.8 Segmental information relating to Turner plc for the year to 30 April 2018 is shown below:

	Software £m	Electronics £m	Engineering £m	Totals £m
Revenues from external customers	250	230	52	532
Inter-segment revenues	45	25	–	70
Interest revenue	18	–	–	18
Interest expense	–	25	–	25
Depreciation	60	35	10	105
Reportable segment profit	10	34	12	56
Other material non-cash items:				
Impairment of assets	–	5	–	5
Reportable segment assets	140	90	34	264
Expenditures for reportable segment:				
Non-current assets	22	12	10	44
Reportable segment liabilities	55	38	4	97

Required:

Analyse the performance of each of the three main business segments for the year and comment on your results.

Chapter 12

GOVERNING A COMPANY

INTRODUCTION

In Chapter 4, we saw that corporate governance, which concerns the way in which companies are directed and controlled, has become an important issue. Strenuous efforts have been made to improve standards of corporate governance, particularly for large listed companies. In this chapter, we consider the framework of rules that has been created to ensure that appropriate checks and balances are in place and that key governance issues are addressed.

We continue our examination of corporate governance matters by considering the role and composition of the board of directors. As part of this examination, we shall explore the roles of chair and non-executive director and the contribution of each role towards good governance. We shall see that each role raises issues which must be resolved if the board is to operate in a smooth and effective manner.

An important aspect of corporate governance is the annual audit. We discussed the audit process briefly in Chapter 5 and saw how it seeks to lend credibility to the financial statements. In this chapter, we take a look at what the audit process involves and the contribution made by each of the key players. We also identify problems that may arise when carrying out, and when reviewing, the audit of a company's financial statements.

For a number of years, the remuneration of directors has been a thorny issue in corporate governance. In this chapter, we discuss the remuneration policies adopted by companies and the performance measures used as a basis for incentivising directors. We also discuss the extent to which the measures identified help align the interests of directors with those of shareholders.

A framework of rules plays an important role in monitoring and controlling the behaviour of directors. However, shareholders also have responsibilities. In the final part of this chapter, we shall consider how shareholders may act to improve accountability and to restrain the excesses of directors.

Learning outcomes

When you have completed this chapter, you should be able to:

- discuss the need for corporate governance rules and the principles upon which these rules are based;

- explain the role and composition of the board of directors and discuss the main issues surrounding the roles of chair and non-executive director;

- describe the audit process and the contribution of the key players to this process;

- explain the main issues and problems associated with the remuneration of directors;

- discuss the importance of shareholder involvement in the corporate governance process and outline the different forms of shareholder involvement that may be found.

CORPORATE GOVERNANCE

With larger companies, ownership is usually separated from day-to-day control of operations. As a result, a conflict of interest may arise between the directors and the shareholders. There is a risk that the directors will pursue their own interests rather than those of the shareholders. If this occurs, it is clearly a problem for the shareholders; however, it may also be a problem for society as a whole.

Activity 12.1

Can you think why directors pursuing their own interests, rather than those of shareholders, may be a problem for society as a whole?

If shareholders believe that their funds will be mismanaged, they will be reluctant to invest. A shortage of funds will lead to companies making fewer investments. Furthermore, the costs of finance will increase as companies compete for what limited funds are available. A lack of concern for shareholders can therefore have a profound effect on the performance of individual companies and, with this, the health of the economy.

To avoid these problems, most competitive market economies have a framework of rules to help monitor and control the behaviour of directors. These rules are usually based around three guiding principles:

- *Disclosure.* This lies at the heart of good corporate governance. Adequate and timely disclosure can help shareholders to judge the performance of the directors. Where performance is considered unsatisfactory this will be reflected in the price of shares. Changes should then be made to ensure the directors regain the confidence of shareholders.

- *Accountability.* This involves setting out the duties of the directors and establishing an adequate monitoring process. In the UK, company law requires that the directors act in the best interests of the shareholders. This means, among other things, that they must not try to use their position and knowledge to make gains at the expense of the shareholders. The law also requires larger companies to have their annual financial statements independently audited. The purpose of an independent audit is to lend credibility to the financial statements prepared by the directors. We shall consider this point in more detail later in the chapter.

■ *Fairness.* Directors should not be able to benefit from access to 'inside' information that is not available to shareholders. As a result in the UK, both the law and the Stock Exchange place restrictions on the ability of directors to buy and sell the shares of the company. This means, for example, that the directors cannot buy or sell shares immediately before the announcement of the annual profits or before the announcement of a significant event such as a planned merger.

These principles are set out in Figure 12.1.

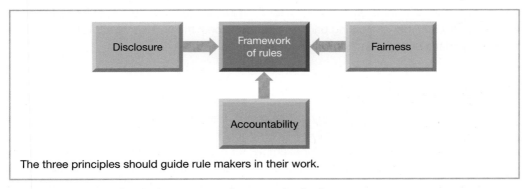

The three principles should guide rule makers in their work.

Figure 12.1 Principles underpinning a framework of rules

Strengthening the framework of rules

The number of rules designed to safeguard shareholders has increased considerably over the years. This has been in response to weaknesses in corporate governance procedures, which have been exposed through well-publicised company failures and frauds, excessive pay increases to directors and evidence that some financial reports were being 'massaged' so as to mislead shareholders.

Many believe, however, that shareholders must shoulder some of the blame for any weaknesses. Ownership, by market value, of the shares listed on the London Stock Exchange is dominated by institutional investors such as insurance businesses, banks and pension funds and so on (see Real World 12.12). They are often massive operations, owning large quantities of the shares of the companies in which they invest. These institutional investors employ specialist staff to manage their share portfolios. Yet, despite their size and expertise, they have often demonstrated little concern with corporate governance matters. As a consequence, directors' behaviour has not been closely monitored. In recent times, however, there has been a significant change. Institutional investors are now engaging much more with the companies in which they invest. We shall return to this point towards the end of the chapter.

THE BOARD OF DIRECTORS

Before we consider corporate governance issues in more detail, it might be helpful to clarify the role and composition of the board of directors. The board governs the company on behalf of the shareholders and is responsible for promoting their interests. It is led by a chair and, for a listed public company, the board will normally include both executive and non-executive directors.

The chair

The **chair** is the senior director. This individual is elected by the other directors and chairs board meetings. We shall discuss the chair's role in more detail a little later in the chapter.

Executive directors

Executive directors are salaried employees with senior management responsibilities. The finance directors of most large companies, for example, are full-time employees. In addition to being a board member and taking part in board decisions, the finance director is responsible for managing the finance function within the company.

Non-executive directors

Non-executive directors act purely as directors; they are not full-time employees of the company. They have often gained experience through their association with other companies or organisations. It is common, for example, for non-executive directors to be executive directors of other companies. In recent years, the role of non-executive director has taken on increasing importance, which, in turn, reflects the increasing attention paid to corporate governance matters.

The **UK Corporate Governance Code**, which we shall discuss shortly, draws a distinction between non-executive directors and *independent* non-executive directors. The term 'independent' in this context implies freedom from other significant links to the company, to its directors or to major shareholders. According to the UK Code, independence may be impaired for a variety of reasons such as where a person had been an employee of the company within the previous five years, or had a significant business relationship with the company within the past three years, or receives remuneration from the company apart from a director's fee.

To try to ensure an effective presence of independent, non-executive directors, the UK Code states that at least half the board, excluding the chair, should consist of independent, non-executive directors. A senior independent non-executive director should be appointed from among the independent non-executive directors to act as a sounding board for the board chair. The chair should also be an independent non-executive director, at the time of being appointed.

Although executive directors are much more deeply involved in running the company than non-executive directors, both have the same legal obligations towards the shareholders of the company. We shall discuss the role of non-executive directors in some detail a little later.

THE UK CORPORATE GOVERNANCE CODE

In recent years, there has been a real effort to address the problems of poor corporate governance. This has led to the creation of a code of best practice, known as the UK Corporate Governance Code. The UK Code is produced by the Financial Reporting Council, an independent regulator that seeks to promote high quality corporate governance and accountability. The first version of the UK Code was published in 1992 and revised versions have been published every few years since then. The 2018 version is divided into five sections and sets out a number of key principles. **Real World 12.1** below describes these principles.

The UK Corporate Governance Code

The UK Code is based on the following key principles:

Board leadership and company purpose

■ A successful company is led by an effective and entrepreneurial board, whose role is to promote the long-term sustainable success of the company, generating value for shareholders and contributing to wider society.

■ The board should establish the company's purpose, values and strategy, and satisfy itself that these and its culture are aligned. All directors must act with integrity, lead by example and promote the desired culture.

■ The board should ensure that the necessary resources are in place for the company to meet its objectives and measure performance against them. The board should also establish a framework of prudent and effective controls, which enable risk to be assessed and managed.

■ In order for the company to meet its responsibilities to shareholders and stakeholders, the board should ensure effective engagement with, and encourage participation from, these parties.

■ The board should ensure that workforce policies and practices are consistent with the company's values and support its long-term sustainable success. The workforce should be able to raise any matters of concern.

Division of responsibilities

■ The chair leads the board and is responsible for its overall effectiveness in directing the company. They should demonstrate objective judgement throughout their tenure and promote a culture of openness and debate. In addition, the chair facilitates constructive board relations and the effective contribution of all non-executive directors, and ensures that directors receive accurate, timely and clear information.

■ The board should include an appropriate combination of executive and non-executive (and, in particular, independent non-executive) directors, such that no one individual or small group of individuals dominates the board's decision-making. There should be a clear division of responsibilities between the leadership of the board and the executive leadership of the company's business.

■ Non-executive directors should have sufficient time to meet their board responsibilities. They should provide constructive challenge, strategic guidance, offer specialist advice and hold management to account.

■ The board, supported by the company secretary, should ensure that it has the policies, processes, information, time and resources it needs in order to function effectively and efficiently.

Company success and evaluation

■ Appointments to the board should be subject to a formal, rigorous and transparent procedure, and an effective succession plan should be maintained for board and senior management. Both appointments and succession plans should be based on merit and objective criteria and, within this context, should promote diversity of gender, social and ethnic backgrounds, cognitive and personal strengths.

$\rightarrow$

- The board and its committees should have a combination of skills, experience and knowledge. Consideration should be given to the length of service of the board as a whole and membership regularly refreshed.
- Annual evaluation of the board should consider its composition, diversity and how effectively members work together to achieve objectives. Individual evaluation should demonstrate whether each director continues to contribute effectively.

Audit, risk and internal control

- The board should establish formal and transparent policies and procedures to ensure the independence and effectiveness of internal and external audit functions and satisfy itself on the integrity of financial and narrative statements.
- The board should present a fair, balanced and understandable assessment of the company's position and prospects.
- The board should establish procedures to manage risk, oversee the internal control framework, and determine the nature and extent of the principal risks the company is willing to take in order to achieve its long-term strategic objectives.

Remuneration

- Remuneration policies and practices should be designed to support strategy and promote long-term sustainable success. Executive remuneration should be aligned to company purpose and values, and be clearly linked to the successful delivery of the company's long-term strategy.
- A formal and transparent procedure for developing policy on executive remuneration and determining director and senior management remuneration should be established. No director should be involved in deciding their own remuneration outcome.
- Directors should exercise independent judgement and discretion when authorising remuneration outcomes, taking account of company and individual performance, and wider circumstances.

Source: Extracts from The UK Corporate Governance Code, Financial Reporting Council, July 2018, pp. 4–13, www. frc.org.uk. © Financial Reporting Council (FRC). All rights reserved. For further information, please visit www.frc.org. uk or call +44 (0)20 7492 2300.

The 2018 UK Code places great emphasis on how the principles described above have been applied in practice. Listed companies are required to provide a statement to shareholders on the approach taken. Because of its importance, this statement should not be produced in a formulaic way. The UK Code states that a 'tick box' approach, which has been a growing trend in corporate governance reporting, is unacceptable.

The UK Code acknowledges there may be circumstances where non-compliance with a particular provision is justified. Nevertheless, a recent survey found that 66 per cent of the largest 350 listed companies declare full compliance with the UK Code provisions. A common reason for non-compliance centres around the independence of the chair and non-executive directors (see Reference 1 at the end of the chapter).

The UK Code has the backing of the London Stock Exchange. This means that companies listed on the London Stock Exchange are expected to comply with the requirements of the UK Code or must give shareholders good reason why they do not. Failure to do one of these can lead to the company's shares being suspended from listing.

It is generally believed that the Code has improved the quality of information available to shareholders. It has also resulted in better checks on the powers of directors, and provided greater transparency in corporate affairs. However, rules can only be a partial answer. Ultimately, good corporate governance behaviour depends on a healthy **corporate culture**. This term refers to the values, attitudes and behaviour displayed towards the company's various stakeholders and to the wider community. To be effective, governance rules rely on corporate decision making that reflect high standards of integrity, openness and accountability.

Rulemaking is a tricky business. Where corporate governance rules are too tightly drawn, entrepreneurial spirit may be stifled and risk taking may be discouraged. However, problems can also arise where rules are too loosely drawn.

Thus, when creating corporate governance rules, a balance must somehow be struck between the need to protect shareholders and other stakeholders and the need to encourage entrepreneurial behaviour.

TASKS OF THE BOARD

To help ensure that the company succeeds in its purpose, the board is charged with various tasks. The main tasks are to:

1 *Decide on the strategic direction of the company.* The degree of involvement in strategy setting tends to vary between boards. In some cases, the full board will establish the strategic aims but will delegate responsibility for developing a strategic plan to an **executive committee**. This is a committee made up of some of the board members, which usually includes the **chief executive officer (CEO)**, who leads the management team, and the

other executive directors. Once the committee has developed a plan, it will be put before the full board for approval.

2 *Exercise control.* To try to ensure that things go according to plan and resources are properly allocated, the board must exercise control. This is often done through board committees. Each committee is made up of some board members who report to the full board on their progress and findings. The key committees are mentioned below.

The main areas over which the board must exercise control include:

- *Carrying out the strategic plan.* Having developed a strategic plan, the executive committee will usually be charged with its successful implementation.
- *Checking the integrity of the financial statements.* The UK Corporate Governance Code states that a separate board committee, known as the **audit committee**, should be set up to promote the reliability of the financial reporting systems.
- *Evaluating and managing risk.* Although a separate **risk management committee** may be formed, the audit committee may take on this responsibility.
- *Nominating and remunerating directors.* The UK Corporate Governance Code states that a **nomination committee** and a **remuneration committee** should each be established to help provide formal and transparent procedures in these areas.
- *Assessing board performance.* Appraisals based on contributions made, or outcomes achieved, should be carried out on individual directors and on the board as a whole.

The control function of the board will be discussed in more detail in later sections.

3 *Maintain external relations.* The board is responsible for promoting the interests of the company and establishing good relationships with shareholders. Relationships with major shareholders are often helped through informal meetings involving key board members. These meetings, which usually involve a free exchange of views between board members and shareholders, may help the shareholders to adopt a long-term perspective on company performance. They may also help in securing support when the board has to make difficult decisions.

The main tasks discussed are summarised in Figure 12.2.

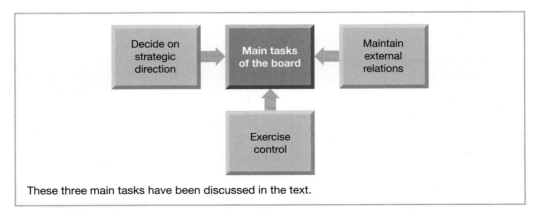

These three main tasks have been discussed in the text.

Figure 12.2 The main tasks of the board of directors

CHAIRING THE BOARD

We have seen that the role of chair is to lead and manage the board of directors. The chair should try to ensure that the board operates as an effective decision-making body and that board meetings are conducted in a business-like manner. To fulfil the role, the chair will normally be expected to:

- hold frequent board meetings so that key issues and problems can be dealt with at the appropriate time;
- try to ensure that the board agenda properly reflects the key issues and problems confronting the company;
- provide board members with relevant, reliable and timely information to help in their deliberations;
- provide enough time at board meetings for key issues and problems to be discussed thoroughly;
- allow all directors the opportunity to voice their opinions at board meetings; and
- guide discussions so that the focus does not deviate from key strategic issues and problems.

The chair should play a crucial role in defining the culture of the board and, through this, the company as a whole. It is important, therefore, that the chair tries to foster a good working relationship between board members by providing a supportive environment where directors feel valued and where a climate of trust prevails.

Activity 12.4

In trying to establish a supportive environment, should the chair try to ensure that board-room conflict is avoided?

No. There are occasions when conflict between board members is beneficial. It can help ensure that issues are thoroughly aired and that important proposals are given proper scrutiny.

The chair will act as an important link between the board and the shareholders. When the board wishes to inform shareholders of its proposals and decisions, the chair will normally take a lead role. Similarly, when shareholders wish to respond to board proposals and decisions, or to raise concerns, they will often relay their views to the board through the chair. Good communication skills are, therefore, a vital ingredient of a successful chair.

Finally, the chair should ensure that board performance is subject to proper scrutiny. The UK Code states that performance of individual directors, board committees and the board, as a whole, should be evaluated on an annual basis. Furthermore, the chair should act on the results. The criteria for assessing board performance will be considered later in the chapter.

Separating the roles of chair and CEO

We have seen that the role of the chair is to lead the board of directors and the role of the chief executive officer is to lead the management team. The UK Corporate Governance Code states that the same individual should not occupy both roles.

What risks are associated with a single individual occupying both roles?

Where the two roles are combined, too much power may be concentrated in the hands of a single individual. This power may be used to dominate the board and to marginalise the contribution of others. It may also be used to plunder the company's resources through excessive pay, bonuses and 'perks'. When the company is performing well, these abuses of power may be overlooked but, when things turn sour, the issue of accountability will inevitably surface.

Having a separate chair may provide a number of benefits. The chair may be a useful source of support for the chief executive when the occasion demands. Where, for example, problems that create controversy among board members arise, they are more likely to be resolved when the chair and chief executive adopt the same stance. A chair can also act as a sounding board for new ideas and provide advice for the chief executive. In many cases, chairs have occupied the position of chief executive at an earlier point in their careers and are older, and more widely experienced, than the chief executive. They are often, therefore, well placed to undertake these supportive roles.

Having a separate chair may also help in smoothing the path of succession. Where a chief executive leaves the company, the continued presence of the chair can help to 'steady the ship' and provide a sense of continuity during the period of transition (see Reference 2 at the end of the chapter). The chair can also help a newly appointed chief executive to settle in and to become familiar with the issues and challenges to be faced.

Finally, a separate chair may help the company to cope more effectively with the demands of modern business. The skills and time required to fulfil both roles are likely to be beyond the capacity of a single individual. It is argued that only by separating the roles can proper attention be given both to corporate governance matters and to managing the company.

Is separation always the best solution?

There is little doubt that a powerful, combined chair and chief executive can create problems for a company. What is less certain, however, is whether a 'one size fits all' approach is the best solution for dealing with this issue. There may be circumstances where combining the roles may be appropriate. A company in difficulties, for example, may benefit from a single, strong leader who has a clear vision and who can act in a decisive and fairly unconstrained manner.

Where a board of directors intends to combine the roles of chair and chief executive, the UK Code requires major shareholders to be consulted prior to any appointment. In addition, the reasons for the decision should be communicated to all shareholders.

Problems in separating the roles

There are potential problems in separating the roles of chair and chief executive, which can be overlooked.

Can you think of potential problems that may arise from separating the two roles?

Responsibilities may become hazy and this, in turn, may result in a lack of clear direction. There is also a risk that the two individuals occupying the roles simply do not get on. They may have conflicting personalities. They may also have conflicting views over the way in which each role should be carried out and the general direction in which the company should be heading. A breakdown in relationships can lead to endless power struggles, which may badly affect the performance of the company.

Perhaps a clinching argument in favour of separating the two roles would be that it leads to a more effective business performance, perhaps evidenced by superior shareholder returns. There is, however, no clear evidence to suggest that this is the case.

Making separation work

Separating the two roles will only be successful if the two individuals concerned strike up a good working relationship. Thus, the board should appoint individuals whose personalities appear to mesh. The board should ideally also appoint two individuals with complementary skills and knowledge (see Reference 3 at the end of the chapter). This will help to fill any gaps and should help to build mutual respect between the chair and the chief executive.

The two roles should be clearly defined and everyone should be made aware of the responsibilities and duties associated with each role. Defining the roles, however, may be difficult. In a fast-changing environment, new issues arise that can result in boundary disputes. Resolving these disputes will depend a great deal on the mutual trust and respect the two individuals have for each other.

The chair, who is often a former chief executive, must resist any temptation to intervene in the management of the company. The role of the chair demands that a different approach be taken. It requires a willingness to operate in the background and to keep ego and ambition firmly in check.

Should the chief executive go on to become chair?

The UK Corporate Governance Code recommends that the chief executive should not go on to become chair of the same company.

Can you think of a potential problem that may arise from allowing the chief executive to relinquish this post and then become the chair?

The main risk here is that the individual will be unable to give up the reins of management easily and will still become involved in operating decisions.

The chair's involvement in day-to-day management issues can create disharmony and can have a detrimental effect on company performance. It can generate confusion and can undermine the decisions of the current chief executive. The chair must not, however, become too detached from management issues. This would allow the chief executive too much freedom in running the company (see Reference 4 at the end of the chapter).

Allowing the chief executive to become chair can also increase the risk of defensive behaviour. The new chief executive may try to score points by criticising the decisions made, and results achieved, when the former chief executive (and now the chair) managed the company. The chair, on the other hand, may try to justify past decisions and actions. This may lead to criticism of the new chief executive and attempts to undermine any proposals for change.

Despite these points, there are possible disadvantages in preventing the chief executive from becoming chair.

Activity 12.8

Can you think what these disadvantages might be?

The most important is the loss to the company of the chief executive's expertise and experience. This loss can be particularly severe where the company's operations are unique or highly complex. In these circumstances, recruiting a suitable outside chair may be extremely difficult. A further disadvantage of not allowing the chief executive to become chair is that a sense of continuity may be lost.

THE ROLE OF NON-EXECUTIVE DIRECTORS

In the past, the image of the non-executive director was that of an avuncular figure offering kindly guidance and advice to the board concerning the direction of the company. This was not seen as an unduly onerous role and any time spent on the company's affairs could be confined to board meetings and in perusing background documents for the various agenda items. Whatever truth such an image may have contained, it is not a faithful portrayal of the current role of the non-executive director of a UK listed public company. An important consequence of strengthening corporate governance standards, which was discussed earlier, has been to increase the demands placed on the non-executive directors.

Non-executive directors are expected to contribute towards each of the functions of the board mentioned above and the contribution they make will largely depend on their background, experience and personal qualities. As we have seen, often non-executive directors of a listed public company are, or have been, executive directors of another listed public company and so will usually have experience of the commercial world as well as expertise in a particular field, such as finance or marketing. As a result, non-executive directors can often play a valuable role in discussions on strategy. They may make useful suggestions and may constructively challenge the assumptions and decisions of the executive directors.

They are more detached from company problems and this allows them to provide a more objective view. This may be of particular value during periods of change or crisis, when an objective view can help executive directors to maintain perspective.

Non-executive directors can also play an important role in monitoring and controlling the activities of the company. In working towards the strategic plan, control mechanisms involving plans, budgets, quality indicators and benchmarking may be used. The experience and skills of non-executive directors may enable them to identify weaknesses in the current control systems and to suggest ways of improving them. They may also be able to highlight areas of poor performance.

Non-executives have an important role in the various board committees that are set up to control the activities of the company. It was mentioned earlier that, to promote the integrity of financial information, an audit committee is usually set up. The UK Corporate Governance Code states that this committee should consist entirely of independent non-executive directors. It was also mentioned that listed companies normally have a remuneration committee that is charged with recommending to the board the remuneration of the executive directors and the chair. The UK Code states that this committee should also consist of independent non-executive directors. This means that non-executives have enormous influence over the remuneration of executive directors and, where there are performance-related elements, will be involved in setting targets and in monitoring the performance of the executive directors. The roles of both the audit committee and the remuneration committee will be considered in more detail later in the chapter.

Finally, the UK Code states that the nomination committee should have a majority of independent non-executive directors as members. We have seen that listed companies normally have such a committee. Its role is to lead the nomination process for new directors. This involves identifying the skills, knowledge and experience required for the board and preparing appropriate job specifications.

The board and large shareholders often maintain a dialogue through informal meetings, which non-executives may attend. This can help them to understand the concerns of shareholders. At times, non-executives may become the shareholders' communications channel to the board of directors. Shareholders may be particularly reliant on this channel if they have already voiced concerns to the chair, or to the executive directors, and have not received satisfactory replies.

Non-executive directors may help to raise the profile of the company. They often enjoy a good reputation within their particular field and may have strong links with a wide range of bodies, including government agencies and foreign companies. These links may be extremely valuable in developing new contacts and in promoting the company's interests.

Role conflict

The different roles that non-executives are expected to play provide potential for conflict. In developing strategy, co-operation between the executive and non-executive directors is essential. All directors are expected to work together as part of a team in pursuit of a common purpose. However, the monitoring role that non-executive directors have means that they must assess the performance of executive directors. Disputes between executive and non-executive directors can easily arise over the company's financial systems, control systems and remuneration systems. Given this potential conflict, non-executive directors must tread carefully and must retain a certain distance from the executive directors to maintain their independence.

Relations with the executive directors

The potential for disputes may make the non-executive and executive directors wary of each other. Executive directors may resent the presence of non-executives on the board because they believe that the non-executives:

- are monitoring their behaviour and, effectively, acting as 'corporate police officers';
- do not fully understand the nature of the company's business; and
- do not devote enough time and effort in carrying out their duties.

Non-executives, on the other hand, may sense that executives are acting in an unhelpful or guarded manner towards them. They may feel that executive directors are seeking to undermine their position by:

- withholding key information or reports;
- failing to provide important information at the required time; and
- holding informal meetings on important matters to which the non-executives are not invited.

The chair of the board can play an important part in overcoming these suspicions and problems.

Activity 12.10

What do you think the chair could do? (Try to think of at least two possible initiatives the chair could take.)

The chair can take various initiatives, such as trying to ensure that the board's procedures are transparent and that informal meetings of cliques are discouraged. Where doubts exist over the competence of particular directors, the chair should see that appropriate training and development opportunities are made available. To allow any suspicions and problems to be aired, the chair should arrange meetings between executive and non-executive directors. Finally, the chair should try to ensure that all directors receive timely and relevant information.

Maintaining independence

There is a danger that non-executive directors will not provide an independent voice. They may come under the influence of the executive directors and fail to challenge decisions and so ensure proper accountability. The fact that non-executives are often executive directors of other companies can result in feelings of empathy with the executive directors on the board.

Activity 12.11

How might shareholders intervene to ensure that the risk of non-executive directors not being sufficiently independent is avoided, or at least reduced?

Shareholders can become involved in the appointment of the non-executive directors, perhaps by identifying and proposing suitable candidates. Once appointed, regular meetings with shareholders may help to strengthen their independence from the executive directors, as well as their commitment to the shareholders' interests.

The role of non-executive directors can be very time-consuming. Despite this, some individuals hold multiple non-executive directorships. This may prevent them from devoting sufficient time to the affairs of each company. The UK Code does not specify a minimum time commitment for non-executive directors, but does state that they should have sufficient time to be able to carry out their duties effectively.

To encourage a diligent attitude, non-executives should be properly rewarded for the time spent on company business and for the responsibilities that they take on. There is a risk, however, of paying non-executives too handsomely for their efforts.

Activity 12.12

What problem may arise from paying non-executive directors large salaries?

It may compromise their independence. Where non-executives are paid fairly modest salaries, based on the time spent carrying out their duties, the amounts will usually form only a small proportion of their total income. This may help them retain a greater degree of independence when making decisions.

Real World 12.2 gives an impression of the remuneration awarded to non-executive directors in the UK's largest listed businesses.

Real World 12.2

Time to get on board

A survey by KPMG, the accountants and management consultants, provides the following average (median) figures for the remuneration of non-executive directors in the UK's 100 listed businesses.

	£000
Basic fees	
Chair	400
Non-executive director	69
Additional fees	
Audit committee chair	23
Remuneration committee chair	20
Nomination committee chair	17
Audit committee member	14
Remuneration committee member	12
Nomination committee member	10

Half of the largest 100 listed businesses pay additional fees for membership of board committees.

Source: Extracts from Guide to Directors' Remuneration 2017, KPMG, pp. 68, 71 and 72.

THE AUDIT PROCESS

External audit

As we saw in Chapter 5, **external audit** forms an important element of corporate governance. To understand what it entails, we must first be clear about the roles and responsibilities of directors and auditors concerning the published financial statements.

Company law requires the directors to prepare annual financial statements that provide a true and fair view of the state of affairs of the company. This will involve:

- selecting suitable accounting policies and applying them consistently;
- making estimates and judgements that are reasonable and prudent;
- stating whether appropriate accounting standards have been adopted;
- presenting information in a way that is relevant, reliable comparable and understandable; and
- applying the going concern convention where it is appropriate to do so.

In addition to preparing the annual financial statements, the law also obliges the directors to keep proper accounting records and to safeguard the assets of the company.

External auditors are appointed by, and report to, the shareholders. They are normally an independent firm of accountants and their role is to form an opinion concerning the integrity of the annual financial statements prepared by the directors. In forming their opinion, the auditors must bring to bear their professional scepticism and judgement. The audit process will involve examining the available accounting records, reviewing the key assumptions and estimates employed and evaluating the internal controls in operation. It will also involve checking to see whether the accounting policies adopted are appropriate, whether key information is adequately disclosed and whether the financial statements are properly presented and structured.

External auditors must inform shareholders of any significant problems that have been unearthed during the audit process. By law, the audit report must include any instances where:

- adequate accounting records have not been kept;
- information and explanations needed to undertake the audit have not been received;
- the financial statements are not in agreement with the underlying accounting records; and
- certain disclosures concerning directors' remuneration are not made.

In addition, there are auditing rules that require auditors to report where other information within the annual report is inconsistent with the financial statements, or is otherwise misleading.

External auditors take on additional responsibilities for Stock Exchange listed companies. These include checking the directors' required statement on the long-term viability of the business and, where the going concern basis for preparing the financial statements is used, that it is appropriate to do so.

Following an examination of all the relevant information, the auditors provide shareholders with an independent opinion as to whether:

- the financial statements provide a true and fair view of the state of affairs of the company and comply with legal and other regulatory requirements;
- information contained within the directors' report and strategic report is consistent with the financial statements and comply with legal requirements; and
- the reporting of certain details concerning directors' remuneration complies with the law.

These opinions are contained within an audit report, which forms part of the published annual report. Where the auditors have no concerns to raise, an 'unmodified opinion' is provided. This should provide reasonable assurance to shareholders that the financial statements are free from any serious misstatements arising from either fraud or error. There is, however, no guarantee that this is the case.

In practice, the audit process does not always operate smoothly. There are times when auditors fail to spot errors and fraud. **Real World 12.3** below reveals one such time.

Real World 12.3

Ringing the changes

BT has appointed KPMG as its new auditor following a review of its accounting practices prompted by a scandal in its Italian division, ending a relationship with rival PwC that lasted more than three decades. The move comes after a whistleblower exposed fraud at BT Italia, triggering a £530 million write-off and wiping a fifth off the telecoms group's market value in January.

The telecoms company was due to carry out a review of its auditors in 2019 but brought the process forward after it became aware of issues at its Italian unit, part of its Global Services division. There was unease from some at the company that PwC had failed to spot the scale of the problems in Italy, which were only brought to the company's attention by a whistleblower and through a subsequent investigation by KPMG.

It was the second time in a decade that auditing problems were uncovered in BT's Global Services division. In 2008–9, the company took a £1.6 billion writedown after optimistic profitability estimates went unchallenged.

 Source: Extracts from Bond, D. and Khan, M. (2017) BT appoints KPMG as auditor after Italian scandal, ft.com, 8 June. © The Financial Times Limited 2017. All rights reserved.

Two key issues have emerged from past audit failures – the gap in expectations between auditors and shareholders and auditor independence. It is to these issues that we now turn.

The expectations gap

Over the years, there has been much discussion of the expectations gap in auditing. This refers to the difference between what external auditors believe their responsibilities and duties to be and what shareholders believe them to be. As seen earlier, external auditors are broadly concerned with checking the integrity of the accounting system and seeing whether the financial statements are properly presented. They are not primarily concerned with the detection of errors and fraud. However, when auditors fail in this respect, the reaction of shareholders suggests that they have a different view of the auditors' role.

From time to time, auditors complain that shareholders do not fully understand the nature and limitations of the audit process. When checking the integrity of accounting systems, for example, auditors often rely on sampling techniques. They do not normally examine every accounting transaction for the period.

Why do you think auditors rely on sampling techniques?

For a company of any size, the huge number of transactions undertaken during a financial period would make an examination of each transaction impossible.

While sampling techniques can help to assess the overall reliability of the accounting system, they cannot guarantee the absence of errors and fraud. Shareholders must, therefore, be realistic about what is achievable from an audit. Narrowing the expectations gap is not, however, simply about educating shareholders. Auditors must understand that shareholders need relevant feedback for their investment decisions.

In recent years, the auditors' report for listed businesses has become much more informative in response to the problems mentioned. It now includes an overview of the scope of the audit. It also describes key audit matters, such as the most significant risks of misstatements that have been identified, including those having the greatest effect on the audit strategy and on how audit resources were allocated. The auditors' report also includes the auditors' response to risks of misstatement and any observations relating to them. Finally, the report includes an explanation as to what the auditors regard as a material amount when performing the audit.

Real World 12.4 explains the view taken by the external auditors of Ocado Group plc, the online grocer, as to the appropriate threshold for what should be considered a material amount for the financial statements as whole.

Real World 12.4

Auditing in the material world

We define materiality as the magnitude of misstatement in the financial statements that makes it probable that the economic decisions of a reasonably knowledgeable person would be changed or influenced. We use materiality both in planning the scope of our audit work and in evaluating the results of our work. Based on our professional judgement, we determined materiality for the financial statements as a whole as follows:

Group materiality	We determined materiality for the group to be £6 million (2016: £5 million).
Basis for determining materiality	We determined materiality to be £6 million based on revenue. As a percentage materiality is 0.4% of revenue (2016: 0.4% of revenue).
	Parent company materiality was determined as less than 0.5% of total assets.
Rationale for the benchmark applied	This has been based on professional judgement and the requirement of auditing standards. We believe revenue to be the financial measure most relevant to users of the financial statements given Ocado's performance, in particular its levels of profitability and the significant investment in technology.
	It also provides a consistent basis to the approach taken by the previous auditor.

Source: Independent Auditors Report, Annual report and Accounts 53 weeks ended 3 December 2017, Ocado plc.

Auditor independence and audit quality

In the past, the external auditors of large UK listed companies were rarely replaced. Instead they tended to enjoy long tenures.

Long tenures, however, run the risk of a cosy relationship developing between the auditors and directors, thereby undermining auditor independence. The external auditors may, for example, be reluctant to revisit earlier decisions relating to accounting policies and processes. In order to maintain good relations, they may feel inhibited from challenging directors on matters about which they have previously agreed. Replacing the auditors avoids this kind of problem. A new chapter begins and earlier decisions can be viewed through fresh eyes. Rather than following a well-trodden path based on previous audit work, a more critical and rigorous approach may be introduced.

To strengthen the independence of auditors, new rules require UK listed companies to change external auditors after a maximum period of 20 years. The audit must, however, be put out to tender at the mid-point of 10 years. A key question is whether strengthening auditor independence in this way will, in turn, lead to an improvement in audit quality. Research carried out to date has usually examined situations where auditor rotations have been carried out on a voluntary basis. The results of this research are mixed. (See Reference 5 at the end of the chapter.) Furthermore, it is already established practice for the partner in the firm of auditors who is responsible for conducting the audit of a large listed business to be rotated every five years. This may pre-empt some of the problems of long audit tenures.

A further issue relating to auditor independence concerns the provision of non-audit services. In the past, auditors have often provided significant non-audit services to client companies. These services, which can take various forms such as tax advice, financial advice and bookkeeping, are often well paid. Whereas it is the shareholders that appoint the auditors in respect of their statutory audit work, the directors have responsibility for making the appointment for the non-audit services.

Providing non-audit services may also involve the auditors carrying out a 'self-review'. This occurs where the auditors make recommendations as part of their non-audit services and then, as part of the audit process, evaluate the validity of these recommendations when implemented.

New rules now prohibit audit firms from providing a wide range of non-audit services to their client-listed businesses. The prohibited services include those relating to bookkeeping, employee payrolls, various human resource, legal and tax services, the design of internal controls and risk management procedures, management decision making and financing matters. Furthermore, the law imposes a cap on fees generated from non-audit services that have not been prohibited.

For some years, concerns have been expressed about the lack of competition within the audit market. The audit of large companies is carried out by only a handful of audit firms and there are doubts that the recent changes to the rules described above will change matters. **Real World 12.5** describes the problems confronted by regulators.

Real World 12.5

Four play

Britain's audit market is overwhelmingly dominated by four firms – EY, Deloitte, KPMG and PwC. Despite new regulation designed to increase choice and competition, the so-called big four audit 98 per cent of FTSE 350 companies. Recent high-profile accounting scandals at UK companies including Rolls-Royce and Tesco – which have involved KPMG and PwC respectively – have meant the continuing concentration is worrying some investors.

Latest market share figures, compiled by PwC, show that 99 of Britain's 100 biggest listed companies are audited by the big four. That is the same as in 2011, before rules were changed to make companies tender their audit every decade, and change auditors every 20. 'It's very clear that tendering has done nothing to improve choice,' says Prof Guy Jubb of Edinburgh Business School's Centre for Accounting and Society and former head of governance at Standard Life.

Audit reform, which sprung from the global financial crisis and took effect in 2014, was supposed to introduce choice and competition in an environment of decades-long, cosy relationships between companies and auditors. Before it appointed a new auditor in 2015, Barclays had been with PwC for 120 years, for example. Last year 68 companies tendered their audit, the highest yearly total since the rule change. But hopes of drawing in new competitors have not materialised and people in the industry say firms outside the big four are increasingly reticent to participate in resource-draining audit tenders for large listed UK companies.

Annual audits for FTSE 100 companies are big catches. PwC, for example, received fees of $111.1 million from HSBC last year, of which $71.3 million were for auditing. But firms argue that switching clients means investing time and money getting to know new businesses, which can hit audit profitability. Mr Persico adds that 'beyond the big four, I don't think there is competition'. He says 'willingness to merge' is the only way smaller players would get to the major leagues. However, Sue Almond, head of audit and assurance at Grant Thornton, says audit tendering processes have helped to increase the group's non-audit work for FTSE 100 companies, which is up by a third since 2013. With scrutiny of Britain's financial accounts in so few hands, there is also a recurring fear one firm will fail. Should one of the big four have 'a crisis of confidence and go into meltdown, because of serious audit quality or reputational issues, you (could) find yourself going rapidly from the big four to the big three,' says Mr Jubb.

Source: Extracts from Cornish, C. (2017) Auditor merry-go-round fails to shake-up cosy market, ft.com, 29 May. © The Financial Times Limited 2017. All rights reserved.

Concerns have also been raised over the quality of audits undertaken by the big four audit firms. Recently, four out of ten audits inspected by the International Forum of Independent Audit Regulators found serious deficiencies in the audits that the big four carried out. (See Reference 6 at the end of the chapter.) Nevertheless, company shareholders rarely show any enthusiasm to change auditors. **Real World 12.6** below provides one example, however, of shareholders sacking one of the big four auditors over the quality of its work.

Real World 12.6

You're fired!

SIG, the building materials group, suffered a large shareholder revolt on Thursday after investors rejected the reappointment of Deloitte as auditor just months after the company admitted repeatedly overstating its profits in previous years.

More than 78 per cent of investors voted against Deloitte's reappointment, in a rare move against an auditor by shareholders. Auditor re-election is usually one of the least controversial aspects of an annual meeting, with the majority of these resolutions gaining support of at least 95 per cent from shareholders.

"The board takes the views of shareholders extremely seriously, and takes this opportunity to inform shareholders that it is committed to carrying out an EU audit regulation compliant audit tender for the role of external auditor, as soon as practicable," a statement from the company said.

"The board intends to consult with shareholders over coming weeks on the timing of that audit tender process and the resulting appointment of a new auditor."

In February, the company said it had discovered misstatements after a whistleblowing allegation about irregularities at its core UK insulation and exteriors business.

It added that a review with auditors at Deloitte and KPMG had found a number of balances related to rebates and other "potential recoveries" from suppliers had been overstated, "in some cases intentionally".

Earlier in the year, the company also said it had overstated its cash balances by around £20m at the end of 2016 and £27m in its 2017 half-year results.

One governance expert described the vote against Deloitte as "unprecedented".

 Source: Mooney, A. (2018) *SIG shareholders reject reappointment of Deloitte as auditors*, ft.com 10 May. © The Financial Times Limited 2018. All rights reserved.

It seems that regulators are losing patience with the big four firms and with the quality of audits being carried out. A thorough review of the audit market, along with the role and responsibilities of auditors, seems imminent. Various changes have been suggested, including:

■ setting a limit to the number of large listed companies the big four firms can audit;
■ requiring larger audit firms to share audits of large listed companies with smaller audit firms;
■ passing responsibility for the appointment of auditors of large listed companies to a regulatory authority, such as the Stock Exchange;
■ encouraging smaller audit firms to merge to enable them to challenge the big four firms;
■ separating audit firms completely from their consulting activities in order to avoid conflicts of interest;
■ ensuring that auditors have a clearer duty to exercise judgement rather than to simply 'tick boxes';
■ imposing larger penalties on auditors that fail to identify significant problems; and
■ expanding the role of auditors to include a responsibility for detecting fraud.

Two points are worth making concerning any further regulatory changes. Firstly, improving the quality of audits will come at a cost. Auditors will have to devote more time and invest in new technology, to further check the accuracy and completeness of financial reports. The additional cost this incurs must be borne by the shareholders. Secondly, some regulation could be avoided if shareholders became more proactive in monitoring the activities of auditors. On the whole, they tend to be passive, even in the face of egregious failures by auditors. There are cases where, following the failure to detect significant fraud or errors, shareholders have overwhelmingly voted to re-appoint the auditors.

Internal audit

Many large companies have an **internal audit** function – although there is no legal requirement to have one. The purpose of an internal audit is to reassure directors about the company's control, risk management and governance procedures. In particular, reassurance is needed about the integrity and reliability of the financial control and accounting systems. An important task of internal audit is, therefore, to review:

- the financial control systems to see whether they are effective in safeguarding the company's assets and in preventing errors and fraud; and
- the accounting systems to see whether they provide reliable information that meets the needs of management and complies with relevant regulations.

The review process will normally highlight areas of weakness and make recommendations based on best practice. It can, therefore, be an important catalyst for improvement.

As internal auditors regularly review the company's accounting and financial control systems, the external auditors may take this into account when planning the scope and nature of the external audit work. External auditors must retain full responsibility for the external audit but may place confidence in the work carried out by competent and experienced internal auditors.

In addition to the risks associated with its accounting systems, a company has to manage many other kinds of risk. How these other risks are managed is vital to good corporate governance.

Activity 12.16

What other kinds of risks may a company face? Try to think of at least three.

They can include:

- risks to its reputation for quality products or fair dealing;
- risks to IT systems from malfunction or security breaches;
- risks of suppliers failing to deliver what is needed on time;
- risks to the health and safety of employees and customers; and
- risks of changes in market demand.

You may have thought of others.

The internal audit function is often charged with reviewing the procedures for managing these other risks. When doing so, a proactive approach may be taken. This means assessing not only how well the procedures cope with managing current risks but also how well they would cope with managing future risks.

Real World 12.7 explains how serious failures in the internal control systems of a well-known car rental business contributed towards investors actively seeking change.

Losing control at Hertz

Carl Icahn, the activist investor, has made a move on Hertz, the US car rental group, revealing an 8.48 per cent stake and saying he could seek seats on the board, a day after the company said it expected this year's earnings to be 'well below' its previous guidance.

Mr Icahn said in a filing to the Securities and Exchange Commission, the US regulator, that his group of companies had a 'lack of confidence in management' at Hertz, but had taken the stake in the belief that the shares were undervalued. He added that his representatives planned to meet Hertz's management and directors to discuss 'shareholder value, accounting issues, operational failures, [and] underperformance relative to its peers'.

The company said it was facing additional costs for the accounting review it has launched to fix the errors in its reporting. Hertz said that these extra costs, and the potential revisions resulting from the accounting review, meant that it was withdrawing its previous guidance that underlying earnings per share this year would be in the range $1.70 to $2.00, which would have been an increase of about 13.5 per cent on the $1.63 reported for 2013.

The company said in June that it would have to restate its 2011 accounts, while the 2012 and 2013 statements would need to be revised to correct errors, and might also need to be withdrawn and formally restated if the accounting review determined that the errors were material. The problems identified included the treatment of depreciation for some assets, and allowances for 'doubtful accounts' in Brazil.

The company said it had uncovered 'at least one material weakness' in its internal control over financial reporting, and that 'disclosure controls and procedures were ineffective at December 31, 2013'.

 Source: Extracts from Crooks, E. (2014) Icahn signals a move on Hertz, ft.com, 20 August.

In carrying out their duties, internal auditors try to be both independent and objective. As employees of the company, however, they cannot enjoy the same degree of independence as external auditors. Nevertheless, their independence can be strengthened where the audit committee, rather than executive directors, determines the nature and scope of their duties. Their independence can be further strengthened where the audit committee takes responsibility for appointing and, where necessary, removing, the head of internal audit.

A little earlier, we mentioned the extent that external auditors may be inclined to rely on the work of internal auditors. Naturally, the external auditors will tend to place more confidence in the work of internal auditors, where the internal auditors have a measure of independence, in the way discussed in the previous paragraph.

We shall now go on to consider the role of audit committees in some detail.

Audit committees

The UK Corporate Governance Code places audit committees at the heart of the financial reporting and control process. The responsibilities of the audit committee have increased in recent years following the introduction of international financial reporting standards and tougher overseas corporate governance rules, such as the Sarbanes–Oxley Act in the US. This Act was introduced in the wake of accounting scandals and applies to a number of large UK listed companies that also list their shares in the US.

The role of the audit committee

The UK Corporate Governance Code recommends that an audit committee should have delegated authority for trying to ensure that financial reporting and internal control principles are properly applied. In essence, the role concerns the oversight and assessment of work carried out by others. Although the committee receives its terms of reference from the board of directors, these tend to be in line with the guidelines set out in **Real World 12.8**.

Real World 12.8

That's the way to do it

The Financial Reporting Council, which is responsible for setting the UK Corporate Governance Code, has set out the following guidelines for the role and responsibilities of audit committees:

- to monitor the integrity of the financial statements and related information such as the strategic report;
- to review the company's internal controls and risk management systems (unless this task has been delegated to other committees);
- to review the need for an internal audit function and, where one exists, to assess its role, resourcing and effectiveness;
- to make formal recommendation to the board of directors for the appointment and removal of the external auditors and to approve their terms of engagement and remuneration;
- to review and monitor the independence, expertise and effectiveness of the external auditors;
- to review the annual work plan of the external auditors;
- to establish and implement policies concerning non-audit services carried out by the external auditors;
- to report to the board of directors on how the committee discharged its responsibilities; and
- to communicate with shareholders its role, the work carried out and any significant issues considered.

Source: Summarised from Guidance on Audit Committees, Financial Reporting Council, April 2016, pp. 6–15. © Financial Reporting Council (FRC). All rights reserved. For further information, please visit www.frc.org.uk or call +44 (0)20 7492 2300.

The audit committee will also review the risk management systems of the company where the board, or a separate risk committee, does not take on this task.

Members of the audit committee do not have to be qualified accountants. The UK Corporate Governance Code imposes only a modest requirement that at least one committee member should have 'recent and relevant financial experience'. To be effective, members must, however, possess integrity, judgement and character. They may need to pursue enquiries when faced with determined opposition from senior managers or directors.

Activity 12.17

Do you think that *all* members of the committee should be qualified accountants? Try to think of the case for and against this idea.

There is an argument for having at least some qualified accountants on the committee. An important part of the committee's role can involve carrying out a detailed examination of complex accounting issues. To deal effectively with these issues, a high level of technical expertise will usually be needed.

The committee must, however, fulfil other roles that do not demand a high level of accounting expertise. These roles may well require other skills, such as those relating to IT, law, risk management and so on. Furthermore, committee members may be put under enormous pressure to agree to controversial accounting policies. When faced with such pressure, the personal qualities mentioned earlier can be more important than formal accounting qualifications.

The UK Code states that the audit committee should consist of at least three or, in the case of smaller companies, two independent non-executive directors. Furthermore, the chair of the board should not be a committee member. To be effective, it should have direct access to key individuals such as the chief executive, the finance director and the heads of the internal and external audit teams. It must also have the authority and resources to carry out its responsibilities.

The audit committee should meet at least three times each year (see Reference 7 at the end of the chapter) and sufficient time should be devoted to each meeting. Only members of the committee are normally entitled to attend these meetings, although others may be invited to attend if needed. Some meetings should be timed to coincide with important events such as the start of the annual audit and the announcement of the annual results. In practice, it seems that audit committees meet at least four times a year, excluding teleconference calls (see Reference 8 at the end of the chapter).

The review process

When reviewing the company's internal controls, the committee should examine the effectiveness of the processes put in place by the internal and external audit teams. The committee must be satisfied that the internal controls are operating smoothly and that recommendations for improvement have been implemented. When reviewing the company's risk management systems, the committee should check that key risk areas are being monitored and that any control failures, or emerging risks, are quickly identified and dealt with. The committee must also be satisfied that risk management is not simply a 'box-ticking' exercise and that everyone appreciates its importance.

When reviewing the internal audit function, the committee should agree the remit that the internal auditors have been given by the board and the resources that they have been allocated. The committee should look at the internal audit work plan and receive regular updates on the work carried out. It should also receive feedback on the responses by management to recommendations provided by the internal auditors. To boost their independence and status, internal auditors are often given direct access to the audit committee and to the chair.

When reviewing the external audit process, the audit committee should consider the experience, expertise and resources of the audit team. It should also review the effectiveness of the audit process. This will usually involve scrutinising audit plans and procedures and seeing how they fit with the work carried out by the internal auditors. It will also involve checking that sufficient time is spent on the audit and that key risk areas are receiving attention. To monitor progress, there should be meetings with the external auditor. Topics for discussion may include any major issues that have been identified and whether they have been resolved. They may also include a review of key audit decisions and any errors that have been unearthed.

To ensure the independence of the auditors is not threatened, the committee should monitor any non-audit services undertaken by the external auditors.

What do you think the audit committee should consider when reviewing the non-audit services provided?

It should consider:

- the type of non-audit work carried out;
- the fees provided for the work carried out;
- whether the external auditors are the most suitable candidates for the work carried out; and
- the regulations concerning the provision of non-audit work.

Each year, the audit committee should recommend to shareholders whether the external auditors should be reappointed. (See Reference 9 at the end of the chapter.)

When reviewing the financial statements, the audit committee should pay particular attention to:

- the accounting policies adopted and whether they conform to the industry norm;
- any changes to accounting policies;
- the estimates and judgements made in key areas such as bad debts, provisions, depreciation and so on;
- any unusual items, such as large write-offs, or unusual relationships, such as very high bad debts to sales revenue figure; and
- any unusual trends in financial performance or position.

This should help to identify irregular accounting practices or fraudulent behaviour.

The committee should also review other information presented in the annual reports that relate to the financial statements, such as the strategic report. It can then advise the board whether the annual reports, as a whole, are fair, balanced and understandable.

The audit committee will produce a report for shareholders to be included within the annual report. The report sets out the main features of the committee including its role, membership and frequency of meetings. It also sets out how the committee has gone about its work. This should include a description of significant issues examined by the committee and how they were addressed. It should also explain how the effectiveness of the external auditors was assessed and how their independence was protected. In practice, the quality of audit committee reports can vary considerably. Not all contain useful information. Some would benefit from a more focused approach that provides more detail concerning key issues and decisions.

Audit committee reports are presented to the annual general meeting of shareholders, which the chair of the audit committee should attend. This allows shareholders the opportunity to question the chair on any matters for which the committee has responsibility.

Problems with audit committees

Over time, the audit committee has had to take on increased responsibilities and its work has been subject to much greater scrutiny. This places committee members under considerable pressure, which may, in turn, promote a cautious approach. A 'compliance' mentality may develop that inhibits creativity and risk taking, which are essential to long-term prosperity (see Reference 10 at the end of the chapter). The pressures mentioned may also discourage individuals from chairing the audit committee, or even becoming a member of it. A great deal of time and effort is normally required to undertake the work involved and an individual's reputation may suffer irreparable damage if things go wrong.

The composition of the audit committee is a contentious issue. We saw earlier that only one committee member is required to have recent and relevant financial experience. Furthermore, no member is required to possess a professional accountancy qualification. This raises the risk that the audit committee will lack the depth and breadth of expertise to handle highly technical accounting issues. Where only one committee member has relevant financial experience, there is also the risk that the burden of dealing with these issues will not be evenly spread. These problems may be mitigated by the committee seeking outside, independent advice; nevertheless, there remains a strong case for requiring a higher minimum level of financial literacy for audit committee members.

Finally, the costs involved in carrying out the tasks of an audit committee are very high. It is not always clear whether the benefits gained outweigh these costs. This is an important issue that has probably not received sufficient attention by researchers.

REMUNERATING DIRECTORS

Setting an appropriate level of remuneration for directors is not an easy task. It can, however, be vitally important to the success of the company. In this section, we consider some key issues that surround this area.

Remuneration policy

The remuneration package of an executive director of a large listed company is usually made up of two elements:

- a fixed element, which is largely in the form of a base salary but will also include benefits such as pension contributions, medical insurance, company car and so on; and
- a variable element, which rewards directors on the basis of both short-term and long-term results.

This latter element is designed to motivate directors to improve performance.

The short-term, variable element usually takes the form of an annual bonus, typically expressed as a multiple of base salary. Not all of the bonus may be paid at the year end; some may be deferred. Deferral may be undertaken on a voluntary or compulsory basis.

Activity 12.19

Why might part of the annual bonus be deferred on a compulsory basis?

One reason is to reduce the risk of paying directors a large sum on the basis of only one year's performance. Instead, a part of the bonus is paid at a later date, subject to satisfactory performance during the deferral period. A further reason for deferral is that it can provide a financial incentive for directors to stay with the company. Directors may become ineligible for the deferred part of a bonus if they leave before the end of the deferral period.

The deferred part of the bonus will normally be invested in company shares during the deferral period, which is often three years. Where part of the bonus is deferred, the directors may receive matching shares to compensate for the deferred amount.

Annual bonuses are paid to directors for achieving prescribed levels of performance. This often relies on the use of profit-based measures (such as operating profit and earnings per share) in conjunction with non-financial measures (such as those relating to personal performance).

The long-term performance reward normally takes the form of a **performance share plan (PSP)**. Under this type of plan, the directors are awarded a specified number of shares in the company. These shares are again awarded for achieving predefined levels of performance. The shares may be awarded on an 'all or nothing basis', that is, all of the shares will be awarded if the performance level is reached and none will be awarded if it is not. Alternatively, shares may be awarded on a sliding scale according to the actual level of performance achieved. Awarding shares, in addition to the number specified, may be used to reward exceptional performance. The shares will be awarded to directors at the end of the performance period, which is typically three to five years.

Under a performance share plan, directors may be awarded **restricted shares**. This type of share is issued to the directors immediately, but the shares are not owned outright. They may be forfeited under certain circumstances, such as where the directors fail to reach the prescribed level of performance, or where they leave the company before the end of the performance period. Restricted shares are rarely issued in the UK.

Share awards will transfer to directors some of the risks and rewards of being a shareholder. This may help directors to think more like shareholders and to strive to enhance shareholder wealth. The process for awarding shares, however, can provoke much head scratching. Finding an appropriate performance measure, setting the appropriate performance level for triggering a bonus award and determining the number of shares to be awarded to directors are all areas fraught with difficulties.

The main elements of the remuneration package for an executive director of a listed public company are summarised in Figure 12.3.

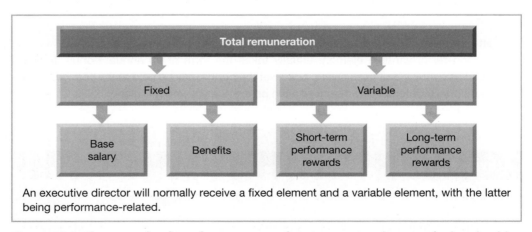

An executive director will normally receive a fixed element and a variable element, with the latter being performance-related.

Figure 12.3 The main elements of remuneration for an executive director of a listed public company

In large listed companies, the variable (performance-related) element typically accounts for a large proportion of the total remuneration for executive directors. In practice, however, the variable element may contain a hidden fixed element. Few directors of large companies receive no annual bonus at all (see Reference 11 at the end of the chapter). The methods used to calculate the variable element of directors' remuneration can be very complicated. This can make it difficult to discover the link between the amounts awarded to directors and the company's financial results.

Real World 12.9 provides an impression of how the total remuneration for executive directors of the UK's largest companies is made up.

Real World 12.9

Just rewards?

KPMG, the accounting and consulting firm, revealed in its 2017 Guide to Directors' Remuneration the following median figures and other details relating to annual basic salaries, annual bonuses and performance share payments for executive directors in the 100 largest listed UK companies.

	Chief Executive	Finance Director	Other executive directors
Basic salary	£871,000	£552,000	£546,000
Total annual bonus received (as percentage of salary)	130%	124%	138%
Maximum permitted bonus deferral (as percentage of salary)	50%	50%	50%
Deferral period	3 years	3 years	3 years
PSP maximum award (as a percentage of salary)	250%	205%	200%
PSP actual award (as percentage of salary)	245%	201%	196%
Total earnings	£3,478,000	£2,128,000	£1,951,000

Source: Guide to Directors' Remuneration 2017, KPMG, Extracts from Summary, p. 2.

A comparison of the data in Real Worlds 12.2 and 12.9 reveals a huge gulf between the remuneration received by part-time, non-executive directors and that received by full-time, executive directors.

The UK Code regards a performance-related element for the remuneration of non-executive directors as inappropriate. It takes the view that non-executive directors should be rewarded on the basis of the time spent and responsibilities undertaken on behalf of the company.

Activity 12.20

Do you agree with this position? Should non-executive directors, as well as executive directors, have a performance-related element to their remuneration?

The view taken is that offering performance-related remuneration may undermine their independence. Not all countries, however, adopt this view.

Tenure and service contracts

The UK Code requires that all directors submit themselves for annual re-election by shareholders. This is designed to encourage greater accountability. There are, however, concerns that it can be disruptive and can encourage short-term thinking among board members. The chair should not remain in position for more than nine years, according to the Code.

Directors are normally given service contracts, but these should not provide immunity against poor performance. Where directors have underperformed, the board must be prepared to terminate their contracts. To prevent the risk of overcompensation when contracts are terminated, the UK Code states that notice periods should be no longer than one year and any compensation awarded should exclude rewards for poor performance. In practice, however, poor performance may prove no obstacle to receiving a handsome payout. **Real World 12.10** provides a recent example of where directors were accused of being rewarded for failure.

Real World 12.10

Rewarding failure?

The main lobby group representing UK bosses has savaged the 'highly inappropriate' pay packets awarded to directors running the now-collapsed construction giant Carillion. Roger Barker, head of corporate governance at the Institute of Directors, said the collapse of the company 'suggests that effective governance was lacking at Carillion'. He added: 'There are some worrying signs. The relaxation of clawback conditions for executive bonuses in 2016 appears in retrospect to be highly inappropriate. It does no good to the reputation of UK business when top managers appear to benefit in spite of the collapse of the organisations that they are responsible for.'

His comments on clawback refer to a change in the company's pay policy made in 2016 that limited the criteria under which the company could demand the repayment of executive bonuses. Previously the firm could ask for cash back if the business went bust but the revised policy said it could only do so in the event of gross misconduct or if the financial results had been misstated.

Much of the criticism has centred on Richard Howson, Carillion's former chief executive from 2012 until a shock profit warning last July resulted in his stepping down. Howson earned £1.5 million in 2016, including £591,000 in bonuses. He continued to work for the firm until last autumn after stepping down as chief executive and is due to stay on the payroll, receiving his £660,000 salary and £28,000 benefits for another year, until October 2018.

Vince Cable, the Liberal Democrat leader and former business secretary, said he hoped that bonuses paid to Carillion's chief executive would be clawed back. In an interview with the BBC's Daily Politics he said it was 'an absolute outrage' that senior executives should receive 'rewards for failure in this way'.

Source: Extracts from Goodley, S. (2018) Carillion's 'highly inappropriate' pay packets criticised, *Guardian*, 15 January.

Remuneration committee

The remuneration committee is the cornerstone of the UK Code's attempt to ensure that directors' rewards are appropriate. The UK Code states that this committee should be responsible for setting remuneration for the chair, executive directors and for senior management. For larger companies, the committee should consist of at least three (and for smaller companies at least two) independent non-executive directors.

Although this committee is meant to prevent executive directors from being over-rewarded, critics point out that, in recent years, directors' pay and benefits have increased at a much faster rate than have corporate profits and sales (or the pay and benefits in other occupations). Furthermore, studies have shown that the relationship between directors' pay and performance is not a very clear one (see Reference 12 at the end of the chapter).

The composition of the remuneration committee means that non-executive directors are responsible for determining the awards of executive directors. We have seen, however, that non-executive directors are often executive directors of other companies, which creates the risk that they will be sympathetic to a high-reward culture. To act as a counterweight, there have been calls for a representative of the workforce to be a member of the remuneration committee.

Activity 12.21

What objections may be raised to having a workforce representative on this committee? Try to think of at least one.

A number of objections have been raised. They include:

- the risk that the representative will not understand the company's strategy and the broader business context with which remuneration decisions are made;
- the difficulty of finding workforce representative that would truly reflect the views of the whole workforce, particularly for large international companies;
- the difficulty of finding a representative willing to challenge the directors and, perhaps, put at risk future career prospects; and
- the risk that the authority of the board will be weakened by having a workforce representative on a board committee.

The revised UK Code does not support the idea of a workers' representative but is sympathetic towards the workforce exerting a greater influence on board decisions generally. It requires the board of directors to engage with the workforce in order to understand its views and states that this should normally be done through one, or more, of the following mechanisms:

- a director appointed from the workforce;
- a workforce advisory panel; and/or
- a designated non-executive director.

Whether this greater engagement provides a moderating influence on directors' remuneration remains to be seen.

In addition to problems of committee membership, there are problems with the way in which the committee operates. It is to these problems that we now turn.

Problems with the process

Various studies have pointed to problems with the way in which remuneration committees operate. One study by Main and others (see Reference 13 at the end of the chapter) interviewed 22 independent non-executive directors with experience of remuneration committees and found that the companies for which they served held, on average, 4.8 committee meetings per year. These meetings were tightly scheduled and often fairly brief (on average 1.5 hours). Despite the importance of their role, it seems that these committees do not devote much time to carrying it out. The study also found that it was quite common for the chief executive officer and chair to be present at remuneration committee meetings.

Why might the presence of the CEO and chair be a problem?

While it may be useful for the committee to receive their input at times, there is a danger that the independence of the committee will be compromised by their presence.

There is some evidence that committee members lack the experience and training to carry out their tasks effectively (see Reference 14 at the end of the chapter). This can be a particular problem when hiring a new chief executive officer. The pool of talent for chief executives is small and it is a 'seller's market'. As a result, to recruit a suitable candidate, the committee may be tempted to offer more than is necessary. Incumbent chief executive officers may also be over-rewarded. They are often powerful personalities with considerable influence over other board members. There is a risk that committee members will be too deferential and will err on the side of generosity in contract negotiations.

There is some concern as to how market data is used by remuneration committees in formulating appropriate reward packages. Too great a focus on market trends and statistics can lead to a 'ratcheting effect' on executive directors' rewards. This occurs when the data is used to justify increases in rewards because companies do not want to be seen paying below-average rewards to directors. The upward pressure on the average level of rewards occurs without a corresponding increase in performance.

Non-executive directors

Setting up a remuneration committee does not deal with the problem of who decides the pay of the non-executive directors.

Who do you think should decide the pay of the non-executive directors?

The UK Corporate Governance Code states that this should be done in accordance with the company's documents of incorporation, or by the board of directors. In the latter case, the executive directors largely decide the pay of the non-executive directors (a point which may not be lost on those non-executive directors serving on the remuneration committee!).

Reporting directors' remuneration

Listed companies are required by law to prepare an annual directors' remuneration report that consists of two parts. The first part is concerned with remuneration policy. It must set out each element of remuneration to which each director is entitled and how it supports the company's strategy and performance. Shareholders are given a binding vote, at least every three years, whether to approve this part of the report. The second part must set out how the remuneration policy was implemented during the financial year. It will contain a figure for the total pay each director receives, which includes all benefits received such as salaries, pension benefits, benefits in kind and share awards. Reporting this single figure should help comparisons to be made over time and between companies. Shareholders are given an advisory vote each year as to whether to approve this part of the report.

The chair of the remuneration committee will normally attend the shareholders' meeting to deal with any issues that may arise.

Activity 12.24

How might these requirements to publish influence the level of directors' remuneration?

Publishing a remuneration report, as well as seeking shareholder approval for remuneration policy and remuneration payments, may help to moderate the level of directors' remuneration.

There is some concern, however, that the reporting requirements could have unintended consequences. It has been suggested, for example, that the disclosure of sensitive, pay-related, information could increase the ratcheting effect on directors' pay.

PERFORMANCE MEASURES

We saw earlier that much of the remuneration received by executive directors is performance-related. Various performance measures can be used as a basis for rewarding directors and we shall go on to consider some of the more popular of these. Before doing so, however, it is useful to identify the characteristics that a good performance measure should possess. Perhaps the key characteristics are that it should:

- be in line with the objectives and strategy of the company;
- lead to a convergence of directors' and shareholders' interests;
- reflect the achievement of the directors; and
- be robust and not easily distorted by particular policies, financing arrangements or manipulative practices.

No single performance measure perfectly encapsulates all of these characteristics. In practice, therefore, companies often employ a combination of measures. When calculating an annual bonus for executive directors, for example, the majority of large UK companies use three or more measures (see Reference 11 at the end of the chapter).

Let us now turn our attention to three of the more popular performance measures found in practice.

Total shareholder return

Total shareholder return (TSR) is a measure that investors employ to assess value created. It is also used as a basis for rewarding directors. The total return from a share is made up as follows:

1 the increase (or decrease) in share value over a period plus (minus); and
2 any dividends paid during the period.

This total return is usually expressed as a percentage of the start-of-period share price.
To illustrate how total shareholder return is calculated, let us assume that a company started trading after issuing shares of £0.50 each at their nominal value (P_0) and by the end of the first

year of trading the shares had increased in value to £0.55 (P_1). Furthermore, the company paid a dividend of £0.06 (D_1) per share during the period. We can calculate the total shareholder return as follows:

$$\text{Total shareholder return} = \frac{D_1 + (P_1 - P_0)}{P_0} \times 100\%$$

$$= \frac{0.06 + (0.55 - 0.50)}{0.50} \times 100\% = 22\%$$

The figure calculated has little information value when taken alone. It can only really be used to assess performance when compared with some benchmark.

Activity 12.25

What benchmark would be most suitable?

Perhaps the best benchmark to use would be the returns made by similar companies operating in the same industry over the same period of time.

Where this benchmark is used, returns generated will be compared with those generated from other investment opportunities with the same level of risk.

TSR and directors' rewards

Using TSR as a basis for rewarding directors has been subject to much criticism. This measure has a number of serious flaws, which include the following:

■ Share prices reflect investors' views concerning future returns. This means that directors receive rewards based on expected future performance rather than on actual performance, though it can be argued that the dividend plus the increase in the share price has actually occurred.

■ Prices quoted for the shares of a listed company may not provide a reliable guide to their 'true' value. There may be times when investors' perceptions about the value of shares become detached from underlying reality.

■ Share price movements may be beyond the control of directors. (For this reason, TSR-based incentives have been described as a lottery for directors.)

■ Directors may achieve higher share returns by simply taking on higher-risk projects. This policy shift may not, however, align with the risk appetite of investors.

■ The contribution of individual directors to changes in TSR cannot normally be determined.

■ Finding similar companies against which to assess relative performance may be difficult. There is also the risk that unsuitable companies will be deliberately selected by directors to make their performance appear better than it is.

■ TSR can be manipulated over the short term (by, for example, the timing of important announcements).

Economic value added (EVA®)

Performance targets based on **economic value added (EVA®)** offer another approach. This measure has been developed and trademarked by a US management consultancy firm, Stern Stewart. EVA®, however, is based on the idea of economic profit, which has been around for many years. The measure reflects the point made earlier that for a company to be profitable in an economic sense, it must generate returns that exceed the returns required by investors. It is not enough simply to make an accounting profit, because this measure does not take full account of the returns required by investors.

EVA® indicates whether the returns generated exceed the returns required by investors. The formula is:

$$EVA® = NOPAT - (R \times C)$$

where:

NOPAT = Net operating profit after tax

R = Returns required by investors (that is, the cost of capital)

C = Capital invested (that is, the net assets of the company).

Activity 12.26

Dena plc has net assets of £250 million and the required return from investors is 10 per cent. The company made a net operating profit of £50 million for the year and the appropriate tax rate is 20 per cent. What is the EVA® for the year?

EVA® will be:

$$(£50 - (20\% \times £50m)) - (10\% \times £250m) = £15m$$

Only when EVA® is positive can we say that the company is increasing shareholder wealth. To maximise shareholder wealth, managers must increase EVA® by as much as possible.

Activity 12.27

What can managers do in order to increase EVA®? (*Hint*: use the formula shown above as your starting point.)

The formula suggests that in order to increase EVA®, managers may try to:

■ Increase NOPAT. This may be done either by reducing expenses or by increasing sales revenue.

■ Use capital invested more efficiently. This means selling off assets that are not generating returns that exceed their cost and investing in assets that do; and/or

■ reduce the required rates of return for investors. This may be achieved by changing the capital structure in favour of long-term borrowing (which tends to be cheaper to service than share capital).

EVA® relies on conventional financial statements to measure the wealth created for shareholders. However, the NOPAT and capital figures shown on these statements are used only as a starting point. They have to be adjusted because of the problems and limitations of conventional measures. According to Stern Stewart, the major problem is that profit and capital are understated because of the conservative bias in accounting measurement. Profit may be understated as a result of arbitrary write-offs such as research and development expenditure written off and as a result of excessive provisions being created (such as allowances for trade receivables). Capital may also be understated because assets are reported at their original cost (less amounts written off), which can produce figures considerably below current market values. In addition, certain assets such as internally generated goodwill and brand names are normally omitted from the financial statements because no external transactions have occurred.

Stern Stewart has identified more than a hundred adjustments that could be made to the conventional financial statements to eliminate the conservative bias. However, it believes that, in practice, only a handful of adjustments to the accounting figures of any particular company tend to be needed. Unless an adjustment is going to have a significant effect on the calculation of EVA®, it is really not worth making.

EVA and directors' rewards

Under EVA®, directors can receive rewards based on achievement over a particular period. Where that period is only one year, directors are given an incentive to increase EVA® over the short term. This may be achieved, however, by cutting back on investment. To encourage a longer-term perspective, rewards should be based on the ability of directors to improve EVA® over a number of years.

The amount of EVA® generated during a period is rarely reported to shareholders. This means that shareholders will be unable to check whether rewards given to directors are appropriate.

Earnings per share

We may recall that the earnings per share (EPS) ratio (considered in Chapter 9) is calculated as follows:

$$\text{Earnings per share} = \frac{\text{Earnings available to ordinary shareholders}}{\text{Number of ordinary shares in issue}}$$

When used as a basis for directors' incentive plans, a particular level of growth in EPS is usually required in order to trigger rewards.

A major difficulty with using this measure for rewarding directors is that an increase in EPS does not necessarily lead to an increase in shareholder wealth. EPS may be increased by embarking on higher risk ventures with higher prospective returns. This higher risk will, however, be reflected in a lower share price. A further difficulty is that EPS can be increased in the short term by changing certain management decisions and accounting policies.

Activity 12.28

Can you think how EPS could be increased in the short term by changes in management decisions and accounting policies?

Management can decide to restrict expenditure on discretionary items such as training, research and nurturing brands. Changes in accounting policies, such as changing the point at which revenue is recognised, and changes in depreciation methods can also increase EPS in the short term.

Other measures of performance, such as return on capital employed, profit before interest and tax or some measure of cash flow generated, are used in practice to reward executive directors. They often suffer, however, from the same sort of problems that afflict EPS.

Real World 12.11 provides some insight to the popularity of the measures discussed among larger UK listed businesses.

Measure for measure

The KPMG survey mentioned earlier found that PSPs continue to be the most common form of LTIP for the largest 100 listed companies. Furthermore, TSR and EPS are the most popular measures for inclusion in PSPs. The findings of the survey are set out in Figure 12.4.

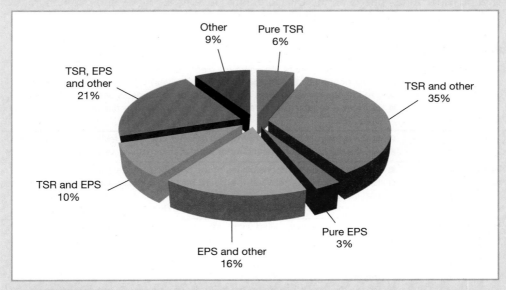

Figure 12.4 Target measures for inclusion in PSPs

The measures falling under the category 'Other' include measures such as profits, cash flow, share price targets and return on capital.

Source: Guide to Directors' Remuneration 2017, KPMG, p. 59.

ASSESSING BOARD PERFORMANCE

It was mentioned earlier that the performance of the board should be subject to regular evaluation. This raises the question as to who should carry out the evaluation. The choice is effectively between the board members themselves or an external party, such as a firm of management consultants. In practice, it seems that boards prefer self-evaluation. The UK Code, however, states that, for larger companies, an external evaluation should be undertaken at least every three years.

What are the advantages and disadvantages of board members, rather than an external party, evaluating board performance?

The main advantage is that the board members have an intimate knowledge of the company's business and of board operations. They should therefore be in a position to ask more searching questions. A further advantage is that there is a low risk that confidentiality will be breached.

A disadvantage is that shareholders might view this as being rather too cosy an arrangement. They may feel that an external party would provide a more objective and a more rigorous assessment of board performance. This may give more credibility to the process (although the cost is likely to be much higher).

A second question raised concerns the areas of performance that should be evaluated. Some possible areas, based on the UK Corporate Governance Code and other sources of good practice, are set out in Table 12.1.

Table 12.1 Evaluating board performance

Company objectives	■ Are the objectives of the company clearly set out? ■ Is the board fully committed to these objectives? ■ Are the objectives used as a framework for board decisions? ■ Is there a regular board review of progress towards the achievement of the objectives?
Controlling the company	■ Is the system of internal control and reporting regularly reviewed by the board? ■ Are the risk management and reporting systems regularly reviewed by the board?
Board structure and roles	■ Are the roles and responsibilities of the board clearly defined? ■ Is the relationship between the board and key board committees appropriate and clear? ■ Are the roles of the chair and non-executive directors appropriate and clear?
Board meetings	■ Are board meetings called with sufficient frequency to permit timely decisions? ■ Is relevant material, including written agendas and minutes of previous meetings, sent to directors prior to a board meeting? ■ Are all directors required to attend board meetings and what is their attendance record? ■ Do the discussions at board meetings focus on strategic rather than operational issues? ■ Are urgent problems arising between board meetings properly managed and reported?
Board composition	■ Is there a separation of the roles of chair and chief executive? ■ Does the board reflect an appropriate balance between executive and non-executive directors? ■ Does the board membership reflect an appropriate mix of age, skills and experience? ■ Is the membership of important board committees, such as remuneration and audit committees, appropriate? ■ Do the tenure agreements of board members provide the opportunity to refresh the board over time?
Board discussions and decisions	■ Does the board work together in an effective manner? ■ Do board discussions result in appropriate decisions being made? ■ Are board decisions implemented and monitored? ■ Are board members given the time and opportunity to express their views on key issues? ■ Is the contribution of all directors at board meetings satisfactory? ■ Are board discussions and decisions dominated by key individuals?
Board relations with shareholders	■ Are there appropriate policies in place for communicating with shareholders? ■ Are the communication channels established between the board and institutional and private shareholders appropriate? ■ Are shareholders satisfied that their views are heard and considered by the board?
Board appointments and development	■ Are rigorous procedures in place for the appointment of new directors? ■ Are there clearly defined and appropriate procedures in place for appraising the performance of individual directors? ■ Are appropriate training and development programmes (including induction programmes) available to board members? ■ Has the board developed clear succession plans?

Improving corporate governance has focused mainly on developing a framework of rules for managing listed companies. Whilst rules are important, it is also important for the shareholders, who own the companies, to play their part by actively monitoring and controlling directors' behaviour. We shall now identify the main shareholders of listed companies and discuss their role in establishing good corporate governance. We also consider why there has been greater shareholder activism in recent years.

Who are the main shareholders?

Real World 12.12 provides an analysis of the ownership of shares in UK listed companies at the end of 2016.

Real World 12.12

Going overseas

The breakdown of ownership of UK listed shares as at 31 December 2016 is shown in Figure 12.5.

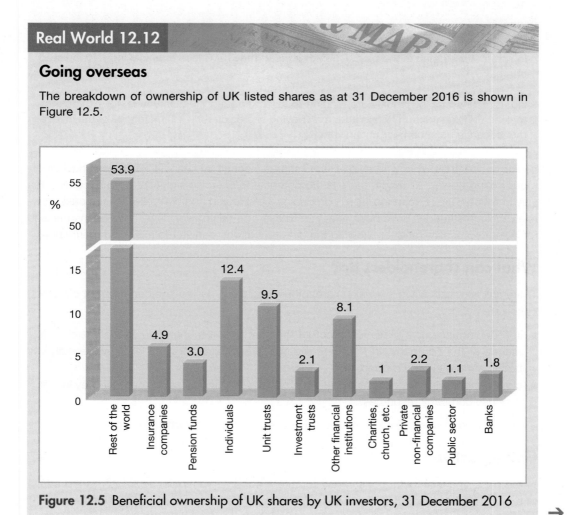

Figure 12.5 Beneficial ownership of UK shares by UK investors, 31 December 2016

Looking at the changes in the ownership of listed shares over the years shows two striking features:

1 the value of listed shares owned by overseas residents has gone up progressively from 30.7 per cent in 1998 to 53.9 per cent in 2016; and
2 the value of listed shares held by UK individuals has fallen from 16.7 per cent in 1998 to 12.3 per cent in 2016.

However, the percentage of shares held by each group appears to have stabilised in the past few years.

There is no reason to believe that the 53.9 per cent of shares owned by non-UK shareholders is any more weighted towards individuals than is the case with UK shareholders.

Source: *Ownership of UK Quoted Shares 2016*, Table 4, Office for National Statistics, 29 November 2017. Office for National Statistics licensed under the Open Government Licence v.3.0.

Activity 12.30

The rise of financial institutions means that private individuals have less direct investment in listed shares than in the past. Does that mean they have less financial interest in listed shares?

No. It means that individuals are tending to invest through the institutions, for example by making pension contributions rather than buying shares directly. Ultimately, all of the investment finance must come from individuals.

The concentration of ownership of listed shares means that financial institutions have enormous voting power. As result, there is the potential to exercise significant influence over the way in which Stock Exchange listed companies are directed and controlled. In the past, however, these institutions have been reluctant to exercise this power. They have been criticised for being too passive and for allowing the directors of companies too much independence.

What can shareholders do?

There are two main ways in which shareholders can try to control the behaviour of directors. These are by:

■ introducing incentive plans for directors that link their remuneration to the share performance of the company. In this way, the interests of directors and shareholders should become more closely aligned; and
■ closely monitoring the actions of the directors and exerting influence over the way in which they use company resources.

The first issue was picked up earlier. It is the second issue to which we now turn.

Getting active

In the past, financial institutions chose to take a non-interventionist approach to the affairs of a company. Instead, they confined their investment activities to deciding whether to buy, hold or sell shares in a particular company. They appear to have taken the view that the costs of actively engaging with directors and trying to influence their decisions are too high in relation to the likely benefits. It is worth pointing out that these costs are borne by the particular financial institution that becomes actively involved, whereas the benefits are spread across all shareholders. (This phenomenon is often referred to as the 'free-rider' problem.)

Waking the sleeping giants

In recent years, financial institutions have begun to play a more active role in corporate governance. More time is being invested in monitoring the actions of directors and in engaging with them over key decisions. This change of heart has occurred for a variety of reasons. One important reason is that the increasing concentration of share ownership has made it more difficult for financial institutions to simply walk away from an investment in a poorly performing company by selling its shares.

Activity 12.31

Why might it be a problem for a financial institution that holds a substantial number of shares in a poorly performing company to simply sell the shares?

Where a substantial number of shares are held, a decision to sell can have a significant impact on the market price, perhaps leading to heavy losses.

A further reason why it may be difficult to disinvest is that a company's shares may be included in a stock market index (such as the FTSE 100 or FTSE 250). Certain types of financial institution, such as investment trusts or unit trusts, may offer investments that are designed to 'track' the particular index and so they become locked into a company's shares in order to reflect the index. In both situations outlined, therefore, a financial institution may have little choice but to stick with the shares held and try to improve performance by seeking to influence the actions and decisions of the directors.

It is also worth mentioning that financial institutions have experienced much greater competitive pressures in recent years. There have been increasing demands from clients for them to demonstrate their investment skills, and so justify their fees, by either outperforming benchmarks or beating the performance of rival financial institutions. This, in turn, has led the institutions to be less tolerant towards underperforming boards of directors.

Finally, the regulatory environment has favoured greater activism on the part of financial institutions. This point will be considered in more detail a little later.

Forms of activism

It is important to clarify the term 'shareholder activism' as it can take various forms. In its simplest form, it involves taking a more active role in voting for or against the resolutions put before the annual general meeting or any extraordinary general meeting of the company. This form of activism is seen by the UK government as being vital to good corporate governance. The government is keen to see much higher levels of participation than currently exist, and expects institutional shareholders to exercise their right to vote. In the past, financial institutions have often indicated their dissent by abstaining from a vote rather than by outright opposition to a resolution. However, they are now more prepared to use their vote to oppose resolutions of the board of directors.

A particularly rich source of contention between shareholders and directors' concerns directors' remuneration. **Real World 12.13** provides an example of a fairly recent falling out.

Revolting shareholders

Ryanair faces a fresh shareholder revolt at its annual meeting this month after adviser groups called on investors to vote against executive pay. An influential trio of advisers – Institutional Shareholder Services, Glass Lewis and Pirc – have recommended investors vote against the low-cost carrier's advisory pay report, flagging concerns about 'poor disclosure' and bonus payments.

Europe's biggest airline by passenger numbers has frequently clashed with shareholders at its annual meetings. Last year, almost a fifth of investors revolted on pay, marking the third year in a row when the airline faced significant protests over its remuneration policies. ISS, Glass Lewis and Pirc, whose recommendations are widely used by asset managers and pension funds when deciding how to vote, said the total pay of Michael O'Leary, Ryanair's chief executive, was not excessive, but expressed concerns about how his bonus was calculated. Mr O'Leary's total pay last year was €3.26 million, including a bonus.

Glass Lewis said it had 'severe reservations about supporting the remuneration report at this time'. 'We believe shareholders should be concerned by the structure of the company's executive remuneration programme and the inadequacy of disclosure regarding several aspects of executive compensation,' it said. ISS said: 'While there has been some improvement, the overall level of disclosure remains lacking and does not allow for visibility between the vigour of targets set against performance achieved by the company.'

Mr O'Leary has repeatedly dismissed concerns about pay structures at the airline and big bonuses at listed companies. 'My view of shareholders voting against my pay package is: if you don't like it, don't vote against it – sell your shares,' Mr O'Leary said last week.

The calls for a rebellion at Ryanair come as institutional investors increasingly show their teeth at annual meetings. Eighteen out of 20 big investors, including BlackRock, cast fewer votes in favour of management recommendations at AGMs in the year to the end of June, compared with the previous 12 months, according to data from Proxy Insight.

The latest version of the UK Code has sought to defuse some of the tensions relating to this issue by laying down various principles concerning how directors' remuneration should be managed and calculated. Thus, when setting directors' remuneration, the remuneration committee must try to promote long-term business success and must take account of wider company pay policy. The UK Code also requires that account be taken, among other things, of the need for clarity and simplicity when calculating rewards and the reputational risk arising from granting excessive rewards. To prevent undue reliance on formulaic calculations, the UK Code expects the remuneration committee to exercise discretion and independent judgement. Finally, it requires the committee to explain, in an annual report, the rationale for the remuneration policies adopted and the level of engagement that took place with shareholders and with the wider workforce concerning these policies.

The UK Code requires boards to be sensitive to shareholder dissatisfaction, which includes dissatisfaction over directors' remuneration. Where 20 per cent, or more, of shareholder votes have been cast against a board resolution, the board should seek feedback from shareholders on the contentious issue. It should also explain in the annual report what impact this feedback had on board decisions and what further action is proposed.

Shareholder revolts over directors' remuneration often catch the headlines but are still fairly unusual occurrences. During 2017, there were only two instances among the largest 350 listed businesses where a majority of votes were cast against the directors' remuneration report. (See Reference 15 at the end of the chapter.) Nevertheless, the benefits for shareholders of flexing their muscles and voting against resolutions put forward by the directors may go beyond their immediate, intended objective: other boards of directors may take note of shareholder dissatisfaction and adjust their behaviour in an attempt to avoid a similar fate. The cost of voting need not be high as there are specialist agencies which offer research and advice to financial institutions on how their votes should be cast.

Another form of activism involves meetings and discussions between representatives of a particular financial institution and the board of directors of a company. At such meetings, a wide range of issues affecting the company may be discussed.

Activity 12.32

What might financial institutions wish to discuss with the directors of a company? Try to think of at least two financial and two non-financial aspects of the company.

Some of the more important aspects that are likely to attract their attention include:

- objectives and strategies adopted;
- trading performance;
- internal controls;
- policies regarding mergers and acquisitions;
- major investments and disinvestments;
- adherence to the recommendations of the UK Corporate Governance Code;
- corporate social responsibility; and
- directors' incentive schemes and remuneration.

This is not an exhaustive list. For shareholders, as owners of the company, anything that might have an impact on their wealth should be a matter of concern.

This form of activism requires a fairly high degree of involvement with the company, and some of the larger financial institutions have dedicated teams for this purpose. This can be, therefore, a costly exercise.

Meetings between financial institutions and the managers of the companies, in which they hold shares, can be a useful mechanism for exchanging views and for gaining a greater understanding of the needs and motivations of each party. This may help to pre-empt public arguments between the board of directors and financial institutions, which is rarely the best way to resolve issues.

The final form of activism involves intervention in the affairs of the company. This, however, can be very costly, depending on the nature of the problem. Where strategic and operational issues raise concerns, intervention can be very costly indeed. Identifying the weaknesses and problems relating to these issues requires a detailed understanding of the nature of the business. This implies close monitoring by relevant experts who can analyse the issues and then propose feasible solutions. The costs associated with such an exercise would normally be prohibitive, although the costs may be mitigated through some kind of collective action by financial institutions.

Not all forms of intervention in the affairs of a company, however, need be costly. Where, for example, there are corporate governance issues to be addressed, such as a failure to adhere to the recommendations of the UK Corporate Governance Code, a financial institution may nominate individuals for appointment as non-executive directors who can be relied upon to ensure that necessary changes are made. This should involve relatively little cost for the financial institution.

The main forms of shareholder activism are summarised in Figure 12.6.

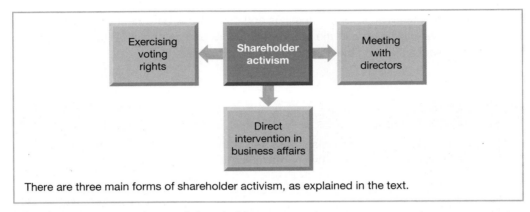

There are three main forms of shareholder activism, as explained in the text.

Figure 12.6 The main forms of shareholder activism

UK Stewardship Code

To improve the quality of engagement between financial institutions and investee businesses, the Financial Reporting Council (FRC) has published the UK Stewardship Code. This sets out key principles concerning the way in which financial institutions should engage with investee businesses. They relate to financial institutions:

■ establishing policies relating to stewardship and voting procedures, along with periodic reporting of how these policies were actioned.
■ checking on investee businesses
■ establishing the circumstances under which stewardship activities are intensified and accepting the need, at times, to act in concert with other shareholders.
■ disclosing conflicts of interest arising from stewardship activities and how they are resolved.

The Code also offers guidance on how these principles should be enacted.

Real World 12.14 describes how Thomas Miller Investment (TMI) will escalate its stewardship activities so as to protect shareholder value. This relates to the fourth requirement of the Code identified above.

The UK Stewardship Code, like the UK Governance Code, operates on a 'comply or explain' basis. It is designed to provide principles and guidance rather than rigid rules. Financial institutions that are signatories to the code are graded, or tiered, by the FRC according to the quality and transparency of the information provided.

Getting active

As a general policy we aim to support the management of the companies in which we invest but our dialogue with companies is a robust one and we will form our own views on the strategy and governance of a business. On occasion our views may differ from those of management or the Board and this may give rise to an escalation in our engagement. Factors taken into account prior to an escalation include an assessment of the materiality of the matter in dispute, the size of our shareholding, the timeframe of the investment thesis and the ownership profile of the business in question. Escalation can also occur when we become aware of differences between directors. Our specific response will always be determined on a case by case basis and there will be instances when we choose to sell our shares.

When escalation is deemed appropriate our first step is often to make contact with other significant shareholders to determine whether they share our views or concerns. Following these conversations, we will speak to the company's advisers and/or independent directors for a further exchange of views. Our strong preference is to achieve our objectives in a consensual and confidential manner but when differences with a company remain we may consider joint engagement with other shareholders, escalating concerns if necessary to regulators and more public forms of dissent, although as a general policy we do not favour using the media to help achieve our objectives. If differences with a company remain unresolved we may vote against the Board in a general meeting or even requisition an extraordinary general meeting to enable all investors to vote on the matter in dispute. We would not normally intervene on an operational matter but topics which have given rise to escalation in the past include the need for management and/or Board change, strategy, capital structure, M&A, protection of shareholder rights, remuneration and other ESG-related issues.

Source: (2018) *Responsible Investment Policy* Fidelity International, February, P.4.

Shareholder activism and short-term behaviour

Shareholder activism is generally regarded as a force for good. There are times, however, when this may not be the case. Some shareholders engage with companies simply in order to extract short-term gains. **Real World 12.15** warns of the problems this can create.

The future of shareholder activism

Shareholder activism appears to be taken an increasing hold. In a study of 400 activist campaigns in the US, McKinsey and Co found that shareholder activism is becoming more frequent and target businesses are becoming larger in size. Perhaps unsurprisingly, the study also found that activism is often provoked by the underperformance of a business in relation to industry peers. While three quarters of activist campaigns began by taking a collaborative approach, almost half of these eventually turned hostile (see Reference 16 at the end of the chapter.)

A key question to be asked is whether shareholder activism makes any real difference to financial performance. Early research in the US was not encouraging for those who urge large investing institutions to take a more active approach. However, a more recent study of 2,000 active interventions found that the operating performance of US businesses was improved for a five-year period following the interventions (see Reference 17 at the end of the chapter). The McKinsey study mentioned above also found a positive effect from activist interventions. The study states:

> Our analysis of 400 activist campaigns (out of 1,400 launched against US companies over the past decade) finds that, among large companies for which data are available, the median activist campaign reverses a downward trajectory in target-company performance and generates excess shareholder returns that persist for at least 36 months. (p. 1)

The key elements required for good corporate governance, which have just been discussed, are summarised in Figure 12.7.

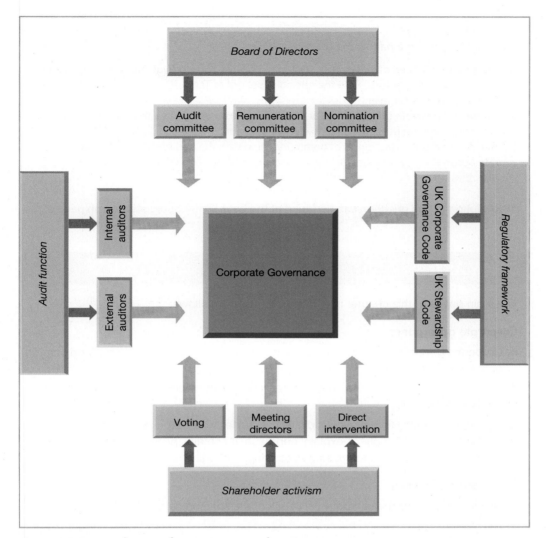

Figure 12.7 Key elements for ensuring good corporate governance

Self-assessment question 12.1

The board of directors of Hexworthy Publishers plc recently endured a stormy annual general meeting of shareholders. During this meeting, the directors were subjected to intense scrutiny and criticism. Two of the non-executive directors were not re-elected for office by shareholders and all members of the remuneration committee resigned when a proposed new long-term performance share plan for directors was comprehensively rejected.

At the meeting, shareholders expressed grave concerns over the way in which the company was being managed and felt that they were not being properly informed of key decisions. They were also concerned that the share price had fallen significantly over the past three years while directors' remuneration had increased significantly over the same period.

The board of directors met to decide how to respond to the anger of shareholders. At this meeting, it was decided to appoint Parix Consulting to carry out a thorough review of board performance. Parix Consulting would also be charged with advising the directors on the composition of the new remuneration committee and the ways in which communications between shareholders and the board could be improved.

→

Required:

Assume that you are a partner in Parix Consulting.

(a) Identify the sources of information that may be used to help evaluate the performance of the board of directors. (Use the checklist set out in Table 12.1 on p. 480 as the basis for carrying out this task.)

(b) Suggest a possible composition for the remuneration committee that may help to restrain excessive pay awards to executive directors.

(c) Set out recommended forms of communication with the shareholders, which incorporate corporate governance rules and good practice, for consideration by the board of directors.

The solution to this question can be found at the back of the book, starting on page 525.

SUMMARY

The main points of this chapter may be summarised as follows:

Corporate governance

- Corporate governance issues arise because of the separation of ownership from control of the company.
- Corporate governance rules are based around the principles of disclosure, accountability and fairness.
- The UK Corporate Governance Code, which applies to UK Stock Exchange listed companies, adopts a 'comply-or-explain' approach. It contains principles and guidance on corporate governance matters as well as annual reporting requirements.

The board of directors

- The board governs the company on behalf of the shareholders.
- It is responsible for setting the strategic direction, exercising control and nurturing relations with shareholders and others.
- The chair must lead and manage the board of directors.
- The chair's role involves ensuring that the board operates effectively, providing advice and support to directors, communicating with shareholders and ensuring that the performance of the board and the directors is subject to regular scrutiny.
- The UK Corporate Governance Code states that the roles of chair and chief executive should not be occupied by the same person. Furthermore, the chief executive should not go on to become chair of the same company.
- The board is made up of executive and non-executive directors, all of which have the same legal obligation to the shareholders of the company.

The role of non-executive directors

- Non-executive directors are part-time and do not engage in the day-to-day running of the company.
- This more detached role allows them to take a more objective view of issues confronting the company.

- Non-executive directors contribute to the main tasks of the board and also play a key role in board committees concerned with the nomination of directors, the remuneration of executive directors and the integrity of financial statements.
- The role of non-executive directors contains the potential for conflict between the need to work with executive directors as part of a team and the need to monitor and assess the performance of executive directors on behalf of the shareholders.

The audit process
- An external audit is required by all but the smallest companies.
- External auditors are appointed by, and report to, the shareholders. Their role is to examine the annual financial statements that have been prepared by the directors.
- Differences in perception can arise between external auditors and shareholders concerning the role of auditors.
- Various measures have been put in place to strengthen the independence of external auditors.
- Many large companies have an internal audit function to provide reassurance to directors about the reliability of the company's control and financial reporting systems.
- The UK Corporate Governance Code states that an audit committee should be created to ensure financial reporting and internal control principles are properly applied and for maintaining an appropriate relationship with the external auditors.
- The terms of reference of the committee will be determined by the board of directors.
- An audit committee report will be prepared for shareholders and presented at the AGM.

Remunerating directors
- The UK Corporate Governance Code states that executive directors' remuneration should be designed to promote strategy and long-term sustainable success of the company.
- The remuneration of executive directors will usually include a fixed element and a variable element, with the latter being linked to the achievement of performance targets.
- The variable element normally rewards short-term performance through an annual bonus and long-term performance through share awards.
- The remuneration committee is the cornerstone of the UK Corporate Governance Code's attempt to ensure that directors' rewards are appropriate.
- Various problems in the way in which a remuneration committee functions may have contributed to excessive rewards being paid to directors.

Performance measures
- Performance targets should be consistent with the objectives and strategy of the company, align the interests of directors with those of shareholders, reflect the achievement of the directors and be robust.
- TSR (total shareholder return) measures changes in shareholder wealth. To assess relative performance, similar companies must be used as a benchmark.

→

- EVA® (economic value added) indicates whether the returns generated exceed the returns required by investors. It relies on conventional financial statements to measure the wealth created but adjusts these to reflect the conservative bias in accounting measurement.

- EPS (earnings per share) can be used as a performance target by setting a particular level of growth required.

- Most listed public companies use a variety of measures and incentives to reward executive directors rather than relying on a single measure.

Assessing board performance

- The board should be subject to regular evaluation, which may be carried out by the board itself or by an external party.

- Areas of performance to be evaluated may include achievement of company objectives, control exercised over the company's activities, board structure and roles, board meetings, board composition, board discussions and decisions, relations with shareholders and board appointments and development.

The rise of shareholder activism

- Institutional shareholders have taken a more active role in the affairs of listed companies in recent years.

- Activism takes the form of using their votes, meetings with directors and intervention in a company's affairs.

- There is some evidence to suggest that activism can improve returns to shareholders.

KEY TERMS

For definitions of these terms, see at the back of the book, starting on page 514.

chair p. 446
executive directors p. 446
non-executive directors p. 446
UK Corporate Governance Code p. 446
corporate culture p. 449
executive committee p. 449
chief executive officer (CEO) p. 449
audit committee p. 450
risk management committee p. 450

nomination committee p. 450
remuneration committee p. 450
external audit p. 458
expectations gap p. 459
internal audit p. 464
performance share plan (PSP) p. 470
restricted shares p. 470
total shareholder return (TSR) p. 475
economic value added (EVA®) p. 476
UK Stewardship Code p. 486

REFERENCES

1 Grant Thornton (2017) *Corporate Governance Review 2017*, www.grantthornton.co.uk.
2 Kimbell, D. and Neff, T. (2006) Separating the roles of chairman and chief executive: Looking at both sides of the debate, *Spencer Stuart Research and Insight*, July, p. 2.
3 Stiles, P. and Taylor, B. (2001) *Boards at Work*, Oxford University Press, p. 108.
4 Owen, G. and Kirchmaier, T. (2006) *The Changing Role of the Chairman: Impact of Corporate Governance Reform in the UK 1995–2005 on Role, Board Compensation and Appointment*, March.

5 Cameran M., Negri G.and Pettinicchio A. (2015) The audit mandatory rotation rule: The state of the art, *Journal of Financial Perspectives*, Vol. 3, issue 2.
6 FT View (2018) What the public should expect from auditors, ft.com, 14 March.
7 Financial Reporting Council (2016) *Guidance on Audit Committees*, April, p. 4, frc.org.uk.
8 KPMG's Audit Committee Institute, *2015 Global Audit Committee Survey*, p. 32.
9 Financial Reporting Council (2016) *Guidance on Audit Committees*, April, p. 10, frc.org.uk.
10 Sulkowicz, K. (2003) New organisational and psychological challenges of the audit committee, *Audit Committee Quarterly*, Audit Committee Institute, issue 8.
11 KPMG (2014), *KPMG's Guide to Directors Remuneration 2014*, kpmg.co.uk, p. 50.
12 Girma, S., Thompson, S. and Wright, P. (2007) Corporate governance reforms and executive compensation determination: Evidence from the UK, *The Manchester School*, Vol. 75, pp. 65–81.
13 Main, B., Jackson, C., Pymm, J. and Wright, V. (2007) Questioning the remuneration committee process, Working Paper, 21 February.
14 Lincoln, D., Young, D., Wilson, T. and Whiteley, P. (2006) *The Role of the Board Remuneration Committee*, PARC Research Report, March.
15 KPMG (2017) *Guide to Directors' Remuneration 2017*, kpmg.co.uk, p. 9
16 Criac, J., De Backer R. and Sanders J. (2014) *Preparing for Bigger, Bolder, Shareholder Activists*, www.mckinsey.com, March.
17 Bebchuk, L., Brav, A. and Jiang, W. (2015) *The Long-term Effects of Hedge Fund Activism*, NBER Working Paper Number 21227, June.

FURTHER READING

If you would like to explore the topics covered in this chapter in more depth, we recommend the following:

Mallin, C. (2016) *Corporate Governance*, 5th edn, Oxford University Press, Chapters 3, 6, 8 and 9.

Millichamp A and Taylor J. (2018) *Auditing*, 11th edn, Cengage Learning, Chapters 1, 2, 7 and 9.

Open University (2016) *Influences on Corporate Governance*, Open University.

Tricker, B. (2015) *Corporate Governance Principles, Policies and Practices*, Oxford University Press, Chapters 13, 14 and 16.

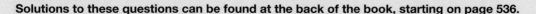

CRITICAL REVIEW QUESTIONS

Solutions to these questions can be found at the back of the book, starting on page 536.

12.1 Assume that you have been asked by the chair of a large listed business to prepare a report highlighting the main areas to be used as a basis for evaluating the performance of the chief executive. Identify and briefly discuss five areas that could be included in the report.

12.2 What are the benefits of separating the roles of chair and chief executive? Should such a separation be made compulsory?

12.3 A large listed business wishes to improve its payroll accounting systems and is seeking outside help to do this. The external auditors are a large firm of accountants that has a consultancy arm. What are the advantages and disadvantages of allowing the external auditors to undertake this task?

12.4 A large listed business has become the target of a shareholder activist. What steps should the board of directors take in response to this event?

Solutions to exercises with coloured numbers can be found at the back of the book, starting on page 545.

Basic-level exercise

12.1 Identify five ways in which the independence of an auditor of a large listed company may be strengthened.

Intermediate-level exercises

12.2 Assume that the chair of the board of directors of a large public listed company has asked you to develop a set of criteria against which the performance of a non-executive director could be appraised. Based on the discussion of the non-executive's role found in the chapter, identify at least six criteria that you might select.

12.3 Reviewing the risk management systems within a company goes beyond the traditional role of internal audit. What changes may have to be made to the internal audit function to enable it to carry out this enhanced role?

12.4 The board of directors of a listed company is likely to place considerable emphasis on maintaining good communications and strong relationships with its institutional shareholders. What are the main benefits and problems of doing this?

Advanced-level exercise

12.5 The newly appointed chair of Vorak plc has been told that considerable tension and suspicion exists between the executive and non-executive directors on the board. The executive directors question the competence of the non-executive directors and the non-executive directors believe that important information is being withheld from them. Assuming that the concerns of each group are well founded, what advice would you give to the chair as to how to ease the tension and promote a better working relationship between the two groups?

Appendix A
RECORDING FINANCIAL TRANSACTIONS

INTRODUCTION

In Chapters 2 and 3, we saw how the financial transactions of a business may be recorded by making a series of entries on the statement of financial position and/or the income statement. Each of these entries had its corresponding 'double', meaning that both sides of the transaction were recorded. However, adjusting the financial statements for each transaction, by hand, can be pretty messy and confusing. Where there are many transactions, as there tends to be even for a fairly small business, it is pretty certain to result in mistakes.

For businesses whose accounting systems are on a computer, this problem is overcome because suitable software can deal with a series of 'plus' and 'minus' entries very reliably. Where the accounting system is not computerised, however, it would be helpful to have some more practical way of keeping accounting records. Such a system not only exists but, before the advent of the computer, was the routine way of keeping accounting records. In fact, the system had been in constant use for recording business transactions since medieval times. It is this system that we shall now examine. We should be clear that the system follows exactly the same rules as those that we have already met. Its distinguishing feature is that it provides those keeping accounting records, by hand, with a methodical approach that allows each transaction to be clearly identified and errors to be minimised.

Learning outcomes

When you have completed this appendix, you should be able to:

- explain the basic principles of double-entry bookkeeping;
- write up a series of business transactions and balance the accounts;
- extract a trial balance and explain its purpose; and
- prepare a set of financial statements from the underlying double-entry accounts.

THE BASICS OF DOUBLE-ENTRY BOOKKEEPING

When we record accounting transactions by hand, we use a recording system known as double-entry bookkeeping. This system does not use plus and minus entries on the face of a statement of financial position and income statement to record a particular transaction, in the way described in Chapters 2 and 3. Instead, individual transactions are recorded in accounts. An account is simply a record of one or more transactions relating to a particular item of asset, claim, revenue or expense, such as:

- cash at bank;
- property, plant and equipment;

- borrowings;
- sales revenue;
- rent payable; and
- equity.

A business may keep few or many accounts, depending on the size and complexity of its operations. Broadly, businesses tend to keep a separate account for each item that appears in either the income statement or the statement of financial position.

An example of an account, in this case the *cash at bank* account, is as follows:

Cash at bank

£	£

We can see that an account, which has a T-shape (and is often known as a *T account*), has three main features:

- a title indicating the item to which it relates;
- a left-hand side, known as the **debit** side; and
- a right-hand side, known as the **credit** side.

One side of an account will record increases in the particular item and the other will record decreases. This, of course, is slightly different from the approach that we used when adjusting the financial statements. When adjusting the statement of financial position, for example, we put a reduction in an asset or claim in the same column as any increases, but with a minus sign against it. However, when T accounts are used, a reduction is shown on the opposite side of the account.

The side on which an increase or decrease is shown will depend on the nature of the item to which the account relates. For example, an account for an asset, such as cash at bank, will show increases on the left-hand (debit) side of the account and decreases on the right-hand (credit) side. However, for claims (that is, equity and liabilities) it is the other way around. An increase in equity or for a liability will be shown on the right-hand (credit) side and a decrease will be shown on the left-hand (debit) side of the relevant account.

To understand why this difference exists, we need to go back to the accounting equation that we first came across in Chapter 2.

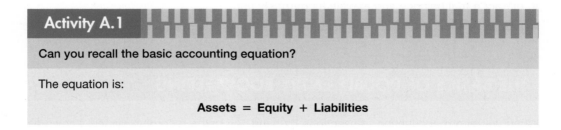

Activity A.1

Can you recall the basic accounting equation?

The equation is:

$$\text{Assets} = \text{Equity} + \text{Liabilities}$$

We can see that assets appear on one side of the equation and equity and liabilities appear on the other. Recording transactions in accounts simply expresses this difference in the recording process. Increases in assets are shown on the debit (left-hand) side of an account and increases in equity and liabilities are shown on the credit (right-hand) side of the account. We should recall the point made in Chapter 2 that each transaction has two aspects. Thus, when we record a particular transaction, two separate accounts will be affected. Recording transactions in this way is known as *double-entry bookkeeping*.

It is worth going through a simple example to see how transactions affecting statement of financial position items would be recorded under the double-entry bookkeeping system. Suppose a new business started on 1 January with the owner introducing initial equity of £5,000 in cash, which was put into a newly opened business bank account. The cash introduced will appear in a separate *cash at bank* account. It represents an increase in an asset and so will be shown on the debit (left-hand) side of the account as follows:

Cash at bank

	£		£
1 January Equity	5,000		

The corresponding entry, which reflects the introduction of equity by the owner, will appear in a separate *equity* account. It represents an increase in equity and so will be shown on the credit (right-hand) side as follows:

Equity

	£		£
		1 January Cash at bank	5,000

It is usual to show, in each account by way of note, where the other side of the entry can be found. Thus, someone looking at the equity account will know that the £5,000 arose from an introduction of cash. This provides potentially useful information, partly because it establishes a 'trail' that can be followed when checking for errors. By including the date of the transaction, additional information is provided to the reader of these T accounts.

Now suppose that, on 2 January, £600 of the cash in the bank is used to buy inventories. This would affect the *cash at bank* account as follows:

Cash at bank

	£		£
1 January Equity	5,000	2 January Inventories	600

This account, in effect, shows 'positive' cash of £5,000 and 'negative' cash of £600 a net amount of £4,400.

What we have seen so far highlights the key rule of double-entry bookkeeping: each left-hand entry must have a right-hand entry of equal size. Using the jargon, we can say that:

Every debit must have a credit

It might be helpful at this point to make it absolutely clear that the words 'debit' and 'credit' are no more than accounting jargon for left and right, respectively. When used outside the context of accounting, people tend to use the word 'credit' to imply something good and 'debit' something undesirable. When used in accounting, however, the words 'debit' and 'credit' have no such implication. Each transaction requires both a debit entry and a credit entry. This is true whether the transaction is 'good', like receiving cash from a credit customer, or 'bad', like having to treat a credit customer's balance as worthless because the customer has gone bankrupt.

RECORDING TRADING TRANSACTIONS

The rules of double entry also extend to 'trading' transactions, which involve making revenues (sales and so on) and incurring expenses. To understand how these transactions are recorded, we should recall that in Chapter 3 the extended accounting equation was set out as follows:

$$\text{Assets} = \text{Equity} + (\text{Revenues} - \text{Expenses}) + \text{Liabilities}$$

This equation can be rearranged as follows:

$$\text{Assets} + \text{Expenses} = \text{Equity} + \text{Revenues} + \text{Liabilities}$$

We can see that increases in expenses are shown on the same side as assets. This means that they will be dealt with in the same way for recording purposes. Thus, an increase in an expense, such as wages, will be shown on the debit (left-hand) side of the *wages* account and a decrease will be shown on the credit (right-hand) side. Increases in revenues are shown on the same side as equity and liabilities and so will be dealt with in the same way. Thus, an increase in revenues, such as sales, will be shown on the credit (right-hand) side of the *sales revenue* account and a decrease will be shown on the debit (left-hand) side.

To summarise, therefore, we can say that:

- Debits (left-hand entries) represent increases in assets and expenses and decreases in equity, liabilities and revenues.
- Credits (right-hand entries) represent increases in equity, liabilities and revenues and decreases in assets and expenses.

Let us continue with our example by assuming that, on 3 January, the business paid £900 to rent business premises for the three months to 31 March. To record this transaction, we should normally open a *rent* account and make entries in this account and in the *cash at bank* account as follows:

Rent			
	£		£
3 January Cash at bank	900		

Cash at bank

	£		£
1 January Equity	5,000	2 January Inventories	600
		3 January Rent	900

The fact that assets and expenses are dealt with in the same way should not be altogether surprising; assets and expenses are closely linked. Most assets transform into expenses as they are 'used up'. Rent, which, as here, is usually paid in advance, is an asset when it is first paid. It represents the value to the business of being entitled to occupy the premises for the forthcoming period (until 31 March in this case). As the three months progress, this asset becomes an expense; it is 'used up'. The debit entry in the rent account does not necessarily represent either an asset or an expense; it could be a mixture of the two. Strictly, by the end of the day on which it was paid (3 January), £30 would have represented an expense for the three days; the remaining £870 would have been an asset. As each day passes, an additional £10 (that is, £900/90 (there are 90 days in January, February and March altogether)) will transform from an asset into an expense. As we have already seen, it is not necessary for us to make any adjustment to the rent account as the days pass. We can, and usually do, separate the expense element from the asset element at the end of the reporting period, as we shall see later in this appendix.

Now let us assume that, on 5 January, the business sold inventories costing £200 for £300 on credit. When we can identify the cost of the inventories sold at the time of sale, we should deal with the sale and the cost of sales separately, with each having its own debits and credits.

First, let us deal with the sale. We need to open separate accounts for both sales revenue and trade receivables – which do not, as yet, exist.

Activity A.3

Can you work out what to do in respect of the sale? Show the entries in the relevant accounts.

The sale gives rise to an increase in revenue and so there is a credit entry in the *sales revenue* account. The sale also creates an asset of trade receivables and so there is debit entry in the *trade receivables* account.

The two accounts will, therefore, be as follows:

Sales revenue

£		£
	5 January Trade receivables	300

Trade receivables

	£		£
5 January Sales revenue	300		

Let us now deal with the inventories sold. Since they have become the expense 'cost of sales', we need to reduce the figure on the inventories account by making a credit entry. We must also make a corresponding debit in a *cost of sales* account, opened for the purpose:

Inventories

	£		£
2 January Cash at bank	600	5 January Cost of sales	200

Cost of sales

	£		£
5 January Inventories	200		

We shall now look at other transactions for our hypothetical business for the remainder of January. They are as follows:

8 January	Bought some inventories on credit costing £800
11 January	Bought some office furniture for £600 cash
15 January	Sold inventories costing £600 for £900, on credit
18 January	Received £800 from trade receivables
21 January	Paid trade payables £500
24 January	Paid wages for the month £400
27 January	Bought inventories on credit for £800
31 January	Borrowed £2,000 from the Commercial Finance Company

We have to open several additional accounts to enable us to record all of these transactions. By the end of January, the set of accounts would appear as follows:

Cash at bank

	£		£
1 January Equity	5,000	2 January Inventories	600
18 January Trade receivables	800	3 January Rent	900
31 January Borrowings	2,000	11 January Office furniture	600
		21 January Trade payables	500
		24 January Wages	400

Equity

	£		£
		1 January Cash at bank	5,000

Inventories

	£		£
2 January Cash at bank	600	5 January Cost of sales	200
8 January Trade payables	800	15 January Cost of sales	600
27 January Trade payables	800		

Rent

	£		£
3 January Cash at bank	900		

Sales revenue

	£		£
		5 January Trade receivables	300
		15 January Trade receivables	900

Trade receivables

	£		£
5 January Sales revenue	300	18 January Cash at bank	800
15 January Sales revenue	900		

Cost of sales

	£		£
5 January Inventories	200		
15 January Inventories	600		

Trade payables

	£		£
21 January Cash at bank	500	8 January Inventories	800
		27 January Inventories	800

Office furniture

	£		£
11 January Cash at bank	600		

Wages

	£		£
24 January Cash at bank	400		

Borrowings

	£		£
		31 January Cash at bank	2,000

All of the transactions from 8 January onwards are similar to those up to that date, which have been discussed in detail. We should, therefore, be able to follow them using the date references as our guide.

BALANCING ACCOUNTS AND THE TRIAL BALANCE

Businesses keeping their accounts, in the way that we have been following, find it helpful to summarise their individual accounts periodically – perhaps weekly or monthly – for two reasons:

- to see at a glance how much is in each account (for example, to see how much cash the business has left); and
- to check the accuracy of the bookkeeping so far.

Let us look at the *cash at bank* account again:

Cash at bank

	£		£
1 January Equity	5,000	2 January Inventories	600
18 January Trade receivables	800	3 January Rent	900
31 January Borrowings	2,000	11 January Office furniture	600
		21 January Trade payables	500
		24 January Wages	400

Does this account tell us how much cash the business has at 31 January? The answer is partly yes and partly no.

We do not have a single figure showing the cash at bank **balance** but we can easily deduce this by adding up the debit (receipts) column and deducting the sum of the credit (payments) column. It would be better, however, if the current balance were clearly shown.

To summarise, or *balance*, this account, we simply add up the column with the larger amount (in this case, the debit side) and put this total on both sides of the account. We then record, on the credit side (in this case), the figure that will make that side add up to the total appearing on both sides of the account. We cannot record this balancing figure just once, as that would contravene the double-entry rule. Thus, to preserve the double entry, we must also *carry down* this figure. This involves putting it on the other side of the same account below the totals, as follows:

Cash at bank

	£		£
1 January Equity	5,000	2 January Inventories	600
18 January Trade receivables	800	3 January Rent	900
31 January Borrowings	2,000	11 January Office furniture	600
		21 January Trade payables	500
		24 January Wages	400
		31 January Balance carried down	4,800
	7,800		7,800
1 February Balance brought down	4,800		

Note that the *balance carried down* (usually abbreviated to 'c/d') at the end of one period becomes the *balance brought down* ('b/d') at the beginning of the next. We can now see at a glance what the cash position is, without having to do any mental arithmetic.

Try balancing the inventories account and then state what we know about the inventories position at the end of January.

The inventories account will be balanced as follows:

Inventories

	£		£
2 January Cash at bank	600	5 January Cost of sales	200
8 January Trade payables	800	15 January Cost of sales	600

Inventories

	£		£
27 January Trade payables	800	31 January Balance c/d	1,400
	2,200		2,200
1 February Balance b/d	1,400		

We can see that the business held inventories costing £1,400 at the end of January. We can also see the movements in inventories during January that led to this figure being the inventories balance by the end of the month.

The remaining accounts can be balanced in a similar way. However, we need not balance accounts that have only one entry (for example, the equity account for our business at this point). This is because they are already in as summarised a form as it is possible for them to be. Following the balancing process, the remaining accounts will appear as shown below:

Equity

	£		£
		1 January Cash at bank	5,000

Rent

	£		£
3 January Cash at bank	900		

Sales revenue

	£		£
		5 January Trade receivables	300
31 January Balance c/d	1,200	15 January Trade receivables	900
	1,200		1,200
		1 February Balance b/d	1,200

Trade receivables

	£		£
5 January Sales revenue	300	18 January Cash at bank	800
15 January Sales revenue	900	31 January Balance c/d	400
	1,200		1,200
1 February Balance b/d	400		

Cost of sales

	£		£
5 January Inventories	200	31 January Balance c/d	800
15 January Inventories	600		
	800		800
1 February Balance b/d	800		

Trade payables

	£		£
21 January Cash at bank	500	8 January Inventories	800
31 January Balance c/d	1,100	27 January Inventories	800
	1,600		1,600
		1 February Balance b/d	1,100

Office furniture

	£		£
11 January Cash at bank	600		

Wages

	£		£
24 January Cash at bank	400		

Borrowings

	£		£
		31 January Cash at bank	2,000

Activity A.5

If we now make a list of all the accounts, showing each one's balance, and separately total the debit balances and the credit balances, what should we expect to find and why?

We should expect to find that these two totals are equal. This must, in theory, be true since every debit entry was matched by an opposite and equal-sized credit entry.

Let us see if our expectation in Activity A.5 works in our example, by listing the debit and credit balances in separate columns as follows:

	Debits £	Credits £
Cash at bank	4,800	
Inventories	1,400	
Equity		5,000
Rent	900	
Sales revenue		1,200
Trade receivables	400	
Cost of sales	800	
Trade payables		1,100
Office furniture	600	
Wages	400	
Borrowings		2,000
	9,300	9,300

This listing is known as a trial balance. The fact that the totals for each column agree provides *some* indication that we have not made any bookkeeping errors.

We cannot, however, have total confidence that there are no errors. Consider, for example, the transaction that took place on 3 January (paid rent for the month of £900). In each of the following cases, all of which are an incorrect treatment of the transaction, the trial balance would still have agreed:

■ The transaction was completely omitted from the accounts, that is, no entries were made at all.

- The amount was misread as £9,000 but then (correctly) debited to the rent account and credited to cash at bank.
- The correct amount of £900 was (incorrectly) debited to cash at bank and credited to rent.

Nevertheless, a trial balance, where the totals agree, provides some assurance that the accounts have been correctly recorded.

PREPARING THE FINANCIAL STATEMENTS (FINAL ACCOUNTS)

Providing the trial balance totals agree and we are not aware of any errors in recording, the next stage is to prepare the income statement and statement of financial position. Preparing the income statement is simply a matter of going through the individual accounts, identifying those amounts that represent revenues and expenses of the period, and transferring them to the income statement, which is itself part of the double-entry system.

We shall now do this for the example that we have been using. The situation is complicated slightly for three reasons:

- As we know, the £900 rent paid during January relates to the three months January, February and March.
- The business's owner estimates that the electricity used during January is about £110. There is no bill yet from the electricity supply business because it normally bills customers only at the end of each three-month period.
- The business's owner believes that the office furniture should be depreciated by 20 per cent each year (straight-line).

These complications will require end-of-period adjustments to be made. This is easily handled, however, in the double-entry accounts. Let us see how it is done.

After completing the transfer to the income statement, the rent account will appear as follows:

Rent

	£		£
3 January Cash at bank	900	31 January Income statement	300
		Balance c/d	600
	900		900
1 February Balance b/d	600		

At 31 January, two months' rent is still unused and so £600 will be an asset of the business. This amount, which is carried down as a debit balance, will appear in the 31 January statement of financial position. The remaining £300 (representing January's rent) is an expense for the period. It is credited to the rent account and debited to a newly opened income statement.

Let us now look at the electricity adjustment. After the transfer to the income statement, the electricity account will be as follows:

Electricity

	£		£
		31 January Income statement	110

As there has been no cash payment or other transaction recorded so far for electricity, an account has not yet been opened. It is, therefore, necessary to open one. We must debit the income statement with the £110 of electricity used during January and credit the electricity account with the same amount. At 31 January, this credit balance reflects the amount owed by this business to the electricity supplier. This balance will, once again, appear on the statement of financial position.

Finally, let us look at the adjustment required regarding the office furniture. The depreciation for the month will be $20\% \times £600 \times \frac{1}{12}$, that is £10. Normal accounting practice is to charge (debit) this to the income statement, with the corresponding credit appearing in a *Depreciation of office furniture* account. The latter entry will be as follows:

Depreciation of office furniture account

	£		£
		31 January Income statement	10

This £10 balance will be shown in the statement of financial position at 31 January. It is deducted from the office furniture asset, as we shall see shortly.

The balances on the following accounts represent straightforward revenue or expenses for the month of January:

- Sales revenue
- Cost of sales
- Wages.

The balances on these accounts will simply be transferred to the income statement.

To transfer these balances to the income statement, we simply debit or credit the account concerned, such that any balance amount is eliminated, and make the corresponding credit or debit in the income statement. Take sales revenue, for example. The sales revenue account has a credit balance (because the balance represents a revenue). We must debit this account with £1,200 and credit the income statement with the same amount. So a credit balance on the sales revenue account becomes a credit entry in the income statement. For these three accounts, then, we have the following:

Sales revenue

	£		£
31 January Balance c/d	1,200	5 January Trade receivables	300
		15 January Trade receivables	900
	1,200		1,200
31 January Income statement	1,200	1 February Balance b/d	1,200

Cost of sales

	£		£
5 January Inventories	200		
15 January Inventories	600	31 January Balance c/d	800
	800		800
1 February Balance b/d	800	31 January Income statement	800

Wages

	£		£
24 January Cash at bank	400	31 January Income statement	400

The income statement will now be as follows:

Income statement

	£		£
31 January Cost of sales	800	31 January Sales revenue	1,200
31 January Rent	300		
31 January Wages	400		
31 January Electricity	110		
31 January Depreciation	10		

We must now transfer the balance on the income statement (a debit balance of £420).

Activity A.7

What does the balance on the income statement represent, and to where should it be transferred?

The balance is either the profit or the loss for the period. In this case it is a loss, as the total expenses exceed the total revenue. This loss must be borne by the owner, and it must therefore be transferred to the equity account.

The two accounts will now appear as follows:

Income statement

	£		£
31 January Cost of sales	800	31 January Sales revenue	1,200
31 January Rent	300		
31 January Wages	400		
31 January Electricity	110		
31 January Depreciation	10	31 January Equity (loss)	420
	1,620		1,620

Equity

	£		£
31 January Income statement (loss)	420	1 January Cash at bank	5,000
31 January Balance c/d	4,580		
	5,000		5,000
		1 February Balance b/d	4,580

The final entry was to balance the equity account.

Now all of the balances remaining on accounts represent either assets or claims as at 31 January. These balances can now be used to produce a statement of financial position, as follows:

Statement of financial position as at 31 January

ASSETS	£
Non-current assets	
Property, plant and equipment	
Office furniture – cost	600
– depreciation	(10)
	590
Current assets	
Inventories	1,400
Prepaid expense	600
Trade receivables	400
Cash at bank	4,800
	7,200
Total assets	7,790
EQUITY AND LIABILITIES	
Owners' equity	4,580
Non-current liability	
Borrowings	2,000
Current liabilities	
Accrued expense	110
Trade payables	1,100
	1,210
Total equity and liabilities	7,790

The income statement could be written in a more stylish manner, for reporting to users, as follows:

Income statement for the month ended 31 January

	£
Sales revenue	1,200
Cost of sales	(800)
Gross profit	400
Rent	(300)
Wages	(400)
Electricity	(110)
Depreciation	(10)
Loss for the month	(420)

THE LEDGER AND ITS DIVISION

The book in which the accounts are traditionally kept is known as the **ledger**, and accounts are sometimes referred to as *ledger accounts*.

The ledger is often divided into separate sections. This is for three main reasons:

- Having all of the accounts in one book means that it is only possible for one person at a time to use the accounts, either to make entries or to extract information.
- It can allow specialisation, thereby allowing individual members of the accounts staff to focus on their own part of the system. This can lead to more accurate and efficient record keeping.
- It can lead to greater security, and so reduce the risk of fraud.

Activity A.8

Can you think how dividing the ledger into various sections could reduce the risk of fraud?

A different member of staff can be responsible for writing up each section so that no one has access to the entire set of accounts. It then becomes much more difficult to conceal irregular transactions. A withdrawal of cash, for example, could be recorded in one section with the corresponding entry appearing in another section of the ledger, by a different person.

There are no universally accepted rules on the division of the ledger, but the following division is fairly common:

- *The cash book.* This tends to be all of the accounts relating to cash either loose (notes and coins – often known as *petty cash*) or in the bank.
- *The sales (or trade receivables) ledger.* This contains the accounts of all of the business's individual trade receivables.
- *The purchases (or trade payables) ledger.* This consists of the accounts of all of the business's individual trade payables.
- *The nominal ledger.* These accounts tend to be those of expenses and revenue, for example, sales revenue, purchases, wages, rent, and so on.
- *The general ledger.* This contains the remainder of the business's accounts, mainly those to do with non-current assets and long-term finance.

SUMMARY

The main points in this appendix may be summarised as follows:

Double-entry bookkeeping

- Double-entry bookkeeping is a system for keeping accounting records by hand, such that a relatively large volume of transactions can be handled effectively and accurately.
- There is a separate account for each item of asset, claim, expense and revenue.
- Each account is T-shaped and often known as a 'T account'.

- Left-hand (debit) side of the account records increases in assets and expenses and decreases in revenues, equity and liabilities.
- Right-hand (credit) side records increases in revenues, equity and liabilities and decreases in assets and expenses.
- The words 'debit' and 'credit' have no implication of good or bad in accounting – they are simply jargon for left and right.
- There is an equal credit entry in one account for a debit entry in another.
- Double-entry bookkeeping is used to record day-to-day transactions.

Double-entry bookkeeping and financial statements

- Double-entry bookkeeping can be used to generate the income statement.
- The statement of financial position is a list of the accounts on which there is a net figure, or balance, after appropriate transfers have been made to the income statement.

Ledgers

- The accounts are traditionally kept in a *ledger,* a term that persists even with computerised accounting.
- The ledger is often broken down into separate sections, each containing particular types of account.

KEY TERMS

For definitions of these terms, see at the back of the book, starting on page 514.

double-entry bookkeeping p. 495
account p. 495
debit p. 496
credit p. 496

balance p. 502
trial balance p. 504
ledger p. 509

FURTHER READING

If you would like to explore the topics covered in this chapter in more depth, we recommend the following:

Benedict, A. and Elliott, B. (2001) *Practical Accounting*, Financial Times Prentice Hall, 2nd edn, Chapters 2 to 5.

Fardon, M. (2013) *Computer Accounting Systems Tutorial*, Osborne Books, Chapters 1 to 12.

Thomas, A. and Ward, A.M. (2015) *Introduction to Financial Accounting*, 8th edn, McGraw-Hill, Chapters 7 to 10.

Wood, F. and Robinson, S. (2017) *Book-keeping and Accounts*, 9th edn, Pearson, Chapters 2 to 8.

Solutions to exercises with coloured numbers can be found at the back of the book, starting on page 545.

A.1 In respect of each of the following transactions, state in which two accounts an entry must be made and whether the entry is a debit or a credit. (For example, if the transaction were buying inventories for cash, the answer would be debit the inventories account and credit the cash at bank account.)

(a) Bought inventories on credit.
(b) Owner made cash drawings.
(c) Paid interest on business borrowings.
(d) Bought inventories for cash.
(e) Received cash from a credit customer.
(f) Paid wages to employees.
(g) The owner received some cash from a credit customer, which was taken as drawings rather than being paid into the business's bank account.
(h) Paid a credit supplier.
(i) Paid electricity bill.
(j) Made cash sales.

A.2 (a) Record the following transactions in a set of double-entry accounts:

1 February	Lee (the owner) put £6,000 into a newly opened business bank account to start a new business
3 February	Bought inventories for £2,600 for cash
5 February	Bought some equipment (non-current asset) for cash for £800
6 February	Bought inventories costing £3,000 on credit
9 February	Paid rent for the month of £250
10 February	Paid fuel and electricity for the month of £240
11 February	Paid general expenses of £200
15 February	Sold inventories for £4,000 in cash; the inventories had cost £2,400
19 February	Sold inventories for £3,800 on credit; the inventories had cost £2,300
21 February	lee withdrew £1,000 in cash for personal use
25 February	Paid £2,000 to trade payables
28 February	Received £2,500 from trade receivables

(b) Balance the relevant accounts and prepare a trial balance (making sure that it agrees).
(c) Prepare an income statement for the month and a statement of financial position at the month end. Assume that there are no prepaid or accrued expenses at the end of the month and ignore any possible depreciation.

A.3 The following is the statement of financial position of David's business at 1 January of last year.

	£	£
ASSETS		
Non-current assets		
Property, plant and equipment		
Buildings		25,000
Fittings – cost	10,000	
– depreciation	(2,000)	8,000
		33,000
Current assets		
Inventories of stationery		140
Trading inventories		1,350
Prepaid rent		500
Trade receivables		1,840
Cash at bank		2,180
		6,010
Total assets		39,010
EQUITY AND LIABILITIES		
Owners' equity		25,050
Non-current liability		
Borrowings		12,000
Current liabilities		
Trade payables		1,690
Accrued electricity		270
		1,960
Total equity and liabilities		39,010

The following is a summary of the transactions that took place during the year:

1 Inventories were bought on credit for £17,220.
2 Inventories were bought for £3,760 cash.
3 Credit sales revenue amounted to £33,100 (cost £15,220).
4 Cash sales revenue amounted to £10,360 (cost £4,900).
5 Wages of £3,770 were paid.
6 Rent of £3,000 was paid. The annual rental amounts to £3,000.
7 Electricity of £1,070 was paid.
8 General expenses of £580 were paid.
9 Additional fittings were purchased on 1 January for £2,000. The cash for this was raised from additional borrowings of this amount. The interest rate is 10% a year, the same as for the existing borrowings.
10 £1,000 of the borrowing was repaid on 30 June.
11 Cash received from trade receivables amounted to £32,810.
12 Cash paid to trade payables amounted to £18,150.
13 The owner withdrew £10,400 cash and £560 inventories for private use.

At the end of the year:

- The electricity bill for the last quarter of the year for £290 had not been paid.
- Trade receivables amounting to £260 were unlikely to be received.
- The value of stationery remaining was estimated at £150. Stationery is included in general expenses.
- Interest on the borrowings (10 per cent a year) was unpaid at the year end.

Depreciation is to be taken at 20% on the cost of the fittings owned at the year end. Buildings are not depreciated.

Required:

(a) Open ledger accounts and bring down all of the balances in the opening statement of financial position.

(b) Make entries to record the transactions 1 to 13 (above), opening any additional accounts as necessary.

(c) Open an income statement (part of the double entry, remember). Make the necessary entries for the bulleted list above and the appropriate transfers to the income statement.

(d) List the remaining balances in the same form as the opening statement of financial position (above).

Appendix B
GLOSSARY OF KEY TERMS

Account A section of a double-entry bookkeeping system that deals with one particular asset, claim, expense or revenue. *p. 495*

Accounting The process of identifying, measuring and communicating information to permit informed judgements and decisions by users of the information. *p. 2*

Accounting convention A generally accepted rule that accountants tend to follow when preparing financial statements. These have evolved over time to deal with practical problems rather than to reflect some theoretical ideal. *p. 54*

Accounting information system The system used within a business to identify, record, analyse and report accounting information. *p. 12*

Accruals accounting The system of accounting that follows the accruals convention. This is the system followed in drawing up the statement of financial position and income statement. *p. 88*

Accruals convention The convention of accounting that asserts that profit is the excess of revenue over expenses, not the excess of cash receipts over cash payments. *p. 88*

Accrued expense An expenses that is outstanding at the end of a reporting period. *p. 84*

Acid test ratio A liquidity ratio that relates the liquid assets (usually defined as current assets less inventories) to the current liabilities. *p. 292*

Allotted share capital *See* Issued share capital. *p. 134*

Allowance for trade receivables An amount set aside out of profit to provide for anticipated losses arising from debts (trade receivables) that may prove irrecoverable. *p. 106*

Amortisation A measure of that portion of the cost (or fair value) of a non-current asset that has been consumed during a reporting period. The word 'amortisation' tends to be used where the particular non-current asset is an intangible one, whereas 'depreciation' is normally used with tangible assets. *p. 89*

Asset A resource controlled by a business that provides a right to potential economic benefits. *p. 38*

Associate company A company over which considerable influence, but not full control, may be exercised by another company. *p. 391*

Audit committee A committee of the board of directors that aims to promote the integrity and reliability of the financial reporting system. *p. 450*

Auditors Independent, professional accountants whose main duty is to report to shareholders whether, in their opinion, the financial statements of a company show a true and fair view of performance and position and comply with statutory and financial reporting standards requirements. *p. 173*

AVCO *See* Weighted average cost. *p. 99*

Average inventories turnover period ratio An efficiency ratio that measures the average period for which inventories are held by a business. *p. 284*

Average settlement period for trade payables ratio An efficiency ratio that measures the average time taken for a business to pay its trade payables. *p. 285*

Average settlement period for trade receivables ratio An efficiency ratio that measures the average time taken for trade receivables to pay the amounts owing. *p. 285*

Bad debt An amount owed to the business that is considered to be irrecoverable. *p. 104*

Balance The net difference between the total debit and credit amounts in an account in a double-entry bookkeeping system. *p. 502*

Bonds See Loan notes. *p. 135*

Bonus shares Reserves that are converted into shares and then issued 'free' to existing shareholders in proportion to their existing shareholdings. *p. 132*

Business entity convention The convention that holds that, for accounting purposes, the business and its owner(s) are treated as quite separate and distinct. *p. 54*

Called-up share capital That part of a company's share capital for which the shareholders have been asked to pay the agreed amount. *p. 135*

Capital reserves Reserves that arise from unrealised 'capital' profits or gains. They arise mainly through issuing shares above their nominal value or through the upward revaluation of non-current assets. *p. 130*

Capitalisation Carrying forward expenditure as an asset as compared with writing it off as an expense. *p. 247*

Carrying amount The difference between the cost (or fair value) of a non-current asset and the accumulated depreciation relating to the asset. The carrying amount is also referred to as the written-down value (WDV) and the net book value (NBV). *p. 92*

Cash generated from operations (CGO) per ordinary share ratio An investment ratio that relates the cash generated from operations and available to ordinary shareholders to the number of ordinary shares. *p. 318*

Cash generated from operations to maturing obligations ratio A liquidity ratio that compares the cash generated from operations to the current liabilities of the business. *p. 293*

Chair The person elected by the board of directors to lead the board so as to provide strategic direction for the business and to act in the best interests of shareholders. *p. 446*

Chief executive officer The senior executive director who leads the management team. *p. 449*

Claim An obligations on the part of a business to provide cash or some other benefit to outside parties. *p. 38*

Common-size financial statements Normal financial statements (such as the income statement, statement of financial position and statement of cash flows) that are expressed in terms of some base figure. *p. 325*

Comparability The quality that helps users to identify similarities and differences between items of information. It enhances the usefulness of accounting information. *p. 8*

Conceptual framework The main concepts, or principles, that underpin accounting, which can help in identifying best practice and in developing accounting rules. *p. 170*

Consistency convention The accounting convention that holds that, when a particular method of accounting is selected to deal with a transaction, this method should be applied consistently over time. *p. 103*

Consolidated financial statements *See* Group financial statements. *p. 360*

Consolidating Changing the nominal value of shares to a higher figure (from, say, £0.50 to £1.00) and then reducing the number of shares in issue so that the total nominal value of shares held by each shareholder remains the same. *p. 129*

Contingent asset A possible asset arising from past events, the existence of which will only be confirmed by future events not wholly within the control of the business. *p. 245*

Contingent liability A possible obligation arising from past events, the existence of which will be only be confirmed by future events not wholly within the control of the business; or a present obligation arising from past events, where either it is not probable that an outflow of resources is needed, or the amount of the obligation cannot be reliably measured. *p. 242*

Conventions of accounting A set of generally accepted rules that accountants tend to follow when preparing financial statements. They have evolved over time in order to deal with practical problems rather than to reflect some theoretical ideal. *p. 16*

Corporate culture The values, attitudes and behaviour displayed towards the company's various stakeholders and to the wider community. *p. 449*

Corporate governance The system of rules and practices that is put in place to direct and control a company. *p. 126*

Corporation tax Taxation that a limited company is liable to pay on its profits. *p. 122*

Cost of sales The cost of the goods sold during a period. Cost of sales can be derived by adding the opening inventories held to the inventories purchases for the period and then deducting the closing inventories held. *p. 78*

Creative accounting Adopting accounting policies to achieve a particular view of performance and position that preparers would like users to see rather than what is a true and fair view. *p. 189*

Credit The right-hand side of an account in double-entry bookkeeping. *p. 496*

Current asset An assets that is held for the short term, including cash itself and other assets that are held for sale or consumption in the normal course of a business's operating cycle. *p. 47*

Current cost accounting (CCA) An approach to preparing financial statements that values assets mainly on the basis of current replacement cost. A key purpose it to help users assess whether the business is able to maintain its scale of operations during a period of inflation. *p. 434*

Current liability A liability that is expected to be settled within the normal course of the business's operating cycle or within twelve months of the statement of financial position date, or which is held primarily for trading purposes, or for which the business does not have the right to defer settlement beyond twelve months of the statement of financial position date. *p. 49*

Current (or constant) purchasing power (CPP) accounting An approach to preparing financial statements that aims to ensure that the general purchasing power of the owners' investment in the business is maintained during a period of inflation. It involves adjusting historic cost figures to reflect changes in a general price index. *p. 433*

Current ratio A liquidity ratio that relates the current assets of the business to the current liabilities. *p. 291*

Debentures See Loan notes. *p. 135*

Debit The left-hand side of an account in double-entry bookkeeping. *p. 496*

Depreciation A measure of that portion of the cost (or fair value) of a non-current asset that has been consumed during a reporting period. *p. 89*

Direct method An approach to deducing the cash flows from operating activities, in a statement of cash flows, by analysing the business's cash records. *p. 213*

Directors Individuals who are appointed (normally by being elected by the shareholders) to act as the most senior level of management of a company. *p. 126*

Directors' report A report containing information of a financial and non-financial nature that the directors must produce as part of the annual financial report to shareholders. *p. 182*

Discrete method An approach to interim profit measurement that treats the interim period as quite separate and distinct from the annual period. *p. 417*

Discriminate function A boundary line, produced by multiple discriminate analysis, which can be used to identify those businesses that are likely to suffer financial distress and those that are not. *p. 332*

Dividend The transfer of assets (usually cash) made by a company to its shareholders. *p. 127*

Dividend cover ratio An investment ratio that relates the earnings available for dividends to the dividend announced to indicate how many times the former covers the latter. *p. 315*

Dividend payout ratio An investment ratio that relates the dividends announced for the period to the earnings available for dividends that were generated in that period. *p. 314*

Dividend yield ratio An investment ratio that relates the cash return from a share to its current market value. *p. 315*

Double-entry bookkeeping A system for recording financial transactions where each transaction is recorded twice, once as a debit and once as a credit. *p. 495*

Dual aspect convention The accounting convention that holds that each transaction has two aspects and that each aspect must be recorded in the financial statements. *p. 56*

Earnings per share ratio An investment ratio that relates the earnings generated by the business during a period, and available to shareholders, to the number of shares in issue. *p. 315*

Economic value added (EVA®) A measure of business wealth generated during a period. It is derived by deducting the cost of finance from the (adjusted) net operating profit after tax. *p. 476*

Efficient capital market A capital market where prices always rationally reflect all that is known about the commodity (for example, shares) traded in that market. *p. 124*

Equity The owners' claim on the business. In the case of a limited company, it comprises the sum of shares and reserves. *p. 41*

Executive committee A committee of directors given delegated responsibility for developing strategic plans. *p. 449*

Executive directors Directors who have senior management responsibilities and are normally full-time employees of the company. *p. 446*

Expectations gap The difference between what external auditors believe their responsibilities and duties to be and what shareholders believe them to be. *p. 459*

Expense A measure of the outflow of assets (or increase in liabilities) incurred as a result of generating revenue. *p. 75*

External audit A review by independent accountants to assess whether, in their opinion, the financial statements of a company show a true and fair view of performance and position and comply with statutory and financial reporting standards requirements. *p. 458*

Fair value The value ascribed to an asset as an alternative to historic cost. It is usually the current market values (that is, the exchange values in an arm's-length transaction). *p. 61*

Faithful representation The ability of information to be relied on to represent what it purports to represent. This is regarded as a fundamental quality of useful accounting information. *p. 6*

Final accounts The income statement, statement of cash flows and statement of financial position taken together. *p. 37*

Finance lease A financial arrangement where the asset title remains with the owner (the lessor) but the lease agreement transfers virtually all the rewards and risks to the business (the lessee). *p. 250*

Financial accounting The identification, measurement and communication of accounting information for external users (those users other than the managers of the business). *p. 13*

Financial gearing The existence of fixed payment-bearing sources of finance (for example, borrowings) in the capital structure of a business. *p. 298*

First in, first out (FIFO) A method of inventories costing which values inventories *as if* the earliest acquired inventories are used (in production or sales) first. *p. 99*

Fully paid shares Shares on which the shareholders have paid the full issue price. *p. 135*

Gearing ratio A ratio that relates long-term, fixed-return finance (such as borrowings) to the total long-term finance of the business. *p. 300*

Going concern convention The accounting convention that holds that a business is assumed to continue operations for the foreseeable future, unless there is reason to believe otherwise. In other words, it is assumed that there is no intention, or need, to liquidate the business. *p. 56*

Goodwill An intangible, non-current asset that lacks a clear and separate identity. The term is often used to cover various positive attributes such as the quality of products, the skill of employees and the relationship with customers. *p. 58*

Goodwill arising on consolidation Anything paid in excess of the underlying net asset value of the subsidiary's shares. *p. 367*

Gross profit The amount remaining (if positive) after the cost of sales has been deducted from trading revenue. *p. 77*

Gross profit margin ratio A profitability ratio that expresses the gross profit as a percentage of the sales revenue for a period. *p. 280*

Group (of companies) A situation that arises where one company is able to exercise control over another or others. *p. 349*

Group financial statements Financial accounting statements that combine the performance, position and cash flows of a group of companies under common control. Also known as *consolidated financial statements. p. 349*

Group income statement An income statement for a group of companies, prepared from the perspective of the parent company's shareholders. *p. 388*

Group statement of cash flows A cash flow statement for a group of companies, prepared from the perspective of the parent company's shareholders. *p. 391*

Group statement of financial position A statement of financial position for a group of companies, prepared from the perspective of the parent company's shareholders. *p. 359*

Historic cost convention The accounting convention that holds that assets should be recorded at their historic (acquisition) cost. *p. 54*

Holding company *See* Parent company. *p. 349*

Horizontal analysis An approach to common-size financial statements where all the figures in equivalent statements over time are expressed in relation to an equivalent figure for the base period (year, month and so on). So, for example, the sales revenue figure for each year will be expressed in terms of the sales revenue figure for the base year. *p. 327*

Impairment loss The amount by which the asset value is reduced as a result of having its value assessed as impaired. *p. 63*

Income statement A financial statement (also known as *profit and loss account*) that measures and reports the profit (or loss) the business has generated during a period. It is derived by deducting from total revenue for a period, the total expenses associated with that revenue. *p. 34*

Indirect method An approach to deducing the cash flows from operating activities, in a statement of cash flows, by analysing the business's other financial statements. *p. 213*

Intangible asset An asset that does not have a physical substance (for example, patents, goodwill and trade receivables). *p. 41*

Integral method An approach to interim profit measurement that regards the interim period as part of the annual reporting period. This means annual expenses are predicted and a proportion is then allocated to the interim period based on the proportion of annual sales revenue arising in the interim period. *p. 417*

Interest cover ratio A gearing ratio that divides the operating profit (that is, profit before interest and taxation) by the interest payable for a period. *p. 301*

Internal audit A review by employees of the company to assess the integrity of the company's internal control and financial reporting systems. It may also involve a review of the risk company's management systems *p. 464*

International Accounting Standards *See* International Financial Reporting Standards. *p. 164*

International Financial Reporting Standards Transnational accounting rules that have been adopted, or developed, by the International Accounting Standards Board and which should be followed in preparing the published financial statements of listed limited companies. *p. 164*

Issued share capital That part of the share capital that has been issued to shareholders. Also known as *allotted share capital. p. 134*

Key performance indicators (KPIs) Measures used by a business to evaluate the degree of success achieved in carrying out its operations. *p. 324*

Last in, first out (LIFO) A method of inventories costing which values inventories *as if* the most recently acquired inventories are used (in production or sales) first. *p. 99*

Ledger The book in which accounts are traditionally kept. *p. 509*

Liability A claim of an individual or organisation, apart from the owner(s), that has arisen from past transactions or events, such as supplying goods or lending money to the business. *p. 42*

Limited company A form of business unit that is granted a separate legal existence from that of its owners. The owners of this type of business are liable for debts only up to the amount that they have agreed to invest. *p. 21*

Limited liability The restriction of the legal obligation of shareholders to meet all of the company's debts. *p. 119*

Loan notes Long-term borrowings usually made by limited companies. *p. 135*

Loan stock See Loan notes. *p. 135*

London Stock Exchange The main stock market for the UK, where shares may be bought and sold. *p. 123*

Management accounting The identification, measurement and communication of accounting information for the managers of a business. *p. 13*

Matching convention The accounting convention that holds that, when measuring income, expenses should be matched to the revenue they helped generate, in the same reporting period as that revenue is recognised. *p. 84*

Materiality Accounting information is material where its omission or misrepresentation will alter the decisions that users make. The threshold of materiality will vary from one business to the next. *p. 6*

Materiality convention The accounting convention that states that, where the amounts involved are immaterial, only what is expedient should be considered. *p. 88*

Minority interests *See* Non-controlling interests. *p. 365*

Monetary items Items appearing on a statement of financial position that have a fixed monetary value assigned to them (for example, cash). *p. 432*

Multiple discriminate analysis (MDA) A statistical technique that can be used to predict financial distress; it involves using an index based on a combination of financial ratios. *p. 332*

Negative goodwill arising on consolidation The amount by which the underlying net asset value of the subsidiary's shares exceeds the amount paid for the shares. *p. 367*

Net book value *See* Carrying amount. *p. 92*

Nominal value The face value of a share in a company. Also called *par value. p. 127*

Nomination committee A committee of the board of directors whose task it is to recommend, to the board, potential new directors. *p. 450*

Non-controlling interests That part of the net assets of a subsidiary company that is financed by shareholders other than the parent company. Also known as *minority interests. p. 365*

Non-current asset An asset held that does not meet the criteria of a current asset. It is held for the long-term operations of the business rather than continuously circulating within the business. Non-current assets can be seen as the tools of the business. They are also known as *fixed assets. p. 48*

Non-current liability A liability of the business that is not a current liability. *p. 50*

Non-executive directors Directors who act purely as directors; they do not have senior management responsibility and are not full-time employees of the company. *p. 446*

Offer for sale An issue of shares that involves a public limited company (or its shareholders) selling the shares to a financial institution that will, in turn, sell the shares to the public. *p. 140*

Operating cash cycle (OCC) The period between the outlay of cash to buy supplies and the ultimate receipt of cash from the sale of goods. *p. 295*

Operating lease An arrangement where a business hires an asset, usually for a short time. Hiring an asset under an operating lease tends to be seen as an operating, rather than a financing, decision. *p. 250*

Operating profit The profit achieved during a period after all operating expenses have been deducted from revenues from operations. Financing expenses are deducted after the calculation of operating profit. *p. 77*

Operating profit margin ratio A profitability ratio that expresses the operating profit as a percentage of the sales revenue for the period. *p. 279*

Ordinary shares Shares that form the main risk capital of a company. Holders of ordinary shares are normally given voting rights and are entitled to any surplus arising from the activities of the company after all other claims have been satisfied. Ordinary shares are also known as *equities. p. 128*

Overtrading The situation arising where a business is operating at a level of activity that cannot be supported by the amount of finance that has been committed. *p. 323*

Paid-up share capital That part of the share capital of a company that has been called and paid. *p. 135*

Par value *See* Nominal value. *p. 127*

Parent company A company that has a controlling interest in another company. *p. 349*

Partnership A form of business unit where at least two individuals, but usually no more than twenty, carry on activities with the intention of making a profit. *p. 20*

Performance share plan A remuneration plan whereby the directors are awarded a specified number of shares in the company for achieving predefined levels of performance. *p. 470*

Preference shares Shares of a company that entitle their owners to the first part of any dividend that a company pays. *p. 128*

Prepaid expense An expenses that has been paid in advance at the end of the reporting period. *p. 87*

Present value The immediate value of a cash flow, or stream of cash flows, to occur at a future time, or times. *p. 253*

Price/earnings (P/E) ratio An investment ratio that relates the market value of a share to the earnings per share. *p. 318*

Private limited company A limited company in which the sale or transfer of shares is restricted. For example, shares cannot be offered for sale to the general public. *p. 120*

Private placing An issue of shares that involves a limited company arranging for the shares to be sold to the clients of particular issuing houses or stockbrokers, rather than to the general investing public. *p. 141*

Profit The increase in wealth attributable to the owners of a business that arises through business operations. *p. 74*

Profit before taxation The result when all appropriately matched expenses have been deducted from the revenue generated for the period, but before the taxation charge is deducted. *p. 147*

Profit for the period The result when all appropriately matched expenses have been deducted from the revenue for the period and, in the case of a limited company, after the taxation charge has also been deducted. *p. 77*

Property, plant and equipment Those non-current assets that have a physical substance (for example, machinery and motor vehicles). *p. 48*

Provision A liability where the timing or amount involved is uncertain. *p. 239*

Prudence convention The accounting convention that holds that caution should be exercised when making accounting judgements. It has been used to defend the practice of reporting actual and expected losses immediately but reporting profits when they arise. *p. 55*

Public issue An issue of shares that involves a public limited company (plc) making a direct invitation to the public to buy shares in the company. *p. 140*

Public limited company A limited company in which there are no restrictions on the sale or transfer of its shares. The shares may be traded on the Stock Exchange *p. 120*

Reducing-balance method A method of calculating depreciation that applies a fixed percentage rate of depreciation to the carrying amount of an asset in each period. *p. 92*

Relevance The ability of accounting information to influence decisions. Relevance is regarded as a fundamental characteristic of useful accounting information. *p. 6*

Remuneration committee A committee of the board of directors whose task it is to recommend to the board the amount of remuneration of the executive directors and the chair. *p. 450*

Reporting period The time span for which a business prepares its financial statements. *p. 45*

Reserves Part of the owners' claim (equity) of a limited company that has arisen from profits and gains, to the extent that these have not been distributed to the shareholders or reduced by losses or taxation. *p. 127*

Residual value The amount for which a non-current asset is sold when the business has no further use for it. *p. 91*

Restricted shares Shares awarded to directors under a performance share plan that are not owned by the directors outright. They may be forfeited under certain circumstances, such as where the directors fail to reach the prescribed level of performance, *p. 470*

Return on capital employed ratio (ROCE) A profitability ratio that expresses the operating profit (that is, profit before interest and taxation) as a percentage of the long-term funds (equity and borrowings) invested in the business. *p. 277*

Return on ordinary shareholders' funds ratio (ROSF) A profitability ratio that expresses the profit for the period available to ordinary shareholders as a percentage of the funds that they have invested. *p. 276*

Revenue A measure of the inflow of assets (for example, cash or amounts owed to a business by credit customers), or a reduction in liabilities, arising as a result of trading operations. *p. 74*

Revenue reserve Part of the owners' claim (equity) of a company that arises from realised profits and gains, including after-tax trading profits and gains from disposals of non-current assets. *p. 127*

Rights issues Issues of shares for cash to existing shareholders on the basis of the number of shares already held. *p. 137*

Risk management committee A committee of the board of directors whose task it is to review the risk management systems in place. *p. 450*

Sales revenue per employee ratio An efficiency ratio that relates the sales revenue generated during a period to the average number of employees of the business. *p. 288*

Sales revenue to capital employed ratio An efficiency ratio that relates the sales revenue generated during a period to the capital employed. *p. 287*

Segmental financial reports Financial reports that break down the overall results of a business according to its different types of business operations. *p. 409*

Shares Portions of the ownership, or equity, of a company. *p. 5*

Share premium account A capital reserve reflecting any amount, above the nominal value of shares, that is paid for those shares when they are issued by a company. *p. 132*

Sole proprietorship A form of business unit where an individual is operating a business on his or her own account. *p. 19*

Splitting Changing the nominal value of shares to a lower figure (from, say, £1.00 to £0.50) and then issuing sufficient shares so that the total nominal value of shares held by each shareholder remains the same. *p. 129*

Statement of cash flows A statement that shows a business's sources and uses of cash for a period. *p. 34*

Statement of changes in equity A financial statement, required by IAS 1, which shows the effect of gains/losses and capital injections/withdrawals on the equity base of a company. *p. 179*

Statement of comprehensive income A financial statement that extends the conventional income statement to include other gains and losses that affect shareholders' equity. *p. 176*

Statement of financial position A statement that shows the assets of a business and the claims on those assets. It is also known as a *balance sheet*. *p. 34*

Stock Exchange A market where 'second-hand' shares may be bought and sold and new capital raised. *p. 123*

Straight-line method A method of accounting for depreciation that allocates the amount to be depreciated evenly over the useful life of the asset. *p. 91*

Strategic report A report designed to provide a fair review of the company's business. Directors must prepare a balanced and comprehensive analysis of financial performance for the year and financial position at the year end. They must also describe the principle risks and uncertainties facing the company. *p. 182*

Subsidiary company A company over which another (parent) company is able to exercise control, usually, but not necessarily, because a majority of its shares are owned by the parent company. *p. 349*

Summary financial statements A summarised version of the full annual financial statements, which are aimed at shareholders who do not wish to receive the full version. *p. 414*

Takeover The acquisition of control of one company by another, usually as a result of acquiring a majority of the ordinary shares of the former. *p. 350*

Tangible asset An asset that has physical substance (for example, plant and machinery, a motor vehicle). *p. 41*

Target company A company that has been identified by another company as a suitable target for a takeover. *p. 353*

Timeliness The provision of accounting information in time for users to make their decision. This quality enhances the usefulness of accounting information. *p. 8*

Total shareholder return (TSR) A measure of the total return from a share, which is made up of two elements: the increase (or decrease) in share value over a period plus any dividends paid during the period. *p. 475*

Trade payable An amount owed to a supplier from whom the business has received goods or services on credit. *p. 43*

Trade receivable An amount outstanding from a customer to whom the business has provided goods or services on credit. *p. 40*

Transfer price The price at which goods or services are sold, or transferred, between divisions of the same business. *p. 411*

Trial balance A list setting out the debit balances and credit balances appearing in the accounts in a double-entry bookkeeping system. The total of debit balances should equal the total of credit balances. *p. 504*

UK Corporate Governance Code A code of practice for companies listed on the London Stock Exchange that deals with corporate governance matters. *p. 446*

UK Stewardship Code A code that sets out good practice concerning the dialogue between financial institutions and investee businesses. *p. 486*

Understandability The quality that enables accounting information to be understood by those for whom the information is primarily compiled. This quality enhances the usefulness of accounting information. *p. 8*

Univariate analysis A statistical technique that can be used to help predict financial distress, which involves the use of a single ratio as a predictor. *p. 331*

Value added statement (VAS) A financial statement that deducts from the revenue for a period the cost of bought-in materials and services to determine the value added by the business. The statement then shows how this value added was distributed among the various stakeholders of the business. *p. 420*

Verifiability The quality that provides assurance to users that the information provided faithfully represents what it is supposed to represent. It enhances the quality of accounting information. *p. 8*

Vertical analysis An approach to common-size financial statements where all of the figures in the particular statement are expressed in relation to one of the figures in that same statement, for example, sales revenue or total long-term funds. *p. 327*

Weighted average cost (AVCO) A method of inventories costing, which values inventories *as if* those inventories on entering the business lose their separate identity and any issues of inventories reflect the weighted average cost of the inventories held. *p. 99*

Working capital Current assets less current liabilities. *p. 215*

Written-down value (WDV) *See* Carrying amount. *p. 92*

Chapter 2

2.1 Simonson Engineering

(a) The statement of financial position should be set out as follows:

Simonson Engineering
Statement of financial position as at 30 September 2018

	£
ASSETS	
Non-current assets	
Property, plant and equipment	
Property	72,000
Plant and machinery	25,000
Fixtures and fittings	9,000
Motor vehicles	15,000
	121,000
Current assets	
Inventories	45,000
Trade receivables	48,000
Cash in hand	1,500
	94,500
Total assets	215,500
EQUITY AND LIABILITIES	
Equity	
Closing balance*	120,500
Non-current liabilities	
Long-term borrowings	51,000
Current liabilities	
Trade payables	18,000
Short-term borrowings	26,000
	44,000
Total equity and liabilities	215,500

* The equity is calculated as follows:	
Opening balance	117,500
Profit	18,000
	135,500
Drawings	(15,000)
Closing balance	120,500

(b) The statement of financial position shows:

- The biggest investment in assets is property, followed by trade receivables and inventories. These, combined, account for more than 76% of the value of assets held.
- The investment in current assets accounts for 44% of the total investment in assets.

- The total long-term finance is divided 70% equity and 30% long-term borrowings. There is, therefore, not excessive reliance on long-term borrowings.
- The current assets (which are cash or near cash) cover the current liabilities (which are maturing obligations) by a ratio of more than 2:1.

(c) The revised statement of position will be as follows:

Simonson Engineering
Statement of financial position as at 30 September 2018

	£
ASSETS	
Non-current assets	
Property, plant and equipment	
Property	115,000
Plant and machinery	25,000
Motor vehicles	15,000
Fixtures and fittings	9,000
	164,000
Current assets	
Inventories	38,000
Trade receivables	48,000
Cash in hand	1,500
	87,500
Total assets	251,500
EQUITY AND LIABILITIES	
Equity	
Closing balance (120,500 + 43,000 − 7,000)	156,500
Non-current liabilities	
Long-term borrowings	51,000
Current liabilities	
Trade payables	18,000
Short-term borrowings	26,000
	44,000
Total equity and liabilities	251,500

Chapter 3

3.1 TT and Co.

Statement of financial position as at 31 December 2017

	£
ASSETS	
Delivery van (12,000 − 2,500)	9,500
Inventories (143,000 + 12,000 − 74,000 − 16,000)	65,000
Trade receivables	
(152,000 − 132,000 − 400)	19,600
Cash at bank (50,000 − 25,000 − 500 − 1,200	750
− 12,000 − 33,500 − 1,650 − 12,000 + 35,000	
+ 132,000 − 121,000 − 9,400)	
Prepaid expenses (5,000 + 300)	5,300
Total assets	100,150
EQUITY AND LIABILITIES	
Equity (50,000 + 26,900)	76,900
Trade payables (143,000 − 121,000)	22,000
Accrued expenses (630 + 620)	1,250
Total equity and liabilities	100,150

Income statement for the year ended 31 December 2017

	£
Sales revenue (152,000 + 35,000)	187,000
Cost of goods sold (74,000 + 16,000)	(90,000)
Gross profit	97,000
Rent	(20,000)
Rates (500 + 900)	(1,400)
Wages (33,500 + 630)	(34,130)
Electricity (1,650 + 620)	(2,270)
Bad debts	(400)
Van depreciation ((12,000 − 2,000)/4)	(2,500)
Van expenses	(9,400)
Profit for the year	26,900

The statement of financial position could now be rewritten in a more stylish form as follows:

Statement of financial position as at 31 December 2017

	£	
ASSETS		
Non-current assets		
Property, plant and equipment		
Delivery van at cost	12,000	
Accumulated depreciation	(2,500)	
	9,500	
Current assets		
Inventories	65,000	
Trade receivables	19,600	
Prepaid expenses	5,300	
Cash	750	
	90,650	
Total assets	100,150	
EQUITY AND LIABILITIES		
Equity		
Closing balance	76,900	
Current liabilities		
Trade payables	22,000	
Accrued expenses	1,250	
	23,250	
Total equity and liabilities	100,150	

Chapter 4

4.1 Dev Ltd

(a) The summarised statement of financial position of Dev Ltd, immediately following the rights and bonus issue, is as follows:

Statement of financial position

	£000
Net assets (235 + 40 (cash from the rights issue))	275
Equity	
Share capital: 180,000 shares @ £1 ((100 + 20) + 60)	180
Share premium account (30 + 20 − 50)	–
Revaluation reserve (37 − 10)	27
Retained earnings	68
	275

Note that the bonus issue of £60,000 is taken from capital reserves (reserves unavailable for dividends) as follows:

	£000
Share premium account	50
Revaluation reserve	10
	60

More could have been taken from the revaluation reserve and less from the share premium account without making any difference to dividend payment possibilities.

(b) There may be pressure from a potential lender for the business to limit its ability to pay dividends. This would place lenders in a more secure position because the maximum buffer, or safety margin, between the value of the assets and the amount owed by the business is maintained. It is not unusual for potential lenders to insist on locking in shareholders' funds in this way as a condition of granting the loan.

(c) The summarised statement of financial position of Dev Ltd, immediately following the rights and bonus issue, assuming a minimum dividend potential objective, is as follows:

Statement of financial position

	£000
Net assets (235 + 40 (cash from the rights issue))	275
Equity	
Share capital: 180,000 shares @ £1 ((100 + 20) + 60)	180
Share premium account (30 + 20)	50
Revaluation reserve	37
Retained earnings (68 − 60)	8
	275

(d) Before the bonus issue, the maximum dividend was £68,000. Now it is £8,000. The bonus issue has therefore locked in an additional £60,000 of assets and thereby restricted the business's ability to pay dividends.

(e) Before the issues, Lee had 100 shares worth £2.35 (£235,000/100,000) each or £235 in total. Lee would be offered 20 shares in the rights issue at £2 each or £40 in total. After the rights issue, Lee would have 120 shares worth £2.2917 (£275,000/120,000) each or £275 in total.

The bonus issue would give Lee 60 additional shares. After the bonus issue, Lee would have 180 shares worth £1.5278 (£275,000/180,000) each or £275 in total.

None of this affects Lee's wealth. Before the issues, Lee had £235 worth of shares and £40 more in cash. After the issues, Lee has the same total wealth but all £275 is in the value of the shares.

(f) The things that we know about the company are as follows:

- It is a private (as opposed to a public) limited company, as it has 'Ltd' (limited) as part of its name, rather than plc (public limited company).
- It has made an issue of shares at a premium, almost certainly after it had traded successfully for a period. (There is a share premium account. It would be unlikely that the original shares, issued when the company was first formed, would have been issued at a premium.)
- Some of the assets in the statement of financial position have been upwardly revalued by at least £37,000. (There is a revaluation reserve of £37,000. This may be only what is remaining after an earlier bonus issue used part of this reserve.)
- The company has traded at an aggregate profit (though there could have been losses in some years), net of tax and any dividends paid. (There is a positive balance on retained earnings.)

Chapter 5

5.1 Comments

(a) Dividends announced between the end of the reporting period and the date at which the financial reports are authorised for publication should *not* be treated as a liability in the statement of financial position at the end of that period. IAS 1 specifically precludes the treatment of such dividends as liabilities.

(b) IAS 1 provides support for three key accounting conventions – accruals, going concern and consistency. It does not specifically support the historic cost convention.

(c) IAS 1 does not permit bank overdrafts to be offset against positive bank balances when preparing the statement of financial position. For the sake of relevance they should be shown separately.

(d) IAS 8 states that accounting policies should be changed if it is required by a new financial reporting standard *or* if it leads to more relevant and reliable information being reported.

(e) IAS 10 states that *significant* non-adjusting events occurring between the end of the reporting period and the date at which the financial statements are authorised should be disclosed by way of note. The standard requires the nature of the event and its likely financial effect to be disclosed.

(f) Preparing a strategic report may present a problem for accountants. For information to be credible to all interested parties, accountants should be as neutral as possible in measuring and reporting the financial performance and position of the business. The strategic report requires some interpretation of results and there is always a risk of bias, or at least the perception of bias among some users, in what items are reported and how they reflect on business performance. The board of directors is charged with running the business and it is logical that the directors accept full responsibility for preparing the report. This should be made clear to users.

Chapter 6

6.1 Touchstone plc

(a)   **Statement of cash flows for the year ended 31 December 2018**

	£m	£m
Cash flows from operating activities		
Profit before taxation (after interest) (see Note 1 below)		60
Adjustments for:		
Depreciation		16
Interest expense (Note 2)		4
		80
Increase in trade receivables (26 − 16)		(10)
Decrease in trade payables (38 − 37)		(1)
Decrease in inventories (25 − 24)		1
Cash generated from operations		70
Interest paid		(4)
Taxation paid (Note 3)		(12)
Dividend paid		(18)
Net cash from operating activities		36
Cash flows from investing activities		
Payments to acquire tangible non-current assets (Note 4)		(41)
Net cash used in investing activities		(41)
Cash flows from financing activities		
Issue of loan notes (40 − 20)		20
Net cash used in financing activities		20
Net increase in cash and cash equivalents		15
Cash and cash equivalents at 1 January 2018		
Cash		4
Cash and cash equivalents at 31 December 2018		
Cash	4	
Treasury bills	15	19

Notes:

1 This is simply taken from the income statement for the year.

2 Interest payable expense must be taken out, by adding it back to the profit before taxation figure. We subsequently deduct the cash paid for interest payable during the year. In this case the two figures are identical.

3 Companies pay 50% of their tax during their accounting year and the other 50% in the following year. Thus the 2018 payment would have been half the tax on the 2017 profit (that is, the figure that would have appeared in the current liabilities at the end of 2017), plus half of the 2018 tax charge (that is, $4 + (1/2 \times 16) = 12$).

4 Since there were no disposals, the depreciation charges must be the difference between the start and end of the year's non-current asset values, adjusted by the cost of any additions:

	£m
Carrying amount at 1 January 2018	147
Additions (balancing figure)	41
	188
Depreciation (6 + 10)	(16)
Carrying amount at 31 December 2018	172

(b)   **Reconciliation of liabilities from financing activities for the year to 31 December 2018**

	£m
Loan notes outstanding at 1 January 2018	20
Cash received from issuing additional loan notes	20
Loan notes outstanding at 31 December 2018	40

Chapter 7

7.1 Prentaxia plc

	Note	£m
Draft profit before tax		87.2
Lease payment adjustment	1	3.0
Depreciation charge	1	(3.8)
Capitalisation of borrowing costs	2	2.0
Increase in existing provision	3	(2.6)
Reversal of provision	4	1.4
Recognition of a provision	5	(4.5)
Development expenditure	6	(1.3)
Revised profit before tax		81.4

Notes:

1 Only the interest charge element of the lease payment should be treated as an expense. The interest charge for the period is £2m. The lease payment incorrectly charged to the income statement is £5m. This means that the net effect of replacing the lease payment with the interest charge will be a £3m (£5m − £2m) increase in profits. However, there should also be a depreciation charge of £3.8m (£19m/5), which will decrease profits.

2 Borrowing costs relating to the construction of an asset should be capitalised.

3 Any increase in the provision should be recognised by a charge to the income statement.

4 The provision should be reversed. There is no present obligation. The obligation to re-line the furnace can be avoided by selling it. The depreciation of the existing lining is appropriate. When the new lining is acquired, it should be capitalised and should be depreciated over its useful lifetime.

5 A provision should be recognised. On the basis of the evidence, there is a present obligation and it is probable that there will be an outflow of resources.

6 The search for new materials is cited in IAS 38 as an example of research expenditure, and should not be capitalised. It must therefore be treated as an expense.

7 There is no present obligation to fit smoke alarms (though there will be next year) and so there is no need to create a provision during the current year.

Chapter 8

8.1 Ali plc and Bhaskar plc

(a) To answer this question, you may have used the following ratios:

	Ali plc	Bhaskar plc
Return on ordinary shareholders' funds ratio	$\dfrac{99.9}{687.6} \times 100 = 14.5\%$	$\dfrac{104.6}{874.6} \times 100 = 12.0\%$
Operating profit margin ratio	$\dfrac{151.3}{1,478.1} \times 100 = 10.2\%$	$\dfrac{166.9}{1,790.4} \times 100 = 9.3\%$
Inventories turnover period ratio	$\dfrac{592.0}{1,018.3} \times 12 = 7.0$ months	$\dfrac{403.0}{1,214.9} \times 12 = 4.0$ months
Settlement period for trade receivables ratio	$\dfrac{176.4}{1,478.1} \times 12 = 1.4$ months	$\dfrac{321.9}{1,790.4} \times 12 = 2.2$ months
Current ratio	$\dfrac{853.0}{422.4} = 2.0$	$\dfrac{816.5}{293.1} = 2.8$
Acid test ratio	$\dfrac{(853.0 - 592.0)}{422.4} = 0.6$	$\dfrac{(816.5 - 403.0)}{293.1} = 1.4$
Gearing ratio	$\dfrac{190}{(687.6 + 190)} \times 100 = 21.6\%$	$\dfrac{250}{(874.6 + 250)} \times 100 = 22.2\%$
Interest cover ratio	$\dfrac{151.3}{19.4} = 7.8$ times	$\dfrac{166.9}{27.5} = 6.1$ times

(Note: It is not possible to use any average ratios because only the end-of-year figures are provided for each business.)

- Ali plc seems more effective than Bhaskar plc at generating returns for shareholders, as indicated by the higher ROSF ratio. This may be partly caused by Ali plc's higher operating profit margin.
- Both businesses have a very high inventories turnover period; this probably needs to be investigated. This ratio is particularly high for Ali plc. Both may suffer from poor inventories management.
- Ali plc has a lower settlement period for trade receivables than Bhaskar plc. This may suggest that Bhaskar plc needs to exert greater control over trade receivables.
- Ali plc has a much lower current ratio and acid test ratio than Bhaskar plc. The acid test ratio of Ali plc is substantially below 1.0: this may suggest a liquidity problem.

- The gearing ratio of each business is quite similar. The ratios indicate that both businesses have good profit coverage for their interest charges. Neither business seems to have excessive borrowing. The interest cover ratio for each business shows Ali plc to be more secure in its gearing that Bhaskar plc, but neither business seems to be at risk.
- To draw better comparisons between the two businesses, it would be useful to calculate other ratios from the financial statements. It would also be helpful to calculate ratios for both businesses over (say) five years as well as key ratios of other businesses operating in the same industry.

Chapter 9

9.1 Achilles plc

(a)

Dividend payout ratio	$(15/46) \times 100 = 32.6\%$
Dividend yield ratio	$((15/200)/3.49) \times 100 = 2.2\%$
Earnings per share	$46/200 = £0.23$
P/E ratio	$3.49/0.23 = 15.2$ times

Without having some information about the business's past ratios, it is difficult to draw very many conclusions. What we can say is that a policy of distributing about a third of the profit for the year is well in line with what many businesses do in practice.

Real World 9.2 showed that the average dividend yield and P/E ratios for all London Stock Exchange listed businesses were 3.78% and 18.72 times. The average dividend payout ratio was 71 per cent. On this basis, Achilles is significantly lower than the average for dividend yield, and a bit higher for P/E. The payout ratio is less than half of the market average.

From a dividend yield perspective, this is not an attractive investment; it yields a return that is lower than can normally be earned from a savings account. The P/E ratio, however, suggests that the market views Achilles as having a brighter than average future.

(b) The Altman-model Z-score is calculated as follows:

$$Z = 0.717a + 0.847b + 3.107c + 0.420d + 0.998e$$

where:
$a =$ Working capital/Total assets
$b =$ Accumulated retained profits/Total assets
$c =$ Operating profit/Total assets
$d =$ Book (statement of financial position) value of ordinary and preference shares/Total liabilities at book (statement of financial position) value
$e =$ Sales revenue/Total assets.

For Achilles plc, the Z-score is

$$0.717[(159 - 161)/812] + 0.847(151/812) + 3.107(97/812) + 0.420[351/(300 + 161)]$$
$$+ 0.998(701/812) = \underline{1.708}$$

According to Altman, those businesses with a Z-score of less than 1.23 tend to fail. The lower the score the greater is the probability of failure. Those with a Z-score greater than 4.14 tend not to fail. Those businesses with a Z-score between 1.23 and 4.14 occupied a 'zone of ignorance' and were difficult to classify. Thus Achilles finds itself in the zone of ignorance and uncomfortably close to the lower limit. It does not look a very healthy business. The problem probably lies with a negative working capital position, plus relatively low turnover and profit given the level of assets involved.

Chapter 10

10.1 Great plc

Group statement of financial position as at 31 December last year

ASSETS	£m
Non-current assets	
Property, plant and equipment (at cost less depreciation)	
Land	99
Plant	53
Vehicles	31
	183
Intangible assets	
Goodwill arising on consolidation (Note 1)	5
	188
Current assets	
Inventories	29
Trade receivables	27
Cash	22
	78
Total assets	266
EQUITY AND LIABILITIES	
Equity	
Called-up share capital: ordinary shares of £1 each, fully paid	100
Retained earnings (Note 2)	81
	181
Non-controlling interests (Note 3)	13
	194
Non-current liabilities	
Loan notes	50
Current liabilities	
Trade payables	22
Total equity and liabilities	266

Notes:

1 Goodwill arising on consolidation: $53 - (80\% \times (20 + 35 + 5)) = 5$.

2

	£m
Great plc's retained earnings balance	77
Great plc's share of Small plc's post-acquisition profits $(40 - 35) \times 80\%$	4
	81

3 Non-controlling interests: $(60 + 5) \times 20\% = 13$

Group income statement for last year

	£m
Revenue	118
Cost of sales	(59)
Gross profit	59
Administration expenses	(11)
Distribution expenses	(8)
Operating profit	40
Interest payable	(3)
Profit before taxation	37
Taxation	(16)
Profit for the year	21
Attributable to non-controlling interests $(20\% \times 5)$	(1)
Profit for the year attributable to Great plc shareholders	20

Chapter 11

11.1 Discussion

The discussion should be along the following lines:

(a) A steward is someone who has custody and control of assets belonging to another or others. In a business context company directors are good examples of stewards. Stewardship accounting is concerned with reporting on how the owners' assets have been deployed and with what effect by the steward. Stewardship accounting may be concerned with bar profits, but is more likely not to be.

(b) The market model of financial reporting has nothing to do with street trading. It is, however, concerned with the theory (broadly confirmed by the evidence) that businesses that provide appropriate information to shareholders and others will be rewarded with a cheaper cost of capital. This is because appropriate disclosure can remove certain doubts and, therefore, risk. Individual businesses can then decide whether the cost of additional disclosure is likely to be adequately rewarded.

(c) IFRS 8 says that segmental information provided with the annual financial statements should be based on a 'management approach'. This means that, for the purposes of segmental external reporting, the business should be segmented along the same lines as it is managed. Thus, if the business is managed on a geographical basis, that basis will be used for segmental reporting – as is the case with Asos plc in real World 11.2. It is true that a segment with less than 10 per cent of the business's combined revenue can be aggregated with that of a similar segment.

(d) In a segmental report, inter-segment trading revenues should be included. Such revenues cannot be included in the revenue figure that appears in the business's income statement, however.

(e) Interim financial statements are not the first draft of the annual financial statements. They are financial statements for shorter periods than the normal one-year reporting period. Interims are usually for a six-month period, though they might be for three months or even some other period.

(f) A business's value added is not usually taken to be its sales revenue. It is usually taken to be the sales revenue less any bought-in goods or services used to generate that revenue.

(g) Current purchasing power financial statements are based on the historic cost ones. An adjustment is made for the movement in the relevant general price index from acquiring an asset and so on to the date of the end of the reporting period.

(h) Monetary items are those that are fixed in monetary terms, like a loan. Other items, say an item of plant, may have a monetary value next to it in the statement of financial position, but it is not a monetary item.

(i) CPP is particularly concerned with shareholders' spending power with reference to general goods and services. CCA is concerned with the ability of a business to continue to trade at the same level as it has recently been doing.

Chapter 12

12.1 Hexworthy and Parix

(a) The sources of information that may be used may include the following:

- documents setting out the:
  - strategic plan of the company;
  - board structure and roles;
  - board appointments procedures;
  - operations of the board;
  - minutes of board meetings;
  - meeting agendas and background information;
  - criteria for directors' appraisal;

- interviews with board members;
- interviews with and/or questionnaires sent to senior management and shareholders;
- attendance and observation at board meetings;
- attendance and observation at meetings with shareholders, including the AGM;
- company website and published material, including the annual reports;
- CVs of board members;
- performance reports (such as monthly budget reports and sales reports) received by the board; and
- information relating to training and development programmes carried out.

This is not an exhaustive list. You may have thought of other sources of information.

(b) The remuneration committee must be sensitive to the needs of shareholders and others with respect to directors' rewards. This has led some to argue that the committee should include an employee representative and, or, a shareholder representative. Perhaps, as a further brake on excessive rewards, the committee should also exclude from membership any non-executive director who is also an executive director of a large listed company. Such suggestions would, however, fly in the face of normal practice and could create various problems. A more conventional suggestion is to ensure that the committee has a chair who has the experience and emotional intelligence required to anticipate problems and to be aware of the risks involved.

(c) Communication with shareholders can take various forms. The following are either required by law or are considered to be good practice:

- distribution of annual reports and interim reports to all shareholders as well as their publication on the company's website;
- timely releases throughout the year concerning major developments;
- a chairman's address at the annual general meeting;
- an address by the chairman of the audit committee and the chairman of the remuneration committee at the annual general meeting;
- an opportunity for shareholders to question the board of directors at the annual general meeting;
- publication of notice of all shareholder meetings on the website;
- dedicated staff to manage the company website and deal with shareholder queries;
- prompt publication of announcements and press releases on the company website;
- briefings for major shareholders and analysts and their publication on the company website;
- regular meetings between major shareholders and the chairman and chief executive;
- regular meetings between non-executive directors and major shareholders; and
- email newsletters setting out new developments, financial results, announcements and so on to major shareholders and analysts.

Appendix D
SOLUTIONS TO CRITICAL REVIEW QUESTIONS

Chapter 1

1.1 Accounting, like a spoken language, is a form of communication. It provides those with an interest in a business with a common means of understanding its financial health and performance. However, while a spoken language is general purpose in nature and can cover a wide range of different issues, the language of accounting is restricted to financial issues. It does not, therefore, have the same breadth of 'vocabulary' as a spoken language.

1.2 The main users of financial information for a university and the purposes for which they need information may be summed up as follows:

Students	Whether to enrol on a course of study. This would probably involve an assessment of the university's ability to continue to operate and to fulfil students' needs.
Other universities and colleges	How best to compete with the university. This might involve using the university's performance in various aspects as a 'benchmark' when evaluating their own performance.
Employees	Whether to take up or to continue in employment with the university. Employees might assess this by considering the ability of the university to continue to provide employment and to reward employees adequately for their labour.
Government/funding authority	How efficient and effective the university is in undertaking its various activities. Possible funding needs that the university may have.
Local community representatives	Whether to allow/encourage the university to expand its premises. To assess this, the university's ability to continue to provide employment for the community, to use community resources and to help fund environmental improvements might be considered.
Suppliers	Whether to supply the university with goods and services on credit. This would involve an assessment of the university's ability to pay for any goods and services supplied.
Lenders	Whether to lend money to the university and/or whether to require repayment of any existing loans. This would involve assessing the university's ability to pay interest and to repay the principal.
Board of governors and managers (faculty deans and so on)	Whether the performance of the university requires improvement. Performance to date would be compared with earlier plans or some other 'benchmark' to decide whether action needs to be taken. Whether there should be a change in the university's future direction. In making such decisions, management will need to look at the university's ability to perform and at the opportunities available to it.

We can see that the users of accounting information and their needs are broadly similar to those of a private sector business.

1.3 Not-for-profit organisations do not pursue profit as their *primary* objective. However, this does not mean that they are indifferent about, or uninterested in, making a profit. By creating wealth (profit), they are usually better placed to pursue their primary objective, such as the relief of suffering or the education of students, more effectively.

A not-for-profit organisation will normally need to account to those with a stake in the organisation how wealth was generated and how it was applied in pursuit of its stated objectives. Hence, it will have a keen interest in monitoring and reporting the inflows and outflows of wealth over time. A good accounting system and sound financial practice can therefore be as vital for this type of organisation as it is for a business.

1.4 We can never be sure what is going to happen in the future, the best we can often do is to make judgements based on past experience. Thus, information concerning past flows of cash and wealth in the recent past may well be useful in helping to form judgements about possible future outcomes.

Chapter 2

2.1 The owner seems unaware of the business entity convention in accounting. This convention requires a separation of the business from the owner(s) of the business for accounting purposes. The business is regarded as a separate entity and the statement of financial position is prepared from the perspective of the business rather than that of the owner. As a result, funds invested in the business by the owner are regarded as a claim that the owner has on the business. In the standard layout of the statement of financial position, this claim will be shown alongside other claims on the business from outsiders.

2.2 A statement of financial position does not show what a business is worth, for two major reasons:

1 Only those items that can be measured reliably in monetary terms are shown on the statement of financial position. Thus, things of value such as the reputation for product quality, skills of employees and so on will not normally appear in the statement of financial position.

2 The historic cost convention results in assets often being recorded at their outlay cost rather than their current value. For certain assets, the difference between historic cost and current value may be significant.

2.3 The statement of financial position is a static financial statement, showing only the situation at a single moment in time, whereas the other two major statements – the income statement and statement of cash flows – are dynamic, showing flows of wealth and cash over time. We saw in Chapter 1 that a business exists in order to generate wealth for its owners. The amount of wealth (profit) generated for a particular period is revealed in the income statements. As a result, this statement tends to be the main focus of attention for many users. The statement of cash flows is also of critical importance. In order to survive over time, a business must have an uninterrupted capacity to pay its debts when they fall due. This means that there must be sufficient cash available when needed.

Apart from its static nature, we saw in the answer to Question 2.2 above, that the statement of financial position provides only a restricted view of financial health. Nevertheless, the statement of financial position still offers important insights and should not be regarded as of secondary importance. To understand the financial health of a business all three major financial statements must be examined.

2.4 Some object to the idea of humans being treated as assets for inclusion on the statement of financial position. It is seen as demeaning for humans to be listed alongside inventories, plant and machinery and other assets. Others argue, however, that humans are often the most valuable resource of a business and that placing a value on this resource will help bring to the attention of managers the importance of nurturing and developing this 'asset'.

Humans are likely to meet the criterion of an asset relating to future potential benefits, otherwise there would be little point in employing them. The criterion relating to exclusive right of control is, however, more problematic. A business cannot control humans in the same way as most other assets, but it can have exclusive rights to their employment services. This makes it possible to argue that this criterion can be met.

The criterion concerning whether the value of humans (or their services) can be measured with any degree of certainty poses the major difficulty. Apart from the unusual circumstances relating to professional footballers mentioned in the chapter, human 'assets' defy reliable measurement.

Chapter 3

3.1 When preparing the income statement, it is not always possible to determine accurately the expenses that need to be matched to the sales revenue for the period. It is perhaps only at some later point that the true position becomes clear. Nevertheless, we must try to include all relevant expenses and so estimates of the future have to be made. These estimates may include accrued expenses, depreciation charges and bad debts incurred. The income statement would lose much of its usefulness if we were to wait for all uncertainties to become clear.

3.2 Depreciation attempts to allocate the cost or fair value, less any residual value, of an asset over its useful life. Depreciation does not attempt to measure the fall in value of the asset during a particular accounting period. Thus, the carrying amount of the asset appearing on the statement of financial position normally represents the unexpired part of its cost, or fair value, rather than its current market value.

3.3 The convention of consistency aims to provide some uniformity in the application of accounting policies. In certain areas, there may be more than one method of accounting for an item, for example inventories. The convention of consistency states that, having decided on a particular accounting policy, a business should continue to apply the policy in successive periods. While this policy helps to ensure that more valid comparisons can be made of business performance *over time,* it does not ensure that valid comparisons can be made *between businesses.* Different businesses may still consistently apply different accounting policies.

3.4 An expense is that element of the cost incurred that is used up during the reporting period. An asset is that element of cost that is carried forward on the statement of financial position and which will normally be used up in future periods. Thus, both assets and expenses arise from costs being incurred. The major difference between the two is the period over which the benefits (arising from the costs incurred) accrue.

Chapter 4

4.1 A private limited company would seem to be more appropriate. The principal advantage of a public limited company is its ability to offer issues of new shares to the general public. This does not seem not to be a consideration for this particular business, since you and your friend feel that you can finance the start up and planned expansion from your own resources. Being a private company means that neither you nor your friend could sell shares to a third party without you both agreeing to it. This may well be something that you would both prefer, at this stage.

4.2 Some businesses arrange, at significant economic cost, to have their shares listed on the London Stock Exchange (LSE). They do this because they see the need for shareholders to have an easy means of selling their shares whenever they choose to do so. Unless investors have the opportunity to sell their shares through the LSE, they will be reluctant to take up shares issued by a business. This will make it more difficult and, probably, more costly for the business to raise equity finance. This means that the LSE barring the business's shares from being traded will be to the great disadvantage of the business.

4.3 This statement is untrue. All that is required for a market to be efficient is active trading by investors researching the various factors affecting each business's economic fortunes. Between them, these investors will generate, through their buying and selling activities, a share price that represents the best estimate of the share's true value. In effect, a business's current share price represents a consensus view among investors of the share's true worth.

4.4 Companies would generally prefer not to issue preference shares because they impose a moral obligation to pay a dividend. Failure to pay a preference dividend may be embarrassing for the company and show it in a bad light to investors. Preference shareholders do not have a right to receive a dividend. They only have a right to receive the first slice of any dividend declared.

From a potential shareholder's perspective, preference shares would not provide the greater certainty of returns that a loan would give. At the same time, preference shares do not give their holders the level of returns associated with ordinary shares.

Chapter 5

5.1 Managers may shy away from an open and meaningful evaluation of the performance and position of a business because of the risk of litigation. If legal action may result from making statements in good faith or making predictions that prove to be inaccurate, managers will be advised by their lawyers to be very guarded and to stick to making only bland statements. To avoid this risk, managers acting in good faith could be awarded some sort of legal protection (safe harbour). This should help to improve the quality of their commentaries. In the UK, the directors' liability for the strategic report is protected by a 'safe harbour' provision.

5.2 Accounting is an evolving subject. It is not static and the conceptual framework that is laid down at any particular point in time may become obsolete. This may occur as a result of changes in our understanding of the nature of accounting information and its impact on users, or as a result of changes in the economic environment within which accounting is employed. We must accept, therefore, that accounting principles will continue to evolve and those currently employed must be regularly reviewed.

5.3 Accounting rules impose an important discipline on managers. They help to ensure that unscrupulous directors do not exploit their position and portray an unrealistic view of financial health. They are also important for the purpose of comparability, both over time and between businesses.

Harmonisation may lead to sovereignty-related problems. Each country has its own tax laws, banking laws, financial regulations and stock exchange rules. International accounting rules may well conflict with these national rules. Furthermore, international rules may not fit well with the local business culture and the way in which businesses operate.

Harmonisation may also lead to some businesses, which operate solely within the confines of its own country, having to comply with international rules.

5.4 The main methods of creative accounting are misstating revenues, massaging expenses, misstating assets, concealing 'bad news' and inadequate disclosure.

Harmonisation of accounting rules will often draw on best practice occurring in highly developed countries. Other countries may well have weaker rules in place, leading to poor quality financial reporting. By harmonising accounting rules, businesses operating within those countries will need to comply with more demanding rules for financial reporting.

Chapter 6

6.1 Cash is normally required in the settlement of claims. Employees, contractors, lenders and suppliers expect to be paid in cash. When businesses fail, it is their inability to find the cash to pay claimants that actually drives them under. These factors lead to cash being the pre-eminent business asset. It is studied carefully to assess the ability of a business to survive and/or to take advantage of commercial opportunities.

6.2 With the direct method, the business's cash records are analysed for the period concerned. The analysis reveals the amounts of cash, in total, that have been paid and received in respect of each category of the statement of cash flows. This is not difficult in principle, or in practice, if it is done by computer, as a matter of routine.

The indirect method takes the approach that, while the profit (loss) for the reporting period is not equal to the net inflow (outflow) of cash from operations, they are fairly closely linked to the extent that appropriate adjustment of the profit (loss) for the period figure will produce the correct cash flow one. The adjustment is concerned with the depreciation charge for, and movements in relevant working capital items over, the period.

The indirect method may help to shed light on the quality of reported profits by reconciling profit with the net cash from operating activities for a period. A business must demonstrate an ability to convert profits into cash. Revealing the link between profits and cash is, therefore, very helpful.

6.3 One reason for tightly defining cash is simply to promote comparability between different businesses or, perhaps, between different time periods for the same business. The more tightly a factor is defined, the greater the possibility of producing comparable financial statements.

A second reason is to avoid the possibility that managers produce a statement of cash flows that could mislead users of the statement, perhaps deliberately. For example, some ordinary shares in another business would not fall within the definition of a cash equivalent because the apparent value of those shares, in terms of cash receivable, is uncertain. Also, a failure to define cash tightly opens the door to all sorts of assets being treated as a cash equivalent. A business might, for example, claim that trade receivables are a cash equivalent, on the grounds that the next step in the business cycle is for the customer to pay. Including receivables in this way simply defeats the whole idea of the statement as being concerned strictly with liquid cash.

6.4 Assuming, an annual reporting period, profit and net cash inflows may well diverge significantly. There are several possible reasons for this, including the following:

- Changes in inventories, trade receivables and trade payables. For example, an increase in trade receivables during a reporting period would mean that the cash received from credit sales would be less than the credit sales revenue for the same period.
- Cash may have been spent on new non-current assets or received from disposals of old ones; these would not directly affect profit.
- Cash may have been spent to redeem or repay a financial claim, or received as a result of the creation or the increase of a claim. These would not directly affect profit.
- Tax charged in the income statement is not normally the same as the tax paid during the same reporting period.

Where the period covers the whole life of the business, the timing differences mentioned would become irrelevant and the profit and net cash flows figures would move together.

Chapter 7

7.1 The threshold for disclosure is higher for a contingent asset than for a contingent liability. A contingent asset is disclosed only when it is probable that there will be an inflow of resources, whereas a contingent liability will be disclosed unless the possibility of an outflow of resources is remote. This asymmetry in disclosure thresholds reflects the influence of the prudence convention in accounting, where anticipated losses and liabilities are recognised at an early stage.

Differences in disclosure thresholds can lead to differences in the way in which two parties to a lawsuit treat a future court decision, which could go either way. The defendant may disclose a contingent liability as a result of a possible obligation whereas the plaintiff may not disclose a contingent asset as it is not expected to lead to a probable inflow of resources.

7.2 IAS 37 *Provisions, Contingent Liabilities and Contingent Assets* adopts a lower threshold of recognition for a provision than its US equivalent. This has been the subject of some criticism. In the case of a lawsuit, there is a risk that by recognising a provision (which arises before the final court decision is made) based on this lower threshold, it may provide valuable information to the plaintiffs in the lawsuit. Creating a provision may reveal a lack of confidence in the defendant's ability to win the case as well as the perceived cost of losing. The higher the threshold for recognition, the less the risk of helping the plaintiffs.

7.3 Research and development expenditure is incurred to generate future economic benefits. As a result, there is an argument for carrying this expenditure forward and charging it to the period(s) when the benefits are ultimately received. This would be in line with the accruals convention. A key problem, however, is that there is normally considerable uncertainty concerning future economic benefits. IAS 38 has therefore decreed that research expenditure should be charged to the period in which it is incurred and that development expenditure, which is incurred at a more advanced stage, can be carried forward to future periods, but only subject to tough conditions. These conditions include the need to demonstrate probable future economic benefits. The IASB has therefore taken a prudent approach to this type of expenditure.

7.4 An operating lease is, in essence, a form of borrowing. We saw that it gives rise to an obligation to make lease payments over time. When these lease payments are treated as an expense in the period incurred, the financial obligation is not recognised in the financial statements. It is possible, therefore, to conceal the true extent of borrowing by entering into operating lease agreements rather than entering into loan agreements (which are shown on the financial statements). Users of financial statements will not be able to make a proper assessment of the level of financial risk associated with the business if the obligation for future operating lease payments is not fully disclosed.

Chapter 8

8.1 The fact that a business operates on a low operating profit margin indicates that only a small operating profit is being produced for each £1 of sales revenue generated. However, this does not necessarily mean that the ROCE will be low. If the business is able to generate sufficient sales revenue during a period, the operating profit may be very high even though the operating profit per £1 of sales revenue is low. If the overall operating profit is high, this can lead, in turn, to a high ROCE, since it is the total operating profit that is used as the numerator (top part of the fraction) in this ratio. Many businesses (including supermarkets) pursue a strategy of 'low margin, high sales revenue'.

8.2 Factors that may affect the average settlement period for trade receivables include changes in:
- the credit terms offered;
- the efficiency with which amounts due from credit customers are recorded and collected;
- the economic environment within which the business operates;
- the number of disputes concerning amounts due or goods/services provided; and
- the type of customer to whom credit is granted.

This is not an exhaustive list. You may have thought of others.

8.3 Three possible reasons for a long inventories turnover period are:
- poor inventories controls, leading to excessive investment in inventories;
- a desire to provide customers with greater choice or, perhaps, speedier supply; and
- inventories building in anticipation of increased future sales.

A short inventories turnover period may be due to:

- tight inventories controls, reducing excessive investment in inventories and/or the amount of obsolete and slow-moving inventories;
- an inability to finance the required amount of inventories to meet sales demand; and
- a difference in the mix of inventories carried by similar businesses (for example, greater investment in perishable goods which are held for a short period only).

These are not exhaustive lists; you may have thought of other reasons.

8.4 Size may well be an important factor when comparing businesses.
- Larger businesses may be able to generate economies of scale in production and distribution to an extent not available to smaller businesses.
- Larger businesses may be able to raise finance more cheaply, partly through economies of scale (for example, borrowing larger amounts) and partly through being seen as less of a risk to the lender.
- Smaller businesses may be able to be more flexible and 'lighter on their feet' than can the typical larger business.

These and other possible factors may lead to differences in performance and position between larger and smaller businesses.

Chapter 9

9.1 A business may prefer not to have its Z-score publicised if the score is a weak one. This is broadly for two reasons:

- The business would prefer to avoid bad publicity for fear that this might damage its reputation and, possibly, brand image.
- A Z-score suggesting that the business may be particularly at risk of financial distress may prove to be a self-fulfilling prediction. A weak Z-score might mean that other businesses and individuals would be reluctant to provide loan finance and/or trade credit. This may make it very difficult for the business to trade, quite possibly leading to its collapse. Similarly, current and potential employees may not wish to work for a business that is in danger of collapse.

9.2 This difference could be for a variety of reasons, including:

- Electricity businesses (EBs) may recently have been more profitable than industrial engineers (IEs) and so have spare cash to pay higher dividends.
- IEs may have the need to invest more than EBs and so have less cash available than EBs.
- The share prices (which form part of the calculation of dividend yields) may be lower for EBs than they are for IEs, relative to their profitability. If this is this the case, it might be because investors do not see as profitable a future for EBs generally than for IEs.

Other possible reasons could be equally valid.

9.3 The P/E ratio may vary between businesses within the same industry for the following reasons:

- *Accounting policies.* Differences in the methods used to compute profit (for example inventories valuation and depreciation) can lead to different profit figures and, therefore, different P/E ratios.
- *Different prospects.* A business may be regarded as having a much brighter future due to factors such as the quality of management, the quality of products, or location. This will affect the market price investors are prepared to pay for the share, and hence it will also affect the P/E ratio.
- *Different asset structures.* A business's underlying asset base may be much higher than the other's, and this may affect the market price of the shares.

9.4 Three ratios that could be affected by overtrading are:

- *Acid test ratio.* This is likely to fall if overtrading is occurring, because the trade payables settlement period is likely to increase and overdraft finance is likely to exist. At the same time, inventories and trade receivables levels could well fall.
- *Cash generated from operations to maturing obligations ratio.* This is likely to fall. Cash generated is likely to rise more slowly than maturing obligations if the business is overtrading.
- *Interest cover ratio.* This is likely to fall despite rising profits because interest, perhaps on short-term borrowing (for instance, overdrafts), is likely to rise more steeply.

  Settlement ratios for both trade payables and receivables could also be affected as the overtrading business delays payment to suppliers and seeks to accelerate receipts from customers.

Chapter 10

10.1 The reason for this is that non-controlling interests alter from one reporting period's end to the next as trading (and other activities) takes place leading to the total value of the subsidiary company's equity rising or falling.

On the other hand, goodwill arising on consolidation is established definitively at the time of the takeover. The goodwill value may be adjusted downwards as the parent company assesses the value of the goodwill annually for impairment. Even so, impairment is very much based on the original value determined at the date of the takeover.

10.2 An attraction of using the 'full' value of goodwill arising on consolidation is that it is more logical than the 'partial' value based on the percentage of the parent's shareholding in the subsidiary. It is more logical because it makes for a consistent approach to the statement of the value of each of the group's assets, that is full value, even where there is not a 100 per cent shareholding. This is justified by the logic that if the parent controls the subsidiary it controls the full value of each asset.

A more practical reason for choosing the full-value approach is that the group's statement of financial position will show a higher value than the partial-value approach. This may cause readers of the statement to form a more positive view of the group. On the other hand, ratios relating profit to capital employed, like ROCE and return on ordinary shareholders' funds, will look less favourable where the full value approach is applied. This is because the relevant profit figure will not be affected by the choice between full and partial, but the capital employed figure will be. Other ratios involving capital employed will be similarly affected.

10.3 The main reason is probably that the group wishes to emphasise that it is a large business, which might give potential suppliers, employees and customers more confidence in it.

This might partially be because the limited liability of each individual subsidiary company is not an issue for these groups. Individual limited liabilities may be attractive to the group and its shareholders, but not to others.

10.4 Although, in theory, it requires more that 50 per cent of the ordinary shares to control a company, in practice the number of shares may be very much less than this. Typically, most shareholders do not attend shareholders' meetings and so an individual (person or company) that owns 20 per cent of the shares could quite easily be able to have resolutions passed. Such a resolution might be to appoint particular individuals as directors. To control the appointment of directors is to control the company. Therefore, to assert, as IFRS 3 does, that 20 per cent ownership gives 'significant influence' seems perfectly reasonable.

Chapter 11

11.1 This criticism may arise because of the problems mentioned in the text. It can be argued that the VAS promotes a view that the business is a coalition of interests. It can be seen as trying to foster a team spirit among key interest groups and trying to get employees 'on side' by treating them as team members. Critics argue that this is mere propaganda, which tries to obscure the underlying conflict between capital and labour. They argue that, as the main purpose of the statement is persuasive rather than informative, the integrity of the financial statements could be damaged in the eyes of users.

Problems relating to team membership and the classification of key items also undermine the usefulness of the statement and this may have a more general adverse effect on the credibility of the financial reports. Supporters of the VAS would dispute these claims. They would argue that value added offers an alternative measure of wealth creation that may provide new insights into business performance. Furthermore, most financial statements have to overcome theoretical or classification problems and the VAS is no exception.

11.2 Inflation may be defined as a general rise in prices or a fall in the general purchasing power of money. The level of inflation is measured by using a general price index, such as the Retail Price Index (RPI). The CPP approach is concerned with maintaining the general purchasing power of the owners' investment in the business and uses the RPI as the basis of making adjustments. It can, therefore, be described as a method of accounting for inflation.

The CCA approach is concerned with specific price changes rather than general price changes. It is concerned with ensuring that a business can maintain its scale of operations. Specific price increases, however, can occur even when there is no inflation. In a dynamic economy there will always be price movements. Thus, even during a period of zero inflation (and deflation) there will be price increases in certain goods and services, which will be offset by price decreases in others. Supporters of CCA, however, would argue that the key issue is not which method is the 'true' method of accounting for inflation, but rather which method is more helpful for decision-making purposes.

11.3 There are a number of possible drawbacks, which include the following:

- The reporting costs may be considerable.
- Reports covering a short period are more likely to be inaccurate because of estimation errors.

- Condensing complex information may result in a distorted portrayal of performance and position.
- It may encourage users to take a short-term perspective when evaluating performance.

11.4 There are various problems associated with the measurement of business segments. These include:

- the definition of a segment;
- the treatment of inter-segmental transactions, such as sales;
- the treatment of expenses and assets that are shared between segments.

There is no single correct method of dealing with these problems, and variations will arise in practice. This, in turn, will hinder comparisons between businesses.

Chapter 12

12.1 The main areas identified to evaluate a chief executive may include:

- setting a vision for the business and communicating the path towards that vision to employees;
- building an effective team of executive directors to manage the business;
- ensuring the business is properly resourced, in terms of finance, human resources and capacity to fulfil the vision that has been set;
- building a culture across the business that promotes openness, participation and high ethical standards; and
- achieving the financial and other targets set to achieve the stated vision.

    You may have thought of others.

12.2 The main benefits of separation are that:

- it ensures that a single individual does not have too much power;
- the chairman can offer support and act as a mentor to the CEO;
- it can smooth the path of succession; and
- it can ensure that the responsibilities of both roles will be carried out more effectively than would be the case if a single individual occupied both roles.

    There may be points in the history of a company when it would benefit from a strong leader with the required authority to be decisive and to overcome strong opposition. However, following this path would carry considerable risk.

12.3 The external auditors may have an intimate knowledge of the accounting and payroll systems that are currently in operation and may be well placed to suggest improvements that suit the company's needs. There may, therefore, be a saving of time and cost if they are given the task. However, there is always a risk that the external auditors will receive too high a proportion of the total fees received from the company in the form of consultancy work. This runs the risk of compromising the auditors' independence. New EU legislation now prohibits this kind of work being undertaken by the external auditors.

12.4 When approached by a shareholder activist, the board of directors should first:

- establish the underlying motivation of the activist, the tactics used and the past history of activism;
- evaluate the proposals that the activist wishes to see implemented; and
- ascertain the degree of support among other shareholders to the proposals.

To deal with the proposals, the board should:

- set up a team of senior directors to create a dialogue with the activist and to advise the board on any developments;
- prepare a detailed response to the proposals raised by the activist;
- establish whether there are any areas where collaboration with the activist is possible; and
- create a dialogue with other shareholders to ensure they are fully informed of the position of the board and the actions taken.

Appendix E
SOLUTIONS TO SELECTED EXERCISES

Chapter 2

2.1 Paul

Statement of cash flows for Thursday

	£
Opening balance (from Wednesday)	59
Cash from sale of wrapping paper	47
Cash paid to purchase wrapping paper	(53)
Closing balance	53

Income statement for Thursday

	£
Sales revenue	47
Cost of goods sold	(33)
Profit	14

Statement of financial position as at Thursday evening

	£
Cash	53
Inventories of goods for resale (23 + 53 − 33)	43
Total assets	96
Equity	96

2.2 Paul (continued)

Equity

	£
Cash introduced by Paul on Monday	40
Profit for Monday	15
Profit for Tuesday	18
Profit for Wednesday	9
Profit for Thursday	14
Total business wealth(total assets)	96

Thus the equity, all of which belongs to Paul as sole owner, consists of the cash he put in to start the business plus the profit earned each day.

2.3 Helen

Income statement for day 1

	£
Sales revenue (70 × £0.80)	56
Cost of sales (70 × £0.50)	(35)
Profit	21

Statement of cash flows for day 1

	£
Cash introduced by Helen	40
Cash from sales	56
Cash for purchases (80 × £0.50)	(40)
Closing balance	56

Statement of financial position as at end of day 1

	£
Cash balance	56
Inventories of unsold goods (10 × £0.50)	5
Total assets	61
Equity	61

Income statement for day 2

	£
Sales revenue (65 × £0.80)	52.0
Cost of sales (65 × £0.50)	(32.5)
Profit	19.5

Statement of cash flows for day 2

	£
Opening balance	56.0
Cash from sales	52.0
Cash for purchases (60 × £0.50)	(30.0)
Closing balance	78.0

Statement of financial position as at end of day 2

	£
Cash balance	78.0
Inventories of unsold goods (5 × £0.50)	2.5
Total assets	80.5
Equity	80.5

Income statement for day 3

	£
Sales revenue ((20 × £0.80) + (45 × £0.40))	34.0
Cost of sales (65 × £0.50)	(32.5)
Profit	1.5

Statement of cash flows for day 3

	£
Opening balance	78.0
Cash from sales	34.0
Cash for purchases (60 × £0.50)	(30.0)
Closing balance	82.0

Statement of financial position as at end of day 3

	£
Cash balance	82.0
Inventories of unsold goods	–
Total assets	82.0
Equity	82.0

2.6 Conversation

(a) The income statement reveals the changes in wealth arising as a result of trading operations. It shows the increase in wealth (revenue) during the period, the decrease in wealth (expenses) in order to generate revenue and the resulting net increase (profit) or decrease (loss) in wealth for the period. While most businesses hold some of their wealth in the form of cash, wealth is also held in other forms, such as non-current assets, receivables and so on.

(b) To be included in a statement of financial position as an asset, a resource must provide potential economic benefits. These benefits may arise from selling the asset in the market, but they may also arise from its use – for example, in production.

There are other conditions that must be met in order for an item to be included in the statement of financial position. These are:

■ the business must control the asset; and
■ the asset must be measurable in monetary terms with a reasonable degree of certainty.

(c) The accounting equation is:

$$\text{Assets} = \text{Equity} + \text{Liabilities}$$

(d) Non-current assets are assets that do not meet the criteria for current assets. They are normally held for the long-term operations of the business. Some non-current assets may be immovable (for example, property) but others are not (for example, motor vans).

(e) Goodwill may or may not have an indefinite life – it will depend on the nature of the goodwill. There are no hard and fast rules that can be applied. Where this asset has a finite life, it should be amortised. Where it is considered to have an indefinite life, it should not be amortised but should be tested annually for impairment.

2.7 Crafty Engineering

(a)

Statement of financial position as at 30 June last year

	£000
ASSETS	
Non-current assets	
Property, plant and equipment	
Property	320
Equipment and tools	207
Motor vehicles	38
	565
Current assets	
Inventories	153
Trade receivables	185
	338
Total assets	903
EQUITY AND LIABILITIES	
Equity(which is the missing figure)	441
Non-current liabilities	
Long-term borrowings (loan from Industrial Finance Company)	260
Current liabilities	
Trade payables	86
Short-term borrowings	116
	202
Total equity and liabilities	903

(b) The statement of financial position reveals a large investment in non-current assets. It represents more than 60% of the total investment in assets (565/903). The nature of the business may require a heavy investment in non-current assets. The current assets exceed the current liabilities by a large amount (approximately 1.7 times). Hence, there is no obvious sign of a liquidity problem. However, the statement of financial position reveals that the business has no cash balance and is therefore dependent on the continuing support of short-term borrowing to meet maturing obligations. When considering the long-term financing of the business, we can see that about 37% (that is, 260/(260 + 441)) of total long-term finance is supplied by borrowings and about 63% (that is, 441/(260 + 441)) by the owners. This level of long-term borrowing seems high but not excessive. However, we need to know more about the ability of the business to service the borrowing (that is, make interest payments and repayments of the amount borrowed) before a full assessment can be made.

Chapter 3

3.1 Comments

(a) Equity does increase as a result of the owners introducing more cash into the business, but it will also increase as a result of introducing other assets (for example, a motor car) and by the business generating revenue by trading. Similarly, equity decreases not only as a result of withdrawals of cash by owners but also by withdrawals of other assets (for example, inventories for the owners' personal use) and through trading expenses being incurred. Generally speaking, equity will alter more as a result of trading activities than for any other reason.

(b) An accrued expense is not one that relates to next year. It is one that needs to be matched with the revenue of the reporting period under review, but that has yet to be met in terms of cash payment. As such, it will appear on the statement of financial position as a current liability.

(c) The purpose of depreciation is not to provide for asset replacement. It is an attempt to allocate, in a systematic way, the cost, or fair value, of the asset (less any residual value) over its useful life. Depreciation provides a measure of the amount of a non-current asset that has been consumed during a period. This amount is then charged as an expense for the period. Depreciation is a book entry (the outlay of cash occurs when the asset is purchased) and does not normally entail setting aside a separate amount of cash for asset replacement. Even if this were done, there would be no guarantee that sufficient funds would be available at the end of the asset's life for its replacement. Factors such as inflation and technological change may mean that the replacement cost is higher than the original cost of the asset.

(d) In the short term, the current value of a non-current asset may exceed its original cost. However, nearly all non-current assets wear out over time through being used to generate wealth. This will be the case for buildings. Thus, some measure of depreciation is needed to reflect the fact that the asset is being consumed. Some businesses revalue their buildings upwards where the current value is significantly higher than the original cost. Where this occurs, the depreciation charge should be based on the revalued amount, which will lead to higher depreciation charges.

3.3 Business owner

Making a profit, while experiencing a downward movement in cash, may arise for various reasons. These include the following:

- the purchase for cash during the period of assets (for example, motor cars and inventories) which were not all consumed during the period and are, therefore, not having as great an effect on expenses as they are on cash;
- the payment of an outstanding liability (for example, borrowings), which will have an effect on cash but not on expenses in the income statement;
- the withdrawal of cash by the owners from the equity invested, which will not affect the expenses in the income statement; and
- the generation of revenue on credit where the cash has yet to be received. This will increase the sales revenue for the period but will not have a beneficial effect on the cash balance until a later period.

3.4 Missing values

(a) Rent payable – expense for period   £9,000
(b) Rates and insurance – expense for period   £6,000
(c) General expenses – paid in period   £7,000
(d) Interest (on borrowings) payable – prepaid   £500
(e) Salaries – paid in period   £6,000
(f) Rent receivable – received during period   £3,000

3.7 WW Associates

Income statement for the year ended 31 December 2017

	£
Sales revenue (211,000 + 42,000)	253,000
Cost of goods sold (127,000 + 25,000)	(152,000)
Gross profit	101,000
Rent (20,000)	(20,000)
Rates (400 + 1,500)	(1,900)
Wages (−1,700 + 23,800 + 860)	(22,960)
Electricity (2,700)	(2,700)
Machinery depreciation (9,360)	(9,360)
Loss on disposal of the old machinery (13,000 − 3,900 − 9,000)	(100)
Van expenses (17,500)	(17,500)
Profit for the year	26,480

The loss on disposal of the old machinery is the carrying amount (cost less depreciation) less the disposal proceeds. Since the machinery had only been owned for one year, with a depreciation rate of 30%, the depreciation to date is £3,900 (that is, £13,000 × 30%). The effective disposal proceeds were £9,000 because, as a result of trading it in, the business saved £9,000 on the new asset.

The depreciation expense for 2017 is based on the cost less accumulated depreciation of the assets owned at the end of 2017.

Statement of financial position as at 31 December 2017

	£
ASSETS	
Machinery (25,300 + 6,000 + 9,000 − 13,000 + 3,900 − 9,360)	21,840*
Inventories (12,200 + 143,000 + 12,000 − 12,700 − 25,000)	15,200
Trade receivables (21,300 + 211,000 − 198,000)	34,300
Cash at bank (overdraft) (8,300 − 23,000 − 25,000 − 2,000 − 6,000 − 23,800 − 2,700 − 12,000 + 42,000 + 198,000 − 156,000 − 17,500)	(19,700)
Prepaid expenses (400 − 400 + 5,000 + 500)	5,500
Total assets	57,140
EQUITY AND LIABILITIES	
Equity (owner's capital) (48,900 − 23,000 + 26,480)	52,380
Trade payables (16,900 + 143,000 − 156,000)	3,900
Accrued expenses (1,700 − 1,700 + 860)	860
Total equity and liabilities	57,140
* Cost less accumulated depreciation at 31 December 2016	25,300
Carrying amount of machine disposed of (£13,000 − £3,900)	(9,100)
Cost of new machine	15,000
Depreciation for 2017 (£31,200 × 30%)	(9,360)
Carrying amount (written-down value) of machine at 31 December 2017	21,840

The statement of financial position could now be rewritten in a more stylish form as follows:

Statement of financial position as at 31 December 2017

	£
ASSETS	
Non-current assets	
Property, plant and equipment	
Machinery at cost less depreciation	21,840
Current assets	
Inventories	15,200
Trade receivables	34,300
Prepaid expenses	5,500
	55,000
Total assets	76,840
EQUITY AND LIABILITIES	
Equity	52,380
Current liabilities	
Trade payables	3,900
Accrued expenses	860
Borrowings – bank overdraft	19,700
	24,460
Total equity and liabilities	76,840

3.8 Nikov and Co.

An examination of the income statements for the two years reveals a number of interesting points, which include:

- An increase in sales revenue and gross profit of 9.9% in 2018.
- The gross profit expressed as a percentage of sales revenue remaining at 70%.
- An increase in salaries of 7.2%.
- An increase in selling and distribution costs of 31.2%.
- An increase in bad debts of 392.5%.
- A decline in profit for the year of 39.3%.
- A decline in the profit for the year as a percentage of sales revenue from 13.3% to 7.4%.

Thus, the business has enjoyed an increase in sales revenue and gross profits, but this has failed to translate to an increase in profit for the year because of the significant rise in overheads. The increase in selling costs during 2018 suggests that the increase in sales revenue was achieved by greater marketing effort, and the huge increase in bad debts suggests that the increase in sales revenue may be attributable to selling to less creditworthy customers or to a weak debt-collection policy. There appears to have been a change of policy in 2018 towards sales, and this has not been successful overall as the profit for the year has shown a dramatic decline.

Chapter 4

4.1 Comment

Limited companies cannot set a limit on the amount of debts they will meet. They must meet their debts up to the limit of their assets, just as private individuals must. Reserves are part of the shareholders' claim against the assets of the company. These assets may, or may not, include cash. Dividends are normally paid in the form of cash but the legal ability of a company to pay dividends is not related to the amount of cash that it holds.

Preference shares do not carry a guaranteed dividend. They simply guarantee that the preference shareholders have a right to the first slice of any dividend that is paid. Shares of many public companies can be bought and sold by investors through the Stock Exchange. These transactions, however, has no direct effect on the company. The company is issuing no new shares. It is simply existing ('second-hand') shares that are being transferred between investors.

4.2 Comments

(a) The first part of the quote is incorrect. Bonus shares should not, of themselves, increase the value of shareholders' wealth. The total amount of shareholders' equity will not change as bonus shares are created through a transfer from reserves to ordinary share capital. Bonus shares, reflecting the amount of the transfer, are then distributed to shareholders in proportion to their existing shareholdings. Each shareholder's stake in the company will be unaffected by this transaction.

(b) This statement is incorrect. Shares can be issued at any price, provided that it is not below their nominal value. Once a company has been trading profitably for a period, its shares will not be worth the same as when the company was first formed (the nominal value). In these circumstances, issuing shares at above their nominal value would not only be legal, but essential to preserve the wealth of the existing shareholders in relation to any new shareholders.

(c) This statement is incorrect. Legally, the company is limited to making a maximum dividend based on the amount of its revenue reserves. These reserves reflect accumulated after-tax profits, or realised gains, remaining after previous dividend payments or trading losses. From a legal viewpoint, cash is not an issue when determining the maximum dividend. It would be perfectly legal for a company without cash to borrow the funds needed to pay a dividend. Whether such action would be commercially prudent is another question.

(d) This statement is partly incorrect. Companies do indeed have to pay tax on their profits. Depending on their financial circumstances, shareholders may also have to pay tax on their dividends.

4.4 Iqbal Ltd

Year	Maximum dividend £	
2014	0	No profit exists out of which to pay a dividend.
2015	0	There remains a cumulative loss of £7,000. Since the revaluation represents a gain that has not been realised, it cannot be used to justify a dividend.
2016	13,000	The cumulative net realised gains are derived as (−£15,000 + £8,000 + £15,000 + £5,000).
2017	14,000	The realised profits and gains for the year.
2018	22,000	The realised profits and gains for the year.

4.6 Pear Limited

Income statement for the year ended 30 September 2018

	£000
Revenue (1,456 + 18)	1,474
Cost of sales	(768)
Gross profit	706
Salaries	(220)
Depreciation (249 + 12)	(261)
Other operating costs (131 + (2% × 200) + 2)	(137)
Operating profit	88
Interest payable (15 + 15)	(30)
Profit before taxation	58
Taxation (58 × 30%)	(17)
Profit for the year	41

Statement of financial position as at 30 September 2018

	£000
ASSETS	
Non-current assets	
Property, plant and equipment	
Cost (1,570 + 30)	1,600
Depreciation (690 + 12)	(702)
	898
Current assets	
Inventories	207
Trade receivables (182 + 18 − 4)	196
Cash at bank	21
	424
Total assets	1,322
EQUITY AND LIABILITIES	
Equity	
Share capital	300
Share premium account	300
Retained earnings (104 + 41 − 25)	120
	720
Non-current liabilities	
Borrowings – 10% loan (repayable 2020)	300
Current liabilities	
Trade payables	88
Other payables (20 + 30 + 15 + 2)	67
Taxation	17
Dividend approved	25
Borrowings – bank overdraft	105
	302
Total equity and liabilities	1,322

4.7 Chips Limited

Income statement for the year ended 30 June 2018

	£000
Revenue (1,850 − 16)	1,834
Cost of sales (1,040 + 23)	(1,063)
Gross profit	771
Depreciation (220 (−2 − 5 + 8) + (94 × 20%))	(240)
Other operating costs	(375)
Operating profit	156
Interest payable (35 + 35)	(70)
Profit before taxation	86
Taxation (86 × 30%)	(26)
Profit for the year	60

Statement of financial position as at 30 June 2018

ASSETS

	Cost £000	Depreciation £000	£000
Non-current assets			
Property, plant and equipment			
Buildings	800	(112)	688
Plant and equipment	650	(367)	283
Motor vehicles (102 − 8);(53 − 5 + 19)	94	(67)	27
	1,544	(546)	998
Current assets			
Inventories			950
Trade receivables (420 − 16)			404
Cash at bank (16 + 2)			18
			1,372
Total assets			2,370

EQUITY AND LIABILITIES

Equity	
Ordinary shares of £1, fully paid	800
Reserves at beginning of the year	248
Retained profit for year	60
	1,108
Non-current liabilities	
Borrowings – secured 10% loan notes	700
Current liabilities	
Trade payables (361 + 23)	384
Other payables (117 + 35)	152
Taxation	26
	562
Total equity and liabilities	2,370

Chapter 5

5.1 Accountants' judgement

The quotation probably overstates the case. It is true that choice has been removed in some areas, but there is still plenty of scope for accountants to make choices and to exercise judgement. Many decisions involving the valuation of assets and liabilities and the treatment of unusual items can involve difficult judgements. We have also seen that some accounting standards require judgements to be made (for example, those dealing with inventories and valuation).

Occasionally, accountants have been criticised for not wishing to exercise judgement. The former chair of the IASB, for example, has stated that accountants often prefer further clarification of certain standards from the IASB to that of exercising judgement.

5.2 Information volume

Apart from increases in accounting regulation, financial reports have increased because of:

- increasing demands by influential user groups, such as shareholders and financial analysts, for financial information relating to the company;
- the increasing sophistication of influential user groups, such as financial analysts, to deal with financial information;
- the increasing complexity of business operations requiring greater explanation; and
- increasing recognition of the need for greater accountability towards certain user groups (such as employees and community groups) requiring the need for additional reports, such as environmental reports and social reports.

5.5   I. Ching (Booksellers) plc

Statement of comprehensive income for the year ended 31 May 2018

	£000
Revenue	943
Cost of sales	(460)
Gross profit	483
Distribution expenses	(110)
Administrative expenses	(212)
Other expenses	(25)
Operating profit	136
Finance charges	(40)
Profit before tax	96
Taxation	(24)
Profit for the year	72
Other comprehensive income	
Revaluation of property, plant and equipment	20
Foreign currency translation differences for foreign operations	(15)
Tax on other comprehensive income	(1)
Other comprehensive income for the year, net of tax	4
Total comprehensive income for the year	76

5.6   Manet plc

Statement of changes in equity for the year ended 31 May 2018

	Share capital £m	Share premium £m	Revaluation reserve £m	Translation reserve £m	Retained earnings £m	Total £m
Balance as at 1 June 2017	250	50	120	15	380	815
Changes in equity for the year						
Profit for the year (see Note 1)					160	160
Other comprehensive income for the year (see Note 2)			30	(5)		25
Dividends (see Note 3)	-	-	-	-	(80)	(80)
Balance at 31 May 2018	250	50	150	10	460	920

Notes:

1 Profit for the year is transferred to retained earnings.
2 The effect of each component of comprehensive income on each component of shareholder equity must be shown. The revaluation gain and loss on exchange translation are each transferred to a specific reserve.
3 Dividends have been shown in the statement rather than in the notes. Either approach is acceptable.

5.7 Accounting regulation

The following points might be made concerning accounting regulation and accounting measurement:

For:

- It seems reasonable that companies, particularly given their limited liability, should be required to account to their members and other. Furthermore, rules should prescribe how this should be done – including how particular items should be measured. It also seems sensible that these rules should try to establish some uniformity of practice. Investors could be misled if identical items appeared in the financial statements of two different companies but had been measured in different ways.
- Companies would find it difficult to attract finance, credit and possibly employees, without publishing information about their financial health. An important measure of financial performance is profit, and investors often wish to make judgements concerning relative performance within an industry sector. Without clear benchmarks by which to judge performance, investors may not invest in a company.

Against:

- It may be argued that companies should decide whether or not they can survive and prosper without publishing information about themselves. If they can, so much the better, as, by not doing so, substantial costs can be avoided. If a company needs to provide financial information so as to attract finance and so on, then it should make the decision as to how much information is required and what forms of measurement should be used.
- Not all company managements view matters in the same way. Allowing companies to select their own approaches to financial reporting enables them to reflect their particular personalities. Thus, a conservative management may adopt conservative accounting policies, such as writing off research and development expenditure quickly. A more risk-oriented management, on the other hand, may adopt less conservative accounting policies, such as writing off research and development expenditure over several years. The choices made concerning accounting policies may give investors an insight to the risk attitudes of the management team.

Chapter 6

6.1 Impact on cash

(a) An increase in the level of inventories would, ultimately, have an adverse effect on cash.
(b) A rights issue of ordinary shares will give rise to a positive cash flow, which will be included in the 'financing' section of the statement of cash flows.
(c) A bonus issue of ordinary shares has no cash flow effect.
(d) Writing off some of the value of the inventories has no cash flow effect.
(e) A disposal for cash of a large number of shares by a major shareholder has no cash flow effect as far as the business is concerned.
(f) Depreciation does not involve cash at all. Using the indirect method of deducing cash flows from operating activities involves the depreciation expense in the calculation, but this is simply because we are trying to find out, from the profit before taxation (after depreciation) figure, what the profit before taxation *and* depreciation must have been.

6.3 Torrent plc

Statement of cash flows for the year ended 31 December 2018

	£m
Cash flows from operating activities	
Profit before taxation (after interest) (see Note 1 below)	170
Adjustments for:	
Depreciation (Note 2)	78
Interest expense (Note 3)	26
	274
Decrease in inventories (41 − 35)	6
Increase in trade receivables (145 − 139)	(6)
Decrease in trade payables (54 − 41)	(13)
Cash generated from operations	261
Interest paid	(26)
Taxation paid (Note 4)	(41)
Dividend paid	(60)
Net cash from operating activities	134
Cash flows from investing activities	
Payments to acquire plant and machinery	(67)
Net cash used in investing activities	(67)
Cash flows from financing activities	
Redemption of loan notes (250 − 150)(Note 5)	(100)
Net cash used in financing activities	(100)
Net decrease in cash and cash equivalents	(33)
Cash and cash equivalents at 1 January 2018	
Bank overdraft	(56)
Cash and cash equivalents at 31 December 2018	
Bank overdraft	(89)

Notes:

1 This is simply taken from the income statement for the year.

2 Since there were no disposals, the depreciation charges must be the difference between the start and end of the year's plant and machinery values, adjusted by the cost of any additions.

	£m
Carrying amount at 1 January 2018	325
Additions	67
Depreciation (balancing figure)	(78)
Carrying amount at 31 December 2018	314

3 Interest payable expense must be taken out, by adding it back to the profit before taxation figure. We subsequently deduct the cash paid for interest payable during the year. In this case the two figures are identical.

4 Companies pay 50% of their tax during their accounting year and 50% in the following year. Thus the 2018 payment would have been half the tax on the 2017 profit (that is, the figure that would have appeared in the current liabilities at the end of 2017), plus half of the 2018 tax charge (that is, $23 + (^1/_2 \times 36) = 41$).

5 It is assumed that the cash payment to redeem the loan notes was simply the difference between the two statement of financial position figures.

It seems that there was a bonus issue of ordinary shares during the year. These increased by £100m. At the same time, the share premium account balance reduced by £40m (to zero) and the revaluation reserve balance fell by £60m.

6.6 Blackstone plc

Statement of cash flows for the year ended 31 March 2018

	£m
Cash flows from operating activities	
Profit before taxation (after interest) (see Note 1)	1,853
Adjustments for:	
Depreciation (Note 2)	1,289
Interest expense (Note 3)	456
	3,598
Increase in inventories (2,410 − 1,209)	(1,201)
Increase in trade receivables (1,173 − 641)	(532)
Increase in trade payables (1,507 − 931)	576
Cash generated from operations	2,441
Interest paid	(456)
Taxation paid (Note 4)	(300)
Dividend paid	(400)
Net cash from operating activities	1,285
Cash flows from investing activities	
Proceeds of disposals	54
Payment to acquire intangible non-current asset	(700)
Payments to acquire property, plant and equipment	(4,578)
Net cash used in investing activities	(5,224)
Cash flows from financing activities	
Bank borrowings	2,000
Net cash from financing activities	2,000
Net decrease in cash and cash equivalents	(1,939)
Cash and cash equivalents at 1 April 2017	
Cash at bank	123
Cash and cash equivalents at 31 March 2018	
Bank overdraft	(1,816)

Notes:
1. This is simply taken from the income statement for the year.
2. The full depreciation charge was that stated in Note 2 to the question (£1,251m), plus the deficit on disposal of the non-current assets. According to Note 2, these non-current assets had originally cost £581m and had been depreciated by £489m, giving a net carrying amount of £92m. They were sold for £54m, leading to a deficit on disposal of £38m. Thus the full depreciation expense for the year was £1,289m (that is, £1,251m + £38m).
3. Interest payable expense must be taken out, by adding it back to the profit before taxation figure. We subsequently deduct the cash paid for interest payable during the year. In this case, the two figures are identical.
4. Many companies pay tax at 50% during their accounting year and the other 50% in the following year. Thus the 2018 payment would have been half the tax on the 2017 profit (that is, the figure that would have appeared in the current liabilities at 31 March 2017), plus half of the 2018 tax charge (that is, $105 + (\frac{1}{2} \times 390) = 300$).

6.7 York plc

Statement of cash flows for the year ended 30 September 2018

	£m
Cash flows from operating activities	
Profit before taxation (after interest) (see Note 1)	10.0
Adjustments for:	
Depreciation (Note 2)	9.8
Interest expense (Note 3)	3.0
	22.8
Increase in inventories and trade receivables (122.1 − 119.8)	(2.3)
Increase in trade payables (82.5 − 80.0)	2.5
Cash generated from operations	23.0
Interest paid	(3.0)
Taxation paid (Note 4)	(2.3)
Dividend paid	(3.5)
Net cash from operating activities	14.2
Cash flows from investing activities	
Proceeds of disposals (Note 2)	5.2
Payments to acquire non-current assets	(20.0)
Net cash used in investing activities	(14.8)
Cash flows from financing activities	
Increase in long-term borrowings	3.0
Share issue (Note 5)	5.0
Net cash from financing activities	8.0
Net increase in cash and cash equivalents	7.4
Cash and cash equivalents at 1 October 2017	
Cash at bank	9.2
Cash and cash equivalents at 30 September 2018	
Cash at bank	16.6

Notes:

1 This is simply taken from the income statement for the year.

2 The full depreciation charge was the £13.0m, less the surplus on disposal (£3.2m), both stated in Note 1 to the question. (According to the table in Note 4 to the question, the non-current assets disposed of had a net carrying value of £2.0m. To produce a surplus of £3.2m, they must have been sold for £5.2m.)

3 Interest payable expense must be taken out, by adding it back to the profit before taxation figure. We subsequently deduct the cash paid for interest payable during the year. In this case, the two figures are identical.

4 Many companies pay 50% of their tax during their accounting year and the other 50% in the following year. Thus the 2018 payment would have been half the tax on the 2017 profit (that is, the figure that would have appeared in the current liabilities at 30 September 2017), plus half of the 2018 tax charge (that is, $1.0 + (\frac{1}{2} \times 2.6) = 2.3$).

5 This issue must have been for cash since it could not have been a bonus issue – the share premium is untouched and 'Reserves' had altered over the year only by the amount of the 2018 retained earnings (profit for the year, less the dividend). The shares seem to have been issued at their nominal value (par). This is a

little surprising since the business has assets that seem to be above that value. On the other hand, if this was a rights issue, the low issue price would not have disadvantaged the existing shareholders since they were also the beneficiaries of the advantage of the low issue price.

6.8 Axis plc

(a) Statement of cash flows for the year ended 31 December 2018

	£m	£m
Cash flows from operating activities		
Profit before taxation (after interest) (see Note 1 below)		34
Adjustments for:		
Depreciation (Note 2)		19
Interest payable expense (Note 3)		2
Interest receivable (Note 4)		(2)
		53
Decrease in inventories (25 − 24)		1
Increase in trade receivables (26 − 16)		(10)
Increase in trade payables (36 − 31)		5
Cash generated from operations		49
Interest paid (Note 3)		(2)
Taxation paid (Note 5)		(15)
Dividend paid		(14)
Net cash from operating activities		18
Cash flows from investing activities		
Interest receivable		2
Proceeds of disposals (Note 2)		4
Payments to acquire non-current assets (Note 6)		(25)
Net cash used in investing activities		(19)
Cash flows from financing activities		
Issue of loan notes		20
Net cash from financing activities		20
Net increase in cash and cash equivalents		19
Cash and cash equivalents at 1 January 2018		
Cash at bank	–	
Short-term investments	–	–
Cash and cash equivalents at 31 December 2018		
Cash at bank	7	
Short-term investments	12	19

Notes:

1 This is simply taken from the income statement for the year.
2 The full depreciation charge for the year is the sum of two figures labelled 'depreciation' and the deficit on disposal of non-current assets (that is, £2m + £16m + £1m = £19m). These were detailed in the income statement.

According to the note in the question, the non-current assets disposed of had a net carrying amount of £5.0m (that is, £15m − £10m). To produce a deficit of £1m, they must have been sold for £4m.

3 Interest payable expense must be taken out, by adding it back to the figure for profit before taxation. We subsequently deduct the cash paid for interest payable during the year. In this case, the two figures are identical.

4 Interest receivable must be taken away to work towards the profit before crediting it, because it is not part of operations but of investing activities. The cash inflow from this source appears under the 'Cash flows from investing activities' heading.

5 Many companies pay 50% of their tax during their accounting year and the other 50% in the following year. Thus the 2018 payment would have been half the tax on the 2017 profit (that is, the figure that would have appeared in the current liabilities at 31 December 2017), plus half the 2018 tax charge (that is, $7 + (\frac{1}{2} \times 16) = 15$).

6 The cost of the newly acquired non-current assets (plant and machinery) can be deduced as follows:

	£m
Cost of plant and machinery at 1 January 2018	70
Plant disposed of	(15)
Plant acquired	25
Cost of plant and machinery at 31 December 2018	80

(b) Reconciliation of liabilities from financing activities for the year to 31 December 2018

	£m
Loan notes outstanding at 1 January 2018	20
Cash received from issuing additional loan notes	20
Loan notes outstanding at 31 December 2018	40

Chapter 7

7.1 Provisions

1 A provision should be recognised because:

- the sale of the motor cars with a warranty gives rise to an obligation; and
- it is probable (based on past experience) that there will be an outflow of resources arising from the warranty.

2 A provision should be recognised because:

- the evidence suggests that there is an obligation; and
- an outflow of resources to compensate the victims is probable.

3 A provision should not be recognised because there is no present obligation. The business can avoid the future costs by selling the aircraft before the point at which the overhauls become due.

7.4 Ondamin plc

	Notes	£m
Draft profit before tax		65.5
Revised amortisation charge for licence	1	(0.5)
Masthead write-off	2	(5.4)
Research write-off	3	(1.6)
General overhead write-off	4	(0.8)
Revised profit before tax		57.2

Notes:

1 As the licence is revalued to fair value, an additional amortisation charge of £0.5m (£1.5m − £1.0m), based on fair value, should be deducted from profit.

2 According to IAS 38, mastheads cannot be capitalised and must be written off immediately. A net adjustment of £5.4m (£6.0m − £0.6m) must therefore be made.

3 According to IAS 38, research expenditure cannot be capitalised and must be written off immediately. A net adjustment of £1.6m (£2.0m − £0.4m) must therefore be made.

4 IAS 38 permits the capitalisation of development expenditure subject to strict conditions. Assuming these conditions have been met, all of the items mentioned can be capitalised, with the exception of the general overhead cost. This must be written off immediately and so a net adjustment of £0.8m (£1.0m − £0.2m) must be made.

7.5 Barchester United Football Club plc

	Notes	£m
Draft profit before tax		48.8
Transfer to restructuring provision	1	5.4
Reversal of previous provision for unfair dismissal	2	2.2
Contingent asset	3	2.0
Research expenditure previously capitalised	4	(1.0)
Capitalisation of borrowing costs	5	3.3
Increase in interest charge	6	(0.3)
Revised profit before tax		60.4

Notes:

1 Restructuring costs should be charged to the relevant provision.

2 As there is now no likelihood of an outflow of resources arising from the court case, the provision should be reversed.

3 As it is now virtually certain that the TV channel will pay the disputed amount, it should be recognised.

4 This research expenditure cannot demonstrate that future probable economic benefits exist. It should therefore be treated as an expense.

5 The borrowing costs should be capitalised as they are directly related to the construction of an asset.

6 The total interest charge is £m (0.8 + 0.6 + 0.4 + 0.2) = £2.0m. The charge in the draft income statement for the first year is therefore £0.5m (£2.0m/4). As the interest charge should be £0.8m, the net effect of replacing the existing interest charge with the correct charge in the income statement will be a £0.3m (£0.8m − £0.5m) decrease in profits.

Chapter 8

8.1 Three businesses

A plc operates a supermarket chain. The grocery business is highly competitive and to generate high sales volumes it is usually necessary to accept low operating profit margins. Thus, we can see that the operating profit margin of A plc is the lowest of the three businesses. The inventories turnover period of supermarket chains also tend to be quite low. They are often efficient in managing inventories and most supermarket chains have invested heavily in inventories control and logistical systems over the years. The average settlement period for receivables is very low as most sales are for cash, although, when a customer pays by credit card, there is usually a small delay before the supermarket receives the amount due. A low inventories turnover period and a low average settlement period for receivables usually mean that the investment in current assets is low. Hence, the current ratio (current assets/current liabilities) is also low.

B plc is the holiday tour operator. We can see that the sales to capital employed ratio is the highest of the three. This is because tour operators do not usually require a large investment of capital: they do not need a large asset base in order to conduct their operations. The inventories turnover period ratio does not apply to B plc. It is a service business, which does not hold inventories for resale. We can see that the average settlement period for receivables is low. This may be because customers are invoiced near to the holiday date for any amounts outstanding and must pay before going on holiday. The lack of inventories held and low average settlement period for receivables leads to a very low current ratio.

C plc is the food manufacturing business. We can see that the sales to capital employed ratio is the lowest of the three. This is because manufacturers tend to invest heavily in both current and non-current assets. The inventories turnover period is the highest of the three. Three different kinds of inventories – raw materials, work in progress and finished goods – are held by manufacturers. The average receivables settlement period is also the highest of the three. Manufacturers tend to sell to other businesses rather than to the public and their customers will normally demand credit. A one-month credit period for customers is fairly common for manufacturing businesses, although customers may receive a discount for prompt payment. The relatively high investment in inventories and receivables usually results in a high current ratio.

8.2 I. Jiang (Western) Ltd

The effect of each of the changes on ROCE is not always easy to predict.

1 On the face of it, an increase in the gross profit margin would tend to lead to an increase in ROCE. An increase in the gross profit margin may, however, lead to a decrease in ROCE in particular circumstances. If the increase in the margin resulted from an increase in sales prices, which in turn led to a decrease in sales revenue, a fall in ROCE can occur. A fall in sales revenue can reduce the operating profit (the numerator (top part of the fraction) in ROCE) if the overheads of the business did not decrease correspondingly.
2 A reduction in sales revenue can reduce ROCE for the reasons mentioned above.
3 An increase in overhead expenses will reduce the operating profit and this in turn will result in a reduction in ROCE.
4 An increase in inventories held would increase the amount of capital employed by the business (the denominator (bottom part of the fraction) in ROCE) where long-term funds are employed to finance the inventories. This will, in turn, reduce ROCE.
5 Repayment of the borrowings at the year end will reduce the capital employed and this will increase the ROCE, assuming that the year-end capital employed figure has been used in the calculation. Since the operating profit was earned during a period in which the borrowings existed, there is a strong argument for basing the capital employed figure on what was the position during the year, rather than at the end of it.
6 An increase in the time taken for credit customers to pay will result in an increase in capital employed if long-term funds are employed to finance the trade receivables. This increase in long-term funds will, in turn, reduce ROCE.

8.3 Amsterdam Ltd and Berlin Ltd

The ratios for Amsterdam Ltd and Berlin Ltd reveal that the average settlement period for trade receivables for Amsterdam Ltd is three times that for Berlin Ltd. Berlin Ltd is therefore much quicker in collecting amounts outstanding from customers. On the other hand, there is not much difference between the two businesses in the time taken to pay trade payables.

It is interesting to compare the difference in the trade receivables and payables settlement periods for each business. As Amsterdam Ltd allows an average of 63 days' credit to its customers, yet pays suppliers within 50 days, it will require greater investment in working capital than Berlin Ltd, which allows an average of only 21 days to its customers but takes 45 days to pay its suppliers.

Amsterdam Ltd has a much higher gross profit margin than Berlin Ltd. However, the operating profit margin for the two businesses is identical. This suggests that Amsterdam Ltd has much higher overheads (as a percentage of sales revenue) than Berlin Ltd. The average inventories turnover period for Amsterdam Ltd is more than twice that of Berlin Ltd. This may be due to the fact that Amsterdam Ltd maintains a wider range of inventories in an attempt to meet customer requirements. The evidence therefore suggests that Amsterdam Ltd is the business that prides itself on personal service. The higher average settlement period for trade receivables is consistent with a more relaxed attitude to credit collection (thereby maintaining customer goodwill) and the high overheads are consistent with incurring the additional costs of satisfying customers' requirements. Amsterdam Ltd's high inventories levels are consistent with maintaining a wide range of inventories, with the aim of satisfying a range of customer needs.

Berlin Ltd has the characteristics of a more price-competitive business. Its gross profit margin is much lower than that of Amsterdam Ltd, that is, a much lower gross profit for each £1 of sales revenue. However, overheads have been kept low, the effect being that the operating profit margin is the same as Amsterdam Ltd's. The low average inventories turnover period and average settlement period for trade receivables are consistent with a business that wishes to minimise investment in current assets, thereby reducing costs.

8.7 Broadbury Ltd

(a)

	2016	2017
1 Operating profit margin	$\dfrac{914}{9,482} \times 100 = 9.6\%$	$\dfrac{1,042}{11,365} \times 100 = 9.2\%$
2 ROCE	$\dfrac{914}{11,033} \times 100 = 8.3\%$	$\dfrac{1,042}{13,943} \times 100 = 7.5\%$
3 Current ratio	$\dfrac{4,926}{1,508} = 3.3{:}1$	$\dfrac{7,700}{5,174} = 1.5{:}1$
4 Gearing ratio	$\dfrac{1,220}{11,033} \times 100 = 11.1\%$	$\dfrac{3,675}{13,943} \times 100 = 26.4\%$
5 Trade receivables settlement period	$\dfrac{2,540}{9,482} \times 365 = 98$ days	$\dfrac{4,280}{11,365} \times 365 = 137$ days
6 Sales revenue to capital employed	$\dfrac{9,482}{(9,813 + 1,220)} = 0.9$ times	$\dfrac{11,365}{(10,268 + 3,675)} = 0.8$ times

(b) The operating profit margin was slightly lower in 2017 than in 2016. Although there was an increase in sales revenue in 2017, this could not prevent a slight fall in ROCE in that year. The lower operating margin and increases in sales revenue may well be due to the new contract. The capital employed by the company increased in 2017 by a larger percentage than the increase in revenue. Hence, the sales revenue to capital employed ratio decreased over the period. The increase in capital employed during 2017 is largely due to an increase in borrowing. However, the gearing ratio is probably still low in comparison with other businesses. Comparison of the premises and borrowings figures indicates possible unused borrowing (debt) capacity.

The major cause for concern has been the dramatic decline in liquidity during 2017. The current ratio for that year is less than half that for 2016. There has also been a similar decrease in the acid test ratio, from 1.7:1 in 2016 to 0.8:1 in 2017. The statement of financial position shows that the business now has a large overdraft and the trade payables outstanding have nearly doubled in 2017.

The trade receivables outstanding and inventories have increased much more than appears to be warranted by the increase in sales revenue. This may be due to the terms of the contract that has been negotiated and may be difficult to influence. If this is the case, the business should consider whether it needs more longer-term finance. If the conclusion is that it does, acquiring more may be a sensible policy.

It would be difficult to conclude that the expansion programme has shown itself to be effective. ROCE has reduced and liquidity is substantially weakened. There may be greater benefits from the expansion in 2017, but this needs to be monitored closely.

8.8 Harridges Ltd

(a)

	2017	2018
ROCE	$\dfrac{310}{1,600} = 19.4\%$	$\dfrac{350}{1,700} = 20.6\%$
ROSF	$\dfrac{155}{1,100} = 14.1\%$	$\dfrac{175}{1,200} = 14.6\%$
Gross profit margin	$\dfrac{1,040}{2,600} = 40\%$	$\dfrac{1,150}{3,500} = 32.9\%$
Operating profit margin	$\dfrac{310}{2,600} = 11.9\%$	$\dfrac{350}{3,500} = 10\%$
Current ratio	$\dfrac{735}{400} = 1.8$	$\dfrac{660}{485} = 1.4$
Acid test ratio	$\dfrac{485}{400} = 1.2$	$\dfrac{260}{485} = 0.5$
Trade receivables settlement period	$\dfrac{105}{2,600} \times 365 = 15$ days	$\dfrac{145}{3,500} \times 365 = 15$ days
Trade payables settlement period	$\dfrac{300}{1,560^*} \times 365 = 70$ days	$\dfrac{375}{2,350^*} \times 365 = 58$ days
Inventories turnover period	$\dfrac{250}{1,560} \times 365 = 58$ days	$\dfrac{400}{2,350} \times 365 = 62$ days
Gearing ratio	$\dfrac{500}{1,600} = 31.3\%$	$\dfrac{500}{1,700} = 29.4\%$

* Used because the credit purchases figure is not available.

(b) There has been a considerable decline in the gross profit margin during 2018. This fact, combined with the increase in sales revenue by more than a third, suggests that a price-cutting policy has been adopted in an attempt to stimulate sales. The resulting increase in sales revenue, however, has led to only a small improvement in ROCE and ROSF.

Despite a large cut in the gross profit margin, the operating profit margin has fallen by less than 2%. This suggests that overheads may have been more tightly controlled during 2018. Certainly, overheads have not risen in proportion to sales revenue.

The current ratio has fallen a little and the acid test ratio has fallen by more than half. Although liquidity ratios tend to be lower in retailing than in manufacturing, the liquidity of the business should now be a cause for concern. However, this may be a passing problem. The business is investing heavily in non-current assets and is relying on internal funds to finance this growth. When this investment ends, the liquidity position may improve quickly.

The trade receivables period has remained unchanged over the two years, and there has been no significant change in the inventories turnover period in 2018. The gearing ratio seems quite low and provides no cause for concern given the profitability of the business.

Overall, the business appears to be financially sound. Although there has been rapid growth during 2018, there is no real cause for alarm provided that the liquidity of the business can be improved in the near future. In the absence of information concerning share price, it is not possible to say whether an investment should be made.

Chapter 9

9.1 Next plc

The Next plc dividend yield is very slightly below that for the retailers' section average. This might imply that Next pays similar dividends to other businesses in the sector. This is despite the fact that Next pays out a smaller proportion of its profit (cover of 3.58 times, compared with the 1.90 average).

Compared to current (most recently reported) earnings, the current market price (P/E ratio) of Next is lower than the average for listed retailers. This implies that the investing public has less confidence in the future prospects of Next than in listed retailers generally. However, both dividend yield and P/E ratios can be difficult to interpret.

9.2 Telford Industrial Services plc

Common-size statement of financial position at 31 December

	2015 £m	2016 £m	2017 £m	2018 £m
Non-current assets	100	83	106	102
Current assets				
Inventories	44	36	38	41
Trade receivables	71	69	56	46
Cash	–	5	–	–
	115	110	94	87
Total assets	215	193	200	189
EQUITY	100	100	100	100
Non-current liabilities	63	49	49	47
Current liabilities				
Trade payables	42	44	41	29
Short-term borrowings	10	–	10	13
	52	44	51	42
Total equity and liabilities	215	193	200	189

[The individual figures are calculated by dividing each of the original figures by the equity value for the year concerned and multiplying the result by 100. For example, the inventories figure for 2015 is 21/48 × 100 = 44. Since the revised values have been expressed in whole numbers (no decimal places), it was necessary to adjust to make the statement of financial position agree, despite rounding errors.]

Summary of income statements for years ended 31 December

	2015 £m	2016 £m	2017 £m	2018 £m
Sales revenue	100	100	100	100
Operating profit	19	24	6	10
Interest payable	(3)	(2)	(4)	(3)
Profit before taxation	16	22	2	7
Taxation	(8)	(9)	–	(3)
Profit for the period	8	13	2	4

[The individual figures are calculated by dividing each of the original figures by the sales revenue value for the year concerned and multiplying the result by 100. For example, the operating profit figure for 2015 is (28/152) × 100 = 19.]

9.3 Delta plc

Dividend payout ratio

(30/65) × 100 = 46.2%

Dividend yield ratio

[30/(2.50 × 200)] × 100 = 6%

Earnings per share

65/200 = 32.5p

Price/earnings ratio

250/32.5 = 7.7 times

The dividend payout ratio is a little lower than the average for the general retailers section, which is 52.6% (that is, 1/1.9). The dividend yield is very much higher than the average; nearly twice as large. The P/E ratio is very low by comparison with the average; it is less than half the average value. Delta seems to be a business whose future is not held in great regard by investors. Compared to its current earnings and dividends, its price is very low. This low price, of course, leads to a relatively high dividend yield.

9.4 Ali plc and Bhaskar plc

(a) The Altman-model Z-score is calculated as follows:

$$Z = 0.717a + 0.847b + 3.107c + 0.420d + 0.998e$$

where:
a = Working capital/Total assets
b = Accumulated retained profits/Total assets
c = Operating profit/Total assets
d = Book (statement of financial position) value of ordinary and preference shares/
Total liabilities at book (statement of financial position) value
e = Sales revenue/Total assets

For Ali plc, the Z-score is:

0.717[(853.0 − 422.4)/1,300.0] + 0.847(367.6/1,300.0) + 3.107(151.3/1,300.0)
+ 0.420[687.6/(190.0 + 422.4)] + 0.998(1,478.1/1,300.0) = <u>2.445</u>

For Bhaskar plc, the Z-score is:

0.717[(816.5 − 293.1)/1,417.7] + 0.847(624.6/1,417.7) + 3.107(166.9/1,417.7)
+ 0.420[874.6/(250.0 + 293.1)] + 0.998(1,790.4/1,417.7) = <u>2.940</u>

(b) The Z-scores for these two businesses are quite close, with Bhaskar looking slightly safer. They are both in the category of businesses in the 'zone of ignorance' and, therefore, difficult to classify (a Z-score between 1.23 and 4.14). This is quite unusual in that the Altman model is able confidently to classify 91 per cent of businesses. Clearly, these two businesses fall into the remaining 9 per cent.

It is questionable whether the Altman model is strictly applicable to UK businesses, since it was derived from data relating to US businesses that had failed. On the other hand, it probably provides a useful insight.

9.8 Genesis Ltd

(a) Current ratio $= \dfrac{232}{550} = 0.42:1$

Acid test ratio $= \dfrac{104}{550} = 0.19:1$

Inventories turnover period $= \dfrac{128}{1,248} \times 365 = 37$ days

Average settlement period for trade receivables $= \dfrac{104}{1,640} \times 365 = 23$ days

Average settlement period for trade payables $= \dfrac{184}{1,260} \times 365 = 53$ days

It is difficult to make a judgement about such matters with no equivalent ratios for past periods, or for other businesses, and without knowledge of the business' own plans. Nevertheless there is some evidence that this business is, overtrading. Both of the liquidity ratios look weak. The acid test ratio should probably be around 1:1. Customers are paying more than twice as quickly as suppliers are being paid. This suggests that pressure may be being applied to the former to pay quickly, perhaps with adverse results. It may also imply that payments are being delayed to suppliers because of a lack of available finance.

(b) Overtrading must be dealt with either by increasing the level of funding to match the level of activity, or by reducing the level of activity to match the funds available. The latter option may result in a reduction in operating profit in the short term but may be necessary to ensure long-term survival.

Chapter 10

10.1 Toggles plc

(a) 1 'Non-controlling interests' represents the portion, either of net assets (statement of financial position) or profit for the year (income statement), which is attributable to minority shareholders. Minority shareholders exist where the parent company does not own all of the shares in its subsidiary. Since, by definition, the parent company is the major shareholder in each of its subsidiaries, any other shareholders must be a minority, in terms of number of shares owned.

2 'Goodwill arising on consolidation' is the difference, at the time that the parent acquires the subsidiary, between what is paid for the subsidiary company shares and what they are 'worth'. 'Worth' normally is based on the fair values of the underlying assets (net of liabilities) of the subsidiary. These are not necessarily, nor usually, the statement of financial position values. Goodwill, therefore, represents the excess of what was paid over the fair values of the (net) assets of the subsidiary. As such, goodwill arising on consolidation is an intangible asset that represents the amount the parent was prepared to pay for the fact that the subsidiary has a workforce in place and any synergies that may arise from the parent and subsidiary having a close relationship.

3 The retained earnings of the parent company will be its own cumulative profits net of tax and dividends paid. When the results of the subsidiaries are consolidated with those of the parent, the parent's share of the post-acquisition retained earnings of its subsidiaries is added to its own retained earnings figure. In this way the parent is, in effect, credited with its share of the subsidiaries' after-tax profit that has arisen since the takeover.

(b) The objective of preparing consolidated financial statements is to reflect the underlying economic reality that the assets of subsidiary companies are as much under the control of the shareholders of the parent, acting through their board of directors, as are the assets owned directly by the parent. This will be true despite the fact that the subsidiary is strictly a company separate from the parent. It is also despite the fact that the parent may not own all of the shares of the subsidiaries.

Consolidated financial statements provide an example where accounting reports substance over form. That is to say, it tries to reflect economic reality rather than the strict legal position. This is done in an attempt to provide more useful information.

10.2 Arnold plc

Group income statement for the year ended 31 December

	£m
Revenue (83 + 47)	130
Cost of sales (36 + 19)	(55)
Gross profit	75
Administration expenses (14 + 7)	(21)
Distribution expenses (21 + 10)	(31)
Profit before taxation	23
Taxation (4 + 3)	(7)
Profit for the year	16
Attributable to non-controlling interests (25% × 8)	(2)
Profit for the year attributable to Arnold plc shareholders	14

10.3 Giant plc

Giant group statement of financial position as at 31 March

	£m
ASSETS	
Non-current assets (at cost less depreciation)	
Property, plant and equipment	
Land	39
Plant	63
Vehicles	25
	127
Current assets	
Inventories	46
Trade receivables	59
Cash	27
	132
Total assets	259
EQUITY AND LIABILITIES	
Equity	
Called-up share capital: ordinary shares of £1 each, fully paid	50
Share premium account	40
Retained earnings	46
	136
Non-current liabilities	
Loan notes	63
Current liabilities	
Trade payables	60
Total equity and liabilities	259

Note that the group statement of financial position is prepared by adding all like items together. The investment in 10 million shares of Jack Ltd (£30m), in the statement of financial position of Giant plc, is then compared with the equity (in total) in Jack Ltd's statement of financial position. Since Giant paid exactly the fair values of Jack's assets *and* bought all of Jack's shares, these two figures are equal and can be cancelled.

10.4 Jumbo plc

The statement of financial position of Jumbo plc and its subsidiary will be as follows:

Statement of financial position as at 31 March

	£m
ASSETS	
Non-current assets (at cost less depreciation)	
Property, plant and equipment	
Land	102
Plant	67
Vehicles	57
	226
Current assets	
Inventories	87
Trade receivables	70
Cash	24
	181
Total assets	407

EQUITY AND LIABILITIES	£m
Equity	
Called-up share capital: ordinary shares of £1 each, fully paid	100
Retained earnings	41
	141
Non-controlling interests	16
	157
Non-current liabilities	
Loan notes	170
Current liabilities	
Trade payables	80
Total equity and liabilities	407

Note that the normal approach is taken with various assets and external claims (that is, adding like items together). The 'non-controlling interests' figure represents the minorities' share (8 million of 20 million ordinary shares) in the equity of Nipper plc (40 per cent of £40 million).

10.5 Apple plc

The statement of financial position of Apple plc and its subsidiary will be as follows:

Statement of financial position as at 30 September

ASSETS	£000
Non-current assets (at cost less depreciation)	
Property, plant and equipment (950 + 320)	1,270
Goodwill arising on consolidation (see Note 2)	24
	1,294
Current assets	
Inventories (320 + 160)	480
Trade receivables (180 + 95)	275
Cash at bank (41 + 15)	56
	811
Total assets	2,105
EQUITY AND LIABILITIES	
Equity	
£1 fully paid ordinary shares	700
Reserves	307
	1,007
Non-controlling interests (see Note 3)	72
	1,079
Non-current liabilities	
Loan notes (500 + 160)	660
Current liabilities	
Trade payables (170 + 87)	257
Taxation (54 + 55)	109
	366
Total equity and liabilities	2,105

Notes:

1 The normal approach is taken with various assets and external claims.
2 The goodwill arising on consolidation is the difference between what Apple plc paid for the shares in Pear Ltd (150,000 × £1.60 = £240,000), less the fair value of the net assets acquired (150,000/200,000 × £288,000 = £216,000), that is, £24,000.
3 The non-controlling interests figure is simply the minority shareholders' stake in the net assets of Pear Ltd. This is (50,000/200,000) × £288,000 = £72,000.

Chapter 11

11.1 Information overload

Some believe that the annual reports of companies are becoming too long and contain too much information. It is quite common for large listed businesses to have annual reports of around 150 pages or more.

There is a danger that users will suffer from information overload if they are confronted with an excessive amount of information. This may, in turn, lead them to:

- fail to distinguish between important and less important information;
- fail to approach the analysis of information in a logical and systematic manner; and
- feel a sense of confusion and avoid the task of analysing the information.

Lengthy annual reports are likely to be a problem for the less sophisticated user. However, for sophisticated users the problem may be that the annual reports are still not long enough. They often wish to glean as much information as possible from the company in order to make investment decisions.

11.3 Summary financial statements

Various problems must be overcome when preparing summary financial statements for shareholders. These include:

- There is no clear view concerning what their content should be. Although shareholders may require less information, the particular content of summary financial statements that would meet their needs is unclear.
- The preparation of summary financial statements will involve the simplification of reality. It can be argued, however, that the full financial statements are already a simplification of complex reality and to try to simplify further is unrealistic. It is also unfair on those who have to prepare such statements.
- By simplifying reality, there is a danger that distortions will occur. This may lead shareholders to arrive at incorrect judgements and conclusions about the performance and position of the business.
- Technical terms will still be required to convey the necessary financial information. Some shareholders may not understand these terms. If so, the summary financial statements may still not provide an effective means of communication. (A glossary of terms could help overcome this problem.)

11.6 Dali plc

A striking feature of the segmental reports is that the car parts segment generates the highest revenue – more than the other two segments combined. Nevertheless, it is the aircraft parts segment that generates the highest profit. We can use some simple ratios at this point to help evaluate performance.

We can start by considering the profit generated in relation to the sales revenue for each operating segment. We can see from the table below that the boat parts segment generates the most profit in relation to sales revenue. Around 21 per cent, or £0.21 in every £1, of profit is derived from the sales revenue generated. The total revenue for this segment, however, is much lower than for the other two segments. Although the car parts segment generates the most revenue, less than 6 per cent, or £0.06 in every £1, of profit is derived from the sales revenue generated. It is worth noting that the aircraft parts segment suffered a large impairment charge during the year, which had a significant effect on profits. The reasons for this impairment charge should be investigated.

We can also compare the profit generated with the net assets employed (that is, total assets minus total liabilities) for each segment. We can see from the table below that the boat parts segment produces the best return on net assets employed by far: around 82 per cent, that is, £0.82 for every £1 invested. Once again, the car parts segment produces the worst results with a return of less than 24 per cent.

The relatively poor results from the car parts segment may simply reflect the nature of the market in which it operates. Compared with car parts segments of other businesses, it may be doing very well. Nevertheless, the business may still wish to consider whether future investment would not be better directed to those areas where greater profits can be found.

The investment in non-current assets during the period in relation to the total assets held is much higher for the boat parts segment. This may reflect the faith of the directors in the potential of this segment.

The depreciation charge as a percentage of segment assets seems to be high for all of the operating segments – but particularly for the car parts division. This should be investigated as it may suggest poor buying decisions.

Table of key results

	Car parts	Aircraft parts	Boat parts
Total revenue	£360m	£210m	£85m
Segment profit	£20m	£24m	£18m
Net assets (assets − liabilities)	£85m	£58m	£22m
Segment profit as a percentage of sales revenue	5.6%	11.4%	21.2%
Segment profit as a percentage of net assets employed	23.5%	41.4%	81.8%
Expenditure on non-current assets	£28m	£23m	£26m
Depreciation as a percentage of segment assets	51.6%	44.0%	34.1%

11.7 Alkrom plc

CPP income statement for the three-month period to 31 March

	CPP £m
Sales revenue (120/120 × £19.2m)	19.2
Cost of sales (120/115 × £16.0m)	16.7
Profit for the period	2.5

CPP statement of financial position as at 31 March

	CPP£m
ASSETS	
Non-current assets	
Property, plant and equipment	
Offices (£4m × 120/115)	4.2
Current assets	
Receivables	19.2
	23.4
EQUITY	
Equity (20.0 × 120/115)	20.9
Retained earnings	2.5
	23.4

11.8 Turner plc

We can see from the table below that the software segment generates the highest revenue, but also generates the lowest profit. We can use some simple ratios at this point to help evaluate segmental performance. We can start by considering the profit generated in relation to the sales revenue for each operating segment. We can see from the table that the engineering segment generates the most profit in relation to sales revenue. Around 23 per cent, or £0.23 in every £1, of profit is derived from the sales revenue generated. However, for the software segment, only 4 per cent, or £0.04 in every £1, of profit is derived from the sales revenue generated.

We can also compare the profit generated with the net assets employed (that is, total assets minus total liabilities) for each segment. We can see from the table that the electronics segment produces the best return on net assets employed: around £0.65 for every £1 invested. Once again, the software segment produces the worst results.

The reasons for the relatively poor results from the software segment need further investigation. There may be valid reasons; for example, it may be experiencing severe competitive pressures. The results for this segment, however, are not disastrous: it is making a profit. Nevertheless, the business may wish to re-evaluate its long-term presence in this market.

It is interesting to note that the software segment benefited most from the investment in non-current assets during the period – as much as the other two segments combined. The reason for such a large investment in such a relatively poorly performing segment needs to be justified. It is possible that the business will reap rewards for the investment in the future; however, we do not have enough information to understand the reasons for the investment decision.

Depreciation charges in the software segment are significantly higher than for the other operating segments. This may be because the segment has more non-current assets, although we do not have a figure for the non-current assets held. The depreciation charge as a percentage of segment assets is also higher and the reasons for this should be investigated.

Table of key results

	Software	Electronics	Engineering
Total revenue	£250m	£230m	£52m
Segment profit	£10m	£34m	£12m
Net assets (assets − liabilities)	£85m	£52m	£30m
Segment profit as a percentage of sales revenue	4.0%	14.8%	23.1%
Segment profit as a percentage of net assets employed	11.8%	65.4%	40.0%
Expenditure on non-current assets	£22m	£12m	£10m
Depreciation as a percentage of segment assets	42.9%	38.9%	29.4%

Chapter 12

12.1 Strengthening the independence of external auditors

Auditor independence may be strengthened in various ways. They include:

- preventing, or restricting, auditing firms from undertaking non-audit work for a client company;
- rotating external auditors on a regular basis (say, every five or ten years);
- rotating the audit partner responsible for overseeing the audit (rather than the audit firm) on a regular basis;
- requiring peer group assessment (where another audit firm reviews the work that has been done for a client company). This type of assessment may be carried out every three years or so;
- establishing audit committees, which monitor and review the work carried out by the audit firm; and
- preventing an audit firm from undertaking an audit where the audit fee would represent a large proportion (say 10 per cent or more) of the total annual fees generated by the audit firm.

12.2 Non-executive directors

The following criteria may be used to evaluate the performance of a non-executive director:

- willingness to spend time in understanding the business and in acquiring additional skills to improve effectiveness;
- contribution made to board discussions on key issues such as strategy development;
- effectiveness in challenging proposals made by identifying key weaknesses and assumptions;
- independence of mind and ability to resist undue pressure from other directors;
- perseverance in following up unresolved issues and in defending positions taken; and
- ability to work as part of a team, when required, and to establish effective relations with key individuals, including other board members.

This is not an exhaustive list.

12.4 Institutional shareholders

The benefits that may accrue from close ties with institutional shareholders are as follows:

- It provides the board of directors with the opportunity to explain the future direction of the company, which may lead to a better understanding of board proposals and decisions that have been made. This may, in turn, make institutional shareholders more willing to offer support during difficult times.
- It may encourage institutional shareholders to take a long-term view. If the board can provide a clear vision and strategy for the company, the shareholders may become less concerned with any short-term setbacks and become more concerned with achieving long-term goals.
- It can impose an external discipline on the board. The directors will be subjected to considerable scrutiny when meeting institutional shareholders. They will have to justify their decisions and be prepared to answer tough questions. This can, however, improve the quality of decisions made.
- It can provide valuable feedback on board proposals. Institutional investors may be sounded out on particular ideas that are under review. Their views can then be taken into account when making a final decision.
- It can help in future funding. Where institutional shareholders have good relations with the board and have confidence in the future direction of the company, they are more likely to be sympathetic to requests for additional funding.

There are various problems that can arise from close links with institutional shareholders. For example, there is a risk that certain commercially sensitive information provided to them will not be treated in confidence. There is also a risk in upsetting small shareholders, who may feel that large institutional shareholders are given undue influence over decisions. Finally, there is a problem in determining what are the acceptable limits to the discussions and information that is offered.

Appendix A

A.1

	Account to be debited	Account to be credited
(a)	Inventories	Trade payables
(b)	Equity (or a separate drawings account)	Cash
(c)	Interest on borrowings	Cash
(d)	Inventories	Cash
(e)	Cash	Trade receivables
(f)	Wages	Cash
(g)	Equity (or a separate drawings account)	Trade receivables
(h)	Trade payables	Cash
(i)	Electricity (or heat and light)	Cash
(j)	Cash	Sales revenue

Note that the precise name given to an account is not crucial so long as it is clear to those who are using the information what each account deals with.

A.2 (a) and (b)

Cash

		£			£
1 Feb	Equity	6,000	3 Feb	Inventories	2,600
15 Feb	Sales revenue	4,000	5 Feb	Equipment	800
28 Feb	Trade receivables	2,500	9 Feb	Rent	250
			10 Feb	Fuel and electricity	240
			11 Feb	General expenses	200
			21 Feb	Equity	1,000
			25 Feb	Trade payables	2,000
			28 Feb	Balance c/d	5,410
		12,500			12,500
1 Mar	Balance b/d	5,410			

Equity

		£			£
21 Feb	Cash	1,000	1 Feb	Cash	6,000
28 Feb	Balance c/d	5,000			
		6,000			6,000
			28 Feb	Balance b/d	5,000
28 Feb	Balance c/d	7,410	28 Feb	Income statement	2,410
		7,410			7,410
			1 Mar	Balance b/d	7,410

Inventories

		£			£
3 Feb	Cash	2,600	15 Feb	Cost of sales	2,400
6 Feb	Trade payables	3,000	19 Feb	Cost of sales	2,300
			28 Feb	Balance c/d	900
		5,600			5,600
1 Mar	Balance b/d	900			

Equipment

		£			£
5 Feb	Cash	800			

Trade payables

		£			£
25 Feb	Cash	2,000	6 Feb	Inventories	3,000
28 Feb	Balance c/d	1,000			
		3,000			3,000
			1 Mar	Balance b/d	1,000

Rent

		£			£
9 Feb	Cash	250	28 Feb	Income statement	250

Fuel and electricity

10 Feb	Cash	240	28 Feb	Income statement	240

General expenses

11 Feb	Cash	200	28 Feb	Income statement	200

Sales revenue

		£			£
28 Feb	Balance c/d	7,800	15 Feb	Cash	4,000
			19 Feb	Trade receivables	3,800
		7,800			7,800
28 Feb	Income statement	7,800	28 Feb	Balance b/d	7,800

Cost of sales

15 Feb	Inventories	2,400	28 Feb	Balance c/d	4,700
19 Feb	Inventories	2,300			
		4,700			4,700
28 Feb	Balance b/d	4,700	28 Feb	Income statement	4,700

Trade receivables

		£			£
19 Feb	Sales revenue	3,800	28 Feb	Cash	2,500
			28 Feb	Balance c/d	1,300
		3,800			3,800
1 Mar	Balance b/d	1,300			

Trial balance as at 28 February

	Debits	Credits
Cash	5,410	
Equity		5,000
Inventories	900	
Equipment	800	
Trade payables		1,000
Rent	250	
Fuel and electricity	240	
General expenses	200	
Sales revenue		7,800
Cost of sales	4,700	
Trade receivables	1,300	
	13,800	13,800

(c)

Income statement

		£			£
28 Feb	Cost of sales	4,700	28 February	Sales revenue	7,800
28 Feb	Rent	250			
28 Feb	Fuel and electricity	240			
28 Feb	General expenses	200			
28 Feb	Equity (profit)	2,410			
		7,800			7,800

Statement of financial position as at 28 February

	£
ASSETS	
Non-current assets	
Equipment	800
Current assets	
Inventories	900
Trade receivables	1,300
Cash	5,410
	7,610
Total assets	8,410
EQUITY AND LIABILITIES	
Equity (owners' claim)	7,410
Current liabilities	
Trade payables	1,000
Total equity and liabilities	8,410

Income statement for the month ended 28 February

	£
Sales revenue	7,800
Cost of sales	(4,700)
Gross profit	3,100
Rent	(250)
Fuel and electricity	(240)
General expenses	(200)
Profit for the month	2,410

A.3 (a) and (b)

Buildings

	£		
£1 Jan Balance b/d	25,000		

Fittings – cost

		£			£
Jan	Balance b/d	10,000	31 Dec	Balance c/d	12,000
31 Dec	Cash	2,000			
		12,000			12,000
Jan	Balance b/d	12,000			

Fittings – depreciation

		£				£
31 Dec	Balance c/d	4,400	1 Jan	Balance b/d		2,000
			31 Dec	Income statement		
				(£12,000 × 20%)		2,400
		4,400				4,400
			1 Jan	Balance b/d		4,400

General expenses

		£			£
1 Jan	Balance b/d	140	31 Dec	Income statement	570
31 Dec	Cash	580		Balance c/d	150
		720			720
1 Jan	Balance b/d	150			

Inventories

		£			£
1 Jan	Balance b/d	1,350	31 Dec	Cost of sales	15,220
31 Dec	Trade payables	17,220		Cost of sales	4,900
	Cash	3,760		Equity	560
				Balance c/d	1,650
		22,330			22,330
1 Jan	Balance b/d	1,650			

Cost of sales

		£			£
31 Dec	Inventories	15,220	31 Dec	Income statement	20,120
	Inventories	4,900			
		20,120			20,120

Rent

		£			£
1 Jan	Balance b/d	500	31 Dec	Income statement	3,000
31 Dec	Cash	3,000		Balance c/d	500
		3,500			3,500
1 Jan	Balance b/d	500			

Trade receivables

		£			£
1 Jan	Balance brought down	1,840	31 Dec	Cash	32,810
31 Dec	Sales revenue	33,100		Income statement (bad debt)	260
				Balance c/d	1,870
		34,940			34,940
1 Jan	Balance b/d	1,870			

Cash

		£			£
1 Jan	Balance b/d	2,180	31 Dec	Inventories	3,760
31 Dec	Sales revenue	10,360		Wages	3,770
	Borrowings	2,000		Rent	3,000
	Trade receivables	32,810		Electricity	1,070
				General expenses	580
				Fittings	2,000
				Borrowings	1,000
				Trade payables	18,150
				Equity	10,400
				Balance c/d	3,620
		47,350			47,350
1 Jan	Balance b/d	3,620			

Equity

		£			£
31 Dec	Inventories	560	1 Jan	Balance b/d	25,050
	Cash	10,400		Income statement (profit)	10,900
	Balance c/d	24,990			
		35,950			35,950
			1 Jan	Balance b/d	24,990

Borrowings

		£			£
30 June	Cash	1,000	1 Jan	Balance b/d	12,000
31 Dec	Balance c/d	13,000		Cash	2,000
		14,000			14,000
			1 Jan	Balance b/d	13,000

Trade payables

		£			£
31 Dec	Cash	18,150	1 Jan	Balance b/d	1,690
	Balance c/d	760	31 Dec	Inventories	17,220
		18,910			18,910
			1 Jan	Balance b/d	760

Electricity

		£			£
31 Dec	Cash	1,070	1 Jan	Balance b/d	270
31 Dec	Balance c/d	290	31 Dec	Income statement	1,090
		1,360			1,360
			1 Jan	Balance b/d	290

Sales revenue

		£			£
31 Dec	Income statement	43,460	31 Dec	Trade receivables	33,100
				Cash	10,360
		43,460			43,460

Wages

		£			£
31 Dec	Cash	3,770	31 Dec	Income statement	3,770

Interest on borrowings

	£			£
		31 Dec	Income statement $((6/12 \times 14,000) + (6/12 \times 13,000)) \times 10\%$	1,350

(c)

Income statement for the year to 31 December

		£			£
31 Dec	Cost of sales	20,120	31 Dec	Sales revenue	43,460
	Depreciation	2,400			
	General expenses	570			
	Rent	3,000			
	Bad debts (Trade receivables)	260			
	Electricity	1,090			
	Wages	3,770			
	Interest on borrowings	1,350			
	Profit (Equity)	10,900			
		43,460			43,460

(d)

Statement of financial position as at 31 December last year

	£	£
ASSETS		
Non-current assets		
Property, plant and equipment		
Buildings		25,000
Fittings – cost	12,000	
– depreciation	(4,400)	7,600
		32,600
Current assets		
Inventories of stationery		150
Inventories		1,650
Prepaid rent		500
Trade receivables		1,870
Cash		3,620
		7,790
Total assets		40,390
EQUITY AND LIABILITIES		
Equity (owners' claim)		24,990
Non-current liabilities		
Borrowings		13,000
Current liabilities		
Trade payables		760
Accrued electricity		290
Accrued interest on borrowings		1,350
		2,400
Total equity and liabilities		40,390

Index

Note: page numbers in **bold** refer to definitions in the glossary